C000103039

20th Edition
WRECKS & RELICS

Ken Ellis

MIDLAND
An imprint of
Ian Allan Publishing

CONTENTS

Preface..3
             Acknowledgements..4 - 5
             Further Reading ....5 - 6
             Lost! and Found! 6
             How to Use *Wrecks & Relics*................................7 - 8
Part One   England... 9 - 96
             Photograph Section ....97 - 128
Part One   England, continued ....129 - 224
             Photograph Section ....225 - 256
Part One   England, continued ....257 - 280
Part Two   Channel Islands 280
Part Three   Scotland...281 - 293
Part Four   Wales...293 - 301
Part Five   Northern Ireland ....301 - 305
Part Six   Ireland ....305 - 310
Part Seven RAF Overseas 310
Appendix A Exports 311
Appendix B *CockpitFest*..312
Index I   Types...313 - 317
Index II   Locations...318 - 320

Front Cover: A section of the 'Milestones of Flight' hall at the RAF Museum, Hendon, Greater London. Blériot XI BAPC.106 'flies' alongside Eurofighter Typhoon FSM BAPC.292. Behind is the very impressive time-line wall.
Anthony Mills

Rear Cover:
Dassault Mystère IVA 64 (with 61 in the background) on the mock runway at Spadeadam, Cumbria. *Mark Harris*

Beagle 206-1X G-ARRM arrived at its birthplace, Shoreham, West Sussex, in May 2005 for a comprehensive restoration. *Ian Haskell*

Title Page: A superb combination, Lightning T.5 XS420 and behind 'The Swan' public house right under the approach at Farnborough. Happy memories! Farnborough Air Sciences, March 2006. *Ken Ellis*

This twentieth edition published by Midland Publishing
(An imprint of Ian Allan Publishing Ltd)
4 Watling Drive, Sketchley Lane Industrial Estate,
Hinckley, Leics, LE10 3EY.

ISBN (10) 1 85780 235 7 and (13) 978 1 85780 235 1

Printed in the UK by Ian Allan Printing Ltd, Riverdene Business Park,
Molesey Road, Hersham, Surrey KT12 4RG

PREFACE

Reasons to be Doleful – Part 20*:
⊙ Increased risk to airliners (unless they used to travel at Mach 2!) in collections and the apparent lack of long term and national vision for them. I predict more scrappings... ⊙ Somebody stole the 'hot jets' that I still consider well-modern – the fabulous Jaguar and the unconquered Sea Harrier. ⊙ Ian Dury. ⊙ More military airfields vaporising: Coltishall... Llanbedr... is St Athan next? ⊙ Being told that *W&R* is a lifeline and that it can't be done without. ⊙ Owners of airframes saying I'm belittling their pride-and-joys by having them in a book about 'wrecks' and 'relics'. ⊙ Not having space for the abbreviations (see page 8 if in need)... ⊙ Douglas Adams. ⊙ Restorers and owners telling me they have someone waving "your book" at that them and saying "they want a quick look"... ⊙ The few bastions protecting our general aviation heritage are in the 'private' and/or 'volunteer' sector. ⊙ Unannounced beings with notebooks and binoculars at my door, asking for directions to so-and-so, or a quick look through my files... (Or 'phoning me at work for the same.) ⊙ Every weekend December to early April spent glued behind a PC - yes, I'm no longer wearing a Mac! ⊙ The dire lack of 'young blood' to keep things going in the preservation 'movement'... ⊙ Thinking of new things to write about in the Preface!

Reasons to be Cheerful – Part 20*:
⊙ Newark Air Museum... the 'Cold War' hall at Cosford... and there are others. ⊙ That there are still people out there who want to preserve aircraft and our aviation heritage. ⊙ Douglas Adams. ⊙ Owners of airframes telling me they are proud to have their pride-and-joy in a book about 'wrecks' and 'relics'. ⊙ Continually hearing that by looking at page so-and-so of the umpteenth edition, aircraft X was acquired and is flying again, or that Y was acquired for display, or that Z 'found' its replacement aileron. ⊙ Ian Dury. ⊙ XH558 and team that are turning back the clock. ⊙ Billie Piper. ⊙ *CockpitFest*. ⊙ Pam taking up golf... ⊙ That there *is* so much still to write about. ⊙ The cats, Rex and Relix, *not* eating the manuscript... ⊙ Every other year, floods of friends (many met, others yet to) sending in their notes, observations, updates and their encouragement. ⊙ Being told that *W&R* is a lifeline and that it can't be done without... ⊙ Having next year 'off'. ⊙ At this moment being the furthest possible distance from another Preface!

Deadlines for the next edition are **31st January 2008** for illustrations and **1st March 2008** for information and comments. If you plan to send 'electric' illustrations (jpegs or tiffs don't you know) please note that Rutland has not long had the electric and that broadband is therefore decades away, although it will probably arrive *before* fresh water does! So please *e-mail before hand* to find out requirements and what buttons are best to be pressed!

Ken Ellis
Surprisingly sunny Rutland
April 2006

Myddle Cottage, Welland Terrace, off Mill Lane, Barrowden,
Oakham, Rutland, LE15 8EH

<u>please note</u> new e-mail address:
wrecksandrelics@kenavhist.wanadoo.co.uk

* In no particular order at all!

Acknowledgements

This book relies on the inputs of a huge spectrum of contributors, each making their mark on the contents in different ways. My many thanks to them all. Overseeing the draft, adding to it and refining it were the following stalwarts: **Alan Allen, Dave Allport, David J Burke, John Coghill, Mick Boulanger** and **Nigel Price**. Dave and Nigel were each having a 'busman's holiday' from working on *Air International / Airforces Monthly* and *FlyPast / Air Enthusiast* respectively. Also pitching from 'the office' were Jarrod Cotter and Mark Nicholls. Without their input, support, encouragement and friendship, this book would just be a set of covers...

Major photographic and other input came from: Tim R Badham, Roger Cook - Pynelea Photo Bureau, Ian Haskell, Alf Jenks, David S Johnstone, Tony (and Brenda) McCarthy, Roger Richards, Sam Tyler, Phil Whalley, David Willis, Andy Wood. Others are credited with their work.

The following **subject and area specialists** made vital inputs: **Gary Adams**, for Northern Ireland; **Peter R Arnold**, Spitfires; **Peter Budden**, Dorset and others; **Michael R Cain**, Southend and others; **Alan Crouchman**, North Weald; **Stephen Dobson**, Shawbury; **Mark Gauntlett**, cockpit 'guru'; **Graham Hall**, Norfolk and area; **Mark Harris**, for notes from his travels; **David S Johnstone** and **David Johnstone Jnr**, Scotland; **Darren Lewington**, Gloucestershire Airport (aka Staverton); **Tony** and **Brenda McCarthy** for extensive notes of equally extensive travels; **Chris Michell**, Isle of Wight; **Seamus Mooney**, Ireland; **Watson J Nelson**, museum policies and funding; **Alistair Ness**, Central Scotland Aviation Group for Scotland; **John Phillips**, rotorcraft and others; **Mike Phipp**, Bournemouth and Dorset; **Geoffrey Pool**, Bruntingthorpe; **Col Pope** Duxford warbirds and others; **Peter Spooner** for a constant flow of notes; **Ian Thompson**, extensive Northern Ireland and Ireland notes; **David E Thompson**, north of England and many other notes; **Francis Wallace**, Buccaneers; **Andy Wood**, Humberside, Lincolnshire and Yorkshire.

A mail-shot is made to the wide array of **organisations working within the heritage movement**. Thanks to the following for taking the time to update items and for their constant help and support: **Tony Albrow**, 95th Bomb Group Hospital Museum; **Bill Baker**, BB Aviation; **Roger Barrell**, East Essex Aviation Museum; **Alan Beattie**, Yorkshire Helicopter Preservation Group; **Phil Bedford**, South East Aviation Enthusiasts Group; **Dave Blackburn**, Jetstream Club; **Kevin Bowen**, formerly of the Trident Preservation Society; **Alec Brew**, Staffordshire Aircraft Restoration Team; **Ben Brown**, Sywell Aviation Museum - and others!; **Ray Burrows**, Ulster Aviation Society; **James Campbell**, Highland Aviation Museum; **Russell Carpenter**, T5 Alive; **Glenn Cattermole**, Buccaneer XT284; **Graham Chaters**, Lincolnshire Aviation Preservation Society; **Richard Clarkson**, Vulcan Restoration Trust; **David Collins**, DH Hornet project; **Graham Crabtree**, Rougham Tower Association; **Ernie Cromie**, Ulster Aviation Society; **Clive Davies**, Gloster Aviation Club; **Lewis Deal**, Medway Aircraft Preservation Society; **Cpl Richie Doel**, Canberras WJ633 and WT525; **Robert Dunnett**, Martlesham Heath Aviation Society; **Bryn Elliott**, North Weald Airfield Museum; **Dr Geoff Edwards**, Stirling Project; **Mark J Evans**, Midland Warplane Museum; **Trevor Flitchett**, Aeropark Volunteers Association; **Ken Fostekew**, Museum of Berkshire Aviation; **John Francis**, RAF Museum Cosford; **Ralph Franklin**, 306th BG Association; **Ron Fulton**, Boscombe Down Aviation Collection; **G/C Pater A Garth**, Airship Heritage Trust; **Graham Gilbert**, Bentwaters Aviation Society; **Nigel Goodall**, Blackburn Buccaneer Society; **Stuart Gowans**, cockpit and Spitfire restorer; **Glynn Griffith**, RAF Millom Museum; **Neil Hallett**, Farnborough Air Sciences; **James Halliday**, Boeing 737 EI-CJF; **Ian Hancock**, Norfolk & Suffolk Aviation Museum; **Roger Hargreaves**, Britannia Aircraft Preservation Trust; **Howard Heeley**, Newark Air Museum; **Dave Hibbert**, Newark Air Museum; **Mike Hodgson**, Thorpe Camp Preservation Group; **Tim Hogben**, Lemming Aerospace; **Stewart Holder**, Jet Aviation Preservation Group; **Daniel Hunt**, Wings Museum; **Sam Hurry**, 100th BG Memorial Museum; **Tony Jeckells**, Station 146 Tower Association; **Roy Jerman**, Military Aircraft Cockpit Collection; **Mark A Jones**, Phantom Preservation Group; **Tim Jones**, cockpit collector; **Ken Fostekew**, Museum of Berkshire Aviation; **Mark A Jones**, Phantom Preservation Group; **Ricky Kelley**, Buccaneer XW550; **Bob Kent**, Balloon Preservation Group; **Mike Killaspy**, East Anglian Aviation Society; **Jack Kirby**, Thinktank; **David Kirkpatrick**, Solway Aviation Museum; **Andrew Lee**, Trident G-AWZI; **Eric Littledike**, Pilcher Hawk; **Trevor Matthews**, Lashenden Air Warfare Museum; **Al McLean**, RAF Museum Cosford; **Angela McLennan**, Royal Engineers Museum; **Vaughan K Meers**, Staffordshire Aircraft Restoration Team; **John S Morgan**, cockpit collector; **Martyn Morgan**, Wolverhampton Aviation Group; **Ross McNeill**, Canberra XH175; **Naylan Moore**, AeroVenture and Classic Aircraft Collection; **Alex Murison**, North East Aircraft Museum; **Dean Nandy**, Queen Air G-KEAB; **Mike North**, Hunter N-302; **Geoff Nutkins**, Shoreham Aircraft Museum; **Dick Nutt**, former Douglas Boston-Havoc UKPG; **Garry O'Keefe**, Victor Association; **Bill O'Sullivan**, Newark Air Museum; **Chris Page**, Northern Aeroplane Workshops; **Richard Parr**, Parallel Aviation; **Tom Perkins**, Parham Airfield Museum; **Steve Petch**, Hunter XE624; **Robin Phipps**, Buccaneer and Sea Vixen cockpits; **Cyril Plimmer**, Boulton Paul Association; **Tony Podmore**, Shuttleworth Collection; **Nigel Ponsford**, Real Aeroplane Museum and his own 'air force'; **Dave Pope**, seasoned collector (!); **Derek Powell**, Wellesbourne Wartime Museum and Vulcan XM655; **Ivor Ramsden**, Manx Aviation Preservation Society; **Elfan ap Rees**, The Helicopter Museum; **Jim Richardson**, Dumfries and Galloway Aviation Museum; **Paul Rose**, Walney Aviation Heritage Museum; **Mark Russell**, Hunter Flying Club; **Elly Sallingboe**, B-17 Preservation; **E Peter G Scoley**, Friends of Metheringham Airfield; **David Shakespeare**, Dove VP-YKF; **Colin Sharp**, Flambards Experience; **Ian Sheffield**, Harrier cockpit; **Kelvin Sloper**, City of Norwich Aviation Museum; **Mike Smith**, Newark Air Museum; **Roger Smith**, Midland Air Museum; **Graham Sparkes**, The Aeroplane Collection; **Dave Stansfield**, The Albemarle Project; **Nick Stone**, Turbulent G-APOL; **Hugh C Stringer**, Dunkeswell Memorial Museum; **Dave Stubley**, Lincolnshire Aircraft Recovery Group; **Andy Taylor**, Suffolk Aviation Heritage Group; **Hal Taylor**, Meteor Flight; **Richard Taylor**, 493rd Bomb Group Museum; **Julian Temple**, Brooklands Museum; **Steve Thompson**, Cotswold Aircraft Restoration Group; **Hugh Trevor**, Lightning Preservation Group and Lightnings in general; **Bob Turner**, Fleet Air Arm Museum; **Tim Turner**, British Balloon Museum and Library; **David Underwood**, gliders and LA-4 G-ASEA; **Peter Vallance**, Gatwick Aviation Museum; **Graham Vale**, Aeropark Volunteers Association; **Peter Vallance**, Gatwick Aviation Museum; **Peter Verdemato**, Spitfire and Hurricane Memorial Museum; **Bill Welbourne**, Fenland and West Norfolk Aviation Museum; **Alistair White**, Acebell Aviation; **Mike Woodley**, Aces High.

Many readers take the time and trouble to send in reports of sightings, snippets and reports – large and small. Without their help this book would not be as topical or authoritative. Also listed here, as ever, are people who have supplied *other* services vital to the production of *W&R!* Thanks to each and every one of you!

Gerry Allen, David Arkle, Martin Addison, Craig Astell, Nigel Bailey-Underwood, Alan G L Barclay, Alan Barley, Len J Batchelor, Alec Berry, John Black, Ken Bruce, Tony Buttler, Paul Carr, Russell Carter, Richard Cawsey, Alan Chapman, Edward Ian Church, Guy Clark, John D Coleman, Glyn Coney, Howard J Curtis, Terry Dann, Clive Davies, John Davis, Russell T Davies, Peter Dawson, Nick Deakin, D Arthur Dent, Patrick Dirksen, Bob Dunn, Andy Durrant, Ian Dury, Don Ellis, Aldon P Ferguson, Daniel Ford, Steve Gardner, Martin Garrett, Richard Giles, Philip Glenister, Mike Goldsmith, Peter Green, Willy Hackett, Peter A Hambelton, Julian Harvey, Ian Haskell, Phil Hewitt, Chris Higginbotham, John Hillier, Jonathan S Horswell, Nigel Howarth; Chris Huggett, Mike Illien, Paul A Jackson, Jim Jobe, Phil Jones, Dave Kimpton, Steve Locke, Ralph Lunt, Chris Mabbott, Dave McNally, Neil McNichol, Andrew Messer, Anthony Mills, Frank Mink, Gary Morris, Mike Morrison, Jan Nelson, Colin O'Neill, Don Nind, Drew Peacock, Robin Phipps, Darren J Pitcher, Laura Pole, Martin Pole, Andrew Powell, Keith Preen, John Richards, Dave Richardson, Norman Roberson, Mark Roberts, Stephen and Julie Robson, Rob Salisbury, Steve Screech, John Simm, Maurice Smith, Paul Snelling, Peter Spooner, Mike 'Stan' Stannard, Nick Stone, Philip J Sudron, David Symington, Gareth Symington, Barry Taylor, David Teninch; Dave Thompson, Ian Thompson, David Underwood, Bob Uppendaun, Bob Vaughn, Mark Vellenoweth, Bob Vendereyt, Colin Walford, Honeysuckle Weeks, Michael Westwood, Mark Whitnall, Les Wild, David Willis, Nick Wilson, Les Woodward...and this edition could not have been created without Thor, the God of IT.

Further Reading

Many references are made while assembling *W&R*, although the over-riding quest is for first-hand information and comment. The following enthusiast-published magazines have proved to be particularly conscientious in their coverage, sticking as much as possible to first-hand reportage and not the ever-increasing recirculation and 'massaging' of other journals, the relentless 'cut-and-paste' from forums and other incestuous 'sources'. I've noted how I find each particularly helpful, as a guide. All offer a variety of other features and articles. Addresses are given for further information.

Air-Britain News, monthly journal of Air-Britain (Historians) Ltd. Good coverage of the civil scene via the *Around and About* section. Barry Collman, 1 Rose Cottages, 179 Penn Road, Hazlemere, Bucks, HP15 7NE e-mail Barry.Collman@air-britain.co.uk www.air-britain.co.uk

Air North, monthly journal of the North-East Branch of Air-Britain. In many ways a ground-breaking 'regional' magazine: detailed civil and military for the north-east of England, and Carlisle. Graeme Carrott, 47 Park Avenue, Grange Park, Gosforth, Newcastle-upon-Tyne, NE3 2HL. e-mail graeme@airnorth1.demon.co.uk www.airnorth.demon.co.uk

Hawkeye, monthly journal of the Gatwick Aviation Society. Excellent, mostly primary, coverage of the UK civil scene in *Around the Dromes* with the emphasis on the south-east. Mike Green, 144 The Crescent, Horley, RH6 7PA. fax / voice-mail 08701 327814 e-mail membership@gatwickaviationsociety.org.uk www.gatwickaviationsociety.org.uk

Humberside Air Review* monthly journal of the Humberside Aviation Society. Civil and military, from Yorkshire to the Wash, covered in exceptional detail. Also published is an excellent additional *Residents Review* annually. Pete Wild, 4 Bleach Yard, New Walk, Beverley, HU17 7HG e-mail pgwild117@aol.com www.focalplane.karoo.net/HAR/has/htm

Irish Air Letter monthly journal published by Paul Cunniffe, Karl Hayes and Eamon Power. Detailed coverage, civil and military, current and historic. 20 Kempton Way, Navan Road, Dublin 7, Ireland e-mail al.magazine@ntlworld.ie

Military Aviation Review, monthly journal published by Military Aircraft Photographs. In-depth UK military and Andy Marden's absolutely excellent *Out of Service* section. Brian Pickering, MAP, Westfield Lodge, Aslackby, near Sleaford, Lincs, NG34 0HG 01778 440760 fax 01778 440060 e-mail brianmap@btinternet.com

Osprey monthly journal of the Solent Aviation Society. Comprehensive coverage of civilian airfields in the regional *Focus On..* section and *Around Britain*, using almost exclusively first-hand information. Paul Chandler, 20 Goring Field, Teg Down, Winchester, Hants, SO22 5NH. e-mail paulchand@hants.gov.uk www.solent-aviation-society.co.uk

Scottish Air News, monthly journal of the Central Scotland Aviation Group. In-depth coverage of Scotland, civil and military, plus Cumbrian aviation. Also publishes a comprehensive residents run-down, *The Scottish Register*, in the form of a supplement. Steve Martin, 3 Pittrichie View, Hattoncrook, Aberdeen, AB21 0UX. e-mail scan.members @btopenworld.com www.scottishairnews.co.uk

SWAG-Mag*, monthly journal (also available as an e-mail subscription) of the South West Aviation Group. Detailed reporting of military happenings in the south-west and on other military concerns. Mike Screech, 4 West Meadow Road, Braunton, EX33 1EB. e-mail michael.screech@virgin.net www http://beehive.thisisnorthdevon.co.uk/swagmag

Ulster Air Mail, monthly journal of the Ulster Aviation Society, civil and military, modern and historic for Northern Ireland. Keith Lloyd, 14d Coolmoyne House, Dunmurry, BT17 9EW. www.ulsteraviationsociety.co.uk

Winged Words monthly journal of The Aviation Society. Detailed and expanding coverage of residents and happenings in the north-west of England. PO Box 26, Manchester M46 9YW 01942 795060 24-hour info hotline 0906 470 0820 e-mail alanbirtles@tiscali.co.uk www.tasmanchester.com

Several of the journals above (marked *) include the ***ELAS Newsletter,*** edited and compiled by Graham Gaff of the **East London Aviation Society**. This covers UK current military by type and is an exceptional piece of work, with painstaking attention to original coverage. 2 Taveners Green Close, Wick Meadows, Wickford, SS12 9RQ. e-mail hammerselas@aol.com

Plus… of course (!):
FlyPast , monthly magazine published by Key Publishing Ltd. PO Box 300, Stamford, Lincs, PE9 1NA. 01780 480404 fax 01780 757812 e-mail subs@keypublishing.com www.flypast.com

A huge array of books have been dipped into, far too many to list completely. The following have been on and off the shelf with great speed and are regarded as trusted friends:

British Civil Aircraft Register 1919-1999, Michael Austin, Air-Britain, 1999
British Military Aircraft Directory, Bob Dunn and Mick Boulanger, Wolverhampton Aviation Group, 2002 and their wonderful monthly updates for WAG members – www.wolverhamptonaviationgroup.co.uk
Combat Codes, Vic Flintham and Andrew Thomas, Airlife, 2003
Fleet Air Arm Fixed-Wing Aircraft since 1946, Ray Sturtivant with Mick Burrow and Lee Howard, Air-Britain, 2004 – a masterpiece!
Jet Airliner Production List, Tony Eastwood and John Roach, The Aviation Hobby Shop, Volume One, Boeing 1997, Volume Two, the rest, 1995
Military Airfields of the British Isles 1939-1945 (Omnibus Edition), Steve Willis and Barry Holliss, self-published, 1987
Phillip's Navigator Road Atlas, Phillip's, 2005
Piston Airliner Production List, Tony Eastwood and John Roach, The Aviation Hobby Shop, 2002
Pooleys Flight Guide, Robert Pooley and Roy Patel, Pooleys Flight Equipment, 2006
Royal Air Force Aircraft XA100 to XZ999, Jim Halley, Air-Britain, 2001 – and others in the series
Royal Air Force Flying Training and Support Units, Ray Sturtivant, John Hamlin and James J Halley, Air-Britain, 1997
Royal Navy Instructional Airframes, Ray Sturtivant and Rod Burden, British Aviation Research Group/Air-Britain, 1997
Squadrons of the Fleet Air Arm, Ray Sturtivant, Air-Britain, 1984
Squadrons of the Royal Air Force 1918-1988, Jim Halley, Air-Britain, 1988
Survivors 2002, Roy Blewett, Gatwick Aviation Society / Aviation Classics, 2002
Turbo-Prop Airliner Production List, Tony Eastwood and John Roach, The Aviation Hobby Shop, 2003
United Kingdom and Eire Civil Registers, Barry Womersley, Air-Britain, 2005
Warbirds Directory, 4th Edition, Geoff Goodall, published by Derek Macphail, 2003
70 Years of the Irish Civil Register, Peter J Hornfeck, Britten-Norman Historians, 1999

LOST and FOUND!

'Evicted' from its traditional slot at the back of the book, this section seeks to get readers scratching around to solve some of the many 'unfinished' stories within the pages of *W&R*. The ultimate aim is to 'find' these, and this mostly takes the form of a confirmed scrapping, or similar. Note that, as with all of the book, the criterion for an aircraft entering LOST! or FOUND! is a *physical* input and not an assumption or interpretation of registration changes etc. Over to YOU!

Lost! G-AFZE Heath Parasol and an anonymous Bensen gyroplane both last noted at **Horley**, Surrey, 11-93; **G-ARBG** Nipper II last noted at **Felthorpe**, Norfolk, 5-91; **G-ASMO** Apache 160G last noted at **Wallington Green**, Gtr Lon, 7-96 – *possibly* to Surrey; **G-ASNN** Cessna 182F para-trainer, last noted at **Tilstock**, Shrop, 1-98; **G-ASUE** Cessna 150D last noted at **West Thurrock**, Essex, 6-94; **G-AXCI** Bensen B.8M; last noted at **Lichfield**, Staffs, 9-93; **G-AXWF** Cessna F.172H hulk last noted at **Clavering**, Essex, 7-95; **G-AYFJ** Rallye Club last noted at **West Thurrock**, Essex, 6-94; **G-BAYV** ('F-OTAN-6') Noralpha last noted at **Eccleston**, Lancs, 1-99; **G-MBTY American Eagle**, last noted at **Camberley**, Surrey, 2-96; Anonymous Mignet HM.21 last noted in the **Hatfield**, Herts, area 10-94; **WH914** Canberra B.92 last noted at **Samlesbury**, Lancs, in deep store 9-91; **'XN493' (XN137)** Jet Provost T.3, last noted at **Camberley**, Surrey, 9-93; **XR436** SARO P.531-2 last noted at **Middle Wallop**, Hants, 7-90; **XR726** Lightning F.6 nose, last noted in the Harrogate, N Yorks, area 3-93; **ES1-16** Jungmeister last noted at **Stretton**, Cheshire, 3-94.

Found! XG544 Sycamore HR.14 last at Lower Tremar, Cornwall, and noted as being sold in 'Wales' 11-00 and sent to lost! in *W&R19*. The direction was way off! It was noted in the static at the opening of the new terminal at Zurich Airport, **Switzerland**, 11-8-04!

About *Wrecks & Relics*

Scope: *Wrecks & Relics* serves to outline, in as much detail as possible, the status and whereabouts of all known PRESERVED (ie in museum or other collections, under restoration etc); INSTRUCTIONAL (ie static airframes in use for training); and DERELICT (ie out of use for a long period of time, fire dump aircraft, scrapped or damaged etc) aircraft in the United Kingdom and Ireland and HM Forces aircraft based on Crown Territory. Where information permits, all aircraft that fall into these categories are included, with the following exceptions:

- Airworthy aircraft not part of a specific collection.
- Aircraft that fall into any of the above categories for only a short period of time - generally less than a year.
- Aircraft without provision for a human pilot, below the size of the GAF Jindivik drone or Fieseler Fi 103 'buzz-bomb'.
- In general, aircraft will only be considered if they are at least a cockpit/nose section.

Locations: Are listed by county/province and then alphabetically. County Boundaries are as given by the Ordnance Survey and as defined by the Local Government Act and include the changes confirmed up to April 2001.
    The entries for both Scotland and Wales are purely an alphabetic listing, primarily to help the English! From 1st April 1996 all of Scotland and all of Wales were wholly divided into 'Single Tier' Unitary Authorities, with their previously-held 'Counties' now having little meaning.
    Directions are given after each place name. Readers should note that these are *to the town or village mentioned* and **not** necessarily to the actual site of the aircraft in question. Directions are *not* given in the following instances:

- Where the location is a large city or town.
- Where specific directions to the site are not fully known.
- At the request of several aircraft owners - who have every right to preserve their peace and quiet as well as their aircraft - some locations have been 'generalised'.

    A form of notation relating to the status of an 'aerodrome' is given. Bearing in mind that in the Air Navigation Order *all* places where flying is conducted are known as aerodromes, a wider interpretation has been employed:
'Aerodrome' signifies a civilian flying ground used by aircraft up to King Air, 'biz-jet' etc size.
'Airfield' is used to signify a flying ground used by the armed forces, test establishments or manufacturers.
'Airport' is used to denote a flying ground that takes 'serious' sized airliners on a regular basis.
Please note: For privacy and security purposes, private strips etc are frequently *not* denoted as such.

Access: Unless otherwise stated, all locations in this work are PRIVATE and access to them *is strictly by prior permission, if at all*. A mention in this book does not imply any right of access. Museum opening times etc are given as a *guide only* and readers are advised to contact the museum in question *before* setting out on a journey.
◆ Used to highlight access and contact details. Details beyond this explain times of admission or who to apply to if prior permission is needed. Occasionally used to draw attention to locations that particularly *do not* allow access or where prior permission is required. Contact details, starting with the postal address for enquiries - a stamped addressed envelope would be most helpful. Then, if applicable, come: *daytime* telephone number(s), faxes, recorded information lines, e-mail addresses and web-sites, where applicable. Note that with web-sites, these are given for information only, no recommendation of content is meant, or to be implied.

Entries and Aircraft Listings: Generally, entries are all dealt with in a standard manner. As W&R covers a two year period, in this case 2004 to 2006, beyond the location header there is a narrative explaining the current status of the entry and outlining any airframes that have moved since the last edition. This narrative frequently and randomly includes discourses on life, the universe and everything! Airframes moving on are given underlined forwarding references, including the county, or province, that reference can be found in. This allows the reader to follow the more energetic examples around the book!
    'Ownership' or 'custodianship' of airframes within this work is not to be inferred as definitive.
    Any aircraft which fall out of any of the four categories above, or are exported, will not have forwarding references and their entry should be considered closed. The LOST! section acts as a 'safety net' for aircraft that have no determined fate. A few sample entries from the main text may help to familiarise readers with the data presented:

Col 1	Col 2	Column 3	3a	Column 4	Column 5	Col 6
❑ G-AFIR*		Luton Minor		ex Cobham, Rearsby. CoA 30-7-71		1-06
❑ DNB	2238	Grunau Baby IIb		ex Bicester, RAFGSA380, D-8039		12-99
❑ –	BAPC.295	Da Vinci 'REP'		built by Skysport, 2003. Stored	[1]	3-04
❑ 5N-AWD		HS.125-1		ex G-ASSI. Fire crews	[1]	10-00
❑ XV140	'K'	Scout AH.1		ex G-KAXL, ex Fleetlands	®	7-03
❑ XV748	'3D'	Harrier GR.3	✈	ex Bedford, 233 OCU, 1, 233 OCU, 1. Sectioned		3-04
❑ –*		Typhoon I		ex Chippenham. Forward fuselage		4-06
❑ –*	TAD.001	Gazelle CIM		ex Middle Wallop. First noted 5-96		12-03
❑ 153008		F-4N-MC		ex VF-154 - USS *Coral Sea*. ABDR		11-01

Columns 1 and 2: Aircraft are listed alpha-numerically, using the following rubric. British civil first (except in Ireland where EI- comes first), followed by British Gliding Association (BGA) and 'B Condition' (or 'trade plate') markings and (from this edition) British Aviation Preservation Council (BAPC) identities for otherwise 'anonymous' airframes. (Please note that, from this edition, the BGA 'tri-gram' identifiers are presented in Column 1 with the BGA number allocation given in Column 2.) Then overseas civil registrations in alpha-numeric order. British military serials follow (with reversal again in Ireland) followed by overseas military listed by country – ie France before Netherlands before USA. Anonymous airframes are inserted where it is thought most logical! Incorrect or fictitious registrations and serials are marked in quotes, eg 'VZ999' or 'G-BKEN'. Codes worn by aircraft are given in column two, eg 'AF-V' or '825'. Entries new to a heading in this edition are marked *. A dash (–) is used to denote an airframe that has no confirmed primary identity.

Registrations or serials, where applicable, are given a two-column treatment. Column 1 gives the *primary* identifier (if applicable). The primary identifier is most often the one *worn* on the airframe. The *secondary* identifier is a way of helping further identification of the airframe, most likely a code letter or number, or another form of identity that will help the reader 'place' the entry. Where space, permits, identities known not to be worn are given in Column 2, frequently leaving Column 1 empty. Note that other identities, present or previous, appear in Column 4.

Column 3 and 3a: Aircraft type/designation, frequently abbreviated. To acquaint readers with the nature of some of the types listed, some abbreviations and a symbol are used:

→ Believed airworthy, at time of going to press.

CIM Purpose-built instructional airframe, not intended for flight – Classroom Instruction Model, or even Module.

EMU Purpose-built test and evaluation airframe, not intended for flight, in most cases using prototype or production jigs and tooling – Engineering Mock-up.

FSM Full-scale model. Faithful external reproduction of an aircraft, but using construction techniques completely unrelated to the original – frequently in fibreglass.

PAX Cockpit for crew emergency egress training, mostly (now retired) Chipmunk T.10s – Passenger (= PAX) Trainer.

REP Reproduction, ie a faithful, or near-faithful copy or a facsimile of an aircraft type. Occasionally built to a different scale, but using construction techniques and proportions in keeping with the original. In the past, the author has used the word 'replica' but in strict usage the only people who can make a replica is the design company involved and in the aviation world, very few such instances exist. (The Yak-3UAs that came out of Orenburg, Russia, from the direct lineage of the Yakovlev OKB, are examples of 'true' replicas.)

Column 4: Where possible, brief historical details of the aircraft listed are given, in a necessarily abbreviated form. In each case, units, operators, previous identities etc are listed in *reverse* order, ie the last user (or identity) is given first. Seasoned readers should have little trouble with these potted histories. Space restrictions this time mean that the **'Abbreviations' section has been jettisoned** to save weight on approach. The 'Abbreviations' section in any previous edition will decode the 'history' section. If any reader needs a decode, please *write in* to the author with an SAE and he'll happily send you a print out of abbreviations used in *W&R* with his compliments. Also given here are other registrations, or maintenance serials applicable to the airframe. Note that Royal Navy maintenance serials, 'A' numbers were reallocated, creating a somewhat confusing vista. Second, third or even fourth allocations are known and are noted in square brackets after the 'A' serial [3]. Readers should refer to the masterful BARG/Air-Britain *Royal Navy Instructional Airframes* for the 'Full Monty'. Where a date is given prefixed 'CoA' (Certificate of Airworthiness), this is the date at which it lapsed and is given as an *indication* of how long the airframe has been flightless. The term 'CoA' is used for all levels of certification, eg Permit to Fly, Ferry Permit etc. Where an airframe has suffered an accident, this is given as 'Crashed' or 'Cr', no attempt has been made to try to delineate the severity, or nature, of the incident.

Column 5: Used to denote an aircraft known to be undergoing a restoration or conservation programme at time of going to press, with the symbol ®. Also used for footnotes – eg [7] – to refer readers back up to the narrative section for specific details on that airframe.

Column 6: 'Last noted' dates are given primarily to help historians to trace the history (or demise) of an airframe and perhaps to alert readers intending to visit the airframe involved as to the 'currency' of the information given. The listing of these dates, it is hoped, will persuade some readers and some of the less enlightened enthusiast and professional magazines to actually note the dates of sightings/reports in future jottings – the *date* of an observation can be a crucial form of evidence in many cases. Physical, first-hand reports – instead of assumptions and handed-on information – are vital for the monitoring of our aviation heritage.

Wrecks & Relics is put together using the best information available to the Author. Every effort is made to be as accurate as possible. However, neither the Author nor Midland Publishing can be held responsible for any errors or changes that may occur in the location or status of aircraft or places listed.

PART ONE
ENGLAND

Bedfordshire 10 - 14
Berkshire 14 - 19
Buckinghamshire 19 - 22
Cambridgeshire 22 - 34
Cheshire 34 - 36
Cornwall 36 - 39
Cumbria 39 - 42
Derbyshire 42 - 43
Devon 43 - 48
Dorset 48 - 51
Durham & Cleveland 52
Essex 52 - 61
Gloucestershire 61 - 68
Hampshire 68 - 80
Herefordshire 80 - 81
Hertfordshire 81 - 84

Isle of Man 84 - 85
Isle of Wight 85 - 86
Kent 86 - 92
Lancashire 92 - 95
Leicestershire 95 - 96, 129 - 135
Lincolnshire 135 - 144
Greater London 145 - 153
Greater Manchester 154 - 157
Merseyside 157 - 158
West Midlands 158 - 160
Norfolk 161 - 168
Northamptonshire 168 - 170
Northumberland
  & Tyneside 171 - 173
Nottinghamshire 173 - 178
Oxfordshire 178 - 180

Shropshire 180 - 190
Somerset 190 - 198
Staffordshire 199 - 202
Suffolk 202 - 209
Surrey 209 - 215
East Sussex 215 - 217
West Sussex 217 - 222
Warwickshire 222 - 224, 257 - 260
Wiltshire 260 - 265
Worcestershire 265 - 267
East Yorkshire 267 - 270
North Yorkshire 270 - 274
South Yorkshire 275 - 279
West Yorkshire 279 - 280

Map by Mary Denton

BEDFORDSHIRE

BEDFORD

Bedford College: Located adjacent to Cauldwell Street. Cessna F.172H G-AVCC was replaced by the Scout. At *least* the tail section moved to Ipswich, Suffolk.

❑ [XM473]	Jet Provost T.3A	ex Norwich Airport 'G-TINY', Halton 8974M, 7 FTS, 1 FTS, 7 FTS, 1 FTS, CFS, 3 FTS, 1 FTS	9-05
❑ XP854	Scout AH.1	ex Ipswich, Wattisham, Middle Wallop TAD.043 / 7898M. Crashed 15-5-65	9-05
❑ XX495*	'C' Jetstream T.1	ex Shawbury, Cranwell, 45, 3 FTS, 45, 6 FTS, METS. First noted 12-05	12-05

Others: Autocrat G-AJUD moved to Doncaster, S Yorks, during the summer of 2005.

❑ G-AGTT	J/1 Autocrat	CoA 11-2-93. Stored	12-97
❑ 1367	Chipmunk T.20	G-BYYW, ex CS-DAR, Spanhoe, Viseu, Port AF. Stored	2-00

BEDFORD AIRFIELD or Thurleigh, north of Bedford, east of the A6

Thurleigh is remembered at the **306th Bomb Group Museum** established in the wartime Small Arms and Ammunition Store and very much worth a visit. There is a wealth of material to see and the location affords great views of what was an astounding airfield.

◆ *Follow 'Bedford Autodrome' and Technology Park signs from A6. Open weekends and Bank Holidays, 1st March to 31st October 10.30am to 4pm, or by prior arrangement. Ralph Franklin, National School Cottage, Mill Hill, Keysoe, MK44 2HP tel 01234 708715 e-mail 306museum@nscmh.fset.co.uk www.306bg.co.uk*

CRANFIELD AERODROME east of Newport Pagnell

Cranfield Institute of Technology (CIT) / **College of Aeronautics** / **Cranfield Aerospace Ltd**: The low-loader based HS.125 has had its registration doctored to read G-DHEA. One possible 'translation' of this could be De Havilland Executive Aircraft! [1] Jetstream G-NFLC was ferried to Perth, Scotland, by December 2004.

❑ G-AWBT	Twin Com' 160B	ex N8508Y. Damaged 10-3-88. Inst airframe		1-06
❑ G-AZXG	Aztec 250D	ex Little Snoring, N6963Y. Crashed 25-10-91. Inst		1-06
❑ 'G-DHEA'	HS.125-3B/RA	G-OHEA, ex Hatfield, G-AVRG, G-5-12. Dump	[1]	1-06
❑ G-RAVL	Jetstream 200	ex G-AWVK, N1035S, G-AWVK. CoA 26-2-94		1-06

T5 Alive: (formerly T5 Projects) Russell Carpenter acquired XS458 from Tony Hulls in 2001. The wonderful machine is kept 'in steam' and regularly taxis.

◆ *Located on an active airfield, visits are not possible without prior arrangement.*

❑ XS458	'T' Lightning T.5	ex Binbrook, LTF, 11, LTF, 5-11 pool, LTF, 5, 226 OCU		1-06

Others: Several references here are now long-in-the-tooth and bound for LOST! [1]

❑ G-BAEW	Cessna F.172M	ex N12798. Crashed 12-11-93. Fuselage	[1]	3-96
❑ G-BALI	DR.400 2+2	ex Meppershall. CoA 3-9-88	[1]	3-96
❑ G-BAUJ	Aztec 250E	ex N14390. CoA 25-7-94. Stored		1-06
❑ G-BCUW*	Cessna F.177RG	ex SE-GKL. CoA 12-5-00. Canx 18-8-04		8-05
❑ G-BDUX	Motor Cadet	CoA 23-2-84. Stored in trailer	[1]	7-90
❑ G-BMSG	SAAB Lansen	ex VAT area, Swedish AF, Malmslatt, Fv32028. Stored		1-06
❑ G-NITA	Cherokee 180C	ex G-AVVG, N7517W. CoA 17-11-97		1-06
❑ G-SADE	Cessna F.150L	ex G-AZJW. CoA 21-9-97		1-06
❑ G-SHIV	GA-7 Cougar	ex N713G. CoA 18-1-98		1-06
❑ BXR	1321 L 13 Blanik	ex G-ATPX. Stored, in trailer	[1]	7-97
❑ CYR	1917 L 13 Blanik	crashed 8-7-90. Original fuselage	[1]	7-97

DUNSTABLE

David Underwood: Acquired a Luton Minor in October 2005. (See also Eaton Bray, Beds.)

❑ G-ASEA*	Luton Minor	CoA 16-8-89. Arrived 12-10-05	10-05

DUNSTABLE AERODROME on the B489 south-east of Dunstable

❏ G-BLGS	Rallye 180T	ex Lasham. CoA 21-5-99. Stripped out		6-05
❏ PH-MSB	Rallye Club	G-OIAN. Canx 2-9-91	off-site	5-01

EATON BRAY west of Dunstable

Peter and **David Underwood**: Kite I ACH (BGA.400) was flying by mid-2004 and is the only genuine World War Two glider still flying in original colours. T.21B BCF was exported to Poland on 12th October 2005, along with another acquired from Camphill, Derbyshire. (See under Dunstable, Beds, for David's Luton Minor.)

❏ AAF*	236	T.6 Kite I	ex Woburn Sands, Dunstable, G-ALUD, BGA.236,		
			BGA.222. Stored		7-04
❏ ALZ	493	Dagling	BAPC.81, Dunstable, Duxford, Warton	®	7-04
❏ DNB	2238	Grunau Baby IIb	ex Bicester, RAFGSA380, D-8039		7-04

HATCH off the B658, south-west of Sandy

Skysport Engineering: Tiger Moth N6720 (G-BYTN) flew following restoration in August 2004. The RAF Museum's Miles Mohawk has returned for a further spell of restoration. Tim Moore and team have a DH.2 REP in its early stages. Skysport built a version of a Leonardo da Vinci hang-glider for the Channel 4 TV documentary *Leonardo's Dream Machines* and this is stored on site [1].

    Notes: Tiger G-ACDA is being worked on for Bryn Hughes [2]. The EoN Primary is stored for the Shuttleworth Collection, it was last noted under Duxford, Cambs, in *W&R15* (p32) [3]. The Demon is for Demon Displays Ltd. It is reported to be a composite with the front end of a former Irish Air Corps Hector. This would almost certainly be the one that was at Cloughjordan, Ireland [4].

◆ *Access strictly by prior permission only.*

❏ G-ACDA	Tiger Moth	ex Chilbolton, BB724, G-ACDA. Crashed 27-6-79	[2]	10-99
❏ [G-AEKW]*	Mohawk	ex Cosford, Hatch, Wyton, USA, Tablada, Spain, HM503,		
		MCCS, Turnhouse SF, G-AEKW. Arrived by 8-04	®	8-04
❏ 'G-AMXA'*	Comet C.2R	XK655, ex Gatwick, Hatch, Carlisle, Maryport, Carlisle,		
		Lutterworth, Strathallan, 51, BOAC, G-AMXA ntu.		
		Nose. BOAC c/s. Arrived 28-1-04 (?)		6-05
❏ G-DINT	Beaufighter I	ex Halton, 3858M, X7688, 29, 153		8-00
❏ G-FORD*	SNCAN SV-4C	ex Chilbolton, F-BBNS. Crashed 16-7-96	®	5-05
❏ AQQ*	580 EoN Primary	ex ?, Duxford, Henlow, Twinwood Farm, G-ALPS. Stored	[3]	12-05
❏ -	BAPC.295 Da Vinci 'REP'	built by Skysport, 2003. Stored	[1]	3-04
❏ F-BGNR	Viscount 708	ex Perth, Air Inter. Stored		11-04
❏ N5595T	C-47A-85-DL	ex Thruxton, Blackbushe, G-BGCG, Spanish AF T3-27,		
		N49V, N50322, 43-15536. Stored		8-00
❏ K8203	Demon I	G-BTVE, ex Cardington, 2292M, 9 BGS, 9 AOS, 64.		
		64 Sqn colours. Rolled-out 5-05	® [4]	5-05
❏ -*	Demon I	frame		2-06
❏ -	Stampe SV-4	ex Spanhoe Lodge, Les Mureaux. Forward fuselage		11-97

HENLOW AIRFIELD on the A6007 south-west of Biggleswade

RAF Henlow: The Hunter guards the station.

❏ WT612	Hunter F.1	ex Halton, Credenhill 7496M, Hawker, AAEE. Gate	3-06

Others: Vampire T.11 XE856 (G-DUSK) moved to <u>Bournemouth</u>, Dorset, on 6th September 2005.

❏ G-AFOB*	Moth Minor	ex Dorchester, Old Warden, X5117, 10 OAFU,		
		StA UAS, 613, G-AFOB. CoA 11-5-93	®	2-02

LONDON (LUTON) AIRPORT

On 12th September 2005 JetStar VP-BLD ended well over a year of external storage when it got up and flew away to Toulouse, France, reportedly for a museum. The fire training area borders Wigmore Valley Park. Last noted with the fire crews in October 2000, HS.125-1 5N-AWD moved to a farm near St Paul's Walden, west of Stevenage, Herts, for a crash rescue exercise, probably in 2002. It is believed it was consumed, and/or scrapped afterwards. But never leave a stone unturned...

❏ G-AOVS	Britannia 312	ex Redcoat, 'G-BRAC', Lloyd, BOAC. CoA 31-7-79.	
		Fuselage. Fire crews	11-05

LOWER STONDON west of the A600/Henlow aerodrome, north of Hitchin

Stondon Transport Museum: A superb collection of 400-plus motor vehicles and other transport artefacts, including a full-scale replica of HMS *Endeavour* and a coffee shop and gift shop.

◆ *Open daily, 10am to 5pm. Signed off the A600. Station Road, Lower Stondon, Henlow, SG16 6JN tel 01462 850339 e-mail info@transportmuseum.co.uk www.transportmuseum.co.uk*

❏ 'G-ADRG'	HM.14 'Flea'	BAPC.77, ex Cheltenham, Long Marston,	
		Innsworth, Ross-on-Wye, Staverton	4-06
❏ G-AXOM	Penn-Smith gyro	wfu 11-10-74	4-06
❏ XN341	Skeeter AOP.12	8002M, ex Luton, St Athan, 4 SoTT, 3 RTR, 651	4-06

LUTON AIRPORT - see under London Airport (Luton) above.

MEPPERSHALL AERODROME south of the A507, west of Stotfold

❏ G-BBTK*	Cessna FRA.150L	ex Bagby. Canx 26-11-03. Stored. First noted 12-04	12-04

OLD WARDEN AERODROME west of Biggleswade, signposted from the A1

Shuttleworth Collection: The former Hangar No.2 has been turned into a very impressive and spacious visitor centre and the already good restaurant further improved. As well as the tremendous aircraft collection, there is the Swiss Garden; the Bird of Prey Centre and Owl Sanctuary; Jubilee Play Centre; Woodland Walk and Conservation Area, making this a great 'all-comers' venue. (Additional entrance fees apply for some of these, but combination tickets are available.)

Notes: Wren G-EBNV is mostly the unregistered No.4 with engine parts from the original G-EBNV (Lympne No.3) [1]. The Aero Vintage Bristol F.2b [2] is resident in readiness for flight – its Rolls-Royce Falcon was installed late in 2005. Provost XF603 carries the markings of an example on delivery to the Sultan of Oman's Air Force [3]. The Me 163B Komet full-scale model includes an original Walter HWK 509A-2 rocket motor [4]. See also Northern Aeroplane Workshops under Batley, W Yorks. See under Hatfield, Herts, for 'another' G-ACSS [5]. Old Warden Airfield Volunteer Fire Service has a Piper Tomahawk fuselage for training [6]. See also under Hatch, Beds, for the collection's EoN Primary.

Several aircraft are on loan to the Shuttleworth Collection: Terry Adams: Turbi G-AOTK; Sir John Allison: Gemini G-AKKH and the Fauvel; Atlantic Connexions: Silvaire G-BSYF; BAE Systems: Moth G-EBLV and Avro XIX G-AHKX; Don Cashmore: Cygnet repro G-CAMM; Pat Donovan: the Po-2 acquired by SVAS for OW??; Peter Holloway: Falcon Major G-AEEG, Hawk Trainer V1075 and Ryan PT-22 '854'; Skysport: the Wallace frame; Andrew Wood: Dove G-EAGA. All are marked ‡.

Departures: Messenger G-AKBO to Enstone, Oxfordshire, by May 2005; Hornet Moth W9385 (G-ADND) flew off to owners in the Bristol area in December 2005.

◆ *Open daily throughout the year, but is closed for up to 14 days covering Xmas Eve, and up to and including New Year's Day. Open April to October 10am to 5pm, November to March 10am to 4pm. Supporting the collection in many ways is the **Shuttleworth Veteran Aeroplane Society** (SVAS) which has an extensive series of activities during the year, is a major fund-raiser for the collection, publishes the excellent Prop-Swing, and welcomes new members. Address as below. Old Warden Aerodrome, Biggleswade, Beds, SG18 9EP tel 01767 627927 fax 01767 927949 e-mail collection@shuttleworth.com www.shuttleworth.org*

❑ G-EAGA		Sopwith Dove ✈	ex Hatch, G-BLOO ntu, Australia, G-EAGA, K-157	‡ 4-04
❑ G-EBHX		Humming Bird ✈	ex Lympne No 8. *L'Oiseau Mouche*	4-06
❑ G-EBIR		DH.51 ✈	ex VP-KAA, G-KAA, G-EBIR. *Miss Kenya*	4-06
❑ G-EBJO		ANEC II ✈	ex Radcliffe on Trent, Old Warden, Lympne No 7. ff 9-3-04	4-06
❑ G-EBLV		DH.60 Moth ✈	ex Hatfield	‡ 4-06
❑ [G-EBNV]	'4'	EE Wren	BAPC.11. CoA 23-6-87	[1] 4-06
❑ G-EBWD		DH.60X Moth ✈	Bought by Richard Shuttleworth in 1932	4-06
❑ G-AAIN		Parnall Elf II ✈	ex Southend, Fairoaks, Badminton	® 4-06
❑ [G-AANG]		Blériot XI ✈	No.14, BAPC.3, ex Ampthill, Hendon	4-06
❑ [G-AANH]		Deperdussin ✈	No.43, BAPC.4, ex Ampthill. CoA 14-5-83	4-06
❑ [G-AANI]		Blackburn Mon ✈	No.9, BAPC.5, ex Wittering	4-06
❑ G-AAPZ		Desoutter I ✈	ex Higher Blagdon, Old Warden	4-06
❑ G-AAYX		Southern Martlet ✈	ex Woodford	4-06
❑ G-ABAG		DH.60 Moth ✈	ex Perth	4-06
❑ G-ABXL*		Archaeopteryx	ex Radcliffe on Trent, Old Warden, Chilwell. CoA 22-9-82. Stored, off-site	12-05
❑ G-ACSS	'34'	DH.88 Comet	ex Hatfield, Farnborough, Old Warden, Leavesden, K5084, G-ACSS. *Grosvenor House.* Damaged 28-10-02	® [5] 4-06
❑ G-ACTF		Comper Swift ✈	ex Rhos, VT-ADO. *The Scarlet Angel.* CoA 6-10-90	4-06
❑ G-AEBB		HM.14 'Flea'	ex Southampton. CoA 31-5-39. Taxies	4-06
❑ G-AEEG		Falcon Major ✈	ex Turweston, SE-AFN, RSwAF Fv913, SE-AFN, G-AEEG, U-20	‡ 4-06
❑ G-AHKX		Avro XIX Srs 2 ✈	ex Woodford, Strathallan, Kemps, Treffield, Smiths	‡ 4-06
❑ G-AKKH*		Gemini 1A ✈	ex Halton, Abingdon, OO-CDO. F/n 6-04	‡ 4-06
❑ G-AOTK*		Druine Turbi ✈	ex Henlow. First noted 6-04	‡ 4-06
❑ [G-ARSG]		Triplane REP ✈	BAPC.1, ex *Those Magnificent Men...* Hants A/C built	4-06
❑ [G-ASPP]		Boxkite REP ✈	BAPC.2, ex *Those Magnificent Men…* Miles-built	4-06
❑ G-BSYF*		Silvaire 8A ✈	ex N71415. First noted 6-04	‡ 6-04
❑ G-CAMM	'6'	Cygnet REP ✈	ex Hucknall, G-ERDB ntu	‡ 4-06
❑ ETE*	2932	Fauvel AV.36C	ex Halton, RAFGSA.53, D-5353, D-8259. *The Budgie.* CoA 6-98. Arrived by 4-04	9-05
❑ –	BAPC.8	Dixon Orni'	–	3-04
❑ D-EGLW		Tomahawk 112	fuselage, fire crews	[6] 3-04
❑ [ZK-POZ]		Po-2 (CSS-13) ✈	ex New Zealand. Soviet colours	‡ ® 4-06
❑ '9917'		Sopwith Pup ✈	G-EBKY, ex 'N6181', N5180. Repaint and Le Prieur rockets by 5-05, first flown 16-7-05.	4-06
❑ 'C4918'		Bristol M.1C REP ✈	G-BWJM. 72 Sqn c/s	4-06
❑ D7889		Bristol F.2b	G-AANM, ex St Leonards-on-Sea, Sandown, St Leonards-on-Sea, Old Warden BAPC.166, Weston-on-the-Green	[2] 4-06
❑ D8096		Bristol F.2b ✈	G-AEPH, ex Filton, Watford, D8096, 208	4-06
❑ F904	'H'	SE.5A ✈	G-EBIA, ex 'D7000', Farnborough, Whitley, G-EBIA, F904 84 Sqn. 56 Sqn colours	4-06
❑ H5199		Avro 504K ✈	G-ADEV, ex G-ACNB, 'E3404' and Avro 504N	4-06
❑ K1786		Tomtit ✈	G-AFTA, ex 5 GCF, 23 GCF, 3 FTS	4-06
❑ 'K3241'		Tutor ✈	G-AHSA, ex K3215, HSA, RAFC. CFS colours	® 4-06
❑ 'K5414'		Hind (Afghan) ✈	G-AENP, BAPC.78. ex 'K5457', Kabul	4-06
❑ N3788		Magister I ✈	G-AKPF, ex 'V1075', Shoreham, Sandown, Shoreham, V1075, 16 EFTS. Complex composite	4-06
❑ 'N6290'		Sop Triplane ✈	G-BOCK, ex Dewsbury. 8 Sqn RNAS c/s, *Dixie II*	4-06
❑ P6382		Magister I ✈	G-AJRS, ex 'G-AJDR', P6382, 3 EFTS, 16 EFTS	® 4-06
❑ T6818	'19'	Tiger Moth II ✈	G-ANKT, ex Aston Down, 21 EFTS	® 4-06
❑ 'V9367'	'MA-B'	Lysander III ✈	G-AZWT, ex 'V9441', Duxford, Strathallan, RCAF 2355. 161 Squadron colours	4-06
❑ Z7015	'7-L'	Sea Hurricane I ✈	G-BKTH, ex Duxford, Staverton, Old Warden, Loughborough, Yeovilton, 759, 880. 880 Sqn c/s	4-06
❑ AR501	'NN-A'	Spitfire V ✈	G-AWII, ex Duxford, Henlow, Loughborough, CGS, 61 OTU, 1 TEU, 58 OTU, 422, 312, 504, 310. 310 c/s	® 4-06

❑ VS610	'K-L'	Prentice T.1		G-AOKL, ex Bassingbourn, VS610, 1 FTS, 22 FTS, RAFC, 22 FTS. CoA 20-9-96	® 4-06
❑ XA241		Grasshopper TX.1		ex Cambridge, Croydon	4-04
❑ XF603		Provost T.1	✈	G-KAPW, ex Cranfield, Filton, Bristol, 27 MU, CAW, RAFC. RAF grey / green camo	[3] 4-06
❑ '18671'		Chipmunk 22		G-BNZC, ex G-ROYS, 7438M, WP905 CFS,	
			✈	664, RAFC. RCAF colours	4-06
❑ '4477'		Jungmann 2000		G-RETA, ex North Weald, Spanish AF E3B-305.	
	'GD+EG'		✈	First flew 8-04	4-06
❑ '191454'		Me 163B FSM		BAPC.271. Wingless	[4] 4-04
❑ '423'		Gladiator I	✈	G-AMRK, ex L8032, 'N2308', L8032, 'K8032',	
and '427'				Gloster, Hamble, 8 MU, 61 OTU, 1624F, 2 AACU. Norwegian AF c/s. '423' port, '427' stb	4-06
❑ 854*	G-BTBH	Ryan PT-22	✈	ex N8541, N50993, 41-20854. Arrived 5-04	‡ 4-06
❑ –		Wallace REP		ex Hatch. Fuselage frame	‡ 4-04

SANDY on the A1 north of Biggleswade

Last noted here in December 1997, Pitts S-1S G-AXNZ is now displayed at Haskoy Dockyard, Istanbul, Turkey.

TWINWOOD FARM near Clapham, off the A6 north of Bedford

Glen Miller Museum and Twinwood Control Tower: The refurbished tower has been turned into a Glen Miller 'shrine' and the top floor into a representation of how it would have been when Miller climbed into the ill-fated Noorduyn Norseman and departed for the Continent in 1944. A series of regular events are staged on the site, including concerts.

◆ *Open weekends and Bank Holidays 10.30am to 4pm. Closed January and February. Twinwood Events, Twinwood Road, Clapham, Beds, MK41 6AB tel 01234 350413 fax 01234 826255 e-mail info@twinwoodevents.com www.twinwoodevents.com*

BERKSHIRE

ARBORFIELD on the A327 south of Reading

Princess Marina College / School of Electrical and Aeronautical Engineering (SEAE - see under Cosford, Shrop, for a glimpse of the future.) Within Hazebrouck Barracks, SEAE maintain a detachment at Middle Wallop, Hants, which see. TAD stands for Technical Aid and Demonstrator – but there are other interpretations! Purpose-built instructional airframes and teaching aids are also known as 'CIMs' – Classroom Instructional Models. By July 2004 Gazelle AH.1 ZB668 had migrated to Middle Wallop, Hants, but had returned by September 2005 +.

Departures: Gazelle AH.1 XZ305 to Middle Wallop, Hants, by 10-04; AH.1 ZB678 was at Middle Wallop, Hants, by 2-04, then Fleetlands, Hants, by 2005, but then moved to Shawbury, Shrop, 29-4-05.

❑ XP848		Scout AH.1	ex Middle Wallop, Wroughton, 659, 669. Gate	9-05
❑ XP855		Scout AH.1	ex Wroughton, 652, 651, 655	9-05
❑ XP899		Scout AH.1	ex Middle Wallop, ARWF. Crashed 1-11-79	9-05
❑ XR601		Scout AH.1	ex BATUS, 657, 665, 666. Damaged 26-8-79	9-05
❑ XT623		Scout AH.1	ex Wroughton, 655, 659, 655	9-05
❑ XT633		Scout AH.1	ex Wroughton, 659, 653, 661, 660, Wroughton	9-05
❑ XV124	'W'	Scout AH.1	ex Middle Wallop, Arborfield, Middle Wallop, Wroughton, 656, 653, 654	9-05
❑ XV141		Scout AH.1	ex Wroughton, 657, 659, 654, 661. REME museum	7-04
❑ [XW838]		Lynx 1-03	TAD.009, ex Middle Wallop, Yeovil	9-05
❑ [XW860]		Gazelle HT.2	TAD.021, ex Middle Wallop, Fleetlands, Wroughton, 705	9-05

❏ [XW863]	Gazelle HT.2	TAD.022, ex Middle Wallop, Wroughton, 705	9-05
❏ [XW888]	Gazelle AH.1	TAD.017, ex Middle Wallop, ARWF, GCF	9-05
❏ XW889	Gazelle AH.1	TAD.018, ex Middle Wallop, ARWF, GCF	9-05
❏ [XW900]	Gazelle AH.1	TAD.900, ex Middle Wallop SEAE, 660. Cr 25-5-76	9-04
❏ XW912	Gazelle AH.1	TAD.019, ex Fleetlands, 655, 3 CBAS, 656, 655, 3 CBAS	5-05
❏ [XX387]	Gazelle AH.1	TAD.014, ex Fleetlands, 651, 661, 657, 16/5 Lancers. Crashed 15-12-95. Avionics and Systems trainer	9-05
❏ [XX454]	Gazelle AH.1	TAD.023, ex Waddington, M' Wallop, 663, 1 Rgt, 662, 656, 657, 4 Rgt, 3 Rgt, 4 Rgt, 659, 669, 664, 654, 4 Rgt, 669, 659	9-05
❏ XZ187*	Lynx AH.7	ex Fleetlands, 655, 667, 655, 667, 655, 651, 654. F/n 3-04	9-05
❏ XZ188	Lynx AH.7	ex Fleetlands, 4 Rgt, 654, 662, 655, 665, 655, LCF, 651	9-05
❏ XZ207*	Lynx AH.7	ex Fleetlands, 652, 9 Rgt, 669, 4 Rgt, 669, 655, 654. Crashed 17-4-00. First noted 3-04	9-05
❏ XZ325	'T' Gazelle AH.1	ex Middle Wallop, 670, 655, 3 Regt	9-05
❏ XZ332	Gazelle AH.1	ex Middle Wallop, 670, ARWF, 656, 664	9-05
❏ XZ333	Gazelle AH.1	ex Middle Wallop, 670, ARWF	9-05
❏ XZ666	Lynx AH.7	ex 669, 655, 665, 655, LCF, 651	9-05
❏ ZA735*	Gazelle AH.1	ex 25 Flt (since new!). First noted 7-04	9-05
❏ ZA769	'K' Gazelle AH.1	ex Middle Wallop, 670, ARWF	9-05
❏ ZB668*	Gazelle AH.1	TAD.015, ex Middle Wallop, Arborfield, Fleetlands, UNFICYP. Crashed 30-11-92. +	9-05
❏ [QP-30]	Lynx HC.28	TAD.013, ex Fleetlands, Almondbank, Wroughton, Qatar Police, G-BFDV	9-05
❏	TAD.001 Gazelle CIM	ex Middle Wallop. Cabin only	9-05
❏	TAD.002 Gazelle CIM	ex Middle Wallop	8-99
❏	TAD.007 Lynx CIM	ex Middle Wallop. Fuselage number TO.42	9-05
❏	TAD.008 Gazelle CIM	ex Middle Wallop. 'Engine/Control Systems' sim	2-01
❏	TAD.010 Lynx CIM	Cockpit. 'Engine/Control Systems' sim	2-01
❏	TAD.011 Lynx CIM	ex Middle Wallop	9-05
❏	TAD.012 Lynx CIM	ex Middle Wallop	9-05

BARKHAM south of the B3349, south-west of Wokingham

Barkham Antiques:

❏ G-KENN	Robinson R-22B	ex Stamford, Sandtoft. Damaged 31-10-94	7-01

BINFIELD north of the B3034, north-west of Bracknell

Amen Corner:

❏ G-ASXF	Brantly 305	ex Thruxton, Biggin Hill, CoA 16-2-79	10-04
❏ G-BJOD	HA-2M Sportster	ex Bracknell. Unflown?	7-01
❏ G-BPCJ	Cessna 150J	ex Solihull, Tattershall Thorpe, N61096. Dam 25-1-90. *Charlie*	10-04

GREENHAM COMMON north of the A339, south-east of Newbury

The former USAF base is now an extensive industrial estate. Within this, the aircraft associated with **Flying 'A' Services / Wizzard Investments Ltd** (that's double 'z') are believed to be kept inside one of the famed cruise-missile bunkers. See under Norwich, Norfolk, for their Seafire III restoration project. An amazing 'discovery' is that US-built SE.5A G-BLXT and once with the late Hon Patrick Lindsay at Booker is stored here. It was thought exported to the USA in 1989, but was cancelled from the UK register on 13th October 2000, with CoA expiry of 25th May 1994. It looks likely it never left these shores [1]. Spitfire XVI RW386 (G-BXVI) was sold and moved to Duxford, Cambs, on 7th July 2005. Contrary to *W&R19* (p15) the nose of Lincoln 2 G-29-1 did *not* come here – see under Martham, Norfolk. See under The Fighter Collection, Duxford, Cambs, for Spitfire XVIII G-BRAF and P-47G N47DG. The former was briefly here before moving onto TFC, while the latter is believed to have been with Warbirds of Great Britain etc since the early 1990s. The TF-51D must be a candidate for TFC [2].

◆ Not *available for public inspection.*

❑ [G-BLXT]*	Eberhart SE.5A	ex ?, ?, N4488, USAAS 22-296. CoA 25-5-94	[1]	6-05
❑ N9950	P-40N Warhawk	ex North Weald, ?, Biggin Hill, USA, USAAF 44-7983		2-04
❑ N33870	PT-19 Cornell	ex North Weald, G-BTNY, N33870, USAAF		1-04
❑ N7098V	TF-51D Mustang	ex North Weald, Biggin Hill, Chino, Israel AF/DF,		
		RCAF 9245, USAAF 44-73871	[2]	2-04
❑ NH238	Spitfire IX	G-MKIX, ex North Weald, ?, Bournemouth, Biggin Hill,		
		Bitteswell, N238V, Harlingen, Hemswell, Winthorpe,		
		Southampton, Andover, OO-ARE, Coxyde, Belg AF SM-36,		
		Dutch AF H-60, Sealand, 76 MU, 9 MU, 49 MU, 84 GSU		6-05

HUNGERFORD on the A4 east of Marlborough
Newbury Aeroplane Company: Des Penrose was at the controls when Hawk Trainer G-ADWT first flew on 7th May 2004. The Tiger is being restored to static condition for the Brooklands Museum [1].

❑ G-AAUP	Klemm L.25	*Clementine*. CoA 21-11-84. Stored		2-98
❑ G-AFGH	Chilton DW.1	ex Billingshurst. CoA 7-7-83	®	2-98
❑ F-BGEQ	Tiger Moth	ex Brooklands, Chessington, Brooklands,		
		Le Mans, French mil, NL846. Stored	® [1]	12-05

LAMBOURN on the B4000 north of Hungerford
In the general area is a *private* strip with several out-of-use or under restoration airframes.

❑ G-BILA		DA-165L Viking	ex Lower Upham, F-PPZE. CoA 14-9-83. Stored		12-05
❑ G-BMJY	'07'	Yak C-18M	ex North Weald, La Ferté Alais, Egyptian AF 627.		
		(SPP)	CoA 27-11-01. Stored		6-03
❑ G-TAFI		Jungmeister	ex North Weald, Breighton, N2210, HB-MIF,		
			Swiss AF U-77. CoA 5-7-01. Stored		6-03
❑ LV-RIE*		Nord 1002	ex North Weald, Duxford, Kersey, Argentina. Stored		12-05
❑ 'DR628'*		Beech D.17S	N18V, ex North Weald, NC18, Bu32898, FT507,		
	'PB1'		44-67761. Stored		8-04
❑ KZ191		Hurricane IV	ex N' Weald, Fowlmere, Israel, 351, 1695F, AFDU.	®	6-03
❑ XW893		Gazelle AH.1	ex Poole (?), Shawbury, Fleetlands, Middle Wallop,		
			665, 657, 658, 660. Pod, spares		6-03
❑ XX388		Gazelle AH.1	ex Poole (?), Shawbury, Fleetlands, 652, 661, 652,		
			661, 657. Pod, spares		6-03
❑ XX393	'W'	Gazelle AH.1	ex Shawbury, Fleetlands, 664, 669, 654, 2F, 6F,		
			GCF, 3 CBAS. Pod, spares		6-03
❑ XX413		Gazelle AH.1	ex Poole (?), Shawbury, Fleetlands, 847, 3 CBAS. Pod		6-03
❑ XX418		Gazelle AH.1	ex Poole (?), Shawbury, Fleetlands, 651, 4 Regt,		
			669, 664, 658. Pod, spares		6-03
❑ XX433		Gazelle AH.1	ex Shawbury, Fleetlands, 685, 3 Regt, 663, 660. Pod		6-03
❑ 152/17		Fokker Dr.I REP	G-ATJM, ex North Weald, Duxford, Rendcomb, North		
			Weald, Duxford, N78001, EI-APY, G-ATJM. CoA 10-9-93		6-03
❑ C4E-88		Bf 109E	ex Tangmere, Stubbington, Spain, SpanAF '6-88'		6-03
❑ J-1758*		Venom FB.54	G-BLSD, ex North Weald, N203DM, Cranfield,		
			G-BLSD, SwAF. Arrived 5-10-05		10-05

Others: The Gannet is reportedly for sale.

❑ XA459	Gannet AS.4	ex Cirencester, Cardiff, Culdrose SAH-7 / A2608,		
		Lee-on-Solent, 831. Stored		12-05

MEMBURY close to the Membury services, east of Swindon on the M4
Southern Sailplanes: The fuselage of Super Cub G-APZJ is the original one [1].

❑ G-AHAG	Dragon Rapide	ex Blandford, Ford, Whitney, RL944. CoA 15-7-73		5-05
❑ G-APZJ	Super Cub 150	crashed 12-6-83. Stored	[1]	9-89

❏	G-AWHX	Beta B.2	ex G-ATEE ntu. *Vertigo.* CoA 14-6-87	5-05
❏	G-BAMT	DR.400 Knight	crashed 8-1-78. Wreck	9-89
❏	G-BAVA	Super Cub 150	ex D-EFKC, ALAT 18-5391. Cr 20-11-77. Frame	1-92
❏	G-BAZC	DR.400 Knight	crashed 21-5-88. Fuselage	7-98
❏	G-BEHS	Pawnee 260C	ex Lancing, OE-AFX, N8755L. CoA 25-6-93	2-95
❏	G-RBIN	DR.400 2+2	crashed 21-5-93. Wreck	7-98
❏	'Z7258'	Dragon Rapide	G-AHGD, ex Old Warden, NR786. *Women of the Empire.*	
			Crashed 30-6-91. Wreck	8-97

NEWBURY on the A34 west of Reading

British Balloon Museum and Library (BBM&L): Envelopes are to be seen at the bi-ennial inflation day (their very active web-site gives details, next one is scheduled for 2008). BBM&L maintains strong links with The Airship Heritage Trust (see below) and looks after the display in the West Berkshire Museum, also see below. Delete the following from those given in *W&R19* (p16/17): G-ATXR Abingdon; G-BBGZ Cambridge; HB-BOU Brighton. Off the balloons listed below, *most* are envelopes and baskets. The envelope of Colt 56SS (special shape) is only loan at Manchester, Gtr Man.

◆ *Tim Turner, 19 Rother Close, West End, Southampton, Hants, SO18 3NJ e-mail tjthafb@aol.com www.britishballoonmuseum.org.uk*

❏	G-ATGN	Thorn Coal Gas	3-06		❏	G-BFAB	Cameron N-56	3-06
❏	G-AVTL	HAG Free	3-06		❏	G-BGAS	Colt 105A	3-06
❏	G-AWCR	Piccard Ax6	3-06		❏	G-BGHS	Cameron N-31	3-06
❏	G-AWOK	Sussex Free Gas	3-06		❏	G-BGOO	Colt 56	3-06
❏	G-AXVU	Omega 84	3-06		❏	G-BGPF	Thunder Ax6-56Z	3-06
❏	G-AXXP	Bradshaw Free	3-06		❏	G-BHKN	Colt 14A	3-06
❏	G-AYAJ	Cameron O-84	3-06		❏	G-BHKR	Colt 14A	3-06
❏	G-AYAL	Omega 56	3-06		❏	G-BIAZ	Cameron AT-165	3-06
❏	G-AZBH	Cameron O-84	3-06		❏	G-BIDV	Colt 17A	3-06
❏	G-AZER	Cameron O-42	3-06		❏	G-BIGT	Colt 77A	3-06
❏	G-AZJI	Western O-65	3-06		❏	G-BIUL	Cameron 60	3-06
❏	G-AZOO	Western O-65	3-06		❏	G-BKES	Cameron SS 57	3-06
❏	G-AZSP	Cameron O-84	3-06		❏	G-BKMR	Thunder Ax3	3-06
❏	G-AZUV	Cameron O-56	3-06		❏	G-BKRZ	Dragon 77	3-06
❏	G-AZYL	Portslade School	3-06		❏	G-BLIO	Cameron R-42	3-06
❏	G-BAMK	Cameron D-96	3-06		❏	G-BLWB	Thunder Ax6-56	3-06
❏	G-BAVU	Cameron A-105	3-06		❏	G-BMEZ	Cameron DP-50	3-06
❏	G-BAXF	Cameron O-77	3-06		❏	G-BMYA	Colt 56A	3-06
❏	G-BAXK	Thunder Ax7-77	3-06		❏	G-BNHN	Colt SS	3-06
❏	G-BBCK*	Cameron O-77	3-06		❏	G-BOGR	Colt 180A	3-06
❏	G-BBFS	Van Bemden Gas	3-06		❏	G-BOTL	Colt 42R	3-06
❏	G-BBLL	Cameron O-84	3-06		❏	G-BPKN	Colt AS-80	3-06
❏	G-BBOD	Cameron O-5	3-06		❏	G-BRZC	Cameron N-90	3-06
❏	G-BBOX	Thunder Ax7-77	3-06		❏	G-BUBL	Thunder Ax8-105	3-06
❏	G-BBYU	Cameron O-65	3-06		❏	G-BUUU	Cameron 77SS	3-06
❏	G-BCAR	Thunder Ax7-77	3-06		❏	G-BVBX	Cameron N-90M -	3-06
❏	G-BCFD	West	3-06		❏	G-BZFG*	Sky 105	3-06
❏	G-BCFE	Portslade School	3-06		❏	G-CHUB	Colt N-51 SS	3-06
❏	G-BCGP	Gazebo Ax-65	3-06		❏	G-ERMS	Thunder AS-33	3-06
❏	G-BDVG	Thunder Ax6-56A	3-06		❏	G-FTFT	Colt 90SS	3-06
❏	G-BEEE	Thunder Ax6-56A	3-06		❏	G-FZZZ	Colt 56A	3-06
❏	G-BEFE	Cameron N-77	3-06		❏	G-HOME	Colt 77A	3-06
❏	G-BEPO	Cameron N-77	3-06		❏	G-HOUS	Colt 31A	3-06
❏	G-BEPZ	Cameron D-96	3-06		❏	G-ICES	Thunder Ax6-56	3-06
❏	G-BETF	Cameron SS	3-06		❏	G-JONO	Colt 77A	3-06
❏	G-BETH	Thunder Ax6-56	3-06		❏	G-LCIO	Colt 240A	3-06
❏	G-BEVI	Thunder Ax7-77A	3-06		❏	G-LOAG	Cameron N-77	3-06

❏ G-NUTS	Cameron 35SS	3-06	❏ – BAPC.258	GQ 5,000ft^3	3-06
❏ G-OBUD	Colt 69A	3-06	❏ EI-BAY	Cameron O-84	3-06
❏ G-ODAY	Cameron N-56	3-06	❏ F-WGGM	T & Colt AS-261	3-06
❏ G-OFIZ	Colt 80SS	3-06	❏ N4990T	Thunder Ax7-65B	3-06
❏ G-OLLI	Cameron O-31	3-06	❏ N12006	Raven S.50	3-06
❏ G-OPKF*	Cameron 90SS	3-06	❏ OY-BOB	Omega 80	3-06
❏ G-PARR	Colt 90SS	3-06	❏ OY-BOW	Colting 77A	3-06
❏ G-PERR	Cameron SS 60	3-06	❏ 5Y-SIL	Cameron A-140	3-06
❏ G-PINT*	Cameron 60SS	3-06	❏ –	Gas balloon	3-06
❏ G-PLUG	Colt 105A	3-06	❏ –	Cam' DG28 Gas	3-06
❏ G-PUBS	Colt SS	3-06	❏ –	Military Gas	3-06
❏ G-ZUMP	Cameron N-77	3-06			

West Berkshire Museum: BBM&L (see above) artefacts are displayed in a special section here.
◆ *At The Wharf in Newbury. Tue to Sat (not Sun and Mon) 10am to 5pm. Also Bank Hols Easter to Aug. Closed Christmas and New Year. The Wharf, Newbury, RG14 5AS tel 01635 30511 fax 01635 519562 e-mail museum@westberks.gov.uk www.westberkshiremuseum.org.uk*

Airship Heritage Trust (AHT): The Trust works closely with BBM&L (see above) and because of this, they are listed here as a 'port of convenience'. In early 2006, negotiations were taking place that hopefully would find a place to display some of the extensive collection. For now, all of the collection is in deep store at a variety of locations - none of them in Berkshire! – and is not available for viewing.
◆ Not available for viewing. General enqiries: G/C Peter A Garth, 5 Orchard Lane, Brampton, PE1 8TF.

❏ G-BECE	AD-500 Skyship	ex Old Warden, Cardington, Kirkbymoorside. Gondola, damaged 9-3-79. Stored	3-06
❏ G-BIHN	Skyship 500	ex Old Warden, Cardington. Dam 27-4-87. Gondola	3-06
❏ –	K88 Airship	ex St Athan, Pensacola, USN. Gondola	3-06

READING

Ben Borsberry: No news on the biplanes believed held in the area.

❏ G-AGNJ	Tiger Moth	ex VP-YOJ, ZS-BGF, SAAF 2366.	®	6-95
❏ G-AZGC	SNCAN SV-4C	ex Hungerford, Booker, F-BCGE, French mil No.120. Damaged 28-5-90. Stored		6-95
❏ G-BRHW	Tiger Moth	ex 7Q-YMY, VP-YMY, ZS-DLB, SAAF 4606, DE671	®	6-95

Kelvin Petty: The MiG-21MF at Boscombe Down, Wilts, was sold in the USA during 2004 - qv. His Lightning F.53 cockpit moved to <u>Bournemouth</u>, Dorset, on 2nd September 2004.

Others: Still stored in the general area is a Provost.

❏ WW447	Provost T.1	ex Exeter, CATCS, CNCS, RAFC. Stored	4-04

THATCHAM or Brimpton, north of the A4, west of Newbury

Sylmar Aviation / Provost Team: Alan House and team operate from a strip in the area.

❏ G-HRLK		Safir	✈ ex G-BRZY, PH-RLK		10-03
❏ G-SAFR		Safir	ex Cranfield, Coventry, Rugby, Bruntingthorpe, PH-RLR RLS	®	1-02
❏ N16403		C34 Airmaster	✈ –		10-03
❏ WV486	'N-D'	Provost T.1	ex Reading, Halton 7694M, 6 FTS. Spares		6-03
❏ XF545	'O-K'	Provost T.1	ex Linton-on-Ouse, Swinderby, Finningley 7957M, Shawbury, 6 FTS, 2 FTS. Fuselage, stored		6-03
❏ XF597	'AH'	Provost T.1	✈ G-BKFW, ex CAW, RAFC		5-05
❏ XF836		Provost T.1	G-AWRY, ex Popham, Old Warden, 8043M, 27 MU, CATCS, CNCS, RAFC, Man UAS. Dam 28-7-87	®	7-03
❏ XF877	'J-X'	Provost T.1	✈ G-AWVF, ex Sandown, CATCS, CNCS, RAFC		7-05
❏ 181		Provost T.51	ex Casement, IAAC. Spares		1-02

WHITE WALTHAM AERODROME south of the A4 south-west of Maidenhead

The Automobile Association keep a travelling composite Enstrom here. It wears their colours and is believed to be based upon the former Somersham, Cambs, hybrid, with the cabin of G-BATU, the tail from G-JDHI and other parts from other machines, including G-BACH [1].

❑ G-AFLW	Miles Monarch	CoA 30-7-98. Stored		6-01
❑ G-ARON*	Colt 108	ex Warminster. CoA 5-7-01	®	5-05
❑ G-BBNY	Cessna FRA.150L	ex Lasham, Blackbushe. Crashed 8-6-86. Wreck		9-96
❑ 'N-NAAS'	Enstrom F-28	composite. Travelling airframe	[1]	6-03

WOODLEY east of Reading

Museum of Berkshire Aviation (MBA): Work continues on the major reconstruction of the Martinet – bringing an otherwise 'extinct' type back to the public gaze. The Elliotts of Newbury gliders were donated by Pat Pottinger [1]; the Gannet is on loan from the Fleet Air Arm Museum [2] and the Gyrodyne from the RAF Museum [3].

Co-operating within the site are the **Royal Berkshire Aviation Society**, **The Herald Society** restoring *Whisky-Alpha* (contact for both K Freeman, 269 Wykeham Road, Reading, Berkshire RG6 1PL, e-mail keith_freeman@uk2.net) and **The Miles Aircraft Collection**. Items on show at MBA from MAC include the Bristol Mercury from the second prototype M.37 JN668 and a 'slice' of upper fuselage of Marathon G-AMEW.

◆ *Sat, Sun and Bank Hols Mar to Oct, 10.30am to 5pm. Wednesdays, all year, 10.30am to 4pm. Mohawk Way (off Bader Way), Woodley, near Reading, Berkshire RG5 4UF tel / answerline 0118 9448089 e-mail museumofberkshireaviation@fly.to www.fly.to/museumofberkshireaviation*

❑ G-APLK		Miles Student 2	ex North Weald, Bruntingthorpe, G-APLK, Cranfield, G-MIOO, Duxford, G-APLK, Glasgow, Shoreham, XS941, G-35-4. Crashed 24-8-85	® 4-06
❑ G-APWA		Herald 100	ex Southend, BAF, PP-SDM, PP-ASV, G-APWA. CoA 6-4-82	4-06
❑ [ANL]	529	EoN Olympia 1	ex RAFGSA.103. Crashed 31-10-57	[1] 4-06
❑ [APW]	562	EoN Olympia 1	ex G-ALJZ, BGA.562. Crashed 20-7-58	[1] 4-06
❑ [AQZ]	589	EoN Primary	ex Farnborough, G-ALMN, BGA.589	[1] 4-06
❑ –	BAPC.233	Wanderlust	ex Farnborough	4-06
❑ –	BAPC.248	McBroom h-g	built 1974	4-06
❑ TF-SHC		Martinet TT.1	ex Reykjavik, Akuereyi, MS902, Reykjavik SF, 251. Crashed 18-7-51. Major reconstruction	® 4-06
❑ 'L6906'		Magister I	BAPC.44, ex Brooklands, Woodley, Wroughton, Frenchay, G-AKKY, T9841, 11 EFTS, 16 EFTS.	4-06
❑ XG883	'773'	Gannet T.5	ex Cardiff, Yeovilton, 849.	[2] 4-06
❑ XJ389		Jet Gyrodyne	ex Cosford, Southampton, G-AJJP, XD759, makers	[3] 4-06

BUCKINGHAMSHIRE

AYLESBURY

Believed still stored in the area is a Luton Minor. Stewart Thornley's Chipmunk is becoming a simulator.

❑ G-AFIR	Luton Minor	ex Cobham, Rearsby. CoA 30-7-71	1-96
❑ WB626	Chipmunk T.10 PAX	ex S Molton, Fownhope, Firbeck, Houghton-on-the-Hill, Southampton, Swanton Morley, Bicester, Kemble, Hendon SF, 5 FTS, 18 RFS	6-01

BLETCHLEY PARK south of the A5, near Milton Keynes

The **Buckinghamshire Aircraft Recovery Group** has been wound up. **No.2366 Squadron Air Cadets** took delivery of a former Cosford Harrier by September 2005.

❑ XV752*	'B' Harrier GR.3	ex Cosford 9078M, 4, 3, 1, 233 OCU, 1, 233 OCU. Arr by 9-05	9-05

HALTON AIRFIELD on the A4011 (camp) and east of the B4544 (airfield), north of Wendover

RAF Halton: Within the station is the **Trenchard Museum** which includes a Cadet glider [1]. (The museum is available for inspection on a prior permission *only* basis, contact 01296 623535, ext 6300.) 'JP' XS215 is used by the **Airman's Command School** and has the wings of XS218 [2]. The Bulldogs are with **2409 Squadron ATC** (Herts & Bucks Wing) with the plan to create one airframe [3]. The Tornado 'guards' the Parade Square [4]. 'JP' T.4 XR672 was no longer in use as a horse-jump on the cross-country course by March 2006 – it seems the 'neddies' have insisted on an upgrade [5]!

Departures: By April 2004 Fauvel ETE had moved to Old Warden, Beds. The fuselage of Chipmunk T.10 WB556 arrived from Bicester, Oxon. It was intended to become another horse jump (see XR672 and XW303) but instead moved on in late 2005 to Northolt, Gtr Lon.

❏	'RA905'		Cadet TX.1	BGA.1143, ex RAFGSA.273, RA905. CoA 14-3-00	[1]	5-04
❏	XF527		Hunter F.6	8680M, ex 1 SoTT, Laarbruch SF, 4 FTS, CFE,		
				19, Church Fenton SF, Linton SF. Gate		2-06
❏	XR672	'50'	Jet Provost T.4	8495M, ex SoRF, 6 FTS, CAW, CATCS, 3 FTS, 1 FTS.	[5]	3-06
❏	[XS215]	'17'	Jet Provost T.4	8507M, ex CAW. Fuselage. GIA	[2]	3-06
❏	XW303*	'127'	Jet Provost T.5A	ex Cosford 9119M, Halton , 7 FTS, 1 FTS. Arr 6-3-06	[5]	3-06
❏	XX665		Bulldog T.1	9289M, ex Newton, E Lowlands UAS, Abn UAS,		
				E Lowlands UAS. Cr 20-9-97. Fuselage	[3]	2-04
❏	XX669	'F'	Bulldog T.1	ex Andover, Llantrisant, Bruntingthorpe, Cosford 8997M,		
				2 FTS, Birm UAS, Man UAS. Damaged 6-9-88. Hulk	[3]	7-04
❏	XZ630		Tornado GR.1	ex St Athan 8986M, Brüggen, BAe, AAEE.	[4]	1-05

HIGH WYCOMBE

Spitfire XIV RM927 moved to Sandown, Isle of Wight, during April 2005. Spitfire XIV RM694 was acquired by a UK private owner and is in storage pending restoration to flying condition – no 'forwarding address'.

IVER HEATH on the A412 west of Uxbridge

Pinewood Film Studios: A series of visits during 2005 found no aviation relics. BAC 111-510ED G-AVMP is thought to have moved out in August 2004. Nothing on the anonymous JetRanger, last noted in January 2004.

LAVENDON on the A428 west of Bedford

Tony and **Nick Collins** :The work of restoring and acquiring cockpit sections continues. As proven at various *CockpitFests*, Tony's workmanship is top-notch. Lightning F.6 XS898 is often displayed at the Lavendon Narrow Gauge Railway, on the A428 between Bedford and Northampton.

❏	WT319		Canberra B(I).6	ex Castle Carey, ?, Filton, Samlesbury, 213,
				Laarbruch SF, 213. Nose	6-05
❏	WT684		Hunter F.1	ex Doncaster, Firbeck, Long Marston, Brize Norton,
				Reading, Halton 7422M, 229 OCU, DFLS. Nose	6-05
❏	XD235*		Scimitar F.1	ex Ingatestone, Welshpool, Southampton, Ottershaw,
				Foulness, FRU, 803. Nose. Arrived by 8-05	8-05
❏	XK627		Vampire T.11	ex Barton, Bacup, Hazel Grove, Woodford,
				Chester, St Athan, 8 FTS, CFS	12-02
❏	XN651		Sea Vixen FAW.2	ex Bletchley Park, Bristol, Culdrose A2616, SAH,
				766, FAW.1, 893. Nose	3-03
❏	XP642		Jet Provost T.4	ex Luton, Bruntingthorpe, Nottingham, Finchampstead
				Ridges, Lasham, Shawbury, 2 FTS, CFS. Nose	3-03
❏	XS898	'BD'	Lightning F.6	ex Bruntingthorpe, Cranfield, Binbrook, 11, 5. Nose	6-05

MILTON KEYNES

No.2532 Squadron, Air Cadets:

❏	XF522		Hunter F.6	ex Aylesbury, Halton, 92, 66, 92. Nose	5-03

Others: Grasshopper TX.1 XA226 moved to Flixton, Suffolk, on 21st April 2004.

NEWPORT PAGNELL on the B526 north of Milton Keynes
Peter R Arnold's Spitfire XII EN224 (G-FXII) and Seafire F.46 LA564 departed here in April 2002 for a private owner and are in store pending restoration to flight. This has left Peter without a Spitfire project for the first time in many decades. He still has the urge to be a member of the 'Spitfire Owners' Club – who knows what's next?

OAKLEY east of the M40, south of the village and north of Worminghall
A paintball 'arena' has been established on a part of the wartime airfield and has a Boeing 727 fuselage. It is reported that 'hi-jack hostage rescue' scenes can be played out. Tasteful! Another portion is used by mircolights.

❏ G-MMKY*	Jordan Duet	canx 1-9-95. Fuselage, stored	1-06
❏ EC-DDX*	Boeing 727-256	ex Bournemouth, Iberia. Fuselage. Arrived by 8-05	1-06

TURWESTON AERODROME north of the A422, east of Brackley
❏ F-BTKO*	HR.100/210	fuselage, first noted 6-05	10-05
❏ F-GMHH*	HR.100/210	ex 3A-MAZ, F-BUHH. fuselage, first noted 6-05	10-05

TWYFORD east of Bicester
Peter Wood:

❏ AD540		Spitfire V	ex Dumfries, Carsphairn, 242, 122. *Blue Peter*. Cr 23-5-42	® 3-06
❏ WK620	'T'	Chipmunk T.10	ex Tattershall Thorpe, Middle Wallop, BFWF, Hull UAS, Mcr UAS, QUAS, Bri UAS, 22 RFS. Dam 19-5-93. Stored	6-01

WOBURN SANDS on the A5130 east of Milton Keynes
Kite I AAF (BGA.236) moved to Eaton Bray, Beds.

WYCOMBE AIR PARK or Booker, on the B482 south-west of High Wycombe
Personal Plane Services (PPS) / **Antique Aero Engines**: Two airframes are being restored or held for US collector Kermit Weeks (KW). The Travelair is bedecked as a Fokker D.VIII [1]. Jungmann I-CABI became G-CCHY and was flying by 2005. Spitfire IX TE517 (G-CCIX) was acquired by a UK owner and is in storage pending restoration to flying condition – no 'forwarding address'.
◆ *Visits possible* only *by prior arrangement.*

❏ G-AZTR	SNCAN SV-4C	ex F-BDEQ. CoA 15-7-94. Dismantled		6-01
❏ [G-BTZE]	Yak C-11	ex OK-JIK. Last flown 12-6-76. Stored		6-03
❏ [OK-JIY]	Yak C-11	ex Czech AF. c/n 172673	off-site	3-96
❏ AR213	Spitfire Ia	G-AIST, ex Patrick Lindsay, Old Warden, *Battle of Britain*, 8 MU, 53 OTU, 57 OTU. CoA 6-9-00	®	3-06
❏ EJ693	Tempest V	N7027E, ex Norfolk (?), USA, Chichester, Henlow, Delft, 486. Crashed 1-10-44	KW ®	3-06
❏ MV262	Spitfire XIV	G-CCVV, ex Winchester, Bitteswell, Blackbushe, Calcutta, Ind AF, ACSEA, 9 MU. Stored	KW	3-06
❏ '626/8'	Travel Air 2000	N6268, ex USA, NC6268	[1]	7-96
❏ –	Pilatus P.2	fuselage. Film mock-up. Luftwaffe colours		8-05
❏ –	BAPC.103 Hulton h-glider	built 1969		3-96

Parkhouse Aviation: T-33A/N G-WGHB moved to Norwich, Norfolk, by late 2004. Three aircraft arrived from Armthorpe, S Yorks, by January 2005: Provost T.1 WW421 (G-BZRE) it then moved to Bournemouth, Dorset, 10th October 2005; Provost T.1 WV499 (G-BZRF) by February 2006 had moved to Exeter, Devon; Vampire T.11 XH313 (G-BZRD) moved quickly to a private owner in 'Surrey'. Hunter F.51 'XF314' (E-412) moved to Brooklands, Surrey, on 10th September 2005. (See also Camberley, Surrey.)

❑	[G-BORM]*		HS.748-2B	ex Exeter, RP-C1043, V2-LAA, VP-LAA, 9Y-TDH.	
				Cockpit. Arrived by 11-05	3-06
❑	XM172	'B'	Lightning F.1A	ex Coltishall 8427M, 226 OCU, 56	4-06
❑	XN549*		Jet Provost T.3	'8235M'/8225M, ex Shawbury, Halton, Shawbury,	
				1 FTS, CFS. Arrived 3-2-06	3-06
❑	430861*		VB-25N-NC	N9089Z, ex North Weald, Duxford, 'HD368', G-BKXW ntu,	
				Southend, Biggin Hill, N9089Z, 44-30861. *Bedsheet Bomber.*	
				Arrived 2-06	2-06

Others: Rutan LongEz G-RPEZ had gone from its resting place up a hangar wall by May 2004 and is believed now to be a 'live' build project elsewhere. All the other wrecks (Warrior II G-BSVF, Tomahawk 112s G-DYOU and G-EORG and Quickie Q.2 G-KUTU) were cleared out by May 2004. Tiger Moth T7404 (G-ANMV), last noted in June 2001, is believed to have been sold in Germany.

CAMBRIDGESHIRE

ALCONBURY AIRFIELD north-west of Huntingdon at the A1/A14 junction
USAF Alconbury: A USAF enclave is still here. The A-10 guards the 'inner' gate [1].

❑	'01532'	F-5E Tiger II	mock up, on 'outer' gate, 527 TFTAS c/s	4-06
❑	80-0219	A-10A	ex 509th TFS, Bentwaters. Accident 4-4-89.	
		Thunderbolt II	10th TFW, 509th TFS-511th TFS c/s. *Phoenix*	[1] 4-06

BASSINGBOURN on the A1198 north of Royston
Tower Museum: Run and maintained by the **East Anglian Aviation Society** (EAAS), the original tower is the basis for a superb museum dedicated to the history of the once resident 91st BG, 11 OTU, 231 OCU, the Army and others. EAAS share joint maintenance of the static 'Army' Canberra preserved within the camp - see below.
◆ *Wed and Sun from 10am to 3pm – other times by prior arrangement. 01763 243500, or Chris Murphy 07808 144328 or Ray Jude 017999 527932 EAAS details from: Mike Killaspy, 3 Sainfoin Close, Sawston, Cambs, CB2 4JY www.bassingbourntowermuseum.co.uk*

Army Training Regiment, Bassingbourn: WJ821 is kept inside the camp, EAAS (see above) help maintain it.
Canberra TT.18 nose WK127 moved to Peterborough, Cambs, circa 2004.

❑	WJ821	Canberra PR.7	8668M, ex RAE Bedford, 13, 58, 82. Displayed	4-06

BOURN AERODROME on the A428 west of Cambridge

❑	G-AZLO	Cessna F.337F	ex Land's End. CoA 22-4-82. Poor state		9-05
❑	G-BEKN	Cessna FRA.150M	ex Peterborough Sport. CoA 8-10-89. Stored		10-05
❑	G-BEZS	Cessna FR.172J	ex Cranfield, Stapleford, I-CCAJ. Cr 15-6-79. Stored		2-02
❑	G-BCJH	Mooney M.20F	ex N9549M. CoA 30-6-91. Engineless		10-05
❑	G-BKOT*	WA.81 Piranha	ex Little Gransden, Glatton, Eversden, F-GAIP. F/n 9-05		10-05
❑	G-BNSV*	Cessna 152 II	ex N5322M. CoA 12-7-97. Crashed 22-3-97	®	10-05
❑	G-BPIL	Cessna 310B	ex N620GS, OO-SEF, N5420A. *Fast Lady*. CoA 28-4-00	®	10-05

BRAMPTON on the A14/A141 south-west of Huntingdon
RAF Brampton / Defence Logistics Organisation:

❑	XT914	'Z'	Phantom FGR.2	ex Leeming, 74, 56, 228 OCU, 92, 228 OCU,	
				56, 228 OCU, 14. 74 Sqn c/s. Gate	3-06

CAMBRIDGE

Arbour College / Cambridge Regional College: In King Hedges Road. The Cessna 310 was up for auction in January 2004 [1]. 'JP' XN582 was back at Cambridge Airport, Cambs, by August 2004. In *W&R17* (p79) under Shobdon, H&W, Cessna F.150L was noted as possibly having gone to Cambridge, Cambs. This was indeed so and it served with the college until 29th June 2004 when it moved to Bruntingthorpe, Leics.

| ☐ G-XITD | Cessna 310G | ex Tattershall Thorpe, Leavesden, Denham, | | |
| | | G-ASYV, HB-LBY, N8948Z. Accident 14-7-88 | [1] | 1-04 |

Others: The Cambridge Strut of the PFA *should* still be working on a 'Flea' in the area.

| ☐ G-ADXS | HM.14 'Flea' | ex East Tilbury, Andrewsfield, Southend, Staverton, | | |
| | | Southend. CoA 1-12-36 | ® | 7-96 |

CAMBRIDGE AIRPORT (TEVERSHAM)

By August 2004 'JP3' XN582 had moved here from Cambridge; this was in preparation for the move to Bruntingthorpe, Leics, on 21st July 2005. TriStar 200 N913PM was scrapped during mid-2001. The nose of Canberra T.4 WJ863 (last noted in December 1999) is believed to have been scrapped.

☐ G-FTAX*	Cessna 421C	ex N8363G, G-BFFM, N8363G. CoA 16-5-01. Stored	1-06
☐ XV201	Hercules C.1K	ex 1312F, LTW. Fuselage, spares	2-06
☐ XV302	Hercules C.3	ex LTW, Fairford Wing, 30/47 Sqns. Fatigue rig	12-05

COMBERTON on the B1046 west of J12 of the M11

The Moth continues to be registered to a local, but no physical sighting this century!

| ☐ G-AANO | DH.60GMW | ex Southampton, N590N, NC590N | ® | 11-91 |

DUXFORD AERODROME south of Cambridge, Junction 10 M11

Imperial War Museum (IWM): Throughout 2005 and 2006, building work on '**AirSpace**' - what some have dubbed the 'Super-Super Hangar' - continued apace. Supporters of the new venture include BAE Systems and it will tell the story of the British aviation industry, although this doesn't seem to fit at all within the IWM's remit. Restoration programmes for the aircraft destined to go on display inside the 'new' building and the aircraft displaced by the construction work meant that there were many aircraft 'movements' on the Duxford site during this time. Aircraft ear-marked at this stage for 'AirSpace' are given a ⇨. (Included are several Duxford Aviation Society airframes – see below. The Bolingbroke that was being restored by the Aircraft Restoration Company now appears not to be included in 'AirSpace' – see below.) Aero Vintage are building a DH.9 for display within 'AirSpace' (see under Historic Aircraft Collection below and under St Leonards-on-Sea, E Sussex). To achieve this Me 163B 191660 is to be passed on to a US warbird group - widely believed to the Paul Allen's Flying Heritage Collection - see 'Departures' below.

Once the hub-bub created by 'AirSpace' has settled down, there will be further shuffling of airframes to take advantage of the gaps created in the other hangars. Some airframes have been loaned out to other collections, some clearly on the edge of the museum's collecting policy, but others – including the F-86A Sabre (see under the American air Museum below) central to it. Other 'settling' may well take place. Further plans for Duxford - not finalised - include yet *another* special building. This would be called 'Airborne Assault' and take in the re-location of the Airborne Forces Museum at Aldershot, Hants – qv.

On 18th May 2005 a founding father of the UK aviation heritage movement died. There are several places in this book where I could pay tribute to **Peter Thomas**, but this seemed the most appropriate as the bulk of his iconic Skyfame Collection can be found here. On 24th March 1961, Sunderland ML824 touched down in Milford Haven, Wales, the result of patience and determination from Peter to bring a Sunderland home. (It can now be found at Hendon, Gtr Lon.)

This success was not enough for Peter. He was determined to establish a museum of 'living' aircraft and this he achieved on 31st August 1963 when the Skyfame Museum opened up at Staverton, Glos. While it might not have seemed it at the time, this was the UK's first *exclusively* aviation museum. Skyfame had to close in 1978 and the bulk of the aircraft were moved to Duxford in an epic rescue operation. Initially they were on loan to IWM but in 1987 it became wholly owned by the Cambridgeshire museum.

Peter's influence on the UK aviation heritage is massive and not confined to the enterprises mentioned here. He was a true pioneer and many collections and individuals took their inspiration from him.

Notes: Hangar 4 contains the 'Air Defence Collection' of fighter types; Hangar 5 is the main restoration hangar; Hangars 2 and 3 continue their traditional role of housing the 'flyers' – see below. The Pilcher Hawk is on loan from Eric Littledike [1]. Hurricane II 'Z2315' could well be BE146 if its upper cowling is anything to go by. BE146 was despatched to Russia on 2nd October 1941 [2]. The F-105, originally intended for the American Air Museum, is stored [3]. IWM Duxford also has the following airframes out on loan: Sea Harrier FA.2 ZA175 (Flixton, Suffolk); Draken Fv35075 (Dumfries, Scotland); F-86A Sabre 0242 (Coventry, Warks).

Departures: The anonymous Hunter F.6 cockpit last used in the kids' play area moved to Wymondham, Norfolk; Me 163B-1 191660 moved to St Leonards-on-Sea, E Sussex, by September 2005 (see above); Draken Fv37075 moved to Dumfries, Scotland, 19-8-05, on loan.

♦ *Open daily 10am to 6pm Apr to Oct and 10am to 4pm the remainder of the year. Last admission 45 minutes before closing. Closed New Year's Day and Dec 24-26. On days other than special events two of the civil airliners are open to inspection free of charge, one of which is normally Concorde. A large SAE will bring a leaflet on special events, airshows etc. Duxford Airfield, Cambs, CB2 4QR tel 01223 835000 fax 01223 837267 www.iwm.org.uk*

❑ G-AFBS		Magister I	ex Staverton, G-AKKU ntu, BB661, G-AFBS.		
			CoA 25-2-63. Rolled-out 4-06	⇨	4-06
❑ G-USUK		Colt 2500A	gondola. *Virgin Atlantic Flyer*.		4-06
❑ –	G-9-185	Hunter F.6	ex Wroughton, South Kensington, Kingston, Dutch AF		
			N-250. Nose. Stored		9-05
❑ –*	BAPC.57	Pilcher Hawk REP	ex St Albans, Wroughton, Hayes, South Lambeth.		
			Built 1930. Arrived by 11-04. Stored	⇨[1]	4-06
❑ –	BAPC.93	Fi 103 (V-1)	ex Cosford. Inside		4-06
❑ E2581	'13'	Bristol F.2b	ex South Lambeth, Cardington (?), Crystal Palace,		
			Eastchurch, 2 GCF, 30 TDS, HQ Flt SE Area, 39.		4-06
❑ F3556		RE.8	ex South Lambeth, Cardington, Crystal Palace,		
			Tadcaster, no service. *[A Paddy Bird from Ceylon]*	® ⇨	4-06
❑ N4877	'MK-V'	Anson I	G-AMDA, ex Staverton, Derby AW, Watchfield		
			SF, 3 FP, ATA, 3 FPP. CoA 14-12-62. 500 Sqn c/s	⇨	4-06
❑ 'R4115'	'LE-X'	Hurricane FSM	BAPC.267, ex South Lambeth. 242 Sqn colours. 'Gate'		4-06
❑ V3388		Oxford I	G-AHTW, ex Staverton, Elstree, Boulton Paul,		
			V3388. CoA 15-12-60. Roll-out 4-06	⇨	4-06
❑ 'V9673'	'MA-J'	Lysander III	G-LIZY, ex RCAF 1558, V9300. 161 Sqn c/s	⇨	4-06
❑ 'Z2315'	'JU-E'	Hurricane IIb	ex TFC, Russia. 111 Sqn colours	[2]	4-06
❑ 'DE998'		Tiger Moth	ex ARC, Stamford, Hooton, Warmingham, 'K2572',		
	'RCU-T'		Hereford, Lutterworth, Holme-on-Spalding Moor.		
			Cam UAS colours. Rolled-out 4-06	⇨	4-06
❑ HM580		Cierva C.30A	G-ACUU, ex Staverton, HM580, 529, 1448 Flt, G-ACUU.		
			CoA 30-4-60		4-06
❑ KB889	'NA-I'	Lancaster X	G-LANC, ex Bitteswell, Blackbushe, RCAF 107 MRU,		
			428. 428 Sqn colours	⇨	4-06
❑ LZ766		Proctor III	G-ALCK, ex Staverton, Tamworth, HQBC, 21 EFTS.		
			CoA 19-6-63		4-06
❑ ML796		Sunderland MR.5	ex La Baule, Maisden-le-Riviere, Aéronavale,		
			27F, 7FE, RAF 230, 4 OTU, 228	⇨	4-06
❑ NF370	'NH-L'	Swordfish III	ex South Lambeth, Stretton, RAF. 119 Sqn c/s		
			Rolled-out 24-10-05	⇨	4-06
❑ TA719		Mosquito TT.35	ex Staverton, G-ASKC, Shawbury, 3/4 CAACU,		
			4 CAACU, Shawbury. Crashed 27-7-64	⇨	4-06
❑ TG528		Hastings C.1A	ex Staverton, 24, 24-36, 242 OCU, 53-99 pool, 47. 24 Sqn c/s	⇨	4-06
❑ VN485		Spitfire F.24	ex Kai Tak 7326M, RHK Aux AF, 80. Rolled-out 10-11-04	⇨	4-06
❑ WH725		Canberra B.2	ex Wroughton, 50, 44. 50 Sqn colours.	⇨	4-06
❑ WJ945	'21'	Varsity T.1	G-BEDV, ex CFS, 5 FTS, AE&AEOS, CFS, 115, 116, 527.		
			CoA 15-10-87		4-06

❑ WK991		Meteor F.8	ex Kemble, 7825M, 56, 46, 13 GCF, NSF.	4-06
❑ WM969	'10'	Sea Hawk FB.5	ex Culdrose, A2530, FRU, 806, 811, 898 ⇨	4-06
❑ WZ590	'19'	Vampire T.11	ex Woodford, Chester, St Athan, 8 FTS, 5 FTS, 228 OCU	4-06
❑ XE627	'T'	Hunter F.6A	ex Brawdy, 1 TWU, TWU, 229 OCU, 1, 229 OCU, 54, 1,	
			54, Horsham St Faith SF, 54, 229 OCU, 92, 65. 65 Sqn c/s	4-06
❑ XF708	'C'	Shack' MR.3/3	ex Kemble, 203, 120, 201. 203 Sqn colours	4-06
❑ XG613		Sea Ven FAW.21	ex Old Warden, RAE, AAEE, RAE	4-06
❑ XG743	'597'	Sea Vampire T.22	ex Wymondham, Duxford, Brawdy SF, 736, 764. Stored	4-06
❑ XG797	'277'	Gannet ECM.6	ex Arbroath, 831, 700, 810. 831 Sqn c/s, 'Flook' logo	4-06
❑ XH648		Victor B.1A (K2P)	ex 57, 55, Honington Wing, 15, 57. 57 Sqn c/s	4-06
❑ XH897		Javelin FAW.9	ex AAEE, 5, 33, 25	4-06
❑ XJ824		Vulcan B.2	ex 101, 9-35, 9, 230 OCU, 27 ⇨	4-06
❑ XK936	'62'	W'wind HAS.7	ex Wroughton, 705, 847, 848, 701, 820, 845 ⇨	4-06
❑ XM135	'B'	Lightning F.1	ex Leconfield, Leuchars TFF, 226 OCU, 74, AFDS. 74 Sqn c/s⇨	4-06
❑ XN239	'G'	Cadet TX.3	ex CGS 8889M	4-06
❑ XP281		Auster AOP.9	ex AFWF, Middle Wallop. MoAF loan. Stored	4-06
❑ XR222		TSR-2 XO-4	ex Cranfield, Weybridge. Unflown. 'Rolled-out' 16-12-05 ⇨	4-06
❑ XS567	'434'	Wasp HAS.1	ex Lee-on-Solent, 829 *Endurance* Flt	4-06
❑ XS576	'125'	Sea Vixen FAW.2	ex Sydenham, 899, Brawdy. 899 Sqn colours	4-06
❑ XS863	'304'	Wessex HAS.1	ex AAEE. Royal Navy colours ⇨	4-06
❑ XV865		Buccaneer S.2B	ex Coningsby 9226M, Lossiemouth, 208, 12, 237 OCU, 208,	
			12, 208, 237 OCU, FAA, 809, 736.208 Sqn c/s.	
			'Rolled out' 14-9-04 ⇨	4-06
❑ XX108		Jaguar GR.1A	ex St Athan, BAe Warton, G-27-313 ntu, DERA, AAEE ⇨	4-06
❑ XZ133	'10'	Harrier GR.3	ex S Lambeth, St Athan, 4, 1, 1417F, 233 OCU. ® ⇨	4-06
❑ ZA465	'FF'	Tornado GR.1B	ex Lossiemouth, 12, 617, 17, 16 ⇨	4-06
❑ –		Typhoon	ex South Lambeth. Cockpit	3-04
❑ A-549		FMA Pucará	ex ZD487 ntu, ex Boscombe Down, Yeovilton, Stanley, FAA	4-06
❑ 18393		CF-100 Mk.4B	ex Cranfield, G-BCYK, RCAF, 440, 419, 409 ⇨	4-06
❑ [3794]		MiG-15 (S-102)	ex Czech AF. Stored	4-06
❑ 57	'8-MT'	Mystère IVA	ex Sculthorpe, FAF 8 Esc, 321 GI, 5 Esc	4-06
❑ 1190		Bf 109E-3	ex Bournemouth, Buckfastleigh, Canada, USA, Canada,	
			White-4 of II/JG.26. Crashed 30-9-40	4-06
❑ 100143		Fa 330A-1	ex Farnborough	4-06
❑ –	'CF+HF'	MS.502	EI-AUY, ex USA, F-BCDG, ALAT	4-06
❑ –	'4V+GH'	Ju 52/3mge	ex Port AF 6316. Luftwaffe c/s. (Amiot AAC.1)	4-06
❑ 96+21		Mi-24D *Hind*	ex Basepohl, WGAF HFS-80, LSK KHG-5 406	4-06
❑ 501		MiG-21PF	ex St Athan, Farnborough, Hungarian AF	4-06
❑ 3685	'Y2-176'	A6M3 *Zeke*	ex Boise, USA, Taroa, Marshall Islands. Stored	9-05
❑ [B2I-27]		CASA 2-111	ex OFMC, Seville, Spanish AF. Stored	9-05
❑ 1133		Strikemaster 80	ex Warton, RSaudiAF, G-BESY, G-27-299 ⇨	4-06
❑ 252983		Schweizer TG-3A	ex AAM, N66630. Stored	9-05
❑ 59-1822		F-105D-6-RE	ex AMARC Virg ANG 192nd TFG, 23rd, 355th,	
			388th, 18th, 23rd, 355th,TFWs, 4520 CCTW. Stored [3]	4-06

American Air Museum (AAM): In a move that totally bewilders the writer, F-86A 48-0242 was placed on loan to the Midland Air Museum for an initial period of at least ten years. No disrespect to MAM, but the F-86A was acquired via a 'must have' shopping list by the IWM which involved the export to the USA of Meteor F.4 VT260 in 1997 (see *W&R16*). Suddenly, the type appears no longer fundamental to their collecting policy (they do bask in the flyable G-SABR on site) and the fact that MAM are keeping the aircraft outside appears to be against 'conventional' national museum loan 'policy'. It moved to <u>Coventry</u>, Warks, on 22nd April 2005.

Notes: P-47 *Oregon's Britannia* was a major reconstruction based upon large elements of P-47D 45-49192 not used in the composite that created The Fighter Collection's machine *No Guts, No Glory* – see below [1]. In store since 2002, the nose section of B-24D Liberator 251457 *Fightin' Sam* left Duxford for the USA on 23rd April 2004, at the end of its loan period.

☐	'S4513'		SPAD XIII REP	G-BFYO, ex 'S3398', Yeovilton, Land's End, Chertsey,		
		'1'		D-EOWM. CoA 21-6-82		4-06
☐	14286		T-33A-1-LO	ex Sculthorpe, FAF CIFAS 328. USAF c/s		4-06
☐	31171		B-25J-30-NC	N7614C, ex Shoreham, Dublin, Prestwick, Luton,		
			Mitchell	44-31171. USMC PBJ-1J colours		4-06
☐	42165	'VM'	F-100D-11-NA	ex Sculthorpe, FAF Esc 2/11, Esc 1/3,		
			Super Sabre	USAF. 352nd TFS, 35th TFW colours		4-06
☐	'46214'	'X-3'	TBM-3E	ex CF-KCG, RCN 326, USN 69327		
			Avenger	'Lt George Bush' titling. Ginny		4-06
☐	60689		B-52D-40-BW	ex 7 BW Carswell and others, USAF		4-06
☐	66692		U-2CT-LO	ex Alconbury, 5 SRTS/9 SRW, Beale		4-06
☐	155529	'114'	F-4J(UK)	ZE359, ex Wattisham, 74, USN 155529.		
			Phantom II	USN VF-74, America colours		4-06
☐	'217786'	'25'	PT-17 Kaydet	ex Swanton Morley, Duxford, CF-EQS, Evergreen,		
				New Brunswick, Canada, 41-8169		4-06
☐	'226413'		P-47D-30-RA	N47DD, ex USA, Peru AF FAP 119 and 545, 45-49192.		
		'UN-Z'	Thunderbolt	Cr 9-2-80. 56th FG c/s, Zemke's a/c. Oregon's Britannia	[1]	4-06
☐	'231983'		B-17G-95-DL	ex IGN F-BDRS, N68269, 44-83735.		
		'IY-G'	Flying Fortress	401st BG colours. Mary Alice		4-06
☐	315509		C-47A-85-DL	G-BHUB, ex Aces High G-BHUB, Airline : 'G-AGIV', 'FD988',		
		'W7-S'	Skytrain	and 'KG418', Spanish AF T3-29, N51V, N9985F, SAS SE-BBH,		
				315 TCG, 316 TCG, 43-15509. 37th TCS / 316th TCG c/s		4-06
☐	'450493'		B-24M-25-FO	44-51228, ex Lackland, EZB-24M. Dugan		4-06
☐	461748	'Y'	TB-29A-45-BN	G-BHDK, ex China Lake, 307th BG, Okinawa.		
			Superfortress	It's Hawg Wild (stb). 307th BG colours		4-06
☐	'463209'	'WZ-S'	P-51D FSM	BAPC.255, ex OFMC, London. 78th FG colours.		4-06
☐	–		Harvard IIB	ex North Weald, Amsterdam, Dutch AF B-168, FE984,		
				RCAF, 2 FIS, 42-12471		4-06
☐	61-17962		SR-71A	ex Palmdale, 9th SRW		4-06
☐	67-0120		F-111E-CF	ex Upper Heyford, 20th TFW. The Chief		4-06
☐	72-1447		F-111F-CF	escape module		4-06
☐	72-21605		UH-1H 'Huey'	ex Coleman Barracks, ATCOM		4-06
☐	76-0020		F-15A-15-MC	ex AMARC Davis-Monthan, Mass ANG 102nd FIW,		
				5th FIS, 33rd TFW, 36th TFW. 'Gate'		4-06
☐	77-0259	'AR'	A-10A	ex Alconbury, 10th TFW, 11th TASG, 128th TFW		4-06

Duxford Aviation Society (DAS): Several of DAS's pioneering airliner collection are destined for 'AirSpace' and are marked ⇨. The cockpit of Beverley C.1 XB261 moved to <u>Winthorpe</u>, Notts, in June 2004.
◆ *Duxford Airfield, Duxford, Cambridge, CB2 4QR tel 01223 836593 www.das.org.uk*

☐	G-AGTO	J/1 Autocrat	✈	on loan		4-06
☐	G-ALDG	Hermes 4		ex Gatwick, Silver City, Britavia, Airwork, BOAC.		
				CoA 9-1-63. BOAC c/s, Horsa. Fuselage. Unveiled 9-3-06	⇨	4-06
☐	G-ALFU	Dove 6		ex CAFU Stansted. CoA 4-6-71	⇨	4-06
☐	G-ALWF	Viscount 701		ex Liverpool, Cambrian, BEIA, Channel, BEA.		
				CoA 16-4-72. BEA colours, Sir John Franklin	⇨	4-06
☐	G-ALZO	Ambassador 2		ex Lasham, Dan-Air, Handley Page, Jordan AF		
				108, BEA. CoA 14-5-72. Dan-Air colours	®	4-06
☐	G-ANTK	York C.1		ex Lasham, Dan-Air, MW232, Fairey, 511, 242.		
				CoA 29-10-64. Dan-Air colours	® ⇨	4-06
☐	G-AOVT	Britannia 312		ex Monarch, British Eagle, BOAC. CoA 11-3-75.		
				Monarch colours		4-06
☐	G-APDB	Comet 4		ex Dan-Air, MSA 9M-AOB, BOAC G-APDB.		
				CoA7-10-74. Dan-Air colours	⇨	4-06
☐	G-APWJ	Herald 201		ex Norwich, Air UK, BIA, BUIA. CoA 21-12-85. Air UK c/s		4-06
☐	G-ASGC	Super VC-10		ex BA, BOAC. CoA 20-4-80. BOAC-Cunard c/s		4-06
☐	G-AVFB	Trident 2E		ex BA, Cyprus 5B-DAC, BEA. CoA 30-9-82. BEA c/s		4-06

❑ G-AVMU	BAC 111-510ED	ex Bournemouth, BA, BEA. CoA 8-1-95.	
		BA c/s. *County of Dorset*	4-06
❑ G-AXDN	Concorde 101	ex BAC/SNIAS. CoA 30-9-77	➪ 4-06
❑ G-OPAS	Viscount 806	ex Southend, Parcelforce/BWA, BAF, BA,	
		BEA G-AOYN. CoA 26-3-97. Nose	4-06

Aircraft Restoration Company (ARC) / **PropShop Ltd**: ARC shares the 'M11-end' hangar in a co-operative arrangement with Historic Flying Ltd (HFL – see below). Long term restoration projects are located in – and listed – under the new facility. Firefly SE-BRG will be rebuilt to flying condition and operated by ARC, SE-CAU will be restored to static condition [1]. Spitfire IX TA805 (G-PMNF) made its first flight on 7th December 2005, with John Romain at the controls. ARC have been fitting it out and completing the restoration on behalf of its owner [2]. The composite 'Blenheim' for the IWM, essentially G-MKIV with the nose of 9893 is held here [3]. See under Stafford, Staffs, and South Kensington, Gtr Lon, for details of a short-term task carried out by ARC on Spitfire F.22 PK664.

Blenheim (Duxford) Ltd, has been set up to restore G-BPIV in Building 66. Great progress has been made with its repair to flying condition. It is intended to mate the nose of Mk.I L6739 (ex 23 Squadron night-fighter) to make the project a *representative* Mk.I in the same way as it previously *represented* a Blenheim IV. As with projects of this magnitude, progress is limited by the amount of funding available as the aircraft is now being restored on a commercial basis rather than the volunteer-led efforts of the previous two restorations [4].

Notes: ARC maintains aircraft on behalf of their owners: including Golden Apple Trust (GA); Invicta Aviation (RA); Radial Revelations (RR - Martin Willing); Spitfire Ltd (SL - Cliff Spink) and T-28 G-TROY. (See also under Flixton, Suffolk for 'another' TD248.)

Departures: Spitfire FSM 'MH415' (BAPC.209) was sold to Ed Russell and went to Canada in April 2005.
◆ *Please note that the ARC/HFL building is not open to public inspection. ARC aircraft can be viewed in other hangars during normal opening hours and during airshows.*

❑ G-AOTR*		Chipmunk 22	ex HB-TUH, D-EGOG, G-AOTR, WB604, ULAS, 18 RFS.		
			Arrived 20-5-05		4-06
❑ G-ASTG		Nord 1002	ex Sutton Bridge, F-BGKI, FAF No.183. CoA 26-10-73		4-06
❑ G-BYNF		NA-64 Yale	ex N55904, Canada, RCAF, 3349	®	4-06
❑ G-BZGK		OV-10B	ex Luftwaffe 99+32, D-9561, 158308	IA	4-06
❑ G-BZGL		OV-10B	ex Luftwaffe 99+26, D-9555, 158302	IA	4-06
❑ G-OTAF*		L 39ZO Albatros	ex '2802' Breighton, North Weald, N40VC, N159JC,		
			N4312X ntu, Chad, Libyan AF 3227. Spares		4-06
❑ SE-BRG		Firefly TT.1	ex Sweden, 766, DT989. Stored	[1]	4-06
❑ SE-CAU		Firefly TT.1	ex Sweden, 827, PP469. Stored	[1]	4-06
❑ -		Bolingbroke IVT	G-BPIV, ex 'R3821', 'L8841', 'Z5722', Strathallan, Canada,		
			RCAF 10201. *Spirit of Britain First*. 82 Sqn c/s.		
			Crashed 18-8-03. Nose of Mk.I L6739	® [4]	4-06
❑ -		Bolingbroke IVT	G-MKIV, ex G-BLHM ntu, RCAF 10038.		
			Crashed 21-6-87. With nose of 9893	[3]	4-06
❑ V9312		Lysander TT.IIIA	G-CCOM, ex N9309K. Florida, Canada, RCAF, RAF, 4,		
			4, 613, 225. Stored, wings being worked on	®	4-06
❑ TA805		Spitfire IX ✈	G-PMNF, ex Sandown, Battle, South Africa,		
	'FX-M'		SAAF, 234, 183. 234 Sqn c/s. First flown 7-12-05	[2]	4-06
❑ TD248	'CR-S'	Spitfire XVI ✈	G-OXVI, ex Audley End, Braintree, Earls Colne, Sealand,		
			Hooton Park 7246M, 610, 2 CAACU, 695. 74 Sqn c/s	SL	4-06
❑ WD373	'12'	Chipmunk T.10 ✈	G-BXDI, ex 2 AEF, S'ton UAS, Leeds UAS, 63 GCF,		
			HCCS, 2 BFTS		4-06
❑ WP859*		Chipmunk T.10 ✈	G-BXCP, ex 8 AEF, 4 AEF, Liv UAS, PFS, AOTS,		
			1 ITS, Bri UAS, 4 SoTT, 663, RAFC. Arrived 23-5-05		4-06
❑ WP929	'F'	Chipmunk T.10 ✈	G-BXCV, ex Shawbury, 8 AEF, Liv UAS, Cam UAS,		
			Wittering SF, RAFTTC, Coningsby SF, 61 GCF, 661		4-06
❑ XP772		Beaver AL.1	G-DHCZ, ex G-BUCJ, Middle Wallop, Beverley, Leconfield,		
			Middle Wallop, 15 Flt, 667, 132 Flt, AFWF	®	4-06
❑ XX543		Bulldog T.1	G-CBAB, ex Shawbury, York UAS, 6 FTS, York UAS,		
			RNEFTS, CFS. *Donna*		4-06

❏	'42161'	Silver Star Mk.3 ✈	G-TBRD, ex N33VC, Switzerland, G-JETT, G-OAHB,		
			CF-IHB, CAF 133261, RCAF 21261	GA	4-06
❏	119	T-28B Fennec ✈	N14113, ex USA, Haiti AF 1236, N14113, FAF		
			(No.119), USAF 51-7545. *Little Rascal*	RR	4-06
❏	1747	Harvard IV ✈	G-BGPB, ex '20385' North Weald, Port AF 1747, WGAF		
			BF+050, AA+050, 53-4619. PortAF c/s. *Taz*		4-06
❏	8178 'FU-178'	F-86A-5-NA ✈	G-SABR, ex B'mouth, N178,N68388,48-0178. 4th FW c/s	GA	4-06
❏	517692	T-28A Fennec ✈	G-TROY, ex F-AZFR, AdA Fennec No.142, 51-7692.		
			EALA 09/72 c/s		4-06
❏	'1164'	Beech 18TM ✈	G-BKGL, ex Prestwick, CF-QPD, RCAF 5193,		
			RCAF 1564. USAAC colours.		4-06

B-17 Preservation Ltd / B-17 Charitable Trust: During the summer of 2004, *Sally B* was used for the Channel 4 TV series *Bomber Crew*, charting the progress of four grand-sons and one grand-daughter of RAF Bomber Command aircrew through simulated training and action. It was festooned with cameras for the filming. The year 2005 marked two anniversaries for the B-17 - her 60th birthday and the 30th year of operation in the UK. However, these 'birthdays' were over-shadowed by the advent of new European Union-inspired insurance categories that put *Sally B* in the same bracket as a Boeing 737! The premiums involved were crippling and a vigorous campaign was initiated that looks set *eventually* to have this daft bit of legislation changed. But *Sally B* faced grounding during the 2005 season until the Virgin Group stepped in to support the season. Then Lloyds underwriters combined to sort out a very beneficial premium for 2006. All of this was *very* welcome support, but the changing of the EU 'ruling' must remain the priority.

Lifeblood of the operation of this flying memorial is the *Sally B* **Supporters' Club** – membership details from the contacts below. The club holds a variety of exclusive events and publishes the excellent *Sally B News*.

◆ PO Box 92, Bury St Edmunds, IP28 8RR tel 01638 721304 fax 01638 720506
   e-mail sallyb@B-17preservation.demon.co.uk www.sallyb.org.uk

| ❏ | '124485' | B-17G-105-VE ✈ | G-BEDF, ex N17TE, IGN F-BGSR, 44-85784. | | |
| | 'DF-A' | | *Sally B* (port), *Memphis Belle* (stb) | | 4-06 |

The Fighter Collection (TFC): In the spring of 2006, TFC announced that it was reviewing the 'fleet'. On the plus side a 'razorback' Curtiss-built P-47G (see below), a TF-51 (see under Greenham Common, Berks, for a good possibility) and Spitfire XVIII G-BRAF (see below) and Pearl Harbor-era P-40B Warhawk would be joining the collection. (The latter, 41-13297, was registered G-CDWH in January 2006 and is thought to be still under restoration in California.) Being disposed of were Hurricane G-HURY [1] and Jungmeister G-AYSJ - cancelled as sold in Canada and the USA respectively during February 2006. *Very likely* going are P-47D/N G-THUN [2] and the yet-to-fly Beaufighter [3]. Not announced at the time, but also *probably* to go as soon as it completes flight test, is the Bristol F.2b G-ACAA [4]; Spitfire IX RK858 is also *believed* to be for sale [5]. B-25D G-BYDR *Grumpy* was finally sold to the Seattle-based Flying Heritage Collection during 2004 and was re-registered as N25644. It is not destined to cross 'The Pond' until mid-2006 but left Duxford on 17th July. Some have expressed horror at these machines moving on. Another out-break of 'Little Englander' disease I'm afraid. Thanks to TFC we have basked in a rich spectrum of warbirds and we continue to. It will be sad to see some of these 'old favourites' go, but great to welcome the new ones. *And* enthusiasts somewhere else in the world (or perhaps the UK) will get to experience 'new' shapes and sounds.

Curtiss Hawk 75A-1 NX80FR first flew following restoration on 13th October 2004 at Chino, California. It arrived at Duxford in April, ready to 'star' in that July's 'Flying Legends' airshow. During December 2005 an exchange took place that brought the 'Staggerwing' to TFC with the P-40 moving to North Weald, Essex [6]. Arriving at TFC's hangar in February 2006 was Fiat CR-42 G-CBLS. Work will continue to complete its restoration to flying condition and the prospect of it and Gladiator G-GLAD flying together is mouth-watering!

Notes: P-47 *No Guts, No Glory* is based upon elements of P-47D N47DD (45-49192), the fuselage of a P-47N and other components. N47DD is also the basis for the static P-47D in the American Air Museum, see above [2]. The P-51C is a heavily-modified Israeli AF/DF P-51D fuselage, fitted with the wings of a P-51B, also found in Israel [7].

Departures: TFC 'hack', Baron D55 G-AWAH was sold in the USA 3-05 becoming N771B with Steve Hinton, no less; Jungmeister G-AYSJ left by road 5-3006 for the USA; Yak-3U G-BTHD was cancelled as sold in the USA in 3-05. P-40M G-KITT to North Weald, Essex, 14-12-05 with 'Staggerwing' G-BRVE coming the other way; Yak-50 '69' (G-BTZB) is registered to a Fareham owner and has been deleted.

W&19 (p27) noted Mosquito T.3 TV959 departing by road for a 'Norfolk workshop' pending export to the USA. It is still at <u>Martham</u>, Norfolk.

◆ *Open to the public during normal museum hours. TFC stages the 'Flying Legends' airshow and operates the Friends of the Fighter Collection support group. c/o IWM, Duxford Airfield, Duxford, CB2 4QR*

❑ G-AYGE		SNCAN SV-4C ✈	ex F-BCGM. CoA 4-6-03		3-04
❑ G-BRVE*		Beech D.17S ✈	ex North Weald, N1139V, NC1139V, FT475,		
			44-67724, 23689 ntu. Arrived 14-12-05	[6]	4-06
❑ 'D8084'	'S'	Bristol F.2b ✈	G-ACAA, ex Hatch, Weston-o-t-Green. 139 Sqn c/s	[4]	4-06
❑ N5903		Gladiator II	G-GLAD, ex Yeovilton, 'N2276', 'N5226', Old Warden,		
			61 OTU	®	4-06
❑ S1581	'573'	Nimrod I ✈	G-BWWK, ex St Leonards-on-Sea, St Just, Henlow, ?,		
			802. 802 Sqn colours		4-06
❑ EP120	'AE-A'	Spitfire V ✈	G-LFVB, ex Audley End, Duxford, St Athan 8070M,		
			Wattisham, Boulmer, Wilmslow, St Athan, 5377M,		
			53 OTU, 402, 501. *City of Winnipeg* , 402 Sqn c/s		4-06
❑ FE695	'94'	Harvard IIB ✈	G-BTXI, ex Vasteras, RSwAF Fv16105, RCAF, 6 SFTS,		
			RAF FE695, 42-892		4-06
❑ 'KD345'	'A-130'	FG-1D Corsair ✈	G-FGID, ex N8297, N9154Z, USN 88297.		
			1850 Sqn, SEAC colours		4-06
❑ KZ321	'JV-N'	Hurricane IV ✈	G-HURY, ex Earls Colne, Biggin Hill, Bitteswell,		
			Blackbushe, Israel, Yugoslav AF, RAF. 6 Sqn c/s	[1]	4-06
❑ 'MV268'	'JE-J'	Spitfire XIV ✈	G-SPIT, ex Sleaford, Blackbushe, G-BGHB ntu, Bangalore,		
			Indian inst T20, IAF, MV293 ACSEA. 'Johnnie' Johnson c/s		4-06
❑ PK624		Spitfire F.22	ex St Athan, Abingdon 8072M, Northolt, Uxbridge,		
			North Weald, 'WP916', 9 MU, 614. Stored		4-06
❑ RK858		Spitfire IX	ex CIS, USSR, RK858 no RAF service. Stored	[5]	4-06
❑ SM969*	'D-A'	Spitfire XVIII	G-BRAF, ex Greenham Common, Australiam Martham,		
			North Weald, ?, Bournemouth, Biggin Hill, Bitteswell,		
			Blackbushe, New Delhi, Indian AF HS877, RAF SM969,		
			47 MU, India, ACSEA, 76 MU. CoA 23-9-93. Stored		**due**
❑ VX653		Sea Fury FB.11	G-BUCM, ex Hendon, Yeovilton, Lee-on-Solent,		
			Lossiemouth, FRU, 811, 738, 736	®	4-06
❑ -	'57-H'	L-4A-PI Cub ✈	G-AKAZ, ex F-BFYL, ALAT, 42-36375. USAAF c/s		9-05
❑ –	'F'	FM-2 Wildcat ✈	G-RUMW, ex USA N4845V, 86711. FAA colours		4-06
❑ 'A19-144'		Beaufighter Mk.21	ex Melbourne, Sydney, RAAF A8-324	® [3]	3-06
❑ No.82*		Hawk 75A-1 ✈	G-CCVH, ex NX80FR, Chino, France, Cazaux, GC 11/5.		
			Arrived 4-05		4-06
❑ -*		Fiat CR-42	G-CBLS, ex Italy, Sweden, RSweAF Fv 2524. Arrived 2-06		4-06
❑		Ki-43 Hyabusa	ex Australia. Stored		1-02
❑ '19'*		Polikarpov I-15 ✈	FLAR-02089. Resident since 7-04		4-06
❑ '20'		Lavochkin La-11	ex Monino, CIS, USSR. Stored		1-02
❑ –		P-40	ex USSR. Substantial remains. Stored		1-02
❑ '40467'	'19'	F6F-5K Hellcat ✈	G-BTCC, ex N10CN ntu, N100TF, Yankee Air Corps,		
			N80142, USMC Museum, 80141		4-06
❑ 21714	'201'	F8F-2P Bearcat ✈	G-RUMM, ex NX700HL, N1YY, N4995V, 121714.		
			VF-20 c/s, Lt/Cdr 'Whiff' Caldwell's a/c		4-06
❑ 80425	'WT-4'	F7F-3P Tigercat ✈	G-RUMT, N7235C, ex Chino, Butler, USN 80425.		
			VMP-254 colours		4-06
❑ 219993		P-39Q-5-BE ✈	N139DP, ex Santa Monica, Australia, New Zealand,		
			New Guinea, 82nd TRS'71st TRG. *Brooklyn Bum*		4-06
❑ 225068*		P-47G	G-THUN, ex N47DG, Greenham Common (?), USA (?),		
			Warbirds of GB, '28476'. N42354, TP-47G, 42-25068.		
			Arrived by container 4-06		4-06
❑ '226671'		P-47D/N ✈	G-THUN, ex N47DD, 45-49192. *No Guts, No Glory.*		
	'MX-X'		78th FG colours	[2]	4-06

❑ '325147'   P-51C   ✈ G-PSIC, ex '2106449', N51PR, Chino. *Princess Elizabeth*
                        352nd FG c/s.First flown 3-6-05   [7] 4-06
❑ 463864   P-51D-20-NA ✈ G-CBNM, ex Sweden SE-BKG, N42805, N251L, IDF/AF 3506
                        RSwAF Fv26158, USAAF 44-63864, 78th FG. *Twilight Tear*   4-06

Historic Aircraft Collection of Jersey (HAC): Following nearly two years of planning and a huge campaign to fund-raise, Hurricane 'Z5140' and Spitfire BM597 flew to Malta on 14th September 2005, flown by Clive Denney and Charlie Brown respectively. This was the 'Merlins over Malta' project designed to show the people of the George Cross Island a Hurricane and Spitfire in the air for the first time since 1945. The Hurricane had adopted the Malta-based colours of 126 Squadron – with the superbly appropriate 'HA-C' codes. For a brief time, the Spitfire took on an overall blue scheme plus the codes 'U-2' to represent a machine launched off the carrier USS *Wasp* during Operation CALENDAR in April 1942. This scheme was removed in early October 2005 [1]. See under St Leonards-on-Sea, East Sussex, for details of HAC's closely-related Aero Vintage Ltd. The MS.505 started life as a German-built airframe (No.1827), before conversion to a Criquet. The intention is to return it to Luftwaffe specification [2]. HAC are building the DH.9 that will go on display in 'AirSpace' - see under St Leonards-on-Sea.

❑ L7181*   Hind I   G-CBLK, ex St Leonards on Sea, Rockliffe, Canada, Kabul,
                             Afghanistan AF, RAF, 211. Stored   9-05
❑ 'Z5140' 'HA-C' Hurricane XII ✈ G-HURI, ex 'Z7381', TFC, Coningsby, Coventry, Canada,
                             71. 126 Sqn colours   4-06
❑ BM597 'JH-C' Spitfire Vb ✈ G-MKVB, ex Audley End, Fulbourne, Church Fenton, Linton-
                             on-Ouse, Church Fenton, St Athan, 5713M, 58 OTU, 317 [1] 4-06
❑ WZ879   '73' Chipmunk T.10 ✈ G-BWUT, ex Newton, CFS, RAFC, CFS, 3 FTS, RAFC,
                             CFS, 2 FTS, Benson SF, PFTS, AOTS, Wales UAS, AOTS,
                             PFS, AOTS, 1 ITS, Leeds UAS, Nott UAS, RAFC, Marham
                             SF, BCCF, Marham SF, BCCF   4-06
❑ 'TA+RC'   MS.505   ✈ G-BPHZ, ex F-BJQC, French mil. Luftwaffe c/s   [2] 4-06

Historic Flying Ltd: HFL's hangar and much of their operational flying is shared with ARC (see above). Only aircraft operated, or being restored by, HFL are given here. Spitfire Tr.9 161 (G-CCCA) first flew in the hands of ARC's John Romain from here on 13th January. Mk.V JG891 should fly in the spring of 2006. It will be unique among its airworthy colleagues, in its configuration with the deep chin cowl associated with the Vokes desert air filter fitment [1]. Mk.XVI RW386 should also be flying before 2006 is out.
   Notes: Spitfire XVI TD248, previously operated by Silver Victory, was acquired by Spitfire Ltd in early 2005 and repainted in 72 Squadron, 2nd TAF colours plus AM Cliff Spink's initials - 'CR-S' - by September 2005. It is now 'based' with ARC - see above.
◆ Not *available to public inspection, although the flyers regularly make appearances at airshows.*

❑ JG891   Spitfire Vc   G-LFVC, ex ZK-MKV, Audley End, Auckland, RAAF
                             A58-178, 79, RAF JG891. Accident 1-44   ⑧ [1] 4-06
❑ RN201   Spitfire XIV ✈ G-BSKP, ex Audley End, Sandown, Audley End, Duxford,
                             Paddock Wood, Audley End, Ludham, Beauvechain 'SG-3',
                             Belg AF SG-31, RAF, 350, 83 GSU, RN201. 41 Sqn c/s   4-06
❑ RW386*'NG-D' Spitfire XVI G-BXVI, ex Greenham Common, North Weald, ?, Audley End,
                             Biggin Hill, Bitteswell, Blackbushe,St Athan, Halton 6944M,
                             58 MU, 604. Arrived 7-7-05   ⑧ 4-06
❑ SM845 'GZ-J' Spitfire XVIII ✈ G-BUOS, ex Audley End, Witney, USA, Ind AF HS687,
                             SM845. 32 Squadron colours   4-06
❑ WB569   Chipmunk T.10 ✈ G-BYSJ, ex SE-BON, WB569, 1 AEF, Cam UAS, Oxf UAS,
                             South Cerney SF, RAFTC CF, 4 SoTT, 22 GCF, 2 SoTT,
                             22 RFS, Cam UAS, 22 RFS.   4-06
❑ WK522   Chipmunk T.10   G-BCOU, ex Audley End, Abn AUS, Liv UAS, Man UAS,
                             Gla UAS, Stn UAS, Bri UAS, 3 RFS, 5 BFTS. *Thunderbird 5.*
                             CoA 30-3-95   ⑧ 4-06
❑ 'UB-424'   Spitfire IX   ex USA, Myanmar, Burma AF UB42̲5, Israel DF/AF
                             20-42, RAF. Stored   4-06
❑ 161   Spitfire Tr.IX ✈ G-CCCA, ex G-TRIX, Goodwood, G-BHGH ntu, IAAC 161,
                             IAAC 161, G-15-174, PV202, 412, 33. IAAC c/s. F/f 13-1-05 4-06

Old Flying Machine Company (OFMC) / **Classic Aviation** (CA): On 2nd December 2005, **Ray Hanna** AFC* died peacefully at his apartment in Switzerland, aged 77. A former leader of the 'Red Arrows'; pilot for major airlines including Cathay Pacific and quite possibly the finest 'warbird' pilot the UK has produced. Despite all of his skills and achievements, it would be difficult to find a more modest person. Extra words to describe an extraordinary life are hardly necessary. We are all the richer for having witnessed Ray fly and for all of the exquisite aircraft that OFMC have brought us over the years.

Several OFMC-operated aircraft owned by others, but are run as a 'stable'. T-28A Fennec 517692 (G-TROY) has been operated by ARC since 2000 and should have been transferred to them long before now – see above.

♦ *Aircraft on show to the public during normal museum hours. OFMC have a support group,* **The Tiger Squadron,** *including newsletter* Tiger Tales. *The Old Flying Machine Co, Duxford Airfield, Duxford, CB2 4QR www.ofmc.co.uk*

❑ LN-AMY		AT-6D Texan	✈ ex Norway, LN-LCS ntu, LN-LCN ntu, N10595, 42-85068	9-05
❑ MH434		Spitfire IX	✈ G-ASJV, ex Booker, COGEA Nouvelle OO-ARA, Belgian AF	
			SM-41, Fokker B-13, Netherlands H-68, H-105 322, MH434,	
			349, 84 GSU, 222, 350, 222.	4-06
❑ TE184	'C'	Spitfire XVI	✈ G-MXVI, ex Halton, North Weald, St Merryn, Holywood,	
			Aldergrove, Finningley, Cranwell, Henlow, Bicester, Royton	4-06
❑ XV474	'T'	Phantom FGR.2	ex Wattisham, 74, 56, 23, 56, 23, 19, 2, 31, 17. 74 Sqn c/s	4-06
❑		A6M *Zeke*	ex Russia (?), USA, Pacific. Stored	4-04
❑ E3B-153		Jungmann	✈ G-BPTS, ex Spanish AF.	4-04
❑ '463221'	'B7-H'	P-51D-25-NA	✈ G-BTCD, ex TFC, N51JJ, N6340T, RCAF 9568, USAAF	
			44-73149. *Ferocious Frankie*	4-06

Plane Sailing Ltd: The 'Cat' flies in the all-white colours of a USAAF OA-10A.

♦ *Duxford Airfield, Duxford, CB2 4QR tel/fax 01223 837011 e-mail 106324.64 @compuserve.com www.catalinabookings.org*

❑ '433915'	Canso A	✈ G-PBYA, ex C-FNJF, CF-NJF, F-ZBBD, CF-NJF, F-ZBAY,	
		CF-NJF,RCAF 11005. USAAF 5th ERS c/s	4-06

Others: A series of aircraft are also resident. Owner/operator decodes are as follows: Carolyn Grace (CG); Classic Wings (CW); Mark Miller and friends (MM). On 19th June 2004 Mark Miller and family celebrated the first flight of their immaculate Dragon Rapide restoration - bedecked in the wartime colours of Scottish Airways Ltd. This has been a painstaking and truly magnificent restoration and is a great addition to the Duxford skyline [1]. The Meteor T.7 is only transiting, as it is reported to have been sold in California, USA [2].

❑ G-ACMN		Leopard Moth	✈ ex X9381, 9GCF, Netheravon SF, 297, 7 AACU,		
			6 AACU, 24, G-ACMN	CG	4-06
❑ G-AGJG		Dragon Rapide	✈ ex X7344, 1 Cam Flt. First flown 19-6-04	MM [1]	4-06
❑ G-APAO		Tiger Moth	✈ ex R4922, 6 FTS, 7 EFTS	CW	4-06
❑ G-AVGG		Cherokee 140	ex Leeds-Bradford. Crashed 10-8-70. Hulk		2-00
❑ HG691		Dragon Rapide	✈ ex AIYR, ex HG691, Yatesbury SF. *Classic Lady.*	CW	4-06
❑ ML407		Spitfire Tr IX	✈ G-LFIX, ex Audley End, Goodwood, St Merryn,		
	'OU-V'		Strathallan, IAAC 162, G-15-175, ML407, 29 MU,		
			332, 485, 349, 341, 485. *Aon.* 485 Sqn colours	CG	4-06
❑ WF877		Meteor T.7 (mod)	G-BPOA, ex Washington, Kemble, North Weald,		
			Higher Blagdon,Blagdon, Tarrant Rushton, Chilbolton,		
			Folland, Gloster, 96, Meteor Flight Wunstorf, 11	[2]	4-06

ELY on the A10 north-east of Cambridge

William Collins: Andover CC.2 XS791 moved to Stock, Essex, by November 2004. Located at the former RAF Hospital, **1094 Squadron, ATC** (e-mail adj@1094sqnatc.org) still have their Chipmunk.

❑ WG362		Chipmunk T.10	8630M/8437M, ex Newton, Swinderby, Filton, Bir UAS, Wales	
		PAX	UAS, Ox UAS, Swanton Morley SF, Carlisle SF, Mildenhall	
			CF, 100, Edn UAS, 3 BFTS, 16 RFS, 3 BFTS, 7 RFS	® 2-06

EVERSDEN on the A603 west of Cambridge

A variety of airframes are stored at a *private* location in the area F.150L G-BAXV was flying again by 2005.

❏ G-AYBV	Tourbillon	unfinished homebuild project. Stored	9-03
❏ G-AZDY	Tiger Moth	ex F-BGDJ, French AF, PG650. CoA 18-8-97	2-01
❏ G-BKKS	Mercury Dart	unfinished homebuild project. Stored	4-95
❏ G-GREG	CEA DR.220	ex F-BOKR. CoA 19-2-91. Stored	2-01

GAMLINGAY on the B1040 south-east of St Neots

❏ G-BBAZ	Hiller UH-12E	ex EC-DOR, G-BBAZ, N31707, CAF CH-112 112276, RCAF 10276. CoA 23-5-91. Stored	2-00

GLATTON on the B660 south of Peterborough

Rainbow Eagle G-MJBN (last noted July 1995) has moved on – no details.

GRANSDEN LODGE AERODROME north of the B1046 north-east of Gamlingay

Grasshopper TX.1 XA243 had gone by September 2005.

HOUGHTON on the A1123 east of Huntingdon

Jon Wilson: Keeps his Canberra nose in the area.

❏ WJ567	Canberra B.2	ex Wyton, 100, 85, MinTech, 45, RNZAF, 45, 59, 149. Nose	9-04

LITTLE GRANSDEN AERODROME south of the B1046, south of Great Gransden

Yak UK Ltd: Jungmann G-BIRI was flying by 2004. By mid-2005 Piranha G-BKOT had moved to Bourn, Cambs. Queen Air 80 G-KEAC was scrapped by late 2005.

◆ *Visits are strictly by prior arrangement only.*

❏ G-AIRI	Tiger Moth	ex N5488, 29 EFTS, 14 EFTS, 20 ERFTS. CoA 9-11-81	4-06
❏ G-TINY	Zlin Z.526F	ex OK-CMD, G-TINY, YR-ZAD. CoA 17-8-98	4-06
❏ LY-ALJ	Yak-52	ex DOSAAF 132. Wreck.	9-03
❏ -*	Stinson 108-2	stored. First noted 8-03.	8-05

LITTLE STAUGHTON AERODROME south of the A45, west of Eaton Socon

❏ G-ARAU	Cessna 150	ex Willingham, Sibson, Land's End, N6494T. Dam 23-5-829-96	
❏ G-ARRG	Cessna 175B	ex Kimbolton, Great Yarmouth, N8299T. Dam 3-11-70	2-00
❏ G-ARSB	Cessna 150A	ex Willingham, N7237X. CoA 10-6-88. Fuselage	2-00
❏ G-BBVG	Aztec 250C	ex ET-AEB, 5Y-AAT. CoA 10-9-88. Derelict	2-00
❏ SE-GVH	Tomahawk 112	ex Chessington. Stored	3-06
❏ 1360	Chipmunk T.20	G-BYYU, ex Bedford, Spanhoe, CS-DAP ntu, PorAF. Stored	4-02

MARCH on the A141 south of Wisbech

No.1220 Squadron Air Cadets: Have their HQ in Gas Road. 'Parent' is Wittering. The entry for the nose of Harrier GR.3 XZ990 being here was 'duff', that has never been so.

❏ –	Cadet TX.3	dismantled and stored outside	1-06

PETERBOROUGH

No.115 Squadron Air Cadets: In the Westwood area, has a Canberra nose.

❏ WK127*	'FO' Canberra TT.18	ex Bassingbourn, Wyton 8985M, 100, 7, 10. Damaged 13-12-88. Nose	2-06

PETERBOROUGH BUSINESS AERODROME (CONINGTON) E of the A1, S of Wansford

❏ G-AVBP	Cherokee 140	Crashed 14-8-96. Stored	4-97

PETERBOROUGH SPORT AERODROME (SIBSON) west of the A1, south of Wansford

Comanche 260 G-ATNV was flying again by 2005. Some of these references are on course for LOST!

❏ G-ARBN	Apache 160	ex EI-AKI, N3421P ntu. Damaged 8-86. Stored	8-03
❏ G-ARMA	Apache 160G	ex Oxford, N4448P. CoA 22-7-77	® 3-06
❏ G-ATMU	Apache 160G	ex Beccles, Southend, N4478P. CoA 14-4-90. Fuselage	8-03
❏ G-AWSD	Cessna F.150J	Damaged 16-10-87. Stored	3-98
❏ G-AYRP	Cessna FA.150L	Crashed 1-8-87. Stored	3-98
❏ G-BDNR	Cessna FRA.150M	Damaged 22-1-92. Rebuild, wings of G-AYRP above	® 10-01
❏ G-BIHE	Cessna FA.152	Damaged 10-3-99. Stored	10-01
❏ G-HUNY	Cessna F.150G	ex G-AVGL. Damaged 16-10-87. Stored	10-97

ST IVES on the A1123 east of Huntingdon

The Stirling Project: Former Stirling navigator Brian Harris and others have established themselves as an active restoration group, dedicated to the education of the public in all matters concerning the Short Stirling. Having almost completed an acclaimed restoration of FN5 nose turret, their attention is now directed to the forward fuselage and work is on hand on the instrument panel, throttle box and rudder pedals. They are fortunate to have the facilities of a workshop within RAF Wyton. The salvage of Mk.III LJ628 from the Peak District courtesy of an RAF Chinook early in 2005 has greatly helped the project.

◆ *Visits by prior arrangement only. Dr Geoff Edwards, Redcroft, St Nicolas Avenue, Cranleigh, GU6 7AQ, tel 01223 894441 e-mail info@stirlingproject.co.uk www.stirlingproject.co.uk*

Others: David Collings *should* still have the B-2.

❏ G-ADFV	Blackburn B-2	ex Breighton, E' Kirkby, Tattershall, Wigan, Caterham, 2893M, 4 EFTS, Hanworth. CoA 26-6-41	off site ®	7-01

UPWOOD south east of Peterborough, west of Ramsey

At the former airfield a Grasshopper is stored.

❏ WZ797*	Grasshopper TX.1 ex Shenington	12-05

WATERBEACH on the A10 north of Cambridge

No.39 Engineers Regiment: The Hunter reminds one and all of a different era at this location.

❏ WN904	Hunter F.2	ex Duxford, Newton 7544M, 257. Gate. 1 Sqn c/s	10-05

WHITTLESEY on the A605 east of Peterborough

❏ G-AOGV	J/5R Alpine	CoA 17-7-72. Stored.	12-97

WITCHFORD south of the A142 south west of Ely

RAF Witchford Museum: The former bomber airfield is now the Lancaster Way Business Park, with access off the A142. An excellent museum dedicated to RAF Witchford and nearby RAF Mepal and the units that served from them has been established within the foyer of the Grovemere Building within the estate. Included in the displays is a Bristol Hercules engine from a 115 Squadron Lancaster II that was recovered in 1995. Also within the business park is a memorial to 115 Squadron.

◆ *Open Mon to Fri (excluding Bank Hols), plus Sundays May to Sep, by kind permission of Grovemere Holdings Ltd. 01353 666666*

WITTERING AIRFIELD on the A1 south of Stamford

RAF Wittering: The Harrier Maintenance Training School (HMTS) cherishes the GR.1.

❑ XV279	Harrier GR.1	8566M, ex Farnborough, Culdrose, AAEE. HMTS	3-06
❑ XV779	Harrier GR.3	8931M, ex 233 OCU, 3, Wittering SF, 3, 20, GR.1, 20, 4, 1.	
		20 Sqn colours. Gate	4-06
❑ XW923	Harrier GR.3	8724M, ex 1417 Flt, 233 OCU, 1, GR.1, 1. Nose. Cr 26-5-81	5-00
❑ XZ146	'S' Harrier T.4	9281M, ex North Luffenham, Shawbury, 20,	
		233 OCU, Gutersloh SF, 233 OCU, 4. 20 Sqn c/s. Displayed	5-04
❑ ZB604*	Harrier T.8	ex Yeovilton, 899. Arrived by road 9-3-06	3-06

Locally: By early 2005 the British Disabled Flying Club former Jordanian Air Force Bulldog 125s had moved on from storage and were flying by July: 408 became G-BDIN; 417 - G-CCZE; 418 - G-CCZF; 420 - G-DISA.

WOODHURST north of St Ives, west of the B1040

Chris Cannon: *Should* still have the Canberra nose.

❑ WE113	Canberra B.2	ex Wyton, 231 OCU, 100, 85, 98, 231 OCU. Nose.	6-00

WYTON AIRFIELD on the B1090 north-west of St Ives

RAF Wyton: The dump was cleared on 14th February 2006; Canberra T.17 WJ633 and PR.7 WT519 being removed by road. The nose of the former was saved by **Cpl Richy Doel** who also has a T.22 nose [1].

❑ WJ633	'EF'	Canberra T.17	ex dump, St Athan, Wyton, 360, 231 OCU, 100. Nose	[1] 3-06
❑ WT525*	'855'	Canberra T.22	ex South Woodham Ferrers, Stock, St Athan, FRADU,	
			17, 80. Nose. Arrived 2003	® [1] 3-06
❑ XH170		Canberra PR.9	8739M, ex 39, RAE, 58. Gate guardian	3-06

CHESHIRE

BURTONWOOD south of the M62, west of Warrington

RAF Burtonwood Heritage Centre: Very little of the once huge USAF Burtonwood air base remains, though cars that hurtle down the M62 are following the course of the main runway. Hangars to the north of the motorway are the most obvious survivors. The centre serves to set this to rights and has amassed an incredible amount of artefacts and images to tell the tale of this great airfield. To further tempt, there is a cafe, shop and a cinema.

◆ *Open weekdays 10.30am to 4.30pm, weekends noon to 4pm. Access off the M62, Junction 8 and signed. Or from Warrington, turn north off the A57 up Whittle Avenue and follow the signs. RAF Burtonwood Heritage Centre, 'Gulliver's World', Shackleton Close, Bewsey Park, Warrington, WA5 9YZ tel 07855 499798or 01925 725469 e-mail ianmrph@aol.com www.burtonwoodbase.org*

CHESTER

Ian Starnes: Vampire T.11 pod XD452 was sold during July 2005 for 'Gloucestershire'.

❑ XR654	Jet Provost T.4	ex Barton, Chelford, Macclesfield, Bournemouth, Coventry,	
		Puckeridge, Hatfield, Shawbury, CAW, 3 FTS, 6 FTS. Nose	3-06

A Vampire is stored, pod in one location and 'metal bits' in another, in this general area.

❑ XH312	'18' Vampire T.11	ex Knutsford, Woodford, Hawarden, St Athan, 8 FTS	3-06

HOOTON PARK south of Junction 6 of the M53, near Eastham Locks

Hooton Park Trust (HPT): The trust manages the site, with other bodies basing themselves. These include the **Griffin Trust** (GT), **The Aeroplane Collection** (TAC - see below) and the **Friends of Hooton Park**.

The project received a major boost with a Heritage Lottery Fund grant for £34,000 towards paying for consultants to examine the full potential of the site and how it can be developed.

Notes: The Tutor and the Spitfire IX FSM are on loan from Peter Storrar for the 610 Squadron Association - 610. Mike Davey owns the Meteor and the Phantom SIM [1]. The Meteor will be finished in the colours of the resident 610 (County of Chester) Squadron. The Hunter is on loan from Graham Sparkes [2].

Departures: Canberra B.2 WF911 was offered for sale by GT (reportedly at £1,500) during June 2004 and moved in August 2004 to Gloucester, Glos. Simon Pulford offered Canberra B.2 nose WJ676 for sale by 12-04 and it moved to South Shields, N&T by 2-05. His anonymous Tornado F.3 FSM departed before the end of 2005.

◆ *By prior arrangement, plus special events. Access off M53, Junction 6 marked 'Eastham Oil Terminal'. Go north to a roundabout then turn right into South Road. The Hangars, South Road, Hooton Park Airfield, Ellesmere Port, CH65 1BQ, tel 0151 327 3565 fax 0151 327 3564 e-mail info@hootonparktrust.co.uk www.hootonparktrust.co.uk*

❏ G-AGPG	Avro XIX Srs 2	ex TAC, Woodford, Brenzett, Southend, Pye, Ekco, Avro.		
		CoA 13-12-71. Hut 27	HPT	4-06
❏ –*	Easy-Riser	ex Manchester. Arrived 9-4-04	GT	4-06
❏ 'P2725' 'TM-B'	Hurricane FSM	BAPC.68, ex 'H3426', Coventry, Great Bridge, Wembley,		
		Lincoln, *Battle of Britain* 'P3975'. Hangar 1	GT ®	4-06
❏ 'RB159'*	Spitfire IX FSM	in 610 Sqn c/s as Mk.V flown by Sqn Ldr Ellis.		
'DW-D'		Hangar 1	610	4-06
❏ VM684	T.8 Tutor	BGA.791, ex VM684. CoA 2-71. 'Flies' in Hut 27	610	4-06
❏ 'WF714'*	Meteor F.8	WK914, ex Scampton, Sandown, Duxford, Rochester,		
		Manston, 85, CAW, 5 CAACU, 19. FR.9 nose.		
		Arrived 26-11-04	[1]	4-06
❏ XE584	Hunter FGA.9	ex Woodford, Barton, Chelford, Macclesfield,		
		Bitteswell, G-9-450, 208, 8, 1. 111 Sqn c/s. Nose	[2]	4-06
❏ –	Phantom SIM	ex Norway, Leuchars	[1]	4-06

The Aeroplane Collection (TAC): TAC is based at Hooton, although it still has a strong presence at the Air and Space Gallery at Manchester, Gtr Man. Much work is being carried out on the two Miles types. The aim is to create a static Gemini (to be 'labelled' G-AKHZ) and a static Messenger (likewise, G-AHUI) - both composites. The Messenger is centred upon Mk.2A G-AHUI, plus Mk.2 G-AILL, Mk.2A G-AJFF, Mk.2A G-AKDF, Mk.1A G-ALUG, Mk.2A EI-AGB (G-AHFP) and Mk.4A VP-KJL (G-ALAR) [1]. The Gemini on: Mk.1A G-AKHZ plus Mk.1 G-AKGD [2]. Anyone interested in helping, or who has leads to parts: please contact: Keith Cooper, 12 Warren Hey, Wirral, CH63 9LF. Apart from the machines noted below, TAC aircraft can be found under the following headings: Barton, Gtr Man (Parker CA-4 G-AFIU); Selby, N Yorks (Fa 330A-1); Manchester, Gtr Man, (Avian, Dragon Rapide, Bensen, 'Flea', Roe Triplane); Wolverhampton, W Mids (Anson).

▶ *Graham Sparkes, 7 Mayfield Avenue, Stretford, M32 9HL tel 07711 407468 e-mail aeroplanecol@aol.com*

❏ G-AJEB	J/1N Alpha	ex Manchester, Hooton, Warmingham, Brize Norton,		
		Wigan, Cosford. CoA 27-3-69. Less wings, Hut 27		4-06
❏ 'G-AHUI'	Messenger	ex Pulborough. Composite	® [1]	4-06
❏ 'G-AKHZ'	Gemini	ex Pulborough. Composite	® [2]	4-06
❏ –	BAPC.204 McBroom hang-g	ex Winthorpe, Hooton Park, Warmingham. Stored		4-06

MACCLESFIELD
Macclesfield College - European Centre for Aerospace Training: The North West Development Agency forked out £250,000 for the Jetstream 31 instructional airframe.

❏ G-BLKP*	Jetstream 3102	ex Humberside, Eastern, G-BLEX ntu, G-31-364.		
		CoA 19-4-03. Fuselage.. Arrived 11-03		6-05

MALPAS west of the A41, north-west of Whitchurch
No.617 Squadron Air Cadets: Whirlwind HAS.7 XK944 was scrapped in November 2002.

NANTWICH west of Crewe

Hack Green Secret Nuclear Bunker: Initially a World War Two radar station, it became a labyrinthine bunker for regional government officials to run to if the 'balloon' went up and is now a three-level visitor centre. Appropriate 'Cold War' exhibit is the **Phantom Preservation Group**'s FGR.2 nose – see also Ruthin, Wales.

◆ *'Brown signed' off the A530 Nantwich to Whitchurch road. Open daily mid-March to end of October. Open most weekends Nov, Jan, Feb, Mar – please check. Closed all Dec. PO Box 127, Nantwich, Cheshire, CW5 8AQ, tel 01270 629219 fax 01270 629218 e-mail coldwar@hackgreen.co.uk www.hackgreen.co.uk*

❑ XV490   Phantom FGR.2   ex Bruntingthorpe, Wattisham, 74, 228 OCU, 92, 56, 22, 92, 56, 23. Nose   ® 3-06

OLLERTON on the A537 south-east of Knutsford

Delta Force Centre: A paint-ball 'battlefield' near here has a camouflaged Aztec to add to the realism of the team-forming, character-enhancing, wallet-emptying, office-as-battleground experience!

❑ [G-SHIP]*   Aztec 250F   ex Hockley Heath, Coventry, Birmingham, N62490. Cr 4-12-83   1-06

SANDBACH on the A534 north-east of Crewe

Sandbach Car and Commercial Ltd: The Yard, Moston Road. Took delivery of a former Cosford Andover in late 2005. The same yard 'processed' the Blackpool, Lancs, Vulcan – qv.

❑ XS641*   'Z' Andover C.1(PR)   ex Cosford 9198M, Shawbury, 60, 115, 46, 84, SAR Flt, 84. First noted 10-05   1-06

STRETTON on the A49 south of Warrington

Last noted in March 1994, former Spanish Air Force Jungmeister ES1-16 has been consigned to LOST!

CORNWALL

BODMIN AERODROME east of the A30, north of Bodmin

W&R19 (p35) had Cessna 152 G-BHJA moving on. It turned up at <u>Biggin Hill</u>, Gtr Lon, by early 2005.

CALLINGTON on the A390 south-west of Tavistock

Complete with over-wing tanks, a Lightning is kept at this *private* location.

❑ XR755   'BA' Lightning F.6   ex Binbrook, 5, 5-11 pool   2-05

CULDROSE AIRFIELD on the A3083 south of Helston

HMS *Sea Hawk:* The **School of Flight Deck Operations** (SFDO) is the main 'user' of *W&R* airframes on the base. With the demise of the incredible Sea Harrier, an influx has arrived here, so it cannot be long before the 'land-lubber' GR.3s move on.

Departures: **Buccaneer** S.2B XV359 to <u>Topsham</u>, Devon, 23-4-05; **Jetstream** T.1 XX491 arrived 5-11-03 from Cranwell, Lincs, to Ipswich, Suffolk, by 9-05 and then <u>Shoreham</u>, W Sussex, on 10-11-05; T.1 XX492 to <u>Winthorpe</u>, Notts, 9-12-04; T.1 XX500 to <u>Ipswich</u>, Suffolk, 29-7-05; **Lynx** HAS.3 XZ243 scrapped circa 2001; **Wessex** HAS.1 XS876 moved via Hixon, Staffs, to <u>Nottingham East Midlands</u> Airport, Leics, in July 2004; HAS.1 XS885 to <u>Predannack</u>, Cornwall, 21-2-06; HC.2 XR528 to <u>Gosport</u>, Hants, 23-2-06; HAS.3 XP137 to <u>Predannack</u>, Cornwall, 12-5-04.

❑ 'AV511'   '511' Merlin EMU   ex Yeovil, avionics test-rig   1-05
❑ XV371   '261' Sea King HAS.1   ex Gosport, A2699[2], Boscombe Down, AAEE.   10-03

❏ XV654	'705'	Sea King HAS.6	ex Gosport, A2698 [2], Fleetlands, 819. Cr 21-7-93	5-05
❏ XV657	'132'	Sea King HAS.5	A2600 [4], ex ETS, Fleetlands, Wroughton, 826.	
			Tail of ZA135	9-05
❏ XV741	'5'	Harrier GR.3	A2608 [3], ex A2607, Cosford, 233 OCU, 3, 233 OCU, 3	9-04
❏ XV753	'4'	Harrier GR.3	A2691 [2], ex Halton, Abingdon, 9075M,	
			St Athan, 233 OCU, 1, 3, 233 OCU	5-05
❏ XV783		Harrier GR.3	A2609 [3], ex Lee-on-Solent, Culdrose SAH, Cosford,	
			233 OCU, 4, 3, 233 OCU, 1, 233 OCU, 1, 233 OCU,	
			1417 Flt, 233 OCU, 4, 20, 4	5-05
❏ XV786	'S'	Harrier GR.3	A2611 [3], A2615, St Athan, 3, 4, 1, 4. Nose	7-05
❏ XV808		Harrier GR.3	A2687 [2], ex 9076M, 233 OCU, 3, 20	5-05
❏ XW271		Harrier T.4	A2692 [2], ex Cosford, 4, 1, 233 OCU	5-05
❏ XX510	'69'	Lynx HAS.2	A2683 [2], ex Gosport, A2601, A2772,	
			Lee-on-Solent, Foulness, Boscombe Down	5-05
❏ XZ145		Harrier T.4	A2610 [4], ex Shawbury, 20, 233 OCU, 3	5-05
❏ XZ440*		Sea Harrier FA.2	ex Yeovilton, 800, BAe, FRS.1, 801, 800, AAEE. Arr 14-2-06	2-06
❏ XZ996	'3'	Harrier GR.3	A2685 [2], ex 1417 Flt, 4, 1417 Flt,	
			233 OCU, 1417 Flt, 233 OCU	5-05
❏ ZD611*	'719'	Sea Harrier FA.2	ex St Athan, 899, 801, 899, 800, 899, 800, 899, 899,	
			800, 899, 801. First noted 9-05	9-05
❏ ZD667		Harrier GR.3	A2684 [2], 9201M, ex 1417 Flt, 233 OCU	2-05
❏ ZE690*	'007'	Sea Harrier FA.2	ex Yeovilton, 801, 899, 801, 800, 801, 800, 801,	
			899, FRS.1, 899. Arrived 29-3-06	3-06
❏ ZE692*	'008'	Sea Harrier FA.2	ex Yeovilton, 899, 801, 899, 800, 801, 899, 801, 899,	
			FRS.1, 801, 899. Arrived 23-2-06	2-06
❏ ZF641		EH-101 PP1	ex Fleetlands, Westland	5-05
❏ ZH797*	'000'	Sea Harrier FA.2	ex Yeovilton, 801, 899. Arrived 23-2-06	2-06
❏ ZH802*	'711'	Sea Harrier FA.2	ex Yeovilton, 899, 800, 899, 800, 801. Arr 21-2-06	2-06
❏ ZH809*		Sea Harrier FA.2	ex Yeovilton, 899, 800. Arrived 7-3-06	3-06

Others: The Sea King HAS.6 is used by the Engineering Training School [1].
◆ *There is a public viewing area with shop and cafe on the B3293 to the south of the base on the way to the village of Gweek. Viewing area open late Mar to end of Oct: Mon to Thu 10am to 5pm, Fri 9.30am to 4.30pm. In association with the Fleet Air Arm Museum there are regular tours of RNAS Sea Hawk staged from the viewing area. Please note: proof of identity required on purchase of tickets; customers may be subject to search; tours do not run during leave periods – late July to late August. Enquiries tel 01326 565085.*

❏ WF225		Sea Hawk F.1	A2623 [2], ex A2645, FRU, 738, 802. Gate	9-05
❏ XV372		SH-3D Sea King	ex Predannack, St Mawgan, Trowbridge, Yeovil,	
			Lee-on-Solent, RAE, Westlands. Hulk	8-02
❏ XV706*	'017'	Sea King HAS.6	ex 820, 810, 706, 810, 706, 814, 819.	[1] 5-05

DAVIDSTOW MOOR on minor road west of the A39 and Camelford

A new museum is being developed on the former airfield's domestic site. Several buildings are to be renovated and plans are to have the former shower block opened by August 2006. Displays will cover the part Cornwall played in World War Two. The squash court and another building will follow.

HELSTON on the A3083 north of Culdrose

The Flambards Experience: There is a huge amount on offer here, but the aviation element is definitely in retreat. As well as the airframes, the 'Britain in the Blitz Experience' is well worth a visit.
◆ *Open most days Easter to end of Oct 10am to 5pm. Call for full details of opening times. Last admission 3.30pm. Signed off the A3083 south of Helston, next to RNAS Culdrose. Clodgey Lane, Helston, TR13 0QA tel 01326 573404 fax 01326 573344, e-mail info@flambards.co.uk www.flambards.co.uk*

❏ WG511		Shackleton T.4	ex Colerne, St Mawgan, MOTU, Kinloss Wing,	
			MOTU, 120, 42. Nose	4-06
❏ XG831	'396'	Gannet ECM.6	ex Culdrose SAH-8, A2539, 831	4-06

| ❑ | XS887 | '403' | Wessex HAS.1 | ex Culdrose A2690, Wroughton, 771 | 4-06 |
| ❑ | – | | Concorde EMU | ex Filton, instrument layout trials | 4-06 |

LAND'S END on the A30 south-west of Penzance

Land's End: Suspended at a dramatic angle within the complex is a Bölkow 105. It has been given a new 'identity' to tie in with the *real* G-CDBS which belongs to the Cornwall Air Ambulance and is based at St Mawgan. G-BCXO was rebuilt with a new pod and flies on as G-THLS [1]. Last noted here in March 2002, Sopwith Baby REP BAPC.137 is reported to have moved to a 'sister' attraction at North Stainley, N Yorks.

◆ *From 10am daily, closing times vary. Sennen, Penzance, TR19 7AA tel 0870 4580044 fax 01736 871812, e-mail info@landsend-landmark.co.uk www.landsend-landmark.co.uk*

| ❑ | 'G-CDBS' | | MBB Bö 105D | G-BCXO, ex 'G-BOND', D-HDCE. wfu 4-3-92 | [1] | 4-06 |

LAND'S END AERODROME or St Just, on the B3306 south of St Just

❑	G-BFNU	BN-2B-21	CoA 18-8-89. Fuselage, stored	6-05
❑	G-SKNT	Pitts S-2A	ex G-PEAL, Plymouth, N81LF, N48KA. Dam 28-6-91	® 6-05
❑	'124'	Fokker D.VIII REP	G-BHCA. Crashed 21-8-81. Fuselage	6-05

LELANT on the A3074 south of St Ives

The Comper is *thought* to still be in store.

| ❑ | G-ABTC | Comper Swift | CoA 18-7-84. *Spirit of Butler*. Stored. | 11-93 |

LISKEARD on the A38 north-west of Plymouth

Castle Motors / Helicopters: The dramatically-posed Lightning graces the car park. The A.109 cabin is regularly hired for film use [1]. Spares-recovered A.109s G-USTA and SX-HCF, last noted in June 2001, are considered to be just that and no longer extant.

| ❑ | N71PT* | A.109A Mk.II | ex N4263A. Cabin | [1] | 6-01 |
| ❑ | XS936 | Lightning F.6 | ex Binbrook, 5, 11, LTF, 5/11, LTF, 5, 11, 23 | | 7-05 |

PREDANNACK AIRFIELD off the A3083 south of Helston

Fleet Air Arm Fire School: Travel back to *W&R16* (p42) where under this heading it was noted that Hunter T.7 XX466 had perished, last noted in May 1995. Well, tenacity will out, as they say. The cockpit is to be found serving the firemen at Guernsey, Channel Islands! The hulk of Harrier GR.3 XV786 here was without its nose and was scrapped by September 2004. (See under Culdrose, Cornwall, for XV786's nose.) By September 2004 there had been a clear-out of Wessex HAS.1 hulks: XM868, XM874, XP160, XS866, XS868 and XS881.

❑	WT308		Canberra B(I).6	A2601, ex Culdrose, DRA Farnborough, AAEE	10-05
❑	XE668	'832'	Hunter GA.11	A2647 [2], Ex A2733, Culdrose SAH,	
				Yeovilton, FRADU, 738, 26, 4	10-05
❑	XM870		Wessex HAS.1	A2634 [2], ex A2712, Gosport, Lee-o-Solent, 772	8-04
❑	XP137*	'711'	Wessex HAS.3	ex Culdrose, A2634 [2], A2712, Culdrose, Lee-on-Solent,	
				Wroughton, 737. Arrived 12-5-04	10-05
❑	XS516	'YQ'	Wessex HU.5	A2652 [2], ex Gosport, A2739, Lee-on-Solent, 845	10-05
❑	XS520*	'YF'	Wessex HU.5	ex Gosport, A2659 [2], A2749, Lee-on-Solent, 845. Arr21-2-06	2-06
❑	XS522	'ZL'	Wessex HU.5	A2663 [2], ex Gosport, A2753, Lee-on-Solent, Wroughton, 848	8-04
❑	XS529	'461'	Wasp HAS.1	A2696 [2], ex A2743, Culdrose, Manadon,	
				Lee-on-Solent, 829,*Galatea* Flt. Poor state	8-04
❑	XS885*	'512'	Wessex HAS.1	ex Culdrose A2631 [2], A2668, 772. Arrived 21-2-06	2-06
❑	XT468	'628'	Wessex HU.5	A2667 [2], ex A2744, ex Culdrose, Gosport,	
				Lee-on-Solent, Wroughton, 772	8-04
❑	XT762		Wessex HU.5	A2661 [2], ex Culdrose A2751, Lee-on-S, Wroughton, RAE	10-05

❑ XX479	'563'	Jetstream T.2	A2611 [4], ex St Athan, 750, CFS, 5 FTS, Sywell, Radlett, G-AXXT	8-04
❑ XZ969		Harrier GR.3	A2612 [3], ex Culdrose, A2610, Manadon, St Athan, 4, 1, 3	10-05
❑ ZD581*	'124'	Sea Harrier F/A.2	ex St Athan,800, FRS.1, 800, 801, 899. Arrived 1-9-04	10-05
❑ ZD631	'66'	Sea King HAS.6	A2621 [2], ex Gosport, Lee-on-Solent	8-04

ST AUSTELL on the A390 north-east of Truro

Henry Orchard and Sons: A consortium of enthusiasts clubbed together and acquired the nose of Shackleton AEW.2 WL756 from this yard. It moved to Caernarfon, Wales, on 10th February 2006.

ST MAWGAN AIRFIELD off the A3059, north-east of Newquay

RAF St Mawgan: As with several others, there is doubt over the future of this base. What units remain are due to move out by 2007 as 'Care and Maintenance' (or is that the estate agents?) move in. There is a sensational 'synthetic' fire trainer here that would appear to be a cross between a Harrier and a Sea King! The Sea King is plinth-mounted for training with the **School of Combat Survival and Rescue** [1].

| ❑ WL795 | 'T' | Shackleton AEW.2 | 8753M, ex 8, 205, 38, 204, 210, 269, 204 | | 9-05 |
| ❑ XV709 | '263' | Sea King HAS.6 | ex Gosport, 810, 706, 820, 826, 820, 814, 706 | [1] | 5-05 |

Barry Wallond: Aviation artist Barry has a Spitfire and other aviation artefacts in his garden and has acquired a Canberra nose.

| ❑ - | 'OU-Z' | Spitfire IX FSM | BAPC.268, ex 'MH978', 'N3317', Duxford, Dark Blue World. 485 Sqn colours | 9-05 |
| ❑ WD954* | | Canberra B.2 | ex Lumb, Hendon area, Rayleigh, East Kirkby, Tattershall, Bicester, 76, Upwood, Hemswell. Nose | 9-05 |

ST MERRYN AERODROME on the B3276 west of Padstow

McCandless G-ARTZ is the second user of the 'reggie' - see under Holywood, N Ireland [1].

❑ G-ARTZ {2}	McCandless M4	Stored. CoA 13-10-69	[1]	10-00
❑ 'G-ATCX'	Cessna 182A	G-OLSC, ex G-ATNU, EI-ANC, N6078B. Cr 6-6-93. Fuse		10-00
❑ G-AXVN	McCandless M4	Stored		10-00
❑ G-MLAS	Cessna 182E	ex Bodmin, OO-HPE, D-EGPE, N2826Y. Dam 14-12-80. Para-trainer		4-99

TORPOINT on the A374, west of Plymouth, across the Tamar

HMS Raleigh:

| ❑ XR523 | 'M' | Wessex HC.2 | ex Fleetlands, Gosport, Shawbury, Fleetlands, 72 | 6-02 |

TREMAR north of the B3254, north of Liskeard

Roy Flood: The Lightning is kept in *private* grounds here. See LOST! for details of a former resident.

| ❑ XR751 | | Lightning F.3 | ex Binbrook, 11, LTF, 29, 226 OCU, EE | 8-03 |

CUMBRIA

BARROW-IN-FURNESS

No news on the BD-5 that was at a night-club here. On finals for LOST!?

| ❑ G-BDTT | | Bede BD-5 | ex Tattershall Thorpe, Bourne | 10-03 |

CARK AERODROME south-west of Grange-over-Sands
North West Parachute Centre: Still have their para-trainer. (www.skydive-northwest.com)
❏ G-AWMZ Cessna F.172H ex Blackpool. Cr 18-1-76. Para-trainer 4-05

CARLISLE or Kingstown, on the A7 north of the City
Another reference that is getting long-in-the-tooth.
❏ G-AKTT Silvaire 8A ex N71852, NC71852. Crashed 6-7-91 1-96

CARLISLE AIRPORT (CROSBY-ON-EDEN)
Solway Aviation Museum operating as the **Edward Haughey Aviation Museum**: Now Lord Ballyedmond, Edward Haughey and his company Haughey Airports, owns Carlisle Airport and is busy setting about its development. The impressive heritage centre is continually up-dated and refined. Improvements have also been made to the workshop and storage areas. The Lightning made the trip from its 'pan' to the museum site during the late summer of 2005. The Vulcan is next!

Notes: Tom Stoddart owns Vulcan XJ823, and a share in the Sea Prince [1]. The Grasshopper is composite, with parts of WZ824 – see Dirleton, Scotland [2]. The Nimrod cockpit is owned by David Price [3].

◆ *Open 1st Apr to end of Oct Sat and Sun, Bank hols and also Fridays July-Aug also Fridays. 10.30am to 5pm. 'Aviation House', Carlisle Airport, Crosby-on-Eden, Carlisle, CA6 4NW tel/fax/info-line 01228 573823 e-mail info@solway-aviation-museum.co.uk www.solway-aviation-museum.co.uk*

❏ G-APLG		J/5L Aiglet	ex Maryport, Bletchley, Romsey, Southend,	
		Trainer	Rettendon, Corringham, Felthorpe. CoA 26-10-68	® 4-06
❏ WE188		Canberra T.4	ex Samlesbury, 231 OCU, 360, 231 OCU, 360,	
			100, 56, 231 OCU, Upwood SF, 231 OCU,	
			Upwood SF, Waddington SF, Hemswell SF	4-06
❏ WP314	'573'	Sea Prince T.1	ex Preston, Hull, Syerston, Halton, 8634M,	
			Kemble, 750, Sydenham SF, 750, Lossiemouth SF,	
			Shorts FU, Brawdy SF, Lossiemouth SF, 750	[1] 4-06
❏ WS832	'W'	Meteor NF.14	ex RRE Pershore, Llanbedr, 12 MU, 8 MU	4-06
❏ WV198	'K'	Whirlwind	G-BJWY ex Firbeck, Warmingham, Chorley,	
		HAR.21	Blackpool, Heysham, Carnforth, Gosport, Lee-on-	
			Solent A2576, Arbroath, 781, 848, USN 130191	4-06
❏ WZ515		Vampire T.11	ex Duxford, Staverton, Woodford, Chester,	
			St Athan, 4 FTS, 8 FTS, 56, 253, 16	4-06
❏ [WZ784]		Grasshopper TX.1	ex Thurrock. Displayed indoors	[2] 4-06
❏ XJ823		Vulcan B.2	ex 50, Wadd Wing, 35, 27, 9/35, Wadd W, 230 OCU, MoA	[1] 4-06
❏ XV259		Nimrod AEW.3	ex Stock, Chattenden, Abingdon, Waddington,	
			Woodford, Kin Wing, St Mawgan Wing. Nose	[3] 4-06
❏ XV406	'CK'	Phantom FGR.2	ex Longtown, Carlisle, 9098M, St Athan, 29,	
			23, 111, HSA, AAEE, HSA. On loan	4-06
❏ ZF583		Lightning F.53	ex Warton, RSaudi AF 53-681, G-27-51. RAF c/s	4-06

HAVERIGG south of Millom
RAF Millom Museum: Run by the **South Copeland Aviation Group**, the museum continues to make great strides and has made the bold move opening daily. A strong association has been struck up with the **Lancashire Aircraft Investigation Team** (LAIT). The former RAF station squash court adjacent to the main museum building has been refurbished and contains an incredible display devoted to the many and varied 'digs' undertaken by LAIT. In July 2004 LAIT did the 'groundwork' for a *Time Team* dig on the remains of a pair of A-26B Invaders (43-22298 and -22336) that collided shortly after take-off from Warton, the wreckage falling in the Ribble Marshes. The salvaged remains are now on show in the museum 'courtyard'. Additionally, the museum is now home to the RAF Mountain Rescue Association's National Archive, another great treasure trove of artefacts.

Notes: Please note that some airframes are being restored or stored within the HM Prison and inspection is *not* a possibility! The rear end of Chipmunk WD377 can also be found in a composite at Dumfries [1]. The wings of Vampire XD425 are on XD547 at Dumfries, Scotland [2]. The Tornado cockpit is on loan from the BAE North West Heritage Group [3].

◆ *On the Bankhead Estate, North Lane, adjacent to HMP Haverigg. Open daily throughout the year 10am to 5pm. Other times by appointment. Glynn Griffith, 21 Holborn Hill, Millom, LA18 5BH, tel 01229 772636 www.rafmillom.co.uk*

❑	'G-ADRX'	HM.14 'Flea'	BAPC.231, ex Torver, Ulverston		4-06
❑	– BAPC.260	HM.280	FAF colours. Touring exhibit		4-06
❑	WD377	Chipmunk T.10	ex Dumfries, 12 AEF, Glas UAS, HCEU, 11 RFS, 2 BFTS. Cr 29-7-66. Cockpit	® [1]	4-06
❑	XD425	'M' Vampire T.11	ex Dumfries, West Freugh, Stranraer, Woodford, Chester, St Athan, 8 FTS, 5 FTS, 7 FTS, 202 AFS. Pod. 6 Sqn c/s	[2]	4-06
❑	XK637	'56' Vampire T.11	ex Royton, Woodford, Chester, St Athan, 4 FTS, 7 FTS	®	4-06
❑	XM660	Whirlwind HAS.7	ex Sunderland, Almondbank, Fleetlands, Lee-on-Solent, Lossiemouth SAR Flt, 737, 700H, 824		4-06
❑	XN597	'X' Jet Provost T.3	7984M, ex Firbeck, Levenshulme, Stamford, Firbeck, Sunderland, Stoke-on-Trent, Bournemouth, Faygate, 2 FTS. Damaged 28-6-67. Nose		4-06
❑	–*	Tornado IDS	ex Warton. Unflown cockpit, RSaudiAF c/s. Arr 4-11-04	[3]	4-06

KENDAL on the A685 south of Brough
The Whirlwind is in a scrapyard and for sale. A collector here *should* still have a 'JP' procedure trainer.

❑	XN387	Whirlwind HAR.9–	ex Spadeadam, Odiham 8564M, Wroughton, Lee-on-Solent SAR Flt, Lossiemouth SF, 846, 719	1-04
❑	–	Jet Provost T.3	ex Welshpool, Elvington, Linton-on-Ouse	7-01

SPADEADAM FOREST north of the B6318, north-east of Carlisle
RAF Spadeadam / Electronic Warfare Tactics Range: The ranges are a complex series of sites centred on the former ballistic missile test/launch facility. Location codes are as follows: Prior Lancey PL; the mock airfield (also known as 'Collinski!') AF; the mock runway RW; revetment R7 RV; Wiley Sike bombing site and used as smoke bomb targets WS. The ranges have issued inventory numbers to most of the targets (and that includes armoured fighting vehicles etc). For completeness, column four gives these. They are prefixed 'SPA117', for example T-33 FT-06 is SPA117-7. Note that both FT-11 and No.180 appear to share the same inventory number! An *unconfirmed* report has a former Iraqi Mi-24 *Hind* arriving here by March 2005.

❑	FT-01		T-33A-1-LO	–	ex Prestwick, Belgian AF, 51-4041	7-04
❑	FT-02	'12'	T-33A-1-LO	–	ex Prestwick, Belgian AF, 51-4043	WS 4-03
❑	FT-06	'10'	T-33A-1-LO	-7	ex Prestwick, Belgian AF, Neth AF M-44, 51-4231	AF 7-04
❑	FT-07	'70'	T-33A-1-LO	-4	ex Prestwick, Belgian AF, Neth AF M-45, 51-4233	AF 7-04
❑	FT-10		T-33A-1-LO	-6	ex Prestwick, Belgian AF, 51-6664	AF 7-04
❑	FT-11		T-33A-1-LO	-8	ex Prestwick, Belgian AF, Neth AF M-47, 51-6661	AF 7-04
❑	FT-29		T-33A-1-LO	–	ex Prestwick, Belgian AF, 53-5753	WS 6-03
❑	61	'38'	Mystère IVA	-2	ex Sculthorpe, FAF. Also coded '8-MI'	RW 7-04
❑	64	'36' + '60'	Mystère IVA	-3	ex Sculthorpe, FAF. Also coded '8-NO'	RW 7-04
❑	81	'8-NU'	Mystère IVA	-9	ex Sculthorpe, FAF	AF 7-04
❑	139	'8-MR'	Mystère IVA	-11	ex Sculthorpe, FAF	AF 7-04
❑	180	'MB'	Mystère IVA	-8	ex Sculthorpe, FAF	AF 7-04
❑	184	'<u>87</u>'	Mystère IVA	-10	ex Sculthorpe, FAF	AF 7-04
❑	207		Mystère IVA	–	ex Sculthorpe, FAF	AF 7-04
❑	282	'8-NW'	Mystère IVA	–	ex Sculthorpe, FAF	AF 7-04
❑	98+10		Su-22M-4	–	ex Farnborough, Boscombe Down, LSK-LV 820	PL 7-04

SPARK BRIDGE on the A5092 north-odf Ulverston

RotAirey Aviation: Neil Airey and Heather Graham have a Lightning cockpit in the area with another due to arrive They are *not* available for inspection, but at least one will be mobile – another reason to visit *CockpitFest!*

❏	XS922*	'BJ' Lightning F.6	ex Stansted, Salisbury, Stock, Wattisham, Binbrook,	
			5-11 pool, 56, 5. Nose.	3-06
❏	XS932*	Lightning F.6	ex Farnborough, Shoreham, Bruntingthorpe, Rossington,	
			Binbrook, 5, 11, 56, 11. Nose	due

WALNEY ISLAND AERODROME on the Isle of Walney, west of Barron-in-Furness

Walney Aviation Heritage Museum (WAHM): With the support of BAE Systems and many other local organisations, WAHM (pronounced Wham) was launched in November 2005 by Paul Rose MBE to bring an aviation museum to this picturesque airfield. Building work is due to begin in July 2006 with opening sometime in late 2007/early 2008. The first airframe was acquired in late March 2006 and others are in the pipeline.

◆ *Not available for public inspection – see above*

❏	XE368*	'200' Sea Hawk FGA.6	ex Market Drayton, Bruntingthorpe, Helston, Culdrose		
			SAH-3, Shotley A2534,738, 806, 803, 899	[1]	due

WINDERMERE on the A592 north of Bowness on Windermere

Windermere Steamboats Museum: As well as the waterglider, two other aeronautical items are within this superb collection; a Sunderland wing float, modified into a 'canoe'; and the MV *Canfly* a 1920s speedboat powered by a Rolls-Royce Hawk from the RNAS airship SST.3.

◆ *Open daily mid-Mar to first week of Nov 10am to 5pm. Special events staged. Rayrigg Road, Windermere, LA23 1BN tel 015394 45565 fax 015394 48769 e-mail post@steamboat.co.uk www.steamboat.co.uk*

❏	–	BGA.266 T.1 Falcon	Modified by Capt T C Pattinson DFC. f/f 3-2-43	3-06

DERBYSHIRE

CHESTERFIELD on the A61 south of Sheffield

4x4 Car Centre: On the Dronfield Road, have a former Finningley 'JP' as an attraction.

❏	XM480	'02' Jet Provost T.3	ex Finningley, Halton 8080M, 6 FTS, 1 FTS	2-04

CLAY CROSS on the A61 south of Chesterfield

Cronifer Metals: The yard here has been very active in the processing of large amounts of scrap from St Athan, Wales, some from Shawbury, Shropshire, and the clear-out of Llanbedr, Wales. 'Processing' is just what happens here, with the hulks hardly languishing. Refer to Llanbedr and St Athan, both Wales, for details.

DERBY

Derby Industrial Museum: Presents a staggering array of aero engines, nearly all of the home-spun Rolls-Royce variety, going from the Eagle to the RB.211 and is a must to visit. The rest of the museum has excellent displays on Derbyshire's industrial past. There are regular exhibitions and special events. The Rolls-Royce Heritage Trust, Derby and Hucknall Branch has many of its engines on show – see also below.

The **Derbyshire Historical Aviation Society** works in support of the museum and stages regular meetings. Contact: Bill Harrison, 71 Mill Hill Lane, Derby, DE3 6SB e-mail williamharrison@tiscali.co.uk)

◆ *Mon 11am to 5pm, Tue to Sat 10am to 5pm. Sun/Bank Hols 2pm to 5pm. Silk Mill Lane, off Full Street, Derby, DE1 3AR tel 01332 255308 fax 01332 716670 e-mail contact@derbymuseum. freeserve www.derby.gov.uk/museums*

Rolls-Royce Heritage Trust: Located within the Rolls-Royce Learning and Development Centre in Willmore Road, the trust has established an incredible heritage exhibition of aero engines and other memorabilia during the autumn of 2001 using engines, artefacts and input from all of the branches. As well as the engines etc, a Canberra B.15 nose is on show. This flew 'ops' during the Suez crisis, 1956.

◆ *Open to groups by prior arrangement only. PO Box 31, Derby DE24 8BJ, tel 01332 249118 fax 01332 249727, e-mail richard.haigh@rolls-royce.com www.rolls-royce.com*

❏ WH960   Canberra B.15   ex Nottingham, Bruntingthorpe, Cosford 8344M,
                                       Akrotiri Wing, 32, 9, 12. Nose   4-06

Rolls-Royce Heritage Trust, Derby and Hucknall Branch and **Coventry Branch** (previously at Mickleover, Derbyshire) share display areas, workshops and storage facilities in the Light Alloy Foundry within a part of the extensive Rolls-Royce complex and are a treasure-trove of aero engine heritage. The building faces re-use and the Trust will need to re-locate in due course – this will be the Coventry Branch's *fifth* move!

◆ *By prior arrangement* only, *and occasional open days – contacts as above.*

❏ 'EN398'*   Spitfire IX FSM   BAPC.184, ex N' Weald, Duxford, Huntingdon. Arr by 10-03   4-06
❏ 0767   MB.339AA   ex Mickleover, Filton, Yeovilton, Stanley, Argentine
                                         Navy. FAAM loan. Stored   4-06

Adrian Marshall: Cleared his store here with Terrier 2 G-ASYN and the anonymous Auster AOP.6 both going to Bruntingthorpe, Leics.

DERBY AERODROME or Egginton, south of the A5132 between Egginton and Hilton

Comet Racer Project Group: make progress with G-ACSP.

◆ *Visits are possible* only *by prior arrangement. Derby Airfield, Hilton Road, Egginton, Derby, DE65 6GU tel 01283 733803 fax 01283 734829 www.cometracer.co.uk*

❏ [G-ACSP]   DH.88 Comet   ex Stoke-on-Trent, Coventry / Staverton, Bodmin,
                                      Chirk, Portugal, CS-AAJ, E-1. *Black Magic*   ®   3-04

Others: Bulldog 120 G-BHZS was flying by 2004.

❏ G-AVLM   Pup 160   ex Shenstone, Tatenhill, Nottingham Airport,
                                      Chippenham. CoA 24-4-69. Stored   1-02
❏ G-SACF   Cessna 152 II   ex G-BHSZ, N47125. Crashed 21-3-97. Wreck   5-03

DEVON

BABCARY east of the A37, east of Somerton

Classic earth-moving – this location is in Somerset!

BARNSTAPLE

Tim A Jones: Tim continues to work on his 'fleet'.

◆ *By prior appointment only via e-mail timjones007@hotmail.com*

❏ XS231   Jet Provost T.5   ex Ipswich, Bruntingthorpe, Bournemouth,
                                       Scampton, Shawbury, AAEE, G-ATAJ ntu. Fuselage   3-06
❏ XX888   Buccaneer S.2B   ex Dundonald, Ottershaw, Shawbury, St Athan, 16, 15.
                                       Sand colours. Nose   3-06
❏ ZD710   Tornado GR.1   ex Welshpool, Robertsbridge, Stock, St Athan, 14.
                                       Crashed 14-9-89. Cockpit   3-06

BERE ALSTON at the end of the B3257 north of Plymouth
Tony Thorne: Previously listed under Ivybridge, Devon, Tony keeps his airframes in the general area.
◆ *Viewing by prior appointment only, tel 01822 840515*

❑ G-ATWT	Napier-Bensen	ex Narborough, G-29-3. wfu 31-1-77		2-06
❑ G-BIVL	Bensen B.8M	ex St Merryn. CoA 29-4-87		2-06
❑ G-MBUZ	Skycraft Scout II	–		2-06
❑ G-STMP	SNCAN SV-4A	ex St Merryn, F-BCKB	®	2-06
❑ –	Hobbycopter	ex 'Leicestershire'		2-06

BRANSCOMBE on a minor road east of Sidmouth
Note that the provenance of Tiger Moth G-ASPV is unknown. The original went to Norway in 1974.

❑ G-ASPV*	Tiger Moth	ex Southampton, Laindon, T7794. CoA 31-8-97	®	11-05
❑ G-ASSY*	Turbulent	ex Dunkeswell, Redhill. Damaged 8-5-83. Stored.		7-05

COBBATON north of the A377 / B3227 west of South Molton
Cobbaton Combat Collection: Within what is described as the largest private collection of military vehicles and wartime memorabilia in the south west can be found a Horsa glider that was used in *A Bridge Too Far*.
◆ *Apr, May, Jun, Sep and Oct, Sunday to Friday; Jul and Aug all week, 10am to 5pm. Open 'most weekdays' during the winter, 'phone first to check. Chittlehampton, Umberleigh, EX37 9RZ tel 01769 540740 fax 01769 540141 e-mail info@cobbatoncombat.co.uk www.cobbatoncombat.co.uk*

❑ –*	Horsa REP	ex *A Bridge Too Far*	6-05

DUNKESWELL AERODROME north of Honiton
Dunkeswell Memorial Museum: The new display hall is dedicated to the history of the airfield and its resident units, including the US Navy's PB4Y-1-equipped FAW-7. The exhibits within are superb and reflect the unique wartime history of this fascinating airfield. With the adoption of the new building the decision was taken – rightly – that the airframes held by other parties were not relevant to the story. Accordingly, the anonymous Gannet cockpit and Vampire T.11 XE982 have been moved to the 'Aerodrome' section
◆ *Mar to Oct, daily except Tues, 10am to 6pm. Nov to Feb weekends, 10am to 5pm. Closed18th Dec to 2nd Jan. Contact the museum for Dec and Jan opening times.Flightway Business Park, Unit C4, Dunkeswell, Honiton, EX14 4PG tel 01404 891943 e-mail dmmsecretary@clara/co.uk www.dunkeswellmemorialmuseum.org.uk*

Aerodrome: An organisation called **Flightaid** bases itself here, raising funds through a travelling 'roadshow' that includes a Wasp marked as XT78? [1]. They have a Cessna 'based' at Croydon, Gtr Lon - qv. The Wasp has also been reported with the **X-Ray Tango Helicopter Group** and they also have (or had) the former Moreton-in-Marsh Sioux [2]. They acquired two Scouts from Bramley, Hants: XP191 and XP853. One of these appeared in the mind-expanding Channel 4 programme *Scrapheap Challenge*, along with what is almost certainly the Cessna from Croydon, Gtr Lon. Both of the Scouts appeared on a well-known internet 'auction' site - a sort of virtual car-car boot sale, but with the humanity removed. XP853 ended up in Sutton, Surrey, while the other went to 'Dave'. Previously on show outside the former museum premises, the anonymous Gannet cockpit section is believed to have been scrapped. Last noted here in May 1993, Turbulent G-ASSY has been tracked down to Branscombe, Devon, having moved at the latest 1998.

❑ G-BJNG	Slingsby T.67AM	CoA 23-7-01. Fuselage, stored		1-06
❑ G-BPRV	Warrior II	ex N4292G. Crashed 29-3-97. Cockpit		7-99
❑ XE982*	Vampire T.11	ex museum, Hereford, St Athan 7564M, RAFC		12-05
❑ XT141*	Sioux AH.1	ex Moreton-in-Marsh, Brize Norton 8509M, Middle Wallop. Frame	[2]	1-05
❑ XT788	'316' Wasp HAS.1	G-BMIR, ex Faygate, Tattershall Thorpe, Wroughton	[1]	3-06
❑ –*	Scout AH.1	ex Bramley. Poor state.	[2]	1-05

EAGLESCOTT AERODROME west of the A377, north of Ashreigney
Aerodrome: The Currie Wot will re-appear in the guise of a scaled-down Pfalz D.VII! [1]

❑ G-ARZW		Currie Wot	Crashed 12-2-88	® [1]	7-05
❑ G-BGBF*		Turbulent	CoA 25-3-04. Stored in roof		7-05
❑ G-BOLD		Tomahawk	ex N9740T. CoA 21-1-96. Stored	®	7-05
❑ N24730		Tomahawk	G-BTIL. Stored, dismantled		7-05
❑ WT744	'868'	Hunter GA.11	ex Yeovilton, FRADU, 738, 247, AFDS		2-06
❑ WT867		Cadet TX.3	ex Syerston, 626 VGS. Stored		2-06
❑ XA289		Cadet TX.3	ex Syerston, 636 VGS. Stored		2-06

EXETER
Arden Family Trust: The late Bertram Arden's airframes are held in careful store in the general area.

❑ G-AALP	Surrey AL.1	CoA 17-5-40	12-97
❑ G-AFGC	BA Swallow II	ex BK893, GTS, CLE, RAE, G-AFGC. CoA 20-3-51	12-97
❑ G-AFHC	BA Swallow II	CoA 20-3-51	12-97
❑ G-AJHJ	Auster V	ex NJ676, 83 GCS, 440. CoA 27-6-49	12-97

Martin Phillips: Spitfire RR232 returned to a *private* workshop in the general area for completion.

❑ RR232*	Spitfire IX	G-BRSF, ex Sandown, Exeter, Lancing, Winchester, Nowra, Bankstown, Point Cook, Cape Town, Ysterplaat, SAAF 5632, RR232, 47 MU, ECFS. *City of Exeter*. Arrived 6-05	®	7-05

Others: Seafire III RX168 had moved by 2002, settling upon <u>Swindon</u>, Wilts.

EXETER AIRPORT
Hunter Flying Club (HFC): During mid-2005 HFC moved into a new hangar and workshop at the airport enabling them to improve and expand their specialist services. HFC operates airworthy Hunters on behalf of a variety of owners: **Alan Fowles** GA.11 XE685 (G-GAII – see below); **Elvington Events** T.8C 'XJ615' (XF357 - G-BWGL); **Global Aviation Services** (GAS) T.7 XL573 (G-BVGH); **Heritage Aviation Developments** F.58A G-PSST *Miss Demeanour*; **SkyBlue Aviation** T.7 G-VETA (arrived 19th Sept 2005); FGA.9 XE601 (G-ETPS) arrived from Boscombe Down, Wilts, on 27th May 2004 making its first post-restoration flight on 21st June 2005; **Stick and Rudder Aviation** WT723 (G-PRII); **Towerdrive Ltd** T.8B WV322 (G-BZSE).

Notes: Hunter GA.11 XE685 (G-GAII) first flew following restoration on 11th February 2006. Hunter T.8C XF358 arrived from Boscombe Down in August 2004. The nose was exported to Canada for Northern Lights on 23rd October 2004. The rest of the airframe is used for spares for Gary Montgomery's XX467 (G-TVII) [1]; Gary also owns XL612 [1]. Hunter T.8M XL602 (G-BWFT) is owned by GAS [2], as is the former Omani T.66B is also owned by GAS and comprises the fuselage of Dutch-built F.6 N-283 (G-9-231) and the nose of T.7 XM123, which also served the Dutch, as N-317, before becoming G-9-164 with HSA [3]. Vampire T.11 pod XE985 is owned by Mark Gauntlett - see also under Cwmbran, Wales [4].

Departures: Hunter T.7 XF321 to <u>Bruntingthorpe</u>, Leics, on 28th May 2004. The following are no longer directly associated with HFC and are listed under 'Airport' below: **F.6A** XJ639; **T.7** XL592; **T.8Cs** WT722; WT799, XE665; **GA.11s** 'WB188' and the red 'WB188'; XE689.

◆ *Visits possible only by prior arrangement. Hangar 52, Exeter International Airport, Exeter, EX5 2BD e-mail info@hunterflyingclub.co.uk www.hunterflyingclub.co.uk*

❑ XE985*	Vampire T.11	ex Bridgend, Cwmbran, Bridgend, London Colney, Woodford, Chester, St Athan, 5 FTS. Pod. Arr 29-1-05	[4]	4-06
❑ XL602	Hunter T.8M	G-BWFT, ex Shawbury, Yeovilton, FRADU, 759, 764	® [2]	4-06
❑ XL612*	Hunter T.7	ex Boscombe Down, ETPS, 8, 1417 Flt, APS Sylt. Arrived 27-5-04	® [1]	4-06
❑ XX467	Hunter T.7	G-TVII, ex Kemble, Perth, 1 TWU, Jordan AF 836, Saudi AF 70-617, G-9-214, XL605, 66, 92. Stored	[1]	4-06
❑ 801*	Hunter T.66B	ex Seeb, Oman AF, Jordan AF 801, RNethAF F.6 N-283 and T.7 N-317. Stored. Arrived 25-1-05	[3]	4-06

Airport: HS.748-2A G-AVXJ moved to <u>Upper Vobster</u>, Somerset, in June 2004. By the end of 2005 the hulk of HS.748-2B G-BORM moved to <u>Wycombe Air Park</u>, Bucks. The Hunters are in store and, as *W&R20* went to press, are reported to be moving on to a new location [1]. The *real* WB188 can be found at Tangmere, W Sussex [2]. Gnat T.1 XM697 moved to <u>Market Drayton</u>, Shrop, by March 2006.

❑ G-BADZ*		Pitts S-2A	CoA 5-6-00. Canx 4-4-02. Fuselage, hung in hangar	12-05
❑ G-BAUR		F.27-200	ex JEA, PH-FEP, 9V-BAP, 9M-AMI, VR-RCZ ntu,	
			PH-FEP. CoA 5-4-96. Fuselage. Fire crews	2-06
❑ G-BSHR*		Cessna F.172N	crashed 3-11-01. Fuselage. Fire crews	2-06
❑ G-BXYU*		Cessna F.152 II	ex Dunkeswell, OH-CKD, SE-IFY. Crashed 2-8-99.	
			Fire crews, first noted 8-01	12-05
❑ G-JEAT*		HS.146-100	ex JEA, N171TR, J8-VBB, G-BVUY, B-2706,	
			G-5-071. CoA 23-10-05. Dump, first noted 8-04	2-06
❑ 'WB188'		Hunter GA.11	G-BZPB, ex WV256, Shawbury, Yeovilton, FRADU	
			738, 229 OCU, 26. Proto (green) c/s. CoA 17-7-03	[1, 2] 3-06
❑ 'WB188'		Hunter GA.11	G-BZPC, ex Shawbury XF300, Yeovilton,	
			FRADU, 130, 234, 71. Red colours	[1, 2] 3-06
❑ WT722	'878'	Hunter T.8C	G-BWGN, ex Shawbury, Yeovilton, FRADU,	
			764, 703, 26, 54. CoA 3-9-97	[1] 2-06
❑ WT799	'879'	Hunter T.8C	ex North Weald, Ipswich, Shawbury, FRADU,	
			FRU, 759, RAE, 4, 11	[1] 2-06
❑ WV499*	'G'	Provost T.1	G-BZRF, ex Wycombe Air Park, Armthorpe, Sandtoft, North	
			Weald, St Athan, Weeton 7698M, 6 FTS. Arrived by 2-06	2-06
❑ XE665	'876'	Hunter T.8C	G-BWGM, ex Shawbury, Yeovilton,	
			FRADU, 764, Jever SF, 118. CoA 24-6-98	[1] 2-06
❑ XE689	'864'	Hunter GA.11	G-BWGK, ex North Weald, Exeter, Shawbury,	
			Yeovilton, FRADU, 234, 130, 67. CoA 11-7-01	[1] 2-06
❑ XJ639	'H'	Hunter F.6A	ex Ipswich, Ipswich aerodrome, Cranwell 8687M,	
			1 TWU, TWU, 229 OCU, 4	[1] 2-06
❑ XL592	'Y'	Hunter T.7	ex Scampton 8836M, 1 TWU, TWU, 229 OCU	[1] 2-06

IVYBRIDGE on the A38 east of Plymouth
This collection of aircraft is located at Bere Alston, Devon – qv.

KINGSBRIDGE on the A381 north of Salcombe

❑ G-AVXB	Bensen B-8	ex Swansea, G-ARTN. CoA 23-6-87.	10-98

NEWTON ABBOT on the A380 south of Exeter
'Flying' within the **Trago Mills** supermarket in the town is the one-off MW.2B [1]. A collector keeps a Sea Vixen cockpit in the general area [2].

❑ G-BDDX		Excalibur	ex Helston. Only flight 1-7-76, built at Bodmin	[1] 8-05
❑ XN650	'456'	Sea Vixen FAW.2	ex Welshpool, Bruntingthorpe, Cardiff, A2639,	
			A2620, A2612, Culdrose, RAE, 892. Nose	[2] 12-02

OKEHAMPTON on the A30 west of Exeter
An airstrip in the general area is home to a large number of 'resting' and recovering Austers. Back in the air are the following: J/5K G-AMMS by May 2005; J/5R G-ANXC by May 2004; J/5G G-AOIY by May 2004; AOP.9 WZ662 (G-BKVK) by May 2005.

❑ G-AIGD	J/1 Autocrat	CoA 6-7-00. Stored	11-05
❑ G-AJAJ	J/1 Autocrat	ex Dunkeswell. CoA 18-4-94. Stored	3-04
❑ G-AMUI*	Auster J/5F	ex Liverpool, Stretton, CoA 15-2-66. F/n 11-04	11-05
❑ G-AVYK	Terrier 3	ex Aboyne, AOP.6 WJ357, 651, 657, 1903 Flt. CoA 28-8-93	7-01

❏	G-AXCZ	SNCAN SV-4C	ex ZS-VFW, G-AXCZ, F-BCFG. CoA 10-7-83. Stored		11-05
❏	G-AYDW*	Terrier 2	ex King's Lynn, Little Gransden, King's Lynn, Camberley,		
			Cranfield, Bushey, G-ARLM, AOP.6 TW568, LAS, AOPS,		
			227 OCU, 43 OTU. CoA 1-7-73. First noted 5-05		11-05
❏	[G-BGKO]	GY-20 Minicab	unfinished project. Stored		11-05
❏	G-BGKZ	J/5K Aiglet Tnr	ex Liverpool, Stretton, F-BGKZ. Cr 30-1-93. Stored		11-04
❏	TJ672*	Auster 5D	G-ANIJ, ex Bournemouth, 227 OCU, 657. CoA 5-5-<u>71</u>.		
			Arrived 2-06		2-06
❏	VX113	Terrier 1	G-ARNO, ex Northampton, Stamford, Nympsfield,		
			Auster AOP.6 VX113, 651, 662. CoA 19-6-81	®	2-06
❏	XK421	Auster AOP.9	ex Doncaster, Firbeck, Thurcroft, Firbeck, Hedge End,		
			Fownhope, Long Marston, Innsworth, Bristol, Caldicote,		
			8365M, St Athan, Detmold, Middle Wallop. Frame		2-06
❏	XP241	Auster AOP.9	ex Middle Wallop, Andrewsfield, Rabley Heath,		
			St Athan, 653, Aden. Frame, stored		11-05
❏	XP286	Auster AOP.9	ex ?, 8044M, Middle Wallop, Hull, 60 MU, 38 GCF,		
			AAC Centre. Frame, stored		9-05

Locally: In the general area are several airframes.

❏	G-ASBH	Airedale	CoA 19-2-99. Stored		5-02
❏	G-BKSX	SNCAN SV-4C	ex F-BBAF, Fr mil. CoA 15-6-89	®	9-02
❏	N6191K	Seabee	(identity believed confirmed). Damaged, stored		5-02

PLYMOUTH
Alan Thompson: Still has his Scout. The anonymous Agusta A109 did *not* come here.

| ❏ | XW281 | Scout AH.1 | G-BYNZ, ex Thruxton. With boom of XP883. Cr 24-9-00 | 2-06 |

PLYMOUTH AIRPORT (ROBOROUGH)

❏	G-BAII	Cessna FRA.150L	ex Bodmin. Cr 9-9-01. Fire crews	8-02
❏	G-BNUY*	Tomahawk 112	CoA 17-8-03. Dismantled	7-05
❏	XN198*	Cadet TX.3	ex Challock. Stored in rafters	7-05

SOUTH MOLTON south of the A361 south east of Barnstaple
A collector in the area took delivery of the former 'Trocadero' Harrier nose. In the exchange that realised this, his anonymous Tiger Moth fuselage moved to the <u>Norwich</u>, Norfolk, area.

| ❏ | ZD670* | Harrier GR.3 | ex Wycombe Air Park, Dagenham, London, | | |
| | | | Bruntingthorpe, Wittering, 233 OCU. Cockpit. Arr 9-04 | 12-04 |

TAVISTOCK AERODROME or Brent <u>Tor</u>, or Burnford Common, north of the town
Dartmoor Gliding Society:

❏	BFP	936 Schleicher Ka-7	crashed 15-11-95. Stored	7-05
❏	FGZ	3262 Schleicher Ka-7	ex D-5376. CoA 9-10-99. Stored	11-05
❏	FTU	3<u>521</u> Schleicher Ka-7	ex HB-599. *Fondue*. Crashed 21-9-02	11-05
❏	HWE	4255 Schleicher K-8B	ex HB-700. Wreck	1-04

TOPSHAM between the M5 and the A376 south of Exeter
Andrew Longden: Keeps three airframes in this *general* area.

❏	XV359*	'035' Buccaneer S.2B	ex Culdrose, A2693 [2], Predannack, Lossiemouth,		
			208, 237 OCU, 12, 208, 12. 809 Sqn c/s. Arrived 23-4-05	1-06
❏	XZ378*	'EP' Jaguar GR.1A	ex Shawbury, 6, 41, 17, 41, 20. Arrived 14-11-05	1-06
❏	ZD612*	'731' Sea Harrier FA.2	ex Yeovilton, ETS, St Athan, 899, 800, 899, 800, 801, 899	1-06

YARCOMBE on the A30 west of Chard
A Tiger Moth arrived by late 2005 for restoration in the general area.

❑ G-ADJJ*	Tiger Moth	ex Chilbolton, Eversden, BB819, 25 RFS, 28 EFTS,		
		1 EFTS, 9 EFTS, G-ADJJ. CoA 20-3-75	®	12-05

YARNSCOMBE north of the B3227, west of Atherington

❑ G-BBAK	MS.894A Rallye	ex D-ENMK ntu. CoA 8-8-98	7-03

DORSET

BOURNEMOUTH

Streetwise Safety Centre: Among the 'attractions' at the awareness training centre in Bournemouth is a Twin Squirrel about to 'land' on a Police helicopter pad.

❑ 'S-WISE'	AS.355 Squirrel	ex PAS Gloucestershire, N354E, F-GIRL	2-04

BOURNEMOUTH AIRPORT (HURN)

Bournemouth Aviation Museum (BAM) Operated by the Bournemouth Aviation Charitable Foundation. BAM currently offers eight cockpits as open to the public. Note that other light aircraft 'lodge' within, but only 'long-termers' are noted here. De Havilland Aviation (DHA, see below) operates within the hangar complex, looking after its own, and other jets. There is a gallery allowing a grandstand view of aircraft within the DHA but access to the engineering 'floor' is not permitted. From this edition DHA-owned aircraft or aircraft under restoration by DHA for other owners are given under their own heading, see below.

Notes: BAM owns Hunter XG160 and Grasshopper WZ798. All others are on loan from individuals or organisations. Some of these are as follows: The newly-arrived Fury ISS by J A D Bradshaw (JB); Dragon Rapide and 'JP5' G-BWOF are owned and operated by Phil Meeson (PM); the BAC 111 is on loan from European Aviation (EAL); Venom 'WR421' from Source Classic Jet (SCJ). The nose of Vulcan XH537 is on loan from Paul Hartley (PH). Paul also owns *two* other Vulcan noses at Bruntingthorpe, Leics, and Wellesbourne Mountford, Warks. Dick Horsfield and Rod Robinson, the Dawn to Dusk Trust, are rebuilding Vampire XE856 at the museum – www.project-vampire.org.uk (DTD). Provost T.1 'WR421' almost certainly has the fuselage of WW450 [1].

Departures: In a '111 shuffle', G-AVMN moved back to the airport site 10-11-04 with G-AZMF taking in place. Auster 5 RT486 (G-AJGJ) flew off to live at Lee-on-Solent, Hants, mid-2004. Gnat T.1 XR537 (G-NATY) is owned by Julian Jones – new owner of DHA and best listed with them below. Hunter F.58 J-4083 (G-EGHH) moved to Kemble, Glos, 10-10-05; Hunter T.68 G-HVIP left for Switzerland 8-3-05.

◆ *Daily Apr to Sep 10am to 5pm, Oct to Mar, 10am to 4pm. Sign-posted from the airport entrance.BAM, Hangar 600, Bournemouth Airport, Christchurch, BH23 6SE tel 01202 580858 www.aviation-museum.co.uk*

❑ G-AGSH	Dragon Rapide 6 ✈	ex Lower Upham, EI-AJO, G-AGSH, NR808.		
		BEA colours, *Gemma Meeson*	PM	3-06
❑ G-AZMF*	BAC 111-530FX	ex European, 7Q-YKJ, G-AZMF, PT-TYY, G-AZMF.		
		CoA 22-1-04. Canx 10-3-06.Arrived 17-11-04		3-06
❑ G-BEYF	Herald 401	ex Channel Express, RMAF FM1022. On loan		3-06
❑ G-BWOF	Jet Provost T.5 ✈	ex N Weald, XW291, Shawbury, 6 FTS, RAFC, CFS	PM	3-06
❑ G-BKRL*	CMC Leopard	ex Old Sarum, Cranfield. CoA 14-12-91. Arr 18-2-05		3-06
❑ G-BRNM	CMC Leopard	ex Old Sarum.		3-06
❑ N7SY	Sea Prince T.1	ex G-BRFC, N Weald, Bourn, WP321,Kemble, 750, 744		3-06
❑ 'K5673'	Isaacs Fury III ✈	G-BZAS. *Spirit of Dunsfold*		3-06
❑ KF488	Harvard IIb	ex Bournemouth, Wimborne, Sandhurst, Avex. Composite	®	3-06
❑ 'WR421'*	Venom FB.50	G-DHTT, ex Source, G-BMOC ntu, ex Swiss AF J-1611.		
		CoA 17-7-99. Red c/s. Arrived 3-12-04	SCJ	3-06

❑ WS776*	'K'	Meteor NF.14		ex Armthorpe, Sandtoft, North Coates, North Luffenham, Lyneham, 7716M, 228 OCU, 85, 25. Arrived 5-2-05		3-06
❑ WT532		Canberra PR.7		ex Airport, Lovaux, Cosford, 8890M / 8728M, RAE Bedford, 13, Wyton SF, 58, 31, 13, 80. Nose		3-06
❑ WW421*	'P-B'	Provost T.1		G-BZRE, ex Wycombe AP, Armthorpe, Sandtoft, Binbrook, Norwich, Lowestoft, East Kirkby, Tattershall, Lytham, St Athan 7688M, 3 FTS. Arr 10-10-05	[1]	3-06
❑ WZ798		Grasshopper TX.1		ex Bournemouth School		3-06
❑ XE856*		Vampire T.11		G-DUSK, ex Henlow, Catfoss, Long Marston, Lasham, Welwyn GC, Woodford, Chester, St Athan, 219, North Weald SF, 226 OCU. Arrived 6-9-05	DTD ®	3-06
❑ XG160	'U'	Hunter F.6A		G-BWAF, ex 'RJAF', Scampton 8831M, 1 TWU, 229 OCU, 111, 43. 111 Sqn colours, black		3-06
❑ XH537		Vulcan B.2MRR		ex Bruntingthorpe, Ottershaw, Camberley, Abingdon 8749M, 27, 230 OCU, MoA. Nose	PH	3-06
❑ XT257*		Wessex HAS.3		ex East Grinstead, Cosford 8719M, Halton, AAEE. Yellow RAF SAR scheme. Arrived 20-1-05		3-06
❑ XX897		Buccaneer S.2B(mod)		ex airfield, DRA Bedford, RAE, RRE. Tornado nose. European Airlines colours		3-06
❑ ZF582*		Lightning F.53		ex Reading. Llantrisant, Luton, Desborough, Portsmouth, Stretton, Warton, RSAF 207, 53-676, G-27-46. Nose. Arrived 21-9-04		3-06
❑ –*	'361'	Fury ISS	→	G-CBEL, ex Kemble, N36SF, Iraqi AF 315. Arr 11-8-04	JB	3-04
❑ C-552		EKW C-3605	→	G-DORN, ex HB-RBJ, SwissAF C-552. CoA 11-11-02		3-06
❑ –		Hunter T.7		ex Biggin Hill, 'G-ERIC', Bournemouth, Leavesden, Elstree, Hatfield. Nose of XJ690		3-06
❑ –		Vanguard SIM		ex Wycombe Air Park, Huntings, East Midlands		3-06

De Havilland Aviation (DHA) / **De Havilland Engineering**: During December 2005, DHA changed hands and is now owned by a new group of shareholders, headed by Julian Jones. Julian owns Gnat T.1 XR537, which should fly during 2006. The storage facility at Bridgend, Wales, has been wound down and all of the DHA airframes are now here. The Vampire Preservation Group's Vampire T.11 WZ507 (G-VTII) flew to North Weald, Essex, on 11th February 2006. Vampire T.55 G-DHZZ is under restoration, reportedly for a Danish owner [1].
◆ *Aircraft viewable during normal museum opening hours from the gallery – see above. www.dehavilland.net*

❑ G-CVIX		Sea Vixen D.3	→	ex XP924, Swansea, Llanbedr, RAE, FRL, RAE, 899. ' Red Bull' colours		3-06
❑ WL505*		Vampire FB.9		G-FBIX, ex Bridgend, Bruntingthorpe, Cranfield, St Athan, Ely, 19, RAFC, 73		3-06
❑ 'WZ589'*		Vampire T.55		G-DHZZ, ex Source, Southampton, Swiss AF U-1230. CoA 4-8-03. 20 Sqn c/s. Arrived by 2-05	® [1]	3-06
❑ XE920	'A'	Vampire T.11	→	G-VMPR, ex Swansea, Chester, Sealand, 8196M Scampton, Henlow, Shawbury, CATCS, 8 FTS, 5 FTS, 1 FTS. 603 Sqn colours		3-06
❑ XR537	'T'	Gnat T.1		G-NATY, ex Cosford 8642M, Reds, 4 FTS	®	3-06
❑ XR954*	'30'	Gnat T.1		ex Source, Ipswich, Halton 8570M, 4 FTS, CFS, 4 FTS. Spares for G-NATY. Arrived 8-05		3-06
❑ 1211		SBLim-5 (MiG-17)		G-MIGG, ex G-BWUF Duxford, Pol AF. Korean c/s	®	3-06

Source Classic Jet Flight / Lindsay Wood Promotions Ltd: On 3rd December 2004 Venom G-DHTT trundled across to the BAM (see above) on loan. It was followed by Gnat T.1 XR954 in August 2005 this one going to DHA. The latter was not a 'trundle' in the true sense of the word, having been in an ISO container for a long period. Vampire T.55 G-DHZZ moved to DHA (above) for restoration, by early 2006.
◆ *Aircraft viewable by prior application only.*

❑ FLV	3354	L-13 Blanik		ex Eaglescott, D-1355. *Jenny.* Fuselage.		2-04
❑ 'VT871'		Vampire FB.6		G-DHXX, ex 'LZ551/G', Southampton, Swiss AF J-1173. CoA 14-8-02. 54 Squadron colours		5-05

❑ 'VV612'		Venom FB.50	G-VENI, ex 'WE402'. Swiss AF J-1523. CoA 25-7-01.
			Prototype colours 5-05
❑ 'WR360'	'K'	Venom FB.50	G-DHSS, ex Swiss AF J-1626. CoA 22-4-03. White 60 Sqn c/s 5-05
❑ 'WR410'		Venom FB.50	G-DHUU, G-BMOD ntu, ex Swiss AF J-1539.
			CoA 24-5-02. 6 Sqn colours, Suez stripes 5-05
❑ 'XE897'		Vampire T.55	G-DHVV, ex Southampton, Swiss AF U-1214.
			CoA 5-6-03. 54 Sqn c/s 5-05
❑ 'XG775'		Vampire T.55 ✈	G-DHWW, ex Southampton, Swiss AF U-1219.
			CoA 23-4-03. Navy FOFT c/s, as Sea Vampire T.22 5-05
❑ J-1573		Venom FB.50	G-VICI, ex HB-RVB, G-BMOB ntu, Swiss AF.
			CoA 24-11-99 5-05

Airliners: More departures: BAC 111-510 G-AVMJ cabin trainer moved to Farnborough, Hants, 30-7-05. BAC 111-501ED G-AVMN was back from the BAM (see above) by 12-04. It was dismantled and left by road for Denmark 11-2-05 destined to become a restaurant. BAC 111-510 G-AVMT moved by road to Cardiff, Wales, on 14th November 2004. *W&R19* (p47) gave BAC 111 G-AVMZ as being scrapped in May-June 2003. It moved to Alton, Hants. BAC 111-501 G-AWYV moved (as a fuselage) to Alton, Hants, by 4-05. BAC 111-530 G-AZMF moved to the BAM above on loan by 12-04. Fokker F.27-500RF G-CEXA and G-CEXD (not 'G as in *W&R19*) were scrapped during 2004. Boeing 727-256 EC-DDX was scrapped with the fuselage moving to Oakley, Bucks, by 8-05. Boeing 737-2H6 XA-TLJ was broken up in mid-2004. The centre fuselage survives for use with FR Aviation for trials. Boeing 737-2K2 EI-CKR fuselage arrived from Prestwick, Scotland, 11-04, it moved to Oldham, Gtr Man, 4-05. Three Channel Express Airbus A300B4s were retired here in late 2005 and may or may not be candidates for *W&R21*: G-CEXK (10-05); G-CEXJ (11-05) and G-CEXI (2-06)

❑ G-BDXG*	Boeing 747-236B	ex Air Namibia, European, BA. Flew in 9-5-04. Breaking 2-062-06	
❑ G-BDXH*	Boeing 747-236B	ex European, BA. Flew in -04. Breaking 2-06	2-06
❑ EC-CFI	Boeing 727-256	ex Iberia. Stored	2-06
❑ EI-CKQ*	Boeing 737-2K2	ex Prestwick, Ryanair, PH-TVU, G-BPLA, PH-TVU,	
		C-FCAV, PH-TVU. Fuselage. Arrived 11-04	2-06
❑ OO-SDK	Boeing 737-229	ex Sabena, G-BYYK ntu. Stored	2-06
❑ 9G-LCA*	CL-44-O	ex 4K-GUP, N447T, EI-BND, N447T, CL-44D4.	
		Last flown 5-05. Stored.	2-06
❑ -*	Boeing 737-2xx	fuselage, arrived by road 3-04. Red c/s. Fire crews	2-06

Others: Cessna F.172M EI-BAS fuselage departed in August 2005. Malibu 350P N44DN was crated and returned to the USA, early 2005.

❑ G-ASOX	Cessna 205A	ex ?, Newcastle, N4856U. CoA 1-8-92	2-04
❑ G-ATPD	HS.125-1B/522	ex 5N-AGU, G-ATPD. CoA 14-10-98. Dump	2-06
❑ G-AXAU	T Comanche 160C	ex N8613Y. CoA 8-3-86. Stored	5-05
❑ G-BAVS	AA-5 Traveler	fuselage. CoA 8-11-94	10-05
❑ G-BBFC	AA-1B Trainer	fuselage. Damaged 9-6-96 ®	10-05
❑ G-BDRB*	AA-5B Tiger	crashed 16-5-94. Fuselage. Arrived 23-6-04	5-05
❑ G-CKCK*	Enstrom 280FX	ex Shoreham, OO-PVL. CoA 14-5-98. Spares. F/n 2-04	5-05
❑ G-GHSI*	Seminole 180T	ex SX-ATA, N8278Z. CoA 1-12-97. F/n 9-04 ®	11-05
❑ [SX-BFM]	Navajo	ex Southampton, N4504J. Cr 23-6-99. Fuselage	10-05
❑ VR-BEB	BAC 111-527FK	ex airliner store, RP-C1181, PI-C1181. Fire dump	2-06
❑ WJ992	Canberra T.4	ex DRA Bedford, RAE, 76. Fire dump	2-06

BOVINGTON off the A352 near Wool, west of Wareham

Tank Museum: Houses the world's finest international collection of armoured fighting vehicles.

◆ Open daily (except Xmas) 10am to 5pm. Special events held throughout the year. Bovington, Dorset, BH20 6JG tel 01929 405096 fax 01929 405360 e-mail admin@tankmuseum.co.uk www.tankmuseum.co

❑ TK718	GAL Hamilcar I	ex Beverley, Christian Malford.	4-06
❑ XM564	Skeeter AOP.12	ex 652, CFS, 12 Flt, 652	4-06

COMPTON ABBAS AERODROME south-east of Shaftesbury

Flying Aces Movie Aircraft Collection: (Note name.) The museum is centred around the airframes and artefacts previously part of the 'Blue Max' museum at Wycombe Air Park, Bucks. Also on show is the tail and top wing from a film mock-up Gotha G.IV ('983/16) used in *Mr Chips' War* in 2002. The airfield is fantastically aspected and there is a superb café affording great views of the flying.

◆ *Open daily other than Xmas week, 10am to 5.30pm.Compton Abbas Airfield, Ashmore, near Shaftesbury, SP5 5AP tel 01747 811767 www.abbasair.com*

❏	–		MF.1 REP	G-BAAF, ex Wycombe AP. Blériot-like. CoA 6-8-96	3-06
❏	–	'10'	Blériot XI REP	G-BPVE, ex Wycombe AP, N1197	3-06
❏	'B2458'	'R'	Camel REP	G-BPOB, ex Wycombe AP, N8997, Tallmantz Av.	3-06
❏	'B5539'		Stampe SV-4 FSM	ex Wycombe AP, The Mummy, *Indiana Jones and the Lost Crusade*. Gun turret, crash scene	3-06
❏	'MS824'		MS 'N' REP	G-AWBU, ex Wycombe APS. CoA 29-6-01	3-06
❏	'422/15'		Fokker E.III REP	G-AVJO, ex Wycombe AP	3-06
❏	'8'	BAPC.238	Ornithopter	ex Wycombe AP, Young *Sherlock Holmes*. PPS-built	3-06

Elsewhere:

❏	G-AZRV	Arrow 200	ex N2309T. Crashed 30-12-00. Dump	1-06

DORCHESTER

Wessex Aviation and Transport: *W&R19* (p48) gave Moth Minor G-AFOB as moving on "thought to Herts". It actually moved by February 2002 to Henlow, Beds. The same page moved Tiger Moth T5672 to 'Wales'. Not so, it is still to be found here [1]. The one that *did* move in that direction was SV-4L G-BMNV, which moved to Haverfordwest, Wales. By mid-2004 PT-13 N4712V had moved on – thought airworthy in Cornwall.

❏	T5672	Tiger Moth	G-ALRI, ex ZK-BAB, G-ALRI, T5672, 7 FTS, 21 EFTS, 7 FTS, RAFC, 4 EFTS. CoA 19-8-94	[1] 5-05

GALLOWS HILL on a minor road between Bere Regis and Wool, north of Bovington Camp

Dorset Gliding Club:

❏	XP492	FSB Grasshopper TX.1	BGA.3480. Ex 2 MGSP, Locking, Taunton, Greater Malvern	10-05

POOLE on the A35 west of Bournemouth

G-DASI is in use as a shed (how appropriate!) on the Nuffield Industrial Estate.

❏	G-BGNG	Short 330-200	ex Bournemouth, Gill, N330FL, G-BGNG. Fuselage	1-02
❏	G-DASI	Short 360	ex Guernsey, Gill, G-14-3606. Fuselage	1-03

SOMERFORD on the A35 north east of Christchurch

The Lobster - The World's Biggest Maize Maze: By the end of 2003 ST-10 G-AYKG had moved on.

STALBRIDGE on the A357 south-west of Shaftesbury

The Moth Minor Coupe is *thought* under restoration to open top format.

❏	G-AFNI	Moth Minor	ex Woodley, W7972, 100 GCF, Foulsham SF, 241, G-AFNI. CoA 26-5-67	® 12-99

DURHAM and CLEVELAND

➤ The unitary authorities of Hartlepool, Middlesbrough, Redcar and Cleveland, Stockton-on-Tees, and Darlington form the region.

DURHAM TEES VALLEY AIRPORT (MIDDLETON ST GEORGE)
(Formerly Teesside Airport)
International Fire Training Centre: As well as the real airframes at the Serco-operated school, there is a convincing mock-up of a Tornado, used for burning practice along with a 747 front fuselage, a 'Boeing 737', a light aircraft and a 'helicopter' mock-up. The Whirlwind is in poor state and the centre is in need of a replacement helicopter fuselage for evacuation training. Offers anyone? (www.iftc.co.uk) Trident 3B G-AWZR gave up the ghost during 2005 and what was left was cut up and removed.

❏ G-ARPO	Trident 1C	ex BA, BEA. CoA 12-1-86. Whole	2-06
❏ G-AVFJ	Trident 2E	ex BA, BEA. CoA 18-9-83. Poor state	2-06
❏ G-AWZS	Trident 3B-101	ex BA, BEA. CoA 9-9-86. Whole	2-06
❏ G-AZLP	Viscount 813	ex BMA, SAA ZS-CDT. CoA 3-4-82. Fuselage	2-06
❏ G-AZLS	Viscount 813	ex BMA, SAA ZS-CDV. CoA 9-6-83. Fuselage	2-06
❏ 'G-JON'	Short 330-100	G-BKIE, ex Newcastle, G-SLUG, G-METP, G-METO,	
		G-BKIE, C-GTAS, G-14-3005. CoA 22-8-93	2-06
❏ XP330	Whirlwind HAR.10	ex Stansted, 21, 32, 230, 110, 225. Poor state	3-06

Others: G-AZNC is used by the fire services for non-destructive training [1]

❏ G-AZNC	Viscount 813	ex BMA, G-AZLW ntu, SAA, ZS-SBZ, ZS-CDZ	[1]	2-06
❏ G-BNGS	Tomahawk 112	ex Carlisle, Tees-side, Carlisle, N2463A. Dam 5-87. Stored		2-06

YEARBY on the B1269 south of Redcar
Aero Engines and Airframes Ltd: During 2005 an unflown Nipper airframe arrived which was originally built at the strip here – details appreciated [1]. Bö 208A-1 D-EFNO listed here as being off-site as spares for G-ASFR is best deleted. It was never a substantial airframe when acquired.

❏ G-APYB	Nipper III	CoA 12-6-96	®	2-06
❏ G-ASFR	Bö 208A-1	ex D-EGMO. CoA 29-3-90		2-06
❏ G-BAMG	Ganagobie	unfinished project. Stored		2-06
❏ G-BHUO	Evans VP-2	unfinished project. Stored		2-06
❏ G-OOSE	Rutan VariEze	unflown project. Damaged, stored		2-06
❏ -*	Nipper	ex Inverness, Stokesley, Yearby.	[1]	2-06

ESSEX

ANDREWSFIELD AERODROME or Great Saling, north of the A120, west of Braintree
Thurston Teal G-OWET test flew in May 2004. Two transitory wrecks of note were Cherokee 140 G-AYWE and Cessna F.150M D-EAWD which were dumped out by May 2005 for spares recovery. They were removed to a local scrapyard in early November 2005.

❏ G-AYUI	Cherokee 180F	ex N8557, G-AYUI. CoA 5-11-93. Fuselage, stored	1-06
❏ 319	'8-ND' Mystère IVA	ex Sculthorpe, French Air Force	4-06

AUDLEY END off the B1383, west of Saffron Walden
❏ F-BGCJ	Tiger Moth	G-BTOG, ex France, French AF, NM192. Stored	4-99

BRAINTREE on the A120 east of Colchester

In a workshop in the general area are salvaged Spitfires - shot down within 72 hours of one another – plus a Seafire from Malta. All three are substantial remains and one day will form restoration projects.

❏ N3200	Spitfire Ia	ex Calais, 19. Shot down 27-5-40. Stored	3-06
❏ P9374	Spitfire Ia	ex Calais, 92. Shot down 24-5-40. Stored	3-06
❏ MB293	Seafire IIc	ex Malta, 879, 887, AAEE. Stored	3-06

Others:

❏ G-MJSP	Tiger Cub 440	ex North Coates, Boston. CoA 31-1-86	3-03

CHELMSFORD

De Havilland Hornet Project: David Collins is hard at work in this area on a long-term project that he calls a 'new-build' DH Hornet, using many original components. David took on material from Mark Reeder's (see under Fyvie, Scotland) project in October 2005 and would like to hear from others who may be able to help. David is using parts gleaned from the de Havilland Heritage Museum (see under London Colney, Herts) including tail sections salvaged by Tony Agar from St Davids, Wales (including NF.21 VW957 '415'). The space-frame cockpit attended *CockpitFest* 2005 at Winthorpe, Notts, and came away with the Best Cockpit, Runner-up award. At this stage this exceptional project does not need a 'formal' listing – but the day cannot be far off!

David also has the former Doncaster Vampire FB.5 which has now been identified thanks to Vampire 'sleuths' Alan Allen, Mick Rogers and David Watkins. David notes that 247 Squadron's CO was "Sqn Ldr Vaughan-Fowler is noted as having an engine blow up while up at 40,000ft in an FB.5. He managed to glide back to Abingdon and make a successful landing. There is only one aircraft that was damaged in the month that this happened, and this turns out to be VZ193!"

◆ *Visits not possible. Enquiries, offers of parts etc: e-mail dcollins103@hotmail.com www.dhhornet50.net*

❏ VZ193*	Vampire FB.5	ex Doncaster, Firbeck, Malmesbury, Hullavington, 229 OCU, 247. Pod. Arrived 10-05	®	2-06

No.276 Squadron Air Cadets: In Meteor Way, off the Chelmsford-Harlow road, keep their T.7.

❏ WH132	'J' Meteor T.7	ex Kemble 7906M, CAW, CFS, CAW, 8 FTS, 207 AFS	6-05

Others: The nose of Hunter F.6 XG209 moved to Kingston-upon-Thames, Gtr Lon.

CHIPPING ONGAR north of the A414, west of the town

Blake Hall 'Ops' Room: The hall is well known for its gardens and tropical house, but also has within it a splendid array of artefacts centred around the hall's history as being the Operations Centre for Sector E, when the 'ops' room at North Weald was dispersed from the airfield.

◆ *Easter to October, Saturday to Wednesday (NB not Sunday) 11am to 5pm. Bobbingworth, Ongar, Essex, CM5 0DG. tel 01277 362502 fax 01277 366947 e-mail / www.blakehall.co.uk*

CLACTON ON SEA

East Essex Aviation Museum (EEAM) **and Museum of the 1940s**: Located within one of the fine Martello towers that dot the coastline, EEAM includes a fine array of recovery items and other memorabilia. Dominating the contents is the fuselage of P-51M *Little Zippie*. Recovered during 1999 and on show is the substantial wreckage of 339th FG P-51D 44-15560 which crashed at Frinton-on-Sea.

◆ *Within Point Clear caravan park. Open Mon 7pm to 10pm and Sun 10am to 2pm Mar to Oct and Bank Holidays 10am to 2pm Jun to Sep. Roger Barrell, c/o 1 Spanbies Road, Stratford St Mary, Colchester, Essex, CO7 6YH, e-mail home@barrellclan.wanadoo.co.uk*

❏ 44-14574	P-51D-10-NA	ex 479th FG *Little Zippie*. Crashed off-shore 13-1-45	2-06

Locally: The Proctor continues its extensive restoration at an airstrip in the area.

❏ G-AHTE	Proctor V	ex Nayland, Llanelli, Cardiff, Swansea, Llanelli, ?, Hereford, Walsall. CoA 10-8-61	®	1-06

CLACTON AERODROME between Clacton on Sea and Jaywick
Super Cub 150G-ARAN was flying again by early 2003 and fellow G-BGWH by December 2003.

CLAVERING on the B1038 south-west of Saffron Walden
As threatened in *W&R19*, the hulk of Cessna F.172H G-AXWF, last noted July 1995, has got LOST!

COLCHESTER
Charleston Aviation Services: The latest example of Craig Charleston's prowess underwent taxi trials at Wattisham, Suffolk, during January 2006. This was Bf 109E-3 1342 (G-BYDS – cancelled in November 2004 as sold in the USA), last listed in *W&R18* (p54) as leaving Earls Colne, Essex, bound for the USA. This was not the case, Craig working his magic to bring it up to full flight status and incredible JG51 colours. Following taxi trials, it was crated and departed for Seattle, Washington, USA, and the Flying Heritage Collection.

❏ –	Sea Fury FB.11	composite.		3-94
❏ LA546	Seafire F.46	ex Newport Pagnell, Newark. Substantial parts.		3-06
❏ 7485	Bf 109F-4	ex Russia.	®	3-02
❏ 8147	Bf 109F-4	ex Lancing, Russia, 6/JG54.	®	3-02
❏ 15458	Bf 109G-2	ex Russia.	®	11-03

EARLS COLNE AERODROME on the B1024 south of Earls Colne, east of Halstead
The wheels may grind slowly, but they *do* grind... Turn to *W&R16* (p60) under this heading and details of the wind-up of the pioneering Rebel Air Museum. PT-26 Cornell N9606H was noted as moving to "a collector in 'Norfolk'" circa 1997. That was, in its own way, spot on. It moved to <u>Martham</u>, Norfolk.

❏ G-AOZL	J/5Q Alpine	ex Southend. CoA 28-5-88.	®	10-05
❏ SE-HXF	Scorpion	-		4-06

EAST TILBURY on a minor road east of Tilbury
Thameside Aviation Museum (TAM): Located within the Coalhouse Fort 1860s Victorian Casemate Fortress, TAM is dedicated to aviation archaeology excavations carried out from the early 1970s, including a huge amount on the Battle of Britain over Essex. Ken Levy is at work on the Chipmunk and the Gnat nose is owned by Darren Wingrave. None of the noses are on public show.

◆ *At Coalhouse Fort, 'brown signed' from A13. TAM open last Sun of the month and Bank Hols, Mar to Oct 11am to 4.30pm. Other times by arrangement. (Details of Coalhouse Fort tel 01375 844203) Coalhouse Fort, East Tilbury, Essex tel 07860 134946 e-mail museum@aviationmuseum.co.uk www.aviationmuseum.co.uk*

❏ WG471	Chipmunk T.10	ex Bury St E, 8210M, Stowmarket, Leeming, Abn UAS, 1 FTS,		
	PAX	6 FTS, 220 OCU, Aston Down CF, MCCS, 4 SoTT, Nott UAS,		
		Leeds UAS, 19 RFS, 24 RFS, 3 BFTS, 16 RFS, 4 BFTS	®	2-06
❏ XM692	Gnat T.1	ex Boscombe Down, Robertsbridge, Salisbury,		
		Southampton, Fareham, Folland. Nose		2-06
❏ 0446	MiG-21UM	ex Salisbury, Farnborough, Egyptian AF. Nose		2-06

FOULNESS ISLAND on a minor road north-east of Great Wakering
Defence Science and Technology Laboratory, Shoeburyness: The range functions in a small enclave, in the north-east of the 'island', beyond Courtsend.

❏ XT895	Phantom FGR.2	ex Valley 9171M, 74, 228 OCU, 92, 228 OCU,		
		111, 6, 228 OCU. Cockpit		3-00
❏ '50' b	MiG-23MF	ex Chester, Latvia, USSR. (023003508)		3-04

FYFIELD on the B184 north of Chipping Ongar
Last noted in June 2001, Skeeter AOP.10 XK482 (G-BJWC) was exported to Australia.

GREAT DUNMOW on the A120 west of Braintree
Paul and **Andy Wood**:.

❏ WP185	Hunter F.5	ex Abingdon, Hendon, Henlow 7583M, 34, 1. Stored	3-06

GREAT WALTHAM on the A130 north of Chelmsford
Messenger 2A G-AKEZ was cancelled as sold in New Zealand in January 2006.

HALSTEAD north-east of Braintree
Tiger Moth G-APBI was flying by 2004 and the restoration of Navion B N3864 was completed by June 2005 at the latest, when it was flying.

❏ G-AJUL	J/1N Alpha	CoA 11-9-81	® 12-90

INGATESTONE on the A12 south west of Chelmsford
Stuart Gowans: Given a public airing at 'CockpitFest' 2004 and 2005 at Winthorpe, Notts, was Stuart's ambitious and lovely Spitfire IX reproduction which will feature a Rolls-Royce Merlin, engine bearers and as many other original parts as possible. Construction/restoration continues and the project is fast becoming an entire fuselage. Vampire XE864 has the wings of XD435 [1]. See under Redhill, Surrey, for details of the fuselage of Blackburn B-2 G-ACBH which transited through here in late 2005. Vampire T.11 XD599 moved to Northampton, Northants, on 10th October 2004 while Scimitar F.1 nose XD235 went to Lavendon, Bucks, by August 2005.

❏ _–*	Spitfire IX REP	see above.	4-06
❏ WF145	Sea Hawk F.1	ex Welshpool, South Molton, Salisbury, Torbay,	
		Brawdy, Abbotsinch, RAE, AAEE. Nose	9-02
❏ WP927*	Chipmunk T.10	ex London Colney, Ashton-under-Lyne, Woodvale,	
	PAX	Ashton-under-Lyne, Crosby, 8216M, Hamble G-ATJK,	
		MCS, Oxf UAS, Lon UAS, Detling SF, Lon UAS	12-05
❏ XE864	Vampire T.11	ex Welshpool, Shobdon, Stretton, Kibworth,	
		Firbeck, Studley, Chester, Woodford, St Athan,	
		8 FTS, 7 FTS, 1 ANS, CFS, 4 FTS	[1] 9-02

LAINDON north of the A127, near Basildon
BA Swallow II G-AFGE flew to its new home in Wiltshire on 18th December 2005. Some parts of the Luton and Jodel are at the strip, will the majority are being worked on in the area.

❏ G-ARXP	Luton Minor	CoA 17-10-95. Stored	off-site 12-05
❏ G-BAGF	Jodel D.92	ex F-PHFC. Stored, off-site	off-site 12-05

LONDON (STANSTED) AIRPORT
W&R19 (p57) recorded HS.125-400B VR-BMB as being parted out here in August 2003. The gutted cockpit section was saved and ultimately moved to Pershore, Worcs, on May 1, 2004. The fire crews have a realistic-looking, steel plate, BAe 146-ish fuselage to torch.

❏ G-IOIT	TriStar 100	ex Classic Airways, G-CEAP, SE-DPM, G-BEAL.	
		Flew in 13-4-98. Stored	7-05

Nearby: *W&R18* (p259) under Salisbury, Wilts, noted the departure of Lightning F.6 nose XS922 to "an Essex-based collector" by March 2002. This was indeed so and the venue was here. By late 2005 it had moved on to Spark Bridge, Cumbria.

NORTH WEALD AERODROME off the A414, junction 7, M11 east of Harlow
- The North Weald site is large and aircraft are listed below under their nominal 'keepers'. It is possible to find aircraft 'owned' by one heading parked in an area 'operated' by another. As with several other venues in the book, airworthy general aviation types based are not listed.

Aces High Flying Museum: PBY-6A N285RA *Spirit of Zvi Avidror* departed en route to Israel and the IDF/AF Museum on 28th May 2004.The DC-4 and the C-54 both arrived in September 2002 for a film on the Berlin Airlift. This has yet to transpire and the pair are in open store [1. The *real* Aztec 250D G-ESKY is airworthy [2]. (See also Dunsfold, Surrey, for Aces High's other facility.)

Departures: Sprint 160 G-SAHI left by road 11-6-05 for restoration to flying condition by a Bedford-based owner; C-47B N3455 left by road for Redhill, Surrey, on 24-7-04, but moved on, by road and ferry to France, on 9-11-04; VB-25N 430861 (N9089Z) moved by road to Wycombe Air Park, Books, during early 2-06. Going back to *W&R19* (p52), CASA 2-111 G-AWHB was recorded as leaving in late 2002 bound for the USA via a 'Norfolk workshop'. It is still to be found at Martham, Norfolk.

◆ Visits strictly by prior appointment *only*.

❑ G-BMPF	OA.7 Optica	ex Bournemouth. CoA 14-1-9<u>3</u>. Stored	2-04
❑ G-BMPL*	OA.7 Optica	ex Dunsfold (?), North Weald, Farnborough,	
		Bournemouth. CoA 2-8-97. Stored, first noted 7-05	7-05
❑ G-BOPR	OA.7 Optica	ex Bournemouth (?). Stored	2-04
❑ 'G-ESKY'	Aztec 250D	G-BADI ex N6885Y. CoA 29-10-92. Hulk	[2] 4-06
❑ G-CSFT	Aztec 250D	ex G-AYKU, N13885. CoA 3-12-94. Hulk	6-05
❑ G-FLSI	Sprint 160	ex Stansted, Bournemouth. Stored	2-04
❑ G-70-503	Sprint 160	G-BXWU, ex Stansted, Bournemouth. Stored	2-04
❑ G-70-505	Sprint 160	G-BXWV, ex Stansted, Bournemouth. Stored	2-04
❑ [D-HGBX]	Enstrom F-280	hulk	2-04
❑ EC-FVM	OA.7 Optica	ex Farnborough, Bournemouth, G-BOPO. Stored	6-05
❑ N47FL	C-47A-20-DK ✈	ex Elstree, EC-FIN, EC-659, N7164E, C-GCTE, C-GXAV,	
		N92A ntu, C-GXAV, CAF 12952, RCAF 968, 42-93203	4-06
❑ N2700	C-119G-FA	ex Manston, 3C-ABA, Belg AF CP-9, 12700. Nose	4-06
❑ N70457 '511'	MD.600N	ex *Tomorrow Never Dies*	2-04
❑ TF-ABP	TriStar	ex Iver Heath, Bruntingthorpe, Air Atlanta Icelandic,	
		VR-HOG Cathay, LTU, Eastern N323EA. Cockpit	4-06
❑ [6W-SAF]	C-47A-65-DL	ex North Weald, Woodley, Kew, Cranfield, F-GEFU,	
		Le Bourget, Senegalese AF, USAF MAAG Brussels,	
		USAAF 42-100611. Nose	6-05
❑ 'FL586'	C-47B-10-DK	ex Pinewood, *Sword of Honour*, OO-SMA, N99346	
	'AI-N'	ntu, Belg AF K-1 OT-CWA, 43-49240. Fuselage	6-05
❑ –*	'NF-A' Dakota 3 ✈	N147DC, ex Dunsfold, North Weald, G-DAKS, Duxford,	
		'10884', 'KG374', *Airline* 'G-AGHY', TS423, RAE,	
		Ferranti, Airwork, Gatow SF, 436, 1 HGSU, 42-100884	4-06
❑ XN437	Auster AOP.9	G-AXWA, ex ?, Lashenden, Welling, Biggin Hill,	
		Luton, Odiham, Maghull, Hoylake, St Athan, Kenya. ®	6-05
❑ 56498	C-54D-1-DC	N44914, ex BuNo 56498, 42-72525. Stored	[1] 4-06
❑ '44-42914'	DC-4-1009	N31356, C-FTAW, EL-ADR, N6404. Stored	[1] 4-06

Hangar 11 Collection: Peter Teichman established a new 'blister' hangar on the 'Squadron' side and the aircraft rolled in on 1st August 2004. The former Soviet Union Spitfire IX is a long-term project and is stored. 'Staggerwing' G-BRVE was involved in the exchange that brought the P-40M here. *Victor-Echo* was ferried to Duxford, Cambs, on 14th December 2005.

◆ Visits strictly by prior appointment *only*.

❑ PL965*	'R' Spitfire PR.XI ✈	G-MKXI, ex Breighton, N965RF, USA, Rochester, Overloon,	
		Brüggen, Overloon, Deelen, Twenthe, 16, 1 PP. Arr 6-9-04	2-06
❑ PT879*	Spitfire IX	G-BYDE, ex Romford, Sandown, Romford, FSU,	
		USSR, SovAF, PT879 no RAF service. Stored	2-06
❑ –*	'49' P-40M-10-CU ✈	G-KITT, ex TFC Duxford, 'P8196', F-AZPJ, Duxford,	
		N1009N, 'FR870', N1233N, RCAF 840, 43-5802.	
		343rd FG c/s. Arrived 14-12-05	2-06
❑ 472035*	P-51D-20-NA ✈	G-SIJJ, F-AZMU, N5306M, HK-2812P, HK-2812X,	
		N5411V, 44-72035. *Jumpin Jacques*	2-06

Kennet Aviation: Seafire F.XVII SX336 moved by road to Turweston, Northants, for spraying in March 2006 courtesy of paint wizard Mick Allen and was expected to have test flown by the time this edition was published. This is an exceptional restoration story and will be a sensation on the airshow circuit [1]. The remains of fellow SX300 was civil registered in December 2005, this is a 'bare bones' project and it its earliest stages [2]. Scout AH.1 XV140 (G-KAXL) left on 21st April 2004, and is thought to have been exported via Tilbury docks.
◆ *Visits strictly by prior appointment* only.

❑ G-FRCE		Gnat T.1	➔ ex North Weald, Halton 8604M, XS104, 4 FTS, CFS, 4 FTS	3-06
❑ G-HUEY		UH-1H	ex Bournemouth, Cranfield, Argentine Army AE-413,	
			73-22077. CoA 12-4-00	6-05
❑ SX300*		Seafire XVII	G-CDTM, ex Twyford, Warwick, Leamington Spa,	
			Warrington, Bramcote A2054/ A646, 728.	[2] 3-06
❑ SX336	'105'	Seafire XVII	G-KASX, ex Nottingham, G-BRMG, Cranfield, Twyford,	
			Newark, Warrington, Stretton A2055, Bramcote, 728.	
			Arrived on-site 30-7-04. 766 Sqn colours ® [1]	4-06
❑ 'WK436'		Venom FB.50	➔ G-VENM, ex Cranfield, J-1614, East Dereham, G-BLIE,	
			Ipswich, Glasgow, Swiss AF. 11 Sqn c/s	3-04
❑ 'XD693'	'Z-Q'	Jet Provost T.1	➔ G-AOBU, ex Cranfield, Winchester, Thatcham, Old	
			Warden, Loughborough, Luton, XM129, G-42-1. 2 FTS c/s	3-06
❑ XF515	'R'	Hunter F.6A	➔ G-KAXF, ex Cranfield, Binbrook, Scampton 8830M,	
			Kemble, 1 TWU, 229 OCU, 43, 247. 43 Sqn c/s	3-06
❑ XF690		Provost T.1	➔ G-MOOS, ex Cranfield, Thatcham, G-BGKA, 8041M,	
			XF690, CATCS, CNCS, 64 GCF, Queens UAS	3-06
❑ XL500*		Gannet AEW.3	G-KAEW, ex Chatham, Culdrose A2701, Lee-on-Solent,	
			Culdrose, Dowty-Rotol, Culdrose, Lossiemouth, 849.	
			Arrived 26-6-04	3-06
❑ XP540	'62'	Gnat T.1	ex Cambridge, Bruntingthorpe, Halton 8608M, 4 FTS	3-04
❑ 'XR993'		Gnat T.1	➔ G-BVPP, ex Cranfield, XP534, Halton 8620M, 4 FTS,	
			CFS, 4 FTS, CFS, 4 FTS. Red Arrows c/s	3-06
❑ 'XS111'		Gnat T.1	➔ G-TIMM, ex 'XM693', Cranfield, Leavesden, Halton	
			8618M, XP504, 4 FTS, CFS, 4 FTS [1]	3-06
❑ XT632*		Scout AH.1	G-BZBD, ex Bruntingthorpe, Oaksey Park, XT632.	
			Crashed 23-8-00. Spares. Arrived 30-10-04	3-06
❑ XV118*	'T'	Scout AH.1	ex Brize Norton 9141M, Wroughton, 657, 658, 652,	
			651, 660. Arrived 2004	12-04
❑ XW289	'73'	Jet Provost T.5A	G-JPVA, ex Cranfield, G-BVXT, Binbrook,	
			➔ Shawbury, 1 FTS, RAFC, CFS	3-06
❑ NZ3905		Wasp HAS.1	➔ G-KAXT, ex Cranfield, Weston-s-M, RNZN, XT787	3-04
❑ NZ3909		Wasp HAS.1	G-KANZ, ex Cranfield, RNZN, XT782.	12-05
❑ 126922		AD-4NA	➔ G-RADR, ex G-RAID, F-AZED, La Ferté Alais, Gabon	
	'AK-402'	Skyraider	AF, FAF No.42, USN 126922. VA-176, *Intrepid* c/s	4-06

Robs Lamplough / Fighter Wing Display Team: In July 2004 P-51D 472216 (G-BIXL) suffered a forced-landing, thankfully with no major injury to the pilot. The aircraft was moved to Filton, Glos, for repair in the hands of Robs' Spitfire team. The story of moving out continues, the hangar having been taken on by another operator. Beech D.17S 'DR628' (N18V) moved to Lambourn, Berks, in August 2004, by which time Nord 1002 LV-RIE had also made the trek. By October 2003 Spitfire IX FSM 'EN398' (BAPC.184) had moved to Derby, Derbyshire. Noralpha '14' (G-BSMD) went to Wycombe Air Park, Bucks, by April 2005 and was flying shortly thereafter. Venom FB.54 J-1758 was the last to move from the site, going to Lambourn, Berks, on 5-10-05. (See also Filton, Glos, for Spitfire VIII 'MT928' – G-BKMI.)

North Weald Airfield Museum: Based at 'Ad Astra' House, located at the former main gate of the station, with a very impressive memorial dedicated to all those who served at 'Weald and another to the Norwegians who flew from there in the foreground. The material on display is superb - an important place of pilgrimage.

◆ *Off Hurricane Way, from North Weald village – ie the B181 – not via the aerodrome. Open Sun noon to 5pm. Other times by arrangement. Tours of the airfield can be arranged. 'Ad Astra House', Hurricane Way, North Weald Aerodrome, Epping, CM16 6AA. tel 07778 296650 e-mail northweald1916@hotmail.co.uk web http://fly.to/northweald*

'The Squadron' / North Weald Flying Services (NWFS): Alcyon G-MSAL left by road for <u>Spanhoe Lodge</u>, Northants, in October 2005. W&R17 (p57) recorded PT-19 Cornell N33870 leaving here for 'Norfolk'. Cosmically speaking, this was spot-on: it went to <u>Martham</u>, Norfolk.
◆ *Visits by prior permission only. A series of fly-ins and events are staged during the season. North Weald Airfield, Epping, Essex, CM16, 6AA tel 01992 52 4510 fax 01992 52 2238*

❑ G-AHUN*	GC-1B Swift	ex Thurrock area, EC-AJK, OO-KAY, NC77764.		
		CoA 4-8-95. Arrived by 7-05	®	2-06
❑ 'G-PRAT'	AA-5A Cheetah	G-BIVV, ex Elstree, N26979. Wreck, fire crews		2-06
❑ N36TH	T-33AN	G-BYOY, N333DV, N134AT, N10018,		
		N134AT,RCAF 21231. 'Thunderbird' c/s		2-06

Others: This includes the newly-erected 'blister' hangar (known as '**Area 39**' close to the 13 threshold). Cherokee G-AVLH departed in November 2004 to Kent for restoration to fly. Newly operating from 'Weald is the **Vampire Preservation Group**'s *India-India* (www.vampirepreservation.org.uk).

❑ G-AKUP	Silvaire 8E	ex N2774K, NC2774K. Stored		2-06
❑ N96240	Beech D.18S	ex Rochester, Spain, Wellesbourne Mountford,		
		Blackbushe, G-AYAH, N6123, RCAF1559		2-06
❑ SP-CHD	PZL.101 Gawron	ex Sandown, Augsburg. In shed	®	2-06
❑ WZ507*	'74' Vampire T.11 ✈	G-VTII, ex Bournemouth, Swansea, Bruntingthorpe,		
		Cranfield, Carlisle, CATCS, 3/4 CAACU, 5 FTS, 8 FTS,		
		229 OCU. Arrived 11-2-06	[1]	3-06

Locally: Two airframes are under restoration nearby.

❑ G-BDXX	SNCAN NC.854	ex airfield, F-BEZQ. CoA 3-7-96	®	2-06
❑ [G-BXIY]	Blake Bluetit	ex Old Warden, BAPC.37, Winchester	®	2-06

PURFLEET on A1090 west of the Dartford Bridge

Purfleet Heritage and Military Centre: Incorporating the **Hornchurch Wing** and housed in the incredible Royal Gunpowder Magazine 18th century arsenal, the centre holds an incredible wealth of aviation artefacts. The section dedicated to Hornchurch is exceptional.
◆ *Just off the A1090, in Centurion Way. Open Thu, Sun and Bank Hols April to October 10am to 4.30pm; Nov to March 10am to 3pm. Closed Christmas and Boxing Day. Alan Gosling, 8 Rapier Close, Purfleet-on-Thames, Essex, RM19 1QQ 01708 523409 www.purfleet5@freeserve.co.uk/heritage.htm*

RAYLEIGH on the A1095 north-west of Southend-on-Sea

The Cockpit Collection: Nigel Towler's collection is located variously within the region. The wings of Vampire WZ608 can be found on WZ518 at Sunderland, N&T [1].
◆ *The collection is scattered in various locations and, accordingly, visits are not possible.*

❑ WZ608	Vampire T.11	ex Market Harborough, Lutterworth, Bitteswell, Woodford,		
		St Athan, 3 CAACU, 5 FTS, 266, Fassberg SF, 11 Vampire Flt,		
		5, Wunstorf SF, 266. Nose	[1]	4-00
❑ 'WZ826'	Valiant BK.1	XD826, ex Cardiff-Wales, Abingdon, Stratford, Cosford,		
		Feltwell 7872M, 543, 232 OCU, 138, 90, 7. Nose		4-00
❑ XH560	Vulcan B.2	ex Marham, Waddington, 50, Wadd W, 27, Akrotiri Wing,		
		Cott W, Wadd W, Cott W, 230 OCU, 12, MoA, 230 OCU.		
		Nose		4-00
❑ XH669	Victor K.2	ex Waddington 9092M, 55, 57, Witt Wing, AAEE. Nose		4-00
❑ XH670	Victor B.2	ex East Kirkby, Tattershall, Woodford, Radlett, MoA. Nose		4-00
❑ XN795	Lightning F.2A	ex Foulness, RAE Bedford, AAEE, BAC. Nose		4-00
❑ XS421	Lightning T.5	ex Foulness, RAE, 23, 111, 226 OCU. Nose		4-00

No.1476 Squadron Air Cadets: In Connaught Road.

☐ G-BOVG	Cessna F.172H	ex Southend, OO-ANN, D-ELTR. Damaged 1991. Fuselage	2-06
☐ XG325	Lightning F.1	ex Southend, Wattisham, Foulness, AAEE. Nose	2-06

RETTENDON on the A1245 south-east of Chelmsford
'The Wheatsheaf': By August 2004, Whirlwind HAR.10 XP399 had gone. Enquiries revealed it "went to Franklins for scrap". No details on this yard have come to light.

RIDGEWELL on the A1017 south-east of Haverhill
Ridgewell Airfield Commemorative Museum / 381st Bomb Group Memorial Museum: Established in USAAF Station No.167's former hospital buildings. A series of displays - including the Tony Ince Collection – are dedicated to the 381st and to the RAF units that operated from the base.
◆ *Second Sun of each month, Apr to Sept, 11am to 5pm. Other times by arrangement. 'White Wings', Ashen Road, Ovington, Sudbury, CO10 8JX tel 01787 277310 or 07881 518572 e-mail jim@381st.com www.381st.com*

SOUTHEND AIRPORT (ROCHFORD)
Vulcan Restoration Trust (VRT): XL426 is kept in fine fettle and regularly ground-run and taxied. Developments at the airport mean that VRT must move its workshops and stores to a new site which (planning permission permitting) will be next to the pan on which XL426 resides.
◆ *Occasional 'up-and-running' days. Other times by appointment. VRT publish the excellent Vulcan News. PO Box 368, Stevenage, Herts, SG1 9BE. e-mail vulcan@avrovulcan.com www.avrovulcan.com*

☐ XL426	Vulcan B.2	ex Waddington, VDF , Waddington SF, 50, 617, 27,	
	G-VJET	617, 230 OCU, 617, 230 OCU, 617, 230 OCU,	
		617, 230 OCU, Scampton Wing, 83	3-06

Airport: As with several other locations within the UK, there are definition problems here relating to airliners here: just *what* is a W&R candidate and what is just 'resting' in between a contract? As well as the aircraft given below, the skyline here carries a strong BAe ATP flavour, some more HS.146s and even a couple of Embraer Brasilias. We must wait and see. Boeing 707 HZ-123 *may* be facing better times. During December 2005 it was surveyed by a team from Australia and it is reported that work will start by the time these words are read on getting the aircraft airworthy, for a ferry flight to Australia in 2007. As VH-EBA it was delivered to QANTAS as *City of Melbourne* on 16th July 1959, becoming the first jet aircraft on the Australian civil register.
   Departures: Viscount 802 G-AOHL scrapped over 12/13-5-04 - replaced by BAC 111 'G-FIRE' - to Stock, Essex; Cherokee 180C G-ATAA cabin removed 2004 for conversion to a flight 'sim', unknown location; Cessna 152 II G-BTYT sold and departed during 2004; Short 330-100 G-SSWP scrapped by 14-5-04 with its cockpit going briefly to Stock, Essex, before settling upon Manston, Kent; Boeing 727-227F EI-PAK became 9L-LEG and then 9L-LFD during 2004 and left 12-2-05; F.27-200MAR 3C-QSB commenced scrapping 12-05 and was removed 2/3-2-06, and was handled by Hainningfield Metals of Stock, Essex.

☐ G-ATRP	Cherokee 140	Damaged 16-10-81. Wreck		1-06
☐ G-AVNP	Cherokee 180C	ex N11C. Crashed 28-4-01. Fuselage, with fire crews		1-06
☐ G-BEPS	Belfast	ex G-27-13, XR368, 53. Last flight 30-3-01	®	3-06
☐ G-BPEL	Warrior 151	ex C-FEYM. CoA 8-2-92. Wreck		1-06
☐ G-BVFS	Motor Cadet III	ex ?? Unflown. Stored, dismantled		1-06
☐ G-CHTT	Varga Kachina	ex Elstree. Crashed 27-4-86. Spares for G-BPVK		1-06
☐ 'G-FIRE'	BAC 111-401AK	5N-HHH, ex HZ-NB2, N5024. To fire crews 3-04		3-06
☐ G-FLTY*	Bandeirante	ex G-ZUSS, G-REGA, N711NH, PT-GMH.		
		Arrived 8-3-05. Stored		3-06
☐ G-OBWD	BAC 111-518FG	9L-LDK ntu, ex G-BDAE, G-AXMI. CoA 14-4-02. Stored		3-06
☐ B-632L*	HS.146-100	N76HN ntu, B-2707, G-5-076. Arrived 6-6-03. Stored		3-06
☐ B-634L*	HS.146-100	G-CCXY, N83HN ntu, B-634L, B-2709, G-5-03.		
		Arrived 30-5-03. Parting out 3-06		3-06

❑ CS-TMY*	Short 360-100	ex G-BLCP, OY-MMA, EI-BYU, OY-MMA,	
		G-BLCP, G-14-3632. Arrived 13-7-04. Stored	3-06
❑ EL-AKJ	Boeing 707-321C	N2NF ntu, ex Omega, PP-BRR, EL-AKJ, 9Q-CSW, 5N-TAS,	
		N864BX, OB-R1243, HK-2473X, N473RN, N473PA. Stored	3-06
❑ HZ-123	Boeing 707-138B	ex N138M, N220M, N138TA, C-FPWV, VH-EBA,	
		N31239. Stored	3-06
❑ N90FL	King Air C90	ex 'N33FL', F-GFLD, HB-GGW, I-AZIO. Stored	1-06
❑ N150JC	Bonanza A35	ex Andover, Wick, N8674A. Dam 18-6-83. Stored	3-06
❑ TF-ELL*	Boeing 737-210C	ex N41026, F-GGFI, N4906. Arrived 7-8-02. Stored ®	3-06
❑ VH-AHL*	HS.748 Srs 2/228	ex RAAF A10-606. Arrived 3-3-05. Stored	3-06
❑ VH-AMQ*	HS.748 Srs 2/228	ex RAAF A10-603. Arrived 20-2-05. Stored	3-06
❑ VH-AYS*	HS.748 Srs 2/228	ex RAAF A10-608. Arrived 14-3-05. Stored	3-06
❑ 3C-QSC	F.27-200MAR	ex M-2 RNethAF, PH-FSI, PH-EXD.Stored	3-06

SOUTHEND-ON-SEA
Adventure Island: On Marine Parade is Lost City Adventure Golf which has a novel putting hazard.

| ❑ G-AZRX | Horizon 160 | ex Great Yarmouth, Tattershall Thorpe (?), F-BLIJ. | |
| | | Crashed 14-8-91. Wreck | 3-06 |

SOUTH WOODHAM FERRERS on the A132 north of Rayleigh
The nose of Canberra T.22 WT525 moved to Wyton, Cambs, in 2003.

STANSTED AIRPORT
Is now best 'parked' under London (Stansted) Airport.

STAPLEFORD TAWNEY AERODROME on the A113 south of the M11/M25 junction
The dump holds a fascinating hybrid. The forward fuselage of Cessna 252 II G-BOTB, coupled to the rear fuselage of Arrow II G-ORDN [1].

❑ G-AZTO	Seneca 200-2	ex Linley Hill, N4516T. Crashed 27-8-92. Spares	6-01
❑ G-BHUP	Cessna F.152	ex Tattershall Thorpe. Crashed 17-5-89. Fuselage	6-01
❑ G-BOIP	Cessna 152 II	ex Tattershall Thorpe, Staverton, N49264. Dam 11-1-90	6-01
❑ G-BOTB*	Cessna 152 II	ex N94571. Crashed 3-7-00. Dump	[1] 5-04

STOCK on the B1007 south of Chelmsford
Hanningfield Metals / H&M Sales: The Andover nose is held in a nearby yard [1].

Departures: HS.748-2A G-AVXI scrapped by 10-04. Bandeirante nose G-OHIG arrived from Alton by 11-04 but moved to Bognor Regis, W Sussex by mid-2005; Canberra PR.9 nose XH175 to Bewdley, Worcs, 15-12-05; Wessex HC.2 XT677 scrapped by 10-04; Phantom FGR.2 nose XV399 exported by 10-04, thought to Norway. HS.125 fuselage ZF130 arrived in late 2002 but left 7-1-03 for a film set in which it was destined to play a Learjet. It returned by August 2003. In late 2005 it moved again, this time to London, Gtr Lon. [1].

❑ G-AOHL*	Viscount 802	ex Southend, BAF, BA, BEA. CoA 11-4-80. Cockpit.	
		Arrived by 7-04	12-05
❑ XS643	Andover E.3A	ex Manston 9278M, Boscombe Down, 32, AAEE,	
		115, 84. Nose	[1] 12-05
❑ XS791*	Andover CC.2	ex Ely, Bruntingthorpe, Northolt, 32, 60, FEAF VIP Flt, 48,	
		FECS, MECS, Abingdon SF. Fuselage. First noted 11-04	12-05

WEST HANNINGFIELD west of the A130, south of Chelmsford
W&R19 (p61) reported Blackburn B-2 G-ACBH moving on perhaps to 'Chelmsford'. This was not a bad stab. It moved to Ingatestone, Essex. Beyond that, to a barn in Kent and in early March 2006 moved to Redhill, Surrey.

WEST HORNDON west of Basildon, south of the A127
Ricky Kelley: Still keeps his Buccaneer nose in the area. Pressures of work have meant that the Buccaneer Preservation Society has had to disband.

◆ *Viewing by prior arrangement only - email rickykelley@aol.com*

❏	XW550	Buccaneer S.2B	ex Stock, St Athan, 16, 15. Nose	3-06

WEST THURROCK near Purfleet, north of the Dartford Bridge
The two airframes listed here – Cessna 150D G-ASUE and Rallye G-AYFJ – were last noted as far back as June 1994 and have been propelled to the realms of LOST!

GLOUCESTERSHIRE

ASTON DOWN AIRFIELD south of the A419 west of Cirencester
Cotswold Gliding Club:

❏	ASR	628 EoN Baby	ex G-ALRU. Crashed 28-5-71. Stored	1-04
❏	CVX	1851 Kestrel 19	stored	7-99
❏	CWV	1873 Rhonlerche II	ex D-8226. CoA 5-94. Stored	1-04
❏	DVW	2424 ASW 20	stored	7-99
❏	EQP	2869 DG-202/17	crashed 12-7-92. Stored	5-04
❏	XA295*	Cadet TX.3	BGA.3336, ex Keevil, Fareham. First noted 7-05	7-05
❏	XP493	Grasshopper TX.1	ex Syerston. Last flight 9-8-84	4-05

BRISTOL
Bristol's City Museum and Art Gallery: The Bristol Boxkite remains the main aeronautical attraction at the museum, although there are other aviation artefacts. It 'flies' in the foyer.

◆ *Daily 10am to 5pm. Queen's Road, Clifton, Bristol, BS8 1RL tel 0117 9223571 fax 0117 9222047, e-mail general_museums@bristol_city.gov.uk www.bristol-city.gov.uk/museums*

❏	–	BAPC.40 Boxkite repro	ex Old Warden, *Those Magnificent Men...*	3-06

Bristol Industrial Museum: Is expected to close for a two-year refurbishment in October 2006.

◆ *Sat to Wed 10am to 5pm all year. But please see above. Prince's Wharf, Bristol BS1 4RN tel 0117 9251470 fax 0117 9297318, e-mail andy_king@bristol-city.gov.uk wwwbristol-city.gov.uk /museums*

❏	–	Concorde EMU	ex Filton. Forward fuselage.	12-05
❏	XL829	Sycamore HR.14	ex 32, MCS, Khormaksar SAR Flight.	12-05

Brunel Technical College: The Beagle 206 is owned by the Midland Air Museum of Coventry, Warks, and is on temporary loan [1]. Although somewhat dated, the entries are *believed* current.

❏	G-ASWJ	Beagle 206-1	ex Halton 8449M, Rolls-Royce. CoA 30-1-75	[1] 2-04
❏	G-ATHA	Apache 235	ex Bristol Airport, N4326Y. CoA 7-6-86	6-91
❏	G-AVDR	Queen Air B80	ex Bournemouth, Shobdon, Exeter, A40-CR, G-AVDR. CoA 30-6-86	6-91
❏	G-AVVW	Cessna F.150H	ex Bristol Airport. CoA 31-5-82	6-91
❏	G-AWBW	Cessna F.172H	ex Bristol Airport, Compton Abbas. Dam 20-5-73	6-91

Others: A long-term project by **Tim Cox** and team at their workshop in the general area is the Miles Sparrowhawk.

❏	G-ADNL	Sparrowhawk	reconstruction	® 9-03
❏	G-AETG	Aeronca 100	ex Hanwell, Booker. Crashed 7-4-69	® 9-01
❏	G-AEWV	Aeronca 100	ex Hanwell. Fuselage frame, other parts. Spares	9-01
❏	–	'252' Cadet TX.1	BGA.427, ex Stoke-on-Trent, Firbeck, Bickmarsh, RAFGSA.258	9-01
❏	EI-ALU	Avro Cadet	ex New Castle, Dublin, G-ACIH	9-01

CHELTENHAM
Nick Parker: Cherishes his Scimitar nose.

❏ XD215	Scimitar F.1	ex Ottershaw, Foulness, Culdrose A2573, 764B, 800, 803, AAEE. Nose	3-04

A Pucará nose has arrived in the general area.

❏ A-533*	FMA Pucará	ex Boscombe Down, Salisbury, St Mary Bourne, Middle Wallop, Boscombe Down, Abingdon, Finningley, ZD486, Stanley, Argentine AF. Nose	12-05

CHIPPING CAMPDEN on the B4081 north of Stow on the Wold
The former Boscombe Down Comet nose is *thought* to be still kept in the area.

❏ XV814	Comet 4	ex Boscombe Down, RAE, BOAC, G-APDF. Nose	6-01

CHIPPING SODBURY
Both Whirlwinds are still to be found here.
◆ *Visits strictly by prior arrangement only – tel 07840 409061*

❏ XK911	'519' Whirlwind HAS.7	ex Adlington, Derby, Colton, Ipswich, Wroughton, Lee-o-S, Arbroath A2603,771, 829, *Ark Royal* Flt, 824, 820, 845	2-06
❏ XR458	'H' Whirlwind HAR.10	ex Moreton Valence, Middle Wallop, Netheravon, Halton 8662M, 2 FTS, CFS, 28, 110, 103	2-06

DURSLEY on the A4135 south-west of Stroud
Retro Track and Air Ltd: A specialist engine overhaul and airframe company, equally as at home with historic Grand Prix racing car restoration. Retro Track and Air have a Gladiator project underway, although it is in the early stages. The Hurricane awaits its turn for restoration.
◆ *Visits strictly by prior arrangement only.*

❏ N5719	Gladiator I	G-CBHO, ex Narvik, 263.	® 12-05
❏ Z5207	Hurricane IIB	G-BYDL, ex Sudbury, Audley End, Russia,151 Wing, 81	12-05
❏ –	Jurca Sirocco	unfinished project. Stored.	6-02

FAIRFORD AIRFIELD south of the A417, east of Cirencester
USAF Fairford: Phantom FGR.2 XV408 moved on 30th November 2005 to Tangmere, W Sussex.

FILTON AIRFIELD south of the M5 at Patchway, north of Bristol
Concorde Visitor Centre: Concorde G-BOAF, on loan from British Airways, was opened to the public in September 2004 but suffered a tragic set-back on the 24th when a visitor fell 15ft to his death as he was boarding the aircraft. *Alpha-Fox* was closed pending an investigation, but quickly re-opened. The centre is run by the Bristol Aero Collection – see under Kemble, Glos, for more details and of the **Filton Heritage Group**.
◆ *Access to Concorde is via the Airbus UK site and for security and safety reasons all visits will need to be pre-booked. Wed to Sun 9.45am to 4.30pm pre-booked. Bristol Aero Collection, Concorde at Filton, PO Box 77, Bristol BS99 7AR tel 0117 9365485 e-mail info@concordeatfilton.org.uk www.concordeatfilton.org.uk*

❏ G-BOAF	Concorde 102	ex BA, G-N94AF, G-BFKX, BOAC	3-06

Rolls-Royce Heritage Trust - Bristol Branch (RRHT): The Branch has an astounding collection of aero engines, centred on two former test-beds that were used for Proteus work within the R-R plant. As well as Bristol and Bristol Siddeley engines and Rolls-Royce (from 1966), de Havilland engines and archive from the former Leavesden Branch are also here.
◆ *By prior permission only. Rolls-Royce Heritage Trust, Peter Pavey, 23 Morley Avenue, Mangotsfield, Bristol, BS16 9JE*

Airfield: By mid-2004 Concorde 100 G-BBDG had moved completely to Brooklands, Surrey. **Rolls-Royce** (RR) bases is Spitfire XIX here and is also hard at work on completing the restoration of its Mk.XIV. Held with Rolls-Royce, the AV-8B Harrier is believed to be as given, but may be 162071 [2]. **Robs Lamplough** (RL) operates his Spitfire from here and his P-51 is licking its wounds on site. Sea Devon XK896 (G-RNAS, last noted in April 2005) and Canberra T.17 WH665 both moved to Tidenham, Glos.

The airfield continues to act as a storage point for out-of-work airliners and during mid-2004 through to 2005 a series of UK-registered HS.146s were to be found biding their time; all have since moved on. By November 2005 former Air Madagascar Boeing 747-2B6B 5R-MFT was being 'parted out' here. Its forward fuselage moved to Tidenham, Glos, by March 2006.

❑	G-AVDS	Queen Air B80	ex Bristol, Bournemouth, Exeter, A40-CS, G-AVDS. CoA 26-8-77. Dump		4-05
❑	'MT928' 'ZX-M'	Spitfire VIII ✈	G-BKMI, ex Huntingdon, Duxford, Australia, RAAF A58-671, MV154, 82 MU, 6MU. 145 Sqn c/s.	RL	3-06
❑	PS853	'C' Spitfire PR.XIX ✈	G-RRGN, ex East Midlands, Filton, G-MXIX, North Weald Coningsby, BBMF, West Raynham, CFE, North Weald SF, Biggin Hill SF, THUM Flt, 16, 268, 16.	RR	7-05
❑	RM689*	Spitfire XIV	G-ALGT, ex Sandown, Filton, Hucknall, East Midlands, 'RM619', Hucknall, 443, 350. Cr 27-6-92. Arr 11-04	® RR	3-06
❑	472216* 'HO-M'	P-51D-20-NA	G-BIXL, ex North Weald, Duxford, Ein-Gedi, Israeli AF/DF 43, RSweAF Fv26116, 44-72216. *Miss Helen*, 352nd FG colours. Force-landing 17-7-04	®	12-04
❑	162074	AV-8B Harrier	ex Wittering, AMARC, VMA-231. Stripped hulk.	RR [2]	2-00

GLOUCESTER

Gloster Aviation Club: Formed in 1998, GAC acquired a clubhouse / workshop in 2001. Two cockpits have been acquired, along with a large amount of other items. The aim is, of course, to obtain a Gloster airframe or cockpit. In the meantime, they are gathering parts towards their 'slow burning' Javelin cockpit project.
◆ Not *open to the public, but happy to be contacted by interested parties.Clive Davies, 1 Severn Road, Gloucester, GL1 2LE tel 07973 768452 e-mail glosteraviationclub@fsmailnet*

❑	WF911*	Canberra B.2	ex Hooton Park, Charnock Richard, Bacup, Preston, Samlesbury, G-27-161,231 OCU. Nose. Arrived 8-04	3-06
❑	XF383*	Hunter F.6	ex Kidlington, North Scarle, Wittering 8706M, Kemble, 12, 216, 237 OCU, 4 FTS, 229 OCU, 65, 111, 263. Nose. 65 Sqn colours. Arrived 6-04	3-06

GLOUCESTERSHIRE AIRPORT (STAVERTON)

Jet Age Museum (JAM) operated by the **Gloucestershire Aviation Collection**. Heritage Lottery Fund announced on December 2 that the museum had been unsuccessful in gaining a grant for its new building. In late December 2005, Jet Age was able to announce a new initiative, in co-operation with Brockworth Enterprise School that would re-locate the entire museum alongside the school in a project estimated to cost £3 million. Located on a section of the former Gloster plant at Brockworth, the school teaches a wide range of skills and sees the co-location as a great way to capitalise on the site's heritage and allow students access to workshop facilities and even to helping in the day to day running of the proposed museum. At the centre of the project would be a 98ft x 196ft display hall. As *W&R20* closed for press, funding possibilities were being investigated.

Notes: The E28/39 FSM uses the mouldings for the Farnborough, Hants, and Lutterworth, Leics, examples [1]. Meteor T.7 WL349 is owned by JAM (previously listed at the airport) and, with modification, will be mated to the nose of F.3 EE425 [2]. Vampire T.11 pod XD616 is stored for the de Havilland Aircraft Heritage Centre, London Colney, Herts [3]. The Vulcan nose is on loan from Gary Spoors and David Price [4].

Departures: Anson C.19 VM325 to Carew Cheriton, Wales, 23-8-05; Sea Venom FAW.22 XG691 left for Luqa, Malta, 12-9-05. (The fuselage etc had been stored at Quedgeley, Glos.)
◆ *Aircraft in store at various locations. Access* not *possible at present. Noel Griffiths, 44 Moselle Drive, Churchdown, GL3 2TA, e-mail noel.griffiths@virgin.net www.jetagemuseum.org*

❑	–	McBroom Arion	ex Hucclecote. Hang-glider. Stored	2-04
❑	– BAPC.259	Gamecock REP	ex Dursley, Staverton. Under construction	off-site ® 2-04
❑	–*	Gloster E28/39 REP	fuselage completed by 12-05	off-site ® [1] 12-05
❑	N5914	Gladiator II	ex Norway, 263. Crashed 2-6-40	off-site 2-04
❑	'V6799'	Hurricane FSM	BAPC.72, ex 'V7767', Bournemouth, Sopley, Bournemouth	
	'SD-X'		Brooklands, North Weald, Coventry, *Battle of Britain*	off-site 2-04
❑	–	Typhoon I	ex Twyford, Chippenham. Cockpit	off-site 2-04
❑	EE425	Meteor F.3	ex Yatesbury, Earls Colne, Andrewsfield, Foulness, MoS,	
			206 AFS, 210 AFS, 206 AFS, 63, 266, 1, 222. Nose , off-site [2]	2-04
❑	WF784	Meteor T.7	ex Bentham, Staverton, Quedgeley, Kemble 7895M,	
			5 CAACU, CAW, FTU, 130, 26	3-06
❑	WH364	Meteor F.8	ex Kemble 8169M, 601, Safi SF, Takali SF, Idris SF,	
			Takali SF, Safi SF, 85. Displayed near main road	3-06
❑	WK126	'843' Canberra TT.18	ex Bentham, Staverton, Hucclecote, N2138J ntu,	
			St Athan, FRADU, 100, 9	3-06
❑	WL349	'Z' Meteor T.7	ex Kemble, 1 ANS, 2 ANS, CFE, 229 OCU	[2] 3-06
❑	WS807	'N' Meteor NF.14	ex Bentham, Staverton, Yatesbury, Watton 7973M,	
			Kemble, 1 ANS, 2 ANS. 46 Squadron c/s	3-06
❑	XD506	Vampire T.11	ex Bentham, Staverton, Thrupp, Staverton, Swinderby,	
			Finningley 7983M, CATCS, CNCS, 5 FTS, 206 AFS	3-06
❑	XD616	Vampire T.11	ex Bentham, Staverton, London Colney, Hoddesdon,	
			Old Warden, Woodford, Chester, St Athan, 8 FTS,	
			1 FTS, 8 FTS, 65. Pod. Stored	[3] 2-04
❑	XE664	Hunter F.4	ex Marlborough, ?, HSA, 26. Nose	off-site 2-04
❑	XG331	Lightning F.1	ex Hucclecote, Barton, Chelford, Long Marston,	
			Innsworth, Staverton, Foulness, AAEE, EE. Nose	off-site 2-04
❑	XH903	'G' Javelin FAW.9	ex Bentham, Staverton, Hucclecote, Innsworth	
			7938M, Shawbury, 5, 33, 29, 33, 23. 33 Sqn c/s	3-06
❑	XM569	Vulcan B.2	ex Bentham, Staverton, Enstone, Cardiff, 44,	
			Wadd Wing, 27, Cott Wing, 27. Nose	[4] 3-06
❑	XW264	Harrier T.2	ex Hucclecote, Innsworth, Dowty, Boscombe	
			Down, HSA. Damaged 11-7-70. Nose	off-site 2-04
❑	XX889	Buccaneer S.2B	ex Bentham, Staverton, Enstone, St Athan,	
			12, 208, 12, 16. 208 Sqn c/s	3-06

Airport: The Learjet is used by **City of Bristol College** and has been joined by an Aztec [1]. KR-2 G-OFMB was donated to the fire crews during 2005 [2]. Dove 8 G-AVVF was broken up during 2004. Pup G-AXPA moved to Glatton, Cambs, and then to <u>Spanhoe Lodge</u>, Northants; it was flying by 2004. Waco UPF-7 G-WACO (last noted in January 1998) was sold in Belgium. Sea Heron C.1 XR442 (G-HRON) was crated on 20th January 2006 for export to the USA. The anonymous BN-2 nose has not been noted since April 1999 and has been deleted.

❑	G-BAUI*	Aztec 250D	ex Bristol, LN-RTS. CoA 15-12-88. Inst	[1] 3-06
❑	G-BHSL*	Jungmann	ex Span AF E3B-286. Crashed 6-7-96	® 3-06
❑	G-OFMB*	Rand KR-2	ex N5337X. Fuselage, fire crews	[2] 3-06
❑	N309LJ	Learjet 25	ex N309AJ, N19FN, N17AR, N3UC, N6GC,	
			N242WT, N954FA, N954GA. Inst	[1] 3-06

INNSWORTH west of the B4063, near Parton, north-east of Gloucester

Cotswold Aircraft Restoration Group (CARG): On 29th April 2004, CARG celebrated its 25th anniversary and was close to clocking up its 750th 'supply mission'. With the impending closure of RAF Innsworth, the future of CARG is uncertain. The Fairey Ultra-Light is for The Helicopter Museum, Weston-super-Mare [1] and the Monospar for the Newark Air Museum, Winthorpe, Notts [2].

◆ Visits *possible by prior application* only. *Steve Thompson, CARG, Kia-Ora, Risbury, Leominster, HR6 0NQ*

❑	G-AOUJ	Fairey ULH	ex Weston-super-Mare, Harlow, White Waltham,	
			XJ928. CoA 29-3-59	® [1] 2-06

| ❑ VH-UTH | Monospar ST-12 | ex Winthorpe, Booker, Biggin Hill, Australia | ® [2] 2-06 |
| ❑ R9371 | Halifax II | ex local, 10. Crashed 9-3-42. Cockpit | off-site 2-06 |

RAF Innsworth: Personnel and Training Command HQ, the Meteor graces the main entrance.

| ❑ VW453 | 'Z' Meteor T.7 | 8703M, ex Salisbury Plain, Hullavington, | |
| | | Ta Qali, 604, 226 OCU, 203 AFS. Gate | 3-06 |

KEMBLE AIRFIELD on the A429 south-west of Cirencester

☛ The Kemble site is large and aircraft are listed below under their nominal 'keepers'. It is possible to find aircraft 'owned' by one heading parked in an area 'operated' by another. As with several other venues in the book, airworthy general aviation types based are not listed.

Bristol Aero Collection (BAC): The collection faces a major move during 2006, re-locating to Hangar E2. For understandable reasons, opening times etc will be somewhat restricted until the process can be achieved. See under Filton, Glos, for a co-operative agreement with Airbus UK and the last-to-fly Concorde. BAC has secured Bolingbroke IVT 9048 from storage in the USA and it will ultimately join the collection. BAC is the leading light in the **Filton Heritage Group** which is striving to establish a museum centred around Concorde G-BOAF on a to-be-determined site at Filton.

Due to the move, BAC regretfully had to terminate the loan agreement whereby they were the custodians of the Britannia Aircraft Preservation Trust's Series 308F G-ANCF. (See below for more on BAPT.) *Charlie Fox* needed to be relocated within 90 days coming on 13th March 2006. Thanks to a very generous offer from Devonair, *Charlie-Fox* and the nose of G-ALRX moved to external storage at their premises (see 'Others' below) for the remainder of 2006 while a long-term solution is considered.

Notes: The Beagle 206 started life as the Bristol 220 design study [1]. The Brigand is on loan from Unimetal Industries via the North East Aircraft Museum [2]. The Bristol 173 is on loan from the RAF Museum [3]. The Harrier used the BSE Pegasus [4], while the Jindivik represents the first application for the BSE (*née* Armstrong Siddeley) Viper [5].

Departures: Britannia 308F G-ANCF and the nose of 101 G-ALRX moved across to the Devonair site (see 'Others' below) during March 2006. Beagle 206 G-ARRM moved to <u>Shoreham</u>, W Sussex, for a five year restoration in late May 2005.

◆ Please check *prior to a visit, due to move. E2 Hangar, Kemble Airfield, Cirencester, GL7 6BA tel 01285 771204, or tel / fax 0117 950 0908 www.bristolaero.com*

❑ 'G-EASQ'	Babe III REP	BAPC.87, ex Banwell, Stoke, Hemswell, Cleethorpes, Selby	12-05
❑ G-ATDD	Beagle 206-1	ex Filton, Wroughton, South Kensington,	
		Leeds. Damaged 6-73. Nose	[1] 12-05
❑	Concorde EMU	ex Brooklands. Test shell, nose. Plus cabin mock-up	12-05
❑ RH746	Brigand TF.1	ex Sunderland, Failsworth, CS(A), ATDU	
		Gosport, Bristol, ATDU, AAEE, Bristol. Fuselage	[2] 3-06
❑ XF785	Bristol 173 Srs 1	ex Cosford, Henlow 7648M, G-ALBN	[3] 12-05
❑ XJ917	'S-H' Sycamore HR.14	ex Banwell, Helston, Wroughton, CFS, 275	12-05
❑ XV798	Harrier GR.1	ex Banwell, Foulness, PCB rig, Dunsfold, 20,	
		233 OCU. Cr 23-4-71. Wing from T.2 XW264	[4] 12-05
❑ A92-708	Jindivik 3	ex Llanbedr	[5] 12-05

Britannia Aircraft Preservation Trust / Bristol Britannia XM496 Preservation Society: XM496 continues its renaissance, following a lot of hard work, internal and external. It is now resplendent in full RAF colours and again carries the name *Regulus*. See above and below for BAPT's airframes. BAPT face an urgent need to find a home for *Charlie-Fox*, if you can help contact Roger Hargreaves on 01444 244613 via email: britboss1@aol.com www.britannia.flyer.co.uk

◆ *e-mail Vsmith817@aol.com www.XM496.com*

| ❑ XM496 | Britannia C.1 | ex Lanseria, EL-WXA, 9Q-CJH, CU-T120, Afrek, G-BDUP, | |
| | | Kemble, XM496 99/511. *Regulus*, RAF c/s | 3-06 |

Delta Jets: A thriving selection of jets, are restored and maintained from this super airfield. As with several other locations within this work, the bulk of the jets here are owner-operated and not part of a collection as such. The listing is restricted to long-term restorations or storage. Hunter T.7 G-BXKF (XL577) made its first post-restoration test flight on 20th September 2004. A composite Hunter, mostly XL578 with the tail of XG290, is used by the fire crews [1]. Please also note that T.7 XL586 is fitted with the rear-end of XL578 [2]!

♦ *Visits by prior arrangement* only. *Occasional open days/airshows staged - www.deltajets.com*

❑ XF995	'K'	Hunter T.8B	G-BZSF, ex Cranwell, 9237M, ex 208, 12, Laarbruch SF		
			237 OCU, Honington SF, 237 OCU, FAA, 229 OCU, 245, 247		7-05
❑ XL578	'77'	Hunter T.7	ex Norwich, Bruntingthorpe, Cranfield, St Athan,		
			1 TWU, TWU, 229 OCU. Dump, composite	[1]	3-06
❑ XL586		Hunter T.7	ex Ipswich, Colsterworth, Shawbury, BAe Warton,		
			1 TWU, 2 TWU, 1 TWU, 229 OCU	[2]	3-06
❑ XP502		Gnat T.1	ex Ipswich, St Athan 8576M, 4 FTS. Red Arrows c/s.		
			Displayed by the tower from 5-05		3-06
❑ [J-4083]*		Hunter F.58	G-EGHH, ex Bournemouth, Swiss AF. Arr 10-10-05		10-05

Others: **Devonair** (you can likely guess what aircraft below they specialise in!) stepped in to aid the BAPT when Britannia *Charlie Fox* needed re-locating. It and the nose of G-ALRX is stored externally on their site for 2006 while a long-term solution is found. (For details of how to contact BAPT see above.) Inside the Devonair hangar can be found a DH Mosquito. This is part of a long-term project by David Hall to create a completely equipped, full-scale model *taxiable* Mosquito [1].

The airfield continues to function as a UK 'Mojave' with a series of airliners parked out. Most of these are awaiting new work and some are broken up for spares ('parting-out') and the bulk of these categories are too transitory to list in this work. Recent scrapping work since *W&R19* has included: Canada 300 A300s; Air India A300 and DC-10 N571RY. By late 2005 the scenery was dominated by HS.146s/BAE RJs and a pair of former BA Boeing 747s (G-BDXE and G-BDXF) but they will likely move on quickly.

Interesting report from here relating to Robinson R-22 G-INTC (wrecked 5th January 1999) was here in October 2003 for conversion to a 'simulator'. Any comments? Also on the rotary front, three former military Sud Pumas (9L-LSA, H.253 and H.255) were noted in store by September 2005 and *may* become *W&R* candidates.

Departures: Auster 5 G-BDFX returned to <u>Oaksey Park</u>, Glos by 7-05; Aircamper G-BSVZ to <u>Haverfordwest</u>, Wales, by 7-05 The fuselage of Boeing 727-223F EI-HCB was broken up by 7-05. Plus, a host of *W&R* types listed here before now were flying by 2005: Messenger 2A G-AJOE; Tiger Moth G-AKUE; J3C-75 Cub G-ATKI; SAN D.117A G-BFEH; Evans VP-2 G-BMSC and Silvaire 8E G-LUST.

❑ G-ALRX*	Britannia 101	ex Banwell, Boscombe Down, WB473 ntu, VX447 ntu.		
		Crashed 4-2-54. Nose, stored	BAPT	3-06
❑ G-ANCF*	Britannia 308F	ex Banwell, Brooklands, Manston, 5Y-AZP, G-ANCF,		
		LV-GJB,LV-PPJ, G-ANCF ntu, G-14-1, G-18-4, N6597C		
		ntu, G-ANCF. CoA 12-1-81. Stored, dismantled	BAPT	3-06
❑ [G-APSO]	Dove 5	ex Coventry, Cumbernauld, Carlisle, Shobdon,		
		N1046T ntu. CoA 8-7-78. Engine test rig		7-05
❑ G-ARJB	Dove 8	ex Cumbernauld, Carlisle, Rocester, East Midlands.		
		CoA 10-12-73. *Exporter*		7-05
❑ G-ASIP	Auster 6A	ex Oaksey Park, Innsworth, Staverton, Nympsfield, Heathrow,		
		VF608, 12 Flt, 652, 1904 Flt, Hague Air Attaché.		
		Damaged 7-5-73. Frame		8-98
❑ G-ASOI*	Terrier 2	ex G-35-11, T.10, AAC, AOP.6, 662, 656. CoA 19-6-<u>98</u>		7-05
❑ G-AXCN	Rallye Club	ex Thruxton. Wrecked 16-10-87		7-99
❑ G-AXRU	Cessna FA.150K	ex Withybush. CoA 10-12-87	®	7-97
❑ G-BAGS*	DR.400-100 2+2	CoA 16-1-03. Stored		7-05
❑ G-BPNL	Quickie Q2	CoA 16-1-96. Stored		5-03
❑ G-OEWA	Dove 8	ex Staverton, Biggin Hill, G-DDCD, G-ARUM. CoA 7-10-91		7-05
❑ SX-BNL*	Bandeirante	first noted, stored 7-05. With the fire crews by 2-06		3-06
❑ V8-RBA*	Boeing 757	ex G-CDMR, Royal Brunei, N6666U. Arrived 13-7-05.		
		Spares by 9-05. Fuselage with fire crews		3-06

❏ N73410	PT-17 Kaydet	ex G-BSGR, Bristol, EC-ATY, N55050, 42-16558	4-02
❏ 'DZ313'	'Mosquito'	fuselage. *Anopheles de Havillandus*	[1] 9-05
❏ VP955	Devon C.2/2	G-DVON, ex Little Staughton, Cranfield, G-BLPD ntu,	
		VP955, 207, 21, C.1 WCS, MCS, 31, Upavon SF,	
		Hendon SF, MEAF, Malta CF. CoA 29-5-96. Stored	7-05
❏ XA880	Devon C.2	G-BVXR, ex RAE, RRE, TRE	11-05
❏ XK895	Sea Devon C.20	G-SDEV, ex Swansea, ex Bruntingthorpe, Cambridge,	
		Culdrose SF, 781Sqn. CoA 17-9-01	9-05
❏ 315211*	C-47A-80-DL	N1944A, ex N5211A ntu, N3239W, RDanAF K-683,	
'JB-Z'		RNorAF, 43-15211. Stored	7-05

MORETON-IN-MARSH on the A44 north-east of Cheltenham
Wellington Aviation Museum: Gerry Tyack's superb collection of artefacts, together with aviation art and prints (many for sale), is always worth a visit. Among the impressive array is the tail section of Wellington L7775 of 20 OTU which crashed near Braemar 23rd October 1940.
◆ *Tue to Sun 10am to 12.30am and 2pm to 5.30pm. On the A44 west of the town, signed. British School House, Moreton-in-Marsh, GL56 0BG tel 01608 650323 www.wellingtonaviation.org*

National Fire College: (formerly the Home Office Fire and Emergency Training Centre) In *W&R18* (p67) the departure of Sioux AH.1 XT141 was reported, but with no 'forwarding address'. It is now known to have gravitated to Dunkeswell, Devon.

❏ G-AZDZ	Cessna 172K	ex Firbeck, Fownhope, Warmingham, Southend,	
		5N-AIH, N1647C, N84508. Crashed 19-9-81	4-05
❏ G-BAPF	Viscount 814	ex Southend, SE-FOY, G-BAPF, D-ANUN.	
		Hot Air colours. CoA 13-6-90	4-05
❏ G-BKRD	Cessna 320	ex Sandtoft, D-IACB, HB-LDN, N2201Q. Cr 5-11-90	4-05
❏ G-BLHL	Emeraude	ex Hooton Park, Warmingham, Wigan, East Kirkby,	
		Tattershall, Chinnor, Booker, F-BLHL, F-OBLM.	
		Crashed 4-8-81. Fuselage frame	8-98
❏ G-BNJJ	Cessna 152 II	ex Stamford area, Spanhoe, Nayland, Cranfield.	
		Damaged 18-5-88. Hulk	6-01
❏ G-BPAD	Seneca 200T	ex N21208. Crashed 15-7-92. Fuselage	6-01
❏ G-BPJT	Cadet 161	ex Oxford, N9156X. Crashed 12-7-92. Wreck	4-03
❏ G-SULL	Saratoga SP	ex Stamford, Spanhoe, N82818. Crashed 1-2-95	8-98
❏ WT804	'831' Hunter GA.11	ex Culdrose A2646, A2732, , Shawbury, FRADU,	
		Lossiemouth, 247. Pole mounted, nose in ground	3-06
❏ XM404	Jet Provost T.3	ex Halton, Newton, 8055BM,Shawbury, 3 FTS, 2 FTS	3-06
❏ XP150	Wessex HAS.3	ex Lee-o-S A2764, Wroughton, 829, *Antrim* Flt	3-06
❏ XP680	Jet Provost T.4	8460M, ex St Athan, CAW, 6 FTS. 'Crash' scene	6-01

NYMPSFIELD AERODROME off the B4066, south-west of Stroud
By July 2005 Cadet TX.3 XE760 had moved to Keevil, Wilts, followed by Grasshopper TX.1 WZ831 by December 2005.

QUEDGELEY east of the A38, south of Gloucester
Historic Aircraft Restorations: The Meteor, will be finished in 2 ANS colours. The team are the owners: John Holder, Sandy Mullen and Sid Griffiths, assisted by Alex Walsh.
◆ *Access by prior permission* only.

❏ WS774	Meteor NF.14	ex Fearn, Ely, Upwood 7959M, Kemble, 1 ANS, 2 ANS	® 2-04

RENDCOMB AERODROME east of the A435 north of Cirencester

The Utterly Butterly Barnstormers 'road-show' has a short-span PT-17 travelling airframe that *may* be based upon one of the frames noted below.

◆ Access on a *strictly* prior permission basis.

| ❑ | [XB-RIY] | PT-17 | ex Hatch, Sudbury. Stored | 7-01 |
| ❑ | – | PT-17 | fuselage frame, stored | 7-01 |

TIDENHAM on the A48 north east of Chepstow

National Diving and Activity Centre: Early in 2005 a Cherokee was 'sunk' into the quarry here (along with an Alvis Stalwart, quite ironic as it's an amphibious lorry!). The Cherokee was quoted as having come from "the local police and had been used as a training aid". Later in the year it was joined by another irony – a *Sea* Devon! Then came the Canberra and a Boeing 747 forward fuselage, both from Filton. A staff member did emphasise that "it's a *very* big quarry!" The Canberra is a composite, with the starboard wing of Q497, see under Dumfries, Scotland [1]. (www.ndac.co.uk)

❑	-*	Cherokee	see above	3-06
❑	5R-MFT*	Boeing 747-2B2B	ex Filton, Air Madagascar. Forward fuselage.	3-06
❑	WH665*	'J' Canberra T.17	ex Filton, Samlesbury, Cosford 8736M, 360, RNZAF, 45, 10. Arrived by 3-06	3-06
❑	XK896*	Sea Devon C.20	G-RNAS, ex Filton, Staverton, North Coates, Staverton, 781, Hal Far SF, 781. CoA 3-7-84. Fuselage.	2-06

HAMPSHIRE

ALDERSHOT on the A325 south of Farnborough

Parachute Regiment and Airborne Forces Museum: Devoted to the exploits of paratroop and glider-borne forces, the museum stages regular special displays and events. A long-term plan envisages this museum relocating to Duxford, Cambs – qv.

◆ *Open Mon to Fri 10am to 4.30pm - last admission 3.45pm. Sat, Sun and Bank Hols 10am to 4pm – last admission 3.15pm. Closed Xmas. Other times by prior arrangement. Photography is* not *permitted inside. Browning Barracks, Aldershot, Hampshire, GU11 2BU tel 01252 349619 fax 01252 349203 e-mail airbornefm@btconnect.com www.army.mod.uk/para/af_museum.index.htm*

❑	KP208	'YS' Dakota IV	ex Kemble, AFNE, Air Adviser New Delhi, AFNE, HCCF, 24, MEAF, USAAF 44-77087	3-06
❑	–	Hotspur II	nose section	2-04
❑	–	Horsa II	nose section	2-04

Keogh Barracks: Have two exit trainers.

| ❑ | XR501 | Wessex HC.2 | ex Gosport, Shawbury, 22, 72, 18, 1 FTU, AAEE | 4-01 |
| ❑ | XS515 | 'N' Wessex HU.5 | ex Gosport, A2658 [2], A2747, Lee-on-Solent, 845 | 4-01 |

ALTON on the A339 south-west of Farnham

Air Salvage International: The yard here specialises in airliner salvage and the moving of them by road – see under Cosford, Shropshire, for their latest challenge. Note that some, or even all, of the aircraft listed here may have only a brief existence before being 'parted-out'. Recent airframes handled on and 'in and out' basis have included a former Norwegian Air Shuttle Fokker 50 and Beech Premier N200PR (crashed at Blackbushe 7th April 2004) both in August 2005. One of the One-Eleven fuselages act as the 'Departure Lounge Cafe' [1]. ASI also has a 'Shed' at nearby Lasham, Hants – qv. Bandeirante cockpit G-OHIG to Stock, Essex, by 11-04; Short 330 fuselage OY-MUB moved to Pocklington, E Yorks.

◆ *Visits strictly by prior arrangement only. Fantastically informative web-site: www.airsalvage.co.uk*

❑ G-ARAY	HS.748-1/100	ex Lasham, Dan-Air, OY-DFV, PI-C784, G-ARAY, PP-VJQ, YV-C-AMC, G-ARAY. Nose		1-02
❑ G-AVMZ*	BAC 111-510ED	ex Bournemouth, European, BA, BEA. CoA 17-2-02. Fuselage. First noted 4-05	[1]	4-05
❑ G-AWYV*	BAC 111-501EX	ex Bournemouth, 5N-OSA ntu, European, BA, BEA. Fuselage. First noted 4-05	[1]	4-05
❑ G-BITW	Short 330-100	ex Coventry, G-EASI, G-BITW ntu, G-14-3070. CoA 9-6-98. Fuselage		1-02
❑ G-BYYI*	Jetstream 3107	ex Jetstream Executive, VH-JSW, G-31-620. Fuselage. Arrived 1-9-04		4-05
❑ G-ODUB	Bandeirante	ex Leeds-Bradford, PH-FVC, G-BNIX, N8536J. CoA 6-2-01. Fuselage		8-05
❑ G-OJEM	HS.748-2B/378	ex Stansted, Emerald, ZK-MCH, G-BKAL, 9N-ADF, G-BKAL, V2-LDK, D-AHSD, G-BKAL. *Tashy's Kite*. Nose. Crashed 31-3-98		1-00
❑ A6-SHK	BAe 146-100	ex UAE Gov, G-BOMA, G-5-091. Fuse, scrapping		4-02
❑ EI-EXP	Short 330-100	ex G-BKMU, SE-IYO, G-BKMU, G-14-3092, EI-BEH, EI-BEG, G-BKMU, G-14-3092. Fuselage		1-00
❑ HB-IZY	SAAB 2000	ex Swiss, SE-047. Crashed 10-7-02. Fuselage		11-03
❑ OY-BNM	Bandeirante	ex Bournemouth, N5071N, G-BFZK		7-00
❑ 5N-BAB	BAC 111-414EG	ex ADC Airlines, EI-BWT, N174FE, G-AZED, N174FE, G-AZED, G-AZDG, D-ANDY, G-16-3. Cockpit		1-02

ANDOVER

Aerofab Restorations: Bulldog 122s G-102 and G-108 moved in April 2004 to Salisbury, Wilts.

❑ G-AVDF	Pup 200	ex St Ives, Brooklands, Shoreham, Duxford, Shoreham. CoA 22-5-68. Stored for owner	4-02
❑ G-AWKM	Pup 100	ex Swansea. CoA 29-6-84. Stored	2-05
❑ G-BGZJ	Tomahawk 112	ex Halfpenny Green. Damaged 5-8-90. Stored	2-03
❑ G-BOPX	Cessna A.152	ex N761BK. CoA 24-1-98	5-04
❑ XX623	'M' Bulldog T.1	ex Newton, CFS, York UAS. EM UAS. Cr 26-7-95	5-03

Durney Collection:

❑ G-ALAX	Dragon Rapide	ex Old Warden, Luton, RL948, ERS, 27 GCF. CoA 8-3-67. Composite. Stored, poor state	2-99

Others:

❑ XX432*	Gazelle AH.1	ex Shawbury, Fleetlands. Arrived 27-4-05	4-05

AWBRIDGE on the B3084 north of Romsey

The nose section of long-lost Pembroke can be found in the area.

❑ WV705	Pembroke C.1	ex Wimborne, Bournemouth, BAC, 60, Wildenrath CS, 2 TAF CS, 152, 78, Khormaksar SF, 1417F,Levant CF, Eastleigh SF, APSF, MECS. Nose	10-02

BASINGSTOKE on the M3 north-east of Winchester

GJD Services Ltd: 'Europe's one-stop shop for all aircraft storage, parting-out, decommissioning, salvage, recovery and transport' is how GJD's web-site explains what they do. Based in the area, the company have been very active parting-out aircraft (see Prestwick, Scotland, for example) and with preservation tasks, including the moving of the Heathrow Trident up to Manchester, among others. In late 2005 they were offering several cockpit sections for sale, most in situ. Those below are listed here as a suitable 'base' for them. The nose of Canberra B.2 WH734 arrived from Llanbedr, Wales, by late 2004, but was exported to New Zealand, by February 2006.

◆ *tel/fax 01252 671251 www.gjdservices.co.uk*

☐	WH849*	'AW'	Canberra T.4	ex Shawbury, 39 Sqn, 1 PRU, 231 OCU, 100, 360, 85, 231 OCU, 232 OCU, Gaydon SF, Binbrook SF, Marham SF. Nose	3-06
☐	WH887*	'847'	Canberra TT.18	ex Llanbedr St Athan, FRADU, Upwood SF, 21, 542, 1323F. Nose	11-04
☐	WT480*	'AT'	Canberra T.4	ex Shawbury, Marham, 1 PRU/39 Sqn, 231 OCU, 360, 7, 231 OCU, 13, 7, 231 OCU, CFS, 102. Nose	3-06
☐	XH174*		Canberra PR.9	ex Shawbury, 1 PRU, 39, 13, 39, MoS, 39, 58. Nose	3-06
☐	ZH807*		Sea Harrier FA.2	ex St Athan, Yeovilton, 809. Arrived 1-9-05	9-05

Others: The Trident nose is though to still be in the area.

| ☐ | G-AWZU | | Trident 3B-101 | ex Stansted, Heathrow, BA, BEA. CoA 3-7-85. *Tina*. Nose | 8-03 |

BLACKBUSHE AERODROME on the A30 west of Yateley.

| ☐ | [G-XIIX] | Robinson R-22 | CoA 21-3-97. Pole-mounted | 12-05 |

BRAMLEY south-east of Tadley, east of the A340

Army Training Estate (ATE) **Home Counties**: Aerial reconnaissance (of the Rule 5 and legal sort!) revealed a Whirlwind, in poor condition, but nevertheless, present. Turn to *W&R18* (p70) and HAR.10 XK970 was 'written out' as having gone by early 2002 and possibly to Devon. This option appears not to have transpired, so that puts XK970 well in the frame – unless *you* know better? [1] What *did* go to Devon were two Scout hulks (most likely XP191 and XP853) the destination being Dunkeswell.

☐	-		Whirlwind	-	[1] 11-04
☐	XP856		Scout AH.1	ex Middle Wallop, AETW	[2] 7-00
☐	XZ300	'L'	Gazelle AH.1	ex Middle Wallop, 670, 664, 662. Crashed 14-2-97.	7-00

CHILBOLTON AERODROME east of the A3057, south of Andover

Hampshire Light Plane Services: Biplanes on the move: Tiger Moth G-ADJJ to Yarcombe, Devon, by late 2005 and SNCAN SV-4C G-FORD to Hatch, Beds, by May 2005.

☐	G-ANFV	Tiger Moth	ex DF155, 25 RFS, 28 EFTS. CoA 4-2-01	® 8-04
☐	G-BEPF	SNCAN SV-4A	ex Warminster, Raveningham, F-BCVD. Stored	9-04
☐	N1134K	Silvaire 8AE	ex NC1134K. Crashed 28-8-96. Spares	5-01
☐	G-NICK*	Super Cub 95	ex Lashenden, PH-CWA, RNethAF R-79, 8A-79, 52-2465. *Josie*. CoA 26-4-89. Canx 3-4-89. Stored. F/n 2-05	2-05

Others:

| ☐ | G-PRIM | Tomahawk 112 | ex N2398A. CoA 25-12-01. Stored | 9-05 |
| ☐ | G-REPM | Tomahawk 112 | ex N2528D. CoA 9-10-95. Cockpit | 9-05 |

COVE on the B3014 north west of Farnborough

Gary Spoors: The cockpit of 707-436 G-APFG moved to Pershore, Worcs, by mid-2004. It was replaced by:

| ☐ | G-AVFM* | Trident 2E | ex Bristol, BA and BEA. CoA 2-6-84. Cockpit | ® 8-04 |

FARNBOROUGH

Whittle Memorial: Dramatically displayed on the Ively roundabout to the north of the airfield, close to the Southwood Golf Course, is a superb Gloster E28/39 as a tribute to Sir Frank Whittle.

| ☐ | - | BAPC.285 Gloster E28/39 FSM | displayed | 4-06 |

Prince's Mead Shopping Centre: The SE.5A still provides 'top cover' for the shoppers.

| ☐ | 'D276' | 'A' | SE.5A REP | BAPC.208, built by AJD Engineering | 4-06 |

FARNBOROUGH AIRFIELD east of the A325, north of Aldershot

Farnborough Air Sciences: The collection continues to make great strides, the, live' Trident cockpit and the One-Eleven fuselage being very significant in their 'people-power' appeal. The fuselage of BAC 111 G-AVMJ was officially opened on 19th November 2005 as a classroom. It is the centre-piece of plans to teach the history and technology of aviation [1]. The mass of material held by the Farnborough Air Sciences Trust is incredible and only the tip of the iceberg can be displayed at any time. The Trust has extensive archives and the almost never-ending task of cataloguing and sorting goes on. Displays are regularly changed and it is hoped to increase the display space available within The Old Balloon School – now renamed Trenchard House in honour of one of its earliest 'bosses'.

Notes: Airframes owned by the FAS trading arm, FAS Ltd are marked FASL. Several airframes are on loan: Trident 3B nose from Andrew Lee [2]; Hunter T.7, Gnat and Jaguar from DERA [3]; Lightning T.5 XS420 from Murray Flint [4]; the Lightning nose from Hugh Trevor [5] but is due to move to Spark Bridge, Cumbria, mid-2006; the 'SHAR' from D&G Aviation Services [6]; the Hunter F.51 from D Johnson [7] and MiG-21 from the Neil Hallett family [8]. Neil also owns Vampire T.11 'U-1215' (XE998) which moved to Southampton, Hants, by mid-2005. Hunter IF-68 is on loan from Parrallel Aviation. It was acquired by HSA in December 1962 and was converted into a T.69 for the Iraqi Air Force, hence its nose became 'spare' [9].

Andrew Lee has put considerable work into the restoration of the Trident cockpit and it is very much a 'live' exhibit. It was opened officially on 8th August 2004. *Zulu-India* is looked after by a dedicated groundcrew, made up largely of former members of Trident Preservation Society members who looked after G-AWZK, now to be found at Manchester Airport, Gtr Man. The cockpit is opened up and 'powered up' most Sundays [2]. (For more details of *Zulu-India*, tel 01483 838378 email G-AWZI@blueyonder.co.uk)

◆ *Sat and Sun 10am to 4pm, other times by arrangement. Trenchard House, 85 Farnborough Road, Farnborough GU14 6TF. tel 01252 375050, e-mail info@fasta.co.uk www.fasta.co.uk*

❑ G-AVMJ*	BAC 111-510ED	ex Bournemouth, Filton, BA, BEA. CoA 17-11-94. Forward fuselage. Arrived 31-7-05 – see above	FASL [1]	4-06
❑ G-AWZI	Trident 3B-101	ex Lasham, Alton, Reigate, Heathrow, BA, BEA. CoA 5-8-85. Cockpit. BEA c/s	[2]	4-06
❑ WT309	Canberra B(I).6	ex Wycombe Air Park, Boscombe Down, Farnborough, Boscombe Down, AAEE, HS. Nose		4-06
❑ WV383	Hunter T.7	ex Boscombe Down, DERA, RAE, 28, Jever SF, Gutersloh SF, RAFFC. *Hecate–Lady of the Night.*	[3]	4-06
❑ WV795*	Sea Hawk FGA.6	ex Bruntingthorpe, Cranfield, Bruntingthorpe, Bournemouth, Bath, Cardiff-Wales, Culdrose A2661, Halton 8151M, Sydenham, 738, 806, 700. 806 c/s. Arrived 26-1-05	FASL	4-06
❑ [XN500]*	Jet Provost T.3A	ex East Midlands, Ipswich, Oxford, 1 FTS, 7 FTS, RAFC, 3 FTS, RAFC. Arrived 19-4-05	FASL	4-06
❑ XP516*	Gnat T.1	ex DS&TL, RAE, 8580M, 4 FTS. Arrived 8-6-04		4-06
❑ XS420	Lightning T.5	ex Walpole St Andrew, West Walton Highway, Narborough, Binbrook, LTF, 5, LTF, 226 OCU	[4]	4-06
❑ XS932	Lightning F.6	ex Shoreham, Bruntingthorpe, Rossington, Binbrook, 5, 11, 56, 11. Nose	[5]	4-06
❑ XV165	Buccaneer S.2B	ex Staverton, Bentham, Staverton, Hucclecote, Heathrow, Stock, Shawbury, 12. Nose. 12 Sqn c/s		4-06
❑ XW566*	Jaguar T.2	ex DS&TL, RAE, AAEE. Arrived 8-6-04	[3]	4-06
❑ ZA195* '002'	Sea Harrier FA.2	ex Wycombe Air Park, Yeovilton, St Athan, Warton, BAE, 899. Arrived 9-3-06	[6]	4-06
❑ -*	Jindivik	ex Llanbedr. Stored, off-site		4-06
❑ [IF-68]*	Hunter F.6	ex Market Drayton, Welshpool, Firbeck, Kexborough, Macclesfield, Bitteswell, Dunsfold, G-9-83, Belgian AF IF-68. Nose . First noted 9-05	[9]	4-06
❑ E-402	Hunter F.51	ex Bournemouth, Kemble, Bournemouth, Macclesfield, Dunsfold, G-9-433, RDanAF Esk.724. Esk 724 c/s	[7]	4-06
❑ 503	MiG-21PF	G-BRAM, ex Bournemouth, North Weald, Hung AF	[8]	4-06

Defence Science and Technology Laboratory / QinetiQ (DS&TL): Gnat T.1 XP516 and Jaguar T.2 XW566 moved to FAST (above) on 8th June 2004. Lynx XZ649 is fitted with the boom of XZ646 [1].

❏ XV344		Buccaneer S.2C	ex Boscombe Down, Farnborough, RAE. *Nightbird*. 'Gate'	4-06
❏ XW241		Puma (SA.330E)	ex RAE Bedford, F-ZJUX. Stored	4-06
❏ XW934	'Y'	Harrier T.4	ex 20, 233 OCU, 1. Stored	4-06
❏ XZ649		Lynx AH.7	ex Boscombe Down, 657. Static tests	[1] 3-03
❏		Mil Mi-24	ex ? Stored	2-02
❏		MiG-23 / -27	ex ? Stored	2-02

Others: Stripped of parts, HS.125-400B G-AXDM was scrapped, but its nose moved to Pershore, Worcs.

FLEETLANDS on the B3334 south of Fareham

Defence Aviation Repair Agency (DARA) **Training Centre:** Gazelle AH.1 XZ318 moved to Shawbury, Shrop, 18th January 2005. CH-47C ZH257 moved to Odiham, Hants, by April 2004.

❏ XS539	'435'	Wasp HAS.1	A2640 [2], ex A2718, Lee, 829 *Endurance* Flt	8-04
❏ XS569		Wasp HAS.1	A2639 [2], ex A2717, Wroughton, NATIU, 703	8-04
❏ XT434	'455'	Wasp HAS.1	A2643 [2], ex A2723, Lee-on-Solent, 829	8-04
❏ XT780	'636'	Wasp HAS.1	A2638 [2], ex A2716, Wroughton, 703	8-04
❏ XW844		Gazelle AH.1	ex Wroughton. 659. 'GAZ.4'	8-04
❏ XX440		Gazelle AH.1	A2702 [2], ex 665, 3 Regt, 12F, 669. 'GAZ.3'	8-04
❏ XZ213		Lynx AH.1	TAD.213, ex Wroughton, Middle Wallop, Wroughton, 659	8-04
❏ XZ307		Gazelle AH.1	A2703 [2], ex 665, 662, 663, 654, GCF. 'GAZ.1'	8-04
❏ ZA733		Gazelle AH.1	A2704 [2], ex 665, 664, BATUS. 'GAZ.2'	8-04
❏ QP31		Lynx HC.28	ex Almondbank, Wroughton, Qatar Police	8-04

GOSPORT on the B3333 south of Fareham

HMS *Sultan*: Air Engineering and Survival School: (See under Cosford, Shrop, for a glimpse of the future.) The wholly fictitious unit, 760 Training Squadron, 'operates' the airframes here and has given some airframes codes in the '2xx' series. Wessex HAS.3 XS122 is used by the medical school at **Fort Grange** (FG). Wessex HC.2 XR508 and Sea King HAS.6 XV677 were both reported to be up for scrapping in November 2005 [1].

Departures: Sea King HAS.6 XV674 sold to Australia for RAN spares use mid-2005; HAS.6 XV701 to Cosford, Shropshire, by 9-05; HU.5 XV705 operational with 771 Sqn by 2-05; HAS.6 ZA126 left 4-8-03 for conversion to HAS.6C; **Wessex** HC.2 XV725 to Cosford, Shrop, 24-1-05; HU.5C XS489 to Redhill, Surrey, 6-3-04; HU.5 XS510 to an Army camp at 'Crowbridge' (details?) by 2-05; HU.5 XS511 to Tangmere, W Sussex by 11-04; HU.5 XS520 to Predannack, Cornwall, 21-2-06; HU.5 XT765 to Yeovilton, Somerset, 29-7-04. The site also handled a couple of Sea King Mk.47s from Egypt in late 2005, for use as spares for the RAN. The hulk of Sea King HAS.6 ZA136 can be deleted, being without its cockpit.

❏ XP110	'55'	Wessex HAS.1	A2636 [2], ex A2714 [2], A2728, Lee-on-Solent, Fleetlands	11-05
❏ XR508	'B'	Wessex HC.2	'XR499', ex Shawbury, 72, 18, 28	[1] 11-05
❏ XR518	'J'	Wessex HC.2	ex Shawbury, 60, 72, 22, 18, 72, 18	4-03
❏ XR528*		Wessex HC.2	ex Culdrose, Predannack, St Mawgan, 60, 28, 240 OCU. Arrived 23-2-06	2-06
❏ XS122	'655'	Wessex HAS.3	A2632 [2], ex A2707, Lee-on-Solent, Manadon, Wroughton, 737. FG	11-05
❏ XS488	'XK'	Wessex HU.5	ex Wattisham, Halton, Wroughton, 846	4-03
❏ XS496		Wessex HU.5	A2675 [2], ex A2763, Lee-on-Solent, 772	4-03
❏ XS507	'627'	Wessex HU.5	A2674 [2], ex A2762, Lee-on-Solent, 772	11-05
❏ XS514	'YL'	Wessex HU.5	A2653 [2], ex A2740, Lee-on-Solent, 845	11-05
❏ XS568	'441'	Wasp HAS.1	A2637 [2], ex A2715, Fleetlands, 829	11-05
❏ XT453	'B'	Wessex HU.5	A2666 [2], ex A2756, Yeovilton, Lee-on-Solent, 845	7-03
❏ XT455	'U'	Wessex HU.5	A2654 [2], ex A2741, Lee-on-Solent. 845	1-04
❏ XT458	'622'	Wessex HU.5	A2679 [2], ex A2768, Lee-on-Solent, 772	11-05
❏ XT466	'XV'	Wessex HU.5	A2617 [4], ex Weeton 8921M, Cosford, Wroughton, 847	11-05
❏ XT484	'H'	Wessex HU.5	A2655 [2], ex A2742, Lee-on-Solent, 845	12-05
❏ XT485	'621'	Wessex HU.5	A2680 [2], ex A2769, Lee-on-Solent, 772	11-05

❑ XT607	'P'	Wessex HC.2	ex Shawbury, Fleetlands, 72	11-05
❑ XT761		Wessex HU.5	A2678 [2], ex A2767, Lee-on-Solent, Wroughton	11-05
❑ XT771	'620'	Wessex HU.5	A2673 [2], ex A2761, Lee-on-Solent, 772	12-05
❑ XV370	'260'	SH-3D Sea King	A2682 [2], ex A2771, Lee-on-Solent, Yeovil, G-ATYU	11-05
❑ XV625	'471'	Wasp HAS.1	A2649 [2], ex A2735, Lee-on-Solent, Culdrose, Manadon, 815	11-05
❑ XV642	'259'	Sea King HAS.2A	A2614 [3], ex A2613, Lee-on-Solent, Yeovil, AAEE,	
			Yeovil, AAEE, Yeovil	11-05
❑ XV655	'270'	Sea King HAS.6	ex 814, 819, 826, 845, 826, 814, 826, 819, 737, 824	4-03
❑ XV660	'269'	Sea King HAS.6	ex Culdrose, 819, 810, 706, 810, 819, 810, 826, 810, 824, 706	4-03
❑ XV663		Sea King HAS.6	ex Fleetlands, 819, 810, 820, 819, 737, 706, 826	4-03
❑ XV665	'507'	Sea King HAS.6	ex 810, 820, 810, 824, 826	4-03
❑ XV669	'410'	Sea King HAS.1	A2602 [4], ex Culdrose, Fleetlands 820. *Mr Walter*	4-03
❑ XV675	'701'	Sea King HAS.6	ex 819, 706, 824, 814, 706, 819, 814, 737, 819	4-03
❑ XV677	'269'	Sea King HAS.6	ex Fleetlands, 814, 820, 810, 819, 814, 820, 819	[1] 11-05
❑ XV696	'269'	Sea King HAS.6	ex Culdrose, 814, 819, 826, 825, 814, 820	11-05
❑ XV708	'501'	Sea King HAS.6	ex 810, 819, 706, 819, 706, 820, 737	11-05
❑ XV711	'515'	Sea King HAS.6	ex 810, 819, 814, 706, 820, 706, 824, 706, 819, 814, 819	11-05
❑ XV712	'266'	Sea King HAS.6	ex 814, 820, 814, 820, 810, 820, 706, 826, 706, 814	6-05
❑ XV713	'018'	Sea King HAS.6	ex Fleetlands, 820, 810, 706, 826, 810, 814, 820	6-05
❑ XV720		Wessex HC.2	A2701 [2], ex Fleetlands, SARTU, 22, 18	11-05
❑ XV724		Wessex HC.2	ex Shawbury, Fleetlands, 22, SARTS, 18	4-03
❑ XZ570		Sea King HAS.5	ex QinetiQ, Yeovil, AAEE	11-05
❑ XZ576		Sea King HAS.6	ex AAEE, Yeovil, 820	6-05
❑ XZ579	'707'	Sea King HAS.6	ex 819, 820, 814, 820, 819, 824, 826, 824	11-05
❑ XZ581	'269'	Sea King HAS.6	ex Fleetlands, 810, 826, 819, 814, 824, 826, 706, 814	4-03
❑ XZ930	'Q'	Gazelle HT.3	ex Shawbury, 2 FTS, CFS	4-03
❑ ZA127	'509'	Sea King HAS.6	ex 810, 706, 810, 826, 810, 706, 820	11-05
❑ ZA128	'010'	Sea King HAS.6	ex 820, 706, 820	11-05
❑ ZA131	'271'	Sea King HAS.6	ex 814, 820, 826, 810, 826	11-05
❑ ZA170		Sea King HAS.5	ex Fleetlands, 706, 810. Black c/s	11-05
❑ ZD607*		Sea Harrier FA.2	ex St Athan, Warton, 800, 801, 800, 801, 800, 801,	
			800, 899. Crashed 17-7-00. Arrived 27-5-05	11-05
❑ ZD630	'012'	Sea King HAS.6	ex Culdrose, 820	11-05
❑ ZD633	'014'	Sea King HAS.6	ex 820, 810, 814, 810, 820, 706	11-05
❑ ZD637	'700'	Sea King HAS.6	ex 819. 814. 810. 819	4-03
❑ ZF649		EH-101 PP5	ex Yeovil	11-05
❑ ZG817	'702'	Sea King HAS.6	ex 819, 810	4-03
❑ ZG818	'707'	Sea King HAS.6	ex Fleetlands, 819, 814	11-05
❑ ZG819	'265'	Sea King HAS.6	ex 814, 820	11-05
❑ ZG875	'013'	Sea King HAS.6	ex Yeovilton, 820, 819, 814. Cr 12-6-99. Wreck	11-05

Bernie Salter: The much-damaged nose of Lancaster B.10 FM118 did *not* come here from Shilo, Canada. Delete all reference to Lancaster nose KB976 being here (*W&R19* p70). This was *not* the case. Bernie's superb Lancaster nose REP was offered for sale in January 2005. It was sold off and left these shores in March. It is reported to have been sold to a German TV company who intended to destroy it at the climax of filming.

HAMBLE south-east of Southampton
Hamble Aerostructures: On the B3397, opposite 'The Harrier' public house, can be found the Gnat, still guarding the former Folland plant.

❑ XM693	Gnat T.1	ex Abingdon, Bicester 7891M, AAEE	3-05

HOOK north of the M3, near Junction 5

❑ G-AJXC	Auster 5	ex TJ343, 652, 655. CoA 2-8-82. Dam 16-10-87	4-06

KINGSCLERE on the A339 north-west of Basingstoke

The UK population of Brochet Pipistrelles has been assembled at a workshop in the area. *Delta-Victor* is close to flight. It *may* be that fellow *Kilo-Bravo* has been used for spares.

❏ G-AVKB*	Brochet MB.50	ex Goodwood, F-PFAL. CoA 30-10-96		9-05
❏ G-BADV*	Brochet MB.50	ex Ludlow, Dunkeswell, F-PBRJ. CoA 9-5-79	®	9-05

LASHAM AERODROME west of Golden Pot, north-west of Alton

Second World War Aircraft Preservation Society (SWWAPS): As well as the aircraft and artefact collection, SWWAPS offers great views of the intensive gliding activity on the airfield. The Meteor NF.13 is a complex composite, with the centre section, wings and tailplane from Israel, the nose from TT.20 WM234, latterly at Arborfield, and rear fuselage of F.8 VZ462 from Biggin Hill [1].

◆ *Located to the east of the gliding headquarters. Open Sun and Bank Hols 10.30am to 5pm (or dusk if first) and other times by arrangement. Bob Coles, 8 Barracane Drive, Crowthorne, RG45 7NU*

❏ 'VH-FDT'	DHA Drover II	G-APXX, ex Blackbushe, Southend, G-APXX,VH-EAS		3-06
❏ 4X-FNA	Meteor NF.13	ex Israel, IDF-AF, WM366, AAEE, RRE	[1]	3-06
❏ VR192	Prentice 1	G-APIT, ex Biggin Hill, Southend, VR192, 1 ASS,		
		6 FTS, CFS, 2 FTS, Blackburn's. CoA 7-9-67		3-06
❏ WF137	Sea Prince C.1	ex Yeovilton, Culdrose SF, Shorts FU,		
		Arbroath SF, 781. 'Admiral's Barge' c/s		3-06
❏ WH291	Meteor F.8	ex Kemble, 229 OCU, 85, CAW, 257. 79 Sqn c/s		3-06
❏ WV798	'026' Sea Hawk FGA.6	ex Chertsey, Culdrose A2557, FRU, 801, 803, 787		3-06
❏ XK418	Auster AOP.9	ex Basingstoke, Thruxton, Middle Wallop 7876M, 654		3-06
❏ XM833	Wessex HAS.3	ex Lasham, Wroughton		3-06
❏ E-423	Hunter F.51	ex Elstree, Bitteswell, Dunsfold G-9-444, Dan AF, Esk 724		3-06
❏ 22+35	F-104G	ex Manching, JbG34, KE+413, DD+105		3-06

Others: The Shorts 360 is held by ASI of Alton, Hants [1].

❏ G-BLGB	Short 360-100	ex BRA / Loganair, G-14-3641. Damaged 9-2-98	[1]	3-06
❏ OO-DHN	Boeing 727-31	ex DHL, N260NE, N97891. Stored		3-06
❏ OO-DHR*	Boeing 727-31	ex DHL, N932FT, N1958. Stored. Arrived 3-02		3-06

LEE-ON-SOLENT AIRFIELD east of the B3385, south of Fareham

Super Catalina Restoration:

◆ *Visits possible* only *by prior permission*

❏ [VR-BPS]	PBY-5A Catalina	ex Lasham, Hamble, Duxford, '9754', G-BLSC, 'JV928',		
		Barkston Heath, South Africa, C-FMIR, N608FF, CF-MIR,		
		N10023, Bu46633. Crashed 27-7-98. Stored	®	5-05
❏ 'JV928'	PBY-5A Catalina	N423RS ex Duxford, Greenpeace, C-FJJG, CF-JJG,		
		N4002A, USN 48423		1-06

Others: C-47 G-DAKK moved on by September 2004 and '292912' (N47FK) was operating from Holland.

❏ G-BNJM	Warrior II	ex Biggin Hill, Carlisle, N8015V. Damaged 18-5-89.	®	9-03

LOWER UPHAM on the A333 near Bishop's Waltham

There are *two* farm strips in the general area.

❏ G-OMOG*	AA-5A Cheetah	ex G-BHWR, N26892. CoA 15-4-02		6-04
❏ G-AWEI*	Condor	CoA 10-11-98. First noted 2-04	®	3-05
❏ G-AWUH*	Cessna F.150H	CoA 16-7-94. Fuselage. First noted 8-05		8-05
❏ G-BXSV*	SNCAN SV-4C	ex N21PM, F-BDDB. First noted 2-04	®	3-05
❏ 44-805942*	L-4J Cub	G-BEDJ, ex F-BDTC, 44-80594. CoA 8-10-96. Stored		3-05

MIDDLE WALLOP AIRFIELD on the A343 south-west of Andover

Museum of Army Flying (MoAF): An extension to the museum building is hoped for in 2007 when many of the artefacts (and some airframes) in store will get an airing.

Notes: The AFEE 10/42 is centred upon an original Jeep and is on loan from the Wessex Aviation Society [1]. Largest Horsa airframe on show is 'KJ351' which is an amalgam of LH208, TL659 and 8569M [2]. Another nose section and other large Horsa sections can be found on display within Hayward Hall. Several other sections are held in store. The battered centre fuselage of TL659 is currently at Shawbury, Shropshire, along with other parts, to act as a reference for a project there. [3]. The GAL Hotspur re-creation has adopted the identity and colours of an example that flew with the Shobdon-based 5 Glider Training School [4]. The Hamilcar (made up of parts from NX836 and TK718) is a 'walk-through' exhibit, currently under restoration [5]. The ML Utility inflatable aircraft had three wing options, 'Clouy', 'Delta' and 'Gadfly', all three are in store [6]. MoAF aircraft out on loan: Gazelle XW276 at Winthorpe, Notts, Pucará A-528 at Sunderland, N&T; and Skeeter AOP.12 XL770 at Southampton.

◆ *Access off the A343, 'brown signed' from the A303. Open 10am to 4.30pm every day - last entry 4pm. 'Choppers' cafe offering views of the activity on the airfield. Middle Wallop, Stockbridge, SO20 8DY tel 01980 674421 fax 01264 781694 e-mail enquiries@flying-museum.org.uk www.flying-museum.org.uk*

❑	G-AXKS		W-Bell 47G-4A	ex Bristow, ARWF, G-17-8. CoA 21-9-82	4-06
❑	'B-415'		AFEE 10/42 REP	BAPC.163, ex Wimborne	[1] 4-06
❑	P-5		Rotachute III	8381M, ex Henlow. On loan from RAF Museum	4-06
❑	'N5195'		Sopwith Pup	G-ABOX, ex Redhill. On loan. CoA 18-6-90	4-06
❑	'T9707'		Magister I	ex Cardington, Manchester, Hendon 8378M, Gaydon, Henlow,	
				G-AKKR, 'T9967', T970<u>8</u>, 51 MU, 16 EFTS, 239. CoA 10-4-65	4-06
❑	'KJ351'		Horsa II	BAPC.80, fuselage	[2] 4-06
❑	–		Horsa II	Fuselage	[3] 4-06
❑	–		Horsa II	Cockpit	[3] 4-06
❑	'HH268'		Hotspur II REP	BAPC.261	[4] 4-06
❑	TJ569		Auster 5	G-AKOW, ex PH-NAD, PH-NEG, TJ569, 652, 660, 659.	
				CoA 26-6-82	4-06
❑	TK777		Hamilcar I	ex Christian Malford. Forward fuselage	[5] 4-06
❑	WG432	'L'	Chipmunk T.10	ex AFWF, LAS, Bri UAS, 19 RFS, Cam UAS,4 BFTS	4-06
❑	WJ358		Auster AOP.6	G-ARYD, ex Perth, WJ358, 651, 657, 1913 Flt	4-06
❑	WZ721		Auster AOP.9	ex 4 RTR, 656, 6 Flt. *Dragon*	4-06
❑	WZ772		Grasshopper TX.1	ex Halton, 1 MGSP, Brentwood. Stored	4-06
❑	XG502		Sycamore HR.14	ex gate, Wroughton, Bristol, JEHU	4-06
❑	XK776		ML Utility Mk 1	ex Cardington, Middle Wallop, AAEE. On loan	[6] 4-06
❑	XL813		Skeeter AOP.12	ex ARWF, 4 Regt, 9 Flt	4-06
❑	'XM819'		Prospector	ex Durrington. Composite	4-06
❑	XP821	'MCO'	Beaver AL.1	ex Shawbury, Kemble, St Athan, Defence Attaché,	
				Laos, 130 Flt, 30 Flt RASC, 656. White/grey c/s	4-06
❑	XP822		Beaver AL.1	ex Duxford, 'Wallop, Shawbury, Kemble, 132 Flt, 667,	
				18 Flt. 'Gate'	4-06
❑	XP847		Scout AH.1	ex AETW, Wroughton, Yeovil	4-06
❑	XP910	'D'	Scout AH.1	ex SEAE. Crashed 13-9-89	® 4-06
❑	XR232		Alouette AH.2	ex Historic Flight, Wroughton, AAEE, Middle	
				Wallop, EW&AU, 656, AAEE, 16 Flt, 6 Flt	4-06
❑	XT108	'U'	Sioux AH.1	ex Duxford, Yeovilton, 'Wallop, D&T Flt, 'Wallop	4-06
❑	XV127		Scout AH.1	ex Fleetlands, Chelsea, Wroughton, 655.	4-06
❑	XX153		Lynx AH.1	ex Yeovil, Wattisham 9320M, Foulness, Westlands	4-06
❑	ZA737		Gazelle AH.1	ex 1 Rgt, 847, Fleetlands 'hack', 670, ARWS	4-06
❑	AE-409	'656'	UH-1H 'Huey'	ex Duxford, Middle Wallop, 656, Stanley,	
				Argentine Army, 72-21506	4-06
❑	111989		L-19A Bird Dog	N33600, ex Fort Rucker, Alabama	4-06
❑	'243809'		CG-4A Hadrian	BAPC.185, ex Burtonwood, Shrewsbury. Fuselage.	4-06
❑	70-15990		AH-1F Cobra	ex US Army. Stored	4-06

Army Air Corps Historic Aircraft Flight / Army Air Corps Reserve Collection Trust (RCT): The Trust supports the Flight and some of their aircraft within the Trust are on loan. Beaver XP772 (G-BUCJ) at Duxford, Cambs was acquired ARC and is no longer part of the Flight. Tiger Moth G-AOHY moved to Spanhoe Lodge, Northants, by mid-2004. Skeeters G-APOI and XL812 moved to storage in the Wattisham, Suffolk, area.
◆ Not *available for public inspection, but does 'do the rounds' of the airshow circuit.*

❏ N6985		Tiger Moth	✈ G-AHMN, ex 2 EFTS, 22 EFTS, Andover SF. Loan		3-98
❏ NX534		Auster III	G-BUDL, ex PH-POL, RNeth AF 8A-2, R-17,		
			NX534, 84 GCS, 4, 130 AF, 658	®	9-04
❏ WD325	'N'	Chipmunk T.10 ✈	ex BFWF, LAS, 12 GCF, 17 RFS		2-04
❏ WZ706		Auster AOP.9	G-BURR, ex 656. First noted 11-03		9-04
❏ XL814		Skeeter AOP.12 ✈	ex 1 Wing, 2 Wing, 651		7-03
❏ XP242		Auster AOP.9 ✈	G-BUCI. Ex AFWF. CoA 19-5-00	RCT	3-98
❏ XP820		Beaver AL.1 ✈	ex 7 Regt, 667, 132 Flt RCT, 130 Flt RCT,		
			30 Flt RASC, 11 Flt, 656		2-04
❏ XP884		Scout AH.1	ex Arborfield, Middle Wallop. Spares		2-04
❏ XR244		Auster AOP.9 ✈	ex AFWF		7-03
❏ XR379		Alouette AH.2 ✈	ex Almondbank, 667, 16F, 6(A) Flt		7-05
❏ XT131	'B'	Sioux AH.1 ✈	ex D&T Flight. Stored		2-04
❏ XT151		Sioux AH.1	ex ARWF. Spares		2-04
❏ XT626	'Q'	Scout AH.1	ex 666, Wroughton, 656, BATUS, 656, 663		2-04

No.2 Training Regiment, Aircrew Technical Training Detachment / No.70 Aircraft Workshops: Technical training here is a detachment of SEAE at Arborfield, Berks, qv. Several airframes serve in this role, within Stockwell Hall. The Sioux on the gate has its complex side. The plate in the cockpit gives it as WA-S-127, which makes it XT827, latterly with the Historic Flight [1]. Long overdue piece of 'house-keeping' needed: SARO P.531-2 XR436 was last noted in use for battle damage repair training in July 1990 – this has gone to LOST!, though it very likely has gone to oblivion. Two BDR airframes have also been deleted, believed long since expired: Scout AH.1 XR630 (last noted June 1998) and Wasp HAS.1 XV629 (May 1994).

❏ WZ724		Auster AOP.9	7432M, ex 'WZ670', 656, FEAF. Tan/brown colours. Gate		11-00
❏ XP893		Scout AH.1	ex Wroughton, Garrison Air Sqn, 3 CBAS, 655, 666, 656		3-00
❏ 'XT123'	'D'	Sioux AH.1	XT827, ex Wroughton, Yeovilton, Coypool, 3 CBAS. Gate	[1]	11-04
❏ XT638	'N'	Scout AH.1	ex Fleetlands, 666. Gate		2-04
❏ XV131	'Y'	Scout AH.1	ex Wroughton, 660, 665,.653, D&TS. ABDR		3-00
❏ XX443	'Y'	Gazelle AH.1	ex 658, 662, 663, 3 Regt, 669, 659. Cr 28-9-97		7-04
❏ XZ305*		Gazelle AH.1	TAD.020, ex Arborfield, 3 Regt, 665, 662, 654, GCF. Arr 10-04		10-04
❏ XZ942*	'42'	Gazelle HT.2	ex Shawbury, 705, Fleetlands. Arrived 10-10-04		10-04
❏ QP32		Lynx HC.28	TAD.016, ex Middle Wallop, Almondbank, Wroughton,		
			Qatar Police		7-04

ODIHAM AIRFIELD on the A32 south of Odiham
RAF Odiham: The Wessex on the dump has the tail of HC.2 XT601 [1]. Chinook ZH257 arrived from Fleetlands, Hants, by April 2004 and went on the dump. During mid-2005 the nose section moved to the Redstone Arsenal, Huntsville, Alabama, USA.

❏ XR453	'A'	Whirlwind HAR.10	8883M, ex Foulness, 2 FTS, CFS, 230, 1563 Flt, CFS. Gate		4-03
❏ XS498	'WK'	Wessex HU.5C	9277M, ex Predannack, Gosport A2641 [3],		
			Shawbury, Akrotiri, 84, FAA. 'Joker'. Dump	[1]	3-04
❏ ZA678	'EZ'	Chinook HC.1	9229M, ex Fleetlands, 7, N37023. Crashed 24-7-89		3-05

Steve Markham: A SIPA is believed stored locally.
❏ G-AWLG	SIPA 903	ex F-BGHG. CoA 22-8-79. Stored.		12-97

POPHAM AERODROME on the A303 west of North Waltham
❏ G-AIPR*	Auster V J/4	CoA 27-5-00. Stored. First noted 8-05		8-05
❏ G-ATKU	Cessna F.172G	ex Hinton-in-the-Hedges. Damaged 20-7-91. Fuselage		1-97

☐ G-BBOH*	Pitts S-1S	CoA 8-9-97. Stored. First noted 8-05	10-05
☐ G-BFHX*	Evans VP-1	CoA 7-4-99. Stored. First noted 8-05	10-05
☐ G-BSTV	Cherokee Six	ex N4069R. Stored	10-05
☐ G-DUST*	Starduster Too	ex N233JP. Cr 22-5-90	® 10-05
☐ G-MTBC	Gemini Flash 2	CoA 11-5-92. Stored	5-98
☐ G-MVDG*	Thruster Mk.1	CoA 26-7-00. Stored. First noted 8-05	1-06
☐ G-RANZ*	S-10 Sakota	CoA 27-6-03. Stored. First noted 10-05	1-06
☐ HA-MKE*	Antonov An-2R	ex White Waltham, Air Foyle, UR-07714, CCCP-07714. Arrived by 10-04	5-05

PORTSMOUTH

Marine Salvage Ltd: Jet Provost T.3 XM369 moved to <u>Lumb</u>, Lancs. Meanwhile, at the **Defence Diving School** (previously the Royal Navy Diving School), the Wessex is kept in a lake off Horsea Island – and is full of eels!

☐ XT760	Wessex HU.5	A2669 [2], ex Fleetlands	2-06

RINGWOOD on the A31 north of Bournemouth

At a *private* house in the area, a former Lydd Aztec has appeared.

☐ G-ASER*	Aztec 250B	ex Lydd, Smeeth, Biggin Hill. Crashed 14-9-72. F/n 8-05	12-05

ROMSEY or Farley, on the A27 north-west of Southampton

A farm strip in this general area has a number of *W&R* inmates.

☐ G-ARBO*	Comanche 250	ex Shipdham, N10F. Crashed 27-4-83	® 2-04
☐ G-ASMA*	Twin Com	ex N10F. Crashed 8-3-02. Stored	8-05
☐ G-AVPS*	Twin Com B	ex N8393Y. Crashed 30-11-04. Stored	8-05
☐ G-AXCX	Pup 150	ex G-35-046. CoA 10-7-94. Stored	5-00
☐ G-BFJJ	Evans VP-1	CoA 23-6-96. Stored	8-05
☐ G-BHDO	Cessna F.182Q	Forward fuselage. Crashed 7-5-89	1-96
☐ G-BNHE	ARV Super 2	CoA 7-8-99. Stored	2-01
☐ D-EGEU*	Colt 108	ex EL-AEU, 5N-AEH. Damaged 27-10-02	8-05
☐ [EC-AOZ]	PA-20-150 Pacer	G-BXBB, ex N1133C	® 8-05
☐ F-BRHN*	Bölkow Junior	ex D-EEAK. Stored. First noted 8-05	8-05
☐ N5052P	Comanche 180	ex Nuthampstead, Panshanger, G-ATFS, N5052P	® 8-05
☐ N8911Y*	Twin Com' C/R	ex Bruntingthorpe, G-AYFT, N8911Y. F/n 8-05	8-05
☐ OO-VPC	Cessna 185A	Stored	1-96

SOPLEY on the B3347 north of Christchurch

One Kraguj (or possibly more) is stored in the area.

☐ 30151	P-2 Kraguj	ex Shoreham, Fordingbridge, Bournemouth, YugAF. Fuselage	2-04

SOUTHAMPTON

Solent Sky: On 12th May 2004, the **Hall of Aviation** was renamed with test-pilot Lt Cdr Peter Twiss and motor racing driver Sir Jack Brabham doing the honours. During 2005 a series of ambitious re-location plans were finally put to bed and instead Solent Sky has decided to stay put and apply for a Heritage Lottery grant to redevelop and expand the current site.

The museum has an excellent relationship with **424 Squadron, Air Cadets** - see separate entry below. The Swift was a great 'catch' having been on the 'shopping list' for a long time. Likewise Dick Melton's exceptional Walrus which is due to arrive during 2006. This is essentially 'coming home' as it was to be found stored in the museum's car park (in its incarnation as a caravan) before being acquired by Dick for return to reality [1].

Notes: The Tiger Moth is a composite, with parts from G-AOAC and G-AOJJ [2]. Several airframes are on loan, the Sandringham from the Science Museum [3], the SR.A.1 from the Imperial War Museum [4], the Sea Vixen and Vampire from Neil Hallett [5]. Noted stored in the roof the museum's library in August 2005 was a Mignet HM.293 fuselage – an unfinished project. It's not known how long it had been there, but it may be on the move to Shoreham, W Sussex [6].

◆ *Open Mon to Sat 10am to 5pm; Sun 12-noon to 5pm. Albert Road South, Southampton, Hants, SO1 1FR tel 023 80635830 fax 023 80223383 e-mail info@spitfireonline.co.uk www.spitfireonline.co.uk*

❏	'G-ADZW'		HM.14 'Flea'	BAPC.253, ex Sandown, Lake, Isle of Wight	1-06
❏	G-ALZE		BN-1F	ex Cosford, Kemble, Bembridge	1-06
❏	–	BAPC.7	SUMPAC	ex Old Warden, Southampton. Man-powered aircraft	1-06
❏	–	BAPC.215	Airwave HG	prototype	1-06
❏	–		HM.14 'Flea'	ex Rayleigh	3-04
❏	–		HM.293	unfinished project, fuselage. First noted 8-05 [6]	3-06
❏	VH-BRC		Sandringham 4	ex Lee-on-Solent, VP-LVE *Southern Cross*, N158C, VH-BRC, ZK-AMH, JM715 [3]	1-06
❏	'C4451'		Avro 504J REP	BAPC.210, built by AJD Engineering	1-06
❏	N248		Supermarine S.6A	ex Cowes, Southampton, Henlow, Southampton Pier, 'S1596', Eastleigh, Calshot, RAFHSF	1-06
❏	'N546'		Wight Quad'plane	BAPC.164, ex Wimborne. Repro	1-06
❏	'K5054'		Spitfire REP	G-BRDV, ex Sandown, Keevil. CoA 18-2-95. off-site	10-03
❏	W2718*		Walrus I	G-RNLI, ex Great Yarmouth, Winchester, Southampton, 276, 751, 764 [1]	due
❏	BB807		Tiger Moth	G-ADWO, ex Wimborne [2]	1-06
❏	PK683		Spitfire F.24	ex Kingsbridge Lane, Kemble, Colerne, Changi 7150M, Singapore Aux AF	1-06
❏	TG263		SARO SR.A.1	ex Duxford, Staverton, Cranfield, G-12-1, TG263 [4]	1-06
❏	WM571		Sea Ven FAW.22	ex Wimborne, Staverton, ADS, 831B, HS. Stored	3-02
❏	WZ753		Grasshopper TX.1	ex Halton, Emanuel School, London	1-06
❏	XD332	'194'	Scimitar F.1	ex Helston, Culdrose SAH-19, Lee-on-Solent A2574, 764B, 736, 807, 804. Stored, outside	10-03
❏	XF114*		Swift F.7	G-SWIF, ex Bicester, Scampton, Bournemouth, Connah's Quay, Aston Down, CS(A), Cranfield	1-06
❏	XJ571	'242'	Sea Vixen FAW.2	ex Brooklands, Dunsfold, Southampton, Cosford 8140M, Halton, Sydenham, 893, 892, 899 [5]	1-06
❏	XK740		Gnat F.1	ex Hamble, Cosford 8396M, Bicester, C' Fenton, MoS, Filton	1-06
❏	XL770		Skeeter AOP.12	ex Middle Wallop, Shrivenham 8046M, Wroughton, 15/19 Hussars, 652, 654	1-06
❏	XN246		Cadet TX.3	ex Syerston, 617 GS	1-06
❏	–		Swift CIM	–	1-06
❏	'U-1215'*		Vampire T.11	XE998, ex Farnborough, Wisbech, Huntingdon, Horley, Charlwood, Biggin Hill, Warmingham, Wigan, Woodford, Chester, St Athan, 8 FTS, 4 FTS, 8 FTS. Arr by 6-05 [5]	1-06

No.424 Squadron, Air Cadets have their headquarters within the museum complex, although not open to the public. All but one of 424's airframes are their own, ie not MoD property. Within their HQ are several impressive procedure trainers, including a three-axis 'JP' cockpit which may be wholly 'synthetic' but may also owe its origins to a Mk.3 or Mk.4, although it is emblazoned 'T Mk 5-A' (sic).

❏	[WK570]	Chipmunk T.10	8211M, ex Bournemouth Airport, Hamble, 663, Hull UAS, 663, RAFC	9-05
❏		PAX		
❏	XD596	Vampire T.11	ex Calmore, St Athan 7939M, CATCS, CNCS, 5 FTS, 4 FTS	10-03
❏	XJ476	Sea Vixen FAW.1	ex Boscombe Down, AAEE. Nose. Stored	3-04
❏	–	Jet Provost CIM	marked 'CRAN 22/2'	3-02
❏	XP542*	'42' Gnat T.1	ex Shrivenham, St Athan 8575M, 4 FTS. Arr by 6-04	1-06

Aero Antiques and AeroTech Ltd: Superbly rebuilt, Wicko G-AFJB (DR613) first flew again on 2nd September 2005. The DH.71 Tiger Moth (monoplane) project has been abandoned. The Dragon project is based on original wings, all else is new build [1]. Tiger Moth G-DHTM is effectively a 'from new' project [2]. Tiger Moth G-AHMM was cancelled as sold in Sweden as far back as 2002. Tiger Moth G-ASPV had moved to <u>Branscombe</u>, Devon, by November 2005.

♦ *Visits possible strictly by prior application* only.

❑ G-ABDX	DH.60G Moth	ex HB-UAS, G-ABDX. CoA 28-7-99. Stored		8-05
❑ G-ACET	DH.84 Dragon	ex Bishop's Stortford, AW171, Ringway SF,		
		6 AACU, G-ACET	® [1]	8-05
❑ G-AERV	Whitney Straight	ex Upper Ballinderry, Newtownards, EM999, Kemble,		
		Abingdon SF, Halton SF, G-AERV. CoA 9-4-66. Stored		8-05
❑ G-AFSW	Chilton DW.2	ex Chilton Manor. Unflown. Stored		1-00
❑ G-ALJL	Tiger Moth	ex T6311, Fairford SF, 38 GCF, Tarrant Rushton		
		SF, 11 OTU, 25 PEFTS. CoA 28-9-50	®	1-00
❑ G-AMIU	Tiger Moth	ex Membury, Wycombe Air Park, T5495, 16 EFTS,		
		54 OTU, Church Fenton SF. Crashed 15-10-69. Stored		11-03
❑ G-ANFP	Tiger Moth	ex Fownhope, London Colney, Denham, Rush Green, N9503,		
		2 RFS, 7 RFS, 2 RFS, 4 RFS, 4 EFTS. CoA 1-7-63. Frame	®	1-00
❑ G-ARTH	Super Cruiser	ex EI-ADO. CoA 21-4-95. Stored	®	8-05
❑ G-DHTM	Tiger Moth	Under construction	[2]	1-00

Frank Lund: Keeps his Canberra nose in the area. Frank has restored not only the airframe but sourced and renovated to working condition all of the photo-recce gear.

❑ WT536	Canberra PR.7	ex Bruntingthorpe, Cosford 8063M 80, 31, 13, 17. Nose	6-04

The World's End: The 'Avro' was last reported in 1999. It (and the venue?) may be heading for LOST!

❑ –	'Avro 504' FSM	–	12-99

Others: A collector in the general area has two Vampires and a Gannet.

❑ WN411	Gannet AS.1	ex Abbotsinch, 820. Cockpit	3-05
❑ 'XD614'	'65' Vampire T.11	WZ572, ex Southampton museum, Leeming, 8 FTS, 7 FTS,	
		202 AFS. Pod	3-05
❑ XH318	'64' Vampire T.11	ex Calmore, Southampton, Ferndown, 7761M, Shawbury,	
		RAFC	3-05

SOUTHAMPTON AIRPORT (EASTLEIGH)

❑ N6NE	JetStar 731	ex VR-CCC ntu, N222Y, N731JS, N227K, N12R,	
		N280R. Damaged 27-11-92. Non-destructive	3-06

THRUXTON AERODROME north of the A303 west of Andover

Classic Aero Engineering: Spitfire IX SM520 is being completed for Paul Portelli and is in two-seater guise [1]. Harvard IV 'KF729' (G-BJST) was flying by September 2005.

❑ G-AOAA	Tiger Moth	ex Chilbolton, DF159, 24 GCF, 1 RS, 1 GTS,		
		20 PAFU, 5 GTS. Crashed 4-6-89	®	5-03
❑ G-BKXP	Auster AOP.6	ex Little Gransden, Royston, Oakington,		
		Belgian AF A-14, VT987	®	5-03
❑ SM520*	Spitfire IX	G-ILDA, ex Sandown, Ramsbottom, G-BXHZ,		
		Oxford, Pretoria, SAAF. Arrived 4-04	® [1]	5-04
❑ –	Tiger Moth	ex Little Gransden, Cranfield, VAT et al	®	5-03
❑ –	Hurricane XII	G-CBOE, ex RCAF 5487	®	5-04

TITCHFIELD on the A27 west of Fareham

Melvyn Hiscock's Rearwin Cloudster G-BVLK became G-EVLE in April 2003 and made its first flight on 9th March 2005, moving on to Popham, Hants.

WINCHESTER east of the M3, north of Southampton
Army Training Regiment, Sir John Moore Barracks: Have a Gazelle training aid.
❑ ZB672*   Gazelle AH.1   ex Shawbury. Arrived 27-7-<u>00</u>   2-06

YATELEY on the B3272 west of Camberley
Mick Long: *Should* still keep cockpits in the general area. The cockpit of Sea Vixen D.3 XN657 has moved on, destination unknown.
❑ WP977   Chipmunk T.10   G-BHRD, ex Crowland, Doncaster, Stamford, Burford,9M-ANA,
                                  VR-SEK, WP977, Malayan Aux AF, Rufforth SF, Man UAS,
                                  Liv UAS,63 GCF, QUAS, Man UAS. Cr 21-1-97   6-01
❑ WZ876   Chipmunk T.10   G-BBWN, ex Twyford, Tattershall Thorpe, Lon UAS,
                                  1 AEF, Lon UAS, Biggin Hill SF, Lon UAS,
                                  Ox UAS, Birm UAS, MCS, 31. Forward cockpit   6-01

HEREFORDSHIRE

BICTON west of the B4361, north west of Leominster
Oaker Wood Leisure: Within a paint-ball 'war zone' is the former Upper Hill Whirlwind.
❑ XP360*   'V' Whirlwind HAR.10 ex Upper Hill, Sunderland, Warmingham, Lasham,
                                  Fawkham Green, CFS, 225. First noted 2-05   2-05

EWYAS HAROLD on the A465 south west of Hereford
No.22 Regiment, Special Air Service: *W&R19* (p77) gave the background on the *likely* identity of the 'Jumbo' forward fuselage here - 747-100 F-BPVE at Bruntingthorpe, Leics. A *possible* is 747-136 G-AWNA also previously at Bruntingthorpe. The *rear* fuselage of *November-Alpha* serves as a cabin services and evacuation trainer at Crawley Down, West Sussex.
❑ –   Boeing 747   forward fuselage in 'airliner' mock-up   7-03

HEREFORD on the A49 south of Leominster
An enthusiast in the general area should still have a pair of Hunters.
❑ XG252   'U' Hunter FGA.9   8840M, ex Cosford, 1 TWU, 2 TWU, 1 TWU,
                                  TWU, 45, 8, Wittering SF, MoA, 54, 66   7-00
❑ XL563   Hunter T.7   9218M, ex Kempston, Farnborough, IAM, MoA, mkrs   3-05

KINGTON west of Leominster, on the A44
Martin Albery: The Edwards is owned by Computair Consultants [1]. The glider was designed in Gloucestershire and is similar to the SG.38, Dagling etc but with a metal frame. It is owned by CARG, see Innsworth, Glos [2].
❑ G-ADPJ*   BAC Drone II   ex Selby, Breighton, Wigan, Bristol, Benson, Thetford.
                                  Damaged 3-4-55. Also parts from G-AEKU   12-05
❑ G-ARIF   OH-7 Coupe   ex Breighton, Wigan   11-03
❑ G-ASDF   Edwards Helic   ex Innsworth, Woking, Coulsdon   [1]   3-02
❑ G-MBWI   Lafayette 1   ex Selby, Leeds, Leigh   11-03
❑ –   Primary glider   ex Innsworth, 'Glos'   [2]   3-02

MADLEY on the B4352 west of Hereford
❑ G-ADWJ   Tiger Moth   ex Shobdon, Defford, BB803, 9 EFTS, 20 EFTS,
                                  12 EFTS, G-ADWJ.   ®   6-97

SHOBDON AERODROME north of the A44 west of Leominster

The anonymous Cessna 150 cockpit had gone from the dump by late 2004.

❏ G-AFGD*	BA Swallow II	ex Exeter, BK897, G-AFGD. CoA expired 9-4-01	1-05
❏ G-BEPN	Pawnee 235D	ex N54877. Crashed 11-2-78. Fuselage frame. Dump	1-06

UPPER HILL between the A4110 and the A49 south of Leominster

Sheppards Surplus and Garden Centre: The Swift guards the entrance to this amazing emporium. Whirlwind HAR.10 XP360 moved to Bicton, Hereford, by February 2005.

❏ WK275	Swift F.4	ex Hatfield, Filton, C(A). Displayed	8-05

HERTFORDSHIRE

BENINGTON on minor road east of Stevenage

❏ G-AXDU	Pup 150	ex G-35-048. Crashed 22-10-96. Fuselage.	1-04

BERKHAMSTED on the A4251 west of Hemel Hempstead

Stuart McKay: Is the driving force of the **de Havilland Moth Club** uniting all who restore, own, operate or just love DH biplanes. As well as the annual Woburn fly-in, they produce by far and away the best magazine of any 'type' organisation anywhere in the UK – *The Moth*.

◆ *De Havilland Moth Club, 23 Hall Park Hill, Berkhamsted, Herts, HP4 2NH.*

❏ G-AVPD	Jodel D.9 Bebe	ex Langley. CoA 6-6-75	3-05

CHESHUNT on the A10 north of Junction 25 of the M25

Autocar G-AOBV moved to Gainsborough, Lincs.

CHIPPERFIELD south of Hemel Hempstead

A Canberra nose was a plaything for children in the area. It was offered for sale in December 2005.

❏ WK122	Canberra TT.18	ex Bruntingthorpe, Helston, Samlesbury, 7,15,61. Nose	2-06

CLOTHALL COMMON on the A507 south-east of Baldock

❏ G-APYU	Tri-Traveler	ex Moreton-in-Marsh. Crashed 23-4-72. Canx 3-4-98. Stored	10-99

ELSTREE AERODROME north of Junction 4, M1

A definitive state-of-the-art on the dump is given below. Kraguj 30146 (G-BSXD) departed by road on 23rd September 2005 – destination unknown, but registered to a Morpeth, Northumberland, owner.

❏ G-ASON	Twin Comanche	ex N7273Y ntu. CoA 30-11-91. Stored	1-00
❏ G-AXGC	MS.880B Rallye	CoA 12-5-88. Stored	9-95
❏ G-BGPK	AA-5B Tiger	ex G-BGRV ntu. Dump	8-04
❏ G-BOVH	Warrior II	ex Bristol, N4311M. Damaged 1-4-94. Dump	8-04
❏ G-BSCR	Cessna 172M	ex N12693. Crashed 19-6-99. Dump	8-04
❏ G-GCNZ	Cessna 150M	ex C-GCNZ. CoA 27-3-98. Fuselage	2-04
❏ G-FLII*	GA-7 Cougar	ex G-GRAC, C-GRAC, N1367R ntu, N730GA.	
		CoA 23-10-04. Stored. First noted 3-05	10-05
❏ G-ODAE	AA-5A Cheetah	ex G-OBSF, G-ODSF, G-BEUW, N6158A. Fuselage. Dump	8-04

❑ C-FQIP	Lake LA-4-200	ex N1068L. Stored	8-05
❑ N320MR	Twin Comanche	ex G-CALV, G-AZFO, N8761Y. Stored	8-05
❑ ST-AHZ	Navajo 310	ex G-AXMR, N6558L. Dump	8-04

HATFIELD
Galleria: The Comet 'flies' inside the mall. (The 'real' G-ACSS can be found at Old Warden, Beds.)

❑ 'G-ACSS'	DH.88 FSM	BAPC.257. *Grosvenor House*.	2-06

Gerry Atwell and **Frank Telling**: As threatened/promised in *W&R19* (p78) the anonymous Mignet HM.21 last noted in October 1994 has been moved to LOST!? **University of Hertfordshire**: The Jetstream test-shell was last to be observed on the campus in August 2001. It was disposed of – no other details – some time after that.

HEMEL HEMPSTEAD on the A414 west of St Albans
The Vampire Collection: Alan Allen's collection is thankfully to be found in this area. Why? I'll quote him: "Despite living under a mile from Buncefield we survived with no damage".
◆ *Visits by prior arrangement* only. *Alan Allen, 201 High Street Green, Hemel Hempstead, HP2 7AA. e-mail alan.allen@lineone.net*

❑ WZ581	'77' Vampire T.11	ex Ruislip, Bushey, Keevil, Exeter, 3/4 CAACU, 229 OCU, 233 OCU, 25. Pod	4-06
❑ XT439	Wasp HAS.1	ex King's Lynn, Bruntingthorpe, Cranfield, Wroughton, 829. Crashed 25-3-86	4-06
❑ 221	Vampire T.55	ex Liss, SAAF	4-06

HITCHIN on the A505 north-east of Luton
Philip Leaver: The GR.1 is thought to have been a 'spare' with the cockpit number FL/R 41H 725624, and – contrary to previous thinking – not a damaged 'flyer'.

❑ –	Harrier GR.1	ex Llantrisant, Welshpool, Stafford, Abingdon, Hamble. Nose	3-02
❑ XV759	'O' Harrier GR.3	ex Bruntingthorpe, Barnstaple (?), Welshpool, Llantrisant, Pendine, St Athan, 233 OCU, 1417F, 233 OCU, 1, 233 OCU, 1, 233 OCU. Nose	3-06

Others: The Martin Monoplane project is still to be found here. The wings are being used on the Humming Bird project, to be found at Hatch, Beds. The yard of **H Williams and Sons** in Wallace Way has a rapid processing policy and during November 2004 were busy with former Italian Air Force Tornado F.3s from St Athan, Wales.

❑ G-AEYY	Martin Mono	ex Bishop's Stortford, Meir	4-05

LEAVESDEN south of Abbots Langley, north of the A41
Studios: Eon Productions have a travelling 'roadshow' dedicated to James Bond. Part of the display should still be the Bede 'Acrostar' (BD-5J) used in *Octopussy*. Three 'stars' from Golden Eye have been seen on the lots/former airfield of late. F-ZWWW was the French prototype Tiger PT1 (or is it Tigre...?) which did become a travelling demonstrator. Is this the real thing or a mock-up? It is *very* convincing…

❑ 'F-ZWWW'*	Eurocopter Tiger	ex *Golden Eye*. First noted 11-02	2-05
❑ –*	Cessna 172	ex *Golden Eye*. Damaged fuselage	2-05
❑ –*	Turbo Porter	ex *Golden Eye*. Damaged fuselage, red star	2-05
❑ –	Bede BD-5J	ex *Octopussy*	1-98

LONDON COLNEY off the A6 between London Colney and South Mimms
De Havilland Aircraft Heritage Centre incorporating the **Mosquito Aircraft Museum** and administered by the De Havilland Aircraft Museum Trust. Bringing back the British Antarctic Survey Otter was an epic recovery. Abandoned on Deception Island since 1967, it is a testament to the 'benefits' of a below-zero existence! The former Rush Green Chipmunk is to be restored in association with local Air Cadets as a museum-led project [1].

Notes: The de Havilland-built Cierva C.24 is on loan from the Science Museum [2]. The stored DH.88 Comet FSM was built in Australia for use in the film *The Great Air Race*. It will re-appear in the colours of G-ACSP *Black Magic* [3]. The Comet SIM is a nose section that was built at the same time as the noses for the first two prototypes and was used for structural tests. It then went to the DH Servicing School and was later converted into a simulator. It is now fitted with Mk.4 instrumentation [4]. The Humming Bird uses the wings of the Martin Monoplane G-AEYY - see under Hitchin, Herts - and is on loan from Mike Russell. [5]. Mosquito FB.6 TA122 is being rebuilt using the wing of TR.33 TW233 acquired in Israel [6]. See under Gloucestershire Airport, Glos, for the pod of Vampire T.11. Chipmunk T.10 PAX WP927 moved to Ingatestone, Essex, during 2005.

♦ *Open from first Sun of Mar to last Sun of Oct, Tue, Thu and Sat 2pm to 5.30pm, Sun and Bank Hols 10.30am to 5.30pm. Last admission 4.30pm. PO Box 107, Salisbury Hall, London Colney, St Albans, AL2 1EX tel/fax/info-line 01727 01727 826400, info-line only 01727 822051 e-mail w4050@dhamt.fsmail.net www.dehavillandmuseum.co.uk*

❑ G-ABLM		Cierva C.24	ex Hatfield. CoA 16-1-35	[2] 3-06
❑ G-ADOT		Hornet Moth	ex Hatfield, Old Warden, Stoke Ferry, Stapleford, Houghton-on-the-Hill, X9326, 5 GCF, 23 OTU, 24 GCF, 6 AONS, Halton SF, 2 CPF, G-ADOT. CoA 5-10-59	3-06
❑ G-AFOJ		Moth Minor	ex Navestock, E-1, E-0236, G-AFOJ. CoA 27-8-69. *Bugs 2* ⑅	3-06
❑ G-AKDW		Dragon Rapide	ex Aviodome, Amsterdam store, F-BCDB, G-AKDW, YI-ABD, NR833. *City of Winchester* ⑅	3-06
❑ G-ANRX		Tiger Moth	ex Belchamp Walter, N6550, SLAW, 25 EFTS, 18 EFTS, 241, 14 EFTS, 56 ERFTS. CoA 20-6-61. Crop duster. *Border City*	3-06
❑ G-AOTI		Heron 2D	ex Biggin Hill, Exeter, G-5-19. CoA 24-6-87 ⑅	3-06
❑ G-AREA		Dove 8	ex Hatfield. CoA 8-9-72	3-06
❑ G-ARYA		HS.125-1	ex Wrexham, Connah's Quay, Hawarden, Connah's Quay, Chester, Hatfield. Nose	3-06
❑ G-ARYC		HS.125 Srs 1	ex Hatfield, Filton, R-R. CoA 1-8-73. RR / BSE colours ⑅	3-06
❑ G-AVFH		Trident 2	ex Heathrow, BA, BEA. Forward fuselage	3-06
❑ –	BAPC.216	DH.88 FSM	ex 'G-ACSS', St Albans, Kings Langley, Wroughton, Aus	[3] 3-06
❑ –	BAPC.232	Horsa I / II	composite fuselage	3-06
❑ –		Comet 2 SIM	ex Wroughton, Crawley	[4] 3-06
❑ D-IFSB		Dove 6	ex Hatfield, BFS, D-CFSB, Panshanger, G-AMXR, N4280V	3-06
❑ F-BGNX		Comet 1XB	G-AOJT, ex Farnborough, F-BGNX. Fuselage	3-06
❑ [VP-FAK]*		Otter	ex Deception Island, British Antarctic Survey. Wfu 26-3-67. Arrived 8-5-05	3-06
❑ J-7326		Humming Bird	G-EBQP, ex Hatch, Audley End, Bishop's Stortford. Fuse	[5] 3-06
❑ W4050 (pt)		Mosquito	ex Hatfield, Chester, Hatfield, Panshanger, Hatfield,	
E-0234 (stb)		prototype	Rolls-Royce, DH, AAEE, E-0234 ⑅	3-06
❑ LF789		Queen Bee	BAPC.186, ex 'K3584', Hadfield, Droylesden, Redhill, St Athan, Pilot-less A/c Unit, Manorbier, St Athan	
'R2-K'				3-06
❑ TA122	'UP-G'	Mosquito FB.6	ex Soesterberg, 4, 2 GCS, 48,4,605,417 ARF. 605 Sqn c/s ⑅	[6] 3-06
❑ TA634		Mosquito TT.35	ex Liverpool, G-AWJV, Aldergrove, 3 CAACU, APS Schleswigland, APS Ahlorn, APS Sylt, 4 CAACU. 571 Sqn c/s	3-06
'8K-K'				
❑ TJ118		Mosquito TT.35	ex Elstree, Exeter, 3/4 CAACU, 3 CAACU. Fuselage	3-06
❑ WM729		Vampire NF.10	ex Gloucestershire, London Colney, Ruislip, Bingley, Bradford, Church Fenton, CNCS, 2 ANS, 25, 151. Nose	1-04
❑ WP790	'T'	Chipmunk T.10	G-BBNC, ex Rush Green, WP790, Bir UAS, Wales UAS, PFTS, AOTS, 1 ITS, RAFC, Man UAS, G&S UAS, Stn UAS, 24 GCF, 5 RFS, 17 RFS ⑅	3-06
❑ WP869*		Chipmunk T.10	ex Rush Green, Firbeck, Stamford, Brierley Hill, Castle Bromwich, 8215M, 8207M, Shawbury, Spitalgate CF, RAFTC, 664 RAFC. Arrived 19-3-06 ⑅	[1] 3-06
❑ WR539		Venom FB.4	ex Gloucestershire, London Colney, Fownhope, Cardiff, 'Midlands', Cosford, 8399M, Kai Tak, 28, 60. Stored ⑅	1-04
❑ WX853		Venom NF.3	ex Debden 7443M, Shawbury, 23. Dismantled ⑅	1-04

❑ XG730	'499' Sea Ven FAW.22	ex Southwick, Portsmouth, Lee-on-Solent, ADS,	
		Sydenham, 893, 894, 891. 894 Sqn colours	3-06
❑ XH328	Vampire T.11	ex Duxford, Bournemouth, Cranfield, Hemel Hempstead,	
		Croxley Green, Bushey, Keevil, Exeter, 3 CAACU, 60	3-06
❑ XJ565	'127' Sea Vixen FAW.2	ex RAE, 899, 893, 766B. '127-E', 899 Sqn c/s	3-06
❑ XJ772	'H' Vampire T.11	ex Brooklands, Wisley, Shawbury, CATCS, 1 FTS, 8 FTS,	
		RAFC, RNorAF 15018 'XP-G'	® 3-06
❑ XK695	Comet C.2(R)	ex Stock, Newton 9164M, Duxford, Wyton, 51, 216,	
		G-AMXH. Nose	3-06
❑ J-1008	Vampire FB.6	ex Hatfield, Swiss AF	3-06
❑ J-1632	Venom FB.50	G-VNOM, ex Cranfield, Bridgend, Bruntingthorpe,	
		Cranfield, Swiss AF. Dismantled	3-06
❑ J-1790	Venom FB.54	G-BLKA, ex 'WR410', 'Norfolk', Bournemouth, B'thorpe,	
		Cranfield, G-VENM ntu, Swiss AF J-1790	3-06

PANSHANGER AERODROME east of Welwyn Garden City, south of the B1000

❑ G-BSKC	Tomahawk 112	ex OY-PJB, N748RM, C-GRQI. Crashed 2-6-96	6-97
❑ G-DTOO	Tomahawk 112	ex Seething. Crashed 9-7-94	9-02
❑ N93938	Ercoupe 415C	Stored	11-04

RUSH GREEN AERODROME east of the B656 west of Stevenage
Chipmunk T.10 WP869 moved to London Colney, Herts, on 19th March 2006.

ST ALBANS
Eric Littledike: Restored Pilcher BAPC.57 moved to Duxford, Cambs, by November 2004.

No news from the **microlight strip**...

❑ G-AZZX	Cessna FRA.150L	damaged 28-2-87. Stored, spares use	1-02
❑ N7263S	Cessna 150H	Stored	1-02
❑ N13253	Cessna 172M	Stored, spares use	1-02
❑ –	Cessna F.150K	ex N5927G. Stored, spares use	6-99

ISLE OF MAN

ISLE OF MAN AIRPORT (RONALDSWAY)
Manx Aviation and Military Museum: Run by the Manx Aviation Preservation Society, the museum charts the island's varied aviation history and occupies wartime buildings on the airport site.
◆ *Open 10am to 4.30pm weekends, Bank Hols and during the TT Races, or by appointment. Ronaldsway Airport, Ballasalla, Isle of Man, IM9 2AT tel 01624 829294 e-mail iramsden@talk21.com www.maps.iofm.net*

| ❑ 9041* | Bolingbroke IVT | ex Canada, RCAF. Cockpit. Arrived by 8-04 | ® 3-06 |

Aeroservice (IoM) Ltd: Only components of the Q.6 moved to Northampton, Northants, the deal having apparently fallen through. The unique project is still to be found here [1]. The three other entries here are probably on their way to LOST!, although the J/1 has owners in north Cheshire and *may* have moved.

❑ G-AFFD	Percival Q.6	ex Sutton Coldfield, Duxford, Redhill, G-AIEY ntu,	
		X9407, MCS, 510, Old Sarum SF, Halton SF, Heston SF,	
		Northolt SF, 6 AACU, G-AFFD. CoA 31-8-56	[1] 1-05

❑ G-AJEE	J/1 Autocrat	ex Compton Abbas. CoA 10-7-89	® 8-92
❑ G-APSZ	Cessna 172	ex Barton, N6372E. Damaged 2-3-84. Stored	6-96
❑ G-BCGA	Seneca 200-2	ex Panshanger, N41975. Crashed 18-12-77. Fuselage	6-96

Airport:

| ❑ G-AZRG | Aztec 250D | ex Aldergrove, N6536Y. CoA 8-7-93. Dump | 7-96 |
| ❑ – | BAPC.282 Eider Duck | Single-seat pusher, unflown. In terminal | 3-06 |

JURBY AERODROME west of Andreas
The taxiable Feggans Brown-built Spitfire is owned by A Saunders [1].

❑ G-ACLL	Leopard Moth	ex AW165, AFEE, 7 AACU, 6 AACU, Ringway SF. CoA 6-12-95. Stored	2-04
❑ –	CEV Bergfalke II	BGA.1492. CoA 12-93. Stored	10-96
❑ –	BAPC.283 Spitfire FSM	ex Farnsfield, Newtown, Kettering, *Piece of Cake*	[1] 2-04

ISLE OF WIGHT

BEMBRIDGE AERODROME on the B3395 south-west of Bembridge
Britten Norman Aircraft Preservation Society:
◆ *Visits* strictly *by prior permission: 32 Budesbury Road, Staines, TW18 2AX e-mail savecn@ bnaps.co.uk www.bnaps.co.uk*

| ❑ G-AVCN | BN-2A | ex Puerto Rico, N290VL, F-OGHG, G-AVCN | ® 1-04 |

B-N Group: The Trislander is a pattern airframe for the proposed Trislander 'line' for China [1].

❑ G-BEVR	Trislander	ex Cumbernauld, JY-JQE, G-BEVR, XA-THE[2], G-BEVR. CoA 6-7-82. Fuselage	[1] 1-04
❑ G-BVHX	BN-2T-4R	Radar-nosed, fuselage. Tests	1-04
❑ G-BVHY	BN-2T-4R	complete, unflown	11-02
❑ G-BWPM	BN-2T-4R	fuselage. Unbuilt kit, stored	11-02
❑ G-RAPA	BN-2T-4R	prototype	1-06
❑ ZG994	Islander AL.1	ex 1 Flt AAC. Crashed 30-6-99. Test rig	5-03

COWES on the A3020, north of the island
Cliftongrade Ltd: The scrap dealers still use the cockpit to advertise their business.

| ❑ XT863 | 'AS' Phantom FG.1 | ex Abingdon, 43, 111, 892, 767. Nose | 1-06 |

NEWPORT on the A3054, middle of the island
Stored in the area in two separate places are two homebuilds. Unconfirmed reports note that the Go-Plane is no more – comments? A collector in the area has acquired a Sea Harrier cockpit.

❑ G-AZJE	Minicab	ex Sandown. CoA 7-7-82. Stored	12-01
❑ G-BCMF	Levi Go-Plane	one and only flight 16-11-74. Stored	1-98
❑ ZH807*	Sea Harrier FA.2	ex Basingstoke, St Athan, accident 1-5-02, 899. Nose	12-05

SANDOWN on the A3055 south of Ryde, east coast
Tipsy Junior G-AMVP moved to <u>Sandown</u> Aerodrome, IoW, for restoration on 12th September 2005.

SANDOWN AERODROME north of the A3056, west of Sandown

Airframe Assemblies: A 'detached unit' from Airframe Assemblies moved, devised the supports, and erected Spitfire F.21 LA198 at its new home in Glasgow, Scotland, during 2005 – qv. Spitfire IX RR232 moved to Exeter, Devon, in June 2005. The fuselage of Spitfire XIV RM689 (G-ALGT) moved to Filton, Glos, in November 2004. Spitfire IX two-seater conversion SM520 (G-ILDA) moved to Thruxton, Hants, in April 2004 for systems fitting out and flight test. Fw 189A-1 2100 returned to Lancing, W Sussex, in June 2004. Spitfire XVI RW382 is with Solent Spitfire Project Ltd [1].

◆ Private *premises - visits strictly by prior permission.*

❑ BH238	Hurricane IIb	ex Front Line Sandown, Russia, Soviet AF. Wreck, stored		3-06
❑ LZ842* 'EF-D'	Spitfire IX	ex Australia, UK, South Africa, SAAF, RAF 232. Arr 7-4-05 ®		3-06
❑ RM927*	Spitfire XIV	ex High Wycombe, USA, Southend, Charnock Richard, Ostend, Belg AF SG-25, RAF, 29 MU, 403. Arr 4-05	®	3-06
❑ RW382	Spitfire XVI	N382RW, ex USA, Audley End, Braintree, Uxbridge 8075M, Leconfield, Church Fenton 7245M, C&RS, 3 CAACU, 604. Wreck, stored	[1]	7-05

Elsewhere: Tipsy G-AMVP is under restoration by Dave French and Tim Buckley of Vectis Aviation.

❑ G-AMVP*	Tipsy Junior	ex Sandown, OO-ULA. CoA 22-6-94. Arr 12-9-05	®	3-06
❑ G-BHMR	Stinson 108-3	ex F-BABO, F-DABO, NC6352M. CoA 23-11-90		3-06
❑ G-BRDN*	Rallye Club	ex OY-DTV. CoA 27-4-02. Spares. First noted 3-05		3-06
❑ G-NRDC	Fieldmaster	ex Old Sarum. CoA 17-10-87. Fuselage		3-06
❑ –	Fieldmaster EMU	ex Old Sarum. Stored		3-06

SHANKLIN

An amusement arcade on the seafront has a Rallye – complete with skeletal pilot! -as an attraction.

❑ G-BIRB	MS.880B Rallye	ex Manston, Firbeck, Carlisle, Hooton Park, Moston, Carlisle, F-BVAQ. CoA 16-6-90	1-06

YARMOUTH on the A3054 west of Newport

A *private* owner here has acquired a damaged Bulldog. One side has been painted as the prototype, G-AXEH.

❑ G-CCOA*	Bulldog 122	ex Ghana AF G-111, G-BCUU. Dam 22-8-01. Arr by 5-04	1-06

Another *private* collector has added a Hunter nose to his Vampire pod.

❑ XE921	'64' Vampire T.11	ex Welshpool, Stoke-on-Trent, Barton, Firbeck, Retford, Firbeck, Keevil, Exeter, 3/4 CAACU, 1 FTS, CFS. Pod	1-06
❑ XL609*	Hunter T.7	ex Boscombe Down, Firbeck, Elgin, Lossiemouth 8866M, 12, 216, 237 OCU, 4 FTS, 56. Nose. 12 Sqn c/s	1-06

KENT

ASHFORD on the M20 west of Folkestone

❑ G-ANFY	Jackaroo	ex NL906, 9 RFS, 23 EFTS, 9 FTS. CoA 25-5-68	1-96
❑ G-ASBY	Airedale	ex St Ives, 'Eversden', Royston. CoA 22-3-80	6-00

BREDHURST or Farthing Corner, south of Junction 4 of the M2, south of Gillingham

This reference looks set for LOST!

❑ G-ARWH	Cessna 172C	ex Golders Green, Fenland, N1466Y. CoA 28-4-86. Spares	5-99

BRENCHLEY east of the B2160, east of Royal Tunbridge Wells
This reference looks set for LOST also!

❑ G-ATKH	Luton Minor	ex Rochester. CoA 24-6-92. Stored	1-96
❑ G-AYXO	Luton Major	ex Beeston Rylands. Stored	1-96

BRENZETT on the A2070 north-west of New Romney
Brenzett Aeronautical Museum Trust: Occupying buildings to the west of the Brenzett (or Ivychurch) Advanced Landing Ground. The Canberra is being restored to its RAE colours.
◆ *Open weekends from Easter to end of Oct, also Bank Holidays, 11am to 5.30pm. Also open Jul, Aug, Sep on Fridays 11am to 5.30pm. Ivychurch Road, Brenzett, Romney Marsh, TN29 0EE tel 01797 344747 or 01233 622721 www.brenzettaero.co.uk*

❑ [G-AMSM]	Dakota 4	ex Booker, Brenzett, Duxford, Brenzett, Lydd, Skyways, Eagle, Starways, KN274, TCDU, 77, St Eval SF, Azores SF, 43-49948. Dam 17-8-78. Nose. Air Freight colours	12-05
❑ V7350	Hurricane I	ex Robertsbridge, 85. Crashed 29-8-40. Cockpit	12-05
❑ WH657	Canberra B.2	ex Godalming, RAE, 231 OCU	® 12-05
❑ XK625	Vampire T.11	ex Firbeck, North Weald, Southend, Woodford, St Athan, 8 FTS, 7 FTS	12-05

CANTERBURY
BB Aviation: Bill Baker and friends have two airframes. *Likely* identity for the Canberra is WJ581 [1].
◆ *Bur Oak, Bossingham, near Canterbury, Kent, CT4 6DX.*

❑ –	BAPC.17 Woodhams Sprite	ex Manchester, Hooton Park, Wigan, Irlam, Wigan, Liverpool, Leamington Spa. Incomplete	® 4-06
❑ –	Canberra PR.7	ex Cardiff-Wales, WAM, CTTS St Athan. Nose	® [1] 4-06

Maypole Air: Stampe SV-4C G-BRXP (formerly N33528) was flying by 2005.

CAPEL LE FERNE on the B2011 north east of Folkestone
National Battle of Britain Memorial: The deeply-moving statue of a pilot sitting, contemplating the English Channel, set against a huge three-bladed propeller akin to the ancient chalk figures found on the South Downs, is well known and a place of pilgrimage for many. There is an excellent visitor centre and small shop. After considerable fund-raising, two 'gate guardians' have joined the centre, both built by GB Replicas. The Hurricane is in the colours of the aircraft flown by P/O Geoffrey Page when he was shot down on 12th August 1940 [1]. Note that the Spitfire is *not* in the colours predicted in *W&R19* (p84) [2].
◆ *Gp Capt Patrick Tootal, 4 The Croft, Leybourne, West Malling, Kent, ME19 5QD tel (9-5) 01732 870809 www.battleofbritainmemorial.org*

❑ 'P2970'	'US-X' Hurricane I FSM	BAPC.291, 56 Squadron colours. *Little Willie*	[1] 4-06
❑ 'R6775'	'YT-J' Spitfire I FSM	BAPC.299, 65 Sqn c/s	[2] 4-06

CHATHAM east of Rochester
The Historic Dockyard Chatham: Gannet AEW.3 XL500 moved to North Weald, Essex, on 26th June 2004.
◆ *North of the A231, signed. Open mid-Feb to late Oct daily 10am to 6pm. Weekends only Nov and closed Dec and Jan. Last entry 3pm up to late Mar thereafter 4pm. Chatham ME4 4TZ tel 01634 823800 fax 01634 823801 e-mail info@chdt.org.uk www.chdt.org.uk*

❑ WG751	'710' Dragonfly HR.3	ex Gosport, Condover, Ramsgreave, Ancoats, *The Last Caravan*, Wisbech, B'bushe, F'lands, 705. 705 Sqn c/s	12-05

Royal Engineers Museum and Library: There is much to interest the aviation enthusiast here including the medals etc of James McCudden VC DSO* MC* MM and many other artefacts. The history of military aviation in the UK from 1880 with balloons, through to man-lifting kites and airships to the Air Battalion of the Royal Engineers of 1912 is all well charted. The wing of a Cody monoplane, on loan from the RAeS, is also on display.

◆ *On the B2004 north of Chatham. Tue to Fri (not Mon) 9am to 5pm, weekends 11.30am to 5pm. Prince Arthur Road, Gillingham, Chatham, ME4 4UG tel 01634 822839 fax 01634 822371 e-mail mail@remuseum.co.uk www.remuseum.org.uk*

❏	–		Vulcan hang-glider –		3-02
❏	XZ964	'D'	Harrier GR.3	ex St Athan, 1417F, 233 OCU, 3, 233 OCU, 1.*Ninja One*	3-06
❏	–		Military balloon	basket only. RAFM loan	3-06

No.1404 Squadron Air Cadets: Chipmunk WZ846 moved to Biggin Hill, Gtr Lon, on 11th December 2004.

CHATTENDEN on the A228 north of Rochester
Defence Explosives Ordnance Disposal School: The 'JP' is in the Lodge Hill Camp site. The Sioux was intended for display at Chatham and is stored [1].

❏	–	BAPC.158	Fieseler Fi 103	held inside the camp		5-00
❏	–	BAPC.159	Ohka 11	held inside the camp		5-03
❏	XM410		Jet Provost T.3	8054AM, ex North Luffenham, Halton, Shawbury, RAFC, 7 FTS, 2 FTS		5-03
❏	XT133		Sioux AH.1	ex Chatham, Arborfield, Middle Wallop 7923M	[1]	5-03
❏	XT907	'W'	Phantom FGR.2	9151M, ex 74, 228 OCU. EOD		5-03

CHISLET north of the A28 south-east of Herne Bay
❏	G-ANWX*	J/5L Aiglet Tr	crashed 1-8-93. First noted 8-05	8-05
❏	G-ASAX*	Terrier 2	ex Auster AOP.6 TW533, 652, LAS, AOPS, 663. CoA 1-9-96. First noted 8-05	8-05
❏	G-ASMT	Linnet 2	CoA 25-9-01. Stored	9-04

DOVER
Dover Museum: Among a wide sweep of exhibits is a V-1 FSM. Other items of interest include a small piece of Blériot's cross-Channel Type XI and a bit from the first bomb ever to drop on the UK - Dover, Christmas 1914.
◆ *Open daily 10am to 5.30pm. Closed Sun, Oct to Apr. Market Square, Dover, CT16 1PB tel 01304 201066 fax 01304 241186 e-mail museumenquiries@dover.gov.uk www.dovermuseum.co.uk*

| ❏ | – | BAPC.290 | Fieseler Fi 103 REP - | 3-06 |

Others: An unknown ATC unit have the former Manston Pup on loan.
| ❏ | HB-NAV | 'A' Pup 150 | ex Stock, Henley-on-Thames, Henlow, Redhill, G-AZCM. Blue/white c/s. Forward fuselage | 3-04 |

GRAVESEND on the A226 east of Dartford
A Buccaneer S.1 nose is with a local collector.
| ❏ | XN928 | Buccaneer S.1 | ex Manston, Bruntingthorpe, Cardiff, St Athan 8179M, 736, 809, 801. Desert pink, *Glenfiddich*, *Jaws* and *Liz* | 12-05 |

Gravesend Police College:
| ❏ | G-AVMK | BAC 111-510ED | ex Bournemouth, BA, BEA. Sections | 1-02 |

HAWKINGE on the A260 north of Folkestone
Kent Battle of Britain Museum: The depth and intensity of the displays is exceptional, especially when remembering that the museum occupies buildings used during the Battle of Britain by the famous RAF station. The Miles Aircraft Collection (see under Pulborough, W Sussex) have passed on a large amount of Miles Master material to the museum for their project to build a Kestrel-engined reproduction.

The prototype Spitfire is an unfinished project started as an all-metal faithful reproduction by Barry Gennard in Luton [1]. The Spitfire IX FSM has a real counterpart, at Coningsby, Lincs, and there is yet *another* MK356 at Cosford, Shrop! [2]. Note that the full-size models are occasionally repainted with new identities and it is not easy to keep track of them!

◆ *Tue to Sun (plus Bank Holidays), Easter to 1st October, 10am to 5pm – last entry 4pm. Signed off the A260. (**Note that** photography and noetbooks are not permitted within the museum.) Aerodrome Road, Hawkinge Airfield, Folkestone, CT18 7AG tel 01303 89140 www.kbobm.org*

❑	'G-AAAH'*		DH.60G REP	BAPC.168, ex Croydon, Gatwick. *Jason*. Stored		5-05
❑	–	BAPC.36	Fi 103 (V-1) FSM	ex Old Warden, Duxford, Old Warden		8-01
❑	–	BAPC.66	'Bf 109' FSM	ex '1480', Chilham Castle, *Battle of Britain*		8-01
❑		BAPC.74	'Bf 109' FSM	ex '6357', '6', Higher Blagdon, *Battle of Britain*		8-01
❑	'D-3-340'		Grunau Baby	ex Ramsgate. True identity unknown		8-01
❑	'K5054'		Spitfire proto REP	BAPC.297, ex Luton, Lowestoft, Luton	[1]	6-00
❑	'N2532'	'GZ-H'	Hurricane FSM	BAPC.272, new build, arr by 4-00. 32 Sqn colours		8-01
❑	'N3289'	'DW-K'	Spitfire FSM	BAPC.65, ex Chilham Castle, *Battle of Britain*. 610 Sqn c/s		8-01
❑	'N3313'	'KL-B'	Spitfire FSM	BAPC.69, ex Higher Blagdon, Stoneleigh, *Battle of Britain*.		
				54 Sqn colours		8-01
❑	'N7033'		Harvard IIb	ex FX442, Bournemouth, Fordingbridge, Bournemouth,		
				Sandhurst, Hullavington, 501, 226 OCU, 203 AFS, 61 OTU		9-02
❑	'P2921'	'GZ-L'	Hurricane FSM	BAPC.273, new build, arr by 4-00. 32 Sqn colours		8-01
❑	'P3059'	'SD-N'	Hurricane FSM	BAPC.64, ex Chilham Castle, *Battle of Britain*, 501 Sqn c/s		4-98
❑	'P3208'	'SD-T'	Hurricane FSM	BAPC.63, ex 'L1592', Higher Blagdon, *Battle of Britain*.		
				501 Sqn colours		8-01
❑	'P3679'	'GZ-K'	Hurricane FSM	BAPC.278. 32 Sqn colours		8-01
❑	'MK356'	'2I-V'	Spitfire IX FSM	–	[2]	8-01
❑	–		Hurricane FSM	ex Lowestoft. 'RF-U' 303 Squadron colours		4-98
❑	–		Tiger Moth	ex Bedford area. Fuselage		12-03
❑	'425/17'		Fokker Dr.I FSM	BAPC.133, ex Winthorpe, Higher Blagdon		8-01
❑	'14'	BAPC.67	'Bf 109' FSM	ex Coventry, North Weald, Newark, *Battle of Britain* .JG52 c/s		8-01

Peter Smith: Typhoon EJ922 will include the rear fuselage of former Malta Sea Fury FB.11 VW589 '106' [1]. The **Hawkinge Airfield Youth Club** are working on the former Manston BE.2 [2]. Peter has a Chipmunk PAX on loan at Brooklands, Surrey - qv.

◆ *Airframes are stored in a variety of places and visits are not possible.*

❑	G-AAXK		Klemm L 25	ex Sevenoaks, CoA 29-11-60. Damaged 3-62. Fuselage		3-02
❑	–	BAPC.117	BE.2c FSM	ex Manston, Sevenoaks, Brooklands,North Weald, *Wings*	[2]	3-02
❑	–	BAPC.190	Spitfire FSM	ex Barton, Chelford, 'K5054', Sevenoaks. Poor state		3-02
❑	EJ922		Typhoon Ib	ex Manston, Brooklands, Sevenoaks, Biggin Hill,		
				Southend, Brooklands, Brownhills, 3. Cockpit	[1]	3-02
❑	–		'SE.5A' FSM	ex Sevenoaks, Coventry. Poor state		3-02
❑	–		Typhoon I	ex Manston, Brooklands, Sevenoaks, Innsworth, Leeds,		
				Cheltenham, Kemble. Cockpit		3-02

IVYCHURCH north of the A259, east of New Romney

| ❑ | G-BEOD | Cessna 180 | ex Errol, OO-SPZ, D-EDAH, SL-AAT, N3294D. Cr 29-6-89 | 3-97 |

LASHENDEN AERODROME or Headcorn, on the A247 south of Headcorn

Lashenden Air Warfare Museum (LAWM): Fund raising for the new museum building continues. The Lightning nose was split vertically for use in the sci-fi film *Wing Commander*. It is on loan from Mike Coleman [1]. The Reichenberg V-1 carries a manually-operated fuel pump and many other fittings that make its provenance certain. LAWM has the remains of the rudder pedals, control column and their cockpit mountings plus the aileron controls and mountings. LAWM believe it originated at Dannenberg. A grant application so that the 'R-IV can be restored at Geisenhausen in Germany should have been submitted by the time *W&R20* is published [2]. See also 'Locally' below for the Vampire project.

◆ *Sun and Bank Hols 10.30am to 6pm, Easter until end of Oct. Sun 10.30am to 3.30pm Nov to Easter. Other times by prior arrangement. Lashenden Aerodrome, Ashford, TN27 9HX tel 01622 890226 or '206783 fax 01622 206783 e-mail lashairwar@blueyonder.co.uk*

☐ ZF587		Lightning F.53	ex Reading, Portsmouth, *Wing Commander*, Portsmouth, Stretton, Warton, RSAF 215, 53-691, G-27-61. Nose	[1] 3-06
☐ 84	'8-NF'	Mystère IVA	ex Sculthorpe, French AF	3-06
☐ 63938	'11-MU'	F-100F-16-NA	ex Sculthorpe, French AF	3-06
☐ 100549		Fa 330A-1	ex Manchester, Liverpool, Blackpool, Lavenham, Hullavington, Biggin Hill, Farnborough	3-06
☐ –	BAPC.91	Fi 103R-IV	ex Rochester, Chattenden, Horsham, Farnborough	[2] 3-06

Aerodrome: Airedale G-AWGA is used for spares for the based and airworthy G-ATCC [1]. The cockpit of an Airbus A300, thought to have come from Filton, Glos, is stored for a collector. Turbulents G-ARBZ, G-ARZM and G-ASAM were scrapped in December 2004/early 2005. SAN D.140C G-BSPC departed in December 2005 for restoration – destination unknown. In *W&R18* (p91) Cub G-NICK was listed as departing for pastures unknown. It can now be found at Chilbolton, Hants.

☐ G-AHAV	J/1 Autocrat	ex HB-EOM ntu. CoA 21-6-75. Canx 28-3-06. Stored	off-site	3-02
☐ G-ARHL	Aztec 250	CoA 23-11-79. Fire dump by 3-04		3-06
☐ G-AWGA*	Airedale	ex Biggin Hill, Sevenoaks, Biggin, Bicester, EI-ATA, G-AWGA, D-ENRU. CoA 3-7-86. Arr by 9-02	[1]	3-06
☐ G-AZVJ*	Seneca 200	ex N4529T. CoA 21-8-03. First noted 8-05		8-05
☐ G-AZZP	Cessna F.172H	ex LN-RTA. Crashed 8-6-97. Stored		3-06
☐ G-BMCS	Tri-Pacer 135	ex 5Y-KMH, VP-KMH, ZS-DJI. CoA 15-7-01. Stored		3-06
☐ G-BLYP*	Robin R3000/120	CoA 5-5-01	®	3-06
☐ G-BOKX*	Warrior II	ex N39709. CoA 21-9-03	®	3-06
☐ G-BSZG*	Starduster	exN70P. CoA 4-7-00. First noted 8-05		3-06
☐ -*	Airbus A300	cockpit. Stored. First noted 12-03	[1]	3-06
☐ A-806	Pilatus P.3-03	G-BTLL, ex Swiss AF. CoA 23-6-94. Stored		3-06

Locally: The Vampire will be restored and mated with wings, tail etc and returned to the museum for display.

☐ WZ450	Vampire T.11	ex LAWM, North Weald, B'ham, Sealand, Wrexham, W'ford, Chester, Shawbury, RAFC, 233 OCU, 202 AFS. Pod	®	9-03

LYDD AIRPORT
Aztec 250B G-ASER moved to Ringwood, Hants, by August 2005.

☐ G-AZLJ	Trislander	ex Coventry, Highland, G-OREG, SX-CBN, G-OREG, G-OAVW, G-AZLJ, G-51-319. CoA 2-2-00. Spares	8-05
☐ G-PIXS*	Cessna 336	ex N86648. CoA 29-1-95. F/n 8-05	8-05

MANSTON AIRPORT
Hurricane and Spitfire Memorial Museum: The superb Hurricane and Spitfire dominate the exhibition – both examples of the workmanship of Medway APS, Rochester. 'BN230' is a composite, with parts from Mk.II Z3687 and Mk.IIc PG593 [1]. There is a wealth of other material to see and the superb 'Merlin Cafeteria' to sample.

◆ *Open daily, summer 10am to 5pm, winter 10am to 4pm.. Closed 25th-27th Dec and 1st Jan. Signed off the A253 Ramsgate road. The Airfield, Manston Road, Ramsgate, Kent, CT12 5DF tel / fax 08143 821940 e-mail spitfire752@btconnect.com www.spitfire.memorial.museum*

☐ 'BN230'	Hurricane II	LF751, ex Rochester, Bentley Priory, Waterbeach		
	'FT-A'		5466M, 27 OTU, 1681 BDTF. 43 Sqn colours	[1] 4-06
☐ TB752	Spitfire XVI	8086M, ex Rochester, Manston 7256M / 7279M, Lyneham,		
	'KH-Z'		5 CAACU, 103, 102 FRSs, 403, 66. *Val* (port). 403 Sqn c/s	4-06

RAF Manston History Museum: In the old MT building, the museum is run by the RAF Manston History Society and concentrates on the 90-year history of Manston, both military and civil. The acquisition of the Flyboys film statics is a major coup as they come with many of the other 'props' as well allowing great scope for diorama building. The build state on some of these machines is exceptional.

The anonymous Auster V frame left for "the Continent" by August 2004. The nose of Valiant BK.1 XD857 moved to Flixton, Suffolk, on 18th October 2005.

◆ *Daily Mar to Oct 10am to 4pm. Nov to Mar Sat and Sun 10am to 4pm. Manston Road, Manston, Ramsgate, CT12 5DF tel 01843 825224 e-mail info@rafmanson.co.uk www.rafmanston.co.uk*

❑	G-SSWP*	Short 330-100	ex Southend, CS-DBY, 5N-OJU ntu, G-BGNB, N330VM, G-BGNB, G-14-3030. Cockpit, arrived 8-04	4-06
❑	–	Huntair Pathfinder	ex Indonesia	4-06
❑	'Bx619'*	Sopwith 1½ Strutter	ex Halton, *Flyboys*. Arrived by 8-05	4-06
❑	'VM791'	Cadet TX.3	XA312/8876M. Ex Kenley	4-06
❑	'WD615'	Meteor TT.20	WD646, ex North Weald, Birmingham, Cosford 8189M, 5 CAACU, 3/4 CAACU, AWA, CSE. 85 Sqn, NF.11 c/s	4-06
❑	WP772	Chipmunk T.10	ex Lyneham, Colerne, Abingdon, St Athan, Middle Wallop, BFWF, QUAS, Hull UAS, 17 RFS	® 4-06
❑	WT205	Canberra B.15	ex Eastwood, Foulness, MoA, 9. Nose. 9 Sqn c/s	4-06
❑	XA231	Grasshopper TX.1	ex Stockport, 'Sealand', Cosford 8888M, Warwick, Kimbolton, Petersfield	4-06
❑	XG226	Hunter F.6A	ex Faversham, Manston, Faygate, Catterick 8800M, 1 TWU, TWU, 229 OCU, 92, 66, 92. Nose	4-06
❑	XJ727	'L' Whirlwind HAR.10	ex Dishforth, Halton 8661M, 2 FTS, CFS, 1310 Flt, 228, 22	® 4-06
❑	XL190	Victor K.2	9216M, ex St Mawgan, 55, 232 OCU, Witt Wing, 139. Nose	4-06
❑	XN380	'67' Whirlwind HAS.7	ex Lashenden, Wroughton, 705, 771, 829, 824, 825. SAR c/s. *Doris*. For the 'gate'	® 4-06
❑	XS482	'A-D' Wessex HU.5	ex DSFCTE, Farnborough, AAEE	4-06
❑	XV352	Buccaneer S.2B	ex Gravesend, Manston, Stock, St Athan, Lossiemouth, 237 OCU, 208. Nose	4-06
❑	-*	Nieuport 17	ex Halton, *Flyboys*. Arrived by 8-05	4-06
❑	-*	Nieuport 17	ex Halton, *Flyboys*. Arrived by 8-05	4-06
❑	-*	Fokker Dr.I	ex Halton, *Flyboys*. Arrived by 8-05	4-06
❑	-*	Gotha G.IV	ex Halton, *Flyboys*. Forward fuselage. Arrived by 8-05	4-06

Defence Fire Services Central Training Establishment (DFSCTE): Operates as an RAF Enclave, 'parented' by Odiham. By November 2005 Harrier GR.3 XW922 was in the training area on its back, but minus its cockpit. As such, it has been deleted. The hulk of F-4J(UK) ZE353 was scrapped by 2002.

❑	WK124	'CR' Canberra TT.18	9093M, ex Wyton, 100, 7, 213, 59, 103.	8-05
❑	XR503	Wessex HC.2	ex Boscombe Down, Gosport A2705 [2], RAE, AAEE, MoA. Tail of XT463.	7-05
❑	XS714	'P' Dominie T.1	9246M, ex Finningley, 6 FTS, RAFC, CAW.	11-05
❑	XV411	'L' Phantom FGR.2	9103M, ex 56, 92, 19, 92, 14. Poor state	11-05
❑	XV864	Buccaneer S.2B	9234M, ex 12, 237 OCU, 16.	8-05
❑	XW870	'F' Gazelle HT.3	ex Shawbury, 2 FTS, CFS.	8-05
❑	XX116*	Jaguar GR.3A	ex St Athan, 16, 226 OCU, 6, 226 OCU, JOCU. Arr 26-9-05	9-05
❑	XX655	'V' Bulldog T.1	ex Colerne, Bri UAS, 2 FTS. Poor state.	7-05
❑	XZ966	'G' Harrier GR.3	9221M, ex Cottesmore, St Athan, 1417 Flt, 4, 1417 Flt, 233 OCU, 1, 1417, 1.	7-05
❑	ZE360	'O' F-4J(UK)	9059M, ex 74, USN 155529.	11-05

Airport:

❑	G-BXVZ	Iskra TS-11	ex Shoreham, SP-DOF	® 8-05
❑	LX-TLB*	DC-8-62	ex Cargo Lion, N922BV, CX-BQN, C-GMXR, N922CL, HB-IDG. Stored, engineless. Arrived 22-9-01	8-05
❑	N218BA*	Boeing 747-245F	ex G-GAFX, N702SW, N812FT, N632FE, N641FE, VP-BXP, N641FE. Arrived by 6-02. Stored	8-05
❑	N812TC	DC-8-55F	ex ST-AJD, N907R, JA8016. Stored	5-04
❑	TF-ABW	Boeing 747-128	ex Iberia, C-GCIS, TF-ABW, F-BPVF. Cockpit	6-03

ROCHESTER AERODROME on the A229 south of Rochester

Medway Aircraft Preservation Society Ltd (MAPS): Harvard IIB G-CTKL made its post-restoration first flight on 30th August 2005 as 'FE788' - another flying triumph for MAPS! Restoration of the cockpit of C-47A N9050T was completed and it moved to <u>Hendon</u>, Gtr Lon, on 19th January 2006. Coming the other was the Fairey Battle for a detailed restoration. The original restoration of this aircraft including elements of P2183 [1].

◆ *The workshop is open to the public on Sun, Mon and Wed 9am to 1pm. Airport rules must be observed – the threshold of Runway 34 needs negotiating via traffic lights.c/o AFIS Unit, Rochester Airport, Maidstone Road, Chatham, ME5 9SD tel / fax 01634 204492*

❑ G-36-1		SB.4 Sherpa	ex Duxford, Staverton, Bristol, Cranfield, G-14-1. Fuselage, stored	2-06
❑ L5343*	'VO-S'	Fairey Battle I	ex Hendon, St Athan, Cardington, Leeming, Iceland, 98, 266. Cr 13-9-40. 98 Sqn c/s. Arr 1-06	® [1] 4-06

BAE Systems: The former Saudi Lightning is displayed at the facility, near the threshold of 20. It made its debut on 20th June 2004. The *Hind-D* moved to <u>Coventry</u>, Warks, on 15th September 2005.

❑ ZF581		Lightning F.53	ex Portsmouth, Wing Commander, Portsmouth, Warton, RSAF 206, 53-675, G-27-45. 56 Sqn c/s	1-06

Others:

❑ WZ589	'19'	Vampire T.11	ex Lashenden, Woodford, Chester, St Athan, 56	9-02
❑ XE956*		Vampire T.11	G-OBLN, ex Pen-Coed, Bridgend, St Albans, Hatfield, CATCS, 1 FTS, 8 FTS, 3 CAACU, APS, 67. Arr 14-5-04	5-04

SEVENOAKS

The reference is long-in-the-tooth, but the Auster is still *believed* to be in the area.

❑ G-APJZ	J/1N Alpha	ex St Albans, 5N-ACY, VR-NDR ntu, G-APJZ. Cr 10-11-75	® 12-97

SHOREHAM west of the A225 north of Sevenoaks

Shoreham Aircraft Museum (SAM): A superb museum based upon SAM's extensive number of 'digs', all beautifully researched and presented. Included in the incredible selection of artefacts, is the rear fuselage skin from Bf 109 *Black 6*. Also on show are some of the paintings of SAM's leading light, Geoff Nutkins. The cockpit of Spitfire XVI TB885 is *not* available for inspection. If further temptation were needed, Geoff wants it pointed out that although this is 'little' Shoreham and no runway, it has *other* virtues – four pubs!

◆ *Open May to Sep Sun only 10am to 5pm, or by prior arrangement. High Street, Shoreham Village, Sevenoaks, Kent, TN14 7TB tel 01959 524416 www.shoreham-aircraft-museum.co.uk*

❑ TB885	Spitfire XVI	ex Kenley, *Reach for the Sky* as 'R1247', Cosford	off-site 3-06

LANCASHIRE

ACCRINGTON on the A679 east of Blackburn

Dean Nandy: Took delivery of Queen Air B80 G-KEAB from Bruntingthorpe, Leics, on 14th June 2004 to convert it into a simulator. He moved to Cyprus in July 2005 and had every intention of taking it with him.

BACUP on the A671 north of Rochdale

Neil Dykes: With no reports on these machines, they are likely turning finals for LOST!

❑ –	BAPC.192	Weedhopper	ex Hooton Park, Warmingham	4-96
❑ –	BAPC.193	Whing Ding	ex Hooton Park, Warmingham	4-96
❑ –		Flexiform h-glider	ex local area	4-96

BLACKPOOL

RavenCockpits: A company, part of Desert Daffodil Ltd, has been established in the area converting cockpits to become computer-driven flight simulators. The 'JP' cockpit has been converted to a single seater - with side consoles - and is their 'demonstrator'. This style of 'sim' is called the 'Raven Privateer'. During 2005 they acquired the nose of a Strikemaster from Warton, Lancs. This is from an unflown BAC.167 and was previously joined to a composite centre section and rear fuselage – see Warton in *W&R19* for more details [1]. They are also developing simulators based on MiG-21 cockpits available 'from the Continent'.

◆ *01253 593042 e-mail sales@ravencockpits.co.uk www.ravencockpits.co.uk*

❑ XN634*	'53' Jet Provost T.3	ex Ipswich, Scampton, 1 FTS, 7 FTS, RAFC, 6 FTS. Cockpit-sim. Arrived by 6-05		2-06
❑ –*	Strikemaster	ex Warton	[1]	2-06

BLACKPOOL AIRPORT (SQUIRES GATE)

Airport: Vulcan XL391 was put up for auction on an the eBay internet site in late 2004 and was snapped up by publican Chris Ollerenshaw of Dukinfield, Gtr Man, for just over £15,000. He intended to move it to his pub, 'The Snipe', and re-erect it as an attraction, but this ambitious plan fell through. The pub gained a Sea Harrier instead – qv. The inevitable came about on 12th January 2006 when it took just 90 minutes to scrap the once-mighty delta. Scrappies from Sandbach, Cheshire, did the deed. The nose and the engines were saved and they were put on a web-based 'auction' site in early February and they *may* have travelled to the Liverpool Docks area. At the same time, the hulk of Cessna 310D G-ARCI was also chopped and removed.

Departures: Cessna 310D G-ARCI - see above; Cherokee G-ATOO flying by 9-05; Gazelle HT.3 G-BXTH was flying (from Southend, Essex) by November 2005; Aztec 250F G-SFHR became G-OSJF was flying by 2005; Cessna 150J G-TAIL was flying by 2005.

❑ G-AIBW*	Auster J/1N	CoA 4-5-97. Stored	12-05
❑ G-APRF*	Auster Alpha 5	ex VR-LAF, G-APRF. CoA 14-11-00. Stored	12-05
❑ G-ATMI	HS.748-2A/225	ex Emerald, VP-LIU, G-ATMI, VP-LIU, G-ATMI, VP-LIU, G-ATMI. *Old Ben*. CoA 18-5-00. Dump	1-04
❑ G-AVWE	Cherokee 140	ex Stanley, Biggin Hill. CoA 22-4-82	8-00
❑ G-AWKP	CEA DR.253	Damaged 8-6-98. Fuselage, stored	8-02
❑ G-AWUA	Cessna P.206D	ex Thruxton, N8750Z. Damaged 16-10-87	8-02
❑ G-BCEO	AA-5 Traveler	Crashed 28-4-02. Wreck	1-04
❑ G-BEJD*	HS.748-1/105	ex Emerald, LV-HHE, LV-PUF. Arrived 13-3-05	3-05
❑ G-BJZX	Grob G-109	ex D-KGRO ntu. Crashed 15-5-98. Stored	10-00
❑ G-BMIY	Great Lakes	ex G-NOME. CoA 27-8-87. Stored	8-02
❑ G-BMJG	Arrow 200	ex ZS-TNS, ZS-FYC, N9345N. Cr 11-10-98. Fuselage	8-02
❑ G-BSPF	T.303 Crusader	ex OY-SVH, N3116C. Wreck	8-02
❑ G-BTEF	Pitts S-1	ex N88PR. CoA 6-6-92. Wreck	8-02
❑ G-LYDD	Navajo 300	ex Lydd, G-BBDU, N6796L. Dam 17-7-91. Dump.	1-04
❑ G-PLAH	Jetstream 31	ex Platinum Air, G-LOVA, G-OAKA, G-BUFM, G-LAKH, G-BUFM, N410MX, G-31-640.CoA 26-7-02. Stored	1-04
❑ ZS-ODJ	HS.748-2A	ex South Africa, F-GHKA, G-BPNJ, 9J-ABW, G-11-4. Stored	7-05
❑ –	ATP	ex Chadderton. c/n 2073. Dump	8-05

BURNLEY on the M65, north-east of Blackburn

The Albemarle Project: Dave Stansfield continues to collect parts for the long-term project. During 2005, Dave found a large section of rear fuselage floor, with sections of the paratroop door in place. Dave has the long-term aim of creating a fitted out cockpit. Also here is the 'tilting' nose of the CG-4A Hadrian at Elvington, N Yorks (qv), the latter wearing a mock-up nose section.

◆ Not *available for public inspection. Enquiries: 54 Hillcrest Avenue, Cliviger, Burnley, BB10 4JA.*

❑ –	Albemarle	ex Bacup, Carlisle, Westnewton. Nose section etc	2-06

CAPENWRAY on the A6 north of Carnforth

Capenwray Diving Centre: While the dates on these airframes may be quite dated, it seems unlikely that they've moved from the depths!

❏	G-BFWL*	Cessna F.150L	ex Barton, Caernarfon, PH-KDC. Crashed 18-12-99	1-02
❏	WP503	'901' Dragonfly HR.3	ex Malton, Storwood, Cleethorpes, Elsham Hall, Stansted,	
			RAE, North Coates, Lee-on-Solent, Lossiemouth SF	4-96
❏	XS491*	'XM' Wessex HU.5	ex Firbeck, Stafford, Wroughton, 845. Arrived 2-00	2-00

CHARNOCK RICHARD on the A49, south-west of Chorley
The Albemarle Project is now listed under Burnley, Lancs.

CHORLEY on the A6 south of Preston
Botany Bay Village: A visit in November found the former mill bereft of airframes, all reported sold off "around Easter time". To clear up the listing: JetRanger G-OBAY (last noted September 2002); Pegasus Q microlight (January 1999); SE.5A scale REP 'A4850' (August 1999).

International Fire Training Centre: At Washington Hall.
❏	–	c/n 2070 ATP	ex Chadderton. Dump.	10-05
❏	XN298	'10' Whirlwind HAR.9	ex Warmingham, Stoke, Bournemouth, Yeovilton, Wroughton,	
			Lee SAR Flt, Fleetlands, Lee, 846, 848	10-05

Others: An Auster is under restoration in the general area.
| ❏ | G-AKSZ | Auster 5C | ex F-BGPQ, G-AKSZ, TJ457, 2 GCF, 666.CoA 9-5-02 | ® | 12-03 |

COCKERHAM on the A588 between Lancaster and Fleetwood
| ❏ | G-ARZE | Cessna 172C | ex Blackpool. Damaged 11-9-76. Para-trainer | 8-01 |
| ❏ | G-MWWE | Team Minimax | CoA 23-7-97. Stored | 7-99 |

ECCLESTON on the B5250 south of Leyland
Bygone Times Antique Warehouse: Noralpha 'F-OTAN-6' (G-BAYV) was not to be seen here in July 2004 and has been moved to LOST!

Delph Scuba Diving Centre: Located to the south of the town, the centre took delivery of a 'JP' in August 2005 and sunk it into the reservoir. (www.thedelph.com)
| ❏ | XP688* | 'E' Jet Provost T.4 | ex Bolton, Chorley, Bruntingthorpe, Halton 9031M, | |
| | | | Shawbury, CATCS, CAW, RAFC. Arrived 8-05 | 2-06 |

LUMB on the B6238 north west of Bacup
Paul Spann: Canberra B.2 nose WD954 was up for sale in August 2004; it moved to St Mawgan, Cornwall.
◆ *Viewing by prior arrangement* only.
| ❏ | XM369* | 'C' Jet Provost T.3 | ex Portsmouth, East Wretham, Halton 8084M, Shawbury, 2 FTS | 2-06 |

LYTHAM ST ANNE'S south of Blackpool.
Donald Campbell Exhibition:
| ❏ | XM708 | Gnat T.1 | ex Bruntingthorpe, Kings Langley, Locking, | |
| | | | Halton 8573M, 4 FTS, CFS, HS | 11-02 |

PRESTON
Marsh Lane Technical School: The composite Harrier has been joined by a Tornado. The Harrier has the nose section of XV281, the centre fuselage of XW272 and the rear of a P.1127 test-rig [1].
❏	XV281	Harrier GR.1	ex Samlesbury, Dunsfold, Boscombe Down,	
			AAEE, BSE, Dunsfold	[1] 4-02
❏	ZA328*	Tornado GR.1	ex BAE. Arrived 19-2-05	2-05

Others: Mike Davey's and Graham Sparkes' Phantom is held in store in this general area.

❑ ZE352	'G' F-4J(UK)	ex Hooton Park area, Stock, Foulness, Pendine,	
		Laarbruch 9086M, 74, USN 153783. Nose, stored	8-03

SAMLESBURY AIRFIELD on the A59 east of Preston

BAE Systems: Canberra B.92 WH914 has been removed to LOST! - long since suspected of being scrapped.

❑ WT537	Canberra PR.7	ex 13, 31, 17. Displayed	3-06
❑ ZF580	Lightning F.53	ex RSAF 53-672, G-27-42. Displayed	3-06

THORNTON-CLEVELEYS north of the A585, north of Blackpool

The 'Chippie' is *believed* to continue its restoration.

❑ WP839	Chipmunk T.10	G-BZXE, ex Newton, 8 AEF, 2 FTS, PFTS, Liv UAS,		
		St A UAS, CUAS, 231 OCU, Birm UAS, 10 AFTS	®	4-97

WARTON AIRFIELD on the A584 west of Preston

BAE Systems North West Heritage Group (NWHG): The group have three airframes on site. Please note that inspection is *not* possible without prior permission. The former Saudi T.55 nose is a mobile exhibit [1]. NWHG also own the Tornado cockpit section at Haverigg, Cumbria and GR.1 ZA354 at Elvington, N Yorks - qv.

◆ *General enquires: 3 Kingsway Avenue, Broughton, near Preston, PR3 5JN .*

❑ XS928	'AD' Lightning F.6	ex BAe, Binbrook, 5-11, 56, 11, 56, 74, 5, 11. 5 Sqn c/s		3-06
❑ XW363	'36' Jet Provost T.5A	ex Samlesbury, Preston, Warton, RAFC, 6 FTS, 1 FTS		2-06
❑ [ZF596]	Lightning T.55	ex Portsmouth, Stretton, Warton, RSAF 233, 55-715,		
		G-27-71. Nose		2-06

BAE Systems: A Tornado serves with the Overseas Customer Training Unit (OCTU) as an instructional airframe, likewise Hawk 200 with the Apprentices School. Blackburn B-2 G-AEBJ flew off to the land of its fathers (Brough, E Yorks) by June 2004. The fuselage of Nimrod AEW.3 XV263 (and a set of wings, from Woodford, Gtr Man) moved to Brough, E Yorks, arriving 20th October 2005 for MRA.4 static tests. The fuselage of Comet 4 c/n 06402, last noted in April 1997, being used for Nimrod development work, can be deleted as long since scrapped. The composite Strikemaster nose on the dump, moved to Blackpool, Lancs, the centre section probably having been scrapped.

❑ ZA359	'B-55' Tornado GR.1	ex TTTE	OCTU	9-01
❑ ZH200	Hawk 200	ex BAe. Apprentice School		10-02

No.967 Squadron Air Cadets: On the Bank Lane site.

❑ WT520	Canberra PR.7	ex Lytham St Annes, Eaglescott, Burntwood, Swinderby,	
		8184M, 8094M, CAW, 31, 17, 1, 17, 31, 80. Nose	3-06

LEICESTERSHIRE and RUTLAND

☛ Within the administrative county boundaries of Leicestershire is the unitary authority - and far from a county - of the People's Republic of Rutland!

BRUNTINGTHORPE AERODROME between the M1 and the A50 south of Leicester

☛ The Bruntingthorpe site is large and aircraft are listed below under their nominal 'keepers'. It is possible to find aircraft 'owned' by one heading parked in an area 'operated' by another. Please note also that admission on the regular Sunday openings need not necessarily provide access to *all* areas.

Cold War Jets Collection / C Walton (Aviation Division) Ltd: With the signing over of the Vulcan to the Vulcan to the Sky Trust XH558 is now listed separately - see below.
Notes: The Boeing 747 is intended to become a conference centre [1]. The Vulcan nose is owned by Paul Hartley, who also has one at Bournemouth, Dorset, and Wellesbourne Mountford, Warks! [2] The Jaguar is on loan from a US owner. It may eventually travel to Florida [3].
◆ *Open every Sunday 10am to 4pm. Other times by prior arrangement – tel Caroline Richmond 0116 2478030. Please note that there are no catering facilities on the airfield. 'Rolling Thunder' days staged when several aircraft are fired up and taxied, in association with other airfield operators. Details published in the aviation press. Bruntingthorpe Airfield, Lutterworth, LE17 5QS. Tel 0116 2478030 fax 0116 2478031 www.tvoc.co.uk www.coldwarjets.co.uk*

❑ G-CPDA		Comet 4C	ex XS235, Boscombe Down, DTEO, AAEE, BLEU.	
			Canopus. Taxiable	4-06
❑ F-BTGV	'1'	Super Guppy 201	ex Airbus Skylink, N211AS	4-06
❑ SX-OAD		Boeing 747-212B	ex Olympic, 9V-SQH. *Olympic Flame.*	[1] 4-06
❑ XH563		Vulcan B.2MRR	ex Banchory, Rotherham, Scampton 8744M, 27, 230 OCU,	
			MoA, 230 OCU, Wadd W, 230 OCU, 12, 83. Nose	[2] 4-06
❑ XM715		Victor K.2	ex 55, 232 OCU, 543, 232 OCU, 100, 139.	
			Teasin' Tina. Taxiable	4-06
❑ XX900		Buccaneer S.2B	ex St Athan, 208, 12, 208, 216, 12, 208. Taxiable	4-06
❑ XZ382		Jaguar GR.1	8908M, ex Coltishall, Halton, Shawbury,	
			14, 17. Jaguar racing green by 3-06. 'Gate'	[3] 4-06
❑ 85	'8-MV'	Mystère IVA	ex East Midlands, Sculthorpe, Fr AF	4-06
❑ 1018		Iskra 100	G-ISKA, ex Polish AF. Taxiable	4-06

Vulcan to the Sky Trust (VTST): The Vulcan to the Sky team was granted their £2,738,000 from the Heritage Lottery Fund in late July 2004 having passed the final hurdle of their Stage One Pass. Work with the team then frantically returned to the matter of the partnership (or 'matching') funding so that the project could receive the 'go' in 2005.Another major milestone in getting XH558 back into the air was achieved on 3rd March 2005 when the Vulcan was signed over from C Walton (Aviation Division) Ltd for a nominal sum. This meant that the Heritage Lottery Funding could 'kick-in' and the process of restoration could begin. To that end, VTST and Marshall Aerospace signed a contract in early May 2005, marking the start of the engineering phase proper.
By the end of 2005, Marshall Aerospace had established a workforce of 20 on site with others involved back at Cambridge Airport. Working parties from several original equipment manufacturers (OEMs) had also established enclaves within the 'Butler' hangar. The CAA cleared the entire operation to A8-20 status and the hangar became a blaze of light as the long-hoped-for work to put the big bird back together started. Flight testing in the second half of 2006 is confidently anticipated. Towards this end, the nose of XM602 has arrived to act as a crew familiarisation trainer, ready for the big day! It is on loan from the Avro Heritage Centre [1].
Supporting XH558 in many important ways is the **Vulcan to the Sky Club** (renamed from the Vulcan 558 Club on 2nd May 2004) which also unites lovers of Vulcans everywhere. They publish a superb journal, *The Vulcan*, and stage meetings and events. Contact: Vulcan to the Sky Club, Denis Parker, 79 Attfield Drive, Whetstone, Leics LE8 6ND info hotline: 07947 702712 www.vulcan558club.com
The summer of 2006 should see the opening of a viewing gallery and visitor centre so that the public can monitor progress on XH558 – we must get used to calling her *Charlie-November!* There are still plenty of ways that readers can help fund-raise for this gargantuan project.
◆ *Refer below for details of public admission. Otherwise inspection by prior permission only. PO Box 3240, Wimborne, Dorset, BH21 4YP, tel/fax 01258 841274 freephone 0800 083 2022 e-mail vulcantothesky@aol.com www.tvoc.co.uk*

❑ XH558	Vulcan	G-VLCN, ex Waddington, VDF, Marham, Waddington,	
	B.2(MRR)	50, Wadd Wing, AAEE, Wadd Wing, 27, 230 OCU,	
		27, Wadd Wing, 230 OCU	® 4-06
❑ XM602*	Vulcan B.2	ex Woodford, St Athan 8771M, 101, Wadd Wing, 35,	
		230 OCU, Wadd W, Cott W, 12. Nose. Arr 11-10-05	[1] 4-06

Tread boldy through the photo-spread for more Leicestershire (and Rutland!) on page 129

BEDFORDSHIRE

Viscount 708 F-BGNR
Hatch, November 2004
Tim R Badham

ANEC II G-EBJO, plus DH.88
G-ACSS and 'Flea' G-AEBB
Old Warden, August 2005
Andy Wood

Fauvel AV.36C BGA.2932
Old Warden, September 2005
Alf Jenks

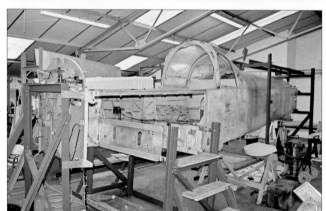

BEDFORDSHIRE

Pup '9917' and Triplane 'N6290'
Old Warden, September 2005
Alf Jenks

Prentice T.1 VS610
Old Warden, August 2005
Andy Wood

BUCKINGHAMSHIRE

Boeing 727-256 EC-DDX
Oakley, January 2006
Ralph Lunt

BUCKINGHAMSHIRE

Robin HR.100s F-GMHH & F-BTKO
Turweston, October 2005
Alf Jenks

CAMBRIDGESHIRE

Cessna F.337F G-AZLO
Bourn, November 2004
Tim R Badham

Phantom FGR.2 XT914
Brampton, April 2005
Francis Wallace

CAMBRIDGESHIRE

Oxford I V3388
Duxford, September 2005
Dave Willis

Mosquito TT.35 TA719
Duxford, February 2005
Col Pope

TSR-2 XR222
Duxford, September 2005
Dave Willis

CAMBRIDGESHIRE

MiG-15 (S-102) 3794
Duxford, October 2004
Col Pope

Bf 109E-3 1190
Duxford, September 2005
Dave Willis

Yale G-BYNF
Duxford, August 2004
Col Pope

CAMBRIDGESHIRE

Firefly TT.1 SE-BRG
Duxford, February 2004
Tim R Badham

Beaver AL.1 XP772
Duxford, December 2005
Col Pope

Hawk 75 No.82
Duxford, July 2005
Phil Whalley

CAMBRIDGESHIRE

Polikarpov I-15 REP '19'
Duxford, September 2005
Dave Willis

Hind I L7181
Duxford, January 2005
Tim R Badham

Hurricane XII 'Z5140'
Duxford, October 2005
Don Nind

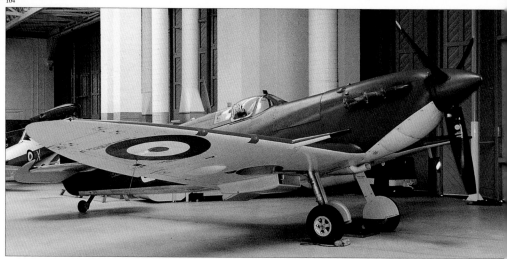

CAMBRIDGESHIRE

Spitfire V BM597
Duxford, October 2005
Don Nind

Spitfire IX 'UB424' and
Spitfire V JG891
Duxford, November 2005
Col Pope

Meteor T.7(mod) WF877
Duxford, October 2004
Col Pope

CAMBRIDGESHIRE

Hunter F.2 WN904
Waterbeach, October 2005
Don Nind

Harrier GR.1 XV279
Wittering, February 2006
Jarrod Cotter

CORNWALL

Hunter GA.11 XE668
Predannack, June 2005
Dave Arkle

CORNWALL

Wessex HU.5 XT762
Predannack, June 2005
Dave Arkle

Harrier GR.3 XZ969
Predannack, June 2005
Dave Arkle

Sea Harrier FA.2 ZD581
Predannack, June 2005
Dave Arkle

DEVON
Excalibur G-BDDX
Newton Abbot, March 2005
Alan G L Barclay

DORSET
Leopard G-BKRL
Bournemouth, December 2005
Peter Budden

Venom FB.50 'WR421'
Bournemouth, December 2004
Ian Haskell

DORSET

Boeing 747-236B G-BDXG
Bournemouth, February 2006
Peter Budden

ESSEX

Mystère IVA 319
Andrewsfield, February 2005
Steve Screech

Hornet REP
Chelmsford, December 2005
David Collins

ESSEX

Scout AH.1 G-BZBD
North Weald, June 2005
Mike Cain

AA-5A Cheetah 'G-PRAT'
North Weald, June 2004
Mike Cain

Lightning F.1 XG325
Rayleigh (here at Southend with
Vulcan B.2 XL426), May 2005
Mike Cain

ESSEX

Cherokee 180 G-AVNP
Southend, October 2005
John D Coleman

BAC 111-401AK 5N-HHH
Southend, October 2005
John D Coleman

BAe 146-100 B-634L
Southend, January 2006
John D Coleman

ESSEX

Boeing 707-138B HZ-123
Southend, December 2005
Phil Whalley

Bandeirante G-OHIG
Stock, December 2005
Mark A Jones

Viscount 802 G-AOHL and
Andover CC.2 XS791
Stock, December 2005
Mark A Jones

112

GLOUCESTERSHIRE

Concorde 102 G-BOAF
Filton, September 2004
Tony McCarthy

Britannia C.1 XM496
Kemble, July 2005
Andrew Powell

Hunter T.7 XL586
Kemble, July 2005
Andy Wood

GLOUCESTERSHIRE

Gnat T.1 XP502
Kemble, July 2005
Andrew Powell

Terrier 2 G-ASOI
Kemble, July 2005
Peter Budden

Boeing 757-2M6 V8-RBA
Kemble, February 2006
Andrew Powell

GLOUCESTERSHIRE

Bandeirante SX-BNL
Kemble, January 2006
Tony McCarthy

Devon C.2 XA880
Kemble, July 2005
Andrew Powell

Cessna 172K G-AZDZ
Moreton-in-Marsh, April 2005
Alf Jenks

GLOUCESTERSHIRE
Viscount 814 G-BAPF
Moreton-in-Marsh, April 2005
Alf Jenks

Cessna 320E G-BKRD
Moreton-in-Marsh, April 2005
Alf Jenks

HAMPSHIRE

BAC-111-510 G-AVMZ (left, nose
to right), BAC-111-501 G-AWYV
Alton, April 2005
Ian Haskell

HAMPSHIRE

Jetstream 31 G-BYYI
Alton, April 2005
Ian Haskell

Clockwise:
Hunter T.7 WV383, Gnat T.1 XP516,
Trident 3B G-AWZI, Buccaneer S.2B
XV165, Canberra B(I).6 WT309,
Lightning F.6 XS932
Farnborough, August 2004
Kevin Bowen

MiG-21PF 503
Farnborough, August 2004
Kevin Bowen

HAMPSHIRE

Wessex HU.5 XT761
Gosport, November 2005
David Symington

Sea King HAS.6 ZA127
Gosport, November 2005
David Symington

PBY-5A Catalina VR-BPS
Lee-on-Solent, May 2005
Anthony Mills

118

HAMPSHIRE

Antonov An-2 HA-MKE
Popham, May 2005
Tim R Badham

Gnat T.1 XP542
Southampton, February 2005
Ian Haskell

GM.1 Wicko G-AFJB
Formerly Southampton (here at
Popham), September 2005
Peter Budden

HERTFORDSHIRE

Moth Minor G-AFOJ
London Colney, April 2005
Roger Richards

Otter VP-FAK
London Colney, May 2005
Tim R Badham

Pilcher Hawk REP BAPC.57
St Albans, October 2004
Eric Littledike

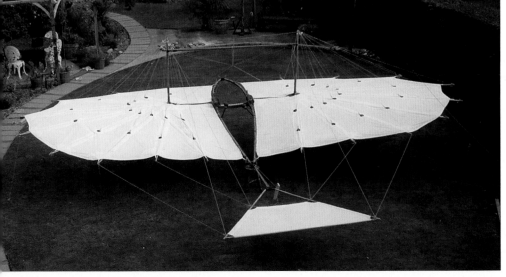

ISLE OF WIGHT

Fieldmaster G-NRDC
Sandown, March 2005
Sam Tyler

KENT

Spitfire FSM 'R6775' and
Hurricane FSM 'P2970'
Capel-le-Ferne, September 2005
Mike Cain

Hurricane II 'BN230'
Manston, September 2004
Roger Richards

KENT

Short 330-100 G-SSWP
Manston, March 2005
Ian Haskell

Chipmunk T.10 WP772
Manston, September 2004
Roger Richards

Dominie T.1 XS714
Manston, November 2005
Francis Wallace

KENT

Phantom FGR.2 XV411
Manston, November 2005
Francis Wallace

Lightning F.53 ZF581
Rochester, September 2004
Roger Richards

LANCASHIRE

Vulcan B.2 XL391
Blackpool, January 2006
Philip Sudron

LEICESTERSHIRE

Comet 4C G-CPDA
Bruntingthorpe, August 2005
Phil Whalley

T-6G Texan 114700
Bruntingthorpe, July 2005
Hugh Trevor

Lightning F.6 XS904
Bruntingthorpe, June 2004
Hugh Trevor

LEICESTERSHIRE

Cessna 150E G-ATAT
Bruntingthorpe, January 2006
Geoffrey Pool

Canberra B.2/6 XH568
Bruntingthorpe, January 2006
Geoffrey Pool

Chipmunk 22 G-BDCC
Husbands Bosworth, July 2005
Alf Jenks

LEICESTERSHIRE

Viscount 807 G-CSZB and
Merchantman G-APES
Nottingham East Midlands Airport,
November 2005
Andrew Powell

Wessex HC.2 XT604, HU.5 XT480
and HAS.1 XS876
Nottingham East Midlands Airport,
November 2005
Andrew Powell

LINCOLNSHIRE

Spitfire XVI TE311
Coningsby, June 2005
Alf Jenks

LINCOLNSHIRE

Sukhoi Su-22M 98+14 and
Buccaneer S.2B XX885
Scampton, October 2005
Hugh Trevor

Vulcan B.2 XM607
Waddington, June 2005
Roger Cook

Phantom FGR.2 XV497
Waddington, June 2005
Roger Cook

GREATER LONDON

Hunter F.1 WT555 and
Lightning F.3 XP745
Greenford, November 2005
Anthony Mills

Auster I LB264
Hendon, December 2004
Dave Willis

'Milestones of Flight' Hall
Hendon, November 2004
Dave Willis

GREATER LONDON

Tempest TT.5 NV778
Hendon, July 2004
Roger Richards

Bf 109G-2 10639
Hendon, November 2004
Dave Willis

Messerschmitt Me 262A-2a 112372
Hendon, July 2004
Roger Richards

BRUNTINGTHORPE, continued from page 96...

Beech Restorations and **Tomcat T6 Restorations**: Adrian Marshall (AM), Philip Turland, Ben Brown and friends are restoring G-BKRN. The former French Air Force T-6G restoration has attracted other similar projects under the 'Tomcat' banner. In Algeria, the French knew armed Texans as 'Tomcats' because of their growl – hence the registration. Harvard IV G-HRVD is being worked on for Dale Featherby (DF) who also owns the 'vintage' Cessna. Harvard II G-CCOY is owned by Phil Earthy – Classic Aero Services [1] Adrian Marshall's Auster 'collection' is now all on site (AM).

◆ *Exhibited at open days, otherwise by prior arrangement only. 14 Hallam Close, Moulton, Northampton, NN3 7LB tel 01604 790901 fax 01604 492946 e-mail philipstudfast@btconnect.com www.beechrestorations.com*

❑ G-AJPZ	J/1 Autocrat	ex Stoke, Sopley, Bournemouth, Wimborne, New Milton, Thruxton, F-BFPE, G-AJPZ. Dam 2-3-84. Frame	AM	2-06
❑ G-ASYN*	Terrier 2	ex Derby, Southend, Sibson, Auster AOP.6 VF519, 661. Damaged 2-1-76. Frame	AM	2-06
❑ [G-ATAT]*	Cessna 150E	ex Norwich, Hull, Shobdon, Billericay, Andrewsfield, Southend, N3041J. CoA 29-7-85. Stored. Arr 4-05	DF	2-06
❑ G-BKRN	Beech D.18S	ex Cranfield, Perth, Prestwick, CF-DTN, RCAF inst A675, RCAF 1500. CoA 26-6-83. US Navy c/s. *Naval Encounter*		2-06
❑ [G-CCOY]*	Harvard II	ex Norwich area, Swansea, 'Exeter', 'FT323', Cranfield, Bushey, East Ham, Port AF 1513, SAAF 7426, EX884, 41-33857. Arrived 4-05	® [1]	2-06
❑ G-HRVD	Harvard IV	ex Felthorpe, Swanton Morley, Wellesbourne, Thruxton, G-BSBC, Mozambique, Port AF 1741, WGAF BF+055, AA+055, 53-4629	® DF	2-06
❑ 51-14700	T-6G-NT Texan	G-TOMC, ex Stoke-on-Trent, Eccleshall, North Weald, Coventry, *Empire of the Sun*, La Ferté Alais, FAF, USAF, USAAF 42-44514. *Texan Tomcat*	®	4-06
❑ – c/n 1908	Auster AOP.6	ex Derby, Shoreham, Hedge End, Warmingham, East Kirkby, Sibson, Wigan, Handforth. Frame	AM	2-06

Blackburn Buccaneer Society: XX894 is owned by Guy Hulme of the Buccaneer Trust.
◆ *Plan to exhibit at open days, otherwise by prior arrangement only. Nigel J Goodall, 32 The Haven, Inkpen Road, Kintbury, Hungerford, RG17 9TY e-mail buccsociety@fsmail.net www.buccsociety.com*

❑ XX894	'020' Buccaneer S.2B	ex Farnborough, Kemble, Bruntingthorpe, St Athan, 208, 16, 12, 208, 12. 809 Sqn c/s. Taxiable	®	3-06

Buccaneer Restorations: XW544 is owned by Rob Goldstone. (e-mail buccrestorations@blueyonder.co.uk)

❑ XW544*	'Y' Buccaneer S.2C	ex Shawbury, Cosford 8857M, Shawbury, 16, 15. Arr 3-10-04	®	3-06

Lightning Preservation Group (LPG): Work continues on keeping their two machines 'live' and LPG undertakes regular 'running' days. Construction work on the former Binbrook QRA shed is well underway.
◆ *Regular open days, otherwise by prior appointment only. 66 Stoneage Close, Bognor Regis, PO22 9QW e-mail htrevorh@tesco.net www.lightnings.org.uk*

❑ XR728	'JS' Lightning F.6	ex Binbrook, 11, LTF, 5, 56, 23, 11, 23. Taxiable	4-06
❑ XS904	'BQ' Lightning F.6	ex BAe Warton, Binbrook, 5-11 pool. Taxiable	4-06

Phoenix Aviation: Sea Vixen XJ494 was powered up and taxied - for the first time in over 30 years - on 27th March 2004 [1]. *W&R19* (p94) noted Whirlwind HAR.10 XP350 moving out in 2002 to a paintball park in the 'West Bromwich' area. Cosmically speaking, that was not bad. The location was actually Basset's Pole, Staffs.

Departures: Buccaneer S.2B nose XZ431 to Market Drayton, Shrop, 31-5-05; **Hunter** FGA.9 XE624 on 19-1-04 for Leicester, Leics; T.7 XF321 from Exeter, Devon, 28-5-04, cut up, nose to Coltishall, Norfolk 9-05; F.51 'XF324' (E-427) to Kidderminster, Worcs, 19-4-05; Jet Provost T.4 XS217 left 7-05 for Germany; **Queen Air** G-KEAB moved to Accrington, Lancs 14-6-04; Provost T.1 XF844 left on 4-12-04 en route to Japan, having been bought by Kunio Yasue of Osaka; **Sea Hawk** FGA.6 WV795 to Farnborough, Hants, 26-1-05; FGA.6 XE368 to Market Drayton, Shrop, by 3-06; **Sea Vixen** FAW.2 nose XN647 to Steventon, Oxfordshire, 11-04.

❏ [G-AYKA]		Baron 55A	ex Shoreham, Elstree, HB-GEW, G-AYKA, D-IKUN,	
	'AY'		N8683M. Cr 18-6-89.Conv to a car, in 2 Sqn marks!	3-06
❏ G-BAXX*		Cessna F.150L	ex Cambridge, Shobdon, Barnstaple. Dam 21-9-78. Arr 29-6-04	3-06
❏ XH136	'W'	Canberra PR.9	ex Cosford 8782M, 1 PRU, AAEE, 39, 13, 58, MoA. Nose	3-06
❏ XH592	'L'	Victor B.1A	ex Cosford 8429M St Athan, 232 OCU, TTF, 232 OCU,	
			Honington Wing, 15. Nose	3-06
❏ XJ494		Sea Vixen FAW.2	ex Kings Langley, Farnborough, FRL, AAEE, HSA,	
			Sydenham, 899, Sydenham, 892	[1] 3-06
❏ XN582*	'95'	Jet Provost T.3A	ex Cambridge Airport, Cambridge, Cambridge Airport,	
			Cosford 8957M, 7 FTS, 1 FTS, 3 FTS, RAFC. Arr 21-7-05	3-06
❏ XP883*		Scout AH.1	ex Oaksey Park, Boscombe Down, 658, 655, 652. Arr 1-4-04	3-06
❏ XT630	'X'	Scout AH.1	G-BXRL, ex Burbage. Crashed 16-10-99.	3-06
❏ XV328	'BZ'	Lightning T.5	ex Cranfield, Binbrook, LTF, 5, LTF, 5, 29. Nose	3-06
❏ J-4091		Hunter F.58	ex FSt7/FSt9, Swiss AF. Taxiable	3-06

Others: A series of machines are held on the aerodrome by private individuals or organisations: Richard Blood (the wings of XN584 are fitted to T.4 XP627 at Sunderland, N&T) [1]; Geoffrey Pool [2]; Roger Wintle and Arthur Perks; WT333 was built as a B(I).8 but was later fitted with the cockpit from B.2 WK135 [3]; Alan Witt and XS209 thought up for sale in February 2006 [4]. Ken Fern is at work on a Percival Mew Gull repro for a US-based owner and is amassing material for a composite P-47 Thunderbolt - both projects are not sufficient yet for a 'formal' entry.

Departures: Harvard IV G-HRVD is with Tomcat T6 - see above. Harvard II FX322 moved to Doncaster, S Yorks. Canberra B.2/6 XH568 (G-BVIC built as a B.6 and then fitted with the cockpit from B.2 WG788) was dismantled during February 2006. The nose was exported to the USA on 28th March 2006. The rest of the airframe was scrapped, with parts going to help WK163 and WT333. Harrier nose XV810 left 13-3-06, presumed to Wigston, Leics. The anonymous Auster frame was sold and left in May 2005.

❏ WT333		Canberra B(I).8	G-BVXC, ex Farnborough, Bedford, RAE, C(A)	[3] 3-06
❏ XL565		Hunter T.7	ex Kemble, Ipswich, Colsterworth, Shawbury, Lossiemouth,	
			FRADU, 237 OCU, 4 FTS, 208, 8, West Raynham SF, 8,	
			1417 Flt, 8, mkrs	[2] 3-06
❏ XM355	'D'	Jet Provost T.3	ex Shobdon, Cambridge, Bruntingthorpe, Halton	
			8229M, Shawbury, 1 FTS, 7 FTS, CFS. Taxiable	[4] 3-06
❏ XN584	'E'	Jet Provost T.3A	ex Halton 9014M, 1 FTS, CFS, RAFC, CFS, RAFC,	
	and '88'		TWU, RAFC. Taxiable	® [1] 3-06
❏ XS209	'29'	Jet Provost T.4	ex Kemble, Staverton, Halton 8409M, St Athan,	
			Kemble, Shawbury, CAW. '5 MU' tail marking	[4] 3-06

Off-site: At a nearby business park is a workshop specialising in Comanche and 'Twin Com' spares. Twin Comanche 160B G-AWBN was active again by 2005. Twin Comanche N8911Y moved to Romsey, Hants, by August 2005.

❏ G-ARIN	Comanche 250	ex N6084P. Crashed 20-5-90	5-03
❏ G-ARUO	Comanche 180	ex N7251P. Crashed 19-3-00	2-04
❏ G-ASCJ	Comanche 250	ex 5N-AEB, N7197P. Crashed 10-9-86	2-04
❏ G-ASYK	Twin Com' 160	ex N7543Y. Crashed 11-5-96	2-04
❏ G-ATFK	Twin Com' 160	ex Romsey, N7642Y. Crashed 12-6-89	2-04
❏ G-ATWR	Twin Com' 160B	ex N8025Y. Crashed 14-9-93	3-04
❏ G-AVCY	Twin Com' 160B	ex N8241Y. Crashed 9-3-91	2-04
❏ G-AVVI	Twin Com' 160B	ex Shipdham, EI-AVD, G-AVVI, N8241Y. Cr 6-4-91	2-04
❏ G-BAWN	Twin Com' 160C	ex N8790Y. Crashed 31-3-98	8-03

COALVILLE on the A511 north-west of Leicester

Snibston Discovery Park: Within can be found a host of fascinating material on the industrial and transport heritage of the county. Items acknowledging aviation in Leicestershire are the Auster AOP.9 and a sectioned Whittle turbojet. Other airframes are in store and listed under this heading as a 'port of convenience'. They are not available for inspection. See under Winthorpe, Notts, for Auster G-AGOH.

◆ *Daily 10am to 5pm, except Xmas and a week in January for maintenance. Signed off the A511. Ashby Road, Coalville, Leicestershire, LE67 3LN tel 01530 278444 fax 01530 813301 info-line 01530 813256 e-mail snibston@leics.gov.uk*

❏ G-AFTN	Taylorcraft Plus C2	ex Heavitree, HL535, 43 OTU, 652, 651, G-AFTN. CoA 1-11-57	®	5-05
❏ G-AIJK	Auster J/4	ex Leicester, Stratford. CoA 24-8-68. off-site		3-02
❏ VZ728	Desford Trainer	G-AGOS, ex Perth, Strathallan, Thruxton, RAE. CoA 28-11-80. Stored		3-02
❏ XP280	Auster AOP.9	ex Leicester, St Athan, 2 Wing, Queen's Dragoon Guards, 2 RTR, 651. On display		5-05

COTTESMORE AIRFIELD north of the B668, north-east of Oakham

RAF Cottesmore: The Spitfire F.21 is owned by the 1 Squadron Association and kept in a hangar [1]. The Hunter is kept in the 4 Squadron hangar [2]. Both appear outside when needed. Harrier XW917 adorns the 'inner' gate and is painted in joint 3 (port) and 4 (starboard) Squadron colours [3], while XW924 is displayed outside the 3 Squadron hangar (the most westerly) in their markings. With 3 Squadron giving up their Harriers in March 2006 and moving on to Coningsby and the Typhoon, XW924 may follow them [4]. Now that Cottesmore is also a Navy base – they'll have the *Ark* on Rutland Water before too long! – a Sea Harrier will be displayed. Its serial reflects the newly-resident unit! It is briefly on show at Greenwich and is scheduled to arrive in October [5]. This is another base to take on a 'synthetic' fire crash rescue rig. In this case it is of the combined 'Harricopter' sort . By October 2005 the fuselage of AV-8B 162068 was scrapped here. The bulk went to the yard at Clay Cross, Derby, while the nose went to Doncaster, S Yorks.

❏ LA255	Spitfire F.21	6490M, ex Wittering West Raynham, Cardington, Tangmere, 1	[1]	3-06
❏ 'XJ673'	Hunter F.6A	XE606, ex Laarbruch 8841M, 1 TWU, TWU, 229 OCU, 92, 74, 65, 54, CFE. 8737M ntu	[2]	11-05
❏ XW917	Harrier GR.3	8975M, ex Laarbruch, 3, 4, 3. SOC 3-4-88. 'Gate'	[3]	3-06
❏ XW924	Harrier GR.3	9073M, ex Laarbruch, Halton, 3, 4, 1, 233 OCU, 4	[4]	3-06
❏ 'ZH801' '001'	Sea Harrier FA.2	ZH800, ex Greenwich, Yeovilton, 800, 899, 801, 899	[5]	**due**

DISEWORTH on the B5401 south of East Midlands Airport

Joe Goy: The Buccaneer is still resident.

❏ XV337	Buccaneer S.2C	ex Stock, St Athan, Abingdon 8852M, AAEE, 208, AAEE, 809, 800. Nose	12-05

DONINGTON CIRCUIT or Donington Park, near to East Midlands Airport

The Spitfire FSM was damaged and is currently being restored. It will return to its mount on a dramatic 'wishbone' plinth over-looking the Craner Curves.

❏ –	'K-W' Spitfire FSM	–	®	3-06

HINCKLEY south-west of Leicester

Former **Douglas Boston-Havoc UK Preservation Trust**: Dick Nutt writes: "Sadly the time has come to close this chapter of the DBHPT. The efforts of Roy [Bonser] and myself to rescue and preserve Boston and Havoc artefacts over the last 30 years are now at an end. Now the reproduction Boston IIIA will go forward in the hands of a younger, more skilled team with a larger workshop and proper facilities." Artefacts amounting to 50% of a Boston IIA that served last with 418 Squadron RCAF at Bradwell Bay are in long-term store. The main item is a skeleton 'birdcage' nose, a 13ft section of forward fuselage, port inner mainplane, main and nose landing gear, Boston-fit Wright Cyclone and rear fuselage and tailplane parts. Also held are the instrument panels, A-20G Havoc 'attack' nose and Martin gun turret. The project remains in the *general* Hinckley area.

◆ *Please note that visits are* only *possible by prior arrangement.*

❏ Z2186	Boston IIA	ex Bethesda, 418, 85, 605, 23. Cr 17-10-42. Stored		3-06
❏ 43-9628	A-20G-30-DO	ex RAAF Museum, Papua New Guinea, USAAF. Forward fuselage	®	3-06

HUSBANDS BOSWORTH AERODROME south of the A427, south of the village

Immaculate Hutter H-17 EPR (BGA.2847) was flying by July 2005. Hiway Skytrike G-MNGO, last noted in June 1998, had gone by May 2005.

| ☐ G-BDCC | Chipmunk 22 | ex WD321, DH. Crashed 29-8-99. Canx 8-4-04 | 7-05 |
| ☐ XK790 | Grasshopper TX.1 | ex Halton. Stored | 5-05 |

LEICESTER

Steve Petch: Took delivery of a former Bruntingthorpe Hunter in January 2005.

◆ Visits *only* possible by prior arrangement e-mail xe624@aviationphotoarchive.com

| ☐ XE624* | 'G' Hunter FGA.9 | ex Bruntingthorpe, Brawdy, 88775M, 1 TWU, 2 TWU, | |
| | | TWU, 229 OCU, West Raynham SF, 1. Arr 19-1-05 | 12-05 |

Others: As well as an Auster, an Aeronca has been under restoration in the area since 1998 and John Poyser has built a full-size Spitfire IX and keeps it in the city.

☐ G-APTU*	Alpha 5	ex Sywell, Leicester. CoA 8-6-98. Stored	® 12-05
☐ G-BRFI*	7DC Champion	ex Londonderry area, Ballymoney, N1058E,	
		NC1058E. Damaged 1990. Arrived 1998	® 6-04
☐ –	'JE-J' Spitfire FSM	fuselage	1-02

LEICESTER AERODROME or Leicester East, or Stoughton, south-east of Leicester

Rans S-10 G-BSNN was flying again by December 2004.

☐ G-AEXZ	J-2 Cub	CoA 2-11-78	off-site ® 8-92
☐ G-AHLK	Auster III	ex NJ889, 43 OTU. CoA 21-9-97	® 6-01
☐ G-AMTD	J/5F Aiglet Tnr	ex EI-AVL, G-AMTD. Crashed 7-8-93. Frame	9-04
☐ G-ARDJ	Auster D.6/180	crashed 30-5-86. Stored	9-04

LOUGHBOROUGH on the A6 north of Leicester

Charnwood Museum: Within the museum the 1956 King's Cup-winning Auster J/1N 'flies' as a memorial to the wonders worked at nearby Rearsby.

◆ *Mon to Sat 10am to 4.30pm, Sun 1pm to 4pm. Granby Street, Loughborough, LE11 3DU tel 01509 233754, fax 01509 268140 www.leics.gov.uk/index/community/museums /charnwood_museum.htm*

| ☐ G-AJRH | '7' J/1N Alpha | ex Leicester area, Harrogate, Wigan. CoA 5-6-69 | 1-05 |

University: Department of Aeronautical, Automotive Engineering and Transport Studies.

| ☐ ZF534 | BAe EAP | ex Warton | 1-06 |

LUTTERWORTH

Lutterworth Museum: Includes much Sir Frank Whittle and Power Jets material and an incredible archive.

◆ *Open Mon, Thu, Fri and Sat, March to November 10am to 4pm. Wycliffe House, Gilmorton Road, Lutterworth, Leics tel 01455 555585*

Whittle Memorial: Dramatically displayed to the south of the town on the A426 roundabout is a superb tribute to the Gloster E28/39 as a tribute to Sir Frank Whittle. This and the similar monument at Farnborough, Hants (qv) were financed and built by the Sir Frank Whittle Commemorative Trust.

| ☐ – | BAPC.284 Gloster E28/39 FSM | displayed | 3-06 |

MARKET HARBOROUGH on the A6 south-east of Leicester

No.1084 Squadron, Air Cadets: The 'JP' spends a lot of its time at Bruntingthorpe, Leics, but is 'based' here.

| ☐ XS181 | 'F' Jet Provost T.4 | ex North Weald, Bletchley, Desborough, Bruntingthorpe, | |
| | | Halton 9033M, Shawbury, CATCS, RAFC, 3 FTS. Nose. | 2-06 |

MELTON MOWBRAY on the A607 north-east of Leicester

Auster Nine Group: Have workshops in the general area.

❑ G-AYUA	Auster AOP.9	ex Bruntingthorpe, Cranfield, Bushey, Luton, Sibson,	
		XK41<u>6</u>, Middle Wallop, 7855M, 651, 19 MU	12-96
❑ XN412	Auster AOP.9	ex Innsworth, Swindon, Dorchester, Middle Wallop,	
		6 Flt, C(A). Stored	1-01
❑ XR267	Auster AOP.9	G-BJXR, ex Innsworth, Staverton, Congresbury,	
		St Athan, 655, 652	® 12-05
❑ XP282	Auster AOP.9	G-BGTC, ex XP282. Damaged 2-10-96. Stored	7-97

David Hall: Is working on an Auster 4 in the general area.

| ❑ G-AJXY | Auster 4 | ex Ipswich, MT243 | ® 12-05 |

NORTH LUFFENHAM north of the A6121 south-west of Stamford

St George's Barracks: Within is an enclave on the eastern side of the former airfield for the **RAF Explosive Ordnance Disposal** unit, a sub-site from EOD at Wittering, Cambs. The Hunter has had the nose cone removed to render it more MiG-looking, aided considerably by the red stars it carries! It is used by EOD to simulate a fully-armed 'defector' complete with 'strange' weaponry to assess and then disarm [1].

❑ [XG194]	'69' Hunter FGA.9	8839M, ex Cosford, 1 TWU, TWU, 229 OCU,	
		1, 92, 111, 43. Soviet red stars	[1] 4-06
❑ XP344	Whirlwind HAR.10	8764M, ex Cranwell, Finningley, Chivenor, 22,	
	'H723'	SAR Wing, CFS. French roundel, olive drab	9-03
❑ [XT905]	'P' Phantom FGR.2	9286M, ex Coningsby, 74, 228 OCU, 29, 228 OCU, 31, 17	4-06
❑ XV804	'O' Harrier GR.3	9280M, ex Winterbourne Gunner, 4, 3,	
		1, 3, 4, 233 OCU, 1417F, 233 OCU	4-04

NOTTINGHAM EAST MIDLANDS AIRPORT (CASTLE DONINGTON)

Aeropark: During the summer of 2004 a 98ft (30m) Romney Hut was acquired to provide internal display space and to act as a base of operations for the AVA - see below. The hut will also act as a workshop and was due to become operational in March 2006.

Supporting the Aeropark is the **East Midlands Airport Volunteers Association** (AVA) (Graham Vale, 76 Springfield Road, Midway, Derbyshire tel 01283 552397 e-mail graham.vale4@btinternet.com) AVA are now staging regular events, including open cockpit days, an aerojumble and a fund-raising air ambulance day. Details in the aviation press and via the number below.

Notes: The Viscount nose is owned by AVA member Colin Jacobs [1]. The Spitfire FSM is believed to have been built by TDL Replicas and portrayed the Dutch Memorial Flight's Mk.IX PH-OUQ. It was acquired by Kevin Wheatcroft, of Donington circuit fame, and is on loan from him [2]. Varsity WL626 is owned by Graham Vale [3] and Wessex XT604 by Mark Lindsey [4]. The pod of recently-arrived XD534 will be used in a composite restoration of XD382. Following this the pod of XD382 will be restored in its own right [5]. Wessex XS876 and XT480 are on loan from Air and Ground Aviation of Hixon, Staffs [6]. Jet Provost T.3A XN500 arrived from Ipswich, Suffolk, during October 2004, but it moved on to Farnborough, Hants, on 19th April 2005.

◆ *Open Thu (10.30am to 5pm), Sat (noon to 5pm) and Sun (10.30am to 7pm) 1st May to 30th Sep, and Sun 10.30am to 5pm or dusk in winter. Also Bank Hols other than Xmas. 'Open cockpit' and special event days. Tel 0776 7313708 - during opening hours www.aeropark.org*

❑ G-APES	Merchantman	ex Hunting, ABC, BEA. CoA 2-10-95. *Swiftsure*. Nose	3-06
❑ G-BEOZ	Argosy 101	ex ABC, N895U, N6502R, G-1-7. CoA 28-5-86	3-06
❑ G-CSZB	Viscount 807	ex Coleorton, Southend, BWA, N141RA ntu, G-CSZB,	
		VQ-GAB, ZK-NAI, SP-LVC, G-AOXU.	
		Viscount Scotland. Cockpit	[1] 3-06
❑ G-FRJB	SA.1 Sheriff	ex Sandown. Incomplete, unflown. Due on site 4-06	® 3-06
❑ 'PL256'*	Spitfire IX	ex Leicester, Donington, Netherlands, 'H-25' *Baby Bee*,	
	'TM-L'	'MK735'. 504 Sqn colours. First noted 8-05	[2] 3-06
❑ WH740	'K' Canberra T.17	ex Cosford 8762M, 360, RNZAF, Upwood SF, 40, 18.	3-06
❑ WL626	'P' Varsity T.1	G-BHDD, ex Coventry, 6 FTS, 1 ANS, 2 ANS, 201 AFS	[3] 3-06

❑ WM224	'X'	Meteor TT.20	ex North Weald 'WM311', East Dereham, Swanton Morley 8177M, 5 CAACU, 3 CAACU, 3/4 CAACU, AWA, 29, 228 OCU. Arrived on site 8-11-05	®	3-06
❑ XD382		Vampire T.11	ex Ripley, Shawbury, Syerston 8033M, CATCS, CNCS, RAFC, 5 FTS, 206 AFS, 208 AFS	[5]	3-06
❑ XD534	'41'	Vampire T.11	ex Welshpool, Barton, Chelford, Hadfield, Wythenshawe, Cheadle Hulme, Woodford, Chester, Shawbury, 7 FTS, CFS, 9 FTS, 10 FTS. Pod	[5]	3-06
❑ XG588		Whirlwind Srs 3	VR-BEP, ex Cuckfield, G-BAMH, Redhill, XG588, 705, 701, Warrior Flt, Albion Flt. SAR c/s	®	3-06
❑ XL569	'N'	Hunter T.7	ex Abingdon, Cosford 8833M, 2 TWU, 1 TWU, 12, 216, 237 OCU, Laarbruch SF, 15, 237 OCU, 12, MinTech, 2 TWU, 1 TWU, TWU, 229 OCU		3-06
❑ XM575		Vulcan B.2	G-BLMC, ex 44, Wadd Wing, Scampton Wing, 617		3-06
❑ XS876*	'523'	Wessex HAS.1	ex Culdrose, Lee-on-Solent A2626 [3], A2695, Wroughton, 771. Arrived 7-04	[6]	3-06
❑ XT480*	'468'	Wessex HU.5	ex Hixon, Fleetlands, A2603 [2], A2617, Wroughton, 847	[6]	3-06
❑ XT604		Wessex HC.2	ex Hixon, Colsterworth, Fleetlands, 22, 103, 78, Muharraq SAR Flt, 78	[4]	3-06
❑ XV350		Buccaneer S.2B	ex Shawbury, Warton, RAE		3-06
❑ ZF588	'L'	Lightning F.53	ex Warton, RSAF 53-693, G-27-63. 74 Sqn c/s		3-06

Airport:

| ❑ [TC-ALM] | Boeing 727-230 | ex Air Alfa, TC-IKO, TC-JUH, TC-ALB, N878UM, D-ABDI. Fire training | 1-06 |

OAKHAM on the A606 west of Stamford
During December 2005 Globe Swift G-BFNM moved to Spanhoe Lodge, Northants, for completion.

SALTBY AERODROME east of the A607 and of the village, north-east of Melton Mowbray
Buckminster Gliding Club: Among the gliders is a well out-of-use FRED.

| ❑ G-BMOO* | FRED Srs 2 | CoA 8-8-91. Stored. First noted 9-05 | 9-05 |

SHAWELL south of Lutterworth, east of the A5
The Wessex is still at the paintball assault course.

| ❑ XT770 | 'P' | Wessex HU.5 | ex Bruntingthorpe, Halton 9055M, Wroughton, 845 | 3-06 |

STANFORD north-east of Rugby, near Swinford
Stanford Hall and **Percy Pilcher Museum**: Within the stables block is a small display devoted to the life and times of Percy Pilcher RN, including a Hawk. As well as the hall itself, there is a small, but impressive, motorcycle museum in the out-buildings.
◆ *Sundays and Bank Hols, Easter to end of Sep 1.30pm to 5.30pm (last admission 5pm). Regular special events in the grounds - SAE for details or hit the 'web'. Lutterworth, LE17 6DH tel 01788 860250 fax 01788 860870 e-mail enquiries@stanfordhall.co.uk www.stanfordhall.co.uk*

| ❑ | BAPC.45 | Pilcher Hawk REP | ex Coventry, Bitteswell | 3-06 |

STONEY STANTON on the B581 east of Hinckley
Stoney Cove: Within the waters of the diving school are a Wessex (down at 70ft); the forward fuselage of a Viscount (23ft) and a Partenavia P.68 (60ft).

❑ G-AWXI	Viscount 814	ex East Midlands, BMA, D-ANOL. forward fuselage	1-05
❑ G-LOUP	P.68B Victor	ex G-OCAL, G-BGMY. Crashed 7-2-93	1-05
❑ XT768	Wessex HU.5	ex Finningley, Wroughton, Westland	1-05

WIGSTON south-east Leicester

Graham Smith: Graham has two Harrier cockpits, both held in different locations within the county.

◆ Private *locations, visits by prior arrangement* only.

❑ XV810*	'K' Harrier GR.3	ex Bruntingthorpe, 9038M, 233 OCU, 4, 20. Nose. Arrived 13-3-06	3-06
❑ XW763	Harrier GR.3	ex Bruntingthorpe, Wigston, Bruntingthorpe, Duxford, St Athan, 9041M / 9002M, 1, 1453 Flt, 3, 4, 3. Nose	2-03

LINCOLNSHIRE

BINBROOK on the B1203 north-east of Market Rasen

Charles Ross: Chairman of the Lightning Association (see below), Charles has an example in his garden and a small museum dedicated to the subject. Charles also owns F.1A XM192 at Woodhall Spa, Lincs, and F.6 nose XS899 at Coltishall, Norfolk.

◆ *Admission by prior arrangement* only - *see below for contact address.*

❑ XR725	'BA' Lightning F.6	ex Rossington, Binbrook, 11, 5, LTF, 5, 56, 74, 5, 23	3-06

BINBROOK AIRFIELD north of the B1203, north of the village

Lightning Association (LA): As well as regular events, the LA publishes *Lightning Review*, their journal covering all aspects of Lightning history and technical documentation. XR724 is kept 'live'.

◆ *Annual open day and other times for LA members. Visits by prior permission only. c/o Charles Ross, Chestnut Farm House, Ludford Road, Binbrook, Market Rasen, LN8 6DR tel 01472 398705, fax 01472 399723, e-mail charles.ross@btconnect.com www.lightning.org.uk*

❑ XR724	Lightning F.6	ex G-BTSY, Shawbury, BAe Warton, 5, 11, 5, 11, 5, LTF, 11	3-06

BOSTON

A *private* workshop in this general area *should* continue to hold some 'long-termers'. Turn to *W&R18* (p135) and you will find reference to Nord 3400 G-ZARA moving from here. It is now known to have moved to <u>Swanton Morley</u>, Norfolk.

❑ G-AXGA	Super Cub 95	ex Tattershall Thorpe, PH-NLE, PH-CUB ntu, RNethAF R-51, 52-2447. Crashed 26-12-86	8-90
❑ G-AYVT	Brochet MB.84	ex Tattershall Thorpe, Sunderland, F-BGLI. Dam 28-6-77	8-90
❑ G-PULL	Super Cub 150	ex Tattershall Thorpe, PH-MBB, ALAT 18-5356. Crashed 13-6-86. Frame	8-90
❑ F-BBGH	Brochet MB.100	ex F-WBGH. Stored	8-90
❑ F-PFUG	Adam RA-14	Stored	8-90

Darren Swinn: Is working on the restoration of the former Coningsby Lightning F.2A in the general area. Darren is also looking after F.1A XM192 at Woodhall Spa, Lincs. Darren also has the cockpit of a long-lost F.3.

❑ XN774	Lightning F.2A	ex Coningsby 8551M, 92, 19. Nose	®	3-04
❑ XP757	Lightning F.3	ex Woodhall Spa, Keighley, Siddal, Binbrook, 29, 23. Cockpit	®	3-04

CLEETHORPES south of Grimsby

❑ G-MJUZ	Dragon 150	ex North Coates. CoA 28-2-87	1-02
❑ G-MMAI	Dragon 150	ex North Coates. CoA 13-7-97	1-02

COLSTERWORTH on the A1 north of Stamford

Witham Specialist Vehicles: Wessex HC.2 XR502 became G-CCUP during November 2004 registered to Kent-based owners – no 'forwarding' address as yet. Sea Harrier FA.2 ZD582 arrived from Shawbury on 9th November 2005. It departed by road on 29th March 2006 to, where else but Shawbury, Shropshire!

❏ ZE696* '124' Sea Harrier FA.2   ex Shawbury, 899, 800, 899, 800, 899, 801, 899, 800.
Arrived 7-11-05   11-05

CONINGSBY AIRFIELD on the B1192, south of Horncastle

Battle of Britain Memorial Flight (BBMF) and **Visitor Centre**: See under Cosford, Shrop, and Hawkinge, Kent, for 'other' MK356s! [1] Spitfire XVI TE311 is under restoration having consumed fellow TB382 as a source of spares [2].

◆ *Open Monday to Friday except Bank Holidays 10am to 4.30pm with the last guided tour at 3.30pm.* **Please note**: *although booking is not required to attend the Visitor Centre, it is advisable as it may be that the Flight in whole or in part are positioning to a show. Lincolnshire's Lancaster Association support the Visitor Centre, the BBMF and PA474 in particular. Something that the compiler did not know was that LLA have owned Shackleton WR977 at the Newark Air Museum since the late 1990s - bizarre. More so, they added Vulcan XM594 in March 2005 - see under Winthorpe, Notts. (Details of them from: 31, Knaton Road, Carlton-in-Lindrick, Worksop, Notts, S81 9HJ.) Battle of Britain Memorial Flight Visits, RAF Coningsby, Lincoln LN4 4SY tel 01526 344041 fax 01526 342330, e-mail bbmf@lincolnshire.gov.uk www.bbmf.co.uk*

❏	P7350	'XT-D'	Spitfire IIa	✈	ex *Battle of Britain* G-AWIJ, Colerne, 57 OTU, CGS, 64, 616, 603, 266. 603 Sqn c/s, *Blue Peter* 4-06
❏	AB910	'IR-G'	Spitfire Vb	✈	ex *Battle of Britain*, BBMF, G-AISU, 29 MU, RWE, 527, 53 OTU, 402, 242, 133, 130, 222. Wg Cdr I R Gleed DFC, 244 Wing c/s by 2-03 4-06
❏	LF363	'YB-W'	Hurricane IIc	✈	ex Audley End, Coningsby, Biggin Hill SF, 41, 41 GCF, Waterbeach SF, Odiham SF, Thorney Island SF, FCCS, Middle Wallop SF, 61 OTU, 41 OTU, 62 OTU, 26, 63, 309, 63. 17 Sqn colours, P/O H A C Bird-Wilson by 4-06 4-06
❏	MK356	'2I-V'	Spitfire IX	✈	ex St Athan, Abingdon, 5690M St Athan, Henlow, Bicester, Hawkinge, Halton, 84 GSU, 443. 443 Sqn c/s [1] 4-06
❏	PA474	'QR-M'	Lancaster I	✈	ex 44, Wroughton, Cranfield College, RAE, FRL, 82. 61 Sqn c/s, *Mickie the Moocher*. H2S scanner 4-06
❏	PM631	'S'	Spitfire PR.XIX		ex THUM Flt, Buckeburg SF, 206 OCU, 203 AFS.
				✈	681 Sqn colours 4-06
❏	PS915		Spitfire PR.XIX	✈	ex Samlesbury, Preston, Brawdy, St Athan, Coningsby, Brawdy, Leuchars 7548M/7711M, West Malling, Biggin Hill, THUM Flt, 2, PRDU, 541. *The Last!*, 81 Sqn colours 4-06
❏	PZ865	'JX-E'	Hurricane II	✈	ex Hawker Siddeley G-AMAU. *Night Reaper*. 1 Sqn colours by 5-05. 4-06
❏	TE311		Spitfire XVI		ex EP&TU, 7241M, 'MK178' 'X4474', France, Abingdon, Henlow, Wattisham, CAACU, 103FRS, 102FRS, 83GSU ® [2] 4-06
❏	WG486	'G'	Chipmunk T.10	✈	ex Newton, Gatow SF, ARWF, 3 AEF, Bri UAS, 3 AEF, Bri UAS, Liv UAS, PFS, 1 FTS, ITS, AOTS, ITS, RAFC, MECS, 114, 651, 657, 2 FTS, 63 GCF, 9 RFS, 5 BFTS 4-06
❏	WK518	'K'	Chipmunk T.10	✈	ex Newton, 1 AEF, Lon UAS, Hull UAS, Leeds UAS, Hull UAS, Coltishall SF, FWS, Cam UAS, Hull UAS, Cam UAS, Mcr UAS, Liv UAS, 63 GCF, RAFC 4-06
❏	ZA947	'AI'	Dakota III	✈	ex DRA, RAE, Farnborough, West Freugh, 'KG661', RCAF 661, 42-24338. 267 Sqn colours 4-06

RAF Coningsby: Lightning F.6 XR753 is for eventual display outside XI Squadron's Typhoon headquarters - see under Tangmere, W Sussex, for its doppelgänger [1]. Wingless Tornado F.3 ZE760 left by road on 22nd June 2004, destination unknown.

❏ XR753* 'XI' Lightning F.6   8969M, ex Leeming, Binbrook, 11, 5-11 pool, 23, FCTU.11 Sqn colours. Arrived 17-11-05   [1] 11-05

❑ XT891	'Z' Phantom FGR.2	9136M, ex 74, 228 OCU, 56, 228 OCU, 29,	
		228 OCU, 29, 228 OCU, 29, 228 OCU, 56,	
		228 OCU, 6, 54, 228 OCU, 54. Gate, 228 OCU c/s	2-06
❑ ZE760	'AP' Tornado F.3	ex St Athan, ItAF MM7206, RAF, 5. 229 OCU c/s. Gate	2-06

CRANWELL AIRFIELD on the A17/B1429 north-west of Sleaford

RAF Cranwell: Jetstream T.1s XX493 and XX498 were removed by truck on 24th May 2004. They went to a scrapyard at North Scarle, Lincs, and were 'processed' very quickly. The Chinook is used by the RAFC **Navigator and Airman Aircrew School** and is located within Trenchard Hall as should be the Harrier nose [TH]. The cockpit of Jetstream G-ATXH (identity confirmed) moved to Doncaster, S Yorks, by mid-2004.

❑ –	BTV DFS Weihe	BGA.1230, ex RAFGGA. CoA 5-93. Stored	2-00
❑ 'P8448'	'UM-D' Spitfire FSM	BAPC.225, ex Swanton Morley. 152 Sqn c/s.	7-01
❑ XW353	'3' Jet Provost T.5A	9090M, ex 3 FTS, RAFC, CFS, 3 FTS, RAFC. 'Gate'	2-06
❑ XZ138	Harrier GR.3	9040M, ex SIF, St Athan, 1, 233 OCU, 1453 Flt,	
		1, 3, 4, 3. Cockpit	[TH] 11-97
❑ ZA717	'C' Chinook HC.1	9238M, ex St Athan, Fleetlands, 78, 7 1310F, 18.	
		Crashed 25-7-89. Fuselage	[TH] 7-01

Aircraft Maintenance Instruction Flight (AMIF) and **Airframe Technology Flight** (ATF): For training, AMIF operates as the fictional '284 (Training) Squadron'.

❑ XX141	'T' Jaguar T.2A	ex 16, 6, Cranwell, 6, 226 OCU, 6 JOCU	11-05
❑ XX396	'N' Gazelle HT.3	8718M, ex EPTT, St Athan, Abingdon,	
		Henlow, 2 FTS. Crashed 30-6-81	7-01
❑ XX747	'08' Jaguar GR.1	8903M, ex Halton, Shawbury, Gibraltar Det,	
		6, 20, 31, 226 OCU. Gulf pink c/s, *Sadman*	ATF 7-01
❑ XX821	'P' Jaguar GR.1	8896M, ex Coltishall, 41, 14, 17, 226 OCU, 17	11-05
❑ XX965	'C' Jaguar GR.1A	ex Coltishall, 16, 226 OCU, 54, 14	7-02
❑ XZ119	'FG' Jaguar GR.1A	ex Coltishall, 41	11-05
❑ XZ132	'C' Harrier GR.3	9168M, ex St Athan, 4, 1, 1351F, 1, 233 OCU, 1, 3	ATF 7-01
❑ XZ358	'L' Jaguar GR.1A	ex Coltishall, 41. 41 Sqn colours	11-05

RAF Exhibition, Production and Transportation Unit (EP&TU): The airframes are based on a former airfield about ten miles to the south-west. EP&TU is 'parented' by the Cranwell-based Directorate of Recruitment and Selection and, for that reason, the 'fleet' is listed under this heading. Access to the 'detached' site is not possible and indeed many of the airframes spend their time in 'transit camps' elsewhere to minimise vehicle usage. As well as the airframes listed below, EP&TU have two Eurofighter Typhoon cockpit mock-ups, both of which include interactive segments. These two and a Hercules exhibit – the latter owing more to Crane Fruehauf than to Lockheed Georgia – are not considered as deserving of a 'formal' listing.

❑ XM191	Lightning F.1	8590M, ex St Athan, Abingdon, 7854M, Wattisham,	
		111.Crashed 9-6-64. Nose. Shark's mouth c/s. Stored	6-05
❑ 'XV238'	'41' Comet 1	ex St Athan, Abingdon, G-ALYW, Farnborough,	
		Heathrow, BOAC. In Nimrod MRA.4 guise	7-00
❑ 'XX226'	'74' Hawk T.1 FSM	BAPC.152, ex St Athan, 'XX262', Abingdon, 'XX162'.	
		74 Sqn c/s	7-00
❑ 'XX253'	Hawk T.1 FSM	BAPC.171, ex St Athan, 'XX297', Abingdon, 'XX262'.	
		'Red Arrows' colours	6-01
❑ XX753	Jaguar GR.1	9087M, ex St Athan, Abingdon, Shawbury, 226 OCU, 6. Nose 6-04	
❑ XZ135	Harrier GR.3	8848M, ex St Athan, Abingdon, 4. Nose	7-04
❑ 'XZ363'	'A' Jaguar GR.1 FSM	BAPC.151, ex St Athan, Abingdon, 'XX824'. Cockpit	7-00
❑ 'ZA556'	'Z' Tornado GR.1 FSM	BAPC.155, ex St Athan, 'ZA368' 'ZA446' Abingdon,	
		'ZA600', 'ZA322'. Grey colours, 13 Sqn c/s	7-04
❑ 'ZH139'	'01' Harrier GR.7 FSM	BAPC.191, ex St Athan, 'ZD472', Abingdon	7-01

Cranwell Aviation Heritage Centre: Located close to the airfield, the centre charts the history of Cranwell and gives notes on the other airfields on the North Kesteven Lincolnshire Airfields Trail. With a souvenir shop, flight simulator and archive film show, it is an excellent stop-off when visiting Cranwell and/or the trail.

◆ *Open May to Sep, 10.30am to 4.30pm, Wed, Thu and Sun. Signed just off the A17 (to the* south *of RAF Cranwell) on the minor road to North and South Rauceby. Tel / fax 01529 488490 during opening times - answerline at other times - or 01529 414294 e-mail tic@n-kesteven.gov.uk www.heartoflincs.com*

❑ [XE946] Vampire T.11 ex Cardington, Henlow 7473M, Habbaniya SF, Nicosia SF. Pod 8-05
❑ XP556 'B' Jet Provost T.4 ex Bruntingthorpe, Halton 9027M, Shawbury, CATCS,
    SoRF, 6 FTS, RAFC 2-06

CROFT west of Skegness

Auster 5 NJ703 moved to Breighton, E Yorks, in September 2005. Nothing on the Tutor's status…
❑ AZK 789 T.8 Tutor ex Skegness, VM650. Stored. 5-93

CROWLAND on the A1073 south of Spalding

The former Russian Hurricane project listed here in *W&R19* (p135) is the former King's Lynn machine – also given in that edition on page 159. This *may* be Mk.IIb BD713.
❑ – Hurricane II ex King's Lynn, Russia. ® 7-05

CROWLAND AERODROME on the A1073 north of the town, south of Spalding

The fuselage of Cherokee 160 G-ARUR had gone by August 2005.

DIGBY east of the B1188 north of Sleaford

RAF Digby: Is guarded by a Spitfire-on-a-stick.
❑ 'MJ832' Spitfire FSM BAPC.229, ex 'L1096', Church Fenton.
  'DN-Y' *City of Oshawa*, 416 Sqn colours. Gate 3-06

Within the historic station the **RAF Digby World War Two Sector Operations Room** has been lovingly restored to its former wartime glory and is a joy to behold.
◆ *Open every Sunday May to Sep, at 11am, guided tours only. Groups by prior arrangement. Tel 01526 327619 weekdays between 8am and 5pm.*

EAST KIRKBY on the A155 west of Spilsby

Lincolnshire Aviation Heritage Centre (LAHC): Run by Fred and Harold Panton as a memorial to their brother Christopher, who was killed on the Nuremberg raid, and as a memorial to Bomber Command as a whole. Other displays include the famous restored and equipped watch tower, the RAF Escaping Society, a blast shelter, 'Blitz' display and much more. There are regular 'in steam' days with the Lancaster and especially moving are the night-time runs - well recommended. The Bayliss Spitfire Tr.IX is based at the airfield and often displays at special events [1]. There is also a great 'NAAFI'!

Two other groups are based within the LAHC: **Lincolnshire Aircraft Recovery Group** (LARG): 'Prize' exhibit is the very substantial Spitfire BL655. LARG have a wide array of artefacts on show. The already impressive collection is ever-increasing, as more aircraft are recovered. (Dave Stubley, 33 Grosvenor Road, Frampton, Boston, PE20 1DB e-mail LARG2DJS@aol.com) **Lincolnshire Aviation Preservation Society** (LAPS): Main project is the painstaking restoration of AE436, the Brian Nicholls Hampden Project and Proctor IV NP294. (Graham Chaters, 154 Park Street, Grimsby, DN32 7NS tel 01472 362285 e-mail chatersgr@grimsby.ac.uk)

Notes: Also here is a convincing looking, but very much steel frame-and-metal panels He 111 cockpit once used for studio sequences in the *Battle of Britain*. In recent years away in New Zealand on a filming assignment. It was back on display by December 2005. The reference to the Colditz Cock REP here needs deleting. The machine here is a scale model used for film-set shots and is not a full-blown example. See under South Lambeth, Gtr Lon, and Flixton, Suffolk, for the two full-size Cocks. (Memo: Could I have worded that differently?)

◆ *Open Easter to Oct Mon to Sat 10am to 5pm, last admission 4pm; Nov to Easter Mon to Sat 10am to 4pm, last admission 3pm. NB not open on Sundays. Acting in support of the taxiable Lancaster is the **East Kirkby Lancaster Association** - subscribing helps in its upkeep and brings benefits, including an annual newsletter. East Kirkby, near Spilsby, Lincs, PE23 4DE tel 01790 763207 fax 01790 763207 e-mail enquiries@lincsaviation.co.uk www.lincsaviation.co.uk*

❑	AE436	'PL-J' Hampden I	ex Coningsby, Henlow, Sweden, 144. Crashed 4-9-42. Forward fuselage, etc	LAPS ®	3-06
❑	BL655	Spitfire Vb	ex Dorrington Fen, 416, 129, 341, 164, 602, 416. Crashed 1-7-43. Substantial fuselage section	LARG	3-06
❑	MJ627	'9G-P' Spitfire Tr.IX ✈	G-BMSB, ex Coningsby, Coventry, G-ASOZ Andover, IAAC 158, G-15-171, MJ627, 1, 441. 441 Sqn c/s	[1]	3-06
❑	NP294	Proctor IV	ex Tattershall, Friskney, Poynton, Andover, Cosford, 4 RS, 2 RS	LAPS ®	3-06
❑	NX611 'DX-C' and 'LE-C'	Lancaster VII	G-ASXX, ex Scampton, 8375M, Blackpool, Hullavington, Lavenham, Biggin Hill, Aéronavale, WU-15, St Athan, Llandow. *Just Jane*, 57 Sqn c/s to stb and 630 Sqn to port. *City of Sheffield*. Taxiable		3-06
❑	WH957	Canberra E.15	ex Bruntingthorpe, Cosford 8869M, 100, 98, Akrotiri Wing, 32, Hemswell SF, Upwood SF, 21, 542, 617. Nose		3-06

Others: A Cessna 170 is under restoration close by.

❑	G-BCLS	Cessna 170B	ex Tees-side, N8094A. CoA 27-1-83	®	3-02

FENLAND AERODROME west of the B1168 and Holbeach St Johns

❑	G-AFVN*	Tipsy Trainer 1	CoA 2-1-03. Stored		12-05
❑	G-BUKO*	Cessna 120	ex N2828N, NC2828N. Cr 28-12-97. Arr 16-9-05	®	12-05
❑	G-GAWA*	Cessna 140	ex Spalding, G-BRSM, N72454, NC72454. CoA 11-6-05. First noted 9-05		12-05

FLEET HARGATE on the A17, east of Holbeach

Harold Payne: Acquired a Hunter during mid-2004. It is displayed within the grounds of the 'Anglia Motel' and is looked after by members of **2430 Squadron, Air Cadets**.

❑	WT680*	'J' Hunter F.1	ex Aberporth, Weeton 7533M, DFLS, West Raynham SF. Arrived 26-7-04		2-06

GAINSBOROUGH north-west of Lincoln

A couple of sites in this general area are the venue for a series of interesting projects. The Shturmoviks will result in a static for the RAF Museum [1]. The C-3605 'Schlepp' is being restored to flying condition for its owner and will be fitted with a T-58 turboprop, at least initially. Terrier 2 G-ASYG was flying (as VX927) by April 2005.

◆ *Visits strictly by prior arrangement only.*

❑	G-AOBV*	J/5P Autocar	ex Cheshunt, Laindon, Stapleford Tawney, Benington. CoA 7-4-71		12-05
❑	G-AOHY*	Tiger Moth	ex Spanhoe Lodge, Middle Wallop, Shobdon, Land's End, Elmdon, N6537, Dyce SF, Ringway SF, 11 RFS, 11 EFTS, 35 ERFTS. CoA 20-8-60. Arr by 6-04	®	3-06
❑	G-BZHL	Harvard IIB	ex Egypt, FT118, USAAF. Arrived 4-01	®	3-02
❑	354 G-BZNK	MS.315E D2	ex France, F-BCNK, French AF	® off-site	1-05
❑	MW763 'HF-L'	Tempest II	G-TEMT, ex Sandtoft, Brooklands, Chichester, India, IAF HA586, RAF MW763	off-site ®	3-06
❑	HA604	Tempest II	G-PEST, ex Sandtoft, Brooklands, Chichester, India, IAF, RAF MW401. Stored	off-site	7-04
❑	'WL505'*	Vampire FB.6	G-MKVI, ex Bridgend, 'VZ304', Bruntingthorpe, Cranfield, Swiss AF J-1167. 614 Sqn c/s. Stored		7-04

❏	G-BZVW	Il-2M3	ex Lancing, Russia	[1] 12-03
❏	G-BZVX	Il-2M3	ex Lancing, Russia	[1] 12-03
❏ –		Il-2	ex Lancing, Russia	[1] 12-03
❏ C-558*		EKW C-3605	G-CCYZ, ex Spanhoe Lodge, N31624, Norwich, Little Gransden, Wycombe AP, Lodrino, Swiss AF. Arr 6-04	® 6-04

GLENTHAM on A631 west of Market Rasen
Alan Ellis: Keeps his Vampire T.11 pod in the area.

❏ XD595	Vampire T.11	ex Altrincham, Woodford, Chester, St Athan, 1 FTS, Oakington SF, 7 FTS, 4 FTS. Pod	5-04

GRAINTHORPE on the A1031 west of North Somercotes
Grimsby-Cleethorpes Aircraft Preservation Group: The nose of T.5 XS457 is with the Lincolnshire Aircraft Preservation Trust (or Lincair). They plan to fit this to the fuselage of Saudi T.55 ZF595, plus F.53 wings [1].
◆ *Visits by prior arrangement* only.

❏ XR757		Lightning F.6	ex New Waltham, Rossington, Binbrook, 5-11 pool, 23, 5. Nose	3-06
❏ XR770	'AA'	Lightning F.6	ex New Waltham, Laceby, Binbrook, 11, 5-11 pool, 56, 23, 74	3-06
❏ XS416	'DU'	Lightning T.5	ex New Waltham, Rossington, Binbrook, 5, LTF, 11, 74, 226 OCU, MoA	3-06
❏ XS457		Lightning T.5	ex North Coates, New Waltham, Laceby, Binbrook, 5, 11, 5, LTF, 11, 226 OCU. Nose	[1] 3-06
❏ A-011		A.35XD Draken	ex New Waltham, Danish AF Esk.729	3-06
❏ 22+57		F-104G	ex New Waltham, Skegness, Laceby, Binbrook, Manching, JbG34, DD+239, KE+438	3-06

HAXEY off the A161, north-west of Gainsborough
Andrew Exton: Still has a Lightning nose.

❏ XR759	Lightning F.6	ex Rossington 'TVI759', Binbrook, 5-11 pool, 56, 74, 5. Nose. 56 Sqn colours	8-05

HEMSWELL on the A631, east of Gainsborough
Bomber County Aviation Museum: for a variety of reasons, the museum threw in the towel during early 2005 and the collection was dispersed: 'Flea' G-AEJZ to <u>Doncaster</u>, S Yorks, by 5-04; Provost T.1 WW388 to <u>Sleap</u>, Shrop, by 9-05; Canberra T.19 WJ975 scrapped, nose to <u>Doncaster</u>, S Yorks; Vampire T.11 XD445 to <u>Abbots Bromley</u>, Staffs; Hunter FGA.9 composite 'XG193' was scrapped on site, the nose (actually GA.11 WT741) going to <u>Doncaster</u>, S Yorks; Lightning F.1A XM192 to <u>Woodhall Spa</u>, Lincs, 3-12-05; Jet Provost T.4 XP557 to <u>Dumfries</u>, Scotland 25-3-05. Not listed in *W&R19*, the Swift SIM moved to <u>Winthorpe</u>, Notts, by 6-05. By September 2004 former Egyptian Air Force SZD Bocian 963 had appeared here, in its own trailer. This also moved on, probably within its mode of transport. Where did it go?

Mystère IVA 101 also moved to Doncaster by December 2005. This move was not for preservation but for scrapping under the aegis of the National Museum of the United States Air Force, at Wright-Patterson, Dayton, Ohio. As *W&R* readers will be well aware, the Mystères, F-100 and T-33As 're-acquired' by the USAF from the French Air Force, are all technically on loan from 'Wright-Patt'. When these airframes arrived (mostly via Sculthorpe, Norfolk) in the early 1980s they were a great 'pump-primer' to the blossoming aviation heritage 'movement'. Bless them, the Mystères are far less relevant than the US-built jets and it has to be said that the UK could do with a few less, and the passing of 101 is not a reason for a wailing and teeth-gnashing bout!

HIBALDSTOW AERODROME on the B1206 south of Brigg
The stored Auster is now identified and is a long out-of-use example.

❏ G-ANHR	Auster 5	ex MT192, 662. CoA 20-7-<u>86</u>. Stored, rafters	2-06
❏ G-AWXY	MS.885 Rallye	ex Sandtoft, EI-AMG. CoA 1-2-97. Stored	7-01

❏ G-BKAB	IS.28M2A	ex Sandtoft. Crashed 19-5-84. Wreck	1-00
❏ G-BWCO	Do 28D-2	ex EI-CJU, N5TK ntu, 5N-AOH, D-ILIF. CoA 19-5-99	2-06

HUMBERSIDE AIRPORT (KIRMINGTON)

Eastern Airways have the fuselage of an unfinished Jetstream 41 kept on the airport site. It was joined by the prototype Jetstream 41 by late 2004. At the Global Aviation facility, several jet 'warbirds' are stored or on their way back to flight. The 'serial' worn on the nose of Gnat XR541 derives from the Paint and Finishing course at St Athan, Wales, that last dealt with it! [1]

❏ G-BIZM*	Nord 3202B	ex N2256K, ALAT No.91. CoA 31-10-00. Stored	12-05
❏ G-BWSH*	Jet Provost T.3A	ex XN498, 1 FTS, 3 FTS, RAFC. CoA 8-7-03	12-05
❏ G-GCJL*	Jetstream 4100	ex Woodford, Prestwick. CoA 29-4-95. Arr by 8-04	6-05
❏ –	Jetstream 41	ex Prestwick, G-4-105. Fuselage	6-03
❏ XM376*	Jet Provost T.3A	G-BWDR, ex XM376, Shawbury, 1 FTS, 7 FTS, RAFC, 1 FTS, 3 FTS, CATCS, RAFC, 2 FTS. CoA 24-10-02	12-05
❏ –	'PF179' Gnat T.1	XR541, ex Binbrook, Ipswich, Worksop, St Athan 8602M, CFS, 4 FTS. Stored	[1] 1-02
❏ OJ-1*	Strikemaster Mk.83	ex Botswana DF, ZG805, Kuwait AF 110, G-27-151. CoA 6-8-02	11-05
❏ 1115*	Strikemaster 80A	ex RSaudi AF, G-27-226. Stored	11-05
❏ 1129*	Strikemaster 80A	ex RSaudi AF, G-27-295. Stored	11-05

KIRTON-IN-LINDSEY on the B1398 north-east of Gainsborough

The Grasshopper is the frame of WZ757, the 'tail feathers' of WZ768 and the wings of XK820 (fuselage at Bridge of Weir, Scotland).

❏ WZ757	Grasshopper TX.1	ex Rufforth, Locking, Chichester. Stored	12-05

LOUTH on the A16 south of Grimsby

The Stewart Ornithopter is *believed* to still be stored in the area.

❏ –	BAPC.161 Stewart Orni'	ex Cleethorpes, South Reston. *Coppelia*. Stored.	8-98

MESSINGHAM on the A159 south of Scunthorpe

❏ XK417*	Auster AOP.9	G-AVXY, ex Melton Mowbray, Tattershall Thorpe, Wisbech, Henstridge, St Athan, 652, 9 Flt, 18 Flt, Middle Wallop. CoA 9-7-00	® 9-05

METHERINGHAM on the B1191 west of Woodhall Spa

Metheringham Airfield Visitor Centre: Based in what was part of the bomber base's communal site is an excellent display showing life at Metheringham and with 106 Squadron in particular. There is a very active **Friends of Metheringham Airfield**. The 'JP' is on loan from Paul Flynn [1].

◆ *At Westmoor Farm, Martin Moor, on the B1189 south-east of Metheringham. Open 12 noon to 4pm Wed and weekends 12 noon to 5pm end of Mar to late Oct. Other times by prior arrangement. Westmoor Farm, Martin Moor, Metheringham, LN4 3BQ tel 01526 378270 e-mail foma_lincs@hotmail.com www.airops.freeserve.co.uk/mavc*

❏ XS186	Jet Provost T.4	ex Ipswich, North Luffenham, Halton 8408M, St Athan, Kemble, Shawbury, CAW	[1] 3-06

NORTH COATES AERODROME north of the A1031, south of Humberston

Stewart Ornithopter BAPC.61 moved to Sibsey, Lincs, during mid-2004.

❏ BMU	1085 Slingsby T.21B (Powered)	ex East Kirkby, 9G-ABD, BGA.1085. *Spruce Goose*. Crashed 22-9-97. Fuselage, spares	4-05

SANDTOFT AERODROME south of the M180, between Sandtoft and Westgate

With a change of management at the aerodrome, the airframes previously held by Imperial Aviation were moved out to a yard near Armthorpe, S Yorks, in October 2004: Lincoln G-29-1; Provosts WV499 and WW421; Meteor WS776; Vampires WZ584 and XH313; TB-25N '151632'. Gannet AEW.3 XL502 moved to Elvington, N Yorks, on 11th March 2005. Cessna F.152 II G-BHCP was flying by 2005 and the dismantled F.152 G-BHSA had moved on (last noted in June 2002).

SCAMPTON AIRFIELD on the A15 north of Lincoln

RAF Scampton: Located within the technical site is the **RAF Scampton Historical Museum**. Visits are *strictly* pre-booked, but include a tour of famous sites on the base and the museum itself is exceptionally well presented. The 'Red Arrows' HQ is guarded by a Gnat within the base.
◆ *Open all year round, occasionally on public holidays, not open during the Christmas season. Visits by prior arrangement only. 01522 879137 e-mail mervhallam@hotmail.com*

❏ XR571	Gnat T.1	8493M, ex Cranwell, Scampton, Cosford, Kemble, Brampton, Kemble, 4 FTS. 'Red Arrows' HQ	3-06

Hawker Hunter Aviation: Operating out of the 'Phantom Sheds' on the perimeter of the RAF base, HHA are a major contractor for the military and industry. As such, much of their fleet is beyond the terms of reference for *W&R* and the listing has been shortened – airframes under restoration or long term store only are mentioned from now on. (The following Hunter F.58s have been deleted: J-4021, G-HHAC; J-4031, G-BWFR; J-4058, G-HHAD; J-4066, G-HHAE; J-4081, G-HHAF – ex G-BWKB; J-4105, G-BWOU; J-4090, G-SIAL.) The CAA granted HHA permission to operate the 'Bucc' as a 'Complex' Permit to Fly aircraft in late 2005. This will make *Alpha-Alpha* the first 'Complex' to fly – the second will be the Bruntingthorpe Vulcan [1].
Departures: Meteor F.8 'WF714' (WK914) to Hooton Park, Cheshire, 26-11-04; Canberra B.2 nose WP515 was refurbished here during 2004 before export to Germany, 1-05 – see under Market Drayton, Shropshire, for details; Hunter F.4 WV276 was offered for disposal 9-04, it was exported to Wernigerode, Germany, 22-7-05.
◆ *Visits only possible by prior appointment. www.hunterteam.com*

❏ XL587	'Z' Hunter T.7	G-HPUX, ex Duxford, Scampton, 8807M, 208, 237 OCU, 1 TWU, 229 OCU		® 11-05
❏ XX885	Buccaneer S.2B	G-HHAA, ex Lossiemouth 9225M, 12, 208, 12, 208, 216, 16		® [1] 1-06
❏ J-4072	Hunter F.58	G-HHAB, ex Speyer, Swiss AF. Dismantled		® 11-05
❏ J-4110*	Hunter F.58	ex Swiss AF. Stored, off-site		11-05
❏ -*	Hunter F.58	ex Swiss AF. Stored, off-site		11-05
❏ 98+14	Sukhoi Su-22M	ex WTD-61 Manching, Luftwaffe, East German AF		® 11-05

SIBSEY on the A16 north of Boston

A Stewart Ornithopter is stored in the area.

❏ -*	BAPC.61 Stewart Ornithopter	ex North Coates, Louth, Tumby Woodside, East Kirkby, Tattershall, Wigan, Irlam, South Reston. *Bellbird II*	6-04

SKEGNESS WATER LEISURE PARK or Ingoldmells, on the A52 north of Skegness

❏ G-AVPI	Cessna F.172H	CoA 30-5-03	9-03
❏ G-AZEE	MS.880B Rallye	ex S Scarle, ?, Shipdham, F-BKKA. CoA 27-9-98. Stored	4-05
❏ G-JENS	MS.880B Rallye	ex G-BDEG, F-OCZU. Crashed 15-6-92. Stored	4-03
❏ G-MJPV	Quicksilver MX	CoA 17-8-04. Stored in rafters	4-05
❏ EI-AOK	Cessna F.172G	ex Abbeyshrule. Spares	9-03
❏ PH-NLK	Geronimo (PA-23)	ex Burgh-le-Marsh, Ipswich, OY-DCG, SE-CKW. Fuselage.	9-03

SLEAFORD on the A15 south of Lincoln

Chrislea Skyjeep G-AKVR flew again following restoration on 30th May 2004 from a strip in the area.

SPALDING west of the A16, north of Peterborough

Skycraft Ltd: The famed 'Chop Shop' continues to process a large number of light aircraft types for spares. Turnaround is swift and it is largely pointless to present any forming of listing in a book with a two-year currency. They have a good web-site where you can virtually shop for that bit or that wotsit you've needed.

◆ *Visits by prior arrangement. 01406 371779 e-mail sales@sky-craft.co.uk www.sky-craft.co.uk*

SPILSBY on the B1195 west of Skegness

Pat Miller: J/1N Alpha G-AJEI moved to Messingham, Lincs, by early 2005 and was flying by June.

❏ G-AHAR	J/1 Autocrat	ex North Weald, F-BGRZ. Frame.		4-03
❏ G-AHSO	J/1N Alpha	CoA 6-4-95.	®	4-03
❏ G-AIGP	J/1 Autocrat	CoA 30-10-73. Lycoming O-320 conversion.	®	4-03
❏ G-AJDW	J/1 Autocrat	ex Luton area. CoA 17-1-77. Frame.		4-03
❏ G-AVOD	D5/180 Husky	crashed 31-7-92.	®	12-03

STAMFORD

Bless him, **Mike Doyle** died on 20th March 2005. Always equipped with a smile and a determination to help anyone, he had recently been busy with the 'JP' nose in and around Stamford raising money for Comic Relief - well XS176 does have a red nose! Mike was that rare commodity - you could not hope to meet a nicer guy. Jet Provost T.4 nose XS176 moved to Inverness, Scotland, on 17th June, 2005. While the 'JP' was northbound, at *CockpitFest* 2005, Winthorpe, Notts, a special award was made in Mike's name – see the Appendix.

Others:

❏ WD335	Chipmunk T.10	G-CBAJ, ex Yateley, Solihull, Wells, Dur UAS, Ox UAS, Gla UAS, Nott UAS, Lon UAS, Gla UAS, Aber UAS, St A UAS, Gla UAS, 11 RFS, 23 RFS. Stored	3-06

STURGATE AERODROME south-east of Gainsborough, near Heapham

❏ G-BHSA*	Cessna 152 II	ex Armthorpe, Sandtoft, N4889B ntu. CoA 11-4-98	8-05
❏ G-BSOE	Silvaire 8A	ex N1604K, NC1604K. Stored	2-06

SUTTON BRIDGE on the A17 west of King's Lynn

A Nord 1002 is stored at a *private* location in the general area.

❏ G-ASUA	Nord 1002	ex Elstree, F-BFDY. Crashed 30-7-64. Stored	12-05

TATTERSHALL THORPE on the B1192 south of Woodhall Spa

Lodge Road Flying Services: The yard was cleared of relics, including the hulk of Whirlwind HAR.10 XP328, by September 2005.

WADDINGTON AIRFIELD on the A607 south of Lincoln

RAF Waddington: The Nimrod MR.2 is believed to be a source of spares for the R.1 'Spook' fleet. F-4J(UK) ZE356 was scrapped on 24th March 2004.

❏ XM607	Vulcan B.2	8779M, ex 44, 101, 35. Display airframe	3-06
❏ XV246*	Nimrod MR.2	ex Kinloss, Kinloss Wing, St Mawgan Wing, 42, Kinloss Wing, 236 OCU, Kinloss Wing. Spares. Arrived 12-1-06	1-06
❏ XV497	'D' Phantom FGR.2	ex Coningsby, 56, 92, 19, 92, 23, 56, 228 OCU, 17. 23 Squadron 'mascot'	7-05

WAINFLEET south-west of Skegness
Aerial Application Collection (AAC):
◆ *Dispersed store, visits are only possible by prior arrangement. Eastside, Eaudyke Road, Friskney, Boston, PE22 8NL e-mail bill@pawnee.demon.co.uk*

❑ G-BFBP	Pawnee 235D	ex Rush Green. Crashed 11-5-78. Cockpit	3-04
❑ G-BFEY	Pawnee 235D	ex Old Buckenham. CoA 19-1-87. Fuselage frame	3-04

Elms Golf Centre: The Lightning T.5 acts as 'gate guardian' for the golf range here.

❑ XS456	'DX' Lightning T.5	ex Binbrook, LTF, 11, 56	6-05

Others:

❑ G-AWLX	J/2 Arrow	ex Gloucester, F-BGJQ, OO-ABZ. CoA 23-4-70	® 4-98
❑ G-BENL	Pawnee 235D	ex Old Buckenham, Sutton Bank, N54893. Crashed 10-7-85. Stored	2-96
❑ RAFGGA.502	L-Spatz 55	ex Brüggen. Identity subject to confirmation	11-93

WICKENBY AERODROME north of the B1399, north east of Lincoln
Lincoln Aviation: Operators of the aerodrome have established a **Visitor Centre** in the former wartime tower and the **RAF Wickenby Memorial Museum**. Among the many items on show are the substantial remains of 97 Squadron Lancaster III JB659 which was shot down on a raid to Berlin on 31st January 1944. It was salvaged from its crash site by members of the Royal Netherlands Air Force and the wreckage arrived here on 16th January 2001. A Nissen Hut is being prepared for a major exhibition. The **Wickenby Register** – 12 and 626 Squadron Association – have placed their archives with the museum.
◆ *Open 9am to 5pm daily except Xmas. The Old Control Tower, Wickenby Aerodrome, Langworth, Lincoln, LN3 5AX tel / fax 01673 885886 e-mail wmm@pipswan.demon.co.uk www.rafwmm.flyer.co.uk*

WISBECH
A Sea Vixen nose owned by a private collector has arrived for storage and then refinishing. It is then due to go on loan to a museum some time during 2006.

❑ XN696*	'751' Sea Vixen FAW.2	ex Walpole, Farnborough, Tarrant Rushton, ADS, 899. Nose. Arrived 6-05	® 11-05

WOODHALL SPA on the B1192 south-east of Woodhall Spa
Thorpe Camp Visitor Centre: The former No.1 Communal Site (or 'Thorpe Camp') of RAF Woodhall Spa is a superb visitor centre. Themes include life in Lincolnshire during the Second World War, the history of Woodhall Spa, including the histories of its resident units, including 617 and 627 Squadrons. A large array of models, artefacts, engines, photos are displayed, including elements of the Fordyce collection, previously at the Torbay Aircraft Museum. In on of the Nissen huts is the Lancaster internal fuselage mock-up made for the TV drama *Night Flight*. The Lightning will make an impressive attraction. It is on loan from Charles Ross [1] and in the care of Darren Swinn (see also under Boston, Lincs).
◆ *On the B1192 south of the former RAF Woodhall Spa. Open Sun and Bank Hols 2pm to 5pm, Easter to Sep plus Wed in Jul and Aug 2pm to 5pm. Other times by appointment. Lancaster Farm, Tumby Woodside, Mareham-le-Fen, Boston, Lincs, PE22 7SP tel 01526 342249 fax 01526 345249 e-mail mjhodgson@lancfile.demon.co.uk www.thorpecamp.org.uk*

❑ XM192*	'K' Lightning F.1A	ex Hemswell, Binbrook, Wattisham 8413M, Wattisham TFF, Binbrook TFF, 226 OCU, 111. 111 Sqn c/s. Arrived 3-12-05	[1] 4-06
❑ –	BAPC.294 Argus REP	ex Southampton. Unfinished, stored.	4-06

Geoff Brown: Cessna 120 G-BUKO moved to <u>Fenland</u>, Lincs, on 16th September 2005. See also Spanhoe Lodge, Northants.

❑ G-ANNN	Tiger Moth	ex Eccleshall, Hatch, T5968, Wattisham SF, 61 GCF, 3 RFS, 28 EFTS, 57 OTU.	® 3-04

GREATER LONDON

☛ Greater London constitutes the following boroughs: Barking and Dagenham, Barnet, Bexley, Brent, Bromley (including Biggin Hill!), Camden, City of Westminster, Croydon, Ealing, Enfield, Greenwich, Hackney, Hammersmith and Fulham, Haringey, Harrow, Havering, Hillingdon, Hounslow, Islington, Kensington and Chelsea, Kingston upon Thames, Lambeth, Lewisham, Livingston, Merton, Newham, Redbridge, Richmond upon Thames, Southwark, Sutton, Tower Hamlets, Waltham Forest, Wandsworth. ...which leads us, of course, to Mornington Crescent.

BENTLEY PRIORY between the A409 and A4140 north of Harrow
RAF Bentley Priory, HQ 11/18 Groups:
☐ 'K9926'	'JH-C'	Spitfire FSM	BAPC.217, 317 Sqn colours	2-02
☐ 'BN230'	'FT-A'	Hurricane FSM	BAPC.218, ex 'P3386', 43 Sqn colours	2-02
☐ XM173	'A'	Lightning F.1A	8414M, ex Binbrook, Binbrook TFF, Leuchars TFF, 226 OCU, 56	4-05

BIGGIN HILL AIRPORT
Airport: Airedale G-AWGA moved to Lashenden, Kent, during 2002. By 2005 Arrow III G-BMOP had moved to Bournemouth, Dorset. Travel Air G-AAOK was flying by 2004 and Tiger Moth N6466 (G-ANKZ) by the following year; Rand KR-2 G-UTSI was flying by 2004. As ever with location, some of the entries have become very long-in-the-tooth and we'll delete the following (last noted dates in brackets): Cessna 150B G-ARWC (2-95); Queen Air A80 G-ASDA (2-95); Cessna F.150H G-AWCO (2-95); Cessna F.152 II G-BFKG (8-97); Cessna FA.152 G-BFZN (2-95); Rallye 110ST G-BLDA; Robin R3000 G-BMTI (6-92); Cessna 152 II G-KAFC (2-95); Cessna 152 II EI-BIB (2-95).

☐ G-AOGE	Proctor III	ex BV651, Halton SF, 2 GCS, FAA. CoA 21-5-84	12-94
☐ G-AOKH	Prentice 1	ex VS251, 3 FTS, CFS, 2 FTS. CoA 2-8-73. Spares	4-01
☐ G-APZR	Cessna 150	ex N6461T. Crashed 14-1-81. Engine test-bed	6-05
☐ G-ATTF	Cherokee 140	ex N11C. Stored	4-01
☐ G-BBNO	Aztec 250E	ex N964PA. CoA 18-1-92. Stored	4-01
☐ G-BFAM	Navajo P	G-SASK, ex SE-GLV, OH-PNF. CoA 30-8-91	12-01
☐ G-BGFX	Cessna F.152 II	ex Nayland. CoA 23-6-91 ®	2-02
☐ G-BHCX	Cessna F.152 II	damaged 16-10-87. Stored	4-01
☐ G-BHJA*	Cessna A 152	ex Bodmin, N4954A. Damaged 21-7-90. Fuselage. F/n 4-05	6-05
☐ G-BHYS	Cherokee 181	ex N8218Y. Crashed 7-12-85. Wreck	4-01
☐ G-BIFB	Cherokee 150C	ex Elstree, 4X-AEC. CoA 17-12-90. Fuselage	4-01
☐ G-BIIF	Fournier RF-4D	ex G-BVET, F-BOXG. CoA 18-3-93. Stored	6-05
☐ G-BNJV	Cessna 152 II	ex N5333B. Crashed 8-3-92. Fuselage	4-01
☐ G-BTES	Cessna 150H	ex N22575. CoA 20-8-00. Stored	4-01
☐ G-BTKT	Warrior 161	ex West Thurrock, Southend, N429FT, N9606N. Cr8-8-95. Fuse	5-03
☐ G-BXPS	Aztec 250C	ex G-AYLY, N6258Y. CoA 16-10-97	4-01
☐ G-MJOI	Tripacer/Demon	wfu 1-11-89. Stored in rafters	5-03
☐ G-OXTC	Aztec 250D	ex G-AZOD, N697RC, N6976Y. CoA 15-6-98. Stored	4-01
☐ G-YUGO	HS.125-1B/522	ex Dunsfold, G-ATWH, HZ-BO1, G-ATWH. Dump	6-05
☐	Civilian Coupe	Unfinished airframe, No.7. Stored	10-95

RAF Memorial Chapel: Is guarded by full-size kits. The Chipmunk is with **2427 Squadron Air Cadets** [1].
☐ 'L1710'	'AL-D' Hurricane FSM	BAPC.219, gate guardian. 79 Sqn colours	5-05
☐ 'N3194'	'GR-Z' Spitfire FSM	BAPC.220, gate guardian. 92 Sqn colours	5-05
☐ WZ846*	Chipmunk T.10	ex Chatham, G-BCSC, 8439M, Bicester, Manston, Wales UAS, AOTS, 202, 228, CFE, W Raynham SF, G&S UAS, Bri UAS, 1 AEF, St Athan, Nott UAS, 63 GCF, Edn UAS, S'tn UAS. Arrived 11-12-04 [1]	11-04

Locally: A Boeing 737 cockpit has arrived.
☐ EI-CJF*	Boeing 737-204	ex Prestwick, Ryanair, G-BTZF, G-BKHF, G-BKGV ntu. Nose section. Arrived by 11-05	12-05

CATFORD south of Greenwich, on the South Circular, A205

Catford Independent Air Force: As well as the more substantial airframes listed, **Alan Partington** has amassed parts from Spitfire Vb AR614 plus others. AR614 was the former G-BUWA, now in the USA. The 'Flea' has a plaque saying 'Made at Capel' [1]. The Harrier is thought to be an unused GR.1 cockpit section and may have come from Richmond Air Cadets. It is 41H/729048 which puts it between GR.1s XV810 and XW630 [2].

◆ *Visits be prior arrangement* only. *Alan Partington, 100 Culverley Road, Catford, London, SE6 2JY e-mail alan.partington@bt.com*

❏	–	HM.14 'Flea'	unfinished		[1]	3-05
❏	–	Spitfire V FSM	built by Feggans Brown for *Piece of Cake*. Cockpit			3-05
❏	–	Harrier	nose section		® [2]	3-05
❏	XH783	Javelin FAW.7	ex Wycombe, Sibson, Aylesbury, Halton 7798M, 64, 25, GWTS, AAEE. Nose			3-05

CROYDON on the A23 in south London

Croydon Airport Visitor Centre: The superb visitor centre within the former terminal building (Airport House) is run in association with the **Croydon Airport Society** (CAS). Heron 2D G-ANUO is painted as 'G-AOXL' of Morton Air Services. The *real* G-AOXL made the last passenger flight from Croydon, on 30th September 1959 [1].The Tiger Moth 'flies' within the historic terminal building. The identity of this Tiger is debatable; G-ANKV was not converted (at Croydon?) and was cancelled from the register in September 1956 [2].

◆ *At Airport House, Purley Way, Croydon. Open on the first Sunday of each month, 11am to 4pm. Group visits at other times by prior arrangement. tel (Croydon Tourist Information) 020 8253 1009 Airport House, Purley Way, Croydon, CRO0 0XZ tel 020 8669 1196 e-mail cas.cavc@hotmail.co.uk CAS enquiries: tel/fax 020 86691196 e-mail croyairsocsec@netscape.net www.croydonairport.org.uk*

| ❏ | 'G-AOXL' | Heron 2D | G-ANUO, ex Biggin Hill, Exeter. CoA 12-9-86 | [1] | 4-06 |
| ❏ | T7793 | Tiger Moth | G-ANKV, ex Redhill. Displayed inside | [2] | 4-06 |

'Aerodrome Hotel': DH.60G Moth REP 'G-AAAH' (BAPC.168) moved to <u>Hawkinge</u>, Kent, for storage.

No.2157 Squadron Air Cadets: The Cessna 'does the rounds' of events on behalf of 'Flightaid' – see also Dunkeswell, Devon. It has also appeared several times on the Channel 4 epic *Scrapheap Challenge* and may therefore have moved on from here, never to return. Perhaps it is now some form of submarine!

| ❏ | G-ATFX | Cessna F.172G | ex Eaglescott, Caterham. CoA 12-2-92 | | 1-00 |

DULWICH on the A205 South Circular, south of Peckham

Dulwich College: *Should* still have their Chipmunk.

| ❏ | WB627 | Chipmunk T.10 | 9248M, ex Cambridge, 5 AEF, 1 AEF, Lon UAS, Cam UAS, 2 SoTT, 22 GCF, Debden SF, Jurby SF, 8 RFS, 18 RFS | 10-96 |

GREENFORD on the A40 west of the city

Vanguard Haulage: By August 2004 the Hunter had re-appeared on the tower to the west of the Hangar Lane Roundabout, on the A40, but by November 2005 it was to be found dismantled and in store inside, alongside the Lightning. By this time a former Air Cadet Vampire T.11 nose was also noted in store – this *could* well be XK632, long lost from Denham, Bucks [1]. Spitfire FSM 'K9962' 'JH-C' (last noted in April 1996) is reported by staff at the premises to have gone a 'long time ago', with 'Duxford' as a likely destination. ('K9926' 'JH-C' at not-so-far away Bentley Priory may throw in *another* possibility – a mis-read and a lack of basic geography!)

❏	WT555	Hunter F.1	ex Cosford, Locking 7499M, AAEE, Dunsfold. Stored		11-05
❏	XP745	'H' Lightning F.3	ex Boulmer 8453M, Leconfield, 29, 56. Stored		11-05
❏	-*	Vampire T.11	pod, first noted 11-05	[1]	11-05

HANWELL on the A4020 east of Uxbridge

The Aeronca is *believed* still to be held in the area.

| ❏ | G-AEXD | Aeronca 100 | CoA 20-4-70. Including parts from G-AESP. Stored | 12-90 |

HENDON north-west London, near the end of the M1

Royal Air Force Museum (RAFM): After the opening of the 'Milestones of Flight' gallery, in December 2003, the emphasis has moved to Cosford, Shropshire, where major developments are in hand – qv. RAF Museum aircraft can also be found at the following locations: **Brooklands**, Surrey: Valiant nose, P.1127; **Cosford**, Shrop: RAF Museum 'North' and the Conservation Centre; **Coventry**, Warks: Meteor WS838 and T-33A; **Kemble**, Glos, Bristol 173 G-ALBN; **Manchester**, Gtr Man, several airframes; **Stafford**, Staffs, 'deep' store; **Tangmere**, W Sussex: Hunter, Meteor, Phantom, Swift; **Woodley**, Berks, Jet Gyrodyne.

◆ *On Grahame Park Way, signposted from the end of the M1 and A41. Open 10am to 6pm all week, except Christmas and New Year. [Please note: The Grahame White Factory building has been known to be subject to closure due to staff shortages - please check before your visit.]. More details of activities on receipt of an SAE, or via the 'hotline'. There is a very active* **Friends of the RAF Museum** *organisation with a variety of activities which also publishes a journal – The Flying M – details of membership from the address below. Hendon, London, NW9 5LL tel 020 82052266 event hotline tel 020 8358 4849 fax 020 8200 1751 www.rafmuseum.org*

❑ 'BE421''XP-G' Hurricane FSM	BAPC.205, 'gate' guard. 174 Sqn colours	4-06
❑ 'MH486''FF-A' Spitfire FSM	BAPC.206, 'gate' guard. 132 Sqn colours	4-06

'Historic Hangars' and **Bomber Command Hall**: (Previously referred to as the 'Main Hall'.)

Notes: The Robinson was gifted from Cabair and used for travelling demos and within the 'Aeronauts' Interactive Gallery [1]. The AA-5B is a 'hands-on' (bum-in, surely?) exhibit and is also in the 'Aeronauts' area [2]. Sections of C-47A N9050T are within the 'Aeronauts' interactive gallery while the cockpits part of a Berlin Airlift exhibition [3]. The Hunter FR.10 (a 'missing' variant in the UK) was a gift from the Sultan of Oman and is on external display [4].

Departures: Battle I L5343 moved for restoration to Rochester, Kent, in January 2006. Valiant BK.1 XD818 left for Cosford, Shrop, in several loads in late August/early September 2005. Sabre F.4 XB812 to Cosford, Shrop, by March 2006.

❑ 'G-RAFM'		Robinson R-22	G-OTHL, ex Redhill. CoA 2-3-00. 'Hands-on'	[1] 4-06
❑ [G-ROWL]		AA-5B Tiger	ex Elstree, N28410 ntu. CoA 9-5-01. Cockpit	[2] 4-06
❑ [N9050T]*		C-47A-10-DK	ex Rochester, Cosford, Fleet, Thruxton, Hal Safi, 5N-ATA, PH-MAG, G-AGYX, KG437, 42-92656. Cockpit. Arr1-06	[3] 4-06
❑ '168'		Tabloid REP	G-BFDE, ex Cardington, Hendon, Cardington. CoA 4-6-83	4-06
❑ '687'		BE.2b REP	BAPC.181, ex Cardington	4-06
❑ 'E2466'	'I'	Bristol F.2b	BAPC.165, ex Cardington, Weston-on-the-Green. Semi-skeletal	4-06
❑ F1010		Airco DH.9A	ex Cardington, Krakow, Berlin, 110	4-06
❑ 'K2227'		Bulldog IIA	ex Hatch, Cardington, Old Warden, Henlow, Filton, G-ABBB, Science Museum, R-11. Cr 13-9-64. 56 Sqn c/s	4-06
❑ K4232		Rota I (C.30A)	ex Spain, Cardington, SE-AZB, K4232, SAC	4-06
❑ K4972		Hart Trainer	ex Cosford, Cardington, Hendon, St Athan, Carlisle, Wigton 1764M, 2 FTS	4-06
❑ K6035		Wallace II	ex Hatch, Henlow, Newark, Cranwell, 2361M, EWS, 502. Uncovered fuselage	4-06
❑ N5628		Gladiator II	ex 263. Lost in Norway 4-40. Forward fuselage	4-06
❑ N9899		Southampton I	ex Cardington, Henlow and Felixstowe. Fuselage	4-06
❑ R5868	'PO-S'	Lancaster I	ex Scampton 7325M, 467, 83. 467 Sqn colours	4-06
❑ W1048	'TL-S'	Halifax II	ex 8465M, Henlow, Lake Hoklingen, Norway, 35, 102. Force-landed 27-4-42. 35 Sqn colours	4-06
❑ 'W2068'	'68'	Anson I	ex Duxford, Australia, VH-ASM, W2068, 4 SFTS, 3 SFTS. Partially uncovered fuselage only on 'Queen Mary' trailer	4-06
❑ BL614	'ZD-F'	Spitfire Vb	ex Rochester, Manchester, St Athan, 'AB871', Colerne, Credenhill 4354M, 118, 64, 222, 242, 611. 222 Sqn c/s	4-06
❑ 'DD931'	'L'	Beaufort VIII	9131M, ex Cardington, Chino, New Guinea. Composite. 42 Sqn colours	4-06
❑ FE905		Harvard IIB	ex Cardington, Winthorpe, Cardington, Royston, London Bridge, Southend, LN-BNM, Danish AF 31-329, RCAF, 41 SFTS, FE905, 42-12392	4-06
❑ 'FX760'	'GA-?'	Kittyhawk IV	ex Cosford 9150M, Wyton, Cardington, Hendon, USA. Composite. 112 Sqn c/s	4-06

❏ 'KL216'	'RS-L'	P-47D-40-RA	ex Cosford 9212M, Duxford, Cardington, Bitteswell, Yugoslavia 13064, USAAF 45-49295. 30 Sqn c/s	4-06
❏ KN751*		Liberator VI	ex Cosford, Colerne, Ind AF 6 Sqn HE807, RAF KN751, 99. Arrived 9-05	4-06
❏ LB264		Auster I	ex Cosford, G-AIXA, Spanhoe, 22 EFTS, 1 EFTS, AAEE	4-06
❏ MF628		Wellington T.10	ex 9210M, Abingdon, St Athan, Biggin Hill, Hendon, Heathrow, Wisley, Vickers, *Dambusters*, 1 ANS	4-06
❏ MN235		Typhoon Ib	ex Shawbury, Smithsonian, USAAF FE-491	4-06
❏ MP425		Oxford I	ex Cardington, Winthorpe, Cardington, G-AITB, Shawbury, Perth, MP425, 7 FTS, 18 (P)AFU, 1536 (BAT) Flt. CoA 24-5-61. 1536 Flt colours	4-06
❏ PK724		Spitfire F.24	ex Finningley 7288M, Gaydon, Norton, Lyneham	4-06
❏ 'PR536'		Tempest II	ex Duxford, Cardington, Chichester, Indian AF	
	'OQ-H'		HA457, RAF. 5 Sqn colours	4-06
❏ RD253		Beaufighter TF.10	ex St Athan 7931M, Portuguese AF BF-13	4-06
❏ VT812	'N'	Vampire F.3	ex Cosford, Wyton, Hendon, Cosford, Shawbury, Colerne 7200M, Cardington, 602, 601, 614, 32.	4-06
❏ WE139		Canberra PR.3	ex 8369M, Henlow, 231 OCU, 39, 69, 540	4-06
❏ WH301		Meteor F.8	ex Henlow 7930M, Kemble, 85, CAW, 609, DFLS	4-06
❏ WP962	'C'	Chipmunk T.10	ex Newton, 3 AEF, Bri UAS, AAC, Lon UAS, 61 GCF, 662	4-06
❏ WV783		Sycamore HR.12	ex Rochester, Wyton, Cardington, Fleetlands, Henlow 7841M, HDU Old Sarum, CFS, ASWDU, G-ALSP. CFS c/s	4-06
❏ WZ791		Grasshopper TX.1	ex 8944M, Syerston, Halton, High Wycombe, Hove	4-06
❏ XA302*		Cadet TX.3	ex Syerston, HAK/BGA.3786. CoA 5-96	4-06
❏ XG154		Hunter FGA.9	ex 8863M, St Athan, 1 TWU, 229 OCU, 54, 43, 54	4-06
❏ XG474	'O'	Belvedere HC.1	ex 8367M, Henlow, 66, 26, 66. 66 Sqn colours	4-06
❏ XL318		Vulcan B.2	ex 8733M, Scampton, 617, 230 OCU, Wadd Wing, 617, 230 OCU, Scamp Wing, 617	4-06
❏ XM463	'38'	Jet Provost T.3A	ex 1 FTS, RAFC. Fuselage. 'Hands-on' exhibit.	4-06
❏ XM555		Skeeter AOP.12	ex Cosford, Shawbury 8027M, Ternhill, CFS, HQ BAOR, 654	4-06
❏ XM717		Victor K.2	ex Cardington, Marham, 55, 57, 55, 543, Witt W, 100. *Lucky Lou*. Nose	4-06
❏ 'XN972'		Buccaneer S.1	XN962, ex Cosford 8183M, St Athan, 'XN972', Abingdon. Nose	4-06
❏ XP299		Whirlwind HAR.10	ex Cosford 8726M, 22, 230, 1563F, Queen's Flt, 230, CFS	4-06
❏ XS925	'BA'	Lightning F.6	ex 8961M, Binbrook, 11, 5-11 pool	4-06
❏ XV424	'I'	Phantom FGR.2	ex 9152M, St Athan, Wattisham, 56, 228 OCU, 29, 92, 228 OCU, 29, 228 OCU, 111, 29	4-06
❏ XV732		Wessex HCC.4	ex Shawbury, Queen's Flight	4-06
❏ XW323	'86'	Jet Provost T.5A	ex 9166M, Shawbury, 1 FTS, RAFC	4-06
❏ XW547	'R'	Buccaneer S.2B	ex Cosford 9169M, Shawbury, 9095M, Gulf Det, 12, 237 OCU, 208, 12, 216, 12, 237 OCU, 12 *Guinness Girl / Pauline / The Macallan*. Pink colours	4-06
❏ XW855		Gazelle HCC.4	ex Shawbury, Fleetlands, 32	4-06
❏ ZA457	'AJ-J'	Tornado GR.1	ex St Athan, 2, 617, RAF Gulf Det, 17, 15, 9, 617, 9, TOEU	4-06
❏ 'IOI'		EH-101 PP8	ZJ116, ex Brize Norton, Yeovil, G-OIOI	4-06
❏ –*		Beaufighter II	ex East Fortune, Hendon, Duxford, Hendon, Cranfield. Nose. Arrived 17-12-04	4-06
❏ A16-199		Hudson IIIA	G-BEOX, ex Strathallan, VH-AGJ, VH-SMM,	
	'SF-R'		A16-199, FH174, 41-36975	4-06
❏ 920	'QN'	Stranraer	ex CF-BXO Queen Charlotte AL, RCAF 920	4-06
❏ 120227	'2'	He 162A-2	ex St Athan 8472M, Colerne, Leconfield, VH513, AM.65, Farnborough, Leck, JG1. JG1 c/s	4-06
❏ 584219	'38'	Fw 190F-8-U1	ex St Athan 8470M, Gaydon, Henlow, Fulbeck, Wroughton, Stanmore, Wroughton, Brize Norton, AM.29, Farn'gh, Karup	4-06
❏ 853		Hunter FR.10	ex Oman, Thumrait, SOAF, RJordanAF 853, XF426, 229 OCU, 2, 208	[4] 4-06

❏ '34037' TB-25N-20-NC ex 8838M, Blackbushe, N9115Z, *Hanover Street*,
Catch 22, USAAF 44-29366   4-06
❏ 44-83868 'N' B-17G-95-DL ex Stansted, N5237V, Andrews AFB, TBM Inc,
Aero Union, USN PB-1W 77233. 94th BG c/s   4-06

Battle of Britain Experience: The audio-visual presentation on the 'Battle' has been upgraded – to sit among such treasures and have them highlighted via a tasteful and stirring presentation is a delight!

❏ K8042 Gladiator I ex 8372M, Biggin Hill 'K8442', 61 OTU, 5 (P)AFU,
AAEE. 87 Squadron colours   4-06
❏ 'L8756' 'XD-E' Bolingbroke IVT ex Boscombe Down, RCAF 10001. 139 Sqn c/s as
Blenheim IV   4-06
❏ N1671 'EW-D' BP Defiant I ex 8370M, Finningley, 285, 307. 307 Sqn c/s 4-06
❏ P2617 'AF-F' Hurricane I ex 8373M, 71 MU, 9 FTS, 9 SFTS, 1, 607, 615. 607 Sqn c/s 4-06
❏ P3175 Hurricane I ex 257. Shot down 31-8-40. Wreck   4-06
❏ R9125 'LX-L' Lysander III ex 8377M, 161, 225. 225 Sqn colours   4-06
❏ T6296 Tiger Moth II ex 8387M, Yeovilton SF, BRNC, RNEC, Stretton,
7 EFTS, 1 EFTS   4-06
❏ X4590 'PR-F' Spitfire I ex Cosford 8384M, Finningley, 53 OTU, 303,
57 OTU, 66, 609. 609 Sqn colours   4-06
❏ ML824 'NS-Z' Sunderland V ex Pembroke Dock, Aéronavale, 330, 201. 201 Sqn c/s 4-06
❏ A2-4 Seagull V ex Cardington, Wyton, VH-ALB, RAAF A2-4   4-06
❏ 4101 '12' Bf 109E-3 ex St Athan 8477M, Henlow, Biggin, Fulbeck,
Wroughton, Stanmore, DG200, 1426 (EA) Flt, AAEE,
DH, Hucknall, RAE. Force-landed 27-11-40   4-06
❏ 360043 Ju 88R-1 ex St Athan 8475M, Henlow, St Athan, Biggin Hill,
'D5+EV' Fulbeck, Wroughton, Stanmore, PJ876, 47 MU, CFE,
1426 (EA) Flt, RAE. Defected 9-5-43   4-06
❏ 494083 Ju 87D-3 ex St Athan 8474M, Henlow, St Athan, Biggin Hill,
'RI+JK' Fulbeck, Wroughton, Stanmore, Eggebek   4-06
❏ 701152 He 111H-23 ex St Athan 8471M, Henlow, Biggin Hill, Fulbeck,
'NT+SL' Stanmore Park, RAE, 56th FG USAAF   4-06
❏ 730301 Bf 110G-4-R6 ex St Athan 8479M, Biggin Hill, Stanmore Park,
'D5+RL' 76 MU, RAE, AM.34, Karup, I/NJG3   4-06
❏ – BAPC.92 Fi 103 (V-1) ex Cardington   4-06
❏ MM5701 Fiat CR-42 ex St Athan 8468M, Biggin Hill, Fulbeck, Wroughton,
'13-95' Stanmore Park, AFDU, RAE, BT474, 95 SCT.
Force-landed Orfordness 11-11-40   4-06
❏ E3B.521 CASA Jungmann ex Spain, Spanish AF. '781-3'   4-06

Grahame-White Factory: While this Grade II listed building may not be the size that it was on its original site at Hendon, the removal and reconstruction has been an incredible operation, bringing visitors the taste and feel of such an early building.
Notes: Avro 504K 'E449' is a composite of G-EBJE (fuselage) and Type 548A G-EBKN (wings), both of which used to ply their joy riding trade from Shoreham, and was originally with the Nash Collection [1].

❏ – Blériot XXVII No.433, BAPC.107, ex Stafford, Cosford, Wyton, Hendon
9202M, Cardington, Nash collection   4-06
❏ '2345' FB.5 Gunbus REP G-ATVP, ex Cardington, Hendon, Weybridge. CoA 6-5-69 4-06
❏ '3066' Caudron G.III ex 9203M, Henlow, Stradishall, Heathrow, Nash,
G-AETA ntu, OO-ELA, O-BELA   4-06
❏ 'A8226' 1½ Strutter REP G-BIDW, ex Cardington, Land's End, '9382'. CoA 29-12-80 4-06
❏ 'C4994' Bristol M.1C REP G-BLWM, ex Cardington, 'C4912', Hucknall. CoA 12-8-87 4-06
❏ 'E449' Avro 504K ex 9205M, Henlow, Abingdon, Heathrow   [1] 4-06
❏ F938 RAF SE.5A ex 9208M, Henlow, Heathrow, 'B4563', Colerne,
Brooklands, G-EBIC, F938, 84 Sqn. CoA 3-9-30   4-06
❏ 'F8614' Vimy REP G-AWAU, ex 'H651'. CoA 4-8-69. *Triple First*   4-06
❏ 'N5182' Sopwith Pup REP ex 9213M, Blackbushe, Old Warden, G-APUP. CoA 28-6-78 4-06

❏ N5912	Sopwith Triplane	ex 8385M, Henlow, 49 MU, 5 MU, Cardington,	
		SAF Redcar, SAF Marske	4-06
❏ HD-75	Hanriot HD.1	ex Cardington, N75, G-AFDX, OO-APJ, Belgian AF	4-06

'Milestones of Flight': P-51 'The Duck' was donated by Bob Tullius of Group 44 Inc, who based it at Sebring, Florida, and takes pride of place on a turntable [1].

❏ G-AAMX		DH.60GM Moth	ex Cosford, Shoreham, NC926M. CoA 7-5-94	4-06
❏ '164'		Blériot XI	BAPC.106, ex Cosford 9209M, Cardington, Hendon,	
			Heathrow, Colerne, Hendon	4-06
❏ F6314	'B'	Camel F.1	ex Cosford 9206M, Wyton, Hendon, Heathrow,	
			Colerne, Hendon, Tring, Waddon	4-06
❏ 'J9941'		Hawker Hart	G-ABMR, ex HSA, 'J9933'. CoA 11-6-57. 57 Sqn c/s	4-06
❏ KK995	'E'	Hoverfly I	ex Henlow, Cranfield, AFEE, 43 OTU, 43-46558	4-06
❏ NV778		Tempest TT.5	ex Cosford, Wyton, Cardington, Hendon, 8386M,	
			Leeming, Middleton St George, North Weald,	
			Foulness, 233 OCU, Napier. 233 OCU c/s	4-06
❏ TJ138	'VO-L'	Mosquito TT.35	ex St Athan 7607M, Swinderby, Finningley, Colerne,	
	'VO-L'		Bicester, Shawbury, 5 CAACU, 98. 98 Sqn colours	4-06
❏ XZ997	'V'	Harrier GR.3	ex 9122M, 233 OCU, 1453F, 4, 1, 4. 4 Sqn colours	4-06
❏ 8417/18		Fokker D.VII	ex 9207M, Cardington, Hendon, Cardington, Hendon,	
			Cardington, Heathrow, Brooklands, Nash,	
			Versailles, OO- ?, Belgian AF (?), Jasta 71	4-06
❏ 10639	'6'	Bf 109G-2	G-USTV, ex Duxford, Benson, Northolt, Lyneham 8478M,	
			Henlow, Wattisham, Stanmore Park, Sealand, CFE-EAF,	
			1426 Flt, RN228, Lydda, 3 Sqn Gambut, III-JG77. Cr 12-10-97	4-06
❏ 112372	'4'	Me 262A-2a	ex Cosford 8482M, St Athan, Cosford, Finningley, Gaydon,	
			Cranwell, Farnborough, VK893 / AM.51, I/KG51	4-06
❏ –	'24'	Ki 100-1b	ex Cosford, St Athan 8476M, Cosford, Henlow,	
BAPC.83			Biggin Hill, Fulbeck, Wroughton, Stanmore, Sealand	4-06
❏ '413317'		P-51D-30-NA	ex N51RT, N555BM, YV-508CP, N555BM, N4409,	
			N6319T, 44-74409. 'VF-B' 4th FG, 336th FS c/s. [1]	4-06
❏ –	BAPC.100	Clarke TWK	ex Wyton, Hendon, Cardington, Hayes, South Ken'. ScM loan	4-06
❏ –	BAPC.292	Typhoon FSM	ex BAE Systems	4-06
❏ –	BAPC.296	*Nulli Secundus I*	repro of Army Balloon Factory airship gondola, 1907	4-06
❏ –	BAPC.293	Spitfire FSM	built by Concepts & Innovations. Entry lobby, wall-mounted	4-06

Locally:

| ❏ WJ731 | Canberra B.2T | ex Dunstable, Willington, Wyton, Wyton SF, 231 | |
| | | OCU, 7, 231 OCU, 50, 90. Nose, trailer-mounted | 8-02 |

ISLINGTON on the A104, North East London
City University: Northampton Square, EC1.

| ❏ G-TORE | '42' | Jet Provost T.3A | ex Ipswich, Cranfield, XM405, 1 FTS, RAFC, | |
| | | | 1 FTS, 2 FTS. CoA 5-5-95 | 9-03 |

KINGSTON-UPON-THAMES
A Hunter nose is kept in the area.

| ❏ XG209* | '66' | Hunter F.6 | ex Chelmsford, Stock, Halton, Cranwell, Halton 8709M, | |
| | | | 12 DFLS, 111, 14. Nose | 12-05 |

LONDON
Andrew Martin International: In Walton Street, SW3. A brightly-polished Gnat forward fuselage is displayed within the showroom and serves more as a lamp standard than anything aeronautical!

❏ XS100 '57' Gnat T.1 ex Fyfield, Bournemouth, Ipswich, Halton 8561M, 4 FTS.
Forward cockpit 12-04

Electroworkz: This nightclub in Islington took delivery of an HS.125 fuselage in late 2005.
❏ ZF130* HS.125-600B ex Stock, Farnborough, St Athan, Cranfield, G-BLUW,
HZ-SJP, HZ-DAC, G-5-19 12-05

'Planet Hollywood': In Coventry Street, Leicester Square. 'Flying' from the ceiling is *Little Nellie*, the famous autogyro from *You Only Live Twice*. This is *not* the original, but has been assembled by Ken Wallis (see under Reymerston Hall, Norfolk) so is doubtless based on one of his 'spares'. (There is yet another *Little Nellie* in 'Planet Hollywood' in Times Square, New York!)
❏ 'G-ARZB' Wallis WA-116 ex Reymerston Hall. *Little Nellie* 8-03

Queen Mary College: Engineering Department, in Bancroft Road, off the Mile End Road.
❏ [G-BVYE] BN-2B-20 ex Bembridge. Over-stressed 28-8-96 11-03

'The Roadhouse': The Piazza, Covent Garden, WC2 (www.roadhouse.co.uk)
❏ 'C-RASH' Robinson R-22 – 1-05

Trocadero: Harrier GR.3 ZD670 left this virtual house of fun in 2002 and moved to a location near Dagenham, Essex. It arrived at Parkhouse Aviation, Wycombe Air Park, Bucks on 28th August 2004 before moving the following month to South Molton, Devon.

LONDON (HEATHROW) AIRPORT
British Airways Archives and Museum Collection:
◆ *In Viscount Way, Hatton Cross. Visits on a prior arrangement only – open Wed and Fri 9.30am to 2.30pm. Building 387 (E.121), British Airways plc, PO Box 10, Heathrow Airport, TW6 2JA tel / fax 020 8562 3124*

Former **Trident Preservation Society** (TPS): Trident 3B G-AWZK left for Manchester Airport, Gtr Man, with the last bit departing on 10th September 2005. With the departure of *Zulu-Kilo* to the frozen north, TPS was wound down. Several TPS members look after the 'live' cockpit of G-AWZI at FAST, Farnborough, Hants – qv.

Others: The Concorde awaits display outside Terminal 5.
❏ G-BOAB Concorde 102 ex BA, G-N94AB, BOAC. CoA 19-9-01. Stored 1-06

LONDON (WESTLAND) HELIPORT, Battersea, north of A3205 east of Wandsworth Bridge
Although far from being an aircraft, bright red helicopter escape training aid previously wearing 'G-DRNT', gets a lot of people 'going', so deserves a mention! Largely based upon a Ford Transit (!) it arrived from Stansted, Essex, in late 2003 and was still there May 2005. By then, it had been 're-registered' as 'G-BMAC' and gained a large yellow 'M' on a red background on the side! (Remember that burgers can be nutritious, particularly if you sprinkle food on them, or just eat the box they come in!)

NORTHOLT AIRFIELD on the A4180 north-west of Northolt
RAF Northolt: The Spitfire is displayed within the camp, near the parade ground, in the colours of W/C Aleksander Gabszewicz, who flew EN526 from Northolt gaining three 'kills' in it.
❏ 'EN526' 'SZ-G' Spitfire FSM BAPC.221, ex 'MH777' 'RF-N'. Displayed. 316 Sqn c/s. 9-05
❏ WB556* Chipmunk T.10 ex Halton, Bicester, Oxf UAS. Fuselage. Arr by 11-05 11-05

ROEHAMPTON on the A306 north of Kingston
Kingston University: School of Engineering, Roehampton Vale campus.
❏ N121EL Learjet 25 ex N121GL ntu, N82UH ntu, N10BF ntu, N102PS,
N671WM, N846HC, N846GA 9-03

SOUTH KENSINGTON on the A4 west of Westminster

Science Museum (ScM): The Avro 504, Lockheed 10A, 'Flying Bedstead' and SC.1 are part of the museum's 'Making the Modern World' (MMW) gallery on the ground floor. The 'hands-on' 'Flight Laboratory', is no more, having been replaced with a series of 'sit-in and ogle' simulators – such is progress. Cessna F.150F G-AWAW is in store, and may be at Wroughton, Wilts [1].During mid-2005 a major exhibition in praise of R J Mitchell was opened. Centre-piece is the 'deconstructed' Spitfire F.22 that had been prepared for its new role by ARCO at Duxford, Cambs [2]. This arrival provides a critical mass of 615 (County of Surrey) Squadron airframes, Hurricane L1592 having also served with the unit.

ScM's 'large object' store is at Wroughton, Wilts. Other ScM airframes can be found at Southampton, Hants (Sandringham VH-BRC) Hendon, Gtr Lon (Clarke TWK); Yeovilton, Somerset (Concorde G-BSST).

◆ *Daily 10am to 6pm. In Exhibition Road, off the Cromwell Road. Nearest tube is South Kensington. South Kensington, London SW7 2DD tel 020 7942 4455 or 020 7942 4454 fax 020 7942 4421 www.sciencemuseum.org.uk*

☐	G-EBIB		RAE SE.5A	ex 'F939', Hendon, G-EBIB, F937, 85 Sqn. CoA 6-6-35		4-06
☐	G-AAAH		DH.60G Moth	CoA 23-12-30. *Jason*. Amy Johnson's machine		4-06
☐	G-ASSM		HS.125-1-522	ex Wroughton, Chester, S'ton, 5N-AMK, G-ASSM		4-06
☐	G-AWAW		Cessna F.150F	ex OY-DKJ. CoA 8-6-92. Stored	[1]	4-04
☐	G-AZPH		Pitts S-1S	ex Meppershall, Chessington, N11CB. *Neil Williams.*		
				Damaged 10-5-91		4-06
☐	DFY	2097	S-Hirth Cirrus	ex Army GA		4-06
☐	–	BAPC.50	Roe Triplane	Roe's second, first flown 13-7-09		4-06
☐	–	BAPC.51	Vickers Vimy IV	Alcock and Brown's machine, 1919		4-06
☐	–	BAPC.53	Wright Flyer REP	Hatfield-built		4-06
☐	–	BAPC.54	JAP-Harding	Blériot-based		4-06
☐	–	BAPC.55	Antoinette	ex Robert Blackburn, Colwyn Bay. 1909 model		4-06
☐		–BAPC.124	Lilienthal REP	built for the Museum		4-06
☐	NC5171N		Lockheed 10A	G-LIOA, ex Wroughton, Orlando, N5171N,		
				NC243 Boston-Maine AW, NC14959 Eastern	MMW	4-06
☐	304		Cody Type V	BAPC.62, with the museum since 1913		4-06
☐	D7560		Avro 504K	ex Middle Wallop, South Ken', Hull, Waddon, 3 TDS	MMW	4-06
☐	J8067		Pterodactyl I	ex Yeovil, Farnborough		4-06
☐	L1592		Hurricane I	ex 9 PAFU, 5 PAFU, 9 AOS, SDF, 615, 43, 152, 17, 43,		
		'KW-Z'		87, 17, 56. 615 Sqn colours		4-06
☐	P9444	'RN-D'	Spitfire IA	ex Sydenham, 53 OTU, 61 OTU, 58 OTU, 72. 72 c/s		4-06
☐	S1595	'1'	Supermarine S.6B	ex RAFHSF. Schneider winner 1931		4-06
☐	W4041/G		Gloster E.28/39	ex Farnborough		4-06
☐	AP507		Cierva C.30A	ex Halton, Sydenham, 76 MU, 5 MU, 529, 1448 Flt,		
		'KX-P'		Duxford Calibration Flt, RAE, G-ACWP. 529 Sqn c/s		4-06
☐	PK664*		Spitfire F.22	ex Stafford, Cosford, Wyton, Cardington, St Athan,		
		'V6-B'		Binbrook, Waterbeach, 7759M, 615. Arr by 5-05	[2]	4-06
☐	XG900		Short SC.1	ex Wroughton, Yeovilton, Wroughton, Hayes,		
				South Kensington, RAE Bedford	MMW	4-06
☐	XJ314		R-R Thrust Rig	ex Wroughton, Yeovilton, East Fortune,		
				Strathallan, Hayes, South Kensington, RAE	MMW	4-06
☐	XN344		Skeeter AOP.12	ex Middle Wallop 8018M, 654, 652		4-06
☐	XP831		Hawker P.1127	ex Hendon 8406M, RAE Bedford, Dunsfold		4-06
☐	–		Short Bros Gas	balloon basket, 1910		4-06
☐	–		Airship No.17	*Beta II*. Gondola, 1910		4-06
☐	–	'448'	Dakota IV	ex Ottawa, RCAF, KN448, 436, 10, 44-76586. Nose		4-06
☐	210/16		Fokker E.III	BAPC.56, captured 8-4-16. Stripped airframe		4-06
☐	191316	'6'	Me 163B-1a	ex Halton, 6 MU, Farnborough, Husum, II/JG.400		4-06
☐	442795		Fi 103 (V-1)	BAPC.199. Sectioned		4-06

SOUTH LAMBETH on the A3203 east of Lambeth Palace

Imperial War Museum (IWM): The gallery in which the large exhibits (tanks to a bus, Polaris to Camel) are displayed is most impressive. The Colditz Cock is within the 'Great Escapes' exhibition. Regular special exhibitions and displays.

◆ *Open 10am to 6pm daily. Closed 24-26th December. Lambeth Road, London SE1 6HZ tel 020 74165320 fax 020 74165374 e-mail mail@iwm.org.uk www.iwm.org.uk*

❑ 2699	RAF BE.2c	ex Duxford, South Lambeth, 192, 51, 50	12-05
❑ N6812	Camel 2F1	ex 'F4043', Yeovilton, Lambeth, 212,	
		Martlesham, Felixstowe. Culley's aircraft	12-05
❑ R6915	Spitfire I	ex Cardiff, RNDU, 57 OTU, 61 OTU, 609	12-05
❑ DV372	Lancaster I	ex 1651 CU, 467. SOC 4-1-45. *Old Fred*. Nose	12-05
❑ PN323	Halifax A.VII	ex Duxford, South Lambeth, Duxford, Staverton,	
		Radlett, Standard Telephones & Cables, 29 MU. Nose	12-05
❑ 120235	'6' He 162A-1	ex Duxford, South Lambeth, Cranwell, Brize	
		Norton, Farnborough AM.68, JG.1, Leck	12-05
❑ [733682]	Fw 190A-8	9211M, ex Duxford, South Lambeth, Biggin Hill,	
		Cranwell, Brize Norton, Farnborough AM.75	12-05
❑ '472218'	P-51D-25-NA	ex Duxford, RCAF 9246, USAAF 44-73979.	
	'WZ-I'	'WZ-I', *Big, Beautiful Doll*, 78th FG colours	12-05
❑ –	A6M5 *Zeke*	ex Duxford, South Lambeth, ATIAU-SEA. Cockpit	12-05
❑ –	BAPC.198 Fi 103 (V-1)	–	12-05
❑ -*	BAPC.90 Colditz Cock REP	ex Duxford, Higher Blagdon, BBC	3-02

TOLWORTH north of the A3, south of Kingston

No.1034 Squadron Air Cadets: Took delivery of a former Cosford Harrier on 6th October 2005.

❑ XZ130*	'A' Harrier GR.3	ex Cosford, 9079M, 4, 3, 233 OCU, 3, 1453F, 1, 4, 20.	
		4 Sqn colours. Arrived 6-10-05	10-05

UXBRIDGE on the A4020 south of the town

RAF Uxbridge: Still displays its Spitfire-on-a-stick. Kept as a 'time capsule' is the wartime **11 Group Operations Room** bunker and it has been turned into a museum. Visits are possible by at least a month's prior arrangement, call 01895 815400 between 8am and 12 noon Monday to Friday to arrange a visit.

❑ 'BR600' 'SH-V' Spitfire FSM		BAPC.222, gate guardian. 64 Sqn colours	4-05

WALLINGTON GREEN at the junction of the A232 and A237 west of Croydon

As threatened in *W&R19* (p151) Apache 160G G-ASMO, last noted in July 1996, has gone to LOST!

WOOLWICH near the A205 South Circular, south-east London

FirePower: Under this title the Royal Regiment of Artillery's international collection of 800 artillery pieces – from bronze guns to missile systems – is displayed. Within the 'Field of Fire' theme can be found experiences of 20th century warfare with the Auster AOP.9 dramatically suspended above.

◆ *Open Wed to Sat, 10am to 5pm. Close to Woolwich ferry and Woolwich Arsenal station. The 'Field of Fire' exhibition is only open twice a day – check for times. Royal Arsenal, Woolwich, London SE18 6ST tel 020 8855 7755 fax 020 8855 7100 e-mail info@firepower.org.uk www.firepower.org.uk*

❑ XR271	Auster AOP.9	ex Larkhill, St Athan, Middle Wallop	12-05

GREATER MANCHESTER

BARTON AERODROME on the A57 south of the M62/M63 junction at Eccles

❑ G-AFIU	Luton Minor	ex Wigan, Stoke, Hooton Park, Wigan, Peel Green,		
		Pembroke. Stored in rafters for TAC		6-05
❑ G-APUY	Turbulent	CoA 10-6-86	®	7-05
❑ G-ASXR	Cessna 210	ex 5Y-KPW, VP-KPW, N6532X. CoA 3-1-93		11-04
❑ G-AZGF*	Pup 150	ex PH-KUF, G-35-076. CoA 2-5-98. F/n 7-04		7-04
❑ G-BECF	Scheibe SF-25A	ex OO-WIZ, D-KARA ntu. CoA 1-3-94		12-03
❑ G-BONG	Enstrom F-28A	CoA 16-8-98. Stored		9-03
❑ G-MMEP	Tiger Cub 440	Canx 4-2-92. Stored		6-01
❑ G-TERY	Archer II	ex G-BOXZ, N22402. CoA 26-6-98. Stored		1-02

BOLTON
Doug Hackins Motorcycles: Jet Provost T.4 XP688 moved to Eccleston, Lancs, by August 2005. Sopwith 1¹/₂ Strutter not-quite-lookalike 'N5177' and Whirlwind HAS.7 XN385 had both gone by September 2005.

CHADDERTON on the A663 north-east of Manchester
BAE Systems: End of an incredible era... manufacturing here at this site during early 2005. The much-reduced site is now home to the Tanker Transport and Reconnaissance Operations support organisation. The existence/fate of the ATP cockpit section is unknown.

❑ –	ATP	cockpit. *Possibly* c/n 2074 or 2076	3-00

DUKINFIELD north of the M67, east Manchester
'The Snipe': Having failed to conquer the logistics of moving Vulcan B.2 XL391 from Blackpool, Lancs, (qv) the publican turned to a much more portable Sea Harrier FA.2.

❑ ZE693*	'717' Sea Harrier FA.2	ex Yeovilton, 899, 800, 801, 800, 801, 800, 801.Arr 29-9-05	2-06

LEVENSHULME on the A6 south-east of Manchester
No.1940 Squadron Air Cadets: In St Oswald's Road. The rear end of WG418 is at London Colney, Herts.

❑ WG418	Chipmunk T.10	8209M, ex Woodvale, Hamble, Jever SF, Lon UAS,	
		61 GCF, QUB UAS, Lon UAS, 3 BFTS, 16 RFS.	1-06
❑ XM474	Jet Provost T.3	8121M, ex Firbeck, Heaton Chapel, Warrington, Shrewsbury,	
		Shawbury, MinTech, 6 FTS, MoA, 6 FTS, CFS. Nose	1-06

MANCHESTER
Imperial War Museum North: While a great hit among visitors, it may well prove to be a let-down to more 'conservative' museum-goers. The building is designed to represent a shattered globe, and three 'shards' of this 'Air', 'Earth' and 'Water' plus the Main Exhibition Space are the main elements.
◆ *Open daily (except Xmas) 10am to 6pm. Signed from the end of the M602. Nearest rail Manchester Oxford Road, closest Metrolink is Harbour City, buses 250, 290 and 291. The Quays, Trafford Wharf Road, Trafford Park, Manchester M17 1TZ tel 0161 836 4000 e-mail info@iwmnorth.org.uk www.iwm.org.uk/north*

❑ 159233	'CG' AV-8A-MC	ex Yeovilton, VMA-231, USMC	3-06

Museum of Science and Industry in Manchester, Air and Space Hall: Initially schemed for 2004, but now looking at 2006/2007 or later, there are plans to radically change the content of the main hall, to be centred around a composite unfinished RJX 100. Some airframes will have to move out to achieve this - remember that the vast majority are on loan. The Shackleton was originally mooted as the first candidate for eviction. On loan from the RAF Museum, this would face massive logistics problems that would probably see it re-locating to Cosford, Shropshire. There, it would just have missed the 'Cold War' hall and would have to ousted other airframes back into the open air.

Replacement of the 'Shack' - with overwhelming local links and meaning - with an airliner type with plenty still in service (as the BAe 146 and RJ) and many years ahead in which to get one, *and* designed and developed in Hertfordshire to boot, would be a crime. (Not to mention the RJX just down the road at Manchester Airport on public display!) During 2005 high MSI management noted that plans *would* include WR960 - we will have to wait and see. Fund raising for the revamp is still underway.

Notes: Airframes on loan from the RAF Museum are marked RAF. Several airframes are on loan from The Aeroplane Collection, and are marked TAC. (See under Hooton Park, Cheshire, for their main entry.) Kieran Medd's HM.14 is stored at the museum [1]. The RJX composite, currently stored off site, is the cockpit, rear fuselage and wings from still-born British European (sorry, flybe.com) Set 396, c/n E3396 [2] plus other sections from the closure of the Woodford line.

Departures: The anonymous Easy Rider moved to Hooton Park, Cheshire, 9th April 2004. Eton TX.1 WP270 moved to Stafford, Staffs, during 2005.

◆ *Open daily from 10am to 5pm, including Bank Holidays but excluding December 23-25/faxLiverpool Road, Castlefield, Manchester M3 4JP tel 0161 832 2244 or 24-hour info line 0161 6060 121 fax 0161 6060 186 www.msim.org.uk*

❑ G-EBZM		Avian IIIA	ex Higher Blagdon, Peel Green, Lymm, Liverpool,		
			Huyton, Manchester, Hesketh Park. CoA 20-1-38	TAC	3-06
❑ G-ABAA		Avro 504K	9244M, ex 'H2311', Henlow, Nash. CoA 11-4-39		3-06
❑ G-ADAH		Dragon Rapide	ex E' Fortune, Peel Green, Booker. CoA 9-6-47. *Pioneer*	TAC	3-06
❑ G-APUD		Bensen B.7M	ex Firbeck, Nostell Priory, Wigan, B' Hill. CoA 27-9-60	TAC	3-06
❑ G-AWZP		Trident 3B-101	ex Heathrow, BA, BEA. CoA 14-3-86. Nose		3-06
❑ G-AYTA		MS.880B Rallye	ex Moston, Wickenby. CoA 7-11-88. 'Hands on'		3-06
❑ G-BLKU		Colt 56 SS	ex Newbury. Loan from BBML. In its bag!		3-06
❑ G-MJXE		Mainair Tri-Flyer	ex Droylesden, Blackpool. Last flew 1995	TAC	3-06
❑ BQT	1156	EoN 460 Srs 1	ex Seighford, Staffs GC, EGC / BGA.2666, BGA.6, BGA.1156		3-04
❑ '14'	BAPC.6	Roe Triplane REP	ex London, Southend, Irlam, Peel Green, Old Warden,		
			Woodford. *Bullseye Avroplane*	TAC	3-06
❑ –	BAPC.12	HM.14 'Flea'	ex East Fortune, Chester-le-Street, Newcastle, Wigan,		
			Stockport, Rishworth	TAC	3-06
❑ –	BAPC.175	Volmer VJ-23	ex Old Warden. David Cook, cross-channel flight		3-06
❑ –	BAPC.182	Wood Ornithopter	ex Hale. Stored	off-site	3-04
❑ –	BAPC.251	Hiway Spectrum	ex Lytham. Built c 1980. Stored		3-06
❑ –	BAPC.252	Flexiform h-g	ex Lancaster. Built Macclesfield c 1982. Stored		3-06
❑ –		HM.14 'Flea'.	under construction. Stored	[1]	3-04
❑ –		Skyhook Safari	stored. From Len Gabriel, London-Paris flight		3-04
❑ –		BAE RJX 100	ex Woodford. Composite, unfinished sections.		
			Mostly Set.396. Stored.	off-site [2]	3-04
❑ MT847		Spitfire XIV	ex Cosford, Weeton, Middleton St George,		
	'AX-H'		Freckleton, Warton, 6960M, 226 OCU, AAEE	RAF	3-06
❑ WG763		EE P.1A	ex Henlow, 7816M, RAE, AAEE, EE.	RAF	3-06
❑ WR960		Shackleton AEW.2	ex Cosford, 8772M, 8, 205, AAEE, 210, 42, 228	RAF	3-06
❑ WT619		Hunter F.1	ex Henlow, St Athan, 7525M, 233 OCU, 222, 43		
			Partially sectioned	RAF	3-06
❑ WZ736		Avro 707A	ex Waddington, Cosford, Finningley, 7868M,		
			Colerne, RAE Bedford, AAEE, Avro	RAF	3-06
❑ XG454		Belvedere HC.1	ex Henlow, 8366M, Abingdon, AAEE, Bristol,		
			Old Sarum, Belvedere Trials Unit	RAF	3-06
❑ XL824		Sycamore HR.14	ex Henlow, 8021M, Wroughton, CFS, 1564 Flt, 103, 284	RAF	3-06
❑ [XS179]	'20'	Jet Provost T.4	ex Salford, Halton '8237M' (8337M), Kemble,		
			Shawbury, CAW, RAFC. Stored	off-site	3-04
❑ [997]		Ohka 11	BAPC.98. Ex 8485M, Henlow, Cottesmore, Cranwell	RAF	3-06

MANCHESTER AIRPORT (RINGWAY)

Aviation Viewing Park (AVP): The Trident finally made its arrival in September 2005. Concorde was opened up for public inspection for the first time on 7th April 2004.

In a co-operative arrangement with Salford University's Department of Aeronautical Engineering, the RJX will also be used as an instructional airframe [1]. The AVP commands great views of the comings and goings at the airport.

◆ *Access off the A538 Wilmslow Road, between Junction 6 of the M56 and the airport tunnels. Open daily from 8.30am to dusk, excluding December 26. The Trident Preservation Society is working to support Zulu-Kilo – more details on www.zulukilo.org.uk and www.hs121.org 01625 534 790 or 0161 489 2443*

❑ G-AWZK*	Trident 3B-101	ex Heathrow, BA, BEA. 14-10-86. BEA c/s. Arr 11-9-05		3-06
❑ G-BOAC	Concorde 102	ex BA, G-N81AC, BOAC		3-06
❑ G-DMCA	DC-10-30	ex Airport, Monarch, N3016Z. CoA 11-3-03. Nose		3-06
❑ G-IRJX	RJX 100	ex Woodford	[1]	3-06
❑ XD624	Vampire T.11	ex Macclesfield, CATCS, CNCS, Church Fenton SF, 19		3-06

Airport: After 24 years with the fire crews, Trident 1C G-ARPK gave up the ghost on 16th March 2006, when it was scrapped and carted away.

❑ 'G-SMOKE'	Trident 2E	G-AVFG, ex Granada TV, Heathrow, BA, BEA CoA 2-7-85. Forward fuselage, green colours	10-05
❑ –	ATP	ex Chadderton, c/n 2072. Fuselage. Fire crews	9-04

MOSTON on the B6393 north of Manchester

The Airbuggy is in need of confirmation, or it will be moved to LOST!

❑ G-AXYX	Ekin Airbuggy	CoA 9-11-77	7-94

OLDHAM

A 737 fuselage has arrived here for use with a college.

❑ EI-CKR*	Boeing 737-2K2	ex Prestwick, Ryanair, PH-TVR, C-FICP, PH-TVR, D-AJAA ntu, PH-TVR. Fuselage. Arrived by 11-04	2-06

RADCLIFFE on the A665 south-west of Bury

No.1005 Squadron Air Cadets: In Knowles Street. The 'JP' nose is 'parented' by RAF Sealand.

❑ XN466	Jet Provost T.3A	ex 1 FTS, 7 FTS, 1 FTS. Nose	3-06

ROYTON on the A671 north of Oldham

No.1855 Squadron Air Cadets: 'Parent' is Sealand, the HQ is located in Park Lane. WS726 will wear 25 Squadron colours when its restoration is completed in mid-2006.

❑ WS726	'G' Meteor NF.14	7960M, ex Kemble, 1 ANS, 2 ANS, 25	®	3-06

SALFORD south-west of Manchester

University of Salford: The Cessna is destined to become a simulator with a 'glass' cockpit.

❑ OO-WIO	Cessna FRA.150L	dismantled – see above	7-03
❑ –	VJ-23 hang-glider	donated by Peter Barlow.	7-99
❑ –	Rotec Rally 2B	ex North Coates, Binbrook	10-03

STOCKPORT on the A6 south-east of Manchester

Peter Rolfe: Is turning the Sea Venom pod into a simulator in the general area.

❑ XG692	Sea Venom FAW.22	ex Baxterley, Hatton, Alcester, Wellesbourne Mountford, Sydenham, Castlereagh, Sydenham, 750. Pod	10-03

WIGAN north-west of Manchester
Ponsford Collection: See Breighton, E Yorks, and Selby, N Yorks, for the bulk of Nigel's 'fleet'.

❑ CHQ	1559 T.31B	ex Bury St Edmunds, Leeds, XN247	3-06
❑ –	BAPC.15 Addyman STG	ex Warmingham, Wigan, Harrogate	3-06
❑ RA848	Cadet TX.1	ex Harrogate, Wigan, Handforth. Cockpit	3-06

WOODFORD AIRFIELD on the A5102 east of Wilmslow
[In answer to a couple of queries received about Woodford's location – county-wise – the majority of the airfield is in Greater Manchester. The threshold of Runway 25 – nearest to Poynton – and about 3,700ft of it is in Cheshire.]
Avro Heritage Centre / The '603 Club: Two static reproductions, an Avro Type F and a Type G were started during 2005 for eventual display. The same team are building a Roe I triplane for eventual display at the Lea Valley Experience. All of these are in their formative stages and do not yet merit a 'formal' listing. The Avro 504L is being rebuilt to flying condition for Geoff New [1].The nose of Vulcan B.2 XM602 moved to Bruntingthorpe, Leics, on 11th October 2005 to act as a crew familiarisation trainer for XH558.
◆ *Open Tue and Thu 10.30am to 4pm, contact the centre on 0161 9554182 to arrange. Note: Cameras not allowed on the site and at least two weeks notice is needed.Avro Heritage Group, c/o BAE Systems, Woodford, Stockport, SK7 1QR tel 0161 9554182*

❑ S-AHAA	Avro 504L	G-EASD, ex Richmond, Sudbury, S-AAP, G-EASD	® [1]	3-04
❑ XM603	Vulcan B.2	ex 44, 101, Wadd Wing, Scampton Wing, 9		3-06

Avro International Aerospace / BAE Systems: By the end of 2004 Jetstream 4100 G-GCJL had moved by road to Humberside Airport, Lincs. It is possible that J61 G-PLXI may go to Liverpool, Merseyside, in due course – qv. (See under Brough, E Yorks, for details of the static test Nimrod AEW.3 XV263.)

❑ G-BTZG	ATP	ex Merpati, G-BTZG, PK-MTV, G-BTZG. Stored	3-06
❑ G-BTZH	ATP	ex Merpati PK-MTW, G-BTZH. Stored	3-06
❑ G-BTZK	ATP	ex Merpati PK-MTZ, G-BTZK. Stored	3-06
❑ G-BUWM	ATP	ex CS-TGB, G-BUWM, CS-TGB, G-11-9. CoA 12-6-93. Stored	3-06
❑ G-6-391	RJX 100	forward fuselage, stored	7-04
❑ G-31-983	Jetstream 32	fuselage, stored	2-04
❑ G-ORJX*	RJX85	unflown, stored	3-06
❑ G-PLXI	ATP(J61)	ex G-MATP, G-OATP ntu. CoA 2-12-92. Stored	3-06
❑ –	c/n 2071 ATP	ex Chadderton. Fuselage, fire crews	3-06
❑ –	c/n 2395 RJX 85	forward and rear fuselage, stored	3-06

MERSEYSIDE

ALTCAR south of Formby, west of the A565
The gunnery ranges still have their Wessex.

❑ XT486	Wessex HU.5	ex Brize Norton 8919M, Wroughton, 845	2-04

BIRKDALE on the A565 south-west of Southport
No.281 Squadron Air Cadets: In Upper Aughton Road, keep a 'Chippax'. 'Parent' is Sealand.

❑ WG477	Chipmunk T.10	8362M, ex Hamble G-ATDP, G-ATDI ntu, Marham SF,		
	PAX	MECS,114, Bri UAS, Abn UAS, 11 RFS, 2 BFTS,		
		25 RFS, Liv UAS, 25 RFS	off-site	3-06

BIRKENHEAD DOCKS
Historic Warship Preservation Trust: Went into liquidation in January 2006. As *W&R20* went to press a rescue bid was being planned, but no public access was possible.

❑ XS570	'445' Wasp HAS.1	ex Glasgow, Plymouth, Lee-on-Solent, A2699.	5-03

HAYDOCK on the A580 north of Newton-le-Willows
'JP' T.3 XN492 was up for sale during August 2004 and it moved to Redhill, Surrey.

LIVERPOOL

Liverpool Marriott Hotel South: On the 'old' airport site, Speke, the superb hotel - a development of the 1930s terminal building - is 'guarded' by a Rapide FSM which was repainted by members of the Jetstream Club during 2004. The Jetstream 41 fourth prototype is owned by **The Jetstream Club** and is kept on the apron alongside the hotel. The Club has developed the J41 as an educational tool - the cockpit having been fitted with a series of flat-screens and a computer flight simulator programme powers up instruments and the rudder pedals, throttles and control yokes are 'live'. The cabin has been fitted out in part-airliner, part-classroom format. During late 2005, the club took delivery of the former Keenair AA-1 fuselage, from the 'new' airport site. The possibility of taking on the Jetstream 61 (aka ATP) prototype at Woodford, Gtr Man (qv) is being examined.

◆ *South of the A561. Open Sat and Sun 11am to 4pm. Other times by prior arrangement. Dave Blackburn, 10 Kirkfield Grove, Birkenhead, CH42 1RY e-mail dave@jetstream-club.org www.jetstream-club.org*

❑ 'G-ANZP'	Rapide FSM	BAPC.280, ex 'G-AEAJ'. Federated Air Transport c/s *Neptune*	4-06
❑ G-JMAC	Jetstream 4100	ex Woodford, Prestwick, G-JAMD, G-JXLI. CoA 6-10-97. *Spirit of Speke.*	4-06
❑ G-SEXY*	AA-1 Yankee	ex G-AYLM. Damaged 11-2-94. Fuselage	4-06

Roy Coates: Has a Sea Hawk cockpit and is restoring it.
◆ Available for inspection by prior arrangement *only.* www.wv838.com

❑ WV838	Sea Hawk FGA.6	ex Bruntingthorpe, Chippenham, Fleetlands, 736, 738, 802. SOC 19-4-59. Cockpit	®	12-05

Others: Reference *W&R19*, page 155, Auster J/5F G-AMUI also moved to Okehampton, Devon.

LIVERPOOL (JOHN LENNON) **AIRPORT** (SPEKE)

Keenair donated the fuselage of AA-1 G-SEXY to the Jetstream Club at the 'old' airport (above) during 2005.

NEWTON-LE-WILLOWS on the A572 north of Warrington

Colin Waterworth:

❑ WB440	Firefly AS.6	ex Manchester, Heaton Chapel, Newton, Salford, Failsworth, Anthorn, 812. Cockpit	1-00

WEST MIDLANDS

☛ Within the administrative regional county boundaries can be found the unitary authorities of Birmingham, Coventry, Dudley, Sandwell, Solihull, Walsall and Wolverhampton.

BERKSWELL between the A452 and the A45 west of Coventry

Ken Woolley: The Dingbat still slumbers...

❑ G-AFJA	Dingbat	ex Headcorn. Crashed 19-5-75. Stored	12-05

BIRMINGHAM

Thinktank – Birmingham Science Museum: Within the Spitfire and Hurricane can be found 'flying'.

◆ *At the Millennium Point Discovery Centre, well signed. Open daily 10am to 5pm, last entry 4pm. Phone to check Xmas season openings.millennium Point, Curzon Street, Birmingham, B4 7XG tel 0121 20222222, e-mail findout@thinktank.ac www.thinktank.ac*

❑ 'P3395'	Hurricane IV	KX829, ex Loughborough, 631, 1606 Flt,	
'JX-B'		137. 1 Sqn, F/L Arthur Clowes DFM colours	12-05
❑ ML427	Spitfire IX	ex Castle Bromwich, St Athan, South Marston,	
'HL-A'		Millfield, Hucknall, 6457M, FLS, 3501 SU. FLS c/s	12-05

BIRMINGHAM AIRPORT (ELMDON)

❑ G-WMCC	Jetstream 3102	ex G-31-601, G-TALL, G-31-601. Fire crews	12-05

BRIERLEY HILL on the A461 south-west of Dudley
No.2156 Squadron Air Cadets: In Hickman Road, Brockmoor. 'Parented' by Cosford.

❑ XZ131	Harrier GR.3	9174M, ex St Athan, 1417 Flt, 233 OCU, 4, 1, 4. Nose	2-06

COVENTRY
Coventry University: As part of a major revamp of the **School of Engineering**, in Alma Street, Hillfields, a pair of airframes from Ipswich have moved in.

❑ XR635*	Scout AH.1	ex Ipswich, Arborfield, Yeovilton, Middle Wallop, 653, 660.	
		Arrived 8-04	8-04
❑ XW270*	Harrier T.4	ex Ipswich, Bruntingthorpe, Cranfield, Wittering, 4, 1, 233	
		OCU, 1, 233 OCU. Wing from XV748. Arrived 14-9-04	9-04

Others: The Chilton is with Roy Nerou [1]. The Mustang Restoration Company's P-51 is reported to be available for sale [2]. **Maurice** and **Peter Bayliss'** Hurricane, most likely a former Canadian example, is *believed* underway locally [3]. See East Kirkby, Lincs, for their Spitfire Tr.IX.

❑ G-AFSV	Chilton DW.1A	CoA 12-7-72	® [1] 7-00
❑ 413954	P-51D-5-NA	G-UAKE, ex Norwich, Ailes Anciennes Le Bourget,	
		Bordeaux, 338th FS, 55th FG. *Da' Quake*	[2] 2-06
❑ –	Hurricane	–	® [3] 12-93

HOCKLEY HEATH south of Solihull, near the M42-M40 interchange
Much camouflaged Aztec G-SHIP moved to Ollerton, Cheshire, by 2004.

SOLIHULL south-east of Birmingham centre
Keith Williams and **Mike Thorn** continue to work on the Bristol Scout.

❑ 'A1742'	Bristol Scout REP	BAPC.38, ex Norwich, Lowestoft, Duxford, Avon area,	
		St Mawgan, St Athan, Colerne, Weeton	® 12-05

WOLVERHAMPTON
Boulton Paul Aircraft Heritage Project (BPAHP): The museum and workshop are run by the **Boulton Paul Association**, courtesy of **Smiths Mechanical Systems**. An extensive exhibition of BP's history has been created and it is also home to the West Midland Aviation Archive. Latest project is the forward fuselage of a BP Overstrand biplane, turret-equipped bomber.

    Notes: Several of the airframes are on loan: ANEC Missel Thrush REP from Bob Trickett [1];. Goevier 3 from Bob Arnold (also part of StART, see below) [2]; the Anson C.19 nose (despite *W&R19!*) is on loan from TAC [3]; the Danish Hunter nose is on loan from Classic Jet of Exeter, Devon [3].

Peter Alcock and Vaughan K Meers' Air Training Heritage Collection has been reformulated into the **Staffordshire Aircraft Restoration Team** (StART). Several airframes (marked St) are on display and on loan here. For main details of StART see the separate entry below. StART's Cadet TX.3 WT877, Grasshopper TX.1 XK822 and Sedbergh TX.1 XN188 moved to local store (see below) during 2005. Motor Cadet G-BPIP is due to move to Abbots Bromley, Staffs, during 2006 [4]. Cadet TX.1 'PD685' has been restored to represent an example that served from Walsall with 43 Gliding School and will be fitted with Grasshopper wings [5] and is expected to move to a local store during 2006.

The Defiant re-creation uses an original turret, and some parts from salvaged remains [6]. The rear fuselage of N3378 and other parts are displayed in a diorama depicting the Bleaklow Moor crash site. These have been joined by the engine and propeller from N1766, on loan from the Night-Fighter Preservation Team.

◆ *Within the Smiths complex, in Wobaston Road, off the A449 Wolverhampton to Stafford road, west of Ford Houses/Oxley. Open Wednesdays and Fridays 2pm to 4pm, May to Oct, by appointment please. For dates of open days – always on Sundays – use the contacts below.Boulton Paul Heritage Project, c/o Smiths Mechanical Systems, Wobaston Road, Wolverhampton. e-mail bpheritagecentre@btopenworld.co.uk www.boultonpaul.com*

❑	G-BPIP*		Motor Cadet III	ex Buckfast Abbey. CoA 27-9-96.	St 3-06
❑	[G-FBPI]		Missel Thrush REP	ex Stoke-on-Trent. Unfinished fuselage	[1] 3-06
❑	CFZ	1759	T.8 Tutor	ex Dowty G/C, Pershore, RAFGSA.178	3-06
❑	DBU	1992	Goevier 3	ex D-5233	St [2] 3-06
❑	'X-25'		B&P P.6 FSM	BAPC.274	3-06
❑	'L7005'	'PS-B'	Defiant recreation	BAPC.281. 264 Sqn colours	[6] 3-06
❑	'PD685'*		Cadet TX.1	ex Wolverhampton, Stoke-on-Trent, ATC	St [5] 3-06
❑	VP519		Anson C.19/2	G-AVVR, ex 'Manchester', Dukinfield, Hadfield, Stockport, Peel Green, Cosford, Wigan, Irlam, Shawbury, FCCS, 11 GCF, MCS, 31, Malta CF, TCDU. Nose	[3] 3-06
❑	WJ576		Canberra T.17	ex Bruntingthorpe, Cardiff, St Athan, 360, MoA, *Swifter* Flight, 231 OCU. Nose	St 3-06
❑	WN149		Balliol T.2	ex Bacup, Salford, Failsworth, RAFC. Mock-up rear fuse	® 3-06
❑	WN534		Balliol T.2	ex Bacup, Salford, Failsworth, 22 MU, RAFC	3-06
❑	WZ755		Grasshopper TX.1	BGA.3481. Ex Gallows Hill, Brunton, Barnstaple	St 3-06
❑	XE799*	'R'	Cadet TX.3	ex Syerston, 8943M, CGS. Arrived by 12-04	St 3-06
❑	XR662	'25'	Jet Provost T.4	ex Bicester, Kemble, Finningley, Halton 8410M, SoRF, CAW, CATCS, RAFC, CAW, 6 FTS, CAW	St ® 3-06
❑	ET-272		Hunter T.7	ex North Weald, Bruntingthorpe, Bournemouth, B'thorpe, Bitteswell, Hatfield, RDanAF, Esk.724, G-9-430. Nose	[4] 3-06

Staffordshire Aircraft Restoration Team (StART): was set up during 2005 based partly on Alec Brew's former Black Country Aircraft Collection and including Air Training Heritage Collection (see Boulton Paul Aircraft Heritage Project above) and more of Vaughan K Meers' airframes. Cadet TX.1 'PD685' has moved to BPAHP for display – see above. Other than these, airframes are in store at a variety of locations in the area ad see also Sleap, Shrop, and Abbots Bromley, Staffs, for more of Vaughan's airframes. Parts are being gathered for a Miles Martinet ('RG907') and a Defiant ('K8310'), both cockpit reproductions.

◆ *Airframes on display at the BPAHP above. Other elements available for inspection only by prior permission. Alec Brew, 35 Blakeley Avenue, Wolverhampton WV6 9HR tel / fax 01902 759696*

❑	G-MMFS*		Tiger Cub 440	ex Otherton. *Black Adder*. CoA 27-7-01. F/n 11-05	1-06
❑	RA-01641	'3'	An-2 Colt	forward fuselage. Crashed 9-99. Stored	1-06
❑	WT877*		Cadet TX.3	ex BPAHP, Walsall, Swinderby, St Athan GC, Syerston, 621 GS	1-06
❑	XK822*		Grasshopper TX.1	ex BPAHP, Kenley, Wimbledon, W Malling, Wimbledon	1-06
❑	XN188*	CJV	Sedbergh TX.1	BGA.1588. Ex BPAHP, 'Wales'	1-06
❑	XP494*		Grasshopper TX.1	ex Rattlesden, Breighton, Stoke-on-Trent, Syerston, Stamford, Cosford, Ratcliffe College, Syerston	1-06
❑	-*		Chipmunk T.10	PAX. Stored	1-06

Michael Boulanger and **Mark Ray** of the Wolverhampton Aviation Group keeps his 'JP' in the area.

◆ *Viewable by prior arrangement only. e-mail mb004a9112@blueyonder.co.uk*

❑	XW315		Jet Provost T.5	ex Long Marston, 'Lincs', CFS, 3 FTS, CFS. Nose	3-06

NORFOLK

ATTLEBOROUGH on the A11 south west of Norwich

Dave Pope: Back from a spell in Malta in April 2005, Dave couldn't give up the collecting 'bug' and set to acquiring a varied 'fleet'. The composite R-22 comprises the bare pod of G-BNGC and the boom of G-BMBX [1]. Another R-22 is supplying spares.

❑ G-PFAG*		Evans VP-1	ex Harthill, Netherthorpe. CoA 30-6-89. Arr 16-7-05	4-06
❑ G-SUMT*		Robinson R-22	ex Spalding, Leeds. Cr 27-5-05. Arr 11-11-05. Spares	4-06
❑ -*		Robinson R-22	ex Ipswich. Composite. Arrived 25-6-05	[1] 4-06
❑ CSA*	1760	T.59F Kestrel	ex Spalding. Cockpit. Arrived 30-6-05	[1] 4-06
❑ FCQ*	3157	Schleicher K8B	ex Spalding, D-0322. Cockpit. Arrived 30-6-05	[1] 4-06

BODNEY CAMP on the B1108 west of Watton

Army Training Estate (ATE) **East**: South of the camp is an extensive training area, centred upon Stanford Water. The two airframes are/were located within the 'drop zone' and are thought to be 'passive' targets (ie they do not get shot at) but as the whole area is huge and access totally restricted, it is not easy to confirm.

❑ WJ775		Canberra B.6RC	ex St Athan, Swanton Morley 8581M, 51, 192	5-96
❑ –		Wessex	–	5-96

COLTISHALL AIRFIELD east of the B1150, north of Coltishall

RAF Coltishall: No.41 Squadron disbanded here on 1st April 2006 and 6 Squadron flew off to Coningsby to start the wind-down that will end in October 2007. A small enclave will remain here, looking after the Jaguar simulator complex, until such time as 'Jags' are also a thing of the past. The base will close in December 2007. The Hurricane up the pole here is not to be confused with the one in similar stance at Farnsfield, Notts! [1] The former Brüggen Jaguar 'guardian' is a composite, based upon the nose and forward fuselage of S.07 XW563 [2]. Jaguar GR.1 XX109 to Norwich Airport, Norwich, 1st September 2004. The cockpit of GR.1A XX979 moved to the cockpit team – see below, the rest was scrapped.

❑ 'V7467'	'LE-D'	Hurricane FSM	BAPC.223, 242 Sqn colours. Gate	[1] 2-06
❑ XW563		Jaguar GR.1	8563M. ex 'XX822', Brüggen. Gate	[2] 2-06
❑ XX846*		Jaguar T.4	ex 16, 41, 16, 41, 226 OCU, RAE, 226 OCU, 6, 226 OCU, 2, 226 OCU. Spares recovery by 8-05	2-06
❑ XZ367	'GP'	Jaguar GR.3	ex Shawbury, 54, 2, 226 OCU, 2, 14. Overstressed. 6 Sqn 90th anniversary colours. WLT	2-06

Mick Jennings and team: The cockpits are looked after by a volunteer team led by CRO Mick Jennings MBE. The Shackleton cockpit is owned by a serviceman based at 'Colt' and it is intended to repaint it during 2006. [1].The Lightning F.3 is on loan from the Lightning PG from Bruntingthorpe, Leics [2]; the F.6 from Charles Ross of Binbrook, Lincs [3].

❑ VP293*	'A'	Shackleton T.4	ex Winthorpe, Coventry, Woodford, Coventry, East Kirkby, Strathallan, RAE, MOTU, 206, 224. Cockpit. Arr 2005	[1] 2-06
❑ XF321*		Hunter T.7	ex Bruntingthorpe, Exeter, Yeovilton A2734, Manadon A2648, RAE, 56, 130. Nose. Arrived 5-05	2-06
❑ XN967*	'233'	Buccaneer S.1	ex Weybourne, Fleckney, Helston, Culdrose A2627, SAH-20, Lossiemouth. Cockpit. Arrived 18-10-04	2-06
❑ XP703		Lightning F.3	ex Bruntingthorpe, Warton, MoD, 29, 56, 74. Cockpit	® [3] 2-06
❑ XS899	'E'	Lightning F.6	ex Bruntingthorpe, Cranfield, Binbrook, 11, 5-11 pool, 23, 5. Nose. 23 Sqn colours	[4] 2-06
❑ XV426	'P'	Phantom FGR.2	ex Coningsby, 56, 23, 228 OCU, 111, 31. Nose	2-06
❑ XX830		Jaguar T.2A	ex Warton, Shawbury, St Athan, ETPS.Nose	2-06
❑ XX979*		Jaguar GR.1A	ex spares recovery, GIA, St Athan, DTEO, AAEE. Cockpit	2-06
❑ XZ375		Jaguar GR.1	ex St Athan, 9255M, 54, 14, 20. *The Guardian Reader*. Nose	2-06

DEOPHAM GREEN north of the A11, north of Attleborough

Turbulent G-ARRZ moved, possibly to Bedfordshire, during 2005. Kensinger G-ASSV to Tibenham, Norfolk.

EAST DEREHAM on the A47 west of Norwich

Russell Dagless: By early 2005 Scout AH.1 XV134 (G-BWLX) had moved to Oaksey Park, Wilts. Wasp HAS.1 XT420 (G-CBUI) moved to Thruxton, Hants, by August 2003 and was flying by 2004.

❏ 5X-UUX	Scout Srs 1	G-BKLJ, ex Tattershall Thorpe, Heysham, Panshanger, Uganda Police Air Wing	7-02
❏ XP166	Scout AH.1	G-APVL, ex Farnborough, RAE, G-APVL	7-02
❏ XV138	Scout AH.1	ex Almondbank, Wroughton, 658	7-02

EAST WINCH AERODROME on the A47 east of King's Lynn
Another entry heading for LOST!

❏ G-BEXK	Pawnee 235D	ex N82424 ntu. Crashed 4-10-92. Frame	8-97

EAST WRETHAM east of the A1075 north of Thetford
Thorpe Camp: See also the 'northern' end of this area, listed under Bodney Camp, Norfolk. The hulk of Scout AH.1 XT643, last noted in November 2003, is believed long since gone.

❏ XM386	'08' Jet Provost T.3	ex St Athan 8076M, Halton, Shawbury, 2 FTS, CFS	2-06

FELTHORPE AERODROME south of the B1149, north-west of Norwich
As threatened/promised in *W&R19*, Nipper II G-ARBG (last noted May 1991) has moved to LOST!

GREAT YARMOUTH
Dick Melton Aviation: Negotiations with Solent Sky came to a successful conclusion early in 2005 and Walrus W2718 moved to Southampton, Hants,

Sea-Front Crazee Golf: The hulk of a Cessna Centurion adorns part of the course.

❏ G-MANT	Cessna 210L II	ex Oxford, G-MAXY, N550SV. Crashed 16-2-92	2-06

HARDWICK or Shelton Common, east of the A140, west of Bungay
93rd Bomb Group Museum: An incredible museum set in three Nissen huts on the former Station 104's Communal Site A with superb displays.

◆ *Open third Sunday of each month, May to Oct. 10am to 5pm. Other times by appointment. Paul Thrower, 12 St David's Close, Long Stratton, Norfolk, NR15 2PP tel 01508 531405 www.93rd-bg-museum.org.uk*

Maurice Hammond: Well-known warbird operator, restorer and engine rebuilder, Maurice is nearing the end of the restoration of his *second* P-51. (He operates G-MSTG from a strip nearby.)

❏ 44-13521	P-51D-20-NT	G-MRLL, ex Etampes, Tech college, USAAF, 339th FG. Crashed 13-8-44.	® 3-06

KING'S LYNN
The former Russian Hurricane moved to Crowland, Lincs, and is one-and-the-same with that listed on page 135 of *W&R19*. The Bristol F.2b and crash site Hurricane previously listed here are now thought either not sufficient to list or no longer here. The ANEC Missel Thrush REP fuselage is at Wolverhampton, W Mids. Terrier 2 G-AYDW moved to Okehampton, Devon, by May 2005.

LITTLE SNORING AERODROME north of the A148, north of the village
Nord 3202B G-BPMU moved to Swanton Morley, Norfolk.

❏ G-FISK	Pazmany PL-4A	CoA 11-4-96. Stored	10-05

LONG STRATTON on the A140, south of Norwich
Stratton Motor Company: In the Thurston Industrial Estate, keep an L39 Albatros.

❑	[28+04]*		L39 Albatros	ex NVA 142. Dismantled. First noted 6-05	9-05

MARHAM AIRFIELD south of the A47 west of Swaffham
RAF Marham: Canberra T.4 'VN799' (WJ874) bowed out on 1st September 2005. This marked the very last of the '1st generation' Canberras serving with the RAF. It was awaiting collection on Christmas Eve 1954, initially joining the Station Flight at Gaydon – an incredible service record. It was put up for tender and was acquired by Air Atlantique, flying off to Coventry, Warks, on 9th November 2005. As *W&R20* closed for press, the official disbandment parade for 39 Squadron was set for July 28, which would also mean the end of the road for the PR.9. With the RAF Museum already having an example (at Cosford) is not known if the fleet – XH131, XH134 and XH135 - will be released for the possibility of preservation. The **Tornado Training School** (TTS) has at least two airframes. Tornados are beginning to be withdrawn, 'lying out' for spares reclamation prior to disposal.

❑	WT509	'BR'	Canberra PR.7	ex 100, 13, MoS, 58, 80, 17, 31. Dump by 11-03		9-04
❑	XH168*		Canberra PR.9	ex 39, 1 PRU, 39, 58. Damaged 8-9-03.		
				Spares recovery by 7-05		1-06
❑	XH169*		Canberra PR.9	ex 39, 1 PRU, 39, 58. Spares recovery by 10-05		3-06
❑	XH673		Victor K.2	8911M, ex 57, Witt Wing, 139, MoA. Outside SHQ.		
				Joint 55 and 57 Sqn colours.		9-04
❑	ZA267		Tornado F.2	9284M, ex Boscombe Down. Inst	TTS	10-02
❑	ZA322	'TAC'	Tornado GR.1	9334M, ex 15. Spares		7-05
❑	ZA356		Tornado GR.1	ex St Athan, 15. Cockpit	TTS	3-04
❑	ZA361*	'TD'	Tornado GR.1	ex 15, TTTE. Spares, first noted 8-4-03		7-05
❑	ZA375	'AJW'	Tornado GR.1	9335M, ex 13, 617. Spares recover, outside 28-4-03		7-05
❑	ZA407		Tornado GR.1	9336M. ex 617, TWCU. Last flew 22-11-01.		
				Plinth-mounted, displayed in the camp. Unveiled 2-11-04		11-05

MARTHAM on the B1152 north of Great Yarmouth
JME Aviation: Jeremy Moore's workshop is working on the Fw 190 and the Me 262 for the Flying Heritage Collection (also known as Vulcan Warbirds Inc) of Seattle, USA, owned by the Microsoft mogul Bill Allen [1]. The Lancaster (previously and wrongly listed under Greenham Common, Berks) nose section is a long-seated 'chestnut'. See under Sandtoft, Lincs, in *W&R18* (pp142/143) for the bulk of the rationale behind this and Armthorpe, S Yorks for the rest of G-29-1. It is now thought that the *extreme* nose (ie from the windscreen forward) comes from Lancaster I TW911 [2]. The Lincoln nose, the CASA 2-111 and the Mosquito are all stored for Flying Heritage. [3]. The Cornells has been in storage since circa 1997 and 1999 respectively. See under Earls Colne and North Weald, both Essex, for more details [4]. Spitfire XVIII SM969 (last noted here in January 2004) moved to Australia, then *back* to the UK at Greenham Common, Berks, and was due to move on to Duxford, Cambs. Clearing up *W&R19* (p160) the Yak-3 did not come here.

◆ *Visits strictly by prior appointment* only.

❑	G-AWHB		CASA 2-111	ex North Weald, Royston, Southend, Battle of Britain,		
				Spanish AF B2I-57. Stored. Arrived late 2002	[3]	2-06
❑	G-29-1		Lincoln B.2	ex North Weald, Bournemouth, Bedford, North Weald,		
				Bitteswell, Blackbushe, Southend, Cranfield, G-APRJ,		
				G-36-3, Napiers G-29-1, G-APRJ, RF342. Nose.		
				Arrived 21-1-04	[2, 3]	2-06
❑	N9606H*		PT-26 Cornell	ex Earls Colne, Andrewsfield, Southend, USA, FH768,		
				42-14361. Stored	[4]	3-06
❑	N33870*		PT-19-FA Cornell	ex North Weald, G-BTNY, N33870, USAAF. Stored	[4]	2-06
❑	TV959*		Mosquito T.3	ex Duxford, Hounslow, Lambeth, Bicester, 3 CAACU,		
		'AF-V'		HCEU, 228 OCU, 13 OTU. Stored. Arrived 12-6-03	[3]	2-06
❑	1227		Fw 190A-5	N19027, ex North Weald, G-FOKW, Biggin Hill,		
				Wycombe Air Park, Russia, 'DG+HO'. Cr 19-7-43	® [1]	3-06
❑	'111617'		Me 262A-1a/U3	N94503, ex Chino, Glendale, Hughes, USAAF,		
				FE-4012 / T2-4012, Lechfeld, 500453	[1]	3-06

NARBOROUGH south of the A47, north west of Swaffham
Wellesley Aviation:

❑ WH850	Canberra T.4	ex Winthorpe, Barton, Chelford, Samlesbury, St Athan, Laarbruch SF, Wildenrath SF, 14,88,Marham SF. Nose	10-02

NEATISHEAD east of the A1151, north of Hoveton, near Horning
Air Defence Radar Museum: The museum is dedicated to every aspect of the history of radar, air defence and battle management. Housed in the original 1942 Operations Building, exhibits include a Battle of Britain 'Ops' Filter Room, a 'Cold War' era 'Ops' Room, ROC Field Post and much more.
◆ *Open 10am to 5pm (last entry 3pm) on the second Saturday of each month, Bank Holidays and every Tues and Thurs, early April to end of Oct. Group visits by prior arrangement. 'Brown signed' off the A1062. Museum Manager, RAF Air Defence Radar Museum, Neatishead, Norwich, NR12 8YB tel 01692 633309 e-mail curator@radarmuseum.co.uk www.radarmuseum.co.uk*

RAF Neatishead: The base was closed during the summer of 2005 and Phantom FGR.2 XV420 was scrapped on site during July. The nose section was kept intact, bound for a yard in Derbyshire, 15th July 2005.

NORWICH
Hull Aero: Ralph Hull is working on a variety of projects. The Seafire is registered to Wizzard (double 'zed') Investments, see under Greenham Common, Berks [1]. The Spitfire IX will return to Canada when completed [2]. Work is also reported underway on the former OFMC Sea Fury, for Kermit Weeks. The fuselage of Spitfire XVI TD135 is reported to have been exported to Belgium. By late 2005, B-26C N4806E and B-26K nose 417657 had moved to Canterbury, Kent.

❑ D-CACY	Sea Fury FB.11	G-BWOL, ex Wycombe (!), Duxford, Uetersen, DLB ES3617, G-9-66, WG599	®	8-02
❑ N4806E*	B-26C Invader	ex Norwich, Manston and area, Southend Airport, Rockford (Illinois), 44-34172, Davis-Monthan, 3 BW, 17 BW, 7 ADW. Stored		2-06
❑ PP972	Seafire III	G-BUAR, ex Martham, Earls Colne, Audley End, East Midlands, Biggin Hill, Thruxton, Biggin Hill, Aéronavale 12F, Bien Hoa, 1F, PP972, FAA, 767, 809	® [1]	1-04
❑ TD314	Spitfire IX	ex Canada, 'N601DA', South Africa, SAAF, 234, 183	® [2]	4-04
❑ 417657*	B-26K Invader	N99218, ex Norwich, Ludham, Booker, Canterbury, Southend, Chino, USAF. Nose. Stored		2-06

Ted Sinclair: *Should* still have two Tempests; the former Ludham example being the most complete.

❑	Tempest V	ex Spanhoe. Cockpit.	®	2-02
❑	Tempest V	ex Ludham, Norwich. Cockpit.	®	4-95

Classic Aero Services: By July 2004 Phil Earthy's Harvard II G-CCOY had arrived from Swansea, Wales. It moved to Bruntingthorpe, Leics, in April 2005. Phil has an anonymous Tiger Moth and a T-33 stored in the area.

❑ G-WGHB*	T-33A/N	ex Wycombe Air Park, Gainsborough, Sandtoft, Portsmouth, Southampton, Coventry, Duxford, Southend, CF-EHB, CAF 21640, 133640. CoA 13-6-77	1-05
❑ -*	Tiger Moth	ex South Molton. Fuselage frame, stored	1-05

Others: Spitfire IX project SM639 moved to Godalming, Surrey.

NORWICH AIRPORT (HORSHAM ST FAITH)
City of Norwich Aviation Museum (CNAM): Internal displays and the aircraft park continue to be refined. A small cafe is also available. The RAF 100 Group Association collection is in a special section devoted to Bomber Command. Other displays show the history of RAF Horsham St Faith, the 8th Air Force, the role of women in aviation and local aviation pioneers. The contents of the History Room at Coltishall will also locate to here.

Canberra nose WH984 and Lightning ZF592 are on loan from John Sheldrake [1]. Hunter F.6A XG172 is on loan from Mick Jennings (of Coltishall, Norfolk, fame) [2]. The Jaguar is courtesy of RAF Coltishall [3].
◆ *Access from the A140, north of the airport, follow 'brown signs'. Apr to Oct: Tue to Sat, 10am to 5pm; Sun and Bank Hols noon to 5pm. Nov to Mar: Wed and Sat 10am to 4pm, Sun noon to 4pm. Closed Christmas and New Year holiday period. Old Norwich Road, Horsham St Faith, Norwich, NR10 3JF tel/fax 01603 893080 e-mail norwichairmuseum@hotmail.com www.cnam.co.uk*

❑ G-ASKK		Herald 211	ex Air UK, PP-ASU, G-ASKK, PI-C910, CF-MCK.	
			CoA 19-5-85	4-06
❑ G-BHMY		Friendship 200	ex KLM uk, Air UK, F-GBDK, F-GBRV ntu,	
			PK-PFS, JA8606, PH-FDL	4-06
❑ WH984*		Canberra B.15	ex Mold, Bruntingthorpe, Hinckley, Bruntingthorpe, Cosford	
			8101M, HS, 9, Binbrook SF, 9. Nose. Arrived 30-11-05	[1] 4-06
❑ WK654	'B'	Meteor F.8	WK654, ex Neatishead 8092M, Kemble, 85, CFE,	
			Odiham SF, AWFCS, 247. 245 Sqn c/s by 12-05	4-06
❑ 'XE683'	'G'	Hunter F.51	E-409, ex 'XF383' Cardiff-Wales, 'WV309', 'XF383',	
			Dunsfold, G-9-437, DanAF Esk.724. 74 Sqn c/s	4-06
❑ 'XG168'	'10'	Hunter F.6A	XG172, ex North Weald, Ipswich, Scampton 8832M,	
			1 TWU, 229 OCU, 263, 19. FR.10 nose. 79 Sqn c/s	[2] 4-06
❑ XM612		Vulcan B.2	ex 44, Wadd Wing, Scampton Wing, 9	4-06
❑ [XP355]		Whirlwind HAR.10	ex G-BEBC, Faygate, 8463M, 38 GCF, 21, CFS. 22 Sqn c/s	4-06
❑ XP458		Grasshopper TX.1	ex Fakenham area. On loan. Stored	4-06
❑ XX109*		Jaguar GR.1	ex Coltishall 8918M, Warton, AAEE. 54 Sqn colours.	
			Arrived 1-9-04	[3] 4-06
❑ –		Scimitar CIM	–	4-06
❑ 121		Mystère IVA	ex Sculthorpe, FAF. '8-MY'. *Patrouille de France* c/s	4-06
❑ 53-686		Lightning F.53	ZF592, ex Portsmouth, Luxembourg, *Wing Commander*,	
			Stretton, Warton, RSAF 223, 53-686, 1305,	
			G-AWON, G-27-56. On loan. RSaudiAF c/s to port	[1] 4-06
❑ –	'TR-999'	T-33A-5-LO	16718, ex Sculthorpe, Turkish AF ntu, FAF. USAF c/s	4-06

Airport: Tomahawk 112 G-BTOM was stripped for spares and scrapped circa 2002.

❑ G-ATIG	Herald 214	ex BAC Express, PP-SDI, G-ATIG. Towing trainer	2-06
❑ G-AVEZ	Herald 210	ex Museum, Air UK, BIA, BUA, PP-ASW,	
		G-AVEZ, HB-AAH. CoA 5-1-81. Fire crews	2-06
❑ G-BCDN	Friendship 200	ex Air UK, PH-OGA, JA8615, LV-PMR ntu,	
		PH-FDP. CoA 19-7-96. Training airframe, fuselage	3-01
❑ G-BCDO	Friendship 200	ex Air UK, PH-OGB, JA8621, PH-FEZ. *Lord Butler*.	
		Fuselage. Damaged 19-7-90. klm UK Tech College	9-99
❑ G-BTAZ*	Evans VP-2	unflown project. Stored, first noted 10-05	2-06
❑ G-OVNE*	Cessna 401A	ex N401XX, N171SF ntu, N71SF, N6236Q. CoA 8-10-92.	
		Canx 8-2-94. Stored, first noted 10-05	2-06
❑ EI-CAZ	FH.227D	ex Iona, SE-KBR, EI-CAZ, SE-KBR, C-FNAK,	
		CF-NAK, N2735R. Dump by 9-95	2-06

Offshore Fire and Survival Training Centre: Page 162 of *W&R19* recorded the Ford Transit-based helicopter training aid 'G-DRNT' moving on (albeit briefly) to Stansted, Essex, by October 2003. Beyond that it moved to London Heliport, Gtr Lon.

❑ [N5880T]	WG.30-100	ex Weston-super-Mare, Yeovil, Air Spur, G-17-31	2-06

REYMERSTON near East Dereham
Wallis Autogiros: See under London, Gtr Lon, for another 'G-ARZB'. (And there's another in 'Planet Hollywood' in Times Square, New York!)
◆ Not *open to public inspection.*

❑ G-ARRT	WA-116/McC	CoA 26-5-83	8-03
❑ G-ARZB	WA-116 Srs 1	ex XR943, G-ARZB. CoA 29-6-93. *Little Nellie*	8-03

❑ G-ASDY	WA-116/F	CoA 30-4-90	8-03
❑ G-ATHM	WA-116/F	ex 4R-ACK, G-ATHM. CoA 23-5-93	8-03
❑ G-AVDG	WA-116 Srs 1	CoA 23-5-92	8-03
❑ G-AVJV	WA-117	CoA 21-4-89	8-03
❑ G-AVJW	WA-118/M	CoA 21-4-83	8-03
❑ G-AXAS	WA-116-T/Mc	CoA 23-5-92	8-03
❑ G-AYVO	WA-120 Srs 1	ex South Kensington. CoA 31-12-78	8-03
❑ G-BAHH	WA-121/Mc	CoA 26-10-93	8-03
❑ G-BGGU	WA-116	–	8-03
❑ G-BGGW	WA-122/RR	CoA 26-10-93	8-03
❑ G-BLIK	WA-116/F-S	CoA 24-4-98	8-03
❑ G-BMJX	WA-116/X	CoA 1-4-89	8-03
❑ G-BNDG	WA-201/R	CoA 3-3-88	8-03
❑ G-SCAN	WA-116-100	CoA 10-7-91	8-03
❑ G-VIEW	WA-116/L	CoA 6-10-85	8-03
❑ [G-VTEN]	WA-117	CoA 3-12-85	8-03
❑ XR944	WA-116/F	G-ATTB, ex XR944, G-ARZC. CoA 23-5-92	8-03

SEETHING AERODROME east of the B1332, north of Bungay

Station 146 Control Tower Museum: The original control tower has been restored and contains a museum dedicated to the history of the aerodrome and the surrounding area. The tower is a living memorial to the Liberator-equipped 448th BG and the brochure sums it up well: @One building, a whole airfield of memories". There is a shop and refreshments are available. A Nissen hut is now also available for viewing.

◆ *Access from the Thwaite St Mary road to the south. First Sun May to Oct, 10am to 5pm. Other times by appointment. Tony Jeckells, 18 Park Close, Thurton, Norwich, NR14 0AU tel 01508 480635 tony.jeckells@bushinternet.com www.seething.org.uk/448-ct.html www.seething-airfield.co.uk*

SHIPDHAM AERODROME off the A1075 south-west of East Dereham

Twin Comanche 160C G-AYAF (last noted in April 1996) and Tiger Cub 440 G-MJUC (September 2003) had moved on by February 2006.

❑ G-AYUM	Slingsby T.61A	ex Swanton Morley. CoA 10-6-02	®	2-06
❑ G-BGRC*	Cherokee 140B	ex Swanton Morley, SE-FHF. CoA 26-10-97. Stored		2-06
❑ G-JDIX	Mooney M.20B	ex G-ARTB. CoA 16-1-00. Stored		2-06
❑ BXR*	1321 Blanik	stored		2-06
❑ DEY*	2067 Blanik	ex RAFGSA R12. Stored		2-06
❑ D-5826	Blanik	BGA.3186, FDV, stored		2-06

SWANTON MORLEY AERODROME east of the B1110, north of East Dereham

A story of migration from the aerodrome: Aircoupe G-ARHF moved to, possibly, the Cromer area; Mong Sport G-BTOA and VP-1 G-BBXZ to Watton, Norfolk, by late 2005; and by mid-2004, Cherokee 140B G-BGRC to Shipdham, Norfolk. **Nearby:** A trio of Nords are stored in the general area.

❑ G-BPMU*	Nord 3202B	ex Little Snoring, High Ham, N22546, G-BIZJ ntu, Liverpool, USA, ALAT No.70. CoA 19-10-90	2-06
❑ No.37*	Nord 3400	G-ZARA, ex Boston, Stixwould, Breighton, Coventry, La Ferté Alais, ALAT F-MMAB.	2-06
❑ No.124*	Nord 3400	G-BOSJ, ex La Ferté Alais, ALAT F-MMAB. Damaged 12-6-94	2-06

TERRINGTON ST CLEMENT north of the A17, west of King's Lynn

Terrington Aviation Collection: Despite the efforts of *W&R19*, the 'JP' is still stored in this area. See under West Walton Highway, Norfolk, for other TAC airframes.

❑ XM468	Jet Provost T.3	ex King's Lynn, Stock, St Athan, Halton 8081M, Shawbury, 6 FTS, RAFC. Stored	2-04

THORPE ABBOTTS off the A140 at Dickleburgh, north of Scole

100th Bomb Group Memorial Museum: Contents of the tower museum are exceptional, offering poignant insights into the life and times of the men and machines of the 'Bloody Hundredth'. As well as the displays, there are refreshments, a shop, visitor centre and picnic area.

◆ *'Brown signed'. Open 10am to 5pm weekends and Bank Hols. Also Wed 10am to 5pm May to Sep. Closed November to end of January. Other times by appointment. Regular special events are staged. Common Road, Dickleburgh, Diss, IP21 4PH tel 01379 740708*

TIBENHAM north of the B1134, north of Diss

Norfolk Gliding Club: On the former wartime airfield. A Tiger Moth is stored here.

❏ N6965*	Tiger Moth	G-AJTW, ex N6965, 13 OTU, 16 EFTS, 13 OTU, 418, Northolt SF, 24, 81, 613. Crashed 7-6-<u>99</u>. Stored	2-06

Black Barn Aviation: At a strip nearby, specialise in US classics. Super Cub 95 G-AYPP (last noted in June 1996) moved on to the Huntingdon area.

❏ G-BRHB*	N2S-3 Kaydet	ex EC-AID, N67955, BuNo 05334. Canx 3-8-05. Stored	2-06
❏ G-FANC	Fairchild 24R-46	ex Felthorpe, N77647, NC77647. Arson attack 18-2-03. Stored	2-06
❏ N1325M	N2S-5 Kaydet	ex USA, BuNo 43390. Stored	2-06
❏ N1328	Fairchild 24KS	ex USA, NC1328. Stored	2-06
❏ N6438C*	L-5 Sentinel	ex USA ®	2-06
❏ N57783*	L-5 Sentinel	ex USA. Frame, stored	2-06
❏ N62842	PT-17D	ex USA. Stored	2-06
❏ N68427	N2S-4 Kaydet	ex USA, BuNo 55771. Stored	2-06

Nearby:

❏ G-ASSV*	Kensinger KF	ex Deopham Green, Brenchley, Deopham Green, Tonbridge, Bobbington, N23S. Crashed 2-7-69. Stored, in trailer.	2-06

TUNSTEAD east of the B1150, north of Hoveton

❏ G-BARD	Cessna 337C	ex North Coates, SE-FBU, N2557S. Cr 12-6-94	9-99

WATTON on the A1075, south of East Dereham

No.611 Volunteer Gliding School:

❏ XP490	Grasshopper TX.1	BGA.4552, ex Swanton Morley, Ipswich, Syerston, Grantham	9-05

Nearby: A workshop in the area has a couple of homebuilds.

❏ G-BBXZ*	Evans VP-1	ex Swanton Morley. CoA 8-3-96.	2-06
❏ G-BTOA*	Mong Sport	ex Swanton Morley, N1067Z. CoA 16-9-94	2-06

WEST WALTON HIGHWAY on the A47 north-east of Wisbech

Fenland and West Norfolk Aviation Museum: Run by the Fenland and West Norfolk Aircraft Preservation Society. The museum has a close association with the **Terrington Aviation Collection** (TAC) and among the latter's artefacts on loan are the Buccaneer and MiG-29 cockpit sections. Note that TAC's 'JP' T.3 XM468 did not come here and remains stored at Terrington St Clement, Norfolk. Grasshopper TX.1 XP488 moved out, initially to Cranwell, Lincs, having been acquired by a helicopter pilot based at Lee-on-Solent, Hants.

◆ *At Bamber's Garden Centre, Old Lynn Road – signed off the A47/B198 junction. Weekends, Bank Hols, Mar and Oct 9.30am to 5pm. (Other times by appointment.) Old Lynn Road, West Walton, Wisbech, PE14 7DA tel 01945 461771 e-mail bill@wwelbourne.freeserve.co.uk*

❏ G-ARNH	Colt 108	ex Chatteris, Elstree. Damaged 1-9-72. Off-site	®	4-06
❏ WR971	'Q' Shackleton MR.3/3	ex Narborough, Cosford 8119M, 120, Kinloss Wing, 201, 120, Kinloss Wing, CA. Fuselage		4-06

❏ XD434	'25'	Vampire T.11	ex Marham, Barton, W'ford, Chester, St Athan, 5 FTS, 7 FTS		4-06
❏ XM402	'J'	Jet Provost T.3	ex Narborough, West Raynham, Halton, Newton		
			8055AM, Shawbury, 6 FTS, 2 FTS		4-06
❏ XN983		Buccaneer S.2B	ex Terrington St Clement, 12, 208, 15, 12. Nose	TAC	4-06
❏ XS459	'AW'	Lightning T.5	ex Narborough, Binbrook, 5, LTF, 56, 29, 226 OCU		4-06
❏ –		Jet Provost	Procedure trainer. On loan from March Air Cadets		4-06
❏ 526		MiG-29 *Fulcrum*	25887, ex Fairford. Crashed 21-7-93. Cockpit	TAC	4-06

WEYBOURNE on the A149 west of Cromer

Muckleburgh Collection: Bannered as Britain's largest working military collection, there is much to fascinate here, including 'live' tank demonstrations during school holidays - check in advance for details. Buccaneer S.1 nose XN967 moved to Coltishall, Norfolk, on 18th October 2004.

◆ *Open Apr to Oct 10am to 5pm daily. Weybourne Military Camp, Weybourne, NR25 7EG tel 01263 588210 fax 01263 588425 e-mail info@muckleburgh.co.uk www.muckleburgh.co.uk*

❏ WD686	'S'	Meteor NF.11	ex Duxford, RAE Bedford, Wroughton,	
			TRE Defford. 141 Sqn colours	12-05
❏ XZ968	'3G'	Harrier GR.3	ex Marham 9222M, St Athan, 233 OCU, 1417F, 1,4	12-05
❏ –		Fi 103 V-1 REP	on ramp	10-04

WYMONDHAM on the A11 south-west of Norwich

No.1986 Squadron Air Cadets: Acquired the former Duxford kids-plaything Hunter nose from the Duxford Aviation Society and during 2005 transformed it into a superb flight simulator. It attended *CockpitFest* 2005 at Winthorpe, Notts, and came away with the *FlyPast* Readers' Best Cockpit and the Mike Doyle Award. A *likely* identity for this nose is XE612.

❏ –*		Hunter F.6	ex Duxford. Cockpit. 74 Sqn c/s	6-05

NORTHAMPTONSHIRE

CORBY

Frank and **Lee Millar**: See under Winthorpe, Notts, for their Canberra PR.9 nose.

❏ XE849	'V3'	Vampire T.11	ex Barton, Shobdon, Mildenhall, Long Marston, Yatesbury,	
			Monkton Farleigh, Conington, Ware, St Athan, 7928M,	
			CNCS, 5 FTS, 7 FTS, 1 FTS, 4 FTS	5-02

'The Works': The 112A *should* still 'fly' from the ceiling.

❏ G-TCSL	Commander 112A	ex Spanhoe, N506CA, N1322J. Crashed 5-12-94.	12-95

CROUGHTON on the B4031 south-west of Brackley

USAF Croughton: The main gate here has been revamped with the 'Thud' and plinth-mounted F-100 displayed much closer to the road and very prominently.

❏ '63000'	'000'	F-100D-11-NA	42212, ex Upper Heyford, Sculthorpe, FAF	4-06
❏ '63428'	'WW'	F-105G-RE	24428, ex Upper Heyford, Davis-Monthan 'FK095',	
			128 TFS, Georgia ANG. 561 TFS, Korat, colours	4-06

HARRINGTON south-east of Market Harborough

'Carpetbagger' Aviation Museum: The museum is centred upon the hardened group operations building of what was once USAAF Station 179, home of the clandestine 492nd and 801st BGs. This building, restored to its wartime state, houses exhibitions describing the covert operations carried out by the US from Harrington and by the RAF from Tempsford, Beds.

Notes: Working in support of the museum is the **Harrington Aviation Museum Society** (Ron Clarke, 43 Greenhill Road, Kettering, NN15 7LP). In the former Paymaster's building, is the **Northants Aviation Museum** run by the Northamptonshire Aviation Society. This benefits from the NAS's extensive 'dig' activity in the county. (Membership enquiries for NAS to 53 Palmerston Road, Northampton, NN1 5EU.) The Harvard is on loan from Gordon King [1].

◆ *Take the minor road south out of Harrington village, towards Lamport, and turn right after the A14 underpass – follow the signs. Open from Easter to October weekends and Bank Holidays, 10am to 5pm. Other times by prior appointment – min 15 people – to the address and number below. Sunny Vale Farm Nursery, off Lamport Road, Harrington, NN6 9PF tel 01604 686608 e-mail cbaggermuseum@aol.com www.harringtonmuseum.org.uk*

❑ 42-12417	Harvard IIB	ex East Tilbury, Windsor, North Weald, Amsterdam, Dutch AF B-163, RCAF FE930, 42-12417. SNJ-2 colours	[1]	8-05
❑ [G-APWK]	Widgeon	ex Corby (?), Sywell, *Eye of the Needle*, Yeovil. Forward fuselage		8-05

HINTON-IN-THE-HEDGES just west of Brackley

❑ G-AZKN	Robin HR.100	ex East Midlands. Crashed 1-9-95. Wreck	10-01
❑ G-AZLL	Cessna FRA.150L	crashed 4-2-99	10-01
❑ G-BONU	T.67B Firefly	CoA 29-6-00. Stored	10-03

KING'S CLIFFE south of the A47, west of Peterborough

John Tempest: About 90% of the parts from the *original* Cosmic Wind G-ARUL are held plus other components. (G-ARUL, as *Ballerina II* is airworthy.)

❑ G-ARUL	Cosmic Wind	ex Halfpenny Green, N22C. Crashed 29-8-66	®	12-05

NORTHAMPTON

Murray Jacobsen: No news on the *Fishbed* cockpit.

❑ 764	MiG-21SPS	ex Wycombe Air Park, Bonn-Hangelar, East GermAF. Cockpit	6-02

NORTHAMPTON AERODROME or Sywell, north-east of Northampton, off the A43

Sywell Aviation Museum: In mid-2004 plans were unveiled for an extension to this already superb museum, situated adjacent to the lovely art-deco 'terminal' building – now 'The Aviator Hotel'. In conjunction with the airport management, Sywell Aerodrome Ltd, and several based operators, planning permission has been gained for a new visitor and education centre alongside the existing building and a 'blister' hangar to house a couple of based 'historics'. Grasshopper WZ820 was due to return to Shoreham, W Sussex, during mid-April 2006 [1].

◆ *Open weekends and Bank Hols 10am to 4.30pm, Easter to end of Sep. Other times by appointment. Car parking for the museum (no charge) doubles as a viewing area for the aerodrome. Sywell Aerodrome, Sywell, Northants, NN6 0BN tel 07968 061708, or 01604 811582 e-mail bbrown@sherwooddunham.com www.sywellaerodrome.co.uk/history*

❑ G-AIJZ	J/1 Autocrat	ex Derby, Hooton Park, Warmingham, Southend, Shobdon. Crashed 25-10-70. Cockpit. Stored		3-06
❑ WZ820	Grasshopper TX.1	ex Shoreham, Lancing College. Stored	[1]	3-06
❑ XD599*	'A' Vampire T.11	ex Ingatestone, Welshpool, Shobdon, Caernarfon, Bournemouth, Blackbushe, Staverton, Stroud, CATCS, RAFC, 1. Arrived 10-10-04. Stored		3-06

Aerodrome: Previously listed under the museum, the **Sywell Messenger Trust** looks after G-AKIN. Owned by the Spiller family since August 1949, *India-November* has been resident at Sywell for over 50 years. The aim of the trust is to keep the Messenger in airworthy condition and to show it off to the public on regular occasions [1]. Matthew Boddington took delivery of BE.2 repro N1914B on 6th May 2005. It was built by Matthew's late father, Charles, so represents a real 'return home' [2].

The 'Vickers Gunbus' film mock-up is displayed within the 'Hangar One' entertainment complex alongside the 'Aviator Hotel'. It is much more DH.2 than FB.5, having been based on Maurice Kirk's flyer – see under Haverfordwest, Wales [3].

Departures: The late Paul Morgan's P-51D G-SUSY was sold to 'Taff' Smith, becoming G-CDHI. It was ferried to <u>Breighton</u>, East Yorks, on 21-3-05. In the end, all of Percival Q.6 G-AFFD that arrived here was the rudder, the deal having apparently fallen through. Accordingly, it can be again listed under Isle of Man Airport, IoM. A tidy-up of airframes listed in recent editions is called for. Three long-listed choppers have been deleted: Hughes 369HS G-AYIA (last noted 2-98); Hughes 269C G-BAUK (2-98) and Robinson R-22 'G-BEAR' (7-97). Alpha 5 G-APTU (12-03) moved to <u>Leicester</u>, Leics. Colson Cassutt G-BWEC (10-98) has moved on to unknown pastures. Firefly G-MNUL (4-02), destination unknown. Tiger Moth NL985 (G-BWIK - 3-03) also moved on, probably to a Wiltshire address.

❑ G-AKIN	Messenger 2A ✈	-		[1] 3-06
❑ [G-AWYI]*	BE.2c REP	ex N1914B, Old Rhinebeck, G-AWYI. Cr 14-6-77. Arrived 6-5-05		® [2] 3-06
❑ –	Aero C-104	ex USA. Spares use		1-04
❑ 'A1452'*	'Gunbus' REP	BAPC.234, ex 'GBH-7', Swindon, Sleap, High Halden, Hawkinge, Manston, Chelford, Coventry, Old Warden, White Waltham, *Sky Bandits, Gunbus. Bombay 3*. Arrived 10-1-06		[3] 3-06
❑ XP454*	G'hopper TX.1	ex Wellingborough, Kimbolton, Holt. Stored		7-04

SPANHOE LODGE AERODROME south-east of Harringworth

Windmill Aviation: Auster J/1 G-AHCN was flying again by 2004; Auster 5 G-AOFJ by 2003 and Cherokee 140 G-AVLC by 2004. C-3605 C-558 moved to <u>Gainsborough</u>, Lincs, by June 2004 along with not long arrived Tiger Moth G-AOHY, previously at Middle Wallop. The Hunter was owned by Paul Smith and is kept as a 'static' but has since changed hands [1]. The EKW D-3801 was a development of the MS.406 single-seat fighter.

❑ G-BFNM*	Globe Swift	ex Oakham, Tatenhill, Nottingham Airport, N78205 Arrived 12-05		® 12-05
❑ EI-AYL	Airedale	ex Abbeyshrule, G-ARRO, EI-AVP ntu, G-ARRO. CoA 1-2-86		4-06
❑ EI-BAL	Airedale	ex Abbeyshrule, G-ARZS. Cancelled 29-6-79		4-06
❑ EI-BBK	Airedale	ex Abbeyshrule, G-ARXB, EI-ATE ntu, G-ARXB. CoA 11-11-83		4-06
❑ XF375	'05' Hunter F.6A	G-BUEZ, ex Duxford, Cranwell, 8736M, ETPS, Warton, AWA, C(A)		[1] 4-06
❑ 143*	MS.733 Alcyon	G-MSAL, ex North Weald, Wycombe AP, F-BLXV, Fr No.143. Arrived 10-05		® 4-06
❑ J-95	EKW D-3801	ex Switzerland, Swiss AF. Fuselage frame		5-05
❑ J-146	EKW D-3801	ex Switzerland, Swiss AF. Fuselage frame		5-05
❑ –	EKW D-3801	ex Switzerland, Swiss AF. Fuselage frame		5-05

Locally: Geoff Brown is working on another Auster. Turner T40A G-BRIO was flying again by mid-2004. See also Woodhall Spa, Lincs.

❑ G-AJDY	J/1 Autocrat	ex Bedford, Cranfield, Northampton, Spanhoe, Cossall, Sherburn. CoA 9-7-71. Canx 13-1-99		® 3-04

WELLINGBOROUGH

Wellingborough School: Grasshopper XP454 moved to <u>Northampton</u>, Northants, by July 2004.

NORTHUMBERLAND and TYNESIDE

- The five unitary authorities of Gateshead, Newcastle-upon-Tyne, Sunderland, North Tyneside and South Tyneside comprise the 'counties'.

BAMBURGH on the B4130 east of Belford and north-west of Seahouses
Bamburgh Castle Aviation Artefacts Museum: There is a small museum within the castle. Run by Derek Walton, two rooms cover local aviation history, including wreckage from local 'digs'.
- ◆ *'Brown signed' off the A1. Open daily Mar to Oct 11am to 5pm – last entry 4.30pm. Bamburgh, NE69 7DF tel 01668 214515 fax 01668 214060 www.bamburghcastle.com*

BOULMER AIRFIELD east of Alnwick
RAF Boulmer: The Phantom which is looked after by NEAM - see Sunderland, below.

❑ XV415	'E' Phantom FGR.2	9163M, ex 56, 74, 228 OCU, 23, 56, 92, 29, 228 OCU, 56, 228 OCU, 31, 228 OCU, 41, 228 OCU, 41, 54, AAEE. Gate	3-06

ESHOTT south of the B6345 north of Morpeth
A Taylorcraft is under restoration off-site. Nick Stone's Turbulent, previously listed under 'Morpeth', N&T, is also to be found in this area. By April 2004 Hiller G-ATKG had moved on, settling at <u>Stannington</u>, N&T.

❑ G-APOL	Turbulent	ex Charterhall. Damaged 24-7-93. Canx 13-9-00	®	9-05
❑ 42-58687	'IY' T'craft DF-65	G-BRIY, ex N59687, NC59687, TG-6 42-58678. CoA 10-7-98	off-site ®	9-04

MORPETH - see Eshott, above.

NEWCASTLE AIRPORT (WOOLSINGTON)
Newcastle Aviation Academy: See under Sunderland, N&T, for a co-operative restoration venture by the academy. Note that the Rye Hill Campus of Newcastle College is also used as a site.
- ▶ Visits possible *only* be prior arrangement. 0191 271 5821 www.newcastleaviation.co.uk

❑ C-GWJO	Boeing 737-2A3	ex Westjet, HR-SHO, CX-BHM, N1797B, N1787B	3-06
❑ 5N-AAN	HS.125-3B/RA	ex Biggin Hill, F-GFMP, G-AVAI, LN-NPA, G-AVAI	3-06

NEWCASTLE UPON TYNE
Military Vehicle Museum: Created by the North East Military Vehicle Club, a wide array of vehicles and other exhibits are on show. John Stelling's Auster is stored here, for eventual display. It comprises: G-ANFU's forward fuselage, a 'spare' rear AOP.6 frame, starboard wing of G-AKPH and port from an AOP.6 [1]. Please note the Auster is *not* available for public viewing.
- ◆ *Off the A167(M) at the junction with the B1318. Open summer 10am to 4pm daily, Nov to March 10am to dusk on weekends and school holidays only. Other times by appointment. Exhibition Park Pavilion, Newcastle upon Tyne, NE2 4PZ tel 0191 281 7222 www.military-museum.org.uk/*

❑ 'NJ719'	Auster 5	G-ANFU, ex NEAM, Bristol, TW385, 663, 227 OCU, 13 OTU. Stored	[1] 2-06

SOUTH SHIELDS on the A1018 north of Sunderland
Karl and Sam Edmondson: The Vampire 'pod' is a restoration to delight the eyes and rightly was an award winner at *CockpitFest* 2004. They've now added a Canberra to the collection.
- ◆ Visits are possible *only* by prior arrangement. e-mail karl.edmondson@btopenworld.com www.karl.edmondson@btinternet.co.uk

❑ WJ676*	Canberra B.2	ex Hooton Park, Heswall, Stock, Wroughton, Colerne, Melksham, 7796M, 245, 35, 50. Nose		3-06
❑ XD602	Vampire T.11	ex Dundonald, Firbeck, Crowland, ?, Brands Hatch, Birmingham, 7737M, Sutton Coldfield, Smethwick, RAFC, 125. RAFC colours, *Carrie May*		3-06

STANNINGTON on the A1 north of Newcastle

A garage and recovery centre here has acquired a Hiller for restoration.

❑ G-ATKG*	Hiller UH-12B	ex Eshott, Thai AF 103. CoA 28-11-69. 'US Army' colours. Trailer-mounted, arrived 12-03	®	10-05

SUNDERLAND site of the former Usworth aerodrome, west of Sunderland

North East Aircraft Museum (NEAM): This excellent collection continues to refine its exhibits – large and small – and remains an absorbing and wholly rewarding visit. Chipmunk T.10 WB685 is currently off-site under restoration by the staff and students of the Newcastle Aviation Academy – a fine example of 'win-win' co-operation [1]. The Pucará (on loan from the Fleet Air Arm Museum) has been relocated to the main exhibition hangar and is fully assembled [2]. NEAM also look after the Phantom at RAF Boulmer's gate – see above.

Notes: Flea 'G-ADVU' (BAPC.207) incorporates parts from an original, built in Congleton, Ches [3]. Work is underway to turn the Short 330 into a 'hands-on' exhibit, including access for wheelchair-users [4]. The exotically-registered Bö 105 pod (c/n S.863) was donated by Rotortech and is being converted into a 'hands-on' cockpit and travelling exhibit by a NEAM member in Surrey [5]. Chipmunk T.10 WB685 is a composite, including the rear fuselage of WP969 (G-ATHC). See above. [1]. The rear fuselage of Firefly AS.5 VT409 is stored, ready for fitment to WD889 in due course [6]. Vampire T.11 WZ518 is fitted with the wings of WZ608, the 'pod' of which can be found at Rayleigh, Essex [7]. 'JP4' XP627 has the wings of Mk.3 XN584, see Bruntingthorpe, Leics, for the fuselage [8]. Sioux AH.1 XT236 moved to Doncaster, S Yorks, during 2005.

◆ *East of Washington on the Old Washington Road between the A1290 and A1231. Signed off the A1290 and the A19. Daily 10am to 5pm (or dusk in winter). Old Washington Road, Sunderland, SR5 3HZ tel 0191 519 0662 e-mail neam_uk@yahoo.com www.neam.org.uk*

❑ 'G-ADVU'	HM.14 'Flea'	BAPC.211, ex Stoke-on-Trent		[3]	3-06
❑ 'G-AFUG'	Luton Minor	BAPC.97, ex Stoke-on-Trent, Sunderland, Sibson, Sywell, Sunderland, Stanley			3-06
❑ G-APTW	Widgeon	ex Helston, Southend, Westlands. CoA 26-9-75			3-06
❑ G-ARAD	Luton Major	ex local, Borgue. Unflown, started 1959			3-06
❑ G-ASOL	Bell 47D-1	ex Weston-s-Mare, Panshanger, N146B. CoA 6-9-71			3-06
❑ G-AWRS	Anson C.19	ex Strathallan, Kemps, Junex, Hewitts, TX213, WCS, 22 GCF, OCTU, 18 GCF, 2 TAF CS, 527, CSE, RCCF. CoA 10-8-73. On loan		®	3-06
❑ G-BEEX	Comet 4C	ex East Kirkby, Tattershall, Woodford, Lasham, Dan-Air, SU-ALM. Nose			3-06
❑ G-MBDL	Lone Ranger	microlight. Stored			3-06
❑ G-OGIL	Short 330-100	ex Gill, G-BITV, G-14-3068. Damaged 1-7-92		[4]	3-06
❑ 'G-BAGJ'	Gazelle 1	ex Carlisle, G-SFTA, HB-XIL, G-BAGJ, XW858 ntu. Crashed 7-3-84		®	3-06
❑ –	BAPC.96 Brown Helicopter	ex Stanley			3-06
❑ –	BAPC.119 Bensen B.7	ex Stanley			3-06
❑ –	BAPC.228 Olympus	hang glider. Stored, in its bag!			3-06
❑ LQ-BLT	MBB Bö 105CBS	ex Bourn, Brazil. Cr 8-6-96. Original pod	off-site	® [5]	3-06
❑ VV217	Vampire FB.5	ex Barnham, Bury St Edmunds, 'VV271', 7323M, Oakington, DH. Stored			3-06
❑ WA577	Sycamore 3	ex King's Heath, Shirley, St Athan 7718M, AAEE, G-ALST ntu			3-06
❑ WB685	Chipmunk T.10	ex Leeds, Irlam, Edn UAS, Lyneham SF, 8 RFS, 1 RFS		[1]	3-06
❑ WD790	Meteor NF.11	ex Darlington, Leeming, 8743M, RAE Llanbedr, RS&RE, RRE, TRE. Nose, travelling exhibit			3-06

❏	WD889		Firefly AS.5	ex Failsworth. Cockpit section	[6]	3-06
❏	WG724		Dragonfly HR.5	ex Chester-le-Street, Moor Monkton, Blackbushe,		
				Lossiemouth SF, Ford SF	®	3-06
❏	WJ639		Canberra TT.18	ex Samlesbury, 7, 57		3-06
❏	WK198		Swift F.4	ex Failsworth, Kirkham, 7428M, Aldergrove, MoS. Fuselage		3-06
❏	WL181	'X'	Meteor F.8	ex Chester-le-Street, Acklington, Kemble, CAW,		
				Tangmere SF, 34		3-06
❏	WN516		Balliol T.2	ex Failsworth, RAFC. Cockpit, stored		3-06
❏	WZ518		Vampire T.11	ex Chester-le-Street, Handforth, Pomona Dock,		
				5 FTS, Oldenburg SF, 2 TAF CF, 14	[7]	3-06
❏	WZ767		Grasshopper TX.1	ex Halton. On loan. Stored		3-06
❏	XG680	'438'	S' Venom FAW.22	ex Sydenham, ADS, 891, Yeovilton SF		3-06
❏	XL319		Vulcan B.2	ex 44, Wadd W, 35, 230 OCU, 617, 230 OCU, Scamp W, 617		3-06
❏	XN258	'589'	Whirlwind	ex Helston, Culdrose SF, Endurance Flt, Culdrose SF		
			HAR.9	Hermes Flt		3-06
❏	XP627		Jet Provost T.4	ex Lon' Colney, Hatfield, Shawbury, 6 FTS, 3 FTS, 1 FTS	[8]	3-06
❏	XT148*		Sioux AH.1	ex Weston-super-Mare, Halton, Panshanger, Wroughton, ARWF		3-06
❏	ZF594		Lightning F.53	ex Warton, RSAF 53-696, G-27-66		3-06
❏	A-522		FMA Pucará	ex Yeovilton, St Athan 8768M, Stanley, Argentine AF.	[2]	3-06
❏	E-419		Hunter F.51	ex Dunsfold, G-9-441, Dan AF Esk.724		3-06
❏	146	'8-MG'	Mystère IVA	ex Sculthorpe, French AF		3-06
❏	42157	'11-ML'	F-100D-16-NA	ex Sculthorpe, French AF		3-06
❏	54439	'WI'	T-33A-1-LO	ex Sculthorpe, French AF		3-06
❏	6171		F-86D-35-NA	ex Hellenikon, Greek AF, USAF 51-6171	®	3-06
❏	26541		F-84F-40-RE	ex Hellenikon, Greek AF, USAF 52-6541		3-06
❏	–*		C-10A	ex Doncaster, Sunderland, Wycombe Air Park, Bushey,		
			Jetstream EMU	W Ruislip, Stanmore, St Albans, Radlett. Nose. Arr by 12-05		3-06

No.2214 Squadron Air Cadets: 'Parented' by Leeming, hold a Vampire and a Phantom nose.

❏	XD622		Vampire T.11	ex Leeming, Barkston Ash 8160M, Shawbury, 118, RAFC	3-06
❏	XV460	'R'	Phantom FGR.2	ex Coningsby, 74, 92, 228 OCU, 29, 228 OCU, 92, 19, 56, 31	3-06

NOTTINGHAMSHIRE

BALDERTON on the A1 south-east of Newark-on-Trent
The only relic on the site of the former A1 Commercials yard is the increasingly distressed Lightning. The site is reported to be due for redevelopment and the inevitable probably awaits XN728...

❏	XN728	'V'	Lightning F.2A	ex Coningsby, 8546M, 92. Poor state	4-06

FARNSFIELD south of the A617, east of Mansfield
Wonderland Pleasure Park: On the A614 and 'brown signed'. The Hurricane up the pole here is not to be confused with the one in similar stance at Coltishall, Norfolk!

❏	'V7467'	'LE-D'	Hurricane FSM	BAPC.288, 242 Sqn colours	8-05
❏	XS919		Lightning F.6	ex Devonport, Lower Tremar, Binbrook, 11, 5, 11, 5, 56, 11	8-05

HUCKNALL AERODROME south of the town
All three are stored off-site. The Drone is composite, with the wings of G-AEJH and tail of G-AEEN [1].

❏	G-AEDB		BAC Drone 2	ex Tadlow, Bishop's Stortford, Duxford,		
				BGA 2731.CoA 26-5-87. Stored	off-site [1]	2-06
❏	G-ARXN		Nipper 2	CoA 19-8-80. Stored		2-06
❏	G-BKOV*		CEA DR.220A	ex F-BOKV. Crashed 22-11-97. Stored		2-06

LANGAR AERODROME east of the A46, south of Whatton
By June 2004, Cessna U.206F G-BATD had moved to Grindale, E Yorks.

MANSFIELD on the A60 north of Nottingham
No.384 Squadron Air Cadets: Have a Canberra nose. 'Parent' is Newton.

| ❑ | WT507 | Canberra PR.7 | 8548M, ex Halton 8131M, St Athan, 31, 17, 58, AAEE, | |
| | | | 58, 527, 58. Nose | 12-02 |

NEWARK-ON-TRENT
Cliff Baker: The J/1N frame originally thought to be the second fuselage used by G-AIGR, is now thought to be from J/1 G-AHHK [1]. A reproduction of the Auster rear-loading ambulance one-off, the B.4, is under way. This will wear the original's identity, 'G-AMKL' [2]; it uses a frame as yet unidentified. Auster 5 G-AOCP is a composite, it includes part from fellow G-AKOT [3]. Now, to the Agricolas. In support of the challenging restoration of G-CBOA is an extensive cache of airframe elements brought in from New Zealand in March 2002. None of these merit a formal listing below but comprise: the centre section of ZK-CCU and three rear fuselage frames. Also here, from Breighton, E Yorks, in 2002, is the rear fuselage of the prototype ZK-BMI (G-ANYG ntu and G-25-3). Delete the reference in *W&R20* (p170)

♦ *The workshop/store is* not *open to the public and visits are strictly by prior permission.*

❑	G-AHHK	J/1 Autocrat	ex Shobdon, Cranfield. Gale damage 3-86.		
			CoA 22-3-70. Frame	[1]	6-05
❑	G-AIJI	J/1N Alpha	ex East Midlands, Elsham Hall, Goxhill,		
			Kirmington. Damaged 12-1-75. Frame, spares		6-05
❑	G-AIKE	Auster 5	ex Portsmouth, NJ728, 661. Crashed 1-9-65		6-05
❑	G-AJAS	J/1N Alpha	CoA 11-4-90		6-05
❑	G-AKWT	Auster 5	ex East Midlands, Elsham Hall, Goxhill, Stroxton		
			Lodge, Tollerton, MT360, 26, 175, 121 Wing,		
			181, 80, 486, 56, 19. Crashed 7-8-48. Frame		6-05
❑	G-ALNV	Auster 5	ex Nottingham, Leicester, RT578, 341, 329. CoA 4-7-50		6-05
❑	'G-AMKL'	Auster 'B.4'	under way by 11-02	[2]	6-05
❑	G-ANHU	Auster 4	ex Shoreham, EC-AXR, G-ANHU, MT255, 659	®	6-05
❑	G-ANHW	Auster 5D	ex Shipdham, TJ320, 664. CoA 9-3-70	®	6-05
❑	G-ANHX	Auster 5D	ex Leicester, TW519, 661, AAEE. Cr 28-3-70		6-05
❑	G-AOCP	Auster 5	ex TW462, 666. Damaged 4-70. Composite	® [3]	6-05
❑	G-APKM	J/1N Alpha	CoA 9-1-89		6-05
❑	G-APTR	J/1N Alpha	CoA 11-4-87		6-05
❑	G-ARGB	Auster 6A	ex Waddington, VF635, 662, 1901F. CoA 21-6-74		6-05
❑	G-AROJ	Airedale	ex Leicester, Thorney, HB-EUC, G-AROJ. CoA 8-1-76		6-05
❑	G-ARTM	Terrier 1	ex Chirk, Auster T.7 WE536, 651, 657,		
			Schwechat SF. Crashed 28-5-70	®	6-05
❑	G-ARXC	Airedale	ex Kirton-in-Lindsey, EI-ATD, G-ARXC. CoA 27-6-76	®	6-05
❑	G-ASWF	Airedale	ex Leicester. CoA 27-4-83		6-05
❑	EI-AMF	Taylorcraft Plus D	ex Abbeyshrule, G-ARRK, G-AHUM, LB286, Coltishall		
			SF, 309, 70 GCF, 84 GCF, 22 EFTS, 43 OTU, 653		6-05
❑	F-BBSO	Auster 5	ex Taunton, G-AMJM, TW452, 62 GCF. Frame		6-05
❑	ZK-BXO	Agricola	G-CBOA, ex New Zealand, ZK-BXO, ZK-BMN	® [4]	6-05
❑	–	Auster D.6-180	ex White Waltham, Rearsby. Frame. c/no 3705		6-05
❑	–	Terrier 3	ex White Waltham, Rearsby. Frame		6-05
❑	WZ729	Auster AOP.9	G-BXON, ex Singapore	®	6-05

Higgins Aviation: Two items from the Higgins' family 'fleet' can be found at the Newark Air Museum, Winthorpe, Notts. Briefly at Newark was their anonymous Hunter nose, acquired from a CCF unit at Harrogate, N Yorks. This transpired to be from F.4 WW664. The rest of this became the prototype T.8B for the Fleet Air Arm and later went to Singapore as a T.75 [1]

| ❑ | WW664* | Hunter F.4 | ex Winthorpe, Newark, Harrogate, HSA, 26. Nose | [1] 12-05 |

NOTTINGHAM AERODROME or Tollerton, south of the A52, east of the city

❏ G-ALVP*	Tiger Moth	ex ?, Shoreham, R4770, 4 RFS, 4 EFTS, 10 FIS,7 EFTS, 11 EFTS, CoA expired 15-2-61. F/n 11-04	1-05
❏ G-BGGF*	Tomahawk	CoA 15-10-94. Stored	10-05
❏ G-GRAY	Cessna 172N	ex N4859D. Ditched 2-4-93. Stored	10-05
❏ N6210K	RC-3 Seabee	ex G-SEAB, Glasgow, N6210K, NC6210K	® 10-05
❏ WB763	Chipmunk T.10	G-BBMR, ex Twyford, Camberley, Feltham, Southall, 2 FTS, 4 FTS, AOTS, 1 ITS, 1 AEF, Bri UAS, 3 AEF, AAC, 652, Odiham SF, 24 RFS, 14 RFS	® 10-05

RADCLIFFE ON TRENT on the A52, east of Nottingham
Archaeopteryx G-ABXL returned to Old Warden, Beds.

RETFORD AERODROME or Gamston, off the B6387 south of East Retford
CEA DR.1050 G-AYGD was flying by 2005.

SYERSTON AIRFIELD off the A46 south-west of Newark-on-Trent
RAF Syerston / Air Cadets Central Gliding School: Sedbergh TX.1 XN185 *may* be donated to the RAF Museum [1]. Be that as it may, by December 2005, Cadet TX.3 XA302 *was* on show at Hendon, Gtr Lon. Cadet TX.3 XE799 moved to Wolverhampton, W Mids, by December 2004.

❏ XN185	Sedbergh TX.1	HNS/BGA.4077, ex 8942M, CGS, 643 VGS, 4 MGSP, 633 VGS, 635 VGS. Stored.	[1]	3-04
❏ ZE686*	Viking TX.1	ex Kirkbymoorside, BGA.3099. First noted 5-04		3-06

TOTON on the A6005 south-west of Nottingham
No.350 Field Squadron HQ, Chetwynd Barracks: In Swiney Way, which links the B6003 and the A6005.

❏ XW267	'SA' Harrier T.4	ex 'Chilwell', Boscombe Down, SAOEU, RAE, AAEE, RAE, 233 OCU	1-06

WINTHORPE SHOWGROUND on the A46 north east of Newark-on-Trent
Newark Air Museum (NAM): On 5th May 2004 the museum celebrated the completion of its 25,834ft^2 (2,400m^2) display hall by rolling in 'JP' XM383 and the T-33A. The most notable roll-in was that of Varsity T.1 WF369 - the first of its type to have a roof put over its head in a UK museum - on 3rd October. The celebrations were completed on 13th November when the hall was officially opened. The new hall vividly illustrates just how far this exceptional museum has come since its foundation in 1973. The site the museum then occupied was just *half* the area of the new hall! Not long afterwards, the museum took delivery of its 70th airframe - the Jetstream. An example of NAM's increasing stature is the presentation of a SAAB Viggen from Sweden to the collection. This fabulous machine – the first to be preserved in the UK - touched down at Cranwell, Lincs, on 7th February 2006 and will move to the museum in a more sedate manner in due course [1]. NAM also own SZD Pirat BGA.1470 CDX which is on loan to the neighbouring gliding club (see below). It first flew after restoration in January 2006. NAM is host to the annual *CockpitFest* gathering -see the Appendix.

During early 2005, Vulcan B.2 XM594 was placed on an internet auction site by its owner. By late February 2005 Lincolnshire's Lancaster Association (LLA) had acquired the airframe and presented it immediately again on loan to NAM. Until this happened, the compiler had no idea that LLA also had owned Shackleton WR977 since the late 1990s. (See under Coningsby, Lincs, for LLA's real purpose.)

Somebody was sorely missed at the opening of the new exhibition hall. NAM founding member **Charlie Waterfall** died on 21st October 2004, aged 76. Charlie and Neville Franklin 'discovered' the frame of Westland Wallace II K6035 in 1963 and this led to the establishment of NAM. (The Wallace fuselage now graces the RAF Museum at Hendon, Gtr Lon.) Charlie was pioneering and inspirational: his legacy can be seen all over the Winthorpe site.

Notes: Several airframes are on loan from outside bodies: the Autocrat from Leicestershire Museum, Arts and Records Service; the Canberra PR.7 from 81 Squadron Associates; the Canberra T.17 nose from Aaron Braid; the Gazelle from the Museum of Army Flying, Middle Wallop, Hants; the Canberra PR.9 nose from Frank Millar; and the *Floggers* from Hawarden Aviation Services. Just prior to *CockpitFest* 2005, Higgins Aviation brought in no less than three of their airframes and placed them on loan to NAM. One of these was an anonymous Hunter but it later returned to <u>Newark</u>, Notts - qv. The others are the Bulldog and Swift CIMs. All these are marked ±.

Tiger Moth 'G-MAZY' is very likely BAPC.21 [2]. Canberra T.19 WH904 was built by Shorts Brothers and Harland as a B.2 and therefore the forward fuselage *should* have a plate reading SHB-0-2388. Inspection found the nose to have the plate EEP71123, which would make it WH651. The logic works out like this... WH651 was issued to English Electric for conversion from a B.2 to a T.4 on 5th July 1956 and in this process it would have been fitted with a new-build T.4 cockpit. It looks as though the old cockpit passed on to Boulton Paul for use in the B.2 to T.11 conversions. WH904 was issued to BP on 17th October 1957 for T.11 fit. It received the cockpit of WH651. (And later was further converted to T.19 status.) [3] The Auster AOP.9 is very probably XR268 or perhaps XS238 [4]. Monospar VH-UTH is at Innsworth, Glos.

Departures: The nose of Shackleton T.4 VP293 moved to <u>Coltishall</u>, Norfolk, during early 2005. The nose of Beverley C.1 XL149 moved to <u>Doncaster</u>, S Yorks, by June 2005.

◆ *Signposted from the A1, on Newark Showground, access off the A46, or A17. Open daily Mar to Oct 10am to 5pm, Nov to Feb daily 10am to 4pm. Closed Dec 24, 25, 26 and Jan 1. Buildings suitable for the disabled. Special events are also staged – SAE for details. Membership includes the excellent journal* The Dispersal. *The Airfield, Winthorpe, Newark, Notts, NG24 2NY tel / fax 01636 707170 e-mail newarkair@lineone.net www.newarkairmuseum.co.uk*

❑ G-AGOH	J/1 Autocrat	ex Leicester. CoA 24-8-95. On loan	±	3-06
❑ G-AHRI	Dove 1	ex Long Marston, East Kirkby, Tattershall, Little Staughton, 4X-ARI, G-AHRI. 'Newark Air Museum'		3-06
❑ G-ANXB	Heron 1	ex Biggin Hill, Fairflight, BEA, G-5-14. CoA 25-3-79. BEA Scottish colours. *Sir James Young Simpson*		3-06
❑ G-APNJ	Cessna 310	ex Shoreham, EI-AJY, N3635D. CoA 28-11-74		3-06
❑ G-APVV	Mooney M.20A	ex Skelmersdale, Barton, N8164E. Cr 11-1-81. Stored		3-06
❑ [G-AXMB]	Motor Cadet Mk2	ex Ringmer, BGA.805, VM590. CoA 9-7-82. Dismantled		3-06
❑ G-BFTZ	Rallye Club	ex Firbeck, Hooton Park, Warmingham, Fownhope, Cardiff-Wales, F-BPAX. CoA 19-9-81		3-06
❑ G-BJAD	FRED Srs 2	ex Retford. Uncompleted project		3-06
❑ G-BKPG	Rattler Strike	ex Egginton, Tatenhill. Stored		3-06
❑ G-CCLT	Powerchute	ex Nantwich. Canx 9-12-03		3-06
❑ 'G-MAZY'	Tiger Moth	ex Innsworth, Staverton, Newark area. Composite, mostly G-AMBB/T6801, ex Scampton SF, 6 FTS, 18 EFTS	[2]	3-06
❑ G-MBBZ	Volmer VJ-24W	ex Old Sarum. CoA 3-9-93		3-06
❑ G-MBUE	Tiger Cub 440	ex Retford, Worksop. *The Dormouse Zeitgeist*		3-06
❑ G-MBVE	Hiway Skytrike	canx 13-6-90		3-06
❑ G-MJCF*	Hill Hummer	canx 24-1-95. Arrived 1-06		3-06
❑ G-MNRT*	Sirocco 377GB	ex Mansfield area. CoA 18-8-01. Arrived 6-05		3-06
❑ – BAPC.43	HM.14 'Flea'	ex East Kirkby, Tattershall, Wellingore		3-06
❑ – BAPC.101	HM.14 'Flea'	ex Tumby Woodside, East Kirkby, Tattershall, Sleaford. Fuselage. (Also G-AFUL's rudder.)		3-06
❑ – BAPC.183	Zurowski ZP.1	ex Burton-on-Trent. Homebuilt helicopter, unflown		3-06
❑ KF532	Harvard IIB	ex 781, 799, 727, 799, 758. Cockpit section		3-06
❑ RA897	Cadet TX.1	Stored		3-06
❑ TG517	Hastings T.5	ex 230 OCU, SCBS, BCBS, 202, 53, 47		3-06
❑ VL348	Anson C.19	G-AVVO, ex Southend, Shawbury, 22 GCF, 24 GCF, Colerne SF, 62 GCF, HCMSU, RCCF		3-06
❑ VR249 'FA-EL'	Prentice T.1	G-APIY, ex 1 ASS, RAFC. CoA 18-3-67		3-06
❑ VZ608	Meteor FR.9	ex Hucknall, Shoreham, MoS, RR. RB.108 test-bed		3-06
❑ VZ634	Meteor T.7	ex Wattisham 8657M, 5 MU, MoA, Leeming SF, Stradishall SF, 41, 141, 609, 247		3-06
❑ WB624	Chipmunk T.10	ex Hooton Park, Firbeck, Long Marston, Warmingham, East Midlands, Wigan, Dur UAS, Abn UAS, Henlow, St Athan, 22 GCF, Debden, Jurby SF, 8 FTS, 18 RFS	®	3-06

☐	WB491		Ashton 2	ex Woodford, Cardiff-Wales, Dunsfold,		
				Farnborough, RAE. Forward fuselage		3-06
☐	WF369	'F'	Varsity T.1	ex 6 FTS, AE&AEOS, AES, 2 ANS, 201 AFS		3-06
☐	WH791		Canberra PR.7	8187M, ex Cottesmore, St Athan 8165M, 8176M, 81, 58, 82, 542	±	3-06
☐	WH863		Canberra T.17	ex Marham 8693M, 360, RAE, IAM. Nose.	±	3-06
☐	WH904	'04'	Canberra T.19	ex Cambridge, 7, 85, West Raynham TFF,		
				228 OCU, 35, 207	[3]	3-06
☐	WK277	'N'	Swift FR.5	ex Cosford, Leconfield 7719M, 2. 2 Sqn colours		3-06
☐	WM913	'456'	Sea Hawk FB.3	ex Fleetwood, Sealand 8162M, Culdrose		
				A2510, Abbotsinch, 736		3-06
☐	WR977	'B'	Shackleton	ex Finningley, 8186M 203, 42, 206, 203, 42,		
			MR.3/3	201, 206, 201, 220	LLA	3-06
☐	WS692	'C'	Meteor NF.12	ex Cranwell, Henlow 7605M, 72, 46		3-06
☐	WS739		Meteor NF.14	ex Misson, Church Fenton 7961M, Kemble,		
				1 ANS, 2 ANS, 25		3-06
☐	WT651	'C'	Hunter F.1	ex Lawford Heath, Halton, Credenhill 7532M,		
				229 OCU, 233 OCU, 229 OCU, 222. 222 Sqn c/s		3-06
☐	WT933		Sycamore 3	ex Sutton, Strensall, Halton 7709M, G-ALSW ntu		3-06
☐	WV606	'P-B'	Provost T.1	ex Halton 7622M, 1 FTS		3-06
☐	WV787		Canberra B.2/8	ex Abingdon 8799M, AAEE. Hefner 'bunny' logo		3-06
☐	WW217	'351'	Sea Ven FAW.21	ex Cardiff, Ottershaw, Culdrose, Yeovilton, ADS, 891, 890		3-06
☐	WX905		Venom NF.3	ex Henlow, Hendon, Yatesbury 7458M, 27 MU, 23.		3-06
☐	XA239		Grasshopper TX.1	ex 'Northampton'		3-06
☐	XB261*		Beverley C.1	ex Duxford Southend, HAM, AAEE. Cockpit. Arrived 6-04		3-06
☐	XD593	'50'	Vampire T.11	ex Woodford, Chester, St Athan, 8 FTS, CFS,		
				FWS, 5 FTS, 4 FTS. CFS colours		3-06
☐	XH177		Canberra PR.9	ex Corby, Stock, Cardiff-Wales, Boscombe, 13, 58. Nose	±	3-06
☐	XH992	'P'	Javelin FAW.8	ex Cosford 7829M, Shawbury, 85. 85 Sqn colours.		3-06
☐	XJ560	'243'	Sea Vixen FAW.2	ex RAE Bedford, Farnborough, Halton 8142M,		
				893, 899, 892, 890		3-06
☐	XL764	'J'	Skeeter AOP.12	ex Nostell Priory, Rotherham, Middle Wallop, Arborfield		
				7940M, Hayes, AAEE, MoA, AAC, Saro, AAC		3-06
☐	XM383	'90'	Jet Provost T.3A	ex Crowland, Scampton, 7 FTS, 1 FTS, RAFC,		
				6 FTS, BSE, 2 FTS, AAEE, 2 FTS		3-06
☐	XM594		Vulcan B.2	ex 44, Scampton Wing, 617, 27	LLA	3-06
☐	XM685	'513'	Whirlwind HAS.7	ex Panshanger area, Elstree, Luton, G-AYZJ ntu,		
				Fleetlands, Lee-o-S, 771, Ark Ship's Flt, 847, 848		3-06
☐	XN573		Jet Provost T.3	ex Blackpool Airport, Kemble, 1 FTS, CFS. Nose		3-06
☐	XN819		Argosy C.1	ex Finningley 8205M, Shawbury, Benson Wing,		
				105, MoA. Cockpit section, in small display hall		3-06
☐	XN964	'613'	Buccaneer S.1	ex Bruntingthorpe, East Midlands, Brough, Pershore, 807		3-06
☐	XP226	'073'	Gannet AEW.3	ex Lee-on-Solent, Southwick, Lee-on-Solent,		
				A2667, Lossiemouth, Ilchester, 849		3-06
☐	XR534	'65'	Gnat T.1	ex Dunholme Bridge, Valley 8578M, 4 FTS, CFS	®	3-06
☐	XS417	'DZ'	Lightning T.5	ex Binbrook, LTF, 5, 11, 5, 11, LTF, 56, 23, 11, 23, 226 OCU		3-06
☐	XT200	'F'	Sioux AH.1	ex Middle Wallop		3-06
☐	XV728	'A'	Wessex HC.2	ex Fleetlands, 72, 2 FTS, CFS, 18. Argonaut.		3-06
☐	XW276		Gazelle 03	ex Sunderland, Wroughton, Southampton, Middle		
				Wallop, Farnborough, Leatherhead, F-ZWRI	±	3-06
☐	XX492*	'A'	Jetstream T.1	ex Culdrose, Cranwell, 45, 3 FTS, 45, 6 FTS, METS.		
				Arrived 9-12-04		3-06
☐	XX634*	'T'	Bulldog T.1	ex Wellesbourne Mountford, Shawbury, Liv UAS, Man UAS,		
				EMUAS, CFS, 3 FTS, CFS, Cam UAS, 2 FTS. Arr 9-1-06		3-06
☐	ZA176*		Sea Harrier FA.2	ex Yeovilton, 801, 800, 801, 899, 801, 899, 800, 801,		
				899, 801, 809, 800, 809, 899. Arrived 21-7-04		3-06
☐	–		TA200 Auster AOP.9	ex Middle Wallop. Stored	[4]	3-06
☐	AR-107		S.35XD Draken	ex Scampton, Esk.729, RDanAF		3-06

❏	83	'8-MS'	Mystère IVA	ex Sculthorpe, French AF		3-06
❏	56321		Safir	G-BKPY, ex Norwegian AF		3-06
❏	Fv37918*		Viggen	ex Cranwell, RSwAF	[1]	due
❏	'04'		MiG-23ML	ex Chester, Latvia, USSR. (024003607)	±	3-06
❏	'71'		MiG-27K	ex Chester, Latvia, USSR. (61912507006)	±	3-06
❏	42223		F-100D-16-NA	ex Sculthorpe, French AF		3-06
❏	51-9036		T-33A-1-LO	19036, ex '5547', Sculthorpe, Fr AF. 48th FIS c/s		3-06
❏	–*		Swift CIM	ex Newark, Hemswell. Arrived 6-05	±	3-06
❏	–		Jet Provost CIM	Procedures trainer.		3-06
❏	–		Gnat T.1 CIM	ex Melton Mowbray. Procedures trainer		3-06
❏	–		Phantom CIM	ex Wattisham. Full-axis simulator		3-06
❏	–*		Bulldog T.1 CIM	ex Newark, Newton. Arrived 6-05	±	3-06

Newark Gliding Club: Sadly, NGC have to move out from their strip opposite the museum. The club have been operating SZD Pirat BGA.1470 CDX since January 2006. This is owned by NAM and is flown by the club in a co-operative agreement. An SF-27MB is under slow restoration in the hangar.

❏	G-BSUM	Scheibe SF-27MB	ex D-KIBE. Canx 21-10-99	®	9-97

OXFORDSHIRE

ABINGDON
A collector in the general area has a Vampire pod.

❏	XH330	'76'	Vampire T.11	ex Camberley, Bridgnorth, Bushey, London Colney, Chester, Woodford, Chester, Shawbury, RAFC. Pod	3-04

BANBURY
John Horton: At this *private* location, there is a Cessna plaything.

❏	G-ARRF	Cessna 150A	ex Perranporth, N7197X. Cr 11-3-88. Fuselage	3-00

BENSON AIRFIELD east of the A4074, east of Wallingford
RAF Benson: Puma HC.1s are being stripped for spares and being disposed of: XW201 by 8-05, left by road 11-1-06; XW202 moved to Shawbury, Shrop, 25-7-05; XW206 being stripped in 8-05.

❏	'EN343'		Spitfire FSM	BAPC.226, gate	3-02
❏	[XT681]	'U'	Wessex HC.2	9279M, ex Shawbury, 72, WTF, 18. ABDR	7-01

BICESTER
Defence and Distribution Centre: *Not* the aerodrome, but signed as 'MoD Bicester' and close to the 'Plough' public house and *not* to be confused with the Defence Logistics Organisation at Caversfield!

❏	ZA319	'TAV'	Tornado GR.1	ex St Athan, 15, TTTE	10-04

BICESTER AERODROME on the A421 north-east of Bicester
The RAF Gliding and Soaring Association Centre closed during early 2004, so much of the list below will have moved on. Falke G-AYUP is believed to have moved to the Cheltenham area. Chipmunk T.10 fuselage WB556 (last noted August 1999) moved to Halton, Bucks. Otherwise, it looks as though *W&R21* will be clearing up here.

❏	BPT	1132	T.49 Capstan	CoA 11-12-95. Stored	3-04
❏	WB645		Chipmunk T.10	8218M, ex Little Rissington, Cottesmore SF, Edn UAS, 8 FTS, 1 CAACU, 17 RFS, 1 RFS. Fuselage. Spares	8-99
❏	WG303		Chipmunk T.10	8208M, ex Shawbury, Kemble, Ox UAS, Gatow SF, Wittering SF, Marham SF, Bir UAS, 5 RFS, 2 BFTS.	8-99

❑ ZE589	Viking T.1	EXT/BGA.3045, ex 634 VGS, Shawbury, Syerston.	
		Crashed 9-7-92. Stored	11-99
❑ –	Chipmunk T.10	cockpit section. Hulk	3-95

Locally: Prior to appearing at the July 2003 International Air Tattoo, Swift F.7 XF114 was purchased by the Southampton Hall of Aviation (now Solent Sky) and it moved to Southampton, Hants.

BRIZE NORTON AIRFIELD on the A4095 south-west of Witney
RAF Brize Norton: The nose of VC-10 ZD234 *should* still serve as a procedures 'sim' [1]. The Air Movements School has become the **Defence Movements School** (DMS) and has a series of airframes to help in loadmaster training. Scout AH.1 XV118 was put up for tender in February 2004 and moved to North Weald, Essex.

❑ XR806	VC-10 C.1K	9285M, ex 10. Dam 18-12-97. Fuselage. ABDR		9-05
❑ XX914	VC-10	8777M, ex RAE, G-ATDJ, BUA. Fuselage	DMS	9-02
❑ XZ994	'O' Harrier GR.3	9170M, ex St A', 1417F, 233 OCU, 1417F, 233'	DMS	9-02
❑ ZB684	Gazelle AH.1	ex Fleetlands, 667, 665, 655	DMS	9-02
❑ ZD234	Super VC-10	8700M, ex Heathrow, G-ASGF, BA, BOAC. Nose	[1]	4-92

CHALGROVE AIRFIELD on the B480 north-west of Watlington
Martin Baker: Meteor T.7 WL419 *Asterix* and T.7(mod) WA638 act as flying test-beds for MB.

❑ EE416	Meteor III	ex Wroughton, South Kensington, MB. Nose	3-03
❑ –	Northrop F-5A	ex Greek AF, 63-8418. Nose. Dump	3-05
❑ –	MiG-19 *Farmer*	ex Pakistan? Nose. Dump	3-05
❑ –	IAI Lavi EMU	Nose. Dump	3-05

CULHAM on the A415 south-east of Abingdon
UKAEA, Lightning Studies Unit: Still have their Hunter in an upstairs lab.

| ❑ WV381 | '732' Hunter GA.11 | ex Kemble, FRADU, FRU, FWS, 222. Fuselage | 3-05 |

ENSTONE AERODROME on the B4030 east of Chipping Norton
Bristol 170 Mk.31M C-FDFC came to grief here on the 18th July 1996. Bits of the 'Biffo' are still to be found here. The nose/cockpit section is now known to have moved to Fleet, Hants, for use as a plaything.

❑ G-AKBO*	Messenger 2A	ex Old Warden. CoA 3-8-03. Canx 24-8-04. Stored. F/n 5-05	5-05
❑ G-AVGJ	SAN DR.1050	ex F-BJYJ. CoA 22-4-85	5-05
❑ G-AWAC*	Horizon 180	Crashed 22-7-03. Dismantled, stored. F/n 5-05	5-05
❑ G-AWSP	Condor	CoA 23-1-95. Stored	5-05
❑ G-AZTD	Cherokee Six 300	ex N8611N. CoA 16-8-98. Stored	6-03
❑ G-BBRY	Cessna 210	ex Cranfield, Blackbushe, Chessington, 5Y-KRZ,	
		VP-KRZ, N7391E. Crashed 2-4-78. Stored	7-02
❑ G-BSGJ	Sonerai II	ex N34WH. CoA 6-9-91. Stored	6-03
❑ G-DKGF	Dragonfly 1	unflown project. Dumped	9-05
❑ G-SION*	Tomahawk 112	ex N32661. Crashed 2-7-97. Stored	9-05

HENLEY-ON-THAMES on the A4155 north of Reading
No.447 Squadron Air Cadets: 'Parented' by Benson. *should* still have their 'JP'.

| ❑ XS218 | Jet Provost T.4 | ex Woodley, Halton 8508M, Shawbury, 3 FTS. Nose | 10-02 |

KIDLINGTON on the A423 north of Oxford
Julian Mitchell: The nose of Hunter F.6 XF383 moved to Gloucester, Glos, in June 2004.

NORTH MORETON south of the A4130, west of Wallingford

❏ G-ARET   Tri-Pacer 160   CoA 20-5-83   ®   5-96

OXFORD

A new Spitfire project as been acquired by an owner in this area. It is very much in the formative stages.

❏ JG668*   Spitfire VIII   ex Australia, RAAF A58-441, JG668.   3-06

OXFORD AIRPORT (KIDLINGTON)

The Apache *may* still be here as an instructional airframe [1]. The hulk of Cessna FR.182RG G-RING was last noted on the dump here in July 1998. The dump itself having gone, *November-Golf* is thought scrapped. JP T.3A XN500 moved briefly to Ipswich, Suffolk, and then to Nottingham East Midlands, Leics, in October 2004. Instructional Sioux AH.1 XT175 moved out, probably as far back as 1994.

❏ G-ARJR   Apache 160G   ex N4447P. CoA 24-10-78   [1] 6-97

SHENINGTON AERODROME west of the A422, west of Banbury

The Grasshopper here was WZ797 and is now to be found at Upwood, Cambs.

SHRIVENHAM east of Swindon, south of the A420

The Defence Academy of the United Kingdom: (formerly, or incorporating) the Royal Military College of Science, The Harrier and Scout are displayed within the grounds, the others are within the Aviation Hall. Gnat T.1 XP542 moved to Southampton, Hants, by June 2004.

❏ XT621		Scout AH.1	ex Wroughton, 655, 656, 666, 664, 666	3-05
❏ XV122	'A'	Scout AH.1	ex Almondbank, Wroughton	7-04
❏ XV744	'3K'	Harrier GR.3	ex St Athan 9167M, 233 OCU, 1, 233 OCU	7-04
❏ XW919	'W'	Harrier GR.3	ex Culdrose A2610 [3], A2609, Cosford, 4, 1, 233 OCU	3-05
❏ 69-16445		AH-1F Cobra	ex US Army, 1/1CAV, Budingen. 'IFOR' markings	3-05
❏ 70-15154		OH-58CR Kiowa	ex Lyneham (transit), US Army	3-05

STEVENTON on the B4017 south of Abingdon

Robin Phipps: Moved his Sea Vixen cockpit to a private location near here during November 2004. Robin's Buccaneer cockpit is displayed at Coventry, Warks.

❏ XN647*   '707'   Sea Vixen FAW.2   ex Bruntingthorpe, Helston, Culdrose SAH-10, A2610, 766,
                                             899. Cockpit. Arrived 11-04   3-06

WITNEY north of the A40 west of Oxford

Witney Technical College: Still no news on this airframe, it seems bound for LOST!

❏ 'G-IRIS'   Aztec / Apache   ex Faringdon?   6-00

SHROPSHIRE

ASTLEY east of the A49 north of Shrewsbury

❏ G-AWGM   Kittiwake II   ex Hanworth, Halton. Damaged 18-1-86. Canx 4-3-99   ®   9-95

CHETWYND AERODROME on the A41 north-west of Newport

Cessna 150F hulk G-ATIE is long since gone, last noted May 1997.

COSFORD AIRFIELD south of Junction 3 of the M54

Royal Air Force Museum: In November 2004, the museum secured the last financial element for their £13 million display hall then entitled 'Divided World: Connected World' to highlight the 'Cold War' years. The huge display building will encompass over 75,000 square feet and will take the form of two enormous triangular-shaped halls. Secretary of State for Defence, Geoff Hoon, performed the first turf cut on 24th February 2005. Construction of the incredible building was due to be completed by early 2006 when the job of fitting out and positioning airframes would start. By the summer of 2005, it was decided to call the new building the **National 'Cold War' Exhibition**, much to the delight of all! Because the new building will be up-and-running during the currency of this edition, the opportunity has been taken to list the airframes under that heading, see below. If types such as the Hastings, the Victor, the Vulcan and the mighty Belfast are to be included, then the scale of this building comes across dramatically. For the first time all three V-bombers will be on show together in complete form. The Sir Michael Beetham Conservation Centre (see below) has been busy working on several of the aircraft destined for the new building, including the Javelin, which has been outside all of its museum life until recently. The re-shuffle of exhibits into the new hall will put other airframes under cover, or bring them out of store. Those *planned* to go on show or indoors as *W&R20* went to press are marked ⊙.

In early January 2006 it was announced that British Airways and the RAF Museum were reviewing the future status of the 'British Airways Collection'. This could not have been unexpected to seasoned *W&R* readers as the museum has been staging a 'holding' operation with them for a long time. (Viscount G-AMOG will have been on external display for 30 years in May 2006.) Comet 1XB G-APAS and Jetstream 200 G-BBYM will be moved indoors with the reshuffle recreated by the 'Cold War' Hall.

STOP PRESS: As *W&R20* went to press, it was announced that the following will be moved to East Fortune, Scotland, as the gifts of BA by ASI of Alton, Hants: Viscount G-AMOG and BAC 111 G-AVMO (both whole) and the following as forward fuselages: 707 G-APFJ and Trident G-ARPH. Additionally the forward fuselage VC-10 G-ARVM would move to Brooklands, Surrey. These are marked ⇨ and also appear under their new headings. No space – at least here, perhaps there will be at East Fortune's entry - for editorial rattlings about this situation.

Notes: The Michael Beetham Conservation Centre is treated separately, as is the new 'Cold War' Hall: see below. Airframes on site, but in 'deep store' and not available for inspection have a separate entry, see below. The T-tail rear fuselage of the Short SB.5 is displayed alongside WG768 [1].

Departures: Liberator VI KN751 moved to Hendon, Gtr Lon, during early September 2005. The following airframes have been prematurely moved to the 'Cold War' Hall listing, most going via attention in the Michael Beetham centre: Dakota KN654, Hastings TG511, York TS798, Meteor XL993, Hunter nose XE670, Lightning XG337, Canberra XH171, Victor XH672, Hunter XL568, Twin Pioneer XL993, Vulcan XM598, Belfast XR371, Phantom nose XV591; Jetstream XX496, MiG-15 01120, Venom J-1704.

◆ *Open daily 10am to 6pm (last admission 4pm) with the exception of Xmas and New Year. Annual airshow in which several museum aircraft (and others from the SoTT) that are not normally outside are displayed - extra charges apply. Near to Junction 3 of the M54 and well signposted. The* **Aerospace Museum Society** *provides a vital link in both the restoration of exhibits and the running of the museum and special events.Cosford, Shifnal, Shropshire, TF11 8UP tel 01902 376200 fax 01902 376211 e-mail cosford@rafmuseum.org www.rafmuseum.org*

☐ G-EBMB	Hawker Cygnet	ex Hendon, Cardington, Henlow, Lympne No.14. CoA 30-11-61		3-06
☐ G-AEEH	HM.14 'Flea'	ex St Athan, Colerne, Bath, Whitchurch		3-06
☐ 'G-AFAP'	CASA 352L	ex Spanish AF T2B-272. British Airways c/s.		3-06
☐ 'G-AJOV'	Dragonfly HR.3	WP495, ex Biggin Hill, Banstead, Warnham, Wimbledon. BEA colours		3-06
☐ G-AMOG	Viscount 701	ex Cardiff-Wales, BOAC, Cambrian, BEA *Robert Falcon Scott*, G-AMNZ ntu. CoA 14-6-77. BEA c/s	⇨	4-06
☐ G-AOVF	Britannia 312F	ex Southend, 9Q-CAZ, G-AOVF, Stansted, Donaldson, British Eagle, BOAC. BOAC c/s		4-06
☐ G-APAS	Comet 1XB	ex Shawbury 8351M, XM823, G-APAS, G-5-23, Air France, F-BGNZ. BOAC c/s	⊙	3-06
☐ G-APFJ	Boeing 707-436	ex British Airtours, BOAC. CoA 16-2-82. Airtours c/s	⇨	4-06
☐ G-ARPH	Trident 1C	ex BA, BEA. CoA 8-9-82. BA colours	⇨	4-06
☐ G-ARVM	VC-10 Srs 1101	ex BA, BOAC. CoA 5-8-80. BA colours	⇨	4-06
☐ G-AVMO	BAC 111-510ED	ex Bournemouth, BA, BEA. *Lothian Region*	⇨	4-06
☐ G-BBYM	Jetstream 200	ex Cranfield, BAe, G-AYWR, G-8-13. CoA 20-9-98		3-06

☐	K9942	'SD-D'	Spitfire I	ex Hendon 8383M, Rochester, Hendon, 71 MU Bicester, Fulbeck, Wroughton, Newark, Cardiff, 53 OTU, 57 OTU, 72. 72 Sqn c/s		3-06
☐	DG202/G		F.9/40 Meteor	ex Yatesbury, Locking 5758M, Moreton Valance.		3-06
☐	'FS628'		Argus II	ex Rochester, G-AIZE, Cosford, Henlow, Hanwell, N9996F, 43-14601. CoA 6-8-66. SEAC colours		3-06
☐	LF738	'UH-A'	Hurricane II	ex Rochester, Biggin Hill, Wellesbourne Mountford, 5405M, 22 OTU, 1682 BDTF. 1682 BDTF colours		3-06
☐	RF398		Lincoln B.2/4A	ex 8376M, Henlow, Abingdon, CSE, BCBS.		3-06
☐	TA639	'AZ-E'	Mosquito TT.35	ex 7806M, CFS, 3 CAACU, Aldergrove TT Flt		3-06
☐	'TB675'*	'4D-V'	Spitfire XVI	RW393, ex Stafford, Cosford, St Athan, Turnhouse 7293M, 602, 3, CAACU, 31, FCCS, 203 AFS. Arrived 19-9-05		3-06
☐	TX214		Anson C.19	ex Henlow 7817M, HCCS, MCS, RCCF, Staff College CF, 1 FU, 16 FU		3-06
☐	VP952		Devon C.2/2	ex St Athan 8820M, 207, 21, WCS, SCS, Upavon SF, TCCF, MCS, BCCS, HCCS, AAEE, MCCF, AAFCE, TCCF, Hendon SF, HS		3-06
☐	WA634		Meteor T.7(mod)	ex St Athan, Martin Baker		3-06
☐	WE600		Auster C4 (T.7 mod)	ex St Athan, Swinderby, Finningley 7602M, Trans-Antarctic Expedition, 663. Skis		3-06
☐	WG760		EE P.1A	ex Binbrook, Henlow, Bicester 7755M, St Athan, Warton, AAEE		3-06
☐	WG768		Short SB.5	ex Topcliffe, Finningley 8005M, ETPS, RAE Bedford, RAE Farnborough, AAEE, RAE Bedford, AAEE	[1]	3-06
☐	WG777		Fairey FD-2	ex Topcliffe, Finningley 7986M, RAE Bedford		3-06
☐	WK935		Meteor F.8(mod)	ex St Athan, Colerne 7869M, RAE. Prone-pilot		3-06
☐	WL679		Varsity T.1	ex 9155M, Farnborough, RAE, BLEU	⊙	3-06
☐	WL732		Sea Balliol T.21	ex Henlow, AAEE, Lossiemouth, Anthorn.		3-06
☐	WP912		Chipmunk T.10	ex Hendon 8467M, Man UAS, RAFC, ITS, Cam UAS, CFS, 2 FTS, Lon UAS, FTCCS, HCCS, 8 FTS		3-06
☐	WV562	'P-C'	Provost T.1	ex Cranwell 7606M, Henlow, 22 FTS. Wears 7606M		3-06
☐	WV746		Pembroke C.1	ex 8938M, 60, 207, 21, WCS, TCCF, FTCCS, BCCS, HS, 2 TAFCF		3-06
☐	WZ744		Avro 707C	ex Topcliffe, Finningley 7932M, RAE, Avro		3-06
☐	XA893		Vulcan B.1	ex Abingdon, Bicester 8591M, AAEE, Avro. Nose		3-06
☐	XD145		SARO SR.53	ex Brize Norton, Henlow, Westcott, AAEE		3-06
☐	XF926		Bristol 188	ex 8368M, Foulness Island, RAE.		3-06
☐	XG225	'S'	Hunter F.6A	ex parade ground, 8713M, Weapons School, 2 SoTT, Kemble, 229 OCU, 92, 74, 20. 'Gate' by 6-04		3-04
☐	XJ918		Sycamore HR.14	ex 2 SoTT 8190M, 32, MCS, Kemble, Wroughton, 110, Seletar, AAEE, 275		3-06
☐	XK724		Gnat F.1	ex Cranwell, Bicester, Henlow 7715M, Folland		3-06
☐	XL703		Pioneer CC.1	ex Manchester, Henlow 8034M, 209, 230. Stored	⊙	3-06
☐	XM351	'Y'	Jet Provost T.3	ex 1 SoTT 8078M, Halton, Shawbury, 3 FTS, 7 FTS, 2 FTS		3-06
☐	XN714		Hunting 126/50	ex RAE Bedford, NASA Ames and Moffett, Holme-on-Spalding Moor, RAE		3-06
☐	XP411		Argosy C.1	ex 2 SoTT 8442M, 6 FTS, Kemble, 70. Stored	⊙	3-06
☐	XR220		TSR-2 XO-2	ex Henlow 7933M, AAEE. Never flown		3-06
☐	XR525*	'G'	Wessex HC.2	ex Shawbury, 72, 60, 72, Benson SF, SAR Wing, Benson SF, 72. Arrived 13-5-04	⊙	3-06
☐	XR977		Gnat T.1	ex 2 SoTT 8640M, Red Arrows, 4 FTS. 'Reds' c/s.		3-06
☐	XS639		Andover E.3A	ex 9241M, Northolt, 32, 115, 32, 46	⊙	3-06
☐	XX654	'3'	Bulldog T.1	ex Shawbury Newton, CFS, 3 FTS, CFS, 3 FTS, Bri UAS, 2 FTS		3-06
☐	XX765		Jaguar GR.1 (mod)	ex Loughborough, Warton, BAe, RAE, AAEE, 226 OCU, 14. ACT 'fly-by-wire' test-bed		3-06
☐	XX946	'WT'	Tornado P.02	ex Hendon, Honington 8883M, Laarbruch, Honington, Warton		3-06
☐	–		BAPC.82 Afghan Hind	ex Hendon, Kabul, RAfghan AF, RAF.		3-06

❑	A-515		FMA Pucará	ex 9245M, ZD485, AAEE, Yeovilton, Stanley, Arg AF A-515	3-06
❑	L-866		PBY-6A Catalina	ex 8466M, Colerne, Danish AF Esk.721, 82-866, BuNo 63993	3-06
❑	420430		Me 410A-1-U2	ex St Athan 8483M, Cosford, Fulbeck, Wroughton,	
		'3U+CC'		Stanmore Park, Brize Norton, Farnborough, AM.72, Vaerlose	3-06
❑	475081		Fi 156C-7	ex St Athan, Coltishall, Bircham Newton, Finningley	
				7362M, Fulbeck, VP546, AM.101, Farnborough	3-06
❑	–		Fa 330A-1	ex 8469M, Henlow, Farnborough	3-06
❑	–		Fi 103 (V-1)	BAPC.94, ex 8583M	3-06
❑	5439		Ki 46 *Dinah*	BAPC.84, ex St Athan 8484M, Biggin Hill, Fulbeck,	
				Wroughton, Stanmore Park, Sealand, ATAIU-SEA.	3-06
❑	–		Ohka 11	BAPC.99, ex St Athan 8486M, Cosford, Westcott	3-06
❑	204		SP-2H Neptune	ex Dutch Navy, 320 Sqn, Valkenburg, 5 Sqn, 321 Sqn	3-06
❑	'413573'	'B6-K'	P-51D-25-NA	ex Hendon 9133M, Halton, N6526D, RCAF 9289,	
				44-73415. Composite. 363rd FS c/s, *Little Friend*	3-06

National 'Cold War' Exhibition: See the introduction for more details on this ambitious and fabulous project. The airframes listed below are all *planned* to go into the hall, and those *due* to be suspended are marked ⇨. A Lockheed C-5 Galaxy delivered the F-111F to Mildenhall, Suffolk, on 9th July 2005 [1].

❑	KN645		Dakota C.4	ex 'KG374', 8355M, Colerne, AFN CF, MinTech, AFN CF,		
				MinTech, AFN HQ, SHAPE CF, Malta CF, BAFO CS,		
				2nd TAF CS, 44-77003. Transport Command c/s	⇨	3-06
❑	TG511		Hastings T.5	ex 8554M, 230 OCU, SCBS, BCBS, 202, 47		3-06
❑	TS798		York C.1	ex 'MW100', Shawbury, Brize Norton, Staverton, 'LV633',		
				G-AGNV, Skyways, BOAC, TS798. CoA 6-3-65		3-06
❑	WS843	'Y'	Meteor NF.14	ex museum, Hendon, St Athan, Henlow 7937M,		
				St Athan, Kemble, 1 ANS, MoA, 228 OCU		3-06
❑	XA564		Javelin FAW.1	ex 2 SoTT, Locking 7464M, Filton	⇨	3-06
❑	XB812*	'U'	Sabre F.4	ex Hendon, 9227M, Duxford, Rome, Italian AF MM19666,		
				XB812, 93, 112, RCAF (no service) 19666. Arrived by 3-06		3-06
❑	XD818*		Valiant BK.1	ex Hendon, Marham 7894M, 49 'A' Flt. Arrived 8/9-05		3-06
❑	XE670		Hunter F.4	ex St Athan 8585M / 7762M, Abingdon, Bicester, 93, 26.		
				Nose		3-06
❑	XG337		Lightning F.1	ex 2 SoTT 8056M, Warton, AAEE, Warton	⇨	3-06
❑	XH171	'U'	Canberra PR.9	ex 2 SoTT 8746M, 39, 13, 39 MoA, 58	⇨	3-06
❑	XH672		Victor K.2	ex 9242M, Shawbury, 55, 57, 543, MoA. *Maid Marion*		3-06
❑	XL568	'C'	Hunter T.7A	ex Cranwell 9224M, Lossiemouth, 12, 74, MoA, 74, HS.		
				74 Sqn colours	⇨	3-06
❑	XL993		T' Pioneer CC.1	ex 8388M, Henlow, Shawbury, 21, 78. Stored		3-06
❑	XM598		Vulcan B.2	ex 8778M, 44, Wadd Wing, Cott Wing, 12		3-06
❑	XR371		Belfast C.1	ex Hucknall, Kemble, 53. *Enceladus*		3-06
❑	XV591		Phantom FG.1	ex St Athan, 111, 43, 892. Trans-Atlantic c/s. Nose.		3-06
❑	XX496	'D'	Jetstream T.1	ex Cranwell, 45, 6 FTS, 3 FTS		3-06
❑	01120		MiG-15*bis*	ex Hendon, Cardington, South Lambeth, Hendon,		
			(Lim-2)	Middlesborough, Polish AF		3-06
❑	J-1704		Venom FB.54	ex Greenham Common and Swiss Air Force		3-06
❑	74-0177*		F-111F	ex Mildenhall, AMARC, 27th TFW, 48th TFW,		
				366th TFW, 347th TFW. Arrived 3-11-05	[1]	3-06

Michael Beetham Conservation Centre: There is a purpose-built viewing gallery that has been described as 'public' but it is accessible only by parties of up to a maximum of 20 who can be accommodated on a prior arrangement basis. Several of the airframes destined for the 'Cold War' Hall were rotated through the centre. The Kestrel's wings are to be found on P.1127 XP984 at Brooklands, Surrey [1].

Departures: Mohawk G-AEKW returned to Hatch, Beds, in August 2004, for work on the wings.
◆ *Viewing on Fridays by prior arrangement only to groups, max 20 persons - tel 01902 376208.*

❑	[F-HMFI]	Farman F.41	ex 9204M, Wyton, Cardington, Henlow, Benson, Nash		3-06
❑	D5329	5F1 Dolphin REP	ex Wyton, Cardington. Using original parts	®	3-06

☐	P1344	'PL-K'	Hampden I	ex 9175M, Wyton, Cardington, Hatch, Petsamo, USSR, 144, 14 OTU. Forced down 6-9-42	®	3-06
☐	XS695		Kestrel FGA.1	ex Wyton, Cardington, Yeovilton, Culdrose A2619, Manadon, Tri-Partite Eval Sqn, AAEE, RAE	[1]	3-06
☐	XT903	'X'	Phantom FGR.2	ex Wyton, Leuchars, 56, 92, 228 OCU, 23, 228 OCU. Nose. Stored		3-06
☐	7198/18		LVG C.VI	ex Old Warden, 9239M, G-AANJ, ex Stanmore, Colerne, Fulbeck		3-06
☐	191614		Me 163B-1a	ex museum 8481M, Biggin Hill, Westcott, Brize Norton, Farnborough, Hussum, II/JG400	®	3-06

Stored: Aircraft listed here are in 'deep store' and not available for inspection. The Canberra B.2 nose carries the c/n EEP.71038 which should make it WD956 (which had no service life, undertaking RED DEAN missile trials), comments? [1]. By June 2004 Hunter F.6A XG225 moved to be 'gate guardian' for the museum - above.

☐	VX573		Valetta C.2	ex 8389M, Henlow, Wildenrath CF, Buckeburg CF. *Lorelei*		3-06
☐	WA346		Vampire FB.5	ex Cardington, Cosford, Henlow, Hendon, 3/4 CAACU, 1 FTS, 7 FTS, 130, 98, 102 FRS. Booms of VX461		3-06
☐	WD931		Canberra B.2	ex Aldridge, Pershore, RRE, RAE. Nose.	[1]	3-06
☐	WE982		Prefect TX.1	ex 8781M, Cardington, Henlow, Syerston, Manston, ACCGS, CGS, 1 GC, 621 GS, 612 GS, 644 GS, 643 GS, 166 GS, 143 GS		3-06
☐	XD674		Jet Provost T.1	ex St Athan, Swinderby, Finningley 7570M, 71 MU	⊙	3-06
☐	-		P.1121	ex Henlow, Cranfield. Fuselage sections		3-06
☐	6130		Ventura II	ex SAAF Museum, SAAF, RAF AJ469		3-06
☐	'6771'		F-84F-51-RE	ex Rochester, Southend, Belgian AF FU-6, 52-7133		3-06

Defence College of Aeronautical Engineering: (DCAE - Formerly 1 School of Technical Training.) Cosford is the centre of the tri-service structure of Defence Training Establishments. Eventually coming into the 'fold' will bet Athan, Wales, Cranwell, Lincs, and the Navy at Gosport, Hants, and the Army at Arborfield, Berks, with everything integrated by 2008. DCAE is split into a series of squadrons and flights, each teaching specialist elements. Please note that this 'order of battle' has changed somewhat since *W&R19*: Aerosystems Mechanical Engineering Squadron; Electrical Trade Training Flight; Mechanical Training Squadron; Survival Equipment, Propulsion and Weapons Training Squadron; and the Line Training Flight. No attempt has been made to delineate which airframes are with which elements in the listing below.

DCAE has four sophisticated Eurofighter Typhoon purpose-built training rigs, called GenFlies. These have the capacity to generate over 100 different faults, to really annoy the trainees. They have been allocated serials not because they are intended to fly, but because they have a maintenance schedule and cost a considerable amount of money... just like any modern-day warplane! [1] Other 'sims' in use with DCAE include ZK006 to ZK008 Tornado Training Aids of unknown pedigree and a barrage of Emulator Test Rigs, AV001 to AV018.

Departures: During December 2005 a large number of airframes were put up for tender and disposal details will doubtless appear in *W&R21*; these are marked ⇨. Other disposals are likely.**Andover** C.1(PR) XS641, long since thought to be going to the HQ Defence Logistics Organisation at Andover (shades of the Beverley and Beverley), was put up for tender 6-05 and moved 10-05 to Sandbach, Cheshire; **Harrier** GR.3 XV752 to Bletchley Park, Bucks, by 9-05; GR.3 XZ130 to Tolworth, Gtr Lon, 5-10-05; **Jaguar** GR.1 XX115 is a centre fuselage only and has been deleted. **Jet Provost** T.5A XW303 (⇨) to Halton, Bucks, 6-3-06; **Sea King** HAS.6 XV710 to Australia as spares late-2005; **Tornado** GR.1 ZA325 to St Athan, Wales, 10-05; **Tornado** P.06 XX948 exported to Hermeskeil, Germany; **Wessex** HU.5 XT773 (l/n 10-03) to Shawbury, Shrop, 4-10-05.

☐	XM362		Jet Provost T.3	8230M, ex Halton, Kemble, Shawbury, 3 FTS, 2 FTS. 'Cutaway' and camouflaged		9-05
☐	XR498	'X'	Wessex HC.2	9342M, ex Shawbury, 72, 60, 72, AAEE		9-05
☐	XR506	'V'	Wessex HC.2	9343M, ex Shawbury, 72, 60, 72, 18		9-05
☐	XR574	'72'	Gnat T.1	8631M, ex Halton, Cosford, Kemble, 4 FTS		9-05
☐	XS177	'N'	Jet Provost T.4	9044M, ex Valley, Shawbury, CATCS, 3 FTS, 2 FTS	⇨	12-05
☐	XS710	'O'	Dominie T.1	9259M, ex Cranwell, 3 FTS, 6 FTS, CAW		9-05
☐	XS726	'T'	Dominie T.1	9273M, ex Cranwell, 3 FTS, 6 FTS, CAW		9-05
☐	XS729	'G'	Dominie T.1	9275M, ex Cranwell, 3 FTS, 6 FTS		6-05
☐	XS733	'Q'	Dominie T.1	9276M, ex Cranwell, 3 FTS, 6 FTS, RAFC, CAW		6-05

❏	XS734	'N'	Dominie T.1	9260M, ex Cranwell, 3 FTS, 6 FTS	6-05
❏	XS738	'U'	Dominie T.1	9274M, ex Cranwell, 3 FTS, 6 FTS	9-05
❏	XV643*	'262'	Sea King HAS.6	ex St Athan, Gosport, Culdrose, 819, 849, 819, 814,	
				820, 824, 814, WHL, AAEE. Arrived 24-1-06	1-06
❏	XV653	'63'	Sea King HAS.6	9326M, ex Gosport, 810, 706	9-05
❏	XV659	'62'	Sea King HAS.6	9324M, ex Gosport, Fleetlands, 810, 814, 819, 706,	
				826, 824, 819, 814, FTU, 824	9-05
❏	XV701*	'64'	Sea King HAS.6	ex Gosport, 814, 820, 706, 810, 819, 706, 814, 824. F/n 9-05	9-05
❏	XV725*	'C'	Wessex HC.2	ex Gosport A2707 [2], Shawbury, 72, 18. Arr 21-1-05	9-05
❏	XW290	'MA'	Jet Provost T.5A	9199M, ex Shawbury, 3 FTS, RAFC, CFS	9-05
❏	XW292	'32'	Jet Provost T.5A	9128M, ex Halton, Shawbury, 3 FTS, RAFC, CFS	⇨ 12-05
❏	XW294	'45'	Jet Provost T.5A	9129M, ex Halton, Shawbury, 3 FTS, RAFC, Leeming SF,	
				1 FTS, CFS	⇨ 12-05
❏	XW299	'MB'	Jet Provost T.5A	9146M, ex Halton, 1 FTS, RAFC, 1 FTS	9-05
❏	XW301	'MC'	Jet Provost T.5A	9147M, ex Halton, 1 FTS	9-05
❏	XW304	'MD'	Jet Provost T.5	9172M, ex 6 FTS, CFS, 1 FTS	5-04
❏	XW309	'ME'	Jet Provost T.5	9179M, ex Shawbury, 6 FTS, 1 FTS	9-05
❏	XW311	'MF'	Jet Provost T.5	9180M, ex Shawbury 6 FTS	9-05
❏	XW312	'64'	Jet Provost T.5A	9109M, ex Halton, 1 FTS	⇨ 12-05
❏	XW318	'MG'	Jet Provost T.5A	9190M, ex 1 FTS, RAFC, CFS, RAFC, CFS, 3 FTS	9-05
❏	XW320	'71'	Jet Provost T.5A	'9015M', ex Halton, 1 FTS, Leeming SF 3 FTS, RAFC.	
				Really 9016M	9-05
❏	XW321	'MH'	Jet Provost T.5A	9154M, ex Shawbury, 1 FTS, 7 FTS, RAFC, 3 FTS	9-05
❏	XW327	'62'	Jet Provost T.5A	9130M, ex Halton, CFS, 7 FTS, 6 FTS, 7 FTS, 1 FTS, CFS, RAFC	9-05
❏	XW328	'MI'	Jet Provost T.5A	9177M, ex 1 FTS, RAFC, CFS, RAFC	5-04
❏	XW330	'MJ'	Jet Provost T.5A	9195M, ex 1 FTS, 7 FTS, 3 FTS, Leeming SF, CFS, RAFC, 3 FTS	9-05
❏	XW335	'74'	Jet Provost T.5A	9061M, ex Halton, Kemble, 3 FTS, RAFC, CFS, RAFC	⇨ 12-05
❏	XW351	'31'	Jet Provost T.5A	9062M, ex Halton, Kemble, 3 FTS, RAFC, 1 FTS, RAFC	⇨ 12-05
❏	XW358	'MK'	Jet Provost T.5A	9181M, ex Shawbury, 1 FTS, RAFC	9-05
❏	XW360	'ML'	Jet Provost T.5A	9153M, ex Shawbury, 1 FTS, RAFC, 7 FTS	9-05
❏	XW361	'MM'	Jet Provost T.5A	9192M, ex 1 FTS, RAFC, 7 FTS, RAFC	9-05
❏	XW364	'MN'	Jet Provost T.5A	9188M, ex Shawbury, 3 FTS, RAFC, CFS, 1 FTS	9-05
❏	XW365	'73'	Jet Provost T.5A	'9015M', ex Halton, 1 FTS, RAFC. Really 9018M	⇨ 12-05
❏	XW366	'75'	Jet Provost T.5A	9097M, ex Halton, 1 FTS, 3 FTS, RAFC	⇨ 12-05
❏	XW367	'MO'	Jet Provost T.5A	9193M, ex 1 FTS, RAFC	9-05
❏	XW370	'MP'	Jet Provost T.5A	9196M, ex 1 FTS, 3 FTS	9-05
❏	XW375	'52'	Jet Provost T.5A	9149M, ex Halton, CFS, 6 FTS, RAFC	9-05
❏	XW405	'MQ'	Jet Provost T.5A	9187M, ex Shawbury, 6 FTS, 1 FTS, 7 FTS, 6 FTS, 1 FTS, RAFC	5-04
❏	XW410	'MR'	Jet Provost T.5A	9125M, ex Shawbury, 1 FTS, RAFC, 3 FTS	9-05
❏	XW413	'69'	Jet Provost T.5A	9126M, ex Halton, 1 FTS, RAFC	⇨ 12-05
❏	XW416	'MS'	Jet Provost T.5A	9191M, ex 1 FTS, RAFC	5-04
❏	XW418	'MT'	Jet Provost T.5A	9173M, ex Shawbury, 1 FTS, 7 FTS, CFS, 3 FTS,	
				Leeming SF, 3 FTS.	9-05
❏	XW419	'125'	Jet Provost T.5A	9120M, ex Halton, 7 FTS, 1 FTS, RAFC.	⇨ 12-05
❏	XW420	'MU'	Jet Provost T.5A	9194M, ex 1 FTS, RAFC	9-05
❏	XW421	'60'	Jet Provost T.5A	9111M, ex PWTS, Halton, Shawbury, CFS, 3 FTS,	
				Leeming SF, 3 FTS	⇨ 12-05
❏	XW425	'MV'	Jet Provost T.5A	9200M, ex CFS, 6 FTS, CFS, 3 FTS, Leeming SF, CFS	9-05
❏	XW427	'67'	Jet Provost T.5A	9124M, ex Halton, 1 FTS, CFS, 3 FTS, CFS, 3 FTS	⇨ 12-05
❏	XW430	'MW'	Jet Provost T.5A	9176M, ex 1 FTS, CFS, 3 FTS, Leeming SF, 3 FTS	9-05
❏	XW432	'MX'	Jet Provost T.5A	9127M, ex Shawbury, 1 FTS, Leeming SF, 3 FTS	9-05
❏	XW434	'MY'	Jet Provost T.5A	9091M, ex Halton, 1 FTS, 7 FTS, 3 FTS, CFS	9-05
❏	XW436	'68'	Jet Provost T.5A	9148M, ex Halton, 1 FTS, CFS, 3 FTS, Leeming SF, 3 FTS, RAFC	9-05
❏	XW768	'N'	Harrier GR.3	9072M, ex Halton, 4, 1, 4, 20	3-06
❏	XW852		Gazelle HT.3	9331M, ex St Athan, Fleetlands, 32	9-05
❏	XX110	'EP'	Jaguar GR.1	8955M, ex Shawbury, 6, AAEE, BAC	9-05
❏	'XX110'		Jaguar GR.1 rig	BAPC.169, ex Halton. Engine systems rig	7-99

❏ XX117*	'ES'	Jaguar GR.3	ex St Athan, 16, 6, RAE, 226 OCU, 54, 6, 54, 226 OCU,	
			JOCU, JCT. Arrived 20-9-05	9-05
❏ XX726	'EB'	Jaguar GR.1	8947M, ex Halton, Shawbury, 6, 54, 14, 54, 6, JOCU	9-05
❏ XX727	'ER'	Jaguar GR.1	8951M, ex PWTS, Shawbury, 6, 54, 6, JOCU	9-05
❏ XX730	'EC'	Jaguar GR.1	8952M, ex Shawbury, 6, JOCU	9-05
❏ XX739	'I'	Jaguar GR.1	8902M, ex Halton, Shawbury, Gibraltar Det, 6	5-04
❏ XX743	'EG'	Jaguar GR.1	8949M, ex Halton, Shawbury, 6	9-05
❏ XX746	'09'	Jaguar GR.1A	8895M, ex Halton, 226 OCU, 14, 17, 6, 31, 226 OCU	9-05
❏ XX751	'10'	Jaguar GR.1	8937M, ex 226 OCU, 14	5-04
❏ XX756	'AM'	Jaguar GR.1	8899M, ex 14, 41, 14, 20, 226 OCU, 14	9-05
❏ XX757	'CU'	Jaguar GR.1	8948M, ex Halton, Shawbury, 20, 226 OCU, 14	9-05
❏ XX766*	'EF'	Jaguar GR.1	ex St Athan, 54, 6, 54, 226 OCU, 54, 226 OCU, 17, 14.	
			Arrived 31-1-06	1-06
❏ XX818	'DE'	Jaguar GR.1	8945M, ex Halton, Shawbury, 31, 20, 17	9-05
❏ XX819	'CE'	Jaguar GR.1	8923M, ex Shawbury, 20, 17	9-05
❏ XX824	'AD'	Jaguar GR.1	9019M, ex Halton, Shawbury, 14, 17, 14	9-05
❏ XX825	'BN'	Jaguar GR.1	9020M, ex Halton, Shawbury, 17, 31, 14	9-05
❏ XX826	'JH'	Jaguar GR.1	9021M, ex Shawbury, 2, 20, 14	⇨ 12-05
❏ XX837	'1'	Jaguar T.2	8978M, ex Halton, Shawbury, 226 OCU	9-05
❏ XX845*	'EV'	Jaguar T.4	ex St Athan, 6, 54, 16, 54, 41, 226 OCU, 2, 14, 17, 31, 17,	
			31, 17, 14, 2, 17. Arrived 17-10-05	10-05
❏ XX956	'BE'	Jaguar GR.1	8950M, ex Halton, Shawbury, 17, 31, 14, 17	9-05
❏ XX958	'BK'	Jaguar GR.1	9022M, ex Shawbury, 17, 14	5-04
❏ XX959	'CJ'	Jaguar GR.1	8953M, ex Shawbury, 20, 14	9-05
❏ XX962	'e'	Jaguar GR.1B	9257M. ex Cranwell, Coltishall, 6, 17, 20, 17	5-04
❏ XX966	'JJ'	Jaguar GR.1A	8904M, ex Halton, Shawbury, 6,54,20, AAEE, 20, 17	5-04
❏ XX967	'AC'	Jaguar GR.1	9006M, ex Shawbury, 14, 31	9-05
❏ XX968	'AJ'	Jaguar GR.1	9007M, ex Shawbury, 14, 31	9-05
❏ XX969	'01'	Jaguar GR.1	8897M, ex 226 OCU, 3, 17, 31, 14, 31	9-05
❏ [XX975]	'07'	Jaguar GR.1A	8905M, ex Halton, 226 OCU, 31, 17, 226 OCU	9-05
❏ XX976	'BD'	Jaguar GR.1	8906M, ex Halton, Shawbury, 17, 31	9-05
❏ XZ104*	'FM'	Jaguar GR.3A	ex St Athan, 41, 6, 2. Arrived 27-10-05	10-05
❏ XZ322*	'N'	Gazelle AH.1	ex St Athan 9283M, Shawbury, 670, ARWS, 6 Flt. Arr 25-1-06	1-06
❏ XZ368	'AG'	Jaguar GR.1	8900M, ex Coltishall, 14, 41, 14, 6, 14	9-05
❏ XZ370	'JB'	Jaguar GR.1	9004M, ex Shawbury, 14,41,54,14,17,41,54,17,54,17	9-05
❏ XZ371	'AP'	Jaguar GR.1	8907M, ex Shawbury, Coltishall SF, 14,41,54,14,17	9-05
❏ XZ374	'JC'	Jaguar GR.1	9005M, ex Shawbury, 14, 20	9-05
❏ XZ383	'AF'	Jaguar GR.1	8901M, ex Colt', 14, 41, 54, 14, 226 OCU, 14, 17	9-05
❏ XZ384	'BC'	Jaguar GR.1	8954M, ex Shawbury, 17, 31, 20	9-05
❏ XZ389	'BL'	Jaguar GR.1	8946M, ex Halton, Shawbury, 17, 31, 20	9-05
❏ XZ390	'DM'	Jaguar GR.1	9003M, ex Shawbury, 2, 20, 31	9-05
❏ XZ935		Gazelle HT.3	9332M, ex St Athan, Fleetlands, 32, CFS	5-04
❏ XZ941*	'B'	Gazelle HT.2	ex St Athan, Shawbury, 2 FTS, Odiham hack, CFS.	
			Arrived 25-1-06	1-06
❏ XZ991*	'3A'	Harrier GR.3	ex St Athan 9162M, 233 OCU, 4, 1417F, 233 OCU, 1,	
			R-R, 1, 3, 1. Arrived 24-1-06	1-06
❏ ZA320	'TAW'	Tornado GR.1	9314M, ex St Athan, 15, TTTE	9-05
❏ ZA323	'TAZ'	Tornado GR.1	ex St Athan, 15, TTTE	9-05
❏ ZA357	'TTV'	Tornado GR.1	ex St Athan, 15, TTTE	9-05
❏ ZA399*	'AJC'	Tornado GR.1	ex St Athan, 617, 20, TWCU. Arrived 10-1-06	1-06
❏ ZA450	'TH'	Tornado GR.1	9317M, ex St Athan, 15, 12, 617, 12, 27, 20, 15	9-05
❏ ZD939	'AS'	Tornado F.2	ex St Athan, Warton, St Athan, 229 OCU. Cockpit	9-05
❏ ZE340	'GO'	Tornado F.3	9298M, ex Coningsby, 56. Rear fuselage of ZE758	5-04
❏ ZJ695	001	GenFly Mk.2	Typhoon training rig	[1] 9-05
❏ ZJ696	002	GenFly Mk.2	Typhoon training rig	[1] 9-05
❏ ZJ697	003	GenFly Mk.2	Typhoon training rig	[1] 9-05
❏ ZJ698	004	GenFly Mk.2	Typhoon training rig	[1] 9-05

PT Flight: Bob Mitchell's aircraft are in the process of relocating to <u>Sleap</u>, Shropshire. Moving during October 2005 were: Monarch G-AFRZ; Stampe G-AWIW; PT-2s 2 N1344 and N56421. The others will follow.

❏ G-AEUJ	Whitney Straight	ex Sutton Coldfield, Marple, East Midlands, Bournemouth. CoA 4-6-70. Stored	5-02
❏ G-AYKZ	SAI KZ-VIII	ex Coventry, HB-EPB, OY-ACB. CoA 17-7-81. Stored	5-02
❏ G-BADW	Pitts S-2A	ex museum. CoA 6-9-95	5-02
❏ G-RIDE	Stephens Akro	ex N81AC, N55NM. CoA 13-8-92	5-02
❏ N49272	'23' PT-23-HO	ex USAAF	5-02
❏ N58566	BT-15 Valiant	ex USAAF	8-04

Others: The Spitfire is 'on guard' in the parade ground - note that the decidedly *real* MK356 can be found at Coningsby, Lincs, while another 'MK356' is at Hawkinge, Kent.

❏ 'MK356'	Spitfire IX FSM	BAPC.298, on parade ground	3-04

Locally: In a field near Junction 3 of the M54 is a Vampire, used by a paintball group.

❏ XE993	Vampire T.11	ex Cosford 8161M, 8, 73. Poor state.	10-02

DONNINGTON south of the A518, north east of Telford
HQ Defence Storage and Disposition Centre: This huge logistics base has a gate guardian.

❏ XZ971	'U' Harrier GR.3	9219M, ex Shawbury, Benson, HOCU, 1417F, 233 OCU. Gate	9-03

LONG MYND AERODROME west of Church Stretton

❏ XN157	FGS Sedbergh TX.1	ex Sealand. CoA 30-7-95. Stored in trailer	8-04

LUDLOW on the A49 north of Leominster
Pipistrelle G-BADV (last noted February 1991) moved to <u>Kingsclere</u>, .Hampshire, by 2000.

❏ G-ABUS	Comper Swift	ex Heathfield. CoA 19-6-79	®	2-91

MARKET DRAYTON on the A53 north-east of Shrewsbury
Parrallel Aviation / Richard Parr: (Please note the 'double-r' based on the patron's surname!) Locally-based Parrallel has been active in providing several airframes for museums and other collections, the Bulldog at Newark Air Museum and the 'Gunbus' at Sywell being good examples. Two former Romanian L29 Delfin noses have arrived and are available. Canberra B.2 nose WP515 moved to Hawker Hunter Aviation at <u>Scampton</u>, Lincs, by May 2004. There it was restored and moved to Berlin on 21st January 2005 for the Luftwaffe Museum. The nose of Hunter F.6 IF-68 moved to <u>Farnborough</u>, Hants, by mid-2005. As *W&R20* closed for press, Sea Hawk FGA.6 XE368 had been acquired to become the founder-member of the Walney Aviation Heritage Museum at <u>Walney Island</u>, Cumbria [1].
◆ *Private location, visits by prior arrangement only. 01630 684040, fax 01630 685467, e-mail rp@parralleltraining.com*

❏ XE368*	'200' Sea Hawk FGA.6	ex Bruntingthorpe, Helston, Culdrose SAH-3, Shotley A2534, 738, 806, 803, 899. Arrived by 3-06	[1]	4-06
❏ [XM697]*	'S' Gnat T.1	G-NAAT, ex Exeter, Bournemouth, Dunsfold, Bournemouth, Woking, HSA, AAEE, HSA. Arrived by 3-06		3-06
❏ XZ431*	Buccaneer S.2B	ex Bruntingthorpe, Marham 9233M, 12, 208, 12, 208. Nose. Arrived 31-5-05		3-06
❏ '29'*	893046 L29 Delfin	ex Romanian AF. Nose. Arrived 3-06		3-06
❏ '53'	395189 L29 Delfin	ex Romanian AF. Nose. Arrived 3-06		3-06

SHAWBURY on the A53 north-east of Shrewsbury
Buccaneer S.2C XW544 moved to <u>Bruntingthorpe</u>, Leics, on 3rd October 2004.

SHAWBURY AIRFIELD on the B5063 north of Shawbury

Assault Glider Trust (AGT - previously the Assault Glider Association): Located within the base, AGT are making exceptional progress with their complete Horsa reproduction and its Dakota tug. AGT have linked up with the Silent Wings Museum at Lubbock, Texas. A second Horsa REP is being built by AGT and will be assembled at Lubbock. The other side of this co-operation became apparent in March 2005 when the fuselage frame of a Waco CG-4 Hadrian arrived and was assembled ready for the official 'unveiling' of the AGT Horsa on 20th March 2005 - to mark the 60th anniversary of Operation VARSITY - the Rhine crossing. A fuselage section of TL659 and other parts have been loaned by the Museum of Army Flying at Middle Wallop, Hants, to act as patterns. The aim is to display the finished gliders, and tug, in the Midlands as a tribute to the Airborne Forces.

◆ *Available for inspection* strictly *by prior permission. Major Ray Conningham, The Manor, Streethay, Lichfield, WS13 8LU e-mail ray@conningham.fsnet.co.uk www.assaultgliderproject.co.uk*

❑ KG651	C-47B-25-DK	G-AMHJ, ex Coventry, SU-AZI, G-AMHJ, ZS-BRW, KG651, 1333 CU, 1383 CU, 24, 109 OTU, 42-108962. CoA 5-12-00		3-06
❑ 'LH291'	Horsa REP	BAPC.279. 'Unveiled' 20-3-05		3-06
❑ –*	CG-4 Hadrian REP	ex Lubbock, Texas. Frame, arrived by 3-05		3-06

Defence Aviation Repair Agency (DARA): As can be readily seen from the 'Departures' section below, the base is **Canberra**-less for the first time in a very long time, although the PR.9s are bound to come through here when 39 Squadron finally calls it a day. In a similar manner, the long-term **Jaguar** store has all but gone. The final retirements from Coltishall will probably go through the disposal sequence much faster. RAF Jetstreams have now almost gone through.

While it may not seem so, most of the **Tucano** store is in a state of 'rotation'. During late 2005, a batch of Tucanos started the spares recovery process, probably in the light of the much smaller requirement for flying training and, perhaps, with the onset of the Military Flying Training System contract, due to be placed in 2006. These have been listed as they are unlikely to go anywhere other than scrap merchants and maybe even museums. As can be seen, some have spent over a decade flightless.

An increasing number of airframes arrive for fast turn-around and disposal (the jargon is 'hot sale'): Sea Harrier FA.2 ZD582 arrived on June 16, 2005, tendered in September 2005 and departed (to Colsterworth, Lincs) November 11, 2005, being typical. (Then, having picked it as 'typical' it came *back* here on 29th March 2006 – see the 'Short-termers' list below!) With the wonderful **Sea Harrier** bowing out of service for good (with 801 Squadron on 28th March 2006), more of the type will go through here, but will very likely be too fleeting for a formal mention in these pages. The Indian Navy are considering purchasing the final six that were in service at the 'bow out'. For completeness 'short-termers' are given separate treatment below.

Wessex disposals are now complete, but the first **Pumas** are beginning to appear. The McDD (Boeing by adoption) **Apaches** are technically in short term storage prior to service issue. From late 2004 an increasing number of Army **Gazelles** have been arriving. Those given below have spent at least a year here but, for completeness 'short-termers' are given separate treatment below.

Departures: Canberra T.4 WH849 scrapped on site 10-05 by Cronifer Metals of Clay Cross, Derbyshire, nose going to Basingstoke, Hants; T.4 WT480 as WH849; PR.9 XH174 nose as WH849; **Gazelle** AH.1 XW892 to Ipswich, Suffolk, 10-10-04; HT.2 XX431 previously listed in this section should appear in 'Others' below; HT.2 XZ942 to Middle Wallop, Hants, 10-10-04; **Hawk** T.1A XX304 nose left 20-5-04 for Thales Training to turn into a simulator; **Jaguar** the following, all to Ipswich, Suffolk: T.2A XX144 on 12-10-05; GR.1A XX741 18-11-05; GR.1A XX745 to Boscombe Down, Wilts, 24-3-04; T.2A XX829 on 6-10-05; T.2A XX832 on 13-10-05; T.2A XX836 on 10-8-05; GR.1A XX955 on 6-9-05; GR.3 XZ361 (arrived 26-6-02) on 15-12-05; GR.1A XZ378 to Topsham, Devon, 14-11-05; **Jetstream** T.1 XX482 and XX497 fuselages only to Hixon, Staffs, 11-5-05; T.1 XX494 tendered 12-04, to Ipswich, Suffolk, 30-3-05; T.1 XX495 tendered 12-04, to Bedford, Beds; **Wessex** HC.2 XR516 was 'adopted' by the resident 60 Squadron in 2004 and is now listed under 'Others'; XR525 to Cosford, Shrop, 13-5-04; XV726 to Hixon, Staffs, 11-5-05.

❑ XW200	Puma HC.1	ex 33, 240 OCU, HOCF. Crashed 9-4-01	3-06
❑ XW202*	Puma HC.1	ex Benson, 33, 230, 33, 27, 230, 1563 Flt, 33, 1563 Flt, 33, 1563 Flt, 33, 240 OCU, 230, AAEE, 230, 240 OCU, 230, 240 OCU. Arrived 25-7-05	3-06
❑ XW849*	Gazelle AH.1	ex 847. Arrived 23-2-05	3-06
❑ XW851*	Gazelle AH.1	ex 847. Arrived 25-11-04	3-06
❑ XW909*	Gazelle AH.1	ex 9 Regt. Arrived 23-2-05	3-06
❑ XX380*	Gazelle AH.1	ex Fleetlands. Arrived 24-1-05	3-06

❑	XX384*	Gazelle AH.1	ex Fleetlands. Arrived 18-1-05	3-06
❑	XX394*	Gazelle AH.1	ex 3 Regt, 4 Regt. Arrived 7-12-04	3-06
❑	XX409*	Gazelle AH.1	ex 4 Regt, 672. Arrived 30-11-04	3-06
❑	XX437*	Gazelle AH.1	ex Wattisham, 3 Regt. Arrived 2-3-05	3-06
❑	XX439*	Gazelle AH.1	ex 4 Regt, 672. Arrived 2-12-04	3-06
❑	XX455*	Gazelle AH.1	ex Fleetlands. Arrived 24-1-05	3-06
❑	XX460*	Gazelle AH.1	ex Fleetlands, Wattisham. Arrived 11-1-05	3-06
❑	XX499	'G' Jetstream T.1	ex Cranwell, 45, 3 FTS, 45, 6 FTS, METS	3-06
❑	XZ312*	Gazelle AH.1	ex Wattisham, 3 Regt. Pod. Arrived 7-1-05	3-06
❑	XZ318*	Gazelle AH.1	ex Fleetlands, Yeovil, Fleetlands. DBR 2-1-97. Pod. Arr 18-1-05	3-06
❑	XZ346*	Gazelle AH.1	ex 5 Regt, 665. Arrived 15-12-04	3-06
❑	ZA774*	Gazelle AH.1	ex Fleetlands. Arrived 18-1-05	3-06
❑	ZD938	'AR' Tornado F.2	ex St Athan, 229 OCU. Forward fuselage	9-05
❑	ZF141*	Tucano T.1	ex Linton-on-Ouse. Arrived 8-9-96. Spares recovery by 11-05	3-06
❑	ZF164*	Tucano T.1	ex Linton-on-Ouse. Arrived 1-10-97. Spares recovery by 11-05	3-06
❑	ZF165*	Tucano T.1	ex Cranwell. Arrived 29-3-95. Spares recovery by 11-05	3-06
❑	ZF200*	Tucano T.1	ex Linton-on-Ouse. Arrived 7-1-98. Spares recovery by 11-05	3-06
❑	ZF201*	Tucano T.1	ex Linton-on-Ouse. Arrived 9-3-98. Spares recovery by 11-05	3-06
❑	ZF245*	Tucano T.1	ex Scampton. Arrived 11-5-95. Spares recovery by 11-05	3-06
❑	ZF265*	Tucano T.1	ex Scampton. Arrived 12-1-95. Spares recovery by 11-05	3-06
❑	ZF267*	Tucano T.1	ex Cranwell. Arrived 2-6-95. Spares recovery by 11-05	3-06
❑	ZF284*	Tucano T.1	ex Cranwell. Arrived 2-5-95. Spares recovery by 11-05	3-06
❑	ZF285*	Tucano T.1	ex Cranwell. Arrived 20-3-95. Spares recovery by 11-05	3-06
❑	ZF340*	Tucano T.1	ex Cranwell. Arrived 11-4-95. Spares recovery by 11-05	3-06
❑	ZF373*	Tucano T.1	ex Linton-on-Ouse. Arrived 15-11-95. Spares recovery by 11-05	3-06
❑	ZF411*	Tucano T.1	ex Linton-on-Ouse. Arrived 9-1-98. Spares recovery by 11-05	3-06
❑	ZF415*	Tucano T.1	ex Linton-on-Ouse. Arrived 14-2-96. Spares recovery by 11-05	3-06
❑	ZF450*	Tucano T.1	ex Linton-on-Ouse. Arrived 7-1-98. Spares recovery by 11-05	3-06

Short-termers: For completeness, the following recent arrivals are briefly listed – serial, type, arrival. Should their stay be longer than a year, they will receive greater attention in *W&R21*.

❑	XW897*	Gazelle AH.1	2-8-05	❑	ZA728*	Gazelle AH.1	1-6-05
❑	XW904*	Gazelle AH.1	27-6-05	❑	ZA775*	Gazelle AH.1	29-9-05
❑	XW913*	Gazelle AH.1	1-6-05	❑	ZA776*	Gazelle AH.1	29-6-05
❑	XX375*	Gazelle AH.1	3-10-05	❑	ZB604*	Sea Harrier T.8	24-11-05
❑	XX381*	Gazelle AH.1	17-5-05	❑	ZB692*	Gazelle AH.1	1-9-05
❑	XX385*	Gazelle AH.1	6-10-05	❑	ZB674*	Gazelle AH.1	15-11-05
❑	XX389*	Gazelle AH.1	23-6-05	❑	ZB665*	Gazelle AH.1	10-1-06
❑	XX392*	Gazelle AH.1	10-7-05	❑	ZD579*	Sea Harrier FA.2	11-1-06
❑	XX412*	Gazelle AH.1	9-6-05	❑	ZD582*	Sea Harrier FA.2	29-3-06
❑	XX416*	Gazelle AH.1	15-8-05	❑	ZH796*	Sea Harrier FA.2	29-3-06
❑	XX417*	Gazelle AH.1	18-8-05	❑	ZH798*	Sea Harrier FA.2	13-12-05
❑	XZ298*	Gazelle AH.1	22-9-05	❑	ZH803*	Sea Harrier FA.2	29-3-06
❑	XZ301*	Gazelle AH.1	27-7-05	❑	ZH804*	Sea Harrier FA.2	29-3-06
❑	XZ313*	Gazelle AH.1	23-6-05	❑	ZH811*	Sea Harrier FA.2	29-3-06
❑	XZ337*	Gazelle AH.1	15-11-05	❑	ZH812*	Sea Harrier FA.2	29-3-06
❑	XZ347*	Gazelle AH.1	22-9-05	❑	ZH813*	Sea Harrier FA.2	8-3-06

Others: Wessex HC.2 XR516 has been 'adopted' by **60 Squadron** (who fly the Bell Griffons from here) [1]. The Wessex on the gate is named *Aries*, shades of the famous Lancaster and Lincolns operated by the resident Central Navigation School and the Empire Air Navigation School, 1943-1949 [2]. The Scout is displayed by **660 Squadron**, AAC (who fly Aerospatiale Squirrels form here) [3]. Both the Scout and the displayed Wessex XT672 are believed to be privately owned. Gazelle HT.2 XX431 is used by the **Airman's' Training School** as an instructional airframe [3]. Jet Provost T.3 XN549 moved from the dump to <u>Wycombe Air Park</u>, Bucks, on 3rd February 2006.

❑	XR516	'WB'	Wessex HC.2	ex Gosport, 9319M, A2709 [2], Shawbury, 2 FTS, 18	[1]	3-06
❑	XT672	'WE'	Wessex HC.2	ex Hixon, Shawbury, 2 FTS, Benson SF, 72. *Aries*	[2]	3-06
❑	XT773*		Wessex HU.5	ex Cosford, 9123M, St Athan, Abingdon, Wroughton,		
				771, 845, 847, 772, 845, 707. Dump. Arrived 4-10-05		3-06
❑	XV123		Scout AH.1	ex Thruxton, Ipswich, Weston-super-Mare, Fleetlands.	[3]	3-06
❑	XX431	'43'	Gazelle HT.2	9300M, ex 705, FONA, 705. Inst airframe	[4]	3-06

SLEAP AERODROME south-west of Wem

Wartime Aircraft Recovery Group Aviation Museum: As well as the airframes there are plenty of aero engines and artefacts recovered from 'digs' - including WAG's 'founder', 61 OTU Spitfire IIa P7304 involved in a mid-air collision near High Ercall on 22nd August 1943 and recovered in 1977. The Fury and Typhoon are on loan from chairman Roger Marley [1]. The Spitfire FSM with *original* instrumentation etc is on loan from Keith Jones [2]. The Provost is owned by Vaughan K Meers (see also Abbots Bromley, Staffs, and Wolverhampton, W Mids) and is being restored [3]. 'Gunbus' FSM 'GBH-7' moved from here and eventually gravitated to Northampton Airport, Northants, via Swindon, Wilts.

◆ *Open the second and fourth Sun in summer, also often open Sat afternoons. Please 'phone to check. Otherwise by prior arrangement. 01630 672969 www.wargroup.homestead.com*

❑	'K7271'		Fury II REP	BAPC.148, ex Market Drayton, Cosford		[1]	3-02
❑	'EN398'	'JE-J'	Spitfire IX FSM	ex Cannock		[2]	3-02
❑	–		Typhoon	ex Market Drayton. Cockpit	off-site [1]		3-02
❑	WW388*		Provost T.1	ex Hemswell, Firbeck, Long Marston, Cardiff-Wales,			
		'O-F'		Llanelli, Chinnor, Chertsey, Cuxwold, Chessington,			
				Halton 7616M, 2 FTS. Arrived by 9-05	® [3]		3-06

Aerodrome: Aircraft from Bob Mitchell's former PT Flight, long-time stored at Cosford, Shropshire, are relocating here – BM.

❑	[G-AFRZ]*		Monarch	ex Cosford, Sutton Coldfield, Shipdham, G-AIDE, W6463,		
				Kemble, 10 GCF, FTCCF, 13 EFTS, G-AFRZ.		
				CoA 29-6-70. Arrived 10-05	BM	3-06
❑	G-AWIW*		SNCAN SV-4B	ex Cosford, F-BDCC. CoA 6-5-73. Arrived 10-05	BM	3-06
❑	G-BLLO		Super Cub 95	ex D-EAUB, Belg AF OL-L25, 53-4699. CoA 12-10-96. Fuse		3-06
❑	G-BLWW		Aerocar Mini-Imp	CoA 4-6-87. Stored		8-03
❑	N1344*		PT-22 Recruit	ex Cosford, 41-20877. Arrived 10-05	BM	3-06
❑	N56421*	'855'	PT-22 Recruit	ex Cosford, 41-15510. Arrived 10-05	BM	3-06

TILSTOCK AERODROME on the A41 south of Whitchurch

Last recorded here in January 1998, para-trainer Cessna 182F G-ASNN has been consigned to LOST!

SOMERSET

AXBRIDGE on the A38 west of Cheddar

See previous issues for clues to the identity of the Robin. Either way it looks set for LOST!

❑	–		HR.100-200B	ex Keynsham. Dismantled, spares.	12-00

BABCARY east of the A37, east of Somerton

Delicately placed in 'Devon' in *W&R19!*

❑	ZA767		Gazelle AH.1	ex Ipswich, Middle Wallop, 25F. Cr 11-9-99. Pod	4-03

BRISTOL AIRPORT (LULSGATE)

Trident 2E G-AVFM and Varsity T.1 WF410 were scrapped during May 2004, with the cockpit of the former going to Cove, Hants. In the fire pits is a convincing helicopter mock-up and a pseudo-767. Dove 6 G-ANAP was scrapped during May 2004, the cockpit going to Pershore, Worcs. Aztec 250D G-BAUI moved to Gloucestershire, Glos, by 2005.

❏ G-AVPK	Rallye Comm	CoA 10-1-92. Stored	11-03
❏ G-BFRL	Cessna F.152 II	Crashed 24-8-92. Stored	2-00
❏ G-BIUO	Commander 112A	ex Staverton, OY-PRH, N1281J. Cr 12-5-84	12-03
❏ G-NERI	Archer II	ex G-BMKO, N31880. Crashed 6-8-98. Wreck	2-00

Paintball Adventure West: On the edge of the airport – they still have their Wessex.

❏ G-AWOX	Wessex 60	ex Weston-super-Mare, Bournemouth, Weston, G-17-2,	
		G-AWOX, 5N-AJO, G-AWOX, 9Y-TFB, G-AWOX,	
		VH-BHE, G-AWOX, VR-BCV, G-AWOX, G-17-1.	
		CoA 13-1-83	2-06

BURNHAM ON SEA south of Weston-super-Mare, on the B3140

A Britannia cockpit is kept in the general area.

❏ 5Y-AYR	Britannia 307F	ex Bournemouth, African Cargo, G-ANCD, Gemini, Lloyd,	
		BUA, Air Charter, 4X-AGE El Al, N6595C ntu,	
		G-ANCD, G-18-3. Cockpit	2-06

CLEVEDON west of Junction 20, M5

A Provost is under restoration in the general area.

❏ WW453	Provost T.1	G-TMKI, ex Cranfield, Thatcham, Strathallan, Perth,	
		Hunting, 1 FTS, 2 FTS.	® 8-05

HENSTRIDGE AERODROME south of the A30, east of Henstridge Marsh

❏ G-ALYG	Auster 5D	ex Charlton Mackrell, Heathrow, Irby-on-Humber,	
		MS968, 661, 653. CoA 19-1-70. Frame. Stored	9-02
❏ G-ANEW	Tiger Moth	ex NM138, Oxf UAS, 8 RFS, 29 EFTS. CoA 18-6-62	3-02
❏ G-ARJD	Colt 108	crashed 17-11-71. Frame. Stored	4-97
❏ G-AWYX	Rallye Club	ex Compton Abbas. CoA 27-6-86. Stored	8-97
❏ G-BFMF*	Cassut IIIM	CoA 24-5-91. Stored	10-05
❏ NC2612	Stinson Junior R	stored, dismantled	9-02

KEW STOKE north of Weston-super-Mare

Mark Templeman: Should still have his Hunter cockpit.

❏ –	Hunter F.4	ex Portishead, Boscombe Down, Salisbury, Cove,	
		Farnborough. Nose. Red c/s	12-01

MARKSBURY on the A39 west of Bath

Hamburger Hill: The paintball wargaming park still has its S-55.

❏ S-887	S-55C	ex Weston-super-Mare, Panshanger, Elstree, RDanAF	2-06

POOLE on minor road north of Wellington

Military Aircraft Spares Ltd: Poole Industrial Estate. Hunter XG164 has the starboard wing of T.7 XL623. The port wing is at Beck Row, Suffolk. The fuselage – with *altogether* different wings – is at Woking, Surrey!

❏ XG164	Hunter F.6	ex Shawbury, Halton 8681M, Kemble, West Raynham SF,	
		74, 111. Composite	3-06

PORTISHEAD west of the M5, Junction 19

Skirmish Paintball Games (Bath): (previously the 1st Twilight Zone) the paintball battleground has an S-55C. (www.skirmishbath.co.uk)

❏ [S-882]	S-55C	ex Weston-super-Mare, Panshanger, Elstree, Dan AF Esk.722	2-06

ROOKS BRIDGE on the A38 south of Weston-super-Mare

❏ G-BHMO	PA-20M Pacer	ex Little Gransden, F-BDRO. Cr 20-8-89. Stored	3-03

UPPER VOBSTER on minor road west of Frome

Vobster Quay: The diving centre acquired the former Exeter HS.748 in June 2004. Split into three sections, those with webbed feet can visit the cockpit and tail at 39ft down, with the centre section at 85ft for those who like to take the 'bends'! For those ones who just *have* to see it (remember a waterproof biro!) there is a mini-submarine available for pleasure dives! (www.vobsterquay.co.uk)

❏ G-AVXJ*	HS.748-2A	ex Exeter, CAAFU. CoA 22-8-98. Arrived 6-04	2-06

WESTON-SUPER-MARE AERODROME on the A371 east of Weston-super-Mare

The Helicopter Museum (THM): Proudly declaring itself as the 'World's Biggest Chopper Collection' (!), THM will only disappoint a very small minority of visitors who have completely mis-interpreted the nature of the venue! They work hard to present an ever-changing collection with plenty of special events: regular helicopter experience flight days; loads of special events, including the incredible 'HeliDays' staged on the beach lawns in late July; tours of the restoration hangar; kids play area with a Lynx to 'fly' and regular 'Open cockpit' days. THM can teach some of the 'nationals' how it's done! The museum have secured a small part of the huge Boeing XCH-62 heavy-lift prototype, 72-2012 which was scrapped at Fort Rucker, Alabama, in October 2005. The main and nose undercarriage units are on their way to Weston – each 17ft high. Expected in April is a an Agusta-Bell AB.204 – no other details at present [1].

Notes: Bö 105D G-PASA was rebuilt in 1993, discarding the original pod (and much else) going on to become G-BUXS which is currently operational [2]. The Frelon started life as SA.321 c/n 116. It is in Olympic Airways colours and the scheme it wore at the 1969 Paris Salon [3]. Airframes on loan from Elfan ap Rees are marked EAR. For Fairey Ultra-Light G-AOUJ see Innsworth, Glos. See also the '**Reserve Collection**' section below.

◆ *All year Wed to Sun 10am to 5.30pm (4.30pm Nov to Mar). Also Bank Hols, Easter fortnight and every day mid-Jul to end of Aug. 'Open Cockpit' days are held every second Sunday, Mar to Oct and the annual 'HeliDays' fly-in is held on the Weston Sea Front on the last weekend of July. Also regular 'Helicopter Experience Flight' days. SAE brings leaflet or hit the web-site. THM run the excellent 'HeliWorld' gift shop, and the great 'Choppers' coffee shop – featuring 'Heliburgers' and 'Belvedere Baguettes'. There is also a* **Friends of the Helicopter Museum** *– which produces its own quarterly bulletin - SAE for information. The Heliport, Locking Moor Road, Weston-super-Mare, BS24 8PP tel 01934 635227 fax 01934 645230 e-mail office@helimuseumfsnet.co.uk www.helicoptermuseum.co.uk*

❏ [G-ACWM]	Cierva C.30A	ex Staverton, Tewkesbury, AP506, 529, 1448 Flt,		
		74 Wing, 5 RSS, G-ACWM. Frame	EAR	3-06
❏ G-ALSX	Sycamore 3	ex Duxford, Staverton, G-48/1, G-ALSX,		
		VR-TBS ntu, G-ALSX. CoA 24-9-65	EAR	3-06
❏ [G-ANFH]	Whirlwind Srs 1	ex Redhill, Gt Yarmouth, Bristow, BEAH. CoA 17-7-71	EAR	3-06
❏ G-AODA	Whirlwind Srs 3	ex Redhill, Bristow, 9Y-TDA, EP-HAC, G-AODA.		
		Dorado. CoA 23-8-91		3-06
❏ G-AOZE	Widgeon 2	ex Cuckfield, Shoreham, 5N-ABW, G-AOZE		3-06
❏ G-ASTP	Hiller UH-12C	ex Biggin Hill, Thornicombe, 'Wales', Thornicombe,		
		Redhill, N9750C. CoA 3-7-82		3-06
❏ G-ATFG	Brantly B.2B	ex East Fortune, Newport Pagnell. CoA 25-3-85.	EAR	3-06
❏ G-AVKE	Gadfly HDW-1	ex Southend, Thruxton. Stored	EAR	3-06
❏ G-AVNE	Wessex 60 Srs 1	ex Bournemouth, Weston-super-Mare, G-17-3, 5N-AJL,		
and G-17-3		G-AVNE, 9M-ASS, VH-BHC, PK-HBQ, G-AVNE.		
		CoA 7-2-83		3-06
❏ G-AWRP	Grasshopper III	ex Blackpool, Heysham, Shoreham, Redhill. CoA 12-5-72		3-06

	Reg	Type	Notes		Date
❑	G-BAPS	Campbell Cougar	ex Weston-super-Mare. CoA 20-5-74		3-06
❑	G-BGHF	WG.30-100	ex Yeovil, Westlands. CoA 1-8-86		3-06
❑	G-BKGD	WG.30-100	ex Yeovil, Penzance, G-BKBJ ntu. CoA 6-7-93		3-06
❑	G-EHIL	EH-101 PP3	ex Yeovil, ZH647		3-06
❑	G-ELEC	WG.30-200	ex Westland W-s-M, Yeovil, G-BKNV. CoA 28-6-85. 'Rescue' and 'Helicopter Museum' titles		3-06
❑	G-HAUL	WG.30-TT300	ex G-17-22, Yeovil. CoA 27-10-86		3-06
❑	G-LYNX	Lynx 800	ZB500 ex Yeovil, ZA500 ntu, G-LYNX		3-06
❑	G-OAPR	Brantly B.2B ✈	ex G-BPST ntu, N2280U	EAR	3-06
❑	G-OTED	Robinson R-22	ex Elstree, G-BMYR, ZS-HLG		3-06
❑	G-PASA	MBB Bö 105D	ex Devon and Cornwall Police, G-BGWP, F-ODMZ, G-BGWP, HB-XFD, N153BB and D-HDAS. Pod	[2]	3-06
❑	G-PASB	MBB Bö 105D	ex Bourn, VH-LSA, G-BDMC, D-HDEC		3-06
❑	–	BAPC.10 Hafner R-II	ex Middle Wallop, Locking, W-s-M, Old Warden, Yeovil		3-06
❑	–	BAPC.60 Murray Helicopter	ex Wigan, Salford		3-06
❑	–	BAPC.128 Watkinson CG-4	ex Horley, Bexhill. Man powered rotorcraft		3-06
❑	–	BAPC.153 WG.33 EMU	ex Yeovil. Ultra-light helicopter. Restored 2001		3-06
❑	–	BAPC.264 Bensen B.8M	ex Westbury-on-Trym. Built 1984. Unflown		3-06
❑	–	BAPC.289 Gyro-Boat	ex Brooklands		3-06
❑	–	Husband Hornet	ex Sheffield. Built 2002, 'hopped'.		3-06
❑	[D-HMQV]	Bö 102 Helitrainer	ground trainer. (c/n 6216)	EAR	3-06
❑	DDR-SPY	Ka-26 *Hoodlum*	ex D-HOAY, Germany, Interflug DDR-SPY	®	3-06
❑	'F-OCMF'	SA.321F Frelon '335'	ex Aérospatiale, Olympic, F-BTRP, F-WKQC, F-OCZV, F-RAFR, F-OCMF, F-BMHC, F-WMHC. Olympic c/s, *Hermes*	[3]	3-06
❑	F-WQAP	SA.365N Dauphin	ex Eurocopter, Marignane, F-WZJJ		3-06
❑	-*	AB.204	see above	[1]	**due**
❑	OO-SHW	Bell 47H-1	ex Thruxton, G-AZYB, LN-OQG, SE-HBE, OO-SHW. Crashed 21-4-84	EAR	3-06
❑	SP-SAY	Mil Mi-2	ex PZL-Swidnik, Hiscso, ZEUS, PZL		3-06
❑	N114WG	WG.30-160	ex Yeovil, Westland Inc, G-EFIS, G-17-8. Boomless		3-06
❑	WG719	Dragonfly HR.5	G-BRMA, ex 'WG718', Shawbury, Weston, Yeovilton, Yeovilton SF, 705	EAR	3-06
❑	XD163 'X'	Whirlwind HAR.10	ex Wroughton, 8645M, CFS, Akrotiri SAR Flt, MoA, 228, 275, 155, MoA	EAR ®	3-06
❑	– XE521	Rotodyne Y	ex Cranfield, White Waltham. Large sections	EAR	3-06
❑	XG452	Belvedere HC.1	G-BRMB, ex Ternhill, 2 SoTT 7997M, Westlands.	®	3-06
❑	XG462	Belvedere HC.1	ex Henlow, Weston-super-Mare, 72, 66. Crashed 5-10-63. Nose	EAR ®	3-06
❑	XG547 'S-T'	Sycamore HR.14	G-HAPR, ex St Athan 8010M, Kemble, CFS	EAR	3-06
❑	XK940 '911'	Whirlwind HAS.7	G-AYXT, ex Tibenham, Redhill, Northampton, Heysham, Carnforth, Panshanger, Elstree, Luton, Blackpool, Fleetlands, 771, Culdrose SF, 705, 825, 824, 845. CoA 4-2-99	EAR	3-06
❑	XL811	Skeeter AOP.12	ex Stoke-on-Trent, Warmingham, Southend, 9/12 Lancers, 17F, 652, 651	EAR	3-06
❑	XM328 '650'	Wessex HAS.3	ex Culdrose, A2644 [2], A2727, Wroughton, 737. *The Sow*		3-06
❑	XM330	Wessex HAS.1	ex Farnborough, RAE		3-06
❑	XP165	Scout AH.1	ex Yeovilton, Weston, HAM Southend, RAE		3-06
❑	XR486	Whirlwind HCC.12	G-RWWW, ex Redhill, Tattershall Thorpe, St Athan, 32, QF, 32, QF. CoA 25-8-96	EAR	3-06
❑	XT190	Sioux AH.1	ex Wattisham, Soest, Middle Wallop, UNFICYP		3-06
❑	XT443 '422'	Wasp HAS.1	ex Oldmixon, Sherborne, *Aurora* Flt		3-06
❑	XV733	Wessex HCC.4	ex Shawbury, Queen's Flight		3-06
❑	XW839	Lynx 00-05 (WG.13)	ex Yeovilton, A2624 [2], A2657, A2710, Manadon, BS Engines		3-06
❑	XX910	Lynx HAS.2	ex DERA/RAE Farnborough, Aberporth, AAEE. Boomless		3-06
❑	ZE477	Lynx 3	ex G-17-24, Yeovil, Westlands		3-06

❏ –	Lynx 3 EMU	ex Yeovil. Built 1984 using Lynx and WG.30 parts	3-06
❏ 622	HUP-3 Retriever	ex N6699D, RCN, 51-16622	3-06
❏ 09147	Mil Mi-4 *Hound*	ex Prague, Sechov, Tabor, Czech AF	3-06
❏ [S-886]	S-55C	ex Panshanger, Elstree, Dan AF Esk.722	EAR 3-06
❏ FR-108 'CDL'	Djinn	ex France, ALAT F-MCDL	3-06
❏ 96+26	Mi-24 *Hind-D*	ex Basepohl, Luftwaffe, E German 421	3-06
❏ 1005 '05'	WSK SM-2	ex Poland	3-06
❏ 2007	Mil Mi-1 (SM-1)	ex Poland. Soviet colours	3-06
❏ 16506	OH-6A Cayuse	ex US Army. (FY67)	3-06
❏ [66-16579]	UH-1H-BF	ex US Army	3-06

THM 'Reserve Collection': Depending on staffing levels, THM are happy to show visitors these airframes, with prior application. Wessex HAS.3 XS149 is fitted with the rear fuselage of Srs 60 G-17-6 [1]. Whirlwind HAS.1 XA862 was exchanged for the former Colerne patriotic Wessex HU.5 which is destined for the main collection in due course [2] and moved to Colerne, Wilts, in early 2005.

❏ [G-ANJV]	Whirlwind Srs 3	ex Redhill, Bristow and VR-BET	3-06
❏ G-ARVN	Grasshopper 1	ex Shoreham, Redhill. CoA 18-5-63. Dismantled	3-06
❏ G-ASCT	Bensen B.8M	ex Hungerford. CoA 11-11-66	3-06
❏ G-ASHD	Brantly B.2A	ex Oxford and area. Crashed 19-2-67. Spares	3-06
❏ G-ATBZ	Wessex 60 Srs 1	ex Bournemouth, G-17-4, Weston. CoA 15-12-81	3-06
❏ G-AXFM	Grasshopper III	ex Blackpool, Heysham, Shoreham, Redhill. Rig	3-06
❏ G-AZAU	Grasshopper III	ex Blackpool, Heysham, Shoreham, Redhill. Rig	3-06
❏ BAPC.212	Bensen B.6	gyroglider	3-06
❏ – BAPC.213	Cranfield Vertigo	ex Yeovil, Cardington, Yeovil. Man-powered helo	3-06
❏ N112WG	WG.30-100	ex Yeovil, Midway	3-06
❏ [N118WG]	WG.30-160	ex Yeovil, PanAm	3-06
❏ [N5820T]	WG.30-100	ex Yeovil, Air Spur, G-BKFD	3-06
❏ [N5840T]	WG.30-100	ex Yeovil, Air Spur, G-BKFF	3-06
❏ [VR-BEU]	Whirlwind Srs 3	ex Redhill, VR-BEU, G-ATKV, EP-HAN, G-ATKV	3-06
❏ VZ962	Dragonfly HR.1	ex Helston, BRNC Dartmouth	3-06
❏ [XG596] '66'	Whirlwind HAS.7	ex Wroughton, A2651, 705, 829, 771, 705, 737. Returned from off-site 8-99	EAR 3-06
❏ [XP404]	Whirlwind HAR.10	ex Finningley, Benson 8682M, 22, SAR Wing, 202, 228	3-06
❏ XR526	Wessex HC.2	ex Yeovil, Sherborne, Farnborough, Odiham 8147M, 72 Damaged 27-5-70. Hydraulics rig	3-06
❏ XS149 '61'	Wessex HAS.3	ex Templecombe, Wroughton, 737	[1] 3-06
❏ XS486* 'F' *and* '524'	Wessex HU.5	ex Colerne 9292M, Bath, Wroughton 9292M, Lee-on-Solent. Union Jack-painted nose.	[2] 3-06
❏ [XT472] 'XC'	Wessex HU.5	ex Hullavington, Netheravon, Wroughton, 845. Spares	3-06
❏	WG.30-300 EMU	ex Yeovil. Transmission rig, using parts from c/n 022	3-06
❏ [S-881]	S-55C	ex Panshanger, Elstree, Dan AF Esk.722. Spares	3-06

WESTON ZOYLAND AERODROME on the A372 east of Bridgwater

Pegasus XL-Q G-MVMA was flying again by 2003. The other example is probably bound for LOST!

❏ G-MNSN	Pegasus Flash 2	CoA 19-4-97. Stored	5-98

YEOVIL AIRFIELD to the west of Yeovil

AgustaWestland: Having restored Lynx XX153 – see Middle Wallop, Hants – the apprentices now have a Lynx HAS.3 for the Fleet Air Arm Museum [1]. The AH.7s are now long-in-the-tooth and may well have moved on.

❏ XX907	Lynx AH.1	ex Farnborough, RAE, Rolls-Royce G-1-1. Dump	4-06
❏ XZ181	Lynx AH.7	ex Arborfield, Fleetlands, 656, 663, 653, 654. Spares	10-99
❏ XZ671	Lynx AH.7	ex Fleetlands, Yeovil, Wroughton, 652. Crashed 24-1-85. With boom of ZE377. Systems trials	10-99
❏ XZ699*	Lynx HAS.3	ex Yeovilton, Fleetlands. Arrived 21-2-06	® [1] 2-06
❏ – '961'	EH.101 EMU	static test airframe. Stored	3-02

Yeovil Technical College: Scout AH.1 'XV137' (XV139) moved to Wattisham, Suffolk, in April 2004.
❏ [XP886]   Scout AH.1   ex Arborfield, Wroughton, 652, 660, 651   2-06

YEOVILTON AIRFIELD on the B5131, south of the A303, north of Yeovil

Fleet Air Arm Museum (FAAM): On 9th August 2005 the museum unveiled the restoration of its Corsair IV to an audience including Fleet Air Arm 'vets' and two pilots who had KD431 in their logbooks. Curator of Aircraft, Dave Morris, and his team set out when the restoration started in 2001 to carefully strip back the aircraft to reveal its exact status in 1944. Investigations into its history showed that in 1963 the Corsair was given a 'top coat' to ready it for the opening of the FAAM but that otherwise, it was a 'time capsule'. So the work involved, in Dave's words, was "carefully removing 1963 to reveal 1944". Accordingly, this is no immaculate restoration; it carries the scuffs and dents of wartime use [1]. Martlet AL246 has been wheeled into the workshop and will receive similar 'treatment'.Aircraft inside the 'Leading Edge' exhibition and the Cobham Hall storage facility are listed separately - see below.

Notes: Several aircraft are on loan and are marked as follows ±. These are: Concorde, Sea Vampire LZ551 and Ohka from the Science Museum; the Short 184 from the Imperial War Museum; the Bristol Scout D REP from Sir George White. Its 'serial' number is actually its US civil registration [2]. Sopwith Baby 'N2078' is a composite, using parts from the sequential 8214 and 8215. Both of these machines, ordered in 1915, were passed on to the Italian government to act as pattern aircraft in July 1916, for production by Macchi. This would go a long way to explaining the Italian tricolour on the rudder of the components acquired by R G J Nash [3]. The long-term restoration of Barracuda II DP872 will use the substantial wreckage of Mk.II LS931 from its crash site on the Scottish Isle of Jura [4]. Visitors to the incredible 'Carrier' exhibition travel to the flight deck 'on board' Wessex XT769 and disembark from XT482 [5]! Firefly Z2033 was displayed in London's St James's Park in early July 2005 as part of the 65th anniversary of the ending of World War Two celebrations [6].

FAAM aircraft can be found at the following: Coventry, Warks, Gannet XA508; East Fortune, Scotland, F-4S 155848; Mickleover, Derby, MB.339 0767; Montrose, Scotland, Sea Hawk XE340; Sunderland, Tyneside, Pucará A-522; Weston-super-Mare, Som, Dragonfly VZ962; Woodley, Berks, Gannet XG883. And, a little further away, Scimitar F.1 XD220 on the USS *Intrepid* in New York!

Wessex HAS.3 XP142 trundled over to Cobham Hall (see below) on 11th February 2005.

◆ *Open every day (other than Xmas) Apr to Oct 10am to 5.30pm and Nov to Mar 10am to 4.30pm. There is a very active Friends of the FAAM. Membership enquiries via the museum. FAAM, in co-operation with RNAS Culdrose run guided coach tours of the Cornish base – see under that heading. RNAS Yeovilton, Ilchester, BA22 8HT tel 01935 840565 fax 01935 842630 e-mail info@fleetairarm.co www.fleetairarm.com*

❏ 8359		Short 184	ex Duxford, South Lambeth, Buncrana, Rosyth,		
			Dundee, Killingholme. Forward fuselage	±	4-06
❏ 'B6401'		Camel REP	G-AWYY, ex 'C1701', N1917H, G-AWYY. CoA 1-9-85		4-06
❏ L2301		Walrus I	ex Arbroath, Thame, G-AIZG, EI-ACC,		
			IAAC N18, Supermarine N18, L2301		4-06
❏ L2940		Skua II	ex Lake Grotli, Norway, 800. Crashed 27-4-40		4-06
❏ N1854		Fulmar II	ex Lossie', Fairey G-AIBE, AAEE. CoA 6-7-59		4-06
❏ 'N2078'		Sopwith Baby	ex Fleetlands, Heathrow, Nash. *The Jabberwock*	[3]	4-06
❏ 'N4389'	'4M'	Albacore	N4172, ex Land's End, Yeovilton		4-06
❏ N5419		Bristol Scout REP	ex Kemble, Banwell, Cardington, USA	± [2]	4-06
❏ 'N5492'		Sopwith Triplane	BAPC.111, ex Chertsey. *Black Maria.*		
		REP	10 (Naval) Sqn, 'B' Flight colours		4-06
❏ 'N6452'		Pup REP	G-BIAU, ex Whitehall. CoA 13-9-89		4-06
❏ 'P4139'		Swordfish II	HS618, ex 'W5984', Manadon A2001, Donibristle.		4-06
❏ 'S1287'		Flycatcher REP	G-BEYB, ex Andover, Middle Wallop, Duxford,		
			Middle Wallop, Yeovilton. 405 Flt colours		4-06
❏ Z2033	'275'	Firefly TT.1	G-ASTL, ex Duxford, Staverton, G-ASTL, SE-BRD,		
			Z2033, 731. 1771 Sqn c/s, *Evelyn Tentions*	[6]	4-06
❏ AL246		Martlet I	ex Loughborough, 768, 802	®	4-06
❏ DP872		Barracuda II	ex Andover area, Yeovilton, Enagh Lough, 769		
			Cr 18-1-44. Forward fuselage. Remainder stored	[4]	4-06
❏ EX976		Harvard IIA	ex Portuguese AF 1657, EX976, 41-33959		4-06

❏ KD431	'E2-M'	Corsair IV	ex Cranfield, 768, 1835, BuNo 14862. 768 Sqn c/s		
			Unveiled 9-8-05	[1]	4-06
❏ KE209		Hellcat II	ex Lossie, Stretton, Anthorn, BuNo 79779		4-06
❏ LZ551/G		Sea Vampire I	ex Waddon, DH, RAE, 778, AAEE, RAE	±	4-06
❏ SX137		Seafire F.17	ex Culdrose, 'W9132', Stretton, 759, 1831, Culham		4-06
❏ VH127	'200'	Firefly TT.4	ex Wroughton, Y'ton, Culdrose, FRU, 700, 737, 812		4-06
❏ WA473	'102'	Attacker F.1	ex Abbotsinch, 736, 702, 800		4-06
❏ WJ231	'115'	Sea Fury FB.11	ex Wroughton, Yeovilton 'WE726', Y'ton SF, FRU		4-06
❏ WN493		Dragonfly HR.5	ex Culdrose, 705, 701, AAEE		4-06
❏ WV856		Sea Hawk FGA.6	ex RAE, 781, 806		4-06
❏ XB446		Avenger ECM.6B	ex Culdrose SF, 831, 751, 820, USN 69502		4-06
❏ XD317	'112'	Scimitar F.1	ex FRU, RAE, 800, 736, 807.		4-06
❏ XL503	'070'	Gannet AEW.3	ex RRE, 849 'D', 'A' Flts, AAEE, 849 HQ Flt, C(A), 849 'A' Flt		4-06
❏ XN957	'630'	Buccaneer S.1	ex 736, 809		4-06
❏ XS527*		Wasp HAS.1	ex Cobham Hall, Wroughton, *Endurance* Flt. Arr 14-2-05		4-06
❏ XS590	'131'	Sea Vixen FAW.2	ex 899, 892		4-06
❏ XT482	'ZM'	Wessex HU.5	A2656 [2], ex A2745, Lee-on-Solent, Wroughton, 848	[5]	4-06
❏ XT596		Phantom FG.1	ex BAe Scampton, Holme-on-Spalding Moor,		
			RAE Thurleigh, Holme, Filton, Hucknall,		
			Patuxent River, Edwards. Dbr 11-10-74		4-06
❏ XT769	'823'	Wessex HU.5	ex Lee-on-Solent, Wroughton, Culdrose, 771, 846, 848	[5]	4-06
❏ XV333	'234'	Buccaneer S.2B	ex 208, 12, 15, 16, FAA, 237 OCU, 12. 801 Sqn c/s		4-06
❏		Fairey IIIF	fuselage frame	®	4-06
❏ 'D.5397'		Albatros D.Va	G-BFXL, ex Leisure Sport, Land's End,		
		REP	Chertsey, D-EGKO. CoA 5-11-91		4-06
❏ '102 /17'		Fokker Dr.I REP	BAPC.88, scale REP, based on a Lawrence Parasol		4-06
❏ 15-1585		Ohka 11	BAPC.58, ex Hayes, South Kensington	±	4-06
❏ 01420		MiG-15*bis*	G-BMZF, ex North Weald, Gamston, Retford,		
		/ Lim-2	Polish AF. North Korean colours		4-06

'Leading Edge': The contents of the inter-active and quite superb Concorde display hangar have been listed separately from this edition.

❏ G-BSST		Concorde 002	UK prototype, ff 9-4-69. CoA 30-10-74	±	4-06
❏ [VR]137		Wyvern TF.1	ex Cranfield. Eagle-powered proto, not flown		4-06
❏ WG774		BAC 221	ex East Fortune, RAE Bedford, Filton		4-06
❏ XA127		Sea Vampire T.22	ex CIFE, 736. Pod		4-06
❏ XL580	'723'	Hunter T.8M	ex FRADU, FOFT, 764		4-06
❏ XP841		HP.115	ex Cosford, Colerne, RAE Bedford		4-06
❏ XP980		P.1127	A2700, ex Culdrose, Tarrant Rushton,		
			RAE Bedford, Cranwell, AAEE		4-06
❏ XZ493	'001'	Sea Harrier	ex Dunsfold, Yeovilton, Lee-on-Solent, 899, 801.		
		FRS.1	Ditched 15-12-94		4-06

Fleet Air Arm Museum Cobham Hall: Home of the FAAM's reserve collection, workshop, archive and much more. Regular open days are staged - details via the FAA Museum contacts above. Wasp HAS.1 XS527 moved to the museum on 14th February 2005.

Notes: Dragonfly HR.1 VX595 is on loan from the RAF Museum [1]. The Jet Provost was donated by a former RN pilot who earned his wings on this very aircraft while with 1 FTS – where a large number of Navy pilots received their training [2]. The Bensen and the Super Eagle hang-glider were offered for disposal in March 2004 [3]. Lynx HAS.3 XZ699 arrived from Fleetlands, Hants, on 5th August 2004 but moved to Yeovil, <u>Somerset</u>, on 21st February 2006 for refurbishment by AgustaWestland. Sea Harrier FA.2 ZA195 complete its spares recovery and moved briefly to Wycombe Air Park, Bucks, in April 2005 before settling on <u>Farnborough</u>, Hants, on 9th March 2006.

◆ Not *open to the public on a regular basis. Enquiries to the contact points above.*

| ❏ 'G-ABUL' | | Tiger Moth | XL717, ex G-AOXG, T7291, 24 EFTS, 19 EFTS | | 4-06 |
| ❏ G-AZAZ | | Bensen B.8M | ex Wroughton, Houndstone, Yeovilton, Manadon | [3] | 4-06 |

❏	[G-BGWZ]		Super Eagle h/g	ex Wroughton, Houndstone, Yeovilton	[3] 4-06
❏	–	BAPC.149	Short S.27 REP	ex Lee-on-Solent. Dismantled	4-06
❏	'N5579'		Sea Gladiator II	ex Dursley, Cardington, Norway. Frame	4-06
❏	VV106		Supermarine 510	ex Wroughton, Lee-on-Solent, Cosford, St Athan, Colerne, Cardington, Halton 7175M	4-06
❏	VX272		Hawker P.1052	ex Wroughton, Lee-on-Solent, Cosford, St Athan, Colerne, Cardington, Halton 7174M	4-06
❏	VX595		Dragonfly HR.1	ex Portland, Gosport, Fleetlands, Henlow, Fleetlands	[1] 4-06
❏	WM292	'841'	Meteor TT.20	ex B'thorpe, Cardiff, Yeovilton, FRU, Kemble, 527	4-06
❏	WP313	'568'	Sea Prince T.1	ex Wroughton, Kemble, 750, Sydenham SF, 750, Lossiemouth SF, 750	4-06
❏	WS103		Meteor T.7	ex Wroughton, Crawley, Wroughton, Lee-on-Solent, FRU, Kemble, Yeovilton Standards Sqn, Anthorn	4-06
❏	WT121	'415'	Skyraider AEW.1	WT983, ex Culdrose, 849, USN 124121	4-06
❏	WV106	'427'	Skyraider AEW.1	ex Culdrose, Helston, Culdrose, 849, Donibristle, Abbotsinch, 124086. 849 Sqn c/s	4-06
❏	WW138	'227'	Sea Ven FAW.22	ex 'Carrier', AWS, 831, 809. Suez stripes	4-06
❏	XA129		Sea Vampire T.22	ex Wroughton, Yeovilton, CIFE, 736	4-06
❏	XA466	'777'	Gannet COD.4	ex Wroughton, Yeovilton, Lee-on-Solent, Lossie', 849	4-06
❏	XA864		Whirlwind HAR.1	ex Wroughton, Y'ton, RAE, AAEE, RAE,CA,G-17-1	4-06
❏	XB480	'537'	Hiller HT.1	ex Wroughton, Yeovilton, Manadon, A2577, 705	4-06
❏	XG574	'752'	Whirlwind HAR.3	ex FAAM, Portland, Wroughton, Yeovilton, Wroughton, Lee-on-S, A2575, 771, 705, 701, *Bulwark* Flt, *Ark Royal* Flt	4-06
❏	XG594	'517'	Whirlwind HAS.7	ex East Fortune, Strathallan, Wroughton, 71, AAEE, 705, 846, 737, 701, RAE Bedford, 700	4-06
❏	XJ481		Sea Vixen FAW.1	ex Fleetlands, Southampton, Ilkeston, Yeovilton, Portland, Yeovilton, Boscombe Down, LRWE	4-06
❏	XK488		Buccaneer S.1	ex museum, BSE Filton and Blackburns	4-06
❏	XL853		Whirlwind HAS.7	ex Portland, Fleetlands, Southampton, Middle Wallop, Lee-on-Solent, A2630, Wroughton, Y'ton SF, 824	4-06
❏	XN332	'759'	SARO P.531	ex FAAM, Portland, Wroughton, Yeovilton, Wroughton, Yeovilton, Manadon, A2579, G-APNV	4-06
❏	XN334		SARO P.531	ex Wroughton, Crawley, Weston-super-Mare, Yeovilton, Arbroath, Lee-on-Solent A2525	4-06
❏	XN462	'17'	Jet Provost T.3A	ex Wroughton, Sharnford, Shawbury, 1 FTS, 2 FTS, CFS, 3 FTS, 7 FTS, 1 FTS	[2] 4-06
❏	XP142*		Wessex HAS.3	ex main museum, Wroughton, Yeovilton, 737. *Humphrey*. Arrived 11-2-05	4-06
❏	XS508		Wessex HU.5	A2677 [2], ex A2766, Lee-on-Solent, Wroughton	4-06
❏	XT176	'U'	Sioux AH.1	ex Wroughton, 3 CBAS	4-06
❏	XT427	'606'	Wasp HAS.1	ex Helston, Yeovilton, Wroughton	4-06
❏	XT778	'430'	Wasp HAS.1	A2642 [2], ex A2722, ex Portland, West Moors, Lee-on-Solent. *Achilles* Flt c/s	4-06
❏	XW864	'54'	Gazelle HT.2	ex Shawbury, 705, Wroughton	4-06
❏	XZ499	'003'	Sea Harrier FA.2	ex St Athan, 801, 800, 801, 899, 800, 801, 800, 809, 801. Tail fin of ZA195	4-06
❏			Sea Vixen CIM	ex Wroughton, Yeovilton. Cockpit	4-06
❏	AE-422		UH-1H Iroquois	ex Wroughton, Yeovilton, Stanley, Arg Army, 74-22520	4-06
❏	0729	'411'	T-34C-1 Turbo Mentor	ex Wroughton, Yeovilton, Stanley, Pebble Island, Arg Navy. Dismantled	4-06
❏	100545		Fa 330A-1	ex Wroughton, Yeovilton, Higher Blagdon, Cranfield, Farnborough	4-06

Royal Navy Historic Flight (RNHF) / **The Swordfish Trust**: The Sea Fury and the Sea Hawk both made first flights in a hectic September 2004. The Trust is a charitable concern designed to support RNHF. Swordfish NF389 is at Brough, E Yorks, under restoration to flying condition.

◆ Not *available for public inspection, but the aircraft are frequently at airshows. RNHF Support Group, RNAS Yeovilton, Ilchester, BA22 8HT tel 01935 456279 www.flynavyheritage.org/uk*

❑ W5856	'A2A'	Swordfish II	✈	G-BMGC, ex Brough, Strathallan, Alabama, RCN,	
				Wroughton, Manston. 810 Sqn c/s. *City of Leeds*	3-06
❑ LS326	'L2'	Swordfish II	✈	ex Westlands, White Waltham, G-AJVH, Worthy	
				Down, 836. 836 Sqn colours. *City of Liverpool* ®	3-06
❑ VR930	'110'	Sea Fury FB.11	✈	ex Brough, Yeovilton, Boscombe Down, Lee-on-Solent,	
				Wroughton, Yeovilton, 8382M, Colerne, Dunsfold, FRU,	
				Lossiemouth, Anthorn, 801, Anthorn, 802. F/f 13-9-04	3-06
❑ VZ345		Sea Fury T.20S		ex Brough, Yeovilton, Boscombe Down, DLB D-CATA,	
				D-FATA, ES.8503, G-9-30, Hawker, Dunsfold, VZ345, 1832.	
				Accident 19-4-85. Stored	5-05
❑ WB657	'908'	Chipmunk T.10	✈	ex BRNC, Leeds UAS, 16 RFS, 25 RFS, Leeds UAS, 25 RFS.	3-06
❑ WK608	'906'	Chipmunk T.10	✈	ex BRNC, Bri UAS, 7 FTS, 3 FTS, Edin UAS,11 RFS. 3-06	
❑ WV908	'188'	Sea Hawk FGA.6		ex Dunsfold, Yeovilton, Dunsfold, Yeovilton, Culdrose SF,	
			✈	Halton 8154M, Sydenham A2660, 738, 806, 898, 807.	
				First flown 15-9-04	3-06
❑ WV911	'115'	Sea Hawk FGA.6		ex Dunsfold, Lee-on-Solent A2622 [2], A2626,	
				Fleetlands, Lee-on-Solent A2526. Stored	3-06

Others: Airframes dealt with by the **Flight Safety and Accident Investigation Unit** (FSAIU) tend to be too transitory to merit inclusion. The **Engineering Training School** (ETS) and the **Heron Gliding Club** (HGC) are also based here. Gazelle XW890 (with the boom of AH.1 ZB668) is displayed outside the DHSA building [1]. The Sea Harrier orientation trainer was made by Ogle Design Ltd of Letchworth, Herts [2].

Departures: Harrier GR.3 XZ129 was exported to the Harrier Acquisition Group in New Zealand early in 2005; **Sea Harrier** FA.2 XZ455 to Ipswich, Suffolk, 30-7-05; FA.2 ZD612 (with the ETS) tendered 12-04, moved to Topsham, Devon, by 11-05.

❑ WV903	'128'	Sea Hawk FGA.4	ex Dunsfold, Lee-on-Solent, Culdrose A2632, Halton 8153M,		
			Sydenham. Dump		3-06
❑ XE339	'149'	Sea Hawk FGA.6	ex Dunsfold, Lee-on-Solent, Culdrose A2635,		
			Halton 8156M. Dump		3-06
❑ XS513		Wessex HU.5	A2681 [2], ex Gosport, A2770, Lee-on-Solent, 772. Dump		3-06
❑ XT653		Swallow TX.1	FUW/BGA.3545, ex Halesland, Syerston, CGS. Stored	HGC	5-98
❑ XT765*	'J'	Wessex HU.5	ex Gosport A2665 [2], A2755, Lee-on-Solent, 845.		
			Arrived 29-7-04. 848 Squadron's 'gate'		3-06
❑ [XV280]		Harrier GR.1	A2700 [2], ex Foulness, Boscombe Down, AAEE,		
			HSA. Nose, Sea Harrier style, trailer-mounted		5-04
❑ XV755	'M'	Harrier GR.3	A2606 [3], ex A2604, 233 OCU, 3, 233 OCU, 3,		
			233 OCU, 1, 233 OCU, 1, 233 OCU. Dump		3-06
❑ XW630		Harrier GR.3	A2671 [2], ex Gosport, A2759 Lee-on-Solent, 3, 4, 3, 20.		
			FAA colours. Dump		3-06
❑ XW890		Gazelle HT.2	ex Fleetlands, Wroughton, 705. Displayed.	[1]	11-03
❑ ZB601		Harrier T.4	ex Dunsfold, St Athan, ETS Yeovilton, 899, 233 OCU. BDRT		3-06
❑ ZD578		Sea Harrier FA.2	ex St Athan, 899, 801, 899, 801, 800, 801, 899, 801,		
			800, 899. Gate. 800 Sqn colours (port), 801 (stb)		3-06
❑ –		Sea Harrier FA.2	EMU, cockpit, orientation trainer	ETS [2]	9-02
❑ –		RG-05 Lynx static rig	ex Weston-super-Mare, Blackpool, Coventry,		
			Yeovil. Fire training, poor state		3-06

STAFFORDSHIRE

ABBOTS BROMLEY on the B5014 south of Uttoxeter
The Vampire is owned by Vaughan K Meers (see Wolverhampton, W Mids) and acts as 'guardian' [1].

❏ G-ARAS*	7FC Tri-Traveler	Crashed 4-5-98. Stored	12-05
❏ XD445*	'51' Vampire T.11	ex Hemswell, Cleethorpes, Hatfield, Woodford, Chester,	
		St Athan, 4 FTS, 5 FTS, Buckeburg SF. 'Gate'	[1] 12-05

BASSET'S POLE at the junction of the A38 and A453, north east of Sutton Coldfield
A paintballing field here has a Whirlwind to shoot at.

❏ XP350*	Whirlwind HAR.10	ex Bruntingthorpe, Helston, Chivenor, 22, 225	5-05

BURSLEM on the A50 north-west of Stoke-on-Trent
Supermarine Aero Engineering: Work is undertaken on SL611 and the Tiger Moth on a time available basis, in between work on purpose-built components for Spitfire projects worldwide.

❏ G-OOSY	Tiger Moth	ex Stoke-on-Trent, Eccleshall, F-BGFI, FAF, DE971	®	1-03
❏ SL611	Spitfire XVI	ex Scafell, 603, 111 OTU. Crashed 20-11-47		6-01

BURTON-UPON-TRENT
No.351 Squadron Air Cadets: On the northern edge of the town, near a railway yard.

❏ XP743	Lightning F.3	ex Stafford, Pendine, Leconfield, 29, 56, 29, 56,	
		Wattisham TFF, 56. Nose	2-04

ECCLESHALL on the A5013 north-west of Stafford
Malcolm Goosey:.

❏ G-ASEF	Auster 6A	ex Arncott, Somerton, Bicester, RAFGSA, VW985,		
		664. CoA 19-12-66	®	2-04
❏ WK638*	Chipmunk T.10	G-BWJZ, ex Stamford, Manston, 9 AEF, RAFC,		
		9 AEF, York UAS, 1 FTS, 1 AEF, Ox UAS, 1 RFS.		
		Crashed 22-8-99. Stored		2-04

HEDNESFORD on the A460 northeast of Cannock
Martyn Jones: *Should* still have his 'JP' nose.

❏ XM417	'D' Jet Provost T.3	ex Fownhope, Halton 8054BM, Shawbury,	
		6 FTS, 7 FTS, 2 FTS. Nose.	8-94

HIXON west of the A51, east of Stafford
Air and Ground Aviation:

❏ XR507	Wessex HC.2	ex Shawbury, 22, SARTU, 22, SARTU, 22, SARTS, 18	8-02
❏ XR511	'L' Wessex HC.2	ex St Athan, 72, 60, 72, 18	1-04
❏ XS674*	'R' Wessex HC.2	ex Ipswich, Fleetlands, 60, 72, 18, 78, 72. F/n 6-04	2-05
❏ XT463	'D' Wessex HU.5C	ex Predannack, Gosport A2624 [3], Shawbury,	
		Akrotiri, 84, FAA. Tail of XR503	12-00
❏ XV722	'WH' Wessex HC.2	ex Shawbury, 2 FTS, CATCS, 18, 72, 18	2-05
❏ XV726*	'J' Wessex HC.2	ex Shawbury, 72, 60, 72, 60, 72, Queen's Flt. Arr 11-5-05	5-05
❏ XX482*	'J' Jetstream T.1	ex Shawbury, Cranwell, 45, 3 FTS, 45, 6 FTS,	
		3 FTS, 5 FTS, CFS. Fuselage. Arrived 11-5-05	5-05
❏ XX497*	'J' Jetstream T.1	ex Shawbury, Cranwell, 45, 3 FTS, 45, 6 FTS, METS	
		Fuselage. Arrived 11-5-05	5-05

LICHFIELD north-west of Tamworth

No.1206 Squadron Air Cadets: Cherry Orchard, near the city railway station. 'Parent' is Stafford.

❑ WK576	Chipmunk T.10	8357M, ex AOTS, 3/4 CAACU, Cam UAS, Oxf UAS, Lon	
	PAX	UAS, Cam UAS, Lon UAS, Cam UAS, Hull UAS, Cam	
		UAS, Bir UAS, Cam UAS, 22 RFS	11-03

Others: As threatened in *W&R19* (p194) Bensen B.8M G-AXCI, last noted in September 1993, is LOST!

LONGTON on the A50 south of Stoke-on-Trent

Motor Clinic: On the Trentham Road, have a 'JP'.

❑ XM425	'88' Jet Provost T.3A	ex King's Lynn, Bruntingthorpe, Halton 8995M, 7 FTS,	
		1 FTS, RAFC, 3 FTS, CFS	10-05

RUGELEY on the A51 east of Stafford

Two airframes are under restoration in the general area. The Provost's entry is now well 'dated'.

❑ WW444	'D' Provost T.1	ex Sibson, Coventry, Bitteswell, Shawbury, CAW, 5 AEF,	
		6 FTS, 3 FTS, 22 FTS.	® 2-96
❑ XD515	Vampire T.11	ex Winthorpe, Misson, Linton-on-Ouse 7998M, 3 FTS,	
		7 FTS, 1 FTS, 5 FTS, 206 AFS.	® 3-04

STAFFORD (Beaconside, west of the city)

Royal Air Force Museum Reserve Collection: Spitfire XVI RW393 went to Cosford, Shropshire, on 16th March 2005 for preparation for display in the 'Living Museum' in St James's Park, London, 4th to 10th July, 2005. Painted as 'TB675' '4D-V' it moved to London on 28th June and then spent a brief while on show outside the RAF Museum, Hendon, Gtr Lon, then returned to <u>Cosford</u>, Shropshire, afterwards. Spitfire F.22 PK664 moved to Duxford, Cambs, on 5th May 2005 for preparation by ARC for a special exhibition at the Science Museum. It moved to <u>South Kensington</u>, Gtr Lon.

◆ *Viewing is possible* only *via prior arrangement*

❑ G-AHED	Dragon Rapide	ex Cosford, Wyton, Cardington, Henlow, RL962,	
		Witney. CoA 17-4-68	2-04
❑ A301	Morane BB	ex Wyton, Cardington, Hendon. Fuselage	2-04
❑ Z7197	Proctor III	ex Hendon 8380M, St Athan, Swinderby, Finningley,	
		G-AKZN, AST, 18 EFTS, 1 RS, 2 SS. CoA 29-11-63	2-04
❑ DG590	Hawk Major	ex Cosford, Wyton, Cardington, Middle Wallop,	
		Henlow, Ternhill, G-ADMW, Swanton Morley SF,	
		Wyton SF, G-ADMW. CoA 4-6-83	2-04
❑ HS503	Swordfish IV	ex Cosford, Wyton, Cardington, Cosford, Henlow,	
BAPC.108		Canada, RCAF, 754, 745	2-04
❑ LA226	Spitfire F.21	ex Cosford, Wyton, Cardington, St Athan, Shawbury,	
		Abingdon, Biggin Hill, South Marston, London, South	
		Marston, Little Rissington, 7119M, 3 CAACU, 122	2-04
❑ PM651	'X' Spitfire PR.XIX	ex Cosford, Wyton, Cardington, St Athan, Hendon,	
		Benson, Bicester, Andover, Hucknall, Leconfield,	
		Church Fenton, 7758M, C&RS, 3 CAACU, 604	2-04
❑ SL674	Spitfire XVI	ex Cosford, Wyton, Cardington, St Athan, 8392M,	
'RAS-H'		Biggin Hill, Little Rissington, 501, 17 OTU	2-04
❑ VX275	Sedbergh TX.1	ex Cosford, Wyton, Cardington, St Athan, BGA.572,	
		8884M, 612 GS, 613 GS, 623 GS, 123 GS	2-04
❑ WP270*	Eton TX.1	ex Manchester Henlow, Hendon, 8598M, 27 MU,	
		61 GCF. Arrived 2005	12-05
❑ XK781*	ML Utility Mk.1	ex Cardington, Middle Wallop. Nacelle, and other bits	3-05
❑ ZJ493*	Jindivik 4A	ex Llanbedr, QinetiQ/DERA, ATA.	
		Last flight 26-10-84. Arrived 29-10-04	3-05

❏	–	FE.2b	ex Wyton, Cardington. Cockpit nacelle		2-04
❏	–*	Lakes Waterbird	ex Cardington, Henlow, Windermere. Damaged		
			17-2-12. Centre section, float and other parts.		3-05
❏	15195	PT-19A Cornell	ex Cosford, Wyton, Cardington, Henlow, Canada		2-04
❏	J-1172	Vampire FB.6	ex Cosford, Wyton, Cardington, Manchester,		
			Cosford, 8487M, Colerne, Swiss AF		2-04
❏	–	BAPC.194 Demoiselle REP	ex Wyton, Cardington, Brooklands, Henlow, Gatow		2-04
❏	–	BAPC.237 Fi 103 (V-1)	ex Wyton, Cardington, St Athan		2-04

Defence Storage and Distribution Centre (DSDC) / Tactical Supply Wing (TSW).

❏	XT469	Wessex HU.5	8920M, ex Wroughton	TSW	3-03
❏	XZ287	Nimrod AEW.3	9140M, ex Abingdon, Waddington, JTU,		
			Woodford. Fuselage. *Fly Suki Airways*	TSW	9-02
❏	XZ987	'C' Harrier GR.3	9185M, ex St Athan, 1417 Flt, 3, 4. Gate		2-05

STOKE-ON-TRENT
The Potteries Museum and Art Gallery:
◆ *Mar to Oct Mon-Sat 10am to 5pm, Sun 2pm to 5pm; Nov to Feb Mon-Sat 10am to 4pm, Sun 1pm to 4pm. Bethesda Street, Hanley, Stoke ST1 3DE tel 01782 232323 fax 01782 232500 e-mail museums@stoke.gov.uk www.stoke.gov.uk/museums*

| ❏ | RW388 | Spitfire XVI | ex Kemble, 'AB917', 71 MU 6946M, 19 MU, 5 MU, | | |
| | | 'U4-U' | Andover, Benson, FC&RS, 612, 667. 667 Sqn c/s | ® | 3-06 |

STONE on the A34 north of Stafford
Alan Simpson:

| ❏ | XG629 | '668' Sea Venom | ex Long Marston, Fleetlands, Higher Blagdon, Culdrose | | |
| | | FAW.22 | ADS, 831, 893 | | 12-05 |

Watson's: The scrapyard had had a clear-out by January 2006 and 'JP' T.3 XN550 had gone.

TAMWORTH
Martyn Morgan: Martyn, of the Wolverhampton Aviation Group, has added a hot-air balloon envelope to his Cadet TX.3 during early 2005. W&R lists envelopes *only* if they come with baskets (the 'fuselage') but, for the record, it's Cameron O-77 G-BPYI, total flights, 338 and total time 362 hours. And it lives in his conservatory!
◆ *Visits by prior arrangement* only.

| ❏ | XE793 | Cadet TX.3 | ex Doncaster, Ringmer, St Athan, 8666M | | 3-06 |

TATENHILL AERODROME south of the B5234, west of Burton-on-Trent
Most of the references here are from another century!

❏	G-ARNN	GC-1B Swift	ex Leicester, VP-YMJ, VP-RDA, ZS-BMX, NC3279K.		
			Crashed 1-9-73	®	7-91
❏	G-AZHE	Slingsby T.61B	ex N61TB, G-AZHE. Damaged 17-6-88. Canx 14-3-99	®	7-91
❏	G-BHIR*	Cherokee Arrow	ex SE-FHP. CoA 6-12-04. Fuselage, dump		3-06
❏	G-BUPJ	Fournier RF-4D	ex N7752	®	6-95
❏	G-BUXM	Quickie TriQ	ex N4435Y. CoA 10-8-95. Stored		7-98
❏	G-BXGE	Cessna 152 II	ex N89283. Crashed 4-8-97. Fuselage, stored		7-04

WOLVERHAMPTON AERODROME, or Halfpenny Green, south of the B4176, east of Bridgnorth
RAF Fire Service Museum: Established in August 2004, the museum aims to collect and present the 'tools of the trade' of the RAFFS and has already acquired a series of fire tenders, rescue vehicles and other items. Re-opening at Halfpenny Green during mid-2006, more details on the web-site: www.raf-fireservicemuseum.org

Aerodrome: Mandark Aviation, respray specialists, have a WAR Fw 190 as an attraction for their business [1]. Cessna 172N II G-BUJN was flying again by 2004.

❏ G-BSYK	Tomahawk 112	ex N23449. Stored		10-01
❏ G-BSYL	Tomahawk 112	ex N91333. Stored		8-03
❏ G-OBEY	Aztec 250C	ex G-BAAJ, SE-EIU. CoA 4-8-86		12-97
❏ G-WULF	WAR Fw 190	CoA 22-6-01	[1]	8-03
❏ –	T.31	BGA.1346, ex Bidford, RAFGSA.297. Air Scouts		2-00

SUFFOLK

BECCLES AERODROME south of the A146 west of Lowestoft

❏ G-ASMY	Apache 160H	ex N4309Y. CoA 25-11-95. Stored	2-06
❏ G-ATHZ	Cessna 150F	ex EI-AOP ntu, N6286R. CoA 27-3-98. Stored	10-05
❏ G-AVPH	Cessna F.150G	ex Blackpool, Woodvale. CoA 9-4-86.	2-06
❏ G-BAOP	Cessna FRA.150L	crashed 22-6-01. Stored	10-05

BECK ROW on the A1101 north of Mildenhall

The Hunter (with the starboard wing of XL572 and XL623 to port) is kept on a farm in the area. (See under Poole, Somerset, for the saga of XL623.)

❏ XG210	Hunter F.6	ex DRA Bedford, BAe Hatfield, CFE, 19, 14	12-05

BENTWATERS AIRFIELD south of the A1152, north-east of Woodbridge

Bentwaters 'Cold War' Museum: centred, initially at least, on the Wing Command Post. Work is at the early stage and it is not yet open to the public. Restoration work has begun on the Meteor and it will be returned to F.8 status. The Navajo had been used for some filming at the airfield and then joined the collection. (It was last noted in *W&R18*, p81, under Fownhope.)

◆ *Control Tower, Rendelsham, Woodbridge, Suffolk IP12 2TW. tel 01394 460655. e-mail museum.help@bentwaters-as.org.uk www.betwaters-as.org.uk*

❏ WH453*	'L'	Meteor D.16	ex Llanbedr, 5 CAACU, 72, 222. Arrived 18-1-05	®	3-06
❏ E18-2*	'42-71'	Navajo	ex ?, Fownhope, Spanish Air Force, N7314L. Fuselage. Here by 11-04		3-06

BURY ST EDMUNDS on the A14 east of Newmarket

Nigel Hamlin-Wright: Has the Chrislea FC.1 Airguard for restoration. Only original components are being used, the reproduction elements having been discarded.

❏ G-AFIN	Chrislea Airguard	ex Wigan, Stoke-on-Trent, Warmingham, Wigan, Finningley	2-06

DEBACH south of the B1078, west of Wickham Market

493rd Bomb Group 'Helton's Hellcats' Museum: The former USAAF Station 152's control tower forms the basis of a growing museum. Things are in their formative days with only special open days at present.

◆ *Last Sunday of Jun, Jul, Aug and Sep, 11am to 4.30pm Richard Taylor, Grove Farm, Clopton, Woodbridge, IP13 6QS e-mail richard@prilly.fsnet.co.uk www.493bgdebach.co.uk*

FELIXSTOWE at the end of the A14, south-east of Ipswich

Glenn Cattermole: Restoration of the Buccaneer cockpit is well in hand.

❏ XT284	'H'	Buccaneer S.2A	ex Stock, St Athan, Abingdon 8855M, St Athan, 237 OCU, 15, 208, 809, 803, 736. Nose	® 3-06

FLIXTON on the B1062 west of Bungay

Norfolk and Suffolk Aviation Museum (N&SAM): This wonderful museum continues to rejoice in its wide collecting policy, making it a haven of exhibits of all shapes and sizes – every turn holds a surprise! The Air-Sea Rescue exhibition is to be increased in size – yet again! The Boulton & Paul-built hangar was officially opened by Wg Cdr Ken Wallis on 25th April 2004. The museum can now boast one of each of all of the V-bombers (as cockpits!). Work is in hand to make them an impressive line-up.

Notes: The following are on loan: Widgeon G-ANLW (from Sloane Helicopters); Friendship 200 G-BDVS; Thunder balloon G-BJZC; Striker G-MTFK; EoN Primary CDN (Norfolk Gliding Club); Colditz Cock JTA (Imperial War Museum); Canberra WG789 (Steve Pickup); Valiant XD857; Victor XL160 (see below); Vulcan XL445; Sea Harrier ZA175 (IWM, Duxford) – all marked ø

Ian Hancock owns several of the airframes - IH. An interesting exhibit of Ian's in the main hangar is a Spitfire XVI fuselage centred on the original skin of TD248 acquired from Historic Flying (HF). The skin, coupled with an original frame No.19, and a fibreglass tail section has created a fuselage that will, ultimately, contain as many original fittings as possible. The fuselage is painted in the colours of 695 Squadron as '8Q-T'. (See under Duxford, Cambs, for the airworthy TD248.) After much thought, this is best termed a 'recreation' [1].

The Victor nose, or Project XL160, is owned by the **HP Victor Association** [2]. The association serves to link all those who flew, worked on, or just love, the Victor and publishes a newsletter. (Details from: Ken McGill, 15 Burnside Flotta, Stromness, Orkney, KW16 3NP e-mail aldaniti@supanet.com)

The Jenny Wren was built using the wings of Luton Minor G-AGEP [3]. The Rooster and Pegasus were donated by the widow of the late John M Lee, who built the wings of the museum's Colditz Cock. The Lightwing Rooster 1 Srs 4 biplane is in unpowered form. [4] The Striker was the last aircraft to fly from Flixton before the runways were broken up [5]. The Penrose Pegasus 2 is a reproduction of the original Harald Penrose example [6]. The Fairchild 24 (pre-Argus) is proving to be a delight in terms of its background. It was the second C8F built and served with the Civil Air Patrol fitted with bomb racks and flare chutes as a sub 'scarer'. It will be finished in this guise [7]. The extreme nose section of a Felixstowe flying-boat, once a potting shed, it amounts to some 10ft, and while not fitting our criteria totally, does represent a singular survivor. Another section of Felixstowe, about 8ft long, is on hand from the RAF Museum [8].Canberra nose WE168 will become a 'hands-on' exhibit [9].

◆ *Open Apr to Oct, Sun to Thu 10am to 5pm (last admission 4pm); Nov to Mar, Tue, Wed and Sun 10am to 4pm (last admission 3pm). The Street, Flixton, near Bungay, NR35 1NZ tel 01986 896644 during opening hours e-mail nsam.flixton@virgin.net www.aviationmuseum.net*

❑	G-ANLW	Widgeon 2	ex Northampton, Blackpool, 'MD497', Wellingborough, Little Staughton, Tattershall Thorpe, *When Eight Bells Toll*, *Eye of the Needle*, Southend. CoA 27-5-81	ø	3-06
❑	G-ASRF*	Jenny Wren	ex Brookmans Park, Panshanger, Brookmans Park. CoA 4-6-71. Arrived 11-9-04	[3]	3-06
❑	G-AZLM	Cessna F.172L	ex Badminton. Cr 23-3-91. Hulk, stored		3-06
❑	G-BABY	JT.2 Titch	CoA 10-10-91		3-06
❑	G-BDVS	Friendship 200	ex Norwich, Air UK, S2-ABK, PH-FEX, PH-EXC, 9M-AMM, PH-EXC, PH-FEX. *Eric Gander Dower*. Nose	ø	3-06
❑	[G-BFIP]	Wallbro Mono REP	ex Shipdham, Swanton Morley. CoA 22-4-82		3-06
❑	G-BJZC*	Thunder Ax7-65Z	ex Lancing. Greenpeace.	ø	3-06
❑	G-MJSU	Tiger Cub	ex Swanton Morley. CoA 31-1-86		3-06
❑	G-MJVI	Rooster 1	ex Littlehampton. Canx 13-6-90	[4]	3-06
❑	G-MTFK	Flexiform Striker	canx 13-6-90	ø [5]	3-06
❑	–	CDN EoN Primary	BGA.1461, ex Tibenham area. CoA 5-69	ø	3-06
❑	–	DUD Grunau Baby III	BGA.2384, ex Bristol, BGA.2074, RAFGSA.374, D-9142		3-06
❑	–	HKJ Pegasus 2 REP	BGA.4002, ex Littlehampton. CoA 15-9-98	[6]	3-06
❑	–	JTA Colditz Cock REP	BGA.4757, ex Duxford. *Spirit of Colditz*	ø	3-06
❑	–	'LHS-1' Bensen B.7	BAPC.147, ex Loddon, Marham, Coltishall		3-06
❑	–	BAPC.115 HM.14 'Flea'	ex Earls Colne, Andrewsfield, Balham, South Wales	IH	3-06
❑	–	Wasp Falcon 4	hang-glider		3-06
❑	–	Antonov C.14	hang-glider		3-06
❑	–*	UFM Icarus II	biplane, tail-less, hang-glider. Arrived 6-11-05		3-06
❑	N16676	Fairchild 24C8F	ex Tibenham, USA, CAP, NC16676	® [7]	3-06
❑	–	Felixstowe F.5	ex Felixstowe. Nose section	[8]	3-06

❑	'P8140'		Spitfire FSM	BAPC.71, ex Chilham Castle, 'P9390' and 'N3317',	
		'ZP-K'		*Battle of Britain. Nuflier.* 74 Sqn c/s	3-06
❑	'TD248'	'8Q-T'	Spitfire XVI	see above. 695 Sqn colours IH [1]	3-06
❑	VL349		Anson C.19	ex Norwich, N5054, G-AWSA, SCS, NCS, North	
		'V7-Q'		Coates SF, WSF, FCCS, HCCS, HCEU, 116, CSE, 1 FU	3-06
❑	VX580		Valetta C.2	ex Norwich, MCS, MEAFCS, 114, HS	3-06
❑	WE168		Canberra PR.3	ex Colchester, Manston 8049M, 231 OCU, 39,	
				69, 540. Nose, minus skin off-site [9]	3-06
❑	WF128	'676'	Sea Prince T.1	ex Honington 8611M, Kemble, Sydenham SF, AAEE, 750	3-06
❑	WF643	'P'	Meteor F(TT).8	ex Coltishall, Kemble, 29, Nicosia SF, 611, 1, 56.	
				56 Squadron colours	3-06
❑	WG789		Canberra B.2/6	ex Mendlesham, Wycombe, Kew, Burgess Hill,	
				Bedford, 231 OCU. Nose ø	3-06
❑	WH840		Canberra T.4	ex Seighford, Locking 8350M, St Athan, Geilenkirchen SF,	
				AAEE, 97, 151, 245, 88, 231 OCU, CFS IH	3-06
❑	WV605	'T-B'	Provost T.1	ex Henlow, Higher Blagdon, 6 FTS, 3 FTS, 22 FTS	3-06
❑	XA226*		Grasshopper TX.1	ex Milton Keynes, Turweston, Ipswich, Halton, Sutton.	
				Arrived 21-4-04	3-06
❑	XD857*		Valiant BK.1	ex Manston, Rayleigh, Foulness, 49. Flightdeck.	
				Arrived 18-10-05 ø	3-06
❑	XG254	'A'	Hunter FGA.9	ex Clacton, Coltishall, Weybourne, Coltishall 8881M,	
				St Athan, 1 TWU, 2 TWU, TWU, 229 OCU, 54, HS, 54.	
				54 Sqn colours IH	3-06
❑	XG329		Lightning F.1	ex Swinderby, Cranwell 8050M, AAEE, Warton IH	3-06
❑	XG518		Sycamore HR.14	ex Sunderland, Balloch, Halton 8009M, Wroughton,	
				Khormaksar SF, El Adem SF, Habbiniya SF, CFS,	
				Amman SF IH	3-06
❑	XG523	'V'	Sycamore HR.14	ex Sunderland, Hayes, Middle Wallop, Ternhill 7793M,	
				CFS, JEHU. Damaged 25-9-62. Nose IH	3-06
❑	XH892	'J'	Javelin FAW.9R	ex Duxford, Colerne 7982M, Shawbury, 29, 64, 23	3-06
❑	XJ482	'713'	Sea Vixen FAW.1	ex Wimborne Minster, A2598, 766, 700Y	3-06
❑	XK624	'32'	Vampire T.11	ex Lytham St Annes, Blackpool, CFS, 3 FTS,	
				7 FTS, 1 FTS, 23 GCF, CFS, 7 FTS	3-06
❑	XL160*		Victor K.2	ex Walpole, Marham 8910M, 57, 55, 57, 55,	
				Witt Wing, 100, MoA. Nose. Arrived 29-7-05 ø [2]	3-06
❑	XL445*		Vulcan K.2	ex Walpole, Lyneham 8811M, 50, 44, 35, 230 OCU,	
				Wadd Wing, Akrotiri Wing, Wadd Wing, 27. Nose.	
				Arrived 29-7-05 ø	3-06
❑	XM279		Canberra B(I).8	ex Firbeck, Nostell Priory, Cambridge, 16, 3. Nose IH	3-06
❑	XN304	'W'	Whirlwind HAS.7	ex Bedford, Henlow, Wroughton, Shrivenham,	
				Wroughton, 705, Old Sarum, 848. 848 Sqn c/s	3-06
❑	XR485	'Q'	Whirlwind HAR.10	ex Wroughton, 2 FTS, CFS	3-06
❑	ZA175*		Sea Harrier FA.2	ex Yeovilton, 899, 800, 899, 800, 899, 801, 800,	
				899, 800, 801, 899. Arrived 27-7-04 ø	3-06
❑	A-528		FMA Pucará	ex Sunderland, Middle Wallop, Cosford, Abingdon	
				8769M, Stanley, Argentine AF, 9th AB, 3rd AB	3-06
❑	79	'2-EG'	Mystère IVA	ex Sculthorpe, FAF, ET.2/8, 314 GE, EC.1/5	3-06
❑	'694'	B'.239	Fokker D.VIII	ex Lowestoft. 5/8th scale reproduction	3-06
❑	42196		F-100D-11-NA	ex Sculthorpe, French AF. EC.4/11, EC.2/11,	
				USAF 48th FBW, 45th FS. 'Skyblazers' colours	3-06
❑	54433		T-33A-5-LO	ex Sculthorpe, French AF, 328 CIFAS, 338	
		'TR-433'		CEVSV, USAF 803rd ABG. 20th FBG c/s	3-06
❑	146289		T-28C Trojan	ex East Ham, France, N99153, Zaire AF FG-289,	
				Congolese FA-289, USN VT-3, VT-5, NABTC	
				146289. Crashed 14-12-77. Fuselage	3-06

FRAMLINGHAM AERODROME or Parham, on the B1116 north of Woodbridge

Parham Airfield Museum: incorporating the **390th Bomb Group Memorial Air Museum** and the **Museum of British Resistance.** The tower here houses a superb museum dedicated to the 390th and Parham, USAAF Station No.153. Within can be found a wide array of engines and many other artefacts. The Resistance Museum is dedicated to the work of the Auxiliary Units - the so-called 'Stay Behind' cells in the event of an invasion.
◆ *Open 11am to 5pm on Sun and Bank Hols Mar to Oct. Also Wed 11am to 4pm in Jun-Sep. Other times by arrangement. Signed from the A12. 37 Stubbs Lane, Braintree, Essex, CM7 3NR tel 01376 320848 e-mail 390bg-bro@suffolkonline.net www.parhamairfieldmuseum.co.uk*

HALESWORTH on the A144 south of Bungay

Halesworth Airfield Memorial Museum and the **56th Fighter Group Museum:** Established on the former 8th Air Force airfield (also known as Holton), this small museum includes a wide range of small exhibits.
◆ *Apr to Oct, Sun and Bank Hols 2pm to 5pm. Other times by prior appointment. 01986 873262, e-mail richie@rspymar.plus.com www.halesworthairfieldmuseum.org.uk*

John Flanagan: *Should* still keep his Carvair cockpit section nearby.
☐ CF-EPV   Carvair   ex Beccles, Thorpe Abbotts, Fritton Lake, Woodbridge,
                                   Southend, EI-AMR, N88819, 42-72343. Cockpit   2-06

HONINGTON AIRFIELD on the A1088 south-east of Thetford

RAF Regiment:
☐ XK526   Buccaneer S.2   8648M, ex RAE Bedford, RRE. Gate   3-06

HORHAM on the B1117 east of Eye

95th Bomb Group Hospital Museum: run by **Tony Albrow** (located to the west of the former airfield, close to Denham Hall) and the **'Red Feather Club'** run the **95th Bomb Group Heritage Association,** are bringing back to life elements of the former USAAF Station 116, once home to the B-17s of the 95th. The restoration of the 'Red Feather Club' (near Denham Corner and Whitehouse Farm) on the former airfield site includes the famous murals painted by S/Sgt Nathan Bindler. At Horham Church there is a striking memorial to the 95th.
◆ *Last Sun of each month, Apr to Oct. Grand open day each May. Otherwise, by prior application. www.95thbg-horham.com Tony Albrow: tel 01379 870514; 95th BG frank.sherman@bushinternet.com*

IPSWICH

Suffolk Aviation Heritage Group: Established in 2002 by a group of worthies previously at the Parham Airfield Museum (see under Framlingham, Suffolk), SAHG signed a licence agreement for use of part of the former Autovon Exchange complex on the south west fringes of Martlesham Heath, on the elements in use by USAFE until the early 1990s. For *W&R20* the project here is in its earliest days, but it would be a shame not to note the feverish activity that has been going on. Phase One of the project plans to see an opening for the public early in 2007, with another two more ambitious phases to follow, in about 18 months following initial 'curtain up' - watch this space!
◆ Andy *Taylor, 8 Brinkley Lane, Highwoods, Colchester, CO4 9XN e-mail andrew@taylor8392.freeserve.co.uk*

Everett Aero: The company continues to very active in acquiring former MoD airframes and trading them on, worldwide. Of airframes received of late, many must have moved on. Please note that several sites are used for storage in the general area and that prior permission to view is *essential.*
    Departures: Harrier T.4 XW270 moved to Coventry, West Mids, 14-9-04; **Jet Provost** T.3 fuselage XN634 to Blackpool, Lancs, by 6-05; T.4 XP558 *cockpit* to Sheffield, S Yorks, by 12-05; **Scout** AH.1 XR627 to Townhill, Scotland (last noted 2-04); AH.1 XR635 moved to Coventry, W Mids, 8-04; **Wessex** HC.2 XS674 to Hixon, Staffs, by 6-04. See under Culdrose, Cornwall and Shoreham, W Sussex for Jetstream T.1 XX491. Several airframes moved in and then out again quickly, but still deserve charting: Jaguar GR.1A XX955 arrived 6-9-05 from Shawbury, Shrop, but quickly moved to Hermeskeil, Germany, for the museum there. Sea Harrier FA.2 XZ439 arrived 12-11-04 and left for the USA (hopefully to fly as a 'warbird' in 1-06).

◆ Strictly *private location, visits* only *possible by prior appointment. www.everettaero.com*

❑	9M-BCR*		Falcon 20	ex Bournemouth. Fuselage	3-06
❑	WZ792		Grasshopper TX.1	ex Falgunzeon, Dishforth, Barnard Castle	2-04
❑	XK788		Grasshopper TX.1	ex Hamois (Belgium), Halton, West Malling, Sevenoaks, Godalming	2-04
❑	XN510	'40'	Jet Provost T.3A	G-BXBI, ex Binbrook, Shawbury, Linton-on-Ouse, 1 FTS, 3 FTS, RAFC, 7 FTS, 1 FTS	3-06
❑	[XN554]		Jet Provost T.3	ex North Luffenham, Halton 8436M, St Athan, Shawbury, CFS	3-06
❑	XN579		Jet Provost T.3A	ex North Luffenham 9137M, ex Shawbury, 1 FTS, 7 FTS, 1 FTS, RAFC,TWU, RAFC	2-04
❑	XP563	'C'	Jet Provost T.4	ex Bicester, Witney, Bruntingthorpe, Halton 9028M, Shawbury, CATCS, SoRF, 6 FTS, CATCS, RAFC	3-06
❑	XP629		Jet Provost T.4	ex North Luffenham 9026M, ex Halton, Shawbury, CATCS, SoRF, CAW, 2 FTS	2-04
❑	XP672	'03'	Jet Provost T.4	G-RAFI, ex North Weald, Bournemouth, Jurby, Halton 8458M, SoRF, CAW, CATCS, CAW, 2 FTS. CoA 11-3-00	3-06
❑	XP686		Jet Provost T.4	ex North Luffenham, Halton 8502M, 8401M, CATCS, 6 FTS, CAW, CATCS, CAW, 3 FTS	2-04
❑	XP888		Scout AH.1	ex Arborfield, Middle Wallop, Wroughton, 651, 652, 14 Flt	2-04
❑	XP905		Scout AH.1	ex Arborfield, Middle Wallop, Wroughton, 656, 655, 652, 654, 652	2-04
❑	XR597		Scout AH.1	ex Wattisham, Arborfield, Middle Wallop, Wroughton, 654, 655, 653, 665, 653. Pod	2-04
❑	XT467	'BF'	Wessex HU.5	ex Bramley, Odiham 8922M, Brüggen, Gütersloh, 'XR504', Wroughton, 771, 707	2-04
❑	XT631*	'D'	Scout AH.1	ex Bolenda Eng, Boscombe Down.	2-04
❑	XT640		Scout AH.1	ex Arborfield, Lee-on-Solent, Middle Wallop, 654, 666, 663	2-04
❑	XW796	'X'	Scout AH.1	ex Wattisham, Middle Wallop, Wroughton, 660, 659	2-04
❑	XW892*		Gazelle AH.1	ex Shawbury, 666, 658, 662, 663, 662, 653, 663, 660. Arrived 10-10-04	10-04
❑	XX139*		Jaguar T.4	ex St Athan, 16, 226 OCU, 6, 54, 226 OCU, JOCU. Arrived 27-10-05	10-05
❑	XX144*	'U'	Jaguar T.2A	ex Shawbury, 16, 226 OCU, 6, 54, 226 OCU, JOCU. Arrived 12-10-05	10-05
❑	XX146*		Jaguar T.2	ex St Athan, 54, SAOEU, 16, 41, 6, 54, 41, 6, 41, 6, 54, 6, 54, 6, 41, 6, 41, 6, 54, 41, 226 OCU, 6, 54, 6, 41, 54, 6, 54, 6, 41, 54, 6, 54, 41, 54, 41, 6, Coltishall SF, 6, 226 OCU, JOCU. Arrived 6-12-05	12-05
❑	XX494*	'B'	Jetstream T.1	ex Shawbury, Cranwell, 45, 3 FTS, 45, 6 FTS, METS. Arrived 30-3-05	6-05
❑	XX500*	'H'	Jetstream T.1	ex Culdrose, Cranwell, 45, 3 FTS, 45, 6 FTS, METS. Arrived 29-7-05	7-05
❑	XX741*	'04'	Jaguar GR.1A	ex Shawbury. 16, 6, 54. Arrived 18-11-05	11-05
❑	XX744	'DJ'	Jaguar GR.1	ex Coltishall 9251M, Cosford, Shawbury, 31, 17, AAEE. Fuselage	2-04
❑	XX829*	'GZ'	Jaguar T.2A	ex Shawbury, St Athan, 54, 16, 6, AAEE, 226 OCU, 6, 54, 6, 54, 6, 54, 41, 54. Arrived 6-10-05	10-05
❑	XX832*	'EZ'	Jaguar T.2A	ex Shawbury, 6, 16, 226 OCU, ETPS, 226 OCU. Arrived 13-10-05	10-05
❑	XX836*	'ER'	Jaguar T.2A	ex Shawbury, 6, 17, 14, 226 OCU, 6, 41, 6, 17, 2, 17, 2, 17, 14, 31, 41. Arrived 18-8-05	8-05
❑	XX974*	'FE'	Jaguar GR.3A	ex St Athan, 16, 54, 16, 54, 41, 6, 31, 17, 31. Arr 25-10-05	10-05
❑	XX977*	'DL'	Jaguar GR.1	ex St Athan, 9132M, Abingdon, Shawbury, 31. Arr 1-11-05	11-05
❑	XZ315		Gazelle AH.1	ex Fleetlands, 665, ARWS	2-04
❑	XZ357*	'FK'	Jaguar GR.3A	ex St Athan, 41. Arrived 27-10-05	10-05
❑	XZ361*		Jaguar GR.3	ex Shawbury, St Athan, 41, 6, 41, 2. Arrived 15-12-05	9-05

❏	XZ455*		Sea Harrier FA.2	ex Yeovilton, FSAIU, 801, 899, 800, 899, 801, 899,	
				700A Crashed 14-2-96. Arrived 30-7-05	7-05
❏	ZB666		Gazelle AH.1	ex Middle Wallop, 9 Regt, 670, ARWS. Pod. Cr 24-2-00	2-04
❏	ZB685		Gazelle AH.1	ex Fleetlands, 665, 655	2-04
❏	ZD350*	'A'	Harrier GR.5	ex St Athan 9189M, Wittering, 1. Cr 7-8-92. Nose	12-05
❏	ZD580	'002'	Sea Harrier FA.2	ex St Athan, Yeovilton, 899, 800, 899, 801. Collision 16-9-96	2-04
❏	ZD614	'122'	Sea Harrier FA.2	ex St Athan, Yeovilton, 800, 801, 800, 801, 800,	
				801, 800. 801, 800. Crashed 8-10-01	2-04
❏	ZD991	'722'	Harrier T.8	ex St Athan, Chadderton, St Athan, 899, RAF, 20,	
				230 OCU, 4. Crashed 24-6-97	2-04
❏	ZE691	'710'	Sea Harrier FA.2	ex St Athan, Yeovilton, 899, 801, 899, 800, 899,	
				801, 800. Crashed 4-2-98	3-06
❏	ZE695	'718'	Sea Harrier FA.2	ex St Athan, Yeovilton, 800, 899. Crashed 26-7-00	2-04
❏	ZH799*		Sea Harrier FA.2	ex St Athan, Yeovilton, 899, 801, 800, 801. Arr 5-10-05	10-05
❏	ZH806*	'730'	Sea Harrier FA.2	ex Shawbury, 899. Arrived 2-2-06	2-06
❏	1125*		Strikemaster 80A	ex RSaudiAF	3-06

Others:

❏	XN351	Skeeter AOP.12	G-BKSC, ex Lossiemouth, Inverness, Shobdon, Cardiff,	
			Higher Blagdon, Old Warden, Wroughton, 3 RTR, 652, 651.	
			CoA 8-11-84	4-03

KESGRAVE on the A12 east of Ipswich
The Super Cub is still to be found in Monument Farm Lane, near Foxhall.

| ❏ | MM54-2372 | Piper L-21B | ex Embry-Riddle, Woodbridge, Italian Army | |
| | | | 'EI-184', I-EIXM, USAF 54-2372. Derelict | 2-06 |

LAKENHEATH AIRFIELD on the A1065 south of Brandon
USAF Lakenheath – Wings of Liberty Memorial Park (MEM).
◆ *Visitor centre and memorial park are viewable only by prior permission.*

❏	'BM631'	'XR-C'	Spitfire V FSM	BAPC.269, 71 'Eagle' Sqn, Chesley Peterson colours	MEM	8-05
❏	'65-777'	'SA'	F-4C-15-MC	37419, ex Alconbury, Texas ANG. 48th TFW c/s	MEM	3-00
❏	30091		F-15A-8-MC	ex Soesterberg. ABDR. 'ABDR'		10-96
❏	'92-048'	'LN'	F-15A-12-MC	40131, ex 122 TFS / Louisiana ANG	MEM	8-05
❏	60029		F-15A-15-MC	ABDR		10-96
❏	60124		F-15B-15-MC	ABDR		8-05
❏	'63319'	'FW-319'	F-100D-16-NA	42269, ex '54048', French AF. Main gate		2-06
❏	-	'LN'	F-111E-CF	68011, ex U' Heyford, 20 TFW. *Miss Liberty*	MEM	8-05

LOWESTOFT
Hannants Model Warehouse: In Harbour Road, Oulton Broad. The two Harriers were cancelled from the UK register in March 2005 as sold in the USA. They are reported to be bound for the Flying Heritage Collection.
◆ *Open Mon to Sat 9am to 5.30pm www.hannants.co.uk*

❏	XZ995	'3G'	Harrier GR.3	G-CBGK, ex Shoreham, Ipswich, St Mawgan 9220M,	
				Chivenor, 1417 Flt, 4, 3, 233 OCU, 3	9-05
❏	ZD668	'3A'	Harrier GR.3	G-CBCU, ex Bruntingthorpe, Wittering, 233 OCU	9-05

MARTLESHAM HEATH south-east of Woodbridge, the A12 runs through the site
Martlesham Heath Control Tower Museum: Run by the Martlesham Heath Aviation Society, the museum was opened in September 2000. A vast amount of material is displayed and there is a 'NAAFI'.
◆ *Look for Eagle Way, then Parkers Place and look for the museum signs. Every Sunday, April to October 2pm to 4.30pm. Other times by appointment. c/o 341 Main Road, Martlesham, IP5 2QU tel 01473 624510 e-mail martleshamtower@hotmail.com www.mhas.org.uk*

MONEWDEN south of the A1120, north of Ipswich

❑ G-ARDZ	SAN D.140A	CoA 29-11-91. Canx 26-2-99. Stored	2-06
❑ G-AVTT	Ercoupe 415D	ex SE-BFZ, NC3774H. CoA 20-1-86. Canx 14-4-02. Stored	2-06
❑ G-BENF	Cessna T.210L	ex Ipswich, N732AE, D-EIPY, N732AE. Cr 29-5-81	2-06

NAYLAND on the B1087 north-west of Colchester
Elster B G-BMWV was flying by 2005.

NEWMARKET on the A1304 east of Cambridge
A private collector has a Hunter in the area.

❑ XG274	'71' Hunter F.6	ex Ipswich, Halton 8710M, 4 FTS, 229 OCU, 66, 14	3-04

RATTLESDEN west of Stowmarket
Grasshopper XP494 moved to Wolverhampton, W Mids, by November 2005.

ROUGHAM north of the A14 east of Bury St Edmunds
Rougham Tower Association: A surprising amount of the former B-17 airfield survives, including the superbly-preserved tower and aviation is still regularly committed here. On the northern perimeter (the Bury St Edmunds to Thurston road) can be found the 'Flying Fortress' public house.

◆ *Turn off A14 east of Bury St Edmunds, follow signs for Rougham Industrial Estate, then pick up signs for the tower/aerodrome. Open May to Oct, Sun 11am to 4pm. The Control Tower, Rougham Industrial Estate, Bury St Edmunds, IP30 9XA tel / answerphone 01359 271471 e-mail tower@rougham.org www.rougham.org*

STOWMARKET on the A14 east of Bury St Edmunds
Giles Howell: The EE P.1B is in this general area for restoration and eventual display.

❑ XA847	EE P.1B	ex Portsmouth, S'ton, Hendon 8371M, Farnboro', AAEE, EE	12-02

SUDBURY on the A134 north-west of Colchester
AJD Engineering / Hawker Restorations Ltd (HRL): Battle of Britain veteran Hurricane I R4118 (G-HUPW) made its first flight at Cambridge, Cambs, on 23rd December 2004 for Peter Vacher. Mk.XII '5429' (G-KAMM) moved to Wattisham, Suffolk, on 2nd March 2006 and with Stuart Goldspink at the controls, made its first flight on the 15th. It is destined for the Seattle-based Flying Heritage Collection. AJD are building a static reproduction of Percival Mew Gull G-AEXF under the commission of Alex Henshaw for eventual display in the RAF Museum [1]. The JN4 'Jenny' is stored for Aero Vintage (see St Leonards-on-Sea, East Sussex) [1].

❑ –*	Mew Gull REP	under construction	[1]	4-06
❑ –	JN4 'Jenny'	ex USA, *Great Waldo Pepper*. Stored	[2]	4-94
❑ P2902	Hurricane I	G-ROBT, ex Dunkirk, P2902, 245. Crashed 3-5-40	®	11-02
❑ P3717	Hurricane I	ex Hinckley, Russia, Mk IIA DR348, 8 FTS, 55 OTU,		
		43, 257, 253, 238. Composite.		3-04
❑ V7497	Hurricane I	G-HRLI, ex 501. Crashed 28-9-40	®	4-02
❑ Z5053	Hurricane II	G-BWHA, ex Cam, Russia, 151 Wing, 402	®	11-02
❑ BW853	Hurricane XIIA	ex G-BRKE, Canada, RCAF. Project		7-99

WALPOLE on the B1117 south-east of Halesworth
Blyth Valley Aviation Collection: The trimming down continues and the airframes that remain on site are no longer available for inspection. Lightning F.3 XR718 left on 26th September 2005 for Dinsdale, N Yorks; Sea Vixen FAW.2 XN696 nose moved to Wisbech, Lincs, in June 2005; Victor K.2 nose XL160 and Vulcan K.2 XL445 both moved to Flixton, Suffolk, on 29th July 2005. The nose of Meteor NF.11 WM267 was sold to a private owner in November 2005. It moved to a location in Norfolk on 30th January 2006 for restoration [1].

◆ Not *available for public inspection.*

❑ WE122	'845'	Canberra TT.18	ex North Weald, Stock, St Athan, FRADU, 7, 98, 245, 231 OCU. Nose	2-06
❑ WE192		Canberra T.4	ex Long Marston, Firbeck, Winsford, Samlesbury, St Athan, 231 OCU, 360, 231 OCU, 39, 231 OCU, 3, 231 OCU. Nose	2-06
❑ WH953		Canberra B.6(M)	ex Lowestoft, Stock, Farnborough, RAE. Nose	2-06
❑ XH165		Canberra PR.9	ex Stock, St Athan, 1 PRU, 39, 13, 58. Nose	2-06
❑ XP919	'706'	Sea Vixen FAW.2	ex Norwich, Chertsey, Halton 8163M, 766, 899, AAEE	2-06

WATTISHAM AIRFIELD north of the B1078, south of Stowmarket

No.3 Regiment, Army Air Corps / 24 Air Mobile Brigade / 7 Battalion, REME: Sioux XT550 was offered for tender in October 2005 with Middle Wallop as its 'address' [1].

❑ XL739		Skeeter AOP.12	ex Detmold, 15/19 Hussars, 1 Wing, 651, AAEE, BATUS, AAEE. Displayed, pole-mounted	1-05
❑ XP852		Scout AH.1	ex Hildesheim, Wroughton, ARWF, 651. Cabin only	2-98
❑ XT550	'D'	Sioux AH.1	ex Detmold, Middle Wallop, Wroughton, 651. Gate	[1] 10-05
❑ XT617		Scout AH.1	ex Almondbank, Wroughton, 653, 660. Displayed	2-06
❑ 'XV137'*		Scout AH.1	XV139, ex Yeovil, Arborfield, Wroughton, 657, 656, 662, 653. Arrived 4-04	4-04
❑ ZA676	'FG'	Chinook HC.1	9230M, ex Odiham, Manston, Fleetlands, N37023. Crashed 15-11-84	6-00
❑ ZA729		Gazelle AH.1	ex Gütersloh, Shawbury, Fleetlands, 658, 1 Regt. 4 Regt, 661, 652. ABDR	8-02

Locally: As well as an Evans, three Skeeters and a Scout are stored in the locality.

❑ G-APOI*	Skeeter Mk.8	ex Middle Wallop, Ipswich. CoA 2-8-00	10-05
❑ G-BICT	Evans VP-1	ex Upavon. Crashed 4-8-96. Canx 30-4-01	1-04
❑ XL812*	Skeeter AOP.12	G-SARO, ex Middle Wallop, Ipswich. CoA 1-8-01	10-05
❑ XM553*	Skeeter AOP.12	ex Middle Wallop, Ipswich.	10-05
❑ XP907*	Scout AH.1	G-SROE, ex Ipswich, Middle Wallop.	10-05

SURREY

BROOKLANDS or Weybridge, on the B374 south of Weybridge

Brooklands Museum: Concorde G-BBDG emerged from its 'tent' during August 2005 with a 'Concorde Experience' due to be fully open during the summer of 2006. Brooklands is a beneficiary of British Airways' largesse in the pull-out from Cosford, Shop. The forward fuselage of VC-10 G-ARVM is due to arrive after the rest has been axed [1]. A new reproduction underway is a White Monoplane – it is too early yet to formally list.

Notes: Several airframes are on loan, as follows: the Ladybird from the estate of the late Bill Manuel; the Harrier and Hunter F.51 from BAE Systems; the Valiant nose from the RAF Museum; the Chipmunk PAX from Peter Smith (see under Hawkinge, Kent); the P.1127 from the RAF Museum and BAE Systems jointly. These are marked ±. The Demoiselle was built by Julian Aubert and friends and uses the original method of construction, employing bamboo and using wing-warping [2]. See also under Bournemouth, Dorset, for *another* K5673 [3]. The P.1127 is fitted with the wing of Kestrel XS695 which is at Cosford, Shrop [4]. See under Shoreham, West Sussex, for Beagle 206 G-ARRM which is on loan to BAC and Hungerford, Berks, for Tiger Moth F-BGEQ which is stored, two-thirds restored. Hunter T.7 XL621 moved to Dunsfold, Surrey, on 29th June 2005.

◆ *On the B374 south of Weybridge, access from Junctions 10 or 11 of the M25 - well signed. Open Tue to Sun 10am to 5pm (last entry 4pm), Easter to Oct. Winter, 10am to 4pm, last entry is 3pm. Note: closed on Mondays. Normally closed Xmas. Pre-arranged guided tours available contact 01932 857381. There is an* **Association of Friends of Brooklands,** *and the* **Brooklands Hurricane Fund** *has been set up. Brooklands Road, Weybridge, KT13 0QN tel 01932 857381 fax 01932 855465 e-mail info@brooklandsmuseum.com www.brooklandsmuseum.com*

❏	'G-EBED'		Viking REP	BAPC.114, ex 'R4', Chertsey, *The Land Time Forgot*	4-06
❏	'G-AACA'		Avro 504K REP	BAPC.177, ex 'G1381', Henlow	4-06
❏	'G-ADRY'		HM.14 'Flea'	BAPC.29, ex Aberdare, Swansea	4-06
❏	G-AEKV		Kronfeld Drone	BGA.2510/DZQ. CoA 6-10-60	4-06
❏	G-AGRU		Viking 1	ex Cosford, Soesterberg, Channel, Kuwait Oil, BWIA, VP-TAX, G-AGRU, BEA. *Vagrant.* CoA 9-1-64	® 4-06
❏	G-APEJ		Merchantman	ex Hunting Cargo, ABC, BEA. *Ajax.* Nose	4-06
❏	G-APEP		Merchantman	ex Hunting Cargo, ABC, BEA. *Superb*	4-06
❏	G-APIM		Viscount 806	ex Southend, BAF, BA, BEA. Damaged 11-1-88. *Viscount Stephen Piercey*	® 4-06
❏	G-ARVM*		VC-10 Srs 1101	ex Cosford, BA, BOAC. CoA 5-8-80. BA c/s. Nose	[1] due
❏	G-ASYD		BAC 111-475AM	ex Filton, BAe, BAC. 'Fly By Light Technology'	4-06
❏	G-BBDG*		Concorde 100	ex Filton. CoA 1-3-82. Arrived from 5-04 to 5-6-04	4-06
❏	[G-LOTI]	'2'	Blériot XI REP	CoA 19-7-82	4-06
❏	G-MJPB		Ladybird	microlight. Dismantled, stored	± 4-06
❏	G-VTOL		Harrier T.52	ex ZA250, Dunsfold. CoA 2-11-86	± 4-06
❏	ATH	643	Slingsby Gull 3	(Hawkridge Kittiwake)	4-06
❏	HFZ	3922	Scud I REP	-	4-06
❏	–	BAPC.187	Roe I Biplane REP	displayed in reproduction of Roe's shed	4-06
❏	–	BAPC.256	Demoiselle REP	taxiable	[2] 4-06
❏	–		Willow Wren	BGA.162, ex Bishop's Stortford. *The Willow Wren*	4-06
❏	–		Voisin scale REP	G-BJHV, ex Old Warden	4-06
❏	–		Vimy repro	cockpit section	4-06
❏	–		VC-10 EMU	test shell, nose section. BOAC colours	4-06
❏	–		Rogallo hang glider	*Aerial.* On loan	4-06
❏	[A4O-AB]		VC-10 1103	ex Sultan of Oman, G-ASIX	4-06
❏	'B7270'		Camel REP	G-BFCZ, ex Land's End, Duxford, Chertsey. CoA 23-2-89. 209 Sqn colours. Ground-runs	4-06
❏	'F5475'	'A'	SE.5A REP	BAPC.250, built on site. *1st Battalion Honourable Artillery Company*	4-06
❏	'K5673'		Fury I FSM	BAPC.249, built on site. 1 Sqn 'A' Flt colours	[3] 4-06
❏	N2980	'R'	Wellington Ia	ex Loch Ness, 20 OTU, 37, 149. Ditched 31-12-40	4-06
❏	Z2389		Hurricane II	ex St Petersburg, Siberia, Sov AF, RAF 253, 136, 247, 71, 249	® 4-06
❏	WF372	'A'	Varsity T.1	ex Sibson, 6 FTS, 1 ANS, RAFC, 201 AFS	4-06
❏	[WP921]		Chipmunk T.10 PAX	ex Croydon, Henley-on-Thames, Benson, G-ATJJ, Colerne SF, Ox UAS, HCMSU, 10 RFS	± 4-06
❏	XD816		Valiant BK.1	ex Henlow, Abingdon, BAC, 214, 148. Nose. 'Stratosphere' chamber	± 4-06
❏	'XF314'*	'N'	Hunter F.51	ex Wycombe Air Park, Sandown, Tangmere, Dunsfold, G-9-439, Danish AF E-412, Esk.724. 43 Sqn c/s. Arrived 10-9-05	4-06
❏	XP984		Hawker P.1127	ex Dunsfold, Lee-on-S, Manadon A2658, RAE	± [4] 4-06
❏	XT575		Viscount 837	ex Bruntingthorpe, DRA Bedford, OE-LAG. Nose	4-06
❏	–		TSR-2 EMU	ex Farnborough. Nose	4-06
❏	E-421		Hunter F.51	ex Brooklands Tech, Kingston, Dunsfold, G-9-443, Aalborg, Esk.724, RDanAF	± 4-06

CAMBERLEY on the M3 south of Bracknell

Parkhouse Aviation: (See also Wycombe, Bucks.)

❏	XL449	'044'	Gannet AEW.3	ex Wycombe Air Park, Camberley, Cardiff, Lossiemouth, 849. Cockpit	2-06

Others: American Eagle G-MBTY (last noted February 1996) and Jet Provost T.3 XN137 (September 1993) are believed long gone. They have been shunted to our version of *Room 101 – LOST!*

CATERHAM west of the A22, north-east of Redhill

Nalson Aviation: The yard has a fast and frequent throughput of light and general aviation types and a listing of these would be mis-leading (and too labour-intensive!). More long term inmates are given below.
◆ *Visits by prior arrangement.*

❏	G-ASSE	Colt 108	ex N5961Z. CoA 12-6-00	6-05
❏	G-BADL	Seneca 200 II	ex N5307T. Crashed 21-10-95	2-04
❏	G-BBEW	Aztec 250E	ex EI-BYK, G-BBEW, N40262. Crashed 20-4-99	1-01
❏	G-BCCP	Robin HR.200	Crashed 9-4-89	1-01
❏	G-BGTP	Robin HR.100	ex G-BGTN ntu, F-BVCP. Crashed 16-10-99. Canx 25-1-00	4-05
❏	G-BIAB	TB-9 Tampico	Crashed 6-8-93	1-04
❏	G-BSIB	Warrior II	ex N8182C. Crashed 3-7-99. Canx 22-11-99	1-01

CHARLWOOD west of the A23/A217 junction, north of Gatwick Airport

Gatwick Aviation Museum: Several airframes are capable of ground-running and visitors are often treated to a 'live' run during open days. The planning dispute with Mole Valley District Council is still in a period of grace. The Sea Hawk is being repainted to Fleet Air Arm colours [1].
◆ *Open Apr to Oct, alt Sundays and holidays, 10am to 4pm. - SAE for details. Otherwise by prior appointment. Lowfield Heath Road, Charlwood, RH6 0BT tel 01293 862915 e-mail gpvgat@aol.com www.gatwick-aviation-museum.co.uk*

❏	VZ638		Meteor T.7	G-JETM, ex North Weald, Bournemouth, Southampton, Southend, Kemble, CAW, RAFC, 237 OCU, 501, Biggin Hill SF, FCCS, 85, 54, 25, 500		3-06
❏	WF118	'569'	Sea Prince T.1	G-DACA, ex Gloucester-Cheltenham, Kemble, 750, AAEE, 727, AAEE, RAE		3-06
❏	WH773		Canberra PR.7	ex Wyton, 8696M, 13, 58, 80, 31, 82, 540		3-06
❏	WK146		Canberra B.2	ex Hull, Wroughton, Abingdon, Bicester, 59, 102. Nose		3-06
❏	WP308	'572'	Sea Prince T.1	G-GACA, ex Staverton, Kemble, 750		3-06
❏	WR974	'K'	Shackleton MR.3/3	ex Cosford 8117M, Kinloss Wing, 203, 42, 203, SWDU, MinTech, ASWDU, CA		3-06
❏	WR982	'J'	Shackleton MR.3/3	ex Cosford 8106M, 201, 206, MoA, 205, 203, 206		3-06
❏	WW442	'N'	Provost T.1	ex Kings Langley, Leverstock Green, Cranfield, Booker, St Merryn, Houghton-on-the-Hill, Kidlington, Halton 7618M, CNCS, 3 FTS		3-06
❏	[XE489]		Sea Hawk FB.5	G-JETH, ex B'mouth, Southend, 'XE364', XE489, FRU, 899	[1]	3-06
❏	XK885		Pembroke C.1	N46EA, ex Staverton, St Athan, 8452M, 60, 21, WCS, Seletar SF, B&TTF, Seletar SF, S&TFF, 209, 267		3-06
❏	XL164		Victor K.2	ex Brize Norton 9215M, 55, 57, 55, 57, MoA. Nose		3-06
❏	XL472	'044'	Gannet AEW.3	ex Boscombe Down, 849 'B', HQ, 'A' Flts.		3-06
❏	XL591		Hunter T.7	ex Kemble, Ipswich, Colsterworth, Shawbury, 237 OCU, 208, 237 OCU, 208, 237 OCU, 4 FTS, RAE, 4 FTS, 229 OCU, FCS		3-06
❏	XN923		Buccaneer S.1	ex Boscombe Down, West Freugh.		3-06
❏	XP351	'Z'	Whirlwind HAR.10	ex Shawbury 8672M, 2 FTS, SAR Wing, 22		3-06
❏	XP398		Whirlwind HAR.10	ex Peckham Rye, Shawbury, 8794M, 22, 1563 Flt, 202, 103, 110, 225		3-06
❏	XS587		Sea Vixen FAW.2	G-VIXN, ex Bournemouth, TT mod, FRL, RAE, 8828M, FRL, ADS, 899		3-06
❏	XV751		Harrier GR.3	ex Bruntingthorpe, Charlwood, Lee-on-Solent A2672, A2760, 3, 1, 3, 20, 233 OCU. Grey c/s, RN titles		3-06
❏	XX734		Jaguar GR.1	ex Park Aviation, Coltishall, Abingdon, 8816M, Indian AF JI014, XX734, 6, JOCU. Damaged hulk		3-06
❏	ZF579		Lightning F.53	ex Portsmouth, Luxembourg, *Wing Commander*, Stretton, Warton, RSAF 203, 53-671, G-27-40		3-06
❏	[E-430]		Hunter F.51	ex Faygate, Chertsey, Dunsfold, G-9-448, Esk.724, Dan AF. FAA colours, GA.11-style		3-06
❏	J-1605		Venom FB.50	G-BLID, ex Duxford, Swiss AF		3-06

Park Aviation Supply / Aerospace Logistics: In Glovers Lane. Have taken on several Sea Harriers.

❑ XX121	'EQ'	Jaguar GR.1	ex Cosford, Shawbury, 6, 54, 226 OCU, JOCU	1-06
❑ XX140		Jaguar T.2	ex Faygate, 226 OCU, 54, JOCU, JCT. Cockpit	4-02
❑ XX223		Hawk T.1	ex Henlow, 4 FTS. Crashed 7-7-86. Cockpit	3-05
❑ XX257		Hawk T.1A	ex St Athan, Red Arrows. Crashed 17-11-98	1-06
❑ XZ459*		Sea Harrier FA.2	ex St Athan, 809, 800, 801, 899, 800, 801, 800, 801, 800,	
			AAEE, 801, 899, 801, 899, 809, 800. Arr 19-10-05	1-06
❑ XZ497*	'126'	Sea Harrier FA.2	ex St Athan, 801, AEE, FRS.1, 899, 801. Arr 23-3-05	1-06
❑ ZD412*		Harrier GR.5	ex St Athan. Fuselage	1-06
❑ ZD608*	'714'	Sea Harrier FA.2	ex St Athan, 899, 800, 899, 801, 899, FRS.1, 801, 899, 801.	
			Arrived by 10-05	1-06
❑ ZD615*		Sea Harrier FA.2	ex St Athan, 801, 899, FRS.1, 800, 801. Arrived 1-11-05	1-06
❑ ZE697*		Sea Harrier FA.2	ex St Athan, 801. 899. 800. 899. 800. 801. 899. FRS.1,	
			801, 800. Arrived 19-10-05	1-06
❑ ZE698*		Sea Harrier FA.2	ex St Athan, 800, FRS.1, 800, 801,899, 801. Arr 20-3-05	1-06
❑ 162730*		AV-8B Harrier II	ex St Athan, Wyton, St Athan, USMC. Fuselage. Arr 25-5-05	1-06

DUNSFOLD AERODROME (or Dunsfold Park) on the A281 south of Guildford
The 'Jumbo' is with film specialists, **Aces High**, who have an office here (see also North Weald, Essex). Kept 'live', the 747 is available for film and TV 'set' work. The Hunter has taken up gate guardian duties at the fast re-developing aerodrome; XL621 first flew from here in 1966. On Guy Fawkes' Day 1985 Sea Harrier FRS.1 (as it then was) ZD610 made its first flight here at Dunsfold. Just 25 days short of its 25th birthday, it returned – by road – for a new life as a display airframe. Dakota 3 N147DC moved back to North Weald, Essex.
◆ *All visits by prior arrangement* only.

❑ G-BDXJ*		Boeing 747-236B	ex Air Atlanta Europe, BA G-BDXJ, N1792B. Arr 25-5-05	3-06
❑ XL621*		Hunter T.7	ex Brooklands, Bournemouth, G-BNCX, RAE, 238 OCU,	
			RAE. ETPS colours. 'Gate'. Arrived 29-6-05	3-06
❑ ZD610*	'006'	Sea Harrier FA.2	ex Yeovilton, 800, 899, 801, 800, 899, 801, 899.	
			Arrived 11-10-05	3-06

Phil Boyden: Keeps the nose of a Harrier GR.3 in the local area. The nose and other parts were left over from the restoration of the Fleet Air Arm Museum's Sea Harrier FRS.1 XZ493.

❑ XV760*		Harrier GR.3	ex Dunsfold, Yeovilton A2605 [2] A2614, Culdrose,	
			St Athan, 3, 4, 233 OCU. Nose	11-04

EGHAM on the A30 west of Staines
Jeremy Hall: Using as many original parts as possible, Jeremy has created the forward fuselage (all 21ft of it) of a Lancaster. It 'does the rounds' of shows and events.

❑ –		Lancaster REP	*Hi Ho!, Hi Ho!* Forward fuselage	6-98

FAIROAKS AERODROME off the A319, east of Chobham
RLM Aviation: Glenn Lacey's expanding collection of Luftwaffe types is based upon this location, although there are off-site workshops and storage areas. (Previously listed under Woking, Surrey. All entries technically 'new' to this heading, but airframes given a * below are new since *W&R19*.)
◆ Strictly *private collection, no access without prior permission.*

❑ G-MESS		Noralpha	ex F-BEEV, F-WZBI, Fr Navy 87. Arrived 7-04	®	4-06
❑ 'D-6292'		Fw 44J Stieglitz ✈	G-STIG, ex Belgium, OO-JKT, D-EHDH, LV-YYX		4-06
❑ OO-EII		Bü 133 J'meister	ex Belgium. Arrived by 3-05		8-05
❑ -*	'NQ+NR'	Klemm Kl 35D ✈	G-KLEM, ex N5050, SE-BGD, RSweAF Fv5050. Arr 5-10-04		4-06
❑ -*	'GL+SU'	Bü 181B-1 ✈	G-GLSU, ex D-EDUB, RSwAF Fv 25071. Arr 12-7-03		4-06
❑ 6234		Ju 87B/R-4	G-STUK, ex Germany, New Zealand, Lancing,		
			Russia, 'L1+FW'. Shot down 24-4-42	off-site	2-06
❑ 1983		Bf 109E-3	G-EMIL, ex 'Essex', Russia, JG5. Shot down 17-7-41	off-site	2-06
❑ 2008		Fi 156A-1	G-STCH, ex Russia?	®	4-06

☐	110451		Fi 156D-0	G-STOR, ex Russia?		2-06
☐	211028	'8'	Fw 190D-9	G-DORA, ex Germany, JG26, JG54	off-site	2-06

Others: The firecrews have a Cherokee fuselage to play with. This is often parked on a trailer in a yard within the aerodrome when it is not being used for an exercise. Its true identity is not known.

☐	'G-DOAT'	Cherokee	fuselage, fire crews	3-06

FARNHAM on the A31 south-west of Aldershot
A collector in the general area has a Lightning nose.

☐	XS933	Lightning F.6	ex Langport, Terrington St Clement, Narborough, Binbrook, 5, 11, BAC, 5, 56, 11. Nose	3-02

FLEET on the A323 north west of Aldershot
The cockpit (or nose section) of a Bristol 170 is in use as a plaything in the area.

☐	C-FDFC*	Bristol 170 Mk.31	ex Enstone, G-BISU Instone, ZK-EPH, NZ5912, ZK-BVI, G-18-194. Crashed 18-7-96. Cockpit	12-05

GODALMING on the A3100, south west of Guildford
A private collector has acquired a Spitfire IX and moved it into the general area.

☐	SM639*	Spitfire IX	ex Norwich, Russia, USSR. Stored	3-06

HASLEMERE on the A286 south-west of Godalming
Sea Vixen Preservation Group: Located in Weyhill, just off the B2131, this is the preservation 'arm' of **1268 Squadron Air Cadets**. A workshop has greatly helped in the restoration work.
♦ *Visits by prior appointment* only. *Flt Lt Kevin Burchett, 43 Beech Road, Waterlooville, PO8 0LN*

☐	XP925	Sea Vixen FAW.2	ex Farnborough, Tarrant Rushton, ADS, 899. Nose	®	3-04
☐		Lightning CIM	ex Farnborough. Cockpit	®	3-04

HORLEY on the A23 south of Reigate
Heath Parasol G-AFZE and the anonymous Bensen gyroplane have been moved to LOST!

MYTCHETT on the B3411 south of Camberley
Defence Medical Services Training Centre:

☐	XG196	'31'	Hunter F.6A	8702M, ex Bracknell, Kemble, 1 TWU,TWU, 229 OCU, 19. Gate	3-05

REDHILL on the A23 east of Reigate
Turbine World: Located on a *private* site in this general area. Some of the references are quite dated.

☐	G-AZBY		Wessex 60 Srs 1	ex Weston-super-Mare, Bournemouth, W-s-Mare, *Full Metal Jacket* 'EM-16', 5N-ALR, G-AZBY. CoA 14-12-82	10-99
☐	'VT-EKG'		Westland WG.30	VT-EKK. Ex Biggin Hill	9-02
☐	XS489*	'R"	Wessex HU.5C	ex Gosport, Ballymena, Odiham, Wroughton, 845, 707, 846, 848. Arrived 6-3-04	3-04
☐	XT671		Wessex HC.2	G-BYRC, ex 72	1-04
☐	XV731		Wessex HC.2	ex Fleetlands, 72, WTF, 240 OCU, 18, 78	9-02

REDHILL AERODROME south of South Nutfield, south-east of Redhill

G-ABNX is looked after by **Acebell Aviation** on behalf of the **Redwing Preservation Trust** [1]. The B-2 is also under Acebell's 'wing'. (Viewing by prior permission *only*: c/o Hangar 8, Redhill Aerodrome, Kingsmill Lane, Surrey, RH1 5JY.). The Scion is owned by the Historic Aircraft Society of Southend, Essex [2].

❏ G-ABNX	Redwing 2	✈	ex Old Sarum, Shoreham	[1]	3-06
❏ G-ACBH*	Blackburn B-2		ex 'Kent', Ingatestone, West Hanningfield, Wickham		
			Bishops, Downham, Ramsden Heath, Brentwood 2895M.		
			CoA 27-11-41. Fuselage. Arrived 3-06		3-06
❏ G-AEZF	Scion II		ex East Tilbury, Southend. CoA 5-5-54. Frame	® [2]	3-06
❏ G-ARDG*	Prospector		ex Washington, Durrington, Middle Wallop, Shoreham,		
			Lympne. 'Pod', poor state. First noted 4-05.		9-05
❏ G-ATBH*	Aero 145		CoA 26-10-<u>81</u>. First noted 11-04	®	1-06
❏ G-BVIH*	Warrior II		CoA 23-1-00. Stored. First noted 9-05	®	9-05
❏ –	Grasshopper TX.1		'fuselage' frame. Stored		7-00

Wings Museum: The **East Surrey Aviation Group**'s collection, run by Daniel and Kevin Hunt, recently changed its name. The Sea Devon project is being worked on by the ESAG and the aim is to display it statically at the aerodrome. The 'JP' nose is now identified [1].

◆ *Visits by prior application only. 28 Windmill Way, Reigate, RH2 0JA e-mail daniel@esag.demon.co.uk*

❏ G-AIUA	Hawk Trainer III	ex King's Lynn, West Chiltington, Benington, Bushey,		
		Old Warden, Duxford, Felthorpe, T9768, 10 AGS,		
		7 FIS, 15 EFTS, Wyton SF. CoA 13-7-67. Fuselage		4-06
❏ G-OJAS	J/1U Workmaster	ex F-BJAS, F-WJAS, F-OBHT ntu. Frame		4-06
❏ BD731	Hurricane II	ex Murmansk, 605, 135. Remains, plus other parts		4-06
❏ VP967	Sea Devon C.2/2	G-KOOL, ex Goodwood, Redhill, East Surrey Tech		
		'G-DOVE', Biggin Hill, VP967, Kemble, 781, 21, 207,		
		SCCS, SCS, WCS, SCS, NCS, SCS, MCS, MoA, MCS,		
		CCCF, 38 GCF, TTCCF, FCCS, 2 TAF CS, MCCS,		
		RAFG CS, 2 TAF CS, Wahn SF, RCCF	®	4-06
❏ XN492	Jet Provost T.3	ex Haydock, Levenshulme, Firbeck, Stock, Odiham,		
		Cosford, Halton 8079M, 6 FTS, RAFC. Cockpit	[1]	4-06
❏ –	Nakajima B5N2	ex Kurile Island. Front fuselage		4-06
❏ –	Mitsubishi A6M2	ex Kurile Island. Front fuselage		4-06
❏ 43-11137	P-63C	ex Kurile Island. Remains		4-06
❏ 44-4315	P-63C	ex Kurile Island. Remains		4-06
❏ –	B-25 Mitchell	ex Kurile Island. Front fuselage		4-06

Others: Mosr references here are now quite dated – offers?

❏ G-BOSC	Cessna U.206F	F-GHEN (ntu?). ex 5N-ASU, N7256N. Fuselage	9-99
❏ G-BOVY	Hughes 269C	ex EI-CIL, G-BOVY, N1096K. Crashed 17-3-99	5-00
❏ G-BXVC	Turbo Arrow IV	ex D-ELIV, N2152V. Crashed 22-8-98. Wreck	9-99
❏ G-FISS	Robinson R-22	ex N40833. Crashed 31-3-96. Pod	9-99
❏ G-OROB	Robinson R-22	ex G-TBFC, N80287. CoA 25-6-95. Pod	9-99
❏ 5N-ALQ	Bell 212	ex Nigeria. Crashed 11-9-95. Stored	3-00
❏ 5N-AQW	Bell 212	ex Nigeria. Crashed 14-1-93. Stored	3-00

REIGATE on the A217 west of Redhill

The Vulcan nose is an 'unplumbed' B.1 with a B.2 'hood'.

❏ –	Vulcan B.1 EMU	ex East Kirkby, Tattershall, Waddington. Nose	®	6-01

SUNBURY-ON-THAMES south of J1 of the M3

J and C Motor Spares: In Fordbridge Road, the B375.

❏ –	Hobbycopter	—	3-06

SUTTON
A Scout cabin has arrived in the general area with a collector.
❏ XP853*   Scout AH.1   ex Dunkeswell, Bramley. Cabin   5-05

WALTON ON THAMES
Adrian Windsor: Still has his Hunter cockpit.
❏ E-420   Hunter F.51   ex Marlow, Ascot, Dunsfold G-9-442, RDanAF. Cockpit   3-02

WEYBRIDGE on the B374 south of the town
Brooklands Technical College: The airframes are believed unchanged.
❏ G-ASSB   Twin Comanche   ex Bournemouth. CoA 6-5-88   10-03
❏ XN586   '91' Jet Provost T.3A   ex Cosford 9039M, 7 FTS, 1 FTS, CFS, 2 FTS, RAFC   3-04

WOKING on the A320 north of Guildford
Big Apple: The Hunter-on-a-stick is still outside. (See under Poole, Somerset, for the saga of XL623.)
❏ XL623   Hunter T.7   8770M, ex Newton, Cosford, 1 TWU, 74, 19, 1,
                                          43, 92, 208, 65. Pole-mounted   4-05

RLM Aviation: The flying base for the collection is Fairoaks, Surrey. All listed under this heading in *W&R19* have moved accordingly.

EAST SUSSEX

BEXHILL on the A259 west of Hastings
❏ G-ACXE   L25cl Swallow   ex 'Hastings', Bagshot, Birmingham. CoA 7-4-40.   ® 10-98

BRIGHTON
No.225 Squadron Air Cadets:
❏ WD370   Chipmunk T.10   ex Hove, 3 AEF, 2 SoTT, 1 AEF, Hull UAS,
                        PAX   2 BTFS. SOC 12-3-75   5-05

Others:
❏ G-AZBT   Western O-65   ex Lancing. *Hermes*. CoA 9-4-76. Stored.   3-98

DEANLAND south of the B2124, west of Hailsham
❏ G-BRKY   Dragonfly II   CoA 8-6-94. Fuselage. Stored.   8-01

HAILSHAM on the A22 north of Eastbourne
Grenville Helicopters: The helipad at the Boship Manor Hotel *should* still have its 'guardian' which carries the tail stabiliser of G-AXKW – to confuse all and sundry!
❏ 'G-AXKW'   Bell 47G   G-AYOE, ex F-OCBF, F-BKQZ, D-HEBO.
                                  Crashed 16-7-77. Composite, including Sioux parts.   10-00

Others: Taylor Titch G-BARN was flying again by 2004 and Isaacs Fury 'K3731' (G-RODI) by 2003.

HOLLINGTON on the B2159 west of Hastings

St Leonard's Motors: In Church Wood Drive, the Meteor was reportedly being offer for disposal in late 2005.

❑ WL345	Meteor T.7	ex Hastings, Kemble, CAW, 8 FTS, 5 FTS, CFE, 229 OCU	12-05

LEWES on the A27 north-east of Brighton

A collector has a Canberra and a Hunter locally [1].

❑ G-AMYL	PA-17 Vagabond	ex N4613H, NC4613H. CoA 20-6-89. *Yankee Lady*		8-00
❑ G-APNS	Fairtravel Linnet	ex Chessington. CoA 6-10-78		8-00
❑ G-AYMU	Wassmer D.112	ex F-BJPB. Damaged 7-1-92		8-00
❑ WH964	Canberra E.15	ex Bruntingthorpe, Cosford 8870M, St Athan, 100,		
		98, Akrotiri Wing, 32, 12. Nose	[1]	5-05
❑ XG195	Hunter FGA.9	ex Sleap, Seighford, Macclesfield, Bitteswell,		
		G-9-453, 208, 1, 19. Nose	[1]	5-05

NEWHAVEN east of Brighton on the A259

Newhaven Fort: Robertsbridge Aviation Society (see below) has an on-going display here. Also within the Fort (but not RAS originated) is a feature on the much-missed Royal Observer Corps.

◆ *Mar to Oct, daily 10.30am to 6.00pm. Weekends in Nov, 10.30am to 4pm. Fort Road, Newhaven, BN9 9DL tel 01273 517622 fax 01273 512059*

ROBERTSBRIDGE on the A21 north-west of Hastings

Robertsbridge Aviation Centre: Operated by the Robertsbridge Aviation Society (RAS), the museum is a barrage of artefacts covering many aspects of aviation. RAS has a close relationship with Newhaven Fort, E Sussex, with a series of displays there.

◆ *Open by appointment only. Membership of RAS includes meetings, trips and a newsletter, Rob Air. Philip Baldock, 53 Wannock Avenue, Willingdon, BN20 9RH tel 01323 483845 e-mail pbaldock@breathermail.net*

❑ WA630	Meteor T.7	ex Newhaven, Robertsbridge, Oakington SF,	
		4 FTS, 205 AFS, RAFC. Nose	2-04
❑ WE173	Canberra PR.3	ex Stock, Coltishall, Farnborough, 231 OCU,	
		39, RAE, 39, 69, 82. Nose	2-04
❑ WN907	Hunter F.2	ex Walpole, Ascot, St Athan, Colerne 7416M, 257. Nose	2-04
❑ XJ488	Sea Vixen FAW.1	ex Nottingham, New Milton, Portsmouth,	
		Boscombe Down, 22 JSTU, AAEE. Nose	2-04
❑ XP701	Lightning F.3	ex High Halden, Hawkinge, Binbrook 8924M,	
		LTF, 5, 11, 56, 29, 111, 29, AAEE. Nose	2-04
❑ XR681	Jet Provost T.4	ex Newhaven, Odiham, Abingdon 8588M,	
		RAFEF, CATCS, 6 FTS, RAFC. Nose	2-04
❑ 7907	Su-7 *Fitter*	ex Farnborough, Egyptian AF. Nose	2-04

ST LEONARDS-ON-SEA west of Hastings

Aero Vintage: DH.9 D5649 is under restoration to static condition for the IWM, Duxford, Cambs – qv [1]. Alongside this 'static' a 'flyer' using similarly sourced components is also underway [2]. The Me 163B is here for preparation prior to departure to the USA [3]. The **Historic Aircraft Collection of Jersey** is closely associated – and see under Duxford, Cambs, for more details. For other AV/HAC aircraft see also: Bristol F.2b at Old Warden, Beds; JN4 'Jenny' at Sudbury, Suffolk. In November 2004, Hind I L7181 moved to Duxford, Cambs, for storage.

❑ D5649	Airco DH.9	ex Hatch, Bikaner, India, RAF/RFC	® [1] 10-05
❑ E8894*	Airco DH.9	G-CDLI, ex India, RAF/RFC	® [2] 10-05
❑ K3661	Nimrod II	G-BURZ, ex 802 Sqn. Other history obscure	® 9-05
❑ K5600	Audax I	G-BVVI, ex 2015M, Kirkham, SAC, 226	off-site ® 4-06
❑ EF545*	Spitfire V	G-CDGY, ex New Zealand, ZK-MKV, RAAF	
		A58-149, EF545.	® 1-05

❏	–		Fury I	G-CBZP, ex SAAF	®	12-03
❏	–		Fury REP	–	®	8-95
❏	191660*	'3'	Me 163B-1	ex Duxford, South Lambeth, Cranwell, 6 MU, RAE,		
				AM.214. Arrived by 9-05	[3]	10-05
❏	1342		Yakovlev Yak-1	G-BTZD, ex Sudbury, Audley End, Paddock Wood,		
				USSR	®	3-04

SEDLESCOMBE AERODROME on the B2244 north of Hastings

❏	G-AXPG	Mignet HM.293	CoA 20-1-77. Stored	11-01
❏	G-BLUL	CEA DR.1051M	ex F-BMPJ. CoA 24-10-91. Stored	11-01
❏	G-BUNS	Cessna F.150K	ex F-BSIL. Stored	11-01

Locally: Spitfire IX UB441 (ML119) was acquired by a UK private owner and is in storage pending restoration to flying condition – no 'forwarding address'.

WANNOCK east of the A22, north of Eastbourne
Foulkes-Halbard Collection: This *private* collection is no longer available for public inspection.

❏	G-BHNG	Aztec 250E	ex Seaford, Shoreham, N54125. Cr 19-12-81. Fuselage		2-04
❏	–	BAPC.127 Halton Jupiter	ex Old Warden, Cranwell, Halton. Stored		2-04
❏	–	IAHC.2 Aldritt Mono REP	ex Portlaoise	®	2-04

WEST SUSSEX

ASHINGTON west of the A24, at the junction of the A283, north of Worthing
Paul Whelland: 'JP' 'XN594' (XN458) was sold and moved to Northallerton, N Yorks, on 8th July 2005.

BOGNOR REGIS
'Prom Bar': Within the 'Bottle Bar and Café' of this emporium can be found a Bandeirante nose.

❏	G-OHIG*	Bandeirante	ex Stock, Alton, G-OPPP, XC-DAI, PT-SAB.	
			CoA 30-4-96. Cockpit. Arrived by 11-04	7-05

BOSHAM north of the A259, south-west of Chichester
Whirlwind HAS.7 XN263 was scrapped during July 2005.

CRAWLEY
Crawley Technical College: Jet provost T.3A XN494 is thought to have moved to Haydock, Lancs, then to the King's Lynn area in 2004 for reduction to spares.

❏	XS463	Wasp HAS.1	XT431, ex Ipswich, Weston-super-Mare,	
			Fleetlands, Lee-on-Solent. Boom of XT431	12-03

EAST GRINSTEAD on the A264 east of Crawley
Sabrewatch: Lingfield Road. This location is *private* property. Wessex HAS.3 XT257 moved to Bournemouth, Dorset, on 20th January 2005.

❏	WF408	Varsity T.1	ex Northolt, 8395M Cosford, 2 SoTT, 6 SS,	
			2 ANS, 1 RS, 11 FTS, 201 AFS. Drab green camo	2-05

No.1343 Squadron Air Cadets: Morton Road, close to Sunnyside Post Office. 'Parent' is Odiham. The anonymous Jaguar GR.1 cockpit had moved to <u>Boscombe Down</u>, Wilts, by June 2004. 'JP' T.4 XP677 was auctioned 'virtually' during December 2004 and is thought to have moved on. **Locally**: Martin Cobb's Sea Vampire is under restoration in the general area.

❏ N6-766   Sea Vampire T.22   G-SPDR, ex Swansea, VH-RAN ntu, RAN, XG766   ®   10-03

FAYGATE on the A264 between Horsham and Crawley

Aerospace Logistics: (formerly Park Aviation Supply / Sheet Metal Products). Jaguar GR.1B XX733 and Sea Harrier FA.1 XZ492 were both minus cockpits by January 2006, so can be deleted.

❏ XW268	'720' Harrier T.4N	ex Yeovilton, 899, 233 OCU	1-06
❏ ZD400	Harrier GR.7	ex Wittering, 1, Dunsfold, Shawbury, 1. Cr 19-5-97	1-06

FORD north of the A259 west of Littlehampton

Peter Hague: Perched atop a lofty plinth on the appropriately-named Hunterford site on the edge of the former entrance of what was HMS *Peregrine*, the famed FAA station, is Peter's Hunter.

❏ WW654   '834' Hunter GA.11   ex Oving, Portsmouth, Culdrose A2664, A2753, SAH,
     FRADU, 738, 229 OCU, 98, 4, 98   7-05

GATWICK AIRPORT - Should these days be London (Gatwick) Airport – so cruise down a bit...

GOODWOOD AERODROME or Westhampnett, north of Chichester

Ercoupe G-COUP was flying again by 2003. Enstrom 280C N281Q, last noted in September 1996 as under spares recovery, is thought to have long since left in little boxes.

❏ [G-BGRN]   Tomahawk 112   ex N9684N. CoA 12-2-00. Dump   5-03

HAYWARD'S HEATH on the A272 north of Brighton

No.172 Squadron, Air Cadets: Inside the TAVR centre in Eastern Road.

❏ XX520   Bulldog T.1   ex Newton 9288M, EM UAS, CFS, RNEFTS, 2 FTS   1-05

LANCING on the A27 east of Worthing

Balloon Preservation Group (BPG) / **Skyart Balloons**: Formed in 1993 by Bob Kent, BPG is the world's largest balloon collection. The majority of the balloons are held in a storage facility in the county. Balloons are occasionally displayed at venues across the country. The group is willing to attend events with balloons on request and has equipment available for long-term loan to museums etc. A number of balloons in the collection have been reduced to spares (see below) and this has helped to return to flight the ones marked ✿ in the list below - most of these are registered to the Balloon Preservation Flying Group. The Sailplane Preservation Group's Ka-4 is stored care of BPG [1].

Departures: The following have been reduced to spares to help other 'aged' balloons: **Avian** N5023U; **Cameron**s G-BMST; G-BRFR; G-BRLX; G-BUKC; G-GURL (in Austria); G-MOLI [1]; G-VOLT; OO-ARK; **Colt**s G-BKOW; G-BONK; G-BOSF; G-BUXA; G-BVFY; G-LBCS plus G-BZYO donated in 2005. **Head** N4519U; **Lindstrand** G-KNOB; **Thunder**s G-BHAT; G-BOTE; G-BTJF; G-BWUR; G-WORK; DQ-PBF plus G-BRXB donated in 2004. The following have been destroyed: Cameron N-180 G-BPSZ; AAC ANR-1 Airship G-MAAC and Cameron N-90 OO-BDO and the following returned to owners: Cameron N-77 G-BXAX and Airtour AH-56 G-OAFC. Thunder Ax7-65 G-BJZC had moved to <u>Flixton</u>, Suffolk and Lindstrand LBL-77 to <u>Doncaster</u>, S Yorks.

◆ *Dispersed storage - visits are not possible. Balloons make frequent appearances at events across the country – see the web-sites for details. 44 Shadwells Road, Lancing, BN15 9EW tel 07906 809515 e-mail bpgballoons@yahoo.co.uk www.litepix.co.uk or www.skyartballoons.co.uk*

❏ CWU   1872 Schleicher Ka-4   ex D-5427. Stored   [1]   3-06

☐	G-AYVA	Cameron O-84	3-06
☐	G-BAKO	Cameron O-84	3-06
☐	G-BAND	Cameron O-84	3-06
☐	G-BAOW	Cameron O-65	3-06
☐	G-BAST	Cameron O-84	3-06
☐	G-BAYC	Cameron O-65	3-06
☐	G-BBDJ ✿	Thunder Ax7-56	3-06
☐	G-BBYL	Cameron O-77	3-06
☐	G-BBYR	Cameron O-65	3-06
☐	G-BCAP	Cameron O-56	3-06
☐	G-BCAS	Thunder Ax7-77	3-06
☐	G-BCCH	Thunder Ax6-56A	3-06
☐	G-BCNR	Thunder Ax7-77A	3-06
☐	G-BCRE	Cameron O-77	3-06
☐	G-BDGO	Thunder Ax7-77	3-06
☐	G-BDMO	Thunder Ax7-77	3-06
☐	G-BEIF ✿	Cameron O-65	3-06
☐	G-BEJB	Thunder Ax6-56	3-06
☐	G-BGST	Thunder Ax7-65	3-06
☐	G-BHYO	Cameron N-77	3-06
☐	G-BKIY	Thunder Ax3	3-06
☐	G-BKOW	Colt 77A (spares)	3-06
☐	G-BKPN	Cameron N-77	3-06
☐	G-BKZB	Cameron 56SS	3-06
☐	G-BLDL	Cameron V-77	3-06
☐	G-BLGX	Thunder Ax7-65	3-06
☐	G-BLIP	Cameron N-77	3-06
☐	G-BLKJ	Thunder Ax7-65	3-06
☐	G-BLSH	Cameron V-77	3-06
☐	G-BLZB	Cameron N-65	3-06
☐	G-BMKX	Cameron 77SS	3-06
☐	G-BMMU	Thunder Ax7-77	3-06
☐	G-BMUJ	Colt SS	3-06
☐	G-BMUK	Colt SS	3-06
☐	G-BMUL	Colt SS	3-06
☐	G-BMWU ✿	Cameron N-42	3-06
☐	G-BNCH	Cameron V-77	3-06
☐	G-BNHL	Colt Beer Glass 90	3-06
☐	G-BNMI	Colt SS	3-06
☐	G-BOCF	Colt 77A	3-06
☐	G-BOGT	Colt 77A	3-06
☐	G-BONV	Colt 17A	3-06
☐	G-BOOP	Cameron N-90	3-06
☐	G-BORA	Colt 77A	3-06
☐	G-BPAH	Colt 69A	3-06
☐	G-BPDF	Cameron V-77	3-06
☐	G-BPFJ	Cameron 90SS	3-06
☐	G-BPFX	Colt 21A	3-06
☐	G-BRDP	Colt SS	3-06
☐	G-BSBM	Cameron N-77	3-06
☐	G-BSGB	Gaertner AX-3	3-06
☐	G-BSWZ	Cameron A-180	3-06
☐	G-BTML	Cameron SS	3-06
☐	G-BTPV ✿	Colt 90A	3-06
☐	G-BTXM ✿	Colt 21A	3-06
☐	G-BUET	Cameron SS	3-06
☐	G-BUEU	Colt 21A	3-06

☐	G-BUIZ	Cameron N-90	3-06
☐	G-BUNI	Cameron SS Bunny	3-06
☐	G-BURX ✿	Cameron N-105	3-06
☐	G-BUXA	Colt 210A	3-06
☐	G-BVBJ	Colt SS Coffee Jar	3-06
☐	G-BVBK	Colt SS Coffee Jar	3-06
☐	G-BVFY	Colt 210A (spares)	3-06
☐	G-BVIO	Colt SS Can	3-06
☐	G-BVWH	Cameron N-90 Bulb	3-06
☐	G-BVWI	Colt 65SS	3-06
☐	G-BWAN ✿	Cameron N-77	3-06
☐	G-BWFK ✿	Lindstrand LBL-77A	3-06
☐	G-BWGA ✿	Lindstrand LBL-105A	3-06
☐	G-BWLA ✿	Colt 69A	3-06
☐	G-BWZP	Cameron SS Home	3-06
☐	G-BXAL	Cameron SS	3-06
☐	G-BXAM	Cameron N-90	3-06
☐	G-BXHM	Lindstrand LBL-25A	3-06
☐	G-BXHN	Lindstrand SS Can	3-06
☐	G-BXIZ ✿	Lindstrand LBL-31A	3-06
☐	G-BXND	Cameron SS Thomas	3-06
☐	G-BXUG ✿	Lindstrand SS Baby Bel	3-06
☐	G-BXUH ✿	Lindstrand LBL-31A	3-06
☐	G-BYFK	Cameron SS Printer	3-06
☐	G-BZIH ✿	Lindstrand 31A	3-06
☐	G-BZTS	Cameron SS Bertie	3-06
☐	G-CBPG	Barnes SS Condom	3-06
☐	G-CFBI	Colt 56A	3-06
☐	G-COLR	Colt 69A	3-06
☐	G-COMP	Cameron N-90	3-06
☐	G-CURE	Colt 77A	3-06
☐	G-DHLI	Colt 90SS	3-06
☐	G-DHLZ	Colt 31A	3-06
☐	G-ENRY	Cameron N-105	3-06
☐	G-ETFT	Colt SS Fin Times	3-06
☐	G-FZZY	Colt 69A	3-06
☐	G-GEUP	Cameron N-77	3-06
☐	G-GOAL ✿	Lindstrand LBL-105A	3-06
☐	G-HELP ✿	Colt 17A	3-06
☐	G-HENS	Cameron N-65	3-06
☐	G-HLIX	Cameron SS	3-06
☐	G-IAMP ✿	Cameron H-34	3-06
☐	G-IBBC	Cameron SS Globe	3-06
☐	G-IGEL	Cameron N-90	3-06
☐	G-IMAG	Colt 77A	3-06
☐	G-JANB	Colt SS	3-06
☐	G-KORN ✿	Cameron 70SS	3-06
☐	G-LBNK	Cameron N-105	3-06
☐	G-LLAI	Colt 21A	3-06
☐	G-LLYD	Cameron N-31	3-06
☐	G-MAPS	Thunder Ax7-77	3-06
☐	G-MHBD	Cameron O-105	3-06
☐	G-NPWR	Cameron RX-100	3-06
☐	G-NWPB	Thunder Ax7-77Z	3-06
☐	G-OBUY ✿	Colt 69A	3-06
☐	G-OCAR	Colt 77A	3-06
☐	G-OCAW	Lindstrand SS Bananas	3-06

❑	G-OCND		Cameron O-77	3-06	❑	G-SCAH	Cameron V-77	3-06
❑	G-OEGG	✿	Cameron SS Egg	3-06	❑	G-SCFO	Cameron O-77	3-06
❑	G-OFLI		Colt 105A	3-06	❑	G-SEGA	Cameron SS	3-06
❑	G-OGGS		Thunder Ax8-84	3-06	❑	G-SEUK	Cameron TV-80SS	3-06
❑	G-OHDC		Colt SS Film Can	3-06	❑	G-TTWO	Colt 56A	3-06
❑	G-OLDV		Colt 90A	3-06	❑	G-UMBO	Colt SS Jumbo	3-06
❑	G-OMXS		Lindstrand LBL-105A	3-06	❑	G-UNIP	Cameron SS Oil Can	3-06
❑	G-OSVY		Sky 31-24	3-06	❑	G-UNRL	Lindstrand RR-21	3-06
❑	G-OVAA	✿	Colt SS Jumbo	3-06	❑	G-USGB	Colt 105A	3-06
❑	G-OXRG		Colt SS Film Can	3-06	❑	G-WATT	Cameron SS	3-06
❑	G-PHOT		Colt SS Film Cassette	3-06	❑	G-WCAT	Colt SS	3-06
❑	G-PNEU		Colt SS Bibendum	3-06	❑	G-WINE	Thunder Ax7-77	3-06
❑	G-PONY		Colt 31A	3-06	❑	C-GYZI	Cameron O-77	3-06
❑	G-POPP		Colt 105A	3-06	❑	D-OPHA	Fire Balloons 3000	3-06
❑	G-PSON	✿	Colt SS	3-06	❑	D-PAMGAS	Cameron N-90	3-06
❑	G-PURE		Colt 70SS Can	3-06	❑	N413JB	Cameron O-84	3-06
❑	G-PYLN		Colt 80SS	3-06	❑	OO-BRM	Thunder Ax7-77	3-06
❑	G-RARE		Thunder Ax5-42	3-06	❑	OO-JAT	Cameron Zero 25	3-06
❑	G-RIPS		Colt 110SS	3-06	❑	VH-AYY	Kavanagh D-77	3-06

Jim Pearce: Another recovery from Russia has arrived and the Fw 189 has returned.

❑	2100*	Fw 189A-1	G-BZKY, ex Sandown, Sandtoft, Lancing, USSR,	
	'V7+1H'		Luftwaffe. Crashed 4-5-43. Stored. Arrived 6-04	6-04
❑	3523	Bf 109E-7	ex Russia, 5/JG5 'CS+ÁJ'. Crashed 3-4-42	12-03
❑	44-2911*	P-39Q Airacobra	ex Russia. Arrived 1-05	1-05

LITTLEHAMPTON on the A259 west of Worthing

Frank Matthews: No update on the Islander project.

| ❑ | VQ-SAC | BN-2A Islander | ex Shoreham. Crashed 4-9-76. Forward fuselage. | ® | 3-94 |

LONDON (GATWICK) AIRPORT

Airport: Comet 4B G-APMB and Tirdent 3B G-AWZX were scrapped in June 2004.

❑	[G-ARWG]	Condor	uncompleted project. Fuselage, stored	6-05
❑	G-AXGU	Condor	crashed 31-3-75. Fuselage, stored	6-05
❑	G-CEXP	Herald 209	ex Skyview, ChanEx, I-ZERC, G-BFRJ, 4X-AHO.	
			Skyview colours. Towing and rescue training	10-05

Skyview Visitors Centre: The nose of Comet C.2R 'G-AMXA' (XK655) was removed from the centre on 28th November 2004 and settled back at Hatch, Beds.

SHOREHAM (BRIGHTON CITY) AIRPORT

(Another airport playing with its name, with the history that this place seeps, it's hardly needed.)

Visitor Centre and **Shoreham Airport Historical Association**: Located near the entrance to the 1930s terminal building, a wide array of archives and artefacts are on show. The 'Flea' was built during 2001 by friends and is used as a travelling exhibit [1]. Construction of the Piffard Humming Bird of 1910 began during early 2004 [2].

◆ *Open daily 10am to 5pm. Guided tours on Tue, Thu and Sat from 1pm - booking essential. 14J Cecil Pashley Way, Shoreham Airport, Shoreham-by-Sea, BN43 5FF. tel 01273 441061 e-mail saha.archive@virgin.net www.thearchivesshoreham.co.uk*

❑	–	BAPC.20	Lee-Richards	ex Winthorpe, *Those Magnificent Men...*		
			Annular REP	350cc Douglas for ground-running		3-06
❑	–	BAPC.277	HM.14 'Flea'	see above	[1]	3-06
❑	–*	BAPC.300	Humming Bird rep	1910 biplane flown from Shoreham	[2]	3-06
❑	WZ820*	Grasshopper TX.1		ex Northampton, Shoreham, Lancing College. Arr 4-06	[1]	**due**

Elsewhere: The prototype Beagle 206 returned to its birthplace in May 2005. Owned by the Brooklands Museum (see Brooklands, Surrey), but recently on loan to the Bristol Aero Collection, it will undertake a five year restoration programme [1]. With the Tornado proudly 'guarding' the Transair shop [2], Wessex HC.2 XR517 made the long trek to Langford Lodge, N Ireland, arriving there on 31st March 2004. *W&R19* (p214) charted the sale of the contents of the **Museum of D-Day Aviation**. Only the Typhoon cockpit is unaccounted for.

Previously on the fire dump, Cessna F.150F G-ATRL was acquired by a military vehicle group to 'help' in their set-pieces. Painted in Luftwaffe markings as 'D+5' and named *Helga*, it is used as a travelling 'exhibit' and backdrop for the vehicles. Does anyone know where it 'lives'? Talking of the fire dump, a Cessna 150 still lingers, but it is not known if it is G-BPRP or N6819F [3].

Departures: Condor G-ASRB is believed to have moved on to Ireland. Aztec 250E G-BAXP on the dump (last noted 5-03) had perished by 2005. Navajo P G-BWDE was exported to the USA in December 2005. Enstrom 280FX G-CKCK departed for Bournemouth, Dorset, by February 2004. Whing Ding II G-MBTS (and its container) moved off, perhaps to the Horsham area. Hughes 269B G-REBL (11-05) thought exported. Strikemaster Mk.80 1107 arrived from Ipswich, Suffolk, on 28th January 2005 for storage. It left in a container on 29th March 2006 – destination unknown.

❏ G-ARRM*	Beagle 206-1X	ex Kemble, Banwell, Brooklands, Shoreham, Duxford, Shoreham. CoA 28-12-64. Arr 23-5-05	® [1]	3-06
❏ G-BAUA*	Aztec 250D	ex N6718Y. CoA 27-7-92. Stored		3-06
❏ G-BHEH	Cessna 310G	ex Bagby, N1720, N8916Z. CoA 9-12-96. Dump		3-06
❏ G-BPRP	Cessna 150E	ex N3569J. CoA 23-5-98. Dump	[3]	3-06
❏ G-THUG*	MD 600N	ex G-RHUG. Crashed 27-8-00. Wreck		3-06
❏ N6819F	Cessna 150F	Dump	[3]	3-06
❏ XX947	Tornado P.03	ex Ipswich, Cosford 8979M, St Athan, Marham, Warton	[2]	3-06

Northbrook College: Located on the airport site. T-6G 51-14526 (G-BRWB) moved to Denmark in 2002. T-6G '2807' G-BHTH became G-TEXN in June 2005 and took to the air again on 1st November 2005. Last noted in March 2000, the fuselage of Archer 181 G-OBUS is thought to have been scrapped.

❏ G-AWKX	Queen Air A65	CoA 25-10-89	3-06
❏ G-BOIU*	TB-10 Tobago	crashed 28-8-04. Cockpit	2-06
❏ G-OBUS	Archer 181	ex G-BMTT, N3002K. Crashed 18-4-89. Fuselage	3-00
❏ G-SACD*	Cessna F.172H	ex G-AVCD. CoA 27-7-00	3-06
❏ G-TOBY	Cessna 172B	ex Sandown, G-ARCM, N6952X. Dam 15-10-83	3-06
❏ WT806	Hunter GA.11	ex Ipswich, Shawbury, Abingdon, Chivenor, FRADU, CFS, 14.	3-06
❏ XX475*	Jetstream T.2	ex Boscombe D, 750, AAEE, N1036S, G-AWVJ.Arr 30-11-05	3-06
❏ XX491*	'K' Jetstream T.1	ex Ipswich, Culdrose, Cranwell, 45, 3 FTS, 45, 6 FTS, METS. Arrived 10-11-05	3-06

TANGMERE south of the A27, east of Chichester

Tangmere Military Aviation Museum: Hunter WP190 and Lightning 'XR753', donated by Raymond and Meryl Hansed, have been in store since their arrival in 2002, pending the completion of a dedicated display building. This was ready in mid-2005 and on 30th June the Hunter was rolled in, followed by the Lightning a month later. The hangar was officially dedicated as the Meryl Hansed Memorial Hall on 1st April 2006. WP190 has been to Tangmere before. It was delivered to 1 Squadron there in August 1955. The Lightning is in the markings of F.6 XR753 'A', 23 Squadron. The *real* XR753 can be found at Coningsby, Lincs [1].

Notes: The Swift, while an operational version, stands handsomely for the record breaking of Mike Lithgow. EE459, WB188, WK281 and the newly-arrived XV408 are on loan from the RAF Museum – [2]. The Meteor F.8 is a complex composite, including items from VZ530, and includes a rare IFR probe [3]. The Hunter F.4 nose is on loan from 1254 Squadron ATC, Godalming. The rest of that Hunter became T.68 J-4201 of the Swiss Air Force and is still extant [4].

◆ *Signposted from the A27. Open daily 10am to 5.30pm from Mar to Oct and 10am to 4.30pm in February and November. Closed Dec and Jan. Parties at other times by arrangement. Tangmere Airfield, Chichester, PO20 6ES tel 01243 775223 fax 01243 789490 e-mail tangmere@aol.com www.tangmere-museum.org.uk*

❏ 'K5054'	Spitfire proto FSM	BAPC.214, ex Southampton, Hendon, Thruxton, Middle Wallop, Thruxton, Andover	4-06
❏ 'L1679' 'JX-G'	Hurricane FSM	BAPC.241, ex Chilbolton, Middle Wallop, Thruxton. 1 Sqn colours. Built by AeroFab	4-06

☐	P3179		Hurricane I	ex Hove, 43. Shot down 30-8-40. Cockpit	4-06
☐	'BL924'	'AZ-G'	Spitfire FSM	BAPC.242, *Valdemar Atterdag*, 234 Sqn colours	4-06
☐	EE549		Meteor IV Special	ex Cosford, St Athan, Abingdon, Hendon, St Athan, Innsworth, Innsworth 7008M, Fulbeck, Cranwell, CFE,FCCS,RAFHSF [2]	4-06
☐	'WA829'	'A'	Meteor F.8	WA984, ex Southampton, Wimborne, Tarrant Rushton, 211 AFS, 19. IFR probe. 245 Sqn colours [3]	4-06
☐	WB188		Hawker P.1067 (Hunter F.3)	ex Cosford, St Athan, Colerne, Melksham, Halton 7154M, Hawker. Hunter prototype [2]	4-06
☐	WK281	'S'	Swift FR.5	ex Hendon, St Athan, Swinderby, Finningley, Colerne 7712M, Northolt, 79. 79 Sqn colours [2]	4-06
☐	WP190	'K'	Hunter F.5	ex Quedgeley, Hucclecote, Stanbridge 8473M, Upwood, Finningley, Bircham Newton 7582M, Nicosia, 1. 1 Sqn colours, Suez stripes [1]	4-06
☐	WV332		Hunter F.4	7673M, ex Godalming, Dunsfold G-9-406, Halton, 234, 112, 67. 234 Squadron colours. Nose [4]	4-06
☐	XJ580	'131'	Sea Vixen FAW.2	ex Christchurch, Bournemouth FRL, RAE Farnborough, Llanbedr, 899. 899 Sqn c/s ®	4-06
☐	XN299	'758'	Whirlwind HAS.7	ex Southsea, Higher Blagdon, Culdrose, JWE Old Sarum, Fleetlands, 847 'B' Flt, 847, Culdrose, 848. 848 Sqn c/s, *Bulwark. The Iron Chicken*	4-06
☐	'XR753'	'I'	Lightning F.53	ZF578, ex Quedgeley, Cardiff-Wales, Warton, RSAF 53-670, G-27-40. 23 Squadron c/s [1]	4-06
☐	XS511*	'YM'	Wessex HU.5	ex Gosport, A2660 [2], A2750, Lee-on-Solent, 845. Arrived by 11-04	4-06
☐	XV408*		Phantom FGR.2	ex Fairford, Halton 9165M, Cranwell, Wattisham, 92, 29, 23, 228 OCU. Arrived 30-11-05 [2]	4-06
☐	19252		T-33A-1-LO	ex Hailsham, Sculthorpe, French AF. USAF c/s	4-06

WASHINGTON east of the A24 north of Worthing
W&R19 (p216) reported Prospector G-ARDG leaving here by road in April 2002, possibly bound for New Zealand. Unless it's gone and come back again, which is doubted, it turned up at <u>Redhill</u>, Surrey, by April 2005.

WEST CHILTINGTON on the B2139 south of Horsham
Adrian Brook: G-AGOY will fly in prototype colours when complete.

☐	G-AGOY		Messenger 3	ex Hatch, Southill, Castletown, EI-AGE, HB-EIP, G-AGOY, U-0247. ®	1-00

WARWICKSHIRE

BAXTERLEY AERODROME south of the A5 near Atherstone
Midland Warplane Museum (MWM) / **Midland Aircraft Recovery Group**: During 2005 the group were presented with a fuselage section from AW Whitley V BD205 which had been used as a goat shelter at a North Wales farm. This joins the centre sections and other parts from Mk.Vs N1498 and BD232. None of this amounts to enough for a 'formal' listing – as yet. The Oxford – identity now confirmed - is stored off-site and is available for exchange or sale [1]. The Harvard has the constructor's number 14-2441 with a build date of 11th January 1944. That would make it *possibly* former 3 FTS Mk.IIB KF741. Comments, folks? [2]
◆ *Visits possible by prior appointment only. Mark J Evans, Spring View, Crackley Lane, Kenilworth, CV8 2JS e-mail mark.evans@coupland.com*

☐	Z1206		Wellington IV	ex Isle of Lewis, 104 OTU, 142. Cr 26-1-44. Forward fuse	3-06
☐	EB518		Oxford V	ex Canada off-site [1]	3-06
☐	–		Harvard IIB	cockpit section. Stored, off site [2]	3-06

Others:

❑ G-AOES*	Tiger Moth	ex T6056, Waddington SF, Benson SF, 18 EFTS.		
		Crashed 26-9-99		10-05
❑ G-APGL	Tiger Moth	ex Fairoaks, NM140, LAS, AOPS, 14 RFS, 8 RFS, 8 EFTS,		
		3 EFTS, 22 EFTS, 3 EFTS, ORTU, Tarrant Rushton SF	®	3-00
❑ –	Tiger Moth	ex Cranfield, VAT et al		7-02

BIDFORD AERODROME or Bickmarsh, north-east of Evesham south of Bidford-on-Avon

Avon Soaring Centre: Rhonadler DYR was flying by early 2004. Of the other *W&R* items, a good search in July 2005 revealed nothing: Rallye G-BAOM (last noted 2-04); Ka.7 DYK (9-99) and Blanik BGA.2121 (5-98).

❑ G-BGKC	Rallye 110ST	CoA 8-9-99. Stored	10-05

COVENTRY (WEST MIDLANDS) AIRPORT (BAGINTON)

Midland Air Museum (MAM), incorporating the **Sir Frank Whittle Jet Heritage Centre**: The arrival of the Sabre, on a minimum of ten years loan from the IWM, Duxford, is quite a coup for MAM. (If somewhat perplexing from an IWM Duxford point of view – see under that heading for some musings.) [1] During mid-2004 Dove G-ALCU was repainted in the colours of a Dove 2B operated locally by Dunlop [2].

Notes: See under Keevil, Wilts, for 'another' BGA.804 [3]. Prentice VS623 is fitted with the wings from G-AONB (VR244) [4]. Meteor NF.14 WS838 is on loan from the RAF Museum [5]. The Gannet T.2 is on loan from FAAM [6]. The Buccaneer nose section, a Gulf War veteran, is on loan from Robin Phipps [7] - see also under Steventon, Oxfordshire. The Beaufighter nose section is possibly Mk.VI T5298. In which case it was previously 4552M and TFU Defford [8]. The HH-43B uses parts from 24538, including the fins [9]. See under Bristol, Glos, for MAM's Beagle 206.

◆ *Well signed from the A45/A423 junction. Open Apr to Oct Mon to Sat 10am to 5pm, Sun and Bank Hols 10am to 6pm. Nov to Mar daily 10am to 4.30pm. Closed Xmas and Boxing Day. Other times by appointment. Coventry Airport, Rowley Road, Baginton, Coventry CV8 3AZ tel / fax 024 76 301033 e-mail midlandairmuseum@aol.com www.midlandairmuseum.org.uk*

❑ G-EBJG	Pixie III	ex Coventry, Stratford. CoA 2-10-36. Remains			4-06
❑ G-ABOI	Wheeler Slymph	ex Coventry, Old Warden. On loan. Stored			4-06
❑ G-AEGV	HM.14 'Flea'	ex Coventry, Knowle, Northampton, Sywell			4-06
❑ 'G-ALVD'	Dove 2	G-ALCU, ex airfield, VT-CEH. Dunlop c/s. CoA 16-3-73		[2]	4-06
❑ G-APJJ	Fairey Ultra Light	ex Heaton Chapel, Coventry, Hayes. CoA 1-4-59.			4-06
❑ G-APRL	Argosy 101	ex ABC/Elan, Sagittair, N890U, N602Z,			
		N6507R, G-APRL. *Edna*. CoA 23-3-87			4-06
❑ G-APWN	Whirlwind Srs 3	ex Cranfield, Redhill, VR-BER, G-APWN,			
		5N-AGI, G-APWN. CoA 17-5-78. Bristows c/s			4-06
❑ G-ARYB	HS.125 Srs 1	ex Hatfield. CoA 22-1-68			4-06
❑ G-MJWH	Vortex 120	hang glider, former microlight			4-06
❑ – BGA.804	Cadet TX.1	ex VM589. Stored		[3]	4-06
❑ – BAPC.9	Humber Mono REP	ex Birmingham Airport, Yeovilton, Wroughton,			
		Yeovilton, Coventry			4-06
❑ – BAPC.32	Tom Thumb	ex Coventry, Bewdley, Coventry, Banbury.			
		Unfinished 1930s homebuild. Stored			4-06
❑ – BAPC.126	Turbulent	ex Shoreham, Croydon. Static airframe			4-06
❑ 'A7317'	Pup REP	BAPC.179, ex Waltham Abbey, North Weald, *Wings*			4-06
❑ EE531	Meteor F.4	ex Bentham, Coventry , Birmingham, Weston			
		Park, B'ham, RAE Lasham, 7090M, AAEE, makers			4-06
❑ VF301	Vampire F.1	ex Stoneleigh, Debden, 7060M, 208 AFS, 595,			
	'RAL-G'	226 OCU. 605 Sqn colours			4-06
❑ VS623	Prentice T.1	G-AOKZ, ex Shoreham, Redhill, Southend,			
		VS623, CFS, 2 FTS, 22 FTS	®	[4]	4-06
❑ VT935	BP P. 111A	ex Cranfield, RAE Bedford			4-06
❑ VZ477	Meteor F.8	ex Kimbolton, 7741M, APS, 245. Nose			4-06
❑ WF922	Canberra PR.3	ex Cambridge, 39, 69, 58, 82. Restn completed mid-2005			4-06

❑	WH646	'EG'	Canberra T.17A	ex Wyton, 360, 45, RNZAF, 45, 10, 50. Nose	4-06
❑	WS838		Meteor NF.14	ex Cosford, Manchester, Cosford, Shawbury,	
				Colerne, RAE Bedford, RRE, MoS, 64, 238 OCU	[5] 4-06
❑	WV797	'491'	Sea Hawk FGA.6	ex Perth, Culdrose A2637, Halton 8155M,	
				Sydenham, 738, 898, 899, Fleetlands, 787	4-06
❑	XA508	'627'	Gannet T.2	ex Yeovilton, Manadon, A2472, 737. 737 Sqn c/s	[6] 4-06
❑	XA699		Javelin FAW.5	ex Cosford, Locking, 7809M, Shawbury, Kemble,	
				Shawbury, 5, 151. 5 Squadron colours	4-06
❑	XD626		Vampire T.11	ex Bitteswell, Shawbury, CATCS, CNCS,	
				5 FTS, RAFC, CFS. Stored	4-06
❑	XE855		Vampire T.11	ex Upton-by-Chester, Woodford, Chester, 27 MU,	
				22 MU, 10 MU, AWOCU. Pod, spares	4-06
❑	XF382	'15'	Hunter F.6A	ex Brawdy, 1 TWU, TWU, 229 OCU, FCS, 65, 63, 92	4-06
❑	'XG190'		Hunter F.51	E-425, ex Dunsfold, G-9-446, DanAF Esk.724	
				111 Sqn 'Black Arrows' colours	4-06
❑	XJ579		Sea Vixen FAW.2	ex Farnborough, AAEE, Llanbedr, 899, 766. Nose	4-06
❑	XK789		Grasshopper TX.1	ex Warwick, Cosford, Stamford	4-06
❑	XK907		Whirlwind HAS.7	ex Bubbenhall, Panshanger, Elstree, Luton,	
				ETPS, RRE, Alvis. Cockpit. Stored	4-06
❑	XL360		Vulcan B.2	ex 44, 101, 35, 617, 230 OCU, Wadd Wing, 230 OCU,	
				Scamp W, 617. *City of Coventry*. 617 Sqn c/s	4-06
❑	XN685		Sea Vixen FAW.2	ex Chester, Cosford, Cranwell, 8173M, 890, 766, 893, HSA	4-06
❑	XR771	'BM'	Lightning F.6	ex Binbrook, 5, 11, 5, 56, 74	4-06
❑	XX899		Buccaneer S.2B	ex Kidlington, Stock, St Athan, Lossiemouth, 208, 12,	
				Gulf Det, 237 OCU, 12, 237 OCU, 12, 237 OCU, 16, 15,	
				12, 208. Nose	® [7] 4-06
❑	ZE694*		Sea Harrier FA.2	ex Yeovilton, 801, 800, 801, 800, 801, 899, 800,801, 800.	
				Arrived 16-2-05	4-06
❑	–		Beaufighter	ex Birmingham, Coventry. Cockpit	[8] 4-06
❑	R-756		F-104G	ex Aalborg, Danish AF, 64-17756	® 4-06
❑	'GN-101'		Gnat F.1	XK741, ex Leamington Spa, Fordhouses, Dunsfold, Hamble,	
				Boscombe Down, Dunsfold. Fuselage. *Kreivi von Rosen*.	
				Finnish AF c/s	4-06
❑	70		Mystère IVA	ex Sculthorpe, Fr AF. *Patrouille de France* colours	4-06
❑	51-4419		T-33A-1-LO	ex Sculthorpe, French AF. Blue with shark's mouth	4-06
❑	17473		T-33A-1-LO	ex Cosford, Sculthorpe, French AF	4-06
❑	54-2174	'SM'	F-100D-16-NA	ex Sculthorpe, French AF. *Mary Jane*. USAF c/s	4-06
❑	280020		Fl 282B V-20	ex Coventry, Cranfield, Brize Norton, Travemünde 'CJ+SN'.	
				Frame	4-06
❑	959		MiG-21SPS	ex Duxford, Cottbus, LSK	4-06
❑	408		Iskra 100	ex airfield, Scampton, Duxford, Polish AF. On loan	4-06
❑	55-713	'C'	Lightning T.55	ex Warton, ZF598, RSAF 55-713, G-27-72. Saudi c/s	4-06
❑	29640	'08'	SAAB J29F	ex Southend, R Swedish AF	4-06
❑	0242*	'FU-242'	F-86A-5-NA	N196B, ex Duxford, Chino, 48-0242. Arrived 22-4-05	[1] 4-06
❑	24535		HH-43B Huskie	ex Woodbridge, 40 ARRS, Det 2. Stored	[9] 4-06
❑	37414		F-4C-15-MC	ex Woodbridge, New York ANG. Stored	4-06
❑	37699	'CG'	F-4C-21-MC	ex Upper Heyford, Fairford, Illinois ANG, 557 TFS,	
				356 TFS, 480 TFS. 366th TFW c/s, MiG 'kill'	4-06
❑	60312		F-101B-80-MC	ex Alconbury, Davis-Monthan, Kentucky ANG	4-06
❑	58-2062		U-6A Beaver	ex Mannheim, US Army	4-06
❑	–*		Mi-24 *Hind-D*	ex Rochester, Chester, Latvia, USSR, '06' red.	
				(353246405029) Arrived 15-9-05	4-06

Warwickshire and Coventry Airport wend their merry way after the second photo-spread, on page 257...

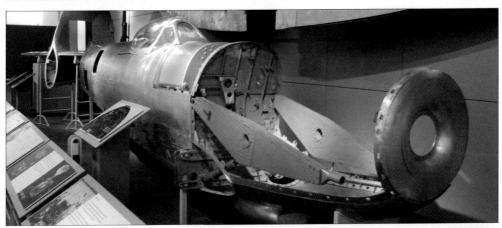

GREATER LONDON

P-51D Mustang '413317'
Hendon, November 2004
Dave Willis

Spitfire F.22 PK664
South Kensington, December 2005
Mark Roberts - Aerobilia

Dakota IV '448'
South Kensington, December 2005
Mark Roberts - Aerobilia

GREATER MANCHESTER

Jet Provost T.3 XM474
Levenshulme (here at *CockpitFest*),
June 2005
Sam Tyler

Trident 3B G-AWZK
Manchester, January 2006
Tim R Badham

Concorde 102 G-BOAC
Manchester Airport, January 2006
Tim R Badham

GREATER MANCHESTER

ATP G-BTZG
Woodford, July 2004
Jon Wickenden

ATP (Jetstream 61) G-PLXI
Woodford, July 2004
Jon Wickenden

MERSEYSIDE

Dragon Rapide FSM 'G-ANZP'
Liverpool, July 2005
Ken Ellis

WEST MIDLANDS

Aztec 250F G-SHIP
Hockley Heath, January 2006
Andrew Powell

NORFOLK

Apache 160H G-ASMY
Beccles, October 2005
Les Wild

Hunter T.7 XF321, Shackleton T.4
VP293 (see Coventry, Warks),
Jaguar T.2A XX830, Jaguar GR.1
XZ375, Lightning F.6 XS899
Coltishall, September 2005
Dave Willis

229

NORFOLK

Tornado GR.1s ZA361, ZA322,
ZA375 and Canberra PR.9 XH168
Marham, July 2005
Don Nind

Jaguar GR.1 XX109
Norwich, October 2005
Don Nind

NORTHAMPTONSHIRE

BE.2 REP G-AWYI
Northampton, October 2005
Alf Jenks

NORTHAMPTONSHIRE

'Gunbus' FSM 'A1452'
Northampton, January 2006
Ben Brown

NOTTINGHAMSHIRE

Lightning F.2A XN728
Balderton, January 2005
Mike Cain

Viking TX.1 ZE686
Syerston, May 2004
Mark Harris

NOTTINGHAMSHIRE

Beverley C.1 XB261
Winthorpe, May 2005
Alf Jenks

Gnat T.1 XR534
Winthorpe, May 2005
Alf Jenks

Sea Harrier FA.2 ZA176
Winthorpe, May 2005
Alf Jenks

NORTHUMBERLAND AND TYNESIDE

Vampire T.11 XD602
South Shields (here at *CockpitFest*)
June 2005
Sam Tyler

OXFORDSHIRE

Harrier GR.3 XV744
Shrivenham, May 2005
Roger Cook

AH-1F Cobra 69-16445
Shrivenham, May 2005
Roger Cook

OH-58C Kiowa

OXFORDSHIRE

OH-58CR Kiowa 70-15154
Shrivenham, May 2005
Roger Cook

SHROPSHIRE

Viscount 701 G-AMOG
Cosford, January 2006
Tim R Badham

Dakota C.4 KN645
Cosford, December 2005
Alf Jenks

234

SHROPSHIRE

Valiant BK.1 XD818
Cosford, January 2006
Tim R Badham

F-111F 74-0177
Cosford, January 2006
Tim R Badham

Farman F.41 F-HMFI (foreground)
LVG C.VI 7198/18
Cosford, January 2006
Tim R Badham

SHROPSHIRE

Gazelle HT.3 XZ935
Cosford, June 2005
Les Wild

Tornado GR.1 ZA323
Cosford, June 2005
Les Wild

Dakota III KG651
Shawbury, November 2004
Tim R Badham

236

SHROPSHIRE

Wessex HU.5 XT773
Shawbury, October 2005
Mark Harris

Jaguars (left to right): GR.1A
XX741, T.2A XX144, GR.1A
XX955 and GR.3 XZ361
Shawbury, July 2005
Mark A Jones

SOMERSET

Husband Hornet
Weston-super-Mare, March 2005
Tony McCarthy

SOMERSET

Kamov Ka-26 DDR-SPY
Weston-super-Mare, July 2004
Andrew Powell

Lynx 3 EMU
Weston-super-Mare, July 2004
Andrew Powell

Part of The Helicopter Museum's
Reserve Collection
Weston-super-Mare, September 2005
Alf Jenks

238

SOMERSET

Corsair IV KD431
Yeovilton, April 2004
Bob Turner

View of Cobham Hall
Yeovilton, April 2005
Peter Budden

Sea Hawk FGA.4 WV903 and
FGA.6 XE339
Yeovilton, June 2005
Steve Screech

SOMERSET

Wessex HU.5 XS513
Yeovilton, February 2004
Bob Turner

Harrier GR.3 XV755
Yeovilton, June 2005
Steve Screech

SUFFOLK

Hunter F.6 XG210
Beck Row, October 2005
Don Nind

SUFFOLK

Jenny Wren G-ASRF
Flixton, July 2005
Alf Jenks

Taylor Titch G-BABY
Flixton, May 2005
Jon Wickenden

Rooster 1 G-MJVI
Flixton, May 2005
Sam Tyler

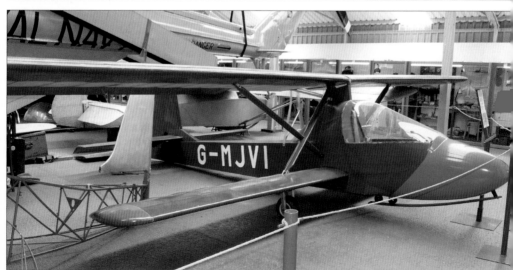

241

SUFFOLK

Felixstowe F.5
Flixton, August 2004
Hugh Trevor

Sea Harrier FA.2 ZA175
Flixton, May 2005
Jon Wickenden

SURREY

Merchantman G-APEP
Brooklands, January 2006
Mark Roberts - Aerobilia

SURREY

TSR-2 EMU
Brooklands, January 2006
Mark Roberts - Aerobilia

Sea Prince T.1s WP308 and WF118
plus Gannet AEW.3 XL472
Sam Tyler

WEST SUSSEX

Condors G-ARWG and G-AXGU
London Gatwick Airport,
January 2005
Alistair Ness

WARWICKSHIRE

Dove 2 'G-ALVD'
Coventry, September 2005
Alf Jenks

Mi-24 Hind-D
Coventry, November 2005
Tim R Badham

Iskra 100 408
Coventry, September 2005
Alf Jenks

WARWICKSHIRE

F-86A 0242
Coventry, November 2005
Tim R Badham

Venom FB.50s J-1629 and J-1649
Coventry, November 2005
Tim R Badham

Scout AH.1 XV136
Netheravon, May 2005
Roger Cook

WILTSHIRE

Scout AH.1 XP859
Boscombe Down, January 2006
David J Burke

Jaguars GR.1 XX761 and
S.06 XW560
Boscombe Down, January 2006
David J Burke

Sea Harrier FA.2 XZ457
Boscombe Down, January 2006
David J Burke

WORCESTERSHIRE

Cessna 150J 'G-BMAF'
Defford, June 2005
Alf Jenks

EAST YORKSHIRE

Hurricane XII G-HURR, Buchón
G-BWUE, P-51D Mustang 472773
Breighton, June 2005
Andy Wood

Delfin '51'
Breighton, June 2005
Tim R Badham

EAST YORKSHIRE

Buccaneer S.2B XV168
Brough, June 2005
Francis Wallace

Cessna U.206Fs G-STAT and
G-BATD
Grindale, June 2004
Andy Wood

Cherokee 160 G-AXRL
(before sinking!)
North Cave, July 2005
Andy Wood

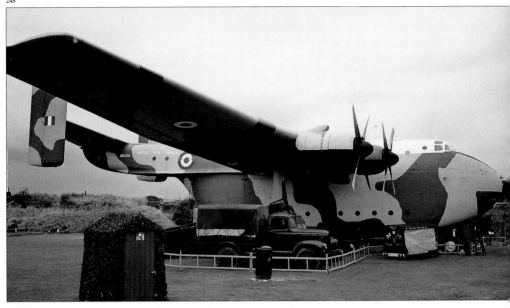

EAST YORKSHIRE

Beverley C.1 XB259
Paull, December 2005
David J Burke

Short 330-200 OY-MUB
Pocklington, October 2005
Andy Wood

NORTH YORKSHIRE

Norecrin II G-BHXJ
Carthorpe, October 2005
Andy Wood

NORTH YORKSHIRE

Spitfire FSM 'AB550' and
Hurricane FSM 'P2793'
Malton, August 2005
Andy Wood

Blackburn Monoplane REP BAPC.130
Elvington, September 2004
Sam Tyler

NORTH YORKSHIRE

Tornado GR.1 ZA354
and GR.4 XZ631
Elvington, July 2005
Ian Haskell

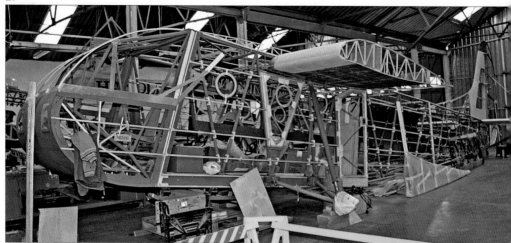

NORTH YORKSHIRE

CG-4A Hadrian '237123'
Elvington, February 2006
Tim R Badham

Jet Provost T.3 XN458
Northallerton, October 2005
Andy Wood

SOUTH YORKSHIRE

Robinson R.22 EI-JWM
Doncaster, December 2005
Roger Richards

SOUTH YORKSHIRE

AV-8B Harrier II 162068
Doncaster, December 2005
Roger Richards

SCOTLAND

Draken Fv 35075
Dumfries, October 2005
David Johnstone jnr

SCOTLAND

Lightning F.53 ZF584
Edinburgh, September 2005
Francis Wallace

SCOTLAND

Harrier T.2 or T.4
Haddington, August 2005
Ian Sheffield

Herald 214 G-ASVO
Inverness, April 2005
Tony McCarthy

Warrior 151 G-BCIE
Perth, April 2004
David S Johnstone

SCOTLAND

Scout AH.1 XR627
Townhill, January 2006
David Johnstone jnr

WALES

Vampire T.11 XE852
Chester, October 2005
David S Johnstone

VFW-614 D-ASDB
St Athan, November 2004
Mark Harris

WALES

Jet Provost T.4 XS180
St Athan, November 2004
Mark Harris

NORTHERN IRELAND

Short 330 G-BDBS and Buccaneer
S.2B XV361
Leaving Langford Lodge,
January 2006
Eric Gray

Sea Hawk FB.3 WN108
Leaving Langford Lodge,
December 2005
Eric Gray

NORTHERN IRELAND

Buccaneer S.2B XV361
Leaving Langford Lodge,
January 2006
Eric Gray

IRELAND

Chipmunk T.20s 199 and 172,
and CM-170-2 221
Casement, August 2005
Mark Harris

Boeing 737-204 EI-CJD
Dublin, July 2005
Ian Haskell

IRELAND

Aircoupe 415C EI-CGG
Weston, August 2004
Seamus Mooney

CYPRUS

Wessex HC.2 XR504
Akrotiri, April 2005
Mark Harris

Lightning F.6 XS929
Akrotiri, April 2005
Mark Harris

COVENTRY AIRPORT, continued from page 224...

Air Atlantique Classic Flight: Classic Aviation Projects operates in association with the Classic Flight under the title **Canberra Display Team** [1]. Proctor V G-AKIU is being restored at Seaton Ross, E Yorks, for the Flight. The **Shackleton Preservation Trust** (formerly known as the **963 Support Group**) have made significant progress with WR963, which regularly ground runs. It has had the radome removed and has been painted as an MR.2. Work is currently in hand to assess its capability for flight [2]. (e-mail shack106.chalk@lineone.net) This is a good place to also 'plug' the **Shackleton Association** who serves to unite air and ground crew and all interested in the 'Shack', producing a house magazine, *The Growler*. (Peter Dunn, *Meadow View*, Parks Lane, Prestwood, Great Missenden, Bucks HP16 0JH.)

◆ *All visits by prior arrangement. For details of visits and of membership of the **Air Atlantique Classic Flight Supporters' Club**: Membership Secretary, AACFC, Dakota House, Coventry Airport, Coventry, CV8 3AZ tel 0870 3304747 www.atlanticdhg.com/aacf*

❏	G-AGTM	Dragon Rapide	✈	ex JY-ACL, OD-ABP, G-AGTM, NF875	4-06
❏	G-AIDL	Dragon Rapide	✈	ex Biggin Hill, Allied Airways, TX310	4-06
❏	G-AJRE	J/1 Autocrat	✈	ex 'Suffolk'	4-06
❏	G-AMPY	C-47B-15-DK		ex EI-BKJ ntu, G-AMPY, N15751, G-AMPY, TF-FIO,	
				G-AMPY, JY-ABE, G-AMPY, KN442, 44-76540. Stored	4-06
❏	G-AMSV	C-47B-25-DK	✈	ex F-BSGV ntu, G-AMSV, KN397, 44-76488. Stored	4-06
❏	G-ANAF	C-47B-35-DK	✈	ex Thales, N170GP, Duxford, G-ANAF, KP220, 44-77104.	
				Radar test-bed	4-06
❏	G-APRS	Twin Pioneer 3	✈	ex Staverton, G-BCWF, XT610, G-APRS, PI-C430 ntu.	
				Primrose. 'Raspberry Ripple' c/s.	4-06
❏	G-APSA	DC-6A	✈	ex 4W-ABQ, HZ-ADA, G-APSA, CF-MCK, CF-CZY	4-06
❏	G-AYWA	Avro XIX Srs 2		ex Bridge of Weir, Lochwinnoch, Strathallan,	
				Thruxton, OO-VIT, OO-DFA. Spares	off-site 3-02
❏	G-AZHJ	Twin Pioneer 3		ex Prestwick, Staverton, Prestwick, G-31-16, XP295, Odiham	
				SF, MoA, 1310F, Odiham SF, 230. CoA 23-8-90	off-site 3-02
❏	G-CONV	CV-440-54		ex Atlantic Group, CS-TML, N357SA, N28KE, N4402	4-06
❏	G-JAYI	J/1 Autocrat	✈	ex OY-ALU, D-EGYK, OO-ABF	4-06
❏	G-SIXC	DC-6A/B	✈	ex N93459, N90645, B-1006, XW-PFZ, B-1006	4-06
❏	KK151	C-47B-15-DK	✈	G-AMRA, ex XE280, G-AMRA, KK151, 43-49474.	4-06
❏	TX226	Anson C.19		ex Duxford, Little Staughton, East Dereham, Colerne 7865M,	
				Shawbury, FTCCF, OCTU Jurby, 187, Hemswell SF,	
				Coningsby CF, CBE. Spares	off-site 3-02
❏	TX235	Anson C.19/2		ex Caernarfon, Higher Blagdon, Andover, Shawbury,	
				SCS, FCCS, CTFU, OCTU, 64 GCS, 2 GCS	off-site 3-02
❏	'VN799'*	Canberra T.4	✈	G-CDSX, ex WJ874, Marham, 39,Gaydon SF, Binbrook SF,	
				Coningsby, SF, 231 OCU, HS, RN, FRU, 231 OCU,Wyton,	
				231 OCU, 39 Sqn. Arrived 9-11-05	4-06
❏	VP959	'L' Devon C.2		N959VP, ex Wellesbourne, Biggin Hill, N959VP ntu,	
				G-BWFB, VP959, RAE. Stored	off-site 3-02
❏	VP981	Devon C.2/2	✈	G-DHDV, ex BBMF VP981, Northolt, 207, 21, WCS,	
				Wildenrath CF, AAFCE, MinTech, AAFCE, Paris	
				Air Attaché, Hendon SF, AFWE.	4-06
❏	VR259	'M' Prentice 1	✈	G-APJB, ex VR259, 1 ASS, 2 ASS, RAFC. 2 ASS c/s	4-06
❏	'WD379'	'K' Chipmunk T.10	✈	G-APLO, ex EI-AHU, WB696, 11 RFS, Ab UAS, 11 RFS	4-06
❏	WD413	Anson C.21	✈	G-VROE, ex G-BFIR, Duxford, Lee-on-Solent, Enstone,	
				Tees-side, Strathallan, Bournemouth, East Midlands,	
				Aldergrove 7881M, TCCS, BCCS, 1 ANS	4-06
❏	WK163	Canberra B.2/6	✈	G-BVWC, ex DRA Farnborough, DRA Bedford, RAE,	
				Napier, ASM, MoA. B.2 nose format. 617 Sqn c/s	[1] 4-06
❏	WM167	Meteor TT.20	✈	G-LOSM, ex Bournemouth, Blackbushe, RAE Llanbedr,	
				228, Colerne CS, 228 OCU	4-06
❏	'WR470'	Venom FB.50	✈	G-DHVM, ex G-GONE, Bournemouth, Chester,	
				Bournemouth, Swiss AF J-1542. 'Ace of Clubs'	4-06

❑ WR963	'X'	Shackleton AEW.2	ex SPT, Waddington, Lossiemouth, 8, 205, 28, 210, 224.		
			Ermintrude. 38 Sqn colours	[2]	4-06
❑ WT711	'833'	Hunter GA.11	ex Culdrose A2645, A2731, Shawbury, FRADU, 14, 54		4-06
❑ WZ553	'40'	Vampire T.11	G-DHYY, ex Bournemouth, Bruntingthorpe, Cranfield,		
			Lichfield, Winthorpe, South Wigston, Bruntingthorpe,		
			Loughborough, East Midlands, Liverpool, Woodford,		
			Chester, St Athan, 4 FTS, 7 FTS, 202 AFS	off-site	11-03
❑ 'XJ771'		Vampire T.55 ✈	G-HELV, ex Bournemouth, '215' Sion, Swiss AF		
			U-1215. RAF colours		4-06
❑ XL929		Pembroke C.1	G-BNPU, ex Shoreham, Sandown, Shawbury, 60,		
			Kemble, 207, SCCS, TCCS, FCCS, BCCS	off-site	4-06
❑ XL954		Pembroke C.1 ✈	G-BXES, ex N4234C, Tatenhill, White Waltham,		
			9042M, Northolt, 60, RAFG CS, 2 TAF CS		4-06
❑ XM223		Dove 7	G-BWWC, ex Cumbernauld, West Freugh, DGTE,		
			T&EE, RAE. Wings from Dove 5 G-APSO	off-site	8-02
❑ [J-1629]		Venom FB.50	ex Bournemouth, Dubendorf, Swiss AF. Stored		4-06
❑ [J-1649]		Venom FB.50	ex Bournemouth, Dubendorf, Swiss AF. Stored		4-06

The Atlantic Group / Air Atlantique / Atlantic Aeroengineering / CFS Aeroproducts: Electra LN-FOI was dismantled during the summer of 2004; the cockpit moving to Pershore, Worcs in September.

❑ G-AVDB	Cessna 310L	ex Popham, Perth, N2279F. CoA 8-7-79. Spares	off-site	3-02
❑ G-BWPG	Robin HR.200	ex Inverness. Crashed 29-10-97. Stored	off-site	3-02
❑ G-LOFA	L.188CF Electra	ex Atlantic, N359Q, F-OGST, N359AC, TI-LRM, N359AC,		
		HC-AVX, N359AC, VH-ECA. CoA 9-2-00.		
		Fire service, sectioned		11-02
❑ G-LOFF	L.188CF Electra	ex Fred Olsen LN-FON, N342HA, N417MA, OB-R-1138,		
		HP-684, N417MA, CF-ZST, N7142C. Spares		2-04
❑ G-OFRT	L.188CF Electra	ex Bournemouth, N347HA, N423MA, N23AF,		
		N64405, SE-FGC, N5537. CoA 28-10-01. Spares		5-03
❑ LN-FOL	L.188CF Electra	G-LOFG, ex Fred Olsen, N669F, N404GN,		
		N6126A. Fire compound		2-04
❑ N2RK	L.188C Electra	ex G-LOFI, Reeve Aleutian, CF-NAX, N851U,		
		N33506, ZK-TEB, ZK-BMQ. Stored.		
		Reeve *Illusion* titles!		4-06
❑ [N4HG]	L.188C Electra	ex G-LOFH, Reeve Aleutian, N9744C. Stored		4-06

Others: By September 2004 Iskra 408 was on loan to MAM - see above. Five long-in-the-tooth entries have been deleted, believed long since scrapped: Sierra G-BBXU (last noted July 1997); Cherokee 140F G-BGTS (December 1992); Cherokee 180 G-BHFL (December 1992); Enstrom F.28A G-BMIU and an anonymous example (both February 1998).

❑ G-BDCL	AA-5 Traveler	ex EI-CCI, G-BDCL, EI-BGV, G-BDCL, N1373R.	
		CoA 29-11-93. Stored	3-00
❑ G-BPJF	Tomahawk 112	ex N9312T. Crashed 20-6-98. Dump	3-02
❑ 70270	F-101B-80-MC	ex MAM, Woodbridge, Davis-Monthan, Texas ANG.	
		Nose. Dump	10-00

KING'S COUGHTON on the A435 north of Alcester

❑ G-BBED	Rallye 220	CoA 13-9-87. Stored	11-05
❑ G-MZDI*	Whittaker MW-6S	CoA 2-02. Stored	11-05

LONG MARSTON AERODROME on the B4632, south-west of Stratford-upon-Avon

Jet Aviation Preservation Group (JAPG): Several airframes are on loan: the Dove and Meteor T.7 from Gordon Yates and the Shackleton, Canberra and Whirlwind from the local land owner. They are marked ±. Composite Chipmunk T.10 WP784 continues to make excellent progress [1].

The single-seat Hunter is a complex beast; with an unused F.6 cockpit from Stafford, the centre section of F.6 XG226, the rear end of a Danish T.7 and the wings from PH-NLH. All of this will be completed as an FR.10 [2]. The Gazelle will ultimately become a complete airframe, JAPG have at least 95% of the helicopter in store [3].

◆ *Open summer months on request, please make contact before before visiting/faxTony Holder, 11 Windsor Road, Evesham, Worcs, WR11 4 QE 01386 45401*

❑	G-ANUW	Dove 6	ex Welshpool, North Weald, Stansted, CAFU. CoA 22-7-81	±	4-06
❑	WL332	Meteor T.7	ex SAC, Cardiff-Wales, Croston, Moston, FRU,		
			Lossiemouth SF, Ford SF	±	4-06
❑	WM367	Meteor NF.13	ex Firbeck, North Weald, Powick, Boscombe Down,		
			AWA, MoA. Nose		4-06
❑	WP784	Chipmunk T.10	ex Hemel Hempstead, Wycombe AP, Boston, Holbeach,		
			Wellingborough, Reading, Benson, Abingdon, 6 AEF, Leeds		
			UAS, Abn UAS, 8 FTS, Man UAS, QUAS, Air Att Paris,		
			5 RFS, 17 RFS	® [1]	4-06
❑	WR985	'H' Shack' MR.3/3	ex SAC, Cosford, 8103M, 201,120,206,203,206, AAEE, 206	±	4-06
❑	WT483	'83' Canberra T.4	ex SAC, Filton, Samlesbury, 231 OCU, 39, 231 OCU, 16,		
			Laarbruch SF, 68, Laarbruch SF, 69	±	4-06
❑	WV382	Hunter GA.11	ex Smethwick, Lee-on-Solent, Shawbury, FRADU, 67		4-06
❑	XD447	'50' Vampire T.11	ex SAC, E Kirkby, Tattershall, Woodford, Chester, St Athan,		
			8 FTS, RAFC, 5 FTS	®	4-06
❑	XG737	Sea Ven FAW.22	ex Cardiff-Wales, Yeovilton, FRU, Sydenham, 894, 893, 891		4-06
❑	'XJ714'	Hunter 'FR.10'	composite	® [2]	4-06
❑	XP346	Whirlwind HAR.10	ex Tattershall Thorpe, Shawbury, 8793M, Lee-on-Solent,		
			Akrotiri, 84, 22, 225	±	4-06
❑	XP568	Jet Provost T.4	ex Faygate, Hatfield, Shawbury, RAFC	®	4-06
❑	XX457	'Z' Gazelle AH.1	ex Arborfield, 2 Flt, 662, 656, ARWF, GCF	[3]	4-06
❑	N-315	Hunter T.7	ex Hucclecote, Batley, Amsterdam, NLS spares,		
			RNethAF, XM121		4-06

Others: The Sea Prince is 'gate guardian' for the aerodrome. Mainair Gemini G-MMIR, last noted in June 1998, is believed to have expired.

❑	G-MNBR*	Gemini Flash	CoA 5-2-94. Stored		7-05
❑	G-MYBZ*	Pegasus XL-Q	CoA 27-9-97. Stored		7-05
❑	G-RACA	'571' Sea Prince T.1	ex WM735, Staverton, Kemble, 750, BTU, AAEE		3-06

NUNEATON on the A444 north of Coventry

Ted Gautrey: Is *thought* to continue to restore his Fox Moth.

❑	G-ACCB	Fox Moth	ex Coventry, Redhill, Blackpool, Southport.		
			Ditched 25-9-56.	®	10-95

RUGBY on the A426 east of Coventry

The identity of XR239 [1] is confirmed. The anonymous, former Kenya, Auster AOP.9 moved out in 2004 – destination unknown.

❑	'5964'	DH.2 repro	BAPC.112, ex Middle Wallop, Chertsey. Wreck		5-05
❑	XP244	Auster AOP.9	ex Middle Wallop, Arborfield 7864M 'M7922'. Fuselage		5-05
❑	XR239	Auster AOP.9	ex Popham. Fuselage frame and wings	® [1]	5-05

STONELEIGH on the B4113 south of Coventry

The anonymous spares ship PT-22 had moved on by 2003.

WARWICK on the A429 west of Royal Leamington Spa

As *W&R20* closed for press, the Fleet was close to air-test. Paul Williams *should* still have his gliders.

❑ G-FLCA		Fleet Canuck	ex Baxterley, Chilbolton, Coventry, Rochester,		
			Blackbushe, CS-ACQ, CF-DQP	®	3-06
❑ –		Hutter H.17a	ex Moreton-in-Marsh	®	1-92
❑ –	BAPC.25	Nyborg TGN.III	ex Moreton-in-Marsh, Stratford. Stored		1-92

WELLESBOURNE MOUNTFORD AERODROME south of the B4086, east of Stratford

Wellesbourne Wartime Museum: Operated by the **Wellesbourne Aviation Group**, the Museum charts the history of the airfield centred on the restored underground Battle Headquarters. The Vulcan nose is owned by Paul Hartley [1]. The nose has been placed on a trestle to allow viewing of the cockpit via the crew entry door. Not content with this Vulcan nose, Paul owns the examples at Bournemouth, Dorset, and Bruntingthorpe, Leics!

◆ *Open every Sunday 10am to 4pm and Bank Holidays, same times. Derek Powell, 167 Colebourne Road, Kingsheath, Birmingham, B13 0HB e-mail d.powell@iclway.co.uk*

❑ –		McBroom Argus	hang-glider, built 1974. Stored		3-06
❑ RA-01378		Yak-52	ex DOSAAF '14'		3-06
❑ WV679	'O-J'	Provost T.1	ex Dunkeswell, Higher Blagdon, Halton 7615M, 2 FTS	®	3-06
❑ XA903		Vulcan B.1	ex Sidcup, Cardiff, Farnborough, RB.199 and		
			Olympus test-bed, Blue Steel trials, Avro. Nose	[1]	3-06
❑ XJ575		Sea Vixen FAW.2	ex Long Marston, Helston, Culdrose, A2611, 766. Nose		3-06
❑ XK590	'V'	Vampire T.11	ex Witney, Brize Norton, CATCS, 4 FTS, 7 FTS		3-06

XM655 Maintenance and Preservation Society: Regularly 'run' XM655 is owned by John Littler of Radarmoor, the airfield owners.

◆ *Occasional ground-running days, otherwise by prior arrangement. Derek Powell, see above. www.xm655.com*

| ❑ XM655 | | Vulcan B.2 | G-VULC, ex N655AV ntu, 44, 101, 50, 12, 35, 9 | 3-06 |

Others: Bulldog T.1 XX634 moved to Winthorpe, Notts, on 9th January 2006.

❑ G-APPA		Chipmunk 22	ex Carlisle, Glasgow, N5703E, G-APPA, WP917, Glas UAS,	
			11 RFS, 8 RFS. CoA 10-11-00. Stored, dismantled	6-01
❑ G-BLLV		Slingsby T.67C	wreck	1-02
❑ G-BNIV*		Cessna 152 II	ex N4972P. CoA 17-8-03. Dumped by 5-05	5-05
❑ G-BRML*		Tomahawk	ex N2510P. CoA 3-6-02. Dumped by 5-05	5-05
❑ G-BSYM		Tomahawk II	ex N2507V. Damaged 27-7-94. Dump	6-05
❑ –		Robinson R-44	cabin. Dump	4-03
❑ 'N3320'	'A'	Spitfire FSM	ex Winthorpe. Stored	7-05
❑ XX671	'D'	Bulldog T.1	ex Shawbury, Birm UAS, 2 FTS	1-06

WILTSHIRE

BOSCOMBE DOWN AIRFIELD south of the A303 at Amesbury

Boscombe Down Aviation Collection: The construction of a BE.2c reproduction has been started. Airframes on loan from QinetiQ and/or MoD are marked Δ. Several items from the **Air Defence Collection** are on loan to the project – marked ADC. The Lightning nose section is on loan from Hugh Trevor [1] and John Sharpe owns the 'JP' and a Canberra nose. [2]. The Scout CIM is a complex composite, including parts from XP859 [3].

Departures: Canberra PR.7 nose WT534 to Doncaster, S Yorks, by 12-04; Hunter F.6 XE601 to Exeter, Devon, 27-5-04; Hunter T.7 XL609 nose moved to Yarmouth, Isle of Wight, by 12-05; MiG-21MF 7708 crated for export to Ohio, USA 9-04; FMA Pucará nose A-533 moved to Cheltenham, Glos. Alpha Jet SIM '4401' was exported to the USA in mid-2005.

◆ *Not open to the public, may be available by prior arrangement. c/o RAF Unit, Boscombe Down, SP4 0JF www.boscombedownaviationcollection.org*

❏	P3554		Hurricane I	ex Salisbury, Swanage, 607, 213, 56, 32.		
				Shot down 5-10-40. *Jessamy*	off-site ADC	3-06
❏	–		Typhoon	ex Salisbury. Cockpit project	off-site ADC	3-06
❏	WH779		Canberra PR.7	ex Farnborough, Marham, RAE, 100,13,31,80,13,542. Nose	[2]	3-06
❏	WH876		Canberra B.2(m)	ex Aberporth, Boscombe Down, AAEE, 73, 207, 115. Nose		3-06
❏	WN890*		Hunter F.2	ex Doncaster, Firbeck, Robertsbridge, Stamford, Hedge		
				End, Boscombe D, AAEE, AWA. Nose. Arr 6-05	ADC	3-06
❏	WT648		Hunter F.1	ex Salisbury, Kexborough, Stock, St Athan		
				7530M, DFLS. Nose	ADC	3-06
❏	WT859		Supermarine 544	ex Long Marston, Brooklands, Ruislip, Foulness, Culdrose,		
				Fleetlands, Culdrose, Lee-on-S A2499, RAE. Nose	®	3-06
❏	[WV910]		Sea Hawk FGA.4	ex DERA, DRA, ETPS, 806. Damaged 2-5-58. Nose		3-06
❏	XF113		Swift F.7	ex Salisbury, Bath, Frome, Farnborough, ETPS,		
				AAEE, HS. Nose	ADC ®	3-06
❏	XF994	'873'	Hunter T.8C	ex Apprentices, Shawbury, Yeovilton, FRADU, 759,		
				229 OCU, AFDS, 66	Δ	3-06
❏	XG290		Hunter F.6	ex Salisbury, Bournemouth, B'thorpe, Swanton Morley, Bentley		
				Priory, Halton 8711M, Laarbruch SF, AAEE. Nose	ADC	3-06
❏	XL564		Hunter T.7	ex ETPS, HS, 229 OCU, Hawker. Crashed 6-8-98. Nose.		
				For spares recovery only		3-06
❏	XN503*		Jet Provost T.3A	ex Haverfordwest, Milford Haven, Salisbury, Firbeck,		
				Coventry, Bicester, Kemble, RAFEF, 4 FTS, 2 FTS,		
				6 FTS, AAEE. Nose. Arrived 10-04	® [2]	3-06
❏	XN726		Lightning F.2A	ex Rayleigh, Foulness, Farnborough, 8545M,		
				Gütersloh, 92, 19. Nose	® [1]	3-06
❏	XP959		Scout AH.1	ex Middle Wallop CIM, AETW. Composite	[3]	3-06
❏	XR650	'28'	Jet Provost T.4	ex DERA, Halton 8459M, SoRF, CAW, CATCS, 3 FTS,		
				CAW, 7 FTS		3-06
❏	XS790		Andover CC.2	ex DERA, Queen's Flight. Nose	®	3-06
❏	XT437	'423'	Wasp HAS.1	ex Lee-on-Solent, *Diomede, Arethusa* and *Olna* Flts. *Del Boy*		3-06
❏	XT597		Phantom FG.1	ex DERA, AAEE	Δ	3-06
❏	XV401	'I'	Phantom FGR.2	ex DERA, Wattisham, 74, 23, 29, 228 OCU, 56, 111, 41	® Δ	3-06
❏	XV784		Harrier GR.3	ex DS&TL, Wittering 8909M, 233 OCU, 4, 1, 4.		
				Damaged 2-4-86. Nose		3-06
❏	XW269	'BD'	Harrier T.4	ex QinetiQ, Wittering, SAOEU, 233 OCU, 3, 1, 233 OCU, 4	Δ	3-06
❏	XW560*		Jaguar S.06	ex East Grinstead, AAEE. Damaged 11-8-72.		
				Cockpit. First noted 6-04	®	3-06
❏	XX105*		BAC 111-201	ex DS&TL, RAE, G-ASJD BCAL, BUA.		
				'Rolled over' by 6-05	Δ	3-06
❏	XX343		Hawk T.1	ex DERA, ETPS. Crashed 8-4-97. Cockpit area	®	3-06
❏	XX761		Jaguar GR.1A	ex airfield, Warton, 226 OCU, 14. *Pudsey*. Accident		
				6-6-78. Nose - superbly restored		3-06
❏	XX919		BAC 111-402	ex DERA, RAE, D-AFWC ntu, PI-C-1121. Nose	®	3-06
❏	XZ457		Sea Harrier FA.2	ex Yeovilton, 899, 800, 801, 800, 899, 800, 899, 700A.		
				Crashed 20-10-95	®	3-06
❏	ZD936	'AO'	Tornado F.2	ex 'Manchester', Bedford, St Athan, 229 OCU. Nose		3-06

Defence Science and Technology Laboratory (DS&TL) / **QinetiQ**: The former Llanbedr Meteor made what was probably the last-ever flight by a manned drone aircraft in the UK when it was ferried here in October 2004. The aircraft will have all the remote control 'gizmos' removed and will also undertake spares reclamation for Martin Baker's 'flyers' at Chalgrove, Oxfordshire. After this, there probably will not be a lot left! Pity, as this aircraft is a Korean era veteran [1]. The 'Chippax' is with **1011 Squadron, ATC** [2].

Departures: Hunter T.8C XF358 to Exeter, Devon, 8-04. Hunter T.7 XL612 moved by road to Exeter, Devon, on 27th May 2004; Harrier GR.3 XV806 (last noted 8-98) was broken up during Life Extension trials in 1999; By June 2005, BAC 111 XX105 was transferred to the Boscombe Down Aviation Collection – see above. The famous Hercules W.2 XV208 was retired on 31st March 2001 and placed into external store. It left on 27th April 2005 for Cambridge, Cambs, to become an engine test-bed for the A400M. Alpha Jet ZJ651 was active by 2005.

☐	WK800*		Meteor D.16	ex Llanbedr, DS&TL, RAE, RAAF A77-876, U.21A,		
				23, 77 RAAF, F.8, RAF. Arrived 11-10-04	[1]	10-05
☐	WP863		Chipmunk T.10	8360M, ex Bournemouth, Marlborough, Chippenham,		
			PAX	Shawbury, G-ATJI, RAFC, 664, RAFC	[2]	1-03
☐	XL629		Lightning T.4	ex ETPS, AAEE. Gate guardian		1-06
☐	XW902	'H'	Gazelle HT.3	ex Shawbury, 2 FTS, 18, CFS		11-01
☐	XW906	'J'	Gazelle HT.3	ex Shawbury, 2 FTS, CFS. Apprentice school		8-01
☐	XX705	'5'	Bulldog T.1	ex S'ton UAS, Birm UAS. Inst		1-03
☐	XX745*	'GV'	Jaguar GR.1A	ex Shawbury St Athan, 54, 16, 6, 16, 226 OCU, 6, 226 OCU,		
				6, 54, 6, 20, 226 OCU. Damaged 31-5-00. Arr 24-3-04		3-04
☐	XZ101	'D'	Jaguar GR.1A	9282M, ex St Athan, Coltishall, 41, 2, 6, 2		4-02
☐	ZA804	'I'	Gazelle HT.3	ex Shawbury, 2 FTS, CFS		11-01
☐	XZ933	'T'	Gazelle HT.3	ex Shawbury, 2 FTS, CFS		11-01
☐	ZJ652		Alpha Jet	ex Furstenfeldbruck, Luftwaffe 41+09		11-01
☐	ZJ653		Alpha Jet	ex Furstenfeldbruck, Luftwaffe 40+22		11-01
☐	ZJ654		Alpha Jet	ex Furstenfeldbruck, Luftwaffe 41+02		11-01
☐	ZJ655		Alpha Jet	ex Furstenfeldbruck, Luftwaffe 41+19		11-01
☐	ZJ656		Alpha Jet	ex Furstenfeldbruck, Luftwaffe 41+40		11-01
☐	–		Scout AH.1	Dump. Pod		6-01
☐	162958		AV-8B Harrier II	ex St Athan, USMC, VMA-214. Fuselage, tests		1-02

CHISELDON or Draycott, west of the A346, south of Swindon
The hulk of Scout AH.1 G-BXSL was exported to Hermeskeil, Germany, by September 2005.

☐	OO-MEL	Piaggio P.149	ex 90+93, AC+470, JC+394, AS+428. Stored	2-06
☐		Spitfire FSM	fuselage	2-06

COLERNE west of Corsham, between the A420 and A4
Wessex HU.5 XS486 moved to Weston-super-Mare, Somerset. Coming the other way was Whirlwind HAS.1 XA862. This was found to be unsuitable for fire training and the cockpit was acquired by YHPG, moving to Doncaster, S Yorks. Bulldog T.1 XX657 became ZK-WUF and is presumed to have been exported.

KEEVIL AERODROME south of the A361, south-west of Devizes
Bannerdown Gliding Club: The airfield is home to a large number of stored gliders . Eton TX.1 FEZ (WP269) was airworthy by mid-2005. Cadet TX.3 XA295 moved to Aston Down, Glos, by July 2005. See under Coventry, Warks, for 'another' BGA.804 [1]. Cadet WT905 is an unfinished Motor Cadet conversion [2].

☐	G-AKXP		Auster 5	ex Hedge End, Hatfield, Claygate, NJ633,		
				29 EFTS, 22 EFTS, 659, HS. Crashed 9-4-70	®	3-05
☐	AYK	765	T.21B	ex Spalding		1-04
☐	BAA	804	T.8 Tutor	ex VM589, XE761. CoA 3-97	[1]	7-05
☐	BJJ	1003	T.45 Swallow	ex Lasham. Wreck		1-04
☐	CHM	1556	Schleicher K.4	ex Lasham, D-5015		1-04
☐	DWF	2433	Grunau Baby	ex AGA.16, RNGSA.1-13, VW743		7-05
☐	EAZ	2543	Schleicher K8B	ex D-5256, D-KANO, D-5256. Crashed 25-7-97		1-04
☐	FRQ	3469	T.45 Swallow	ex XT653		1-04
☐	GEQ	3776	SZD-12A Mucha	ex SP-2001, Bury St Edmunds, Tibbenham	®	1-04
☐	WB981	FFZ	Sedburgh TX.1	BGA.3238. Ex Aston Down, Sealand, 635 VGS. Fuse	®	1-06
☐	WE992	EHE	Prefect TX.1	BGA.2692		1-04
☐	WT905		Cadet TX.3	ex Stour Row	[2]	7-05
☐	WZ793		Grasshopper TX.1	ex Croydon, Basingstoke, Taunton	®	7-05
☐	WZ831*		Grasshopper TX.1	ex Nympsfield, Locking, Reading, Halton, Lightwater		12-05
☐	XA240	JJS	Grasshopper TX.1	BGA.4556, ex Yeovilton, Locking, Radley		7-05
☐	XA244		Grasshopper TX.1	ex Lasham, Cosford, Walsall		7-05
☐	XA310	KBP	Cadet TX.3	BGA.4963, ex Fareham		1-06
☐	XE760*		Cadet TX.3	BGA.1745, ex Nympsfield, VM539. Arrived by 7-05	®	7-05

LYNEHAM AIRFIELD west of the A3102, south-west of Wooton Bassett

RAF Lyneham: The Dakota is displayed outside 47 Air Despatch Squadron, Royal Logistics Corps. The dump is occupied by a large, all-steel 'DC-10' look-alike.

❏ 'FZ625' 'YS-DH'	C-47B-30-DK	ex G-AMPO, Coventry, Air Atlantique, LN-RTO, G-AMPO KN566, Oakington SF, 77, 62, Waterbeach SF, 1381 CU, 133 CU, 238, 44-76853. CoA 29-3-97. 271 Sqn c/s		3-06
❏ XK699	Comet C.2	7971M, ex Henlow, Lyneham, 216. Gate		3-06

MALMESBURY

Martin Painter: Continues on the restoration of his Nimrod cockpit.

❏ XV148	Nimrod proto	ex Guildford, Woodford, AAEE, HSA. Cockpit	®	2-04

MELKSHAM on the A350 south of Chippenham

Adrian Brimson and **John Phillips**: Restoration of the Skeeter continues. Documents and photographs relating to this airframe would be most welcome.

◆ *Viewing by prior permission only. tel 01225 702485 or e-mail Heli1jp@aol.com*

❏ XL765	Skeeter AOP.12	ex Northants, Clapham, Leverstock Green, Leamington Spa, Leeds, Rotherham, Wroughton, 17F, 654, 651, SARO	®	3-06

NETHERAVON AIRFIELD on the A345 north of Amesbury

No.7 Regiment, AAC:

❏ XT150	Sioux AH.1	7883M, ex Middle Wallop, comp with 7884M. Gate	7-05
❏ XV136	Scout AH.1	ex Almondbank, Wroughton. Gate	7-05

OAKSEY PARK AERODROME south of Cirencester, east of the A429

Scout AH.1 XT632 (G-BZBD) moved to Bruntingthorpe, Leics, on 1st April 2004, but moved quickly to <u>North Weald</u>, Essex, by November 2004. Last noted here in May 2003, Scout AH.1 XP883 moved to <u>Bruntingthorpe</u>, Leics, on 1st April 2004.

❏ G-AZMN	Airtourer T5	ex Kemble, Oaksey Park, Bristol, Glasgow. Cr 23-6-87	9-03
❏ G-BDFX*	Auster 5	ex Kemble, Oaksey Park, F-BGXG, TW517, 661. Crashed 10-10-93. First noted 7-05	7-05
❏ XV134* 'P'	Scout AH.1	G-BWLX, ex East Dereham, Ipswich, Fleetlands, Middle Wallop. Stored. First noted 3-05	6-05
❏ 91	Wasp HAS.1	ex SAAF. Forward fuselage	7-03

OLD SARUM AERODROME east of the A345 north of Salisbury

Tiger Moth G-ACDI has been listed under this heading in previous editions, but has been off-site for a while [1]. CMC Leopard 001 G-BKRL moved to <u>Bournemouth</u>, Dorset, on 18th February 2005. PT-13D G-BRTK had moved on – destination unknown – by early 2005. A full-size, static, Loening Air Yacht is being built here [2].

❏ G-ACDI*	Tiger Moth	ex Shoreham, BB742, 29 EFTS, 21 EFTS, 13 EFTS, 4 EFTS, 13 EFTS, G-ACDI.	® [1]	5-05
❏ G-BJBY	PA-28 Warrior 161	ex N8415L. Crashed 23-11-97. Wreck		9-05
❏ G-BKHR*	Luton Minor	CoA 6-1-04. Stored		9-05
❏ -*	Air Yacht	static rep. First noted 8-03	[2]	9-05

SALISBURY

A pair of Bulldogs has moved into the general area for storage.

❏ G-102*	Bulldog 122	ex Andover, Ghana AF. Stored. Arrived 4-04	4-04
❏ G-108*	Bulldog 122	ex Andover, Ghana AF, G-BCUP. Stored. Arrived 4-04	4-04

SWINDON

Richard Galazka: Is still at work on his Harvard.

❑ KF435	Harvard IIB	ex Guildford, Duxford, Ottershaw, Wycombe AP, Camberley, Sandhurst, 1 FTS, 2 FTS, 22 SFTS, 20 FTS, 11 (P)AFU	®	7-04
❑ WT899	Cadet TX.3	ex Rush Green, Benington, Syerston, 661 VGS, 643 VGS, Cosford, St Athan		4-99

Others:

❑ RX168*	Seafire III	G-BWEM, ex Exeter, Andover, Norwich, Battle, Dublin, IAAC 157, RX168	6-05

UPAVON AIRFIELD on the A342 south-east of Devizes

Wyvern Gliding Club:

❑ D-4019	Bergfalke II	last flown 1996. Stored	1-04
❑ XA225	Grasshopper TX.1	ex Keevil, Petersfield. Stored	3-05

WARMINSTER on the A36 east of Frome

Restoration of the Stampe is *assumed* to continue, but this reference is well long-in-the-tooth.

❑ G-AYDR	SNCAN SV-4C	ex Raveningham, F-BCLG. CoA 27-3-75	®	8-93

WROUGHTON AIRFIELD on the A4361 south of Swindon

Science Museum: The Air Transport Collection remains largely elusive to the public.

◆ Occasional *open days and special events, otherwise visits by prior arrangement. Wroughton Airfield, Swindon, SN4 9NS tel 01793 814466 www.sciencemuseum.org.uk/wroughton*

❑ G-AACN	HP Gugnunc	ex Hayes and K1908	3-06
❑ G-ACIT	DH.84 Dragon	ex Southend, Beagle, ANT Blackpool, BEA, Scottish, Highland. CoA 25-5-74	3-06
❑ G-AEHM	HM.14 'Flea'	ex Hayes, Whitchurch, Bristol	3-06
❑ G-ALXT	Dragon Rapide	ex Strathallan, Staverton, 4R-AAI, CY-AAI, G-ALXT, NF865, 5 MU, 18 MU, MCS	3-06
❑ G-ANAV	Comet 1A	ex South Kensington. CF-CUM. Nose	3-06
❑ G-APWY	Piaggio P.166	ex Southend, Marconi. CoA 14-3-81	3-06
❑ G-APYD	Comet 4B	ex Dan-Air, Olympic SX-DAL, G-APYD, BEA. CoA 3-8-79	3-06
❑ G-ATTN	Piccard HAB	ex South Kensington, Hayes, South Kensington	3-06
❑ G-AVZB	Z-37 Cmelak	ex Southend, OK-WKQ. CoA 5-4-84	3-06
❑ G-AWZM	Trident 3B-101	ex Heathrow, BA, BEA. CoA 13-12-85	3-06
❑ G-BBGN	Cameron A-375	ex South Kensington, Hayes, South Ken'. Gondola. *Daffodil II*	3-06
❑ G-BGLB	Bede BD-5B	ex Booker. CoA 4-8-81	3-06
❑ G-MMCB	Pathfinder II	microlight	3-06
❑ G-RBOS	Colt AS-105	hot air airship. CoA 6-3-87	3-06
❑ –	BAPC.52 Lilienthal Glider	ex South Ken, Hayes, South Ken, Oxford. Original of 1895	3-06
❑ –	BAPC.162 Manflier MPA	major parts	3-06
❑ –	BAPC.172 Chargus Midas	powered hang glider	3-06
❑ –	BAPC.173 Grasshopper	hang glider	3-06
❑ –	BAPC.174 Bensen B.7	gyroglider	3-06
❑ –	BAPC.188 Cobra 88	hang glider	3-06
❑ –	BAPC.276 Hartman Orni'	ex Cranfield. Stored	3-06
❑ EI-AYO	DC-3A-197	ex Shannon, N655GP, N65556, N225JB, N8695SE, N333H, NC16071	3-06
❑ N18E	Boeing 247	ex Wings and Wheels, Orlando, Sky Tours, NC18E, NC18, NC13340 CAA, United/National A/T	3-06
❑ N7777G	L-749A-79	G-CONI, ex Dublin, Lanzair, KLM PH-LDT, PH-TET	3-06

☐ OO-BFH	Piccard Gas	ex South Kensington, Hayes, South Ken'. Gondola	3-06
☐ VP975	Devon C.2/2	ex RAE Farnborough, AAEE, CCCF, 19 GCF, CPE	3-06
☐ XP505	Gnat T.1	ex South Kensington, RAE, MinTech, Dunsfold, CFS	3-06
☐ 100509	Fa 330A-1	ex South Kensington, Farnborough	3-06

YATESBURY north of the A4, east of Calne

Meteor Flight: Having amassed a huge spares holding, including over a dozen engines, the group continues to make good progress towards the restoration of T.7 WA591 as a 'two-stick' flyer. The group is actively seeking CAA A8-20 status.

◆ *Visits possible by prior arrangement* only *to Max Tapper tel 01249 812557. General correspondence: Hal Taylor, Sunfield House, Townsend Road, Streatley, RG8 9LH tel/fax 01491 872205 www.meteorflight.com*

☐ WA591	Meteor T.7	G-BWMF, ex Woodvale, St Athan 7917M, Kemble, CAW, 8 FTS, 5 FTS, CAW, 12 FTS, 215 AFS, 208 AFS, 203 AFS, 226 OCU, CFE	® 3-06
☐ WF825	'A' Meteor T.7	ex Malmesbury, Monkton Farleigh, Lyneham 8359M, Kemble, CAW, 33, 603. Stored	3-06
☐ WL360	'G' Meteor T.7	ex Staverton, Hucclecote, Locking 7920M, 229 OCU, 1, Wattisham SF, 211 AFS, 210 AFS, 215 AFS. Stored	3-06
☐ WL405	Meteor T.7	ex Chalgrove, Farnborough, BCCS, 1 GCF, 231 OCU, Wittering SF, JCU, Hemswell CF. Stored	3-06
☐ WS760	Meteor NF.14	ex Loughborough, Cranfield, Bushey, Duxford, Brampton, Upwood, 7964M, 1 ANS, 64, 237 OCU. Stored	3-06

WORCESTERSHIRE

BEWDLEY on the A456, west of Kidderminster

Ross McNeill: Took delivery of a Canberra nose during December 2005. It is kept in the general area.

◆ *Visits possible* only *by prior arrangement.*

☐ XH175*	'AR' Canberra PR.9	ex Stock, St Athan, 1 PRU, 39, 58. Nose. Arrived 15-12-05	® 12-05

BIRLINGHAM on the A4104, east of the B4080 to the west of Evesham

Graham Revill: This *private* collection is unchanged.

☐ [WF299]	Sea Hawk FB.3	WF299, ex 'WN105', Helston, St Agnes, Topcliffe, Catterick 8164M, Lee-on-Solent, A2662, A2509, Culdrose SAH-8, 802, 738, 736. Composite	3-06
☐ WH166	Meteor T.7	ex Digby 8052M, CFS, 5 CAACU, CAW, 4 FTS, 205 AFS, 210 AFS, 208 AFS	3-06
☐ WZ425	Vampire T.11	ex Cardiff-Wales, Woodford, Chester, St Athan, 5 FTS, RAFC, 229 OCU, CGS	3-06
☐ XE979	'54' Vampire T.11	ex Standish, Woodford, Chester, St Athan, 1 FTS, 8 FTS, RAFC	3-06
☐ XF526	'78' Hunter F.6 and 'E'	ex St Athan, Halton 8679M, Laarbruch SF, 4 FTS, 229 OCU, 56, 43, 56, 63, 66	3-06
☐ XN632	Jet Provost T.3	ex Eaglescott, Chivenor, St Athan 8352M, Kemble, Shawbury, 3 FTS	3-06

BROMSGROVE on the A448 north-west of Redditch

Bob Dunn, Brian Barrett and Mick Boulanger of the **Wolverhampton Aviation Group** keep two cockpits locally. See also under Wolverhampton, W Mids, for Mick's 'JP'.

❑	WJ865	Canberra T.4	ex Stamford, Stock, Farnborough, ETPS. Nose	3-06
❑	XE597	Hunter FGA.9	8874M, ex Moreton-in-Marsh, Halton, Bentley Priory, Brawdy, 1 TWU, 2 TWU, TWU, 229 OCU, West Raynham SF, 1, 54, MoA, 208, 56, 63, 66. Nose	3-06

DEFFORD on the A4104 south-west of Pershore

The Cessna 150 'tail-dragger' is used by the Missionary Aviation Fellowship (hence the 'registration') as a fund-raising aid [1]. The other references here are well long-in-the-tooth.

❑	G-BOKW	Bö 208C Junior	ex G-BITT, F-BRHX, D-EEAL. CoA 3-11-95	4-98
❑	'G-BMAF'*	Cessna 150J	G-BOWC, ex N60626. First noted 6-05	[1] 12-05
❑	G-BPAO	Air Command 503	CoA 8-8-91. Stored	4-98
❑	G-MNAF	Pegasus XL-R	CoA 3-95. Stored	4-98

ECKINGTON on the B4080 south of Pershore

A private owner keeps the cockpit of an Arrow in the general area. It is being turned into a simulator.

❑	G-TOBE	Cherokee Arrow II	ex Lashenden, G-BNRO, N40979. Crashed 6-3-92	12-03

EVESHAM on the A435 south of Redditch

HMS *Explorer:* Shinehill Lane, South Littleton.

❑	XS886	'27' Wessex HAS.1	ex Birmingham, Lee-on-Solent A2685, Wroughton, 771	3-06

KIDDERMINSTER

During April 2005 a private owner in the area took delivery of a Hunter F.51.

❑	'XF324'*	Hunter F.51	E-427, ex Bruntingthorpe, Brough, Holme-on-Spalding Moor, Brough, Dunsfold, G-9-447, Danish AF, Esk.724. RAF 92 Sqn 'Blue Diamonds' c/s. Arr 19-4-05	4-05

MALVERN WELLS on the A449 south of Great Malvern

Peter Ward: A 'Flea' is kept in the area.

❑	'G-ADYV'	HM.14 'Flea'	BAPC.243, ex 'A-FLEA', Leigh-on-Sea	8-03

PERSHORE on the A44 west of Evesham

John S Morgan: John is co-owner of Buccaneer S.2 XX893 – see Portmoak, Scotland and has also gained a taste for silent flight. The Grunau is a long term restoration [1]. John also has several other gliders either airworthy, about to be or at other locations – these are not listed here. The nose of Electra LN-FOI was exported to New Zealand in February 2006 (where it once served as ZK-TEA). John located a Piper Tomahawk and presented it to the local Air Cadet unit – see below.

◆ *Viewable by prior arrangement only - jsmorgan@btconnect.com*

❑	G-ANAP*		Dove 6	ex Bristol, CAFU Stansted. CoA 6-9-73. Cockpit		3-06
❑	G-APFG*		Boeing 707-436	ex Cove, Bruntingthorpe, Cardington, Stansted, British Airtours, BOAC. CoA 24-5-81. Nose		3-06
❑	G-AXDM*		HS.125-400B	ex Farnborough, Edinburgh, BAE Systems, GEC-Marconi. CoA 7-6-03. Cockpit		3-06
❑	G-BNCY		F.27-500F	ex Bournemouth, Guernsey, Air UK, VH-FCE, PH-EXH. *Friendship Lilly Langtree*. Damaged 7-12-97. Nose	®	3-06
❑	G-CHNX		Electra 188AF	ex Bournemouth, Channel Express, EI-CHO, G-CHNX ntu, N5535. Nose		3-06
❑	CMY*	1663	Grunau Baby IIIC	ex Bidford, RAFGSA.373, D-1090.	® [1]	3-06
❑	VR-BMB		HS.125-400B	ex Stansted, VR-BKN, I-GJBO, G-AYLI, G-5-11. Cockpit.		3-06

❏ WK128*	Canberra B.2	ex Llanbedr, FRL. Cockpit. Arrived 12-04	3-06
❏ XM144	Lightning F.1	ex Wycombe AP, Eaglescott, Burntwood, Leuchars 8417M,	
		Leuchars TFF, 23 Leuchars TFF, 226 OCU, 74. 74 Sqn c/s.	
		Nose, trailer-mounted	3-06
❏ –*	Hawk SIM	ex Farnborough. Arrived 14-5-04	3-06

No.233 Squadron Air Cadets: Have a Tomahawk, care of John Morgan.

| ❏ –* | Tomahawk 112 | cockpit | 3-06 |

REDDITCH

❏ G-ARMD	Chipmunk 22A	ex WD297, 666, 1 BFTS. CoA 5-6-76. Stored	2-04
❏ 'WZ868'	'H' Chipmunk T.10	G-ARMF, ex Wellesbourne, Twyford, WG322, 63 GCF,	
		Leeds UAS, 22 RFS. Damaged 19-6-96. Stored	2-04

WORCESTER

John Hancock: *Should* still have his Canberra nose.

| ❏ WK118 | Canberra TT.18 | ex Stock, Wyton, 100, 7, 59, 103. Nose | 3-96 |

EAST YORKSHIRE

BEVERLEY

Former **Museum of Army Transport**: Beverley C.1 XB259 left by road for <u>Paull</u>, E Yorks, on 23rd May 2004.

BREIGHTON AERODROME in between Bubwith and Breighton, east of Selby

Real Aeroplane Company and **Museum**: Rob Fleming acquired Nigel Ponsford's Aeronca in 2004 [1]. Spitfire PR.XI PL965 (N965RF) returned on 12th June. It did not stay long, flying to <u>North Weald</u>, Essex, on 6th September 2004. The Spitfire I, as flown by 'Al' Deere, is a long term restoration project and is held off site [2]. The Delfin is displayed at the main entrance, but may also be kept 'in steam' [3].

Notes: Aircraft owned and operated by 'Taff' Smith or Rob Fleming plus the collection assembled by Nigel Ponsford (NHP) and any other aircraft under long-term restoration are listed here. (See also under Wigan, Gtr Man, and Selby, N Yorks, for other elements of Nigel's collection.) L-18C Cub G-CUBJ was sold to a local operator and remains based.

◆ *Signed from Bubwith on the A163. Open 10.30am to 4pm, weekends and Bank hols, Easter to October. Other times by prior arrangement. Different admission rates apply to fly-ins/airshows. The Aerodrome, Breighton, Selby, YO8 7DH tel / fax 01757 289065 www.realaero.com*

❏ G-ABVE	Active II	✈ ex Old Warden, Tiger Club		3-06
❏ G-AEVS	Aeronca 100	✈ Composite, inc parts from G-AEXD. *Jeeves*	[1]	3-06
❏ G-AEXF	Mew Gull	✈ ex Old Warden, Sudbury, Old Warden, ZS-AHM		3-06
❏ G-AMAW	Luton Minor	ex Batley, Old Warden, Hitchin. CoA 6-8-88	NHP	3-06
❏ G-AOBG	Somers-K SK.1	ex Benington, Eaton Bray, Cranfield. CoA 6-6-58	NHP	3-06
❏ G-AXEI	Ward Gnome	ex East Kirkby, Tattershall	NHP	3-06
❏ G-BVGZ	Fokker Dr.I REP ✈	ex Netheravon		3-06
❏ G-BWUE	'1' HA-1112-M1L	ex Sandown, Breighton, Duxford, N9938, *Battle of Britain*,		
	Buchón	G-AWHK, SpanAF C4K-102. Werner Schroer, JG27 c/s	®	3-06
❏ G-MJLK	Dragonfly 250	Stored, dismantled		3-06
❏ G-MMUL	Ward Elf	ex Newark area. Citroen Ami	NHP	3-06
❏ G-TAFF	CASA I-131E	ex Sherburn, Breighton, G-BFNE, SpanAF E3B-148	®	3-06
❏	'F50' HM.14 'Flea'	taxiable. Built by Mick Ward. Citroen Ami	NHP	3-06
❏ T9738	Magister I	✈ G-AKAT, ex F-AZOR, G-AKAT, T9738, 24 EFTS, 15 EFTS		3-06

❑	X4276*		Spitfire I		G-CDGU, ex 54. Crashed 28-12-40	[2]	3-06
❑	'52024'	'LK-A'	Hurricane XII	✈	G-HURR, ex Duxford, Brooklands, RCAF 5589. 87 Sqn c/s		3-06
❑	472773*		P-51D-25-NA	✈	G-CDHI, ex Northampton, G-SUSY, N12066, Nica AF		
		'QP-M'			GN120,USAAF 44-72773. *Susy*. 354th FG c/s. Arr 21-3-05		3-06
❑	U-99		Jungmeister	✈	G-AXMT, ex N133SJ, G-AXMT, HB-MIY, Swiss AF U-99		3-06
❑	491273*	'51'	L29 Delfin		ex Chester, YL-PAG, SovAF. Arr 7-4-05, on 'gate' 18-7-05	[3]	3-06
❑	100502*		Fa 330A-1		ex Selby, Breighton, East Kirkby, Tattershall, Wigan.		
					TAC loan		3-06

Others: A helicopter workshop has acquired a former Romanian 1973 IAR-built Alouette III for rebuild.

❑	G-AYFC*		D.62B Condor		CoA 26-12-02	®	3-06
❑	[G-CDSJ]*		Alouette III		ex Romanian AF 21. First noted 1-05	®	3-06
❑	EC-FQI*		Alouette III		hulk, spares. First noted 1-05		3-06
❑	WB555*		Chipmunk T.10		ex Canada (?), Woodvale 7924M, Liv UAS, Bir UAS,		
					2 SoTT, Debden, 4 SoTT, Gla UAS, 43 GCF, MCCF,		
					Ox UAS. Cockpit. Arrived 6-3-06		3-06
❑	WG458*		Chipmunk T.10		N458BG, ex 1 AEF, 5 AEF, Cam UAS, 3 BFTS	®	3-06
❑	WK622*		Chipmunk T.10		G-BCZH, Yeovilton, 2 FTS, Wattisham TFF, Bri UAS,		
					3 AEF, Bri UAS, Leeds UAS, 24 GCF, Ox UAS, 18 RFS,		
					22 RFS. Crashed 6-9-87. Arrived 6-3-06	®	3-06
❑	XZ299*		Gazelle AH.1		G-CDXE, ex Fleetlands. Arrived 19-11-04	®	3-06

Tony Brier: Has a workshop nearby and took delivery of an Auster 5 during September 2005.

| ❑ | NJ703* | | Auster 5 | | G-AKPI, ex Skegness, Humberside, 652, 660. | | |
| | | | | | CoA 1-12-85. Arrived 9-05 | ® | 3-06 |

BROUGH AIRFIELD south of the A63 west of Hull

BAE Systems: In August 2002 the B-2 flew off to Warton, Lancs, but it has now returned. The Nimrod fuselage is to be coupled with a set of wings (from Woodford, Gtr Man?) for static tests for the MRA.4 programme.

❑	G-AEBJ*		Blackburn B-2	✈	ex Warton, Brough. Returned by 6-04		6-04
❑	NF389		Swordfish III		ex Yeovilton, Brough, Lee-on-Solent	® [1]	3-02
❑	XV168		Buccaneer S.2B		ex Lossiemouth, 12, 208, 12, FAA. 12 Sqn c/s		12-05
❑	XV263*		Nimrod AEW.3		ex Woodford/Warton, Bournemouth, Finningley 8967M,		
					Waddington, JTU, Woodford, St M Wing, 203.		
					Static testing. Arrived 20-11-05		11-05
❑	XX736		Jaguar GR.1		9110M, ex Coltishall, Shawbury, Warton, G-27-327,		
					Indian AF JI013, 6, 226 OCU, JOCU. Fatigue tests		3-02
❑	ZD353	'H'	Harrier GR.5		ex Dunsfold, Brough, Wittering, 233 OCU, 1.		
					Damaged 29-7-91. Undercarriage test rig		3-02
❑	–		Jaguar GR.1		nose		3-02
❑	–		Hawk		fatigue rig. T.1A life extension test		3-02
❑	–		Hawk Mk.203		forward fuselage		3-02
❑	–		Harrier GR.5		fatigue rig		3-02
❑	–		Eurofighter 2000		fatigue rig, two-seater variant. Nose only		3-02
❑	–		Eurofighter 2000		fatigue rig, single-seater cockpit only		3-02
❑	[LL-5313]		Hawk T.53		ex Bournemouth, Indonesian Air Force. Gate		12-05

GRINDALE north-west of Bridlington

British Skysports: The former para-trainer G-BRID is being used in a complex composite restoration.

❑	G-BATD*		Cessna U.206F		ex Langar, Isle of Man, Sibson, Shobdon, N60204.		
					Crashed 5-4-80. First noted 6-04	®	6-04
❑	G-BRID		Cessna U.206A		ex N4874F. CoA 20-5-93	®	6-04
❑	G-STAT*		Cessna U.206F		ex Strathallan, Hibaldstow. A6-MAM, N8732Q		
					Crashed 24-8-03. First noted 6-04	®	6-04

HULL
Streetlife Museum of Transport: BAE Systems are Brough, E Yorks refurbished the Blackburn Lincock FSM over the winter of 2005/2006, it was due to be 'hung' again here in mid-March 2006.
◆ *Open Mon to Sat 10am to 5pm; Sun 1.30pm to 4.30pm; open Bank Hols, Closed Xmas and Easter. 36 High Street, Hull, HU1 1NQ, 01482 613902 fax 01482 613710, www.hullcc.gov.uk/ museums/streetlife/index.php*
❑ 'G-EBVO'*   Lincock FSM   BAPC.287, ex Brough   3-06

W&R19 (p262) noted the hulk of Cessna 150E leaving here for the 'Norwich area'. It moved to Norwich Airport, and then in April 2005 to Bruntingthorpe, Leics.

LINLEY HILL AERODROME or Beverley, west of Leven, off A165 north-east of Beverley.
❑ G-AYBW   Cessna FA.150K   ex Perth. Crashed 8-10-72. Fuselage   7-05
❑ G-BAIP   Cessna F.150L   Crashed 30-5-95. Dismantled   7-05
❑ G-MYJY*   S.6 Coyote II   CoA 28-7-03. First noted 7-05. Stored   7-05

MARFLEET on the A1033 east of Kingston upon Hull
Humbrol Ltd: The Hunter guards the factory.
❑ XF509   Hunter F.6   ex Chivenor 8708M, Thurleigh, 4FTS, MoA, AFDS, 54   12-05

NORTH CAVE on the B1230 west of Hull
Eight Acre Dive Site: or Mires Lane Lake. On 21st July 2005 the Cherokee was sunk into the waters (all 42ft of it) for the divers to play 'Find'! They are hoping for a Boeing 727 fuselage next. www.eightacrelake.8m.com
❑ G-AXRL*   Cherokee 160   ex PH-CHE, D-EFRI, N11C. CoA 20-2-86.   2-06

OTTRINGHAM on the A1033 east of Hull
The strip here was closed and ploughed up several years ago. The two inmates (both last noted in July 1999) are unaccounted for: Mooney M.20F G-AWLP and Cessna 120 G-BRPG.

PAULL on minor road south of Hedon
Fort Paull Armouries: The team did not rest from moving the giant to its new location. On 30th April 2005 the re-assembled and re-opened XB259 was toasted by a VIP gathering. The 'Paull' in XB259's history was the now long-defunct aerodrome not far from its new resting place. Part of a set-piece scene from World War Two includes a Bulldog cockpit.
◆ *Open Nov to Mar, Tues to Sun, 11am to 4pm. Apr to Oct, all week 10am to 6pm. Battery Road, Paull, HU12 8F tel / fax 01482 896236 www.fortpaull.com*
❑ XB259*   Beverley C.1   ex Beverley, Paull, Luton, RAE, Blackburns, G-AOAI.
                                    Arrived 23-5-04   3-06
❑ [XX557]   Bulldog T.1   ex Topcliffe, Linton-on-Ouse, St Athan, Gla UAS,
                                    CFS. Crashed 11-9-75. Cockpit   12-05

POCKLINGTON AERODROME east of the A1079, west of the village
Wolds Gliding Club: Took delivery of a distinctive briefing room during March 2005.
❑ BPX   1136 T.45 Swallow   ex XS859. CoA 5-7-98. Stored   1-06
❑ [OY-MUB]*   Short 330-200   ex Alton, Bournemouth, Muk Air, G-BITX, G-14-3069.
                                    Fuselage. Arrived 3-05   1-06

PRESTON on the B1239 north of Hedon
Wright's Garage: Staithes Road. The Varsity nose is still kept at the filling station-cum-scrapyard.
❑ WL627   Varsity T.1   ex Hull, Newton 8488M, 6 FTS, 2 ANS, 1 ANS, BCBS   12-05

SEATON ROSS north-west of Holme-on-Spalding-Moor
Hornet Aviation: Are restoring a Proctor for the Air Atlantique Classic Flight.

❏ G-AKIU	Proctor V	ex Coventry, Nottingham, Bedford, Houghton-on-the-Hill, North Weald, Southend, Edenbridge. CoA 24-1-65	off site ®	2-04
❏ G-AYZI*	SNCAN SV-4C	ex F-BBAA, French mil. Damaged 13-6-04	®	9-04

STORWOOD south of the B1228, south-east of York
Melbourne Autos: Yorkshire Helicopter Preservation Group moved their 'spares ship' Whirlwind HAR.10 XD165 to <u>Doncaster</u>, S Yorks, during November 2005.

WITHERNSEA on the A1033 east of Hull
Oblivion: Within the night-club could be found a 'crashed' Cessna. Perhaps this is still the case…

❏ G-BDEW	Cessna FRA.150M	Crashed 13-8-96.	2-02

NORTH YORKSHIRE

BAGBY AERODROME on the A19 south-east of Thirsk
T.67B G-BLLP moved to Eshott, N&T, in May 2003 but was sold on and moved to <u>Leeds</u>, W Yorks. The Cessna 152 was 'written out' of *W&R18*, but is made of stronger stuff! [1]

❏ G-ARLR*	Terrier 2	ex VW996, AAC, 663. CoA 9-9-01		2-06
❏ G-AVGZ*	CEA DR.1050	ex F-BKPR. CoA 13-7-<u>97</u>. Stored		2-06
❏ G-BCUL	Rallye 100ST	ex F-OCZL. CoA 8-5-00		3-05
❏ G-BDGM*	Warrior 151	ex N41307. Crashed 28-10-04. First noted 8-05		2-06
❏ G-BRBF*	Cessna 152 II	ex N67748. CoA 5-7-98. Stored	[1]	2-06
❏ G-BTFP*	Tomahawk 112	ex N6201A. CoA 6-8-<u>00</u>. First noted 2-06		2-06
❏ N10053*	Boeing A75N1	ex Mexico. First noted 10-05	®	2-06

CARLTON MOOR on minor road south-east of Carlton-in-Cleveland
Carlton Moor Gliding Club: Rhonlerche II EAL moved 'south' during 2005.

❏ DUC	2383 Carmam M.100S	ex F-CCSA. CoA 5-88. Stored	2-06

CARTHORPE west of the A1, south-east of Bedale
Camp Hill Activity Centre:
◆ *Access by prior arrangement only. tel 01845 567788 fax 01845 567065 www.camphill.co.uk*

❏ [G-BHXJ]	Norecrin II	ex 'London', F-BEMX	10-05

DINSDALE on a minor road south of Middleton St George
Anthony Harker: Took delivery of the former Blyth Valley Lightning at a location in the area.

❏ XR718*	'DA' Lightning F.3	ex Walpole, Wattisham 8932M, ABDR, LTF, 11, LTF, 11, 5, LTF, 5, 11, LTF, 5, LTF, 5, 226 OCU, 29, 56. Arrived 26-9-05	2-06

DISHFORTH alongside the A1(M), east of Ripon
9 Regiment AAC: Took delivery of a Gazelle in 2004 that is destined to be displayed at the gate.

❏ ZB670*	Gazelle AH.1	ex Arborfield, 665. Stored	2-06

ELVINGTON off the A1079 south-east of York

Yorkshire Air Museum (YAM): Now with a 'matching' pair of Tornados, YAM continues to expand the aircraft collection and to refine the facilities on site. The famed 'NAAFI' remains a 'must do'.

Notes: The Bf 109G FSM was built by Danny Thornton of Garforth, W Yorks [1]. The PV.8 Eastchurch Kitten REP WAS built by Bill Sneesby [2]. The Spitfire FSM 'guards' the memorial room of the **609 (West Riding) Squadron Association** [3]. The Mosquito is on loan from **Tony Agar** and is a complex composite, using the nose section of HJ711; the rear fuselage of TT.35 RS715 from Elstree; the centre section from Mk XVI PF498 from Leyland; and the outer wings of T.3 VA878 from St Davids [4]. The Halifax re-creation is a complex composite: using the centre section from former 58 Squadron Mk II HR792 which came to grief in a take-off accident at Stornoway on 13th January 1945; the wings from Hastings C.1 TG536 from Catterick; myriad Halifax detail parts; Hercules engines courtesy of the French Air Force and ex-Noratlas, plus new-build nose and rear section and many other elements [5]. Buccaneer S.2B XX901 is owned by the **Buccaneer Aircrew Association** (Dave Herriott, 84 Lees Gardens, Maidenhead, SL6 4NT). BAA serves to link all former Buccaneer aircrew [6]. Tornado ZA354 on loan from the North West Aircraft Heritage Group [7]. The original nose of the Hadrian is still to be found at Bacup, Lancs [8]. Several airframes are on loan and are marked ±: the 'Flea' from Dave Allan; the Dragonfly from Ray McElwain; the Victor from André Tempest and team, which regularly taxies (they also have a Victor procedure trainer); and the Lightning from Peter Chambers.

◆ *Signed from the A64 southern York ring, at the A64/A166/A1079 junction. Open late Oct to late Mar 10am to 3.30pm daily, summer 10am to 5pm daily. Elvington, York, YO41 4AU tel 01904 608595 fax 01904 608246 www.yorkshireairmuseum.co.uk*

☐ 'G-AAAH'	DH.60 Moth FSM	BAPC.270, *Jason*		4-06
☐ 'G-AFFI'	HM.14 'Flea'	BAPC.76, ex Hemswell, Cleethorpes, Nostell, Rawdon	±	4-06
☐ [G-AJOZ]	Argus II	ex Woodhall Spa, Tattershall, Wigan, Market Drayton, Wigan, Southend, Sywell, FK338, Kemble, ATA 2 FP, 42-32142. Crashed 16-8-62. Stored		4-06
☐ G-AVPN	Herald 213	ex Channel Express, I-TIVB, G-AVPN, D-BIBI, HB-AAK ntu. CoA 14-12-99		4-06
☐ G-MJRA	Mainair Tri-Flyer	ex Wetherby. Demon 175 wing		4-06
☐ G-TFRB	Air Command 532	ex Hartlepool. CoA 6-8-98		4-06
☐ G-YURO	Europa 001	ex Wombleton. CoA 9-6-95	off-site	4-06
☐ –	BAPC.28 Wright Flyer REP	ex Leeds, Eccleston, Cardington, Finningley		4-06
☐ –	BAPC.41 BE.2c REP	ex St Athan, '6232'. Halton		4-06
☐ –	BAPC.89 Cayley REP	ex Manchester, Hendon, Lasham.		4-06
☐ –	BAPC.130 Blackburn 1911 R	ex Stoke, Helston, *Flambards*		4-06
☐ –	BAPC.240 Bf 109G FSM	ex Garforth	[1]	4-06
☐ 'F943'	SE.5A REP	G-BKDT, ex Selby, Elvington, Selby		4-06
☐ 'H1968'	Avro 504K REP	BAPC.42, ex St Athan, Halton		4-06
☐ [N540]	PV Kitten REP	ex Selby. Stored	[2]	4-06
☐ 'P3873' 'YO-H'	Hurricane I FSM	BAPC.265, 1 Sqn RCAF colours		4-06
☐ 'R6690' 'PR-A'	Spitfire I FSM	BAPC.254, 609 Sqn colours	[3]	4-06
☐ HJ711 'VI-C'	Mosquito NF.II	ex Huntington. 169 Sqn c/s. *Spirit of Val*	® [4]	4-06
☐ 'KG427''	C-47B-30-DK	G-AMYJ, ex Coventry, Air Atlantique, SU-AZF, G-AMYJ, XF747, G-AMYJ, KN353, 110, 96, 243, 44-76384. CoA 4-4-97. (Wings of G-ANAF.)	®	4-06
☐ 'LV907' and 'NP763'	Halifax II	ex Isle of Lewis. 'NP-F', *Friday 13th*, 158 Sqn c/s to post, 'H7-N' 346 Sqn c/s to stb	[5]	4-06
☐ RA854	Cadet TX.1	ex Wigan, Woodford, RAFGSA, Woodvale, 41 GS. Stored		4-06
☐ 'TJ704' 'JA'	Terrier 2	G-ASCD, ex Holme-on Spalding Moor, Nympsfield, Blackbushe, PH-SFT, G-ASCD, Auster AOP.6 VW993, 651, 663. CoA 26-9-71	®	4-06
☐ VV901	Anson T.21	ex Bacup, Burtonwood, Cosford, Irton Holme, Leconfield, CFCCU, Dur UAS, 1 RFS	®	4-06
☐ WH846	Canberra T.4	ex Samlesbury, St Athan, Laarbruch SF, 231 OCU		4-06
☐ WH903	Canberra B.2	ex 100, 85, MoA, 85, W Raynham TFF, 228 OCU, 102, 617. Nose		4-06

☐ WH991		Dragonfly HR.5	ex Storwood, Tattershall Thorpe, Tattershall, Wisbech, Taunton, Fleetlands, Culdrose SF, 705, 700, Eglinton SF, *Centaur* Flt, 705, *Illustrious* Flt	± 4-06
☐ 'WK864'	'C'	Meteor F.8	WL168 ex Finningley, 'WH456', St Athan, Swinderby, Finningley, Heywood 7750M, Sylt, 604, 111. 616 c/s	4-06
☐ WS788	'Z'	Meteor NF.14	ex Leeming 'WS844', Patrington 7967M, 1 ANS, 2 ANS, 152	4-06
☐ XH278	'42'	Vampire T.11	ex Felton, Henlow 8595M, Upwood 7866M, 27 MU, RAFC. RAFC colours	4-06
☐ XH767		Javelin FAW.9	ex Norwich, Monkton Farleigh, Worcester 7955M, Shawbury, 228 OCU, 11, 25. 23 Sqn colours	4-06
☐ XL231		Victor K.2	ex 55, 57, Witt Wing, Victor TF, Witt Wing, 139. *Lusty Lindy* ±	4-06
☐ XL502*		Gannet AEW.3	G-BMYP, ex Sandtoft, Carlisle, Leuchars 8610M, 849, MinTech, Pershore, 849. CoA 29-9-89. Arr 11-3-05	4-06
☐ 'XL571'	'V'	Hunter T.7	XL572 / G-HNTR, ex Brough, Bournemouth, Cosford 8834M, 1 TWU, 2 TWU, TWU, 229 OCU. 92 Sqn, 'Blue Diamonds' colours	4-06
☐ XN974		Buccaneer S.2	ex Warton, Holme on Spalding Moor, AAEE, 803	4-06
☐ XP640	'M'	Jet Provost T.4	ex Halton 8501M, CATCS, 6 FTS, CAW, CFS, 3 FTS	4-06
☐ XS903	'BA'	Lightning F.6	ex Binbrook, 11, 5-11 pool	± 4-06
☐ XV748	'3D'	Harrier GR.3	ex Cranfield, Bedford, 233 OCU, 1, 233 OCU, 1	4-06
☐ XX901		Buccaneer S.2B	ex Kemble, St Athan, Lossiemouth, 208, 12, 237 OCU, 208. *Kathryn - The Flying Mermaid*. Pink c/s	[6] 4-06
☐ XZ631*		Tornado GR.4	ex Warton, Panavia, AAEE. Arrived 22-3-05	4-06
☐ ZA354*		Tornado GR.1	ex Warton. Arrived 29-4-05	[7] 4-06
☐ –	'1'	Jet Provost T.3	ex Linton-on-Ouse. Procedure trainer	4-06
☐ –	'2'	Jet Provost T.3	ex Linton-on-Ouse. Procedure trainer	4-06
☐ –		Victor	ex Navenby. Procedure trainer	± 4-06
☐ 21417		CT-133 S' Star	ex Sollingen, CAF	4-06
☐ 538	'3-QH'	Mirage IIIE	ex Chateaudun, 3 *Esc*, FAF	4-06
☐ 'N-2'		Hunter FGA.78	N-268. ex Bournemouth, Qatar AF QA-10, G-9-286, Dutch AF N-268. Dutch colours	4-06
☐ '237123'		CG-4A Hadrian	BAPC.157, ex Bacup, Ormskirk	® [8] 4-06

GREAT AYTON on the A173 south-east of Middlesbrough
The nose of Buccaneer S.2B XV867 moved to Inverness, Scotland, by April 2005 followed by the nose of Meteor NF.11 WM145 and Vampire T.11 WZ557 during February 2006.

HARROGATE on the A61 north of Leeds
As warned in *W&R19*, the nose of Lightning F.6 XR726 – last noted here March 1993 – has been sent to LOST!

INGLEBY ARNCLIFFE between the A19 and A172 north east of Northallerton
☐ G-BHNV	W-Bell 47G-3B1	ex F-GHNM, G-BHNV, XW180. CoA 28-5-89	10-02
☐ G-MMKM	Gemini/D Striker	CoA 11-6-99. Stored	10-02

KIRKBYMOORSIDE AERODROME on the A170 west of Pickering, south of the town
Slingsby Aviation: By February 2005, Viking TX.1 ZE686 had moved to Syerston, Notts.
☐ –	c/n 2006 T.67 Firefly	static test airframe	3-02

LEEMING AIRFIELD east of the A1, west of Bedale
RAF Leeming: Lightning F.6 XR753 followed 11 Squadron to the land of the Typhoon, Coningsby, Lincs, on 17th November 2005. By October 2005 several Tornado F.3s were being stripped of spares ready for scrapping: eg ZE293, ZG770 and ZG796.

☐	XA634	'L'	Javelin FAW.4	7641M, ex Shawbury, Colerne, Melksham, Gloster.	
				228 OCU markings	9-05
☐	XV499		Phantom FGR.2	ex 74, 92, 228 OCU, 29, 23, 19, 92, 41, 6	6-05
☐	ZD934	'AD'	Tornado F.2	ex St Athan, 229 OCU. Nose. ABDRT	1-04

LINTON-ON-OUSE AIRFIELD west of the A19, north-west of York
RAF Linton-on-Ouse: Tours of the **Memorial Room**, held on a number of Sundays each year, remain popular. They *must* be booked in advance on 01347 848261, ext 7660.

| ☐ | XN589 | '46' | Jet Provost T.3A | 9143M, ex 1 FTS, RAFC. 1 FTS c/s. Gate | 12-05 |

MALTON off the A64 north of Malton at A169 junction
Eden Camp Modern History Theme Museum: Each hut in this former prisoner of war camp has a different theme and the level of presentation is breath-taking. There is much to fascinate the aviation follower, including a Link trainer display, plotting room, items on 617 Squadron, the Comete escape line and much more. The Hurricane was built by G B Moulders of Norfolk, the Spitfire and V-1 by TDL Replicas of Lowestoft. The Spitfire's serial number was changed in honour of one of the former staff who flew the type during the war.
◆ *Daily 10am to 5pm, last admission 4pm. (Extended closure Xmas and New Year, call for details.) Malton, YO17 6RT tel 01653 697777 fax 01653 698243 e-mail admin@edencamp.co.uk www.edencamp.co.uk*

☐	–		BAPC.235	Fi 103 (V-1) FSM	–	1-04
☐	'P2793'	'SD-M'	Hurricane FSM	BAPC.236. 501 Sqn colours	8-05
☐	'AB550'	'GE-P'	Spitfire FSM	BAPC.230, ex 'AA908'. 349 Sqn colours	[1] 8-05

NEWBY WISKE north-west of Thirsk, near South Otterington
Jungmann E3B-369 (G-BPDM, last noted October 2002) had moved by March 2004, for the Durham area.

| ☐ | G-BBBW* | | FRED II | CoA 2-4-03. Stored | 3-04 |
| ☐ | G-BGFK | | Evans VP-1 | Canx 7-4-99. Stored | 3-04 |

NORTHALLERTON on the A168/A684 east of Leeming Bar
'The Standard': A consortium of 12 owners acquired the 'JP' and moved it to the pub. It will be restored, probably to its 1 FTS scheme.

| ☐ | XN458* | '19' | Jet Provost T.3 | ex Ashington, 'XN594' WAM Cardiff, St Athan 8334M, | |
| | | | | Halton, Shawbury, 1 FTS. Arrived 8-7-05 | ® 10-05 |

NORTH STAINLEY on the A6109 north west of Ripon
Lightwater Valley Theme Park / Lightwater Village: The former Land's End, Cornwall, Sopwith Baby is *reported* to have come here, the two sites being owned by the same organisation.
◆ *North Stainley, Ripon, HG34 3HT tel 0870 4580040 fax 01765 635359 e-mail leisure@lightwatervalley.co.uk www.lightwatervalley.co.uk*

| ☐ | –* | | BAPC.137 | Sopwith Baby REP | ex Land's End, Chertsey | 1-06 |

RUFFORTH AERODROME south of the A1237, west of York
McLean's Sailplanes: A donation to local charity allows a look inside this busy workshop when operating conditions permit. The rafters hold a series of gliders, the more long-term and the substantial are listed here. (www.mclean-aviation.com) Cadet TX.3 XA286 was sold in Holland by March 2004.

☐	G-ATSY		Super Baladou IV	ex Newcastle. CoA 23-11-91. Spares	2-06
☐	G-BCHX		SF-23A Sperling	ex Netherthorpe, D-EGIZ. Damaged 7-8-82. Frame	2-06
☐	G-BVNI*		JT.2 Titch	unflown. Stored. First noted 3-02	2-06
☐	AUJ	668	T.21B	damaged 16-7-85. Stored	3-02
☐	DPT*	2278	L-Spatz 55	ex RAFGGA.510. Damaged 28-3-97. Stored	2-06
☐	EJD*	2715	T.65D Vega	ex RAFGSA. Stored. First noted 3-02	2-06

❑ GAC*	3670	Schleicher	ex RAFGGA.510. Damaged 28-3-97. Stored		2-06
❑ XA290		Cadet TX.3	ex Syerston, Dishforth, 661 VGS, 643 VGS. Fuselage		2-06
❑ XP463*		Grasshopper TX.1	dismantled. First noted 3-<u>02</u>		2-06

Others: The elements of Elster C G-LUFT held for spares for G-APVF here are not substantial enough to formally list; they have been deleted.

SCARBOROUGH

❑ G-AHCK	J/1N Alpha	ex Thwing, Spilsby, Croft, Skegness. Dam 14-9-91	® 12-03
❑ G-AJRC	J/1 Autocrat	ex Thwing. CoA 14-7-02	® 12-03

SELBY on the A19 south of York

Anne Lindsay and **Nigel Ponsford**: See also under Breighton, E Yorks and Wigan, Gtr Man, for other elements of the collection. Drone G-ADPJ moved to <u>Kington</u>, Hereford. Fa 330A-1 100502 moved to <u>Breighton</u>, E Yorks.
◆ *Airframes listed held in deep storage or restoration in and around the area and visits are not possible.*

❑ G-AEFG		HM.14 'Flea'	BAPC.75, ex Breighton, Leeds, Harrogate, Kirkby Overblow, Accrington		® 3-06
❑ G-APXZ		Knight Twister	ex Breighton, Tumby Woodside, Loughborough, Biggin Hill. Frame		3-06
❑ ALX	491	Dagling	ex Leeds, Great Hucklow		3-06
❑ AQY	588	EoN Primary	ex Breighton, Hemel Hempstead. Stored		3-06
❑ BVM	1269	Dart 17R	ex Breighton, Rufforth		3-06
❑ –		Hutter H.17a	ex Leeds, Accrington		3-06
❑ –		Dickson Primary	ex Leeds, Harrogate		3-06
❑ –	BAPC.14	Addyman STG	ex Leeds, Harrogate, Wigan		3-06
❑ –	BAPC.16	Addyman UL	ex Leeds, Harrogate, Wigan		3-06
❑ –	BAPC.18	Killick Gyroplane	ex Leeds, Harrogate, Irlam		3-06
❑ –	BAPC.39	Addyman Zephyr	ex Leeds, Harrogate. Substantial parts		3-06
❑ XK819		Grasshopper TX.1	ex Breighton, Warmingham, Stoke-on-Trent, Cosford, Malvern, 2 MGSP, Kimbolton		® 3-06

SHERBURN-IN-ELMET AERODROME on the B1222 east of the town, east of Leeds

LongEz G-BNCZ moved to a new owner in Northamptonshire for rebuild.

❑ G-SACU	Cadet 161	ex N9162X. Crashed 29-6-96	5-05

THIRSK on the A19 north-east of Ripon

A local strip may well still contain to Evans homebuilds.

❑ G-BEKM	Evans VP-1	ex Eaton Bray. CoA 23-3-95. Stored	11-03
❑ G-BFFB	Evans VP-2	ex Eaton Bray. Unflown. Stored	11-03

Calverts: The famous scrapyard here, last mentioned in *W&R17* (p263) staged a major clear-up in late 2005. The two Buccaneer *rear* fuselages (XV867 plus another) were fully exposed as was the wing of Lightning F.2A XN774. The latter led to some web-site 'reporting' that the original wings of the Fairey FD.2 WG774 (which was considerably rebuilt as the BAC 221, see under Yeovilton, Somerset) had been found. The yard was due to cleared by mid-2006.

TOPCLIFFE on the A168 south west of Thirsk

645 VGS: Have the forward fuselage of a Cadet.

❑ XE797*	Cadet TX.3	ex Dishforth, Catterick, Dishforth. Crashed 28-9-78. Nose	12-05

SOUTH YORKSHIRE

ARMTHORPE on the A630 north of Doncaster
No.1053 Squadron Air Cadets: Keep a 'Chippax' in Church Street. 'Parent' is Waddington.

❏ WG419	Chipmunk T.10	8206M, ex Finningley, MoA, Laarbruch SF, Gütersloh SF,	
	PAX	Ahlhorn SF, Oldenburg SF, CFS, Abn UAS, Bir UAS,	
		15 RFS, 4 BFTS, 6 RFS	12-05

Others: A yard here handled the former Sandtoft 'museum' airframes. See under Martham, Norfolk, for the nose section of Lincoln 2 G-29-1. Negotiations are reported to be in hand to take the Lincoln to Australia [1]. The Mitchell might well go to Brussels, Belgium [2]. Provost T.1s WV499 and WW421 plus Vampire T.11 XH313 moved to Wycombe Air Park, Bucks by 1-05; Meteor NF.14 WS776 to Bournemouth, Dorset, 5-2-05

❏ G-29-1*	Lincoln 2	ex Sandtoft, North Coates, North Weald, Bournemouth,	
		Bedford, North Weald, Bitteswell, Blackbushe, Southend,	
		Cranfield, G-APRJ / G-36-3, Napier G-29-1, G-APRJ,	
		RF342. Plus cockpit area of Lancaster X KB994	
		(G-BVBP) and rear section(s) of Lancaster X	
		KB976 (G-BCOH). Dismantled	[1] 12-05
❏ WZ584*	'K' Vampire T.11	G-BZRC, ex Sandtoft, North Coates, St Albans, Hatfield,	
		CATCS, 1 FTS, 2 CAACU, 32. Dismantled	12-05
❏ '151632'*	TB-25N-NC	G-BWGR, ex Sandtoft, North Coates, North Weald,	
		NL9494Z,Coventry, Blackbushe, 44-30925.	
		Gorgeous George-Ann. Dismantled	[2] 12-05

ASKERN on the A19 north of Doncaster

❏ XX477	Jetstream T.1	ex Finningley 8462M, Little Rissington, CFS,	
		G-AXXS. Crashed 1-11-74. Fuselage, stored	12-05

BAWTRY on the A638 south of Doncaster
No.216 Squadron Air Cadets:

❏ WK584	Chipmunk T.10	7556M, ex Church Fenton, Linton-on-Ouse, Edzell SF,	
	PAX	Ox UAS, Glas UAS, 11 RFS	3-03

Bawtry Paintball: Located to the north of the town, the arena has a 'chopper' for he-men to assault.

❏ [XL840]	Whirlwind HAS.7	ex Long Marston, Norwich, Sibson, Blackpool, Fleetwood,	
		Wroughton, 705, Brawdy SF, Culdrose SF, 705, 820	3-06

DONCASTER

AeroVenture: Expansion and refinement of the museum continued during 2005 with yet another display hall inaugurated and the shop/café being refurbished. Gannet AS.4 XA460 is owned by the local **750 Squadron, Air Cadets**, and is to be kept and restored in a co-operative arrangement with AeroVenture [1]. Working with AeroVenture and co-based is the **Yorkshire Helicopter Preservation Group** - see below.

Notes: Airframes on loan: Dave Charles, marked DC; Bill Fern - BF; AeroVenture curator Naylan Moore via his **Classic Aircraft Collection**, CAC. Naylan is restoring Harvard FX322 for Phillip Jarvis [2]. During 2005, Naylan took on the nose of the former Hemswell, Lincs, composite Hunter FGA.9. Being from GA.11 WT741, the opportunity has been taken to drop the rest of the identity [3]. Naylan is also at work on a Typhoon or Tempest cockpit section from Gloucestershire. See under Hemswell, Lincs, for notes on Mystère IVA 101. C.150H G-WCL is owned by Robert Ward [4]. HS.125 nose G-BOCB and Hunter T.7 nose N-302 are owned by Mike North [5]. The Tiger Moth fuselage will be restored to the colours of the locally-based 9 RFS [6]. The identity of the Venom FB.1 is now confirmed [7]. Bill Fern's new Cadet is fitted with the wings of WT917 [8]. Venom NF.3 WX788 is on loan from Steve Hague [9]. The Valetta nose came from Cardington and Henlow before that and is said to have been with an ATC unit before joining the museum. During strip-down it revealed a CFS badge [10].Vampire T.11 XD459 has the wings and booms from XE872 and is owned by Dave Hardy [11]. Lightning F.6 XP703 is owned by Scott Clayton [12] while XS897 is owned by two museum members [13].

Departures: Hunter F.2 cockpit WN890 to Boscombe Down, Wilts, 17-6-05; the anonymous Vampire FB.5 pod to Chelmsford, Essex, 10-05; the Jetstream EMU to Sunderland, N&T, by late 2005. The hulk of Cessna F.152 II G-BISB arrived by July 2004, it was stripped of spares and scrapped as the cabin area was beyond use.

◆ *At the Doncaster Lakeside Leisure Park. Access off the A638 beyond 'The Dome' or follow signs off the M18/ A6182 for 'Yorkshire Outlet'. Open Wed to Sun, 10am to 5pm, and Tue, school holidays. AeroVenture are happy to offer 'back lot' tours of the storage area - apply in advance. Dakota Way, Doncaster Leisure Park, Doncaster, DN4 7FP tel 01302 761616 www.aeroventure.org.uk*

❏ 'K-158'	Whippet REP	BAPC.207, ex Sunderland, Stoke-on-Trent	DC	3-06
❏ G-AEJZ*	HM.14 'Flea'	BAPC.120, ex Hemswell, Cleethorpes, Brough.		
		Stored. Arrived by 5-04		3-06
❏ G-AJUD*	J/1 Autocrat	ex Bedford, Camberley, Tongham. CoA 18-5-74	CAC ®	3-06
❏ G-ALYB	Auster 5	ex Firbeck, Bristol, White Waltham, RT520,		
		85 GCS, 84 GCS. CoA 26-5-63. Frame	®	3-06
❏ G-AOKO	Prentice 1	ex Coventry, Southend, VS621, CFS, 2 FTS, 22 FTS.		
		CoA 23-10-72. Stored		3-06
❏ G-APMY	Apache 160	ex Firbeck, Connah's Quay, Halfpenny Green,		
		EI-AJT. CoA 1-11-81		3-06
❏ G-ARGI	Auster 6A	ex Newark-on-Trent, Chirk, Heathfield, VF530, 661.		
		CoA 4-7-76. Frame, stored	CAC	3-06
❏ G-ARHX	Dove 8	ex Sunderland, Booker, Southgate, Leavesden. CoA 8-9-78		3-06
❏ [G-ATXH]*	Jetstream 200	ex Cranwell, Finningley, Prestwick, Filton. Cockpit		3-06
❏ G-AVAA	Cessna F.150G	ex Firbeck, Shobdon, Bournemouth. CoA 5-7-96. Fuselage		3-06
❏ G-AWCL	Cessna F.150H	Canx 2-2-88	[4]	3-06
❏ G-BAML*	JetRanger	ex Walton Wood, N7844S. Crashed 30-5-03. Arrived by 5-04		3-06
❏ G-BOCB	HS.125-1B/522	ex Cardiff, Hatfield, G-OMCA, G-DJMJ, G-AWUF,		
		5N-ALY, G-AWUF, HZ-BIN. CoA 16-10-90. Nose	[5]	3-06
❏ G-DELB	Robinson R-22B	ex Firbeck, Sherburn, Retford, N26461. Cr 27-12-94. Stored		3-06
❏ –	Beagle Pup	ex Stamford. Unfinished cockpit	CAC	3-06
❏ –	Jetstream 41	ex Woodford, Prestwick. Unfinished cockpit		3-06
❏ G-MJKP	Hiway Skytrike	CoA 31-12-86, canx 9-12-94		3-06
❏ G-MJPO	Goldwing	canx 9-4-02		3-06
❏ G-MVRS*	CFM Shadow BD	Cancelled 5-7-90. Fuselage, stored. First noted 4-04		3-06
❏ EI-JWM*	Robinson R-22	ex G-BSLB. First noted 7-04		3-06
❏ N3188H	Ercoupe 415C	ex Chislet, NC3188H. Damaged 7-92		3-06
❏ N4565L	DC-3-201A	ex Framlingham, Ipswich, Dublin, LV-GYP, LV-PCV,		
		N129H, N512, N51D, N80C, NC21744. *Aisling*		3-06
❏ FX322*	Harvard II	ex Bruntingthorpe, Stoke, ?, French AF, FX322.	CAC ® [2]	3-06
❏ 'NM145'	Tiger Moth	fuselage	CAC ® [6]	3-04
❏ WA662	Meteor T.7	ex Firbeck, Willington, Chalgrove, Llanbedr, Farnborough,		
		FCCS, 3, Wildenrath SF, Gütersloh SF, 3	®	3-06
❏ WB560	Chipmunk T.10	ex Firbeck, Fownhope, St Athan, Oxf UAS, 242 OCU, 2 SoTT,		
	PAX	South Cerney SF, ITS, 7 AEF, Nott UAS, 4 AEF	CAC	3-06
❏ WB733	Chipmunk T.10	ex Firbeck, Sevenoaks, Shawbury SF, Hamble CoAT,		
		Marham SF, 4 SoTT 'hack', Lyneham SF, Upavon SF,		
		HUAS, 11 RFS		3-06
❏ [WB969]	Sedbergh TX.1	BGA.2036. ex Wroot		3-06
❏ WD935	Canberra B.2	ex Birdlip, Bridgnorth, Ottershaw, Egham, 8440M, St Athan,		
		360, 97, 151, CSE, EE, BCDU, RAAF A84-1 ntu. Nose	CAC	3-06
❏ [WE987]	Prefect TX.1	BGA.2517, ex Newport Pagnell	BF	3-06
❏ WF122 '575'	Sea Prince T.1	ex Bruntingthorpe, Helston, Culdrose A2673, 750,		
		Sydenham SF, Arbroath SF, Lossiemouth SF, 700Z Flt,		
		Lossiemouth SF, FOFT, 750, Eglinton SF, 744		3-06
❏ WJ565	Canberra T.17	ex Harrington, North Coates, Coventry, North Coates, Binbrook,		
		Bruntingthorpe, Cosford 8871M, St Athan, 360, CA. Nose		3-06
❏ WJ903	Varsity T.1	ex Firbeck, Dumfries, Glasgow Airport, 6 FTS,		
		AE&AEOS, 1 ANS, 2 ANS, 3 ANS. Nose		3-06

❑	WJ975*	'S' Canberra T.19	ex Hemswell, Cleethorpes, Cambridge, 100, 7, 100, 85, West Raynham TFF, 228 OCU, 44, 35, 231 OCU.Nose. F/n 12-05	BF	3-06
❑	WK393	Venom FB.1	ex CGS, FWS, Silloth, Firbeck, Dumfries, Silloth. Pod	BF [7]	3-06
❑	WK626	Chipmunk T.10	ex Firbeck, Salisbury, Welling, White Waltham, Bicester, 8213M, Odiham SF, Ox UAS, South Cerney SF, 1 FTS, Bicester SF, Odiham SF, FTCCS, Lon UAS, Cam UAS, Colerne SF, Leeds UAS, Nott UAS, 16 FRS, 18 RFS. Fuse	BF	3-06
❑	WL131	Meteor F.8	ex Firbeck, Guernsey 7751M, APS Sylt, 601, 111. Nose	BF	3-06
❑	WP255	Vampire NF.10	ex Haverigg, Firbeck, Ecclesfield, Bingley, Church Fenton, 27 MU, CNCS, 1 ANS, CNCS, 23. Pod	CAC	3-06
❑	WT534*	Canberra PR.7	ex Boscombe Down, Solihull, Halton 8549M, St Athan, 17. Nose. Arrived by 12-04	CAC	3-06
❑	WT741*	Hunter GA.11	ex Hemswell, Macclesfield, Bitteswell, HAS, 738. 'Black Arrows' c/s, nose.	[3]	3-06
❑	WT913	FGA Cadet TX.1	BGA.3239, ex Strubby. CoA 21-7-96	BF [8]	3-06
❑	WX788	Venom NF.3	ex Elvington, Kenilworth, Long Marston, Cardiff, Bledlow Ridge, Connah's Quay, DH. Stored	[9]	3-06
❑	[WZ822]	Grasshopper TX.1	ex Firbeck, Robertsbridge, Halton, London. Stored		3-06
❑	–	Valetta	ex Cardington, Henlow (?), ATC unit (?). Nose	[10]	3-06
❑	XA460	'768' Gannet AS.4	ex Connah's Quay, Brawdy, 849	[1]	3-06
❑	XD377	'A' Vampire T.11	ex Firbeck, Barton, Elvington, Cosford, B'ham, Shawbury 8203M, Hawarden, 66. Pod, stored	BF	3-06
❑	XD459	'63' Vampire T.11	ex East Mids, B'thorpe, Long Marston, Bennington, Cranfield, Bushey, Keevil, 3/4 CAACU, 229 OCU, 233 OCU, 151, 253, 56	® [11]	3-06
❑	XE317	'S-N' Sycamore HR.14	ex Firbeck, Winthorpe, Portsmouth, CFS, 275, G-AMWO	®	3-06
❑	XE935	'30' Vampire T.11	ex Firbeck, Sibson, Hitchin, Woodford, Chester, St Athan, 8 FTS		3-06
❑	XG297	'Y' Hunter FGA.9	ex Firbeck, Newton-le-Willows, Bacup, Macclesfield, Bitteswell, HSA, 20, 28, 20, 4. 20 Sqn c/s. Nose	BF	3-06
❑	XH584	Canberra T.4	ex Firbeck, Sunderland, Marham, 231 OCU. Nose		3-06
❑	XL149*	Beverley C.1	ex Winthorpe, Finningley 7988M, 84, 30, 84, 242 OCU. Cockpit. Stored. Arrived by 6-05		3-06
❑	XL388	Vulcan B.2	ex Walpole, Honington 8750M, 50, Wadd Wing, Scampton Wing,9. Nose		3-06
❑	XM350	'89' Jet Provost T.3A	ex Firbeck, Church Fenton 9036M, 7FTS,1FTS,RAFC,AAEE		3-06
❑	[XM411]	'X' Jet Provost T.3	ex Firbeck, Otterburn, Halton 8434M, St Athan, Shawbury, Kemble, CFS. Nose section		3-06
❑	XM561	Skeeter AOP.12	ex Firbeck, East Kirkby, Tattershall, Moston, Middle Wallop, Arborfield 7980M, Wroughton, HQ 1 Wing, HQ 2 Wing, 651		3-06
❑	XN238	Cadet TX.3	ex Firbeck, Robertsbridge, St Athan, 622 VGS. Nose	BF	3-06
❑	XN386	'435' Whirlwind HAR.9	ex Lancaster, Blackpool, Heysham, Wroughton, Yeovilton A2713, Fleetlands, *Endurance* Flt, 846, 814. Cockpit		3-06
❑	XN511	'12' Jet Provost T.3	ex Firbeck, Robertsbridge, 'XM426', Lutterworth, Liversedge, Kemble, CFS, 1 FTS, CFS. Nose	BF	3-06
❑	XN979	Buccaneer S.2	ex Stamford, Croydon, Popham, Stanbridge, Henlow, Cranfield, 801.Ditched 9-6-66. Nose	®	3-06
❑	XP190	Scout AH.1	ex Firbeck, Wroughton, Arborfield		3-06
❑	XP703	Lightning F.3	ex Hemswell, Strubby, Binbrook 8925M, LTF, 11, 5, LTF, 23, 111, 74	[12]	3-06
❑	XP902	Scout AH.1	ex Firbeck, Otterburn, Edinburgh, Dishforth, Netheravon, Wroughton, Garrison Air Sqn, 3 CBAS. Cockpit		3-06
❑	XR754	Lightning F.6	ex Firbeck, Walpole, King's Lynn, Stock, Honington, Binbrook 8972M, 11, 5-11, 23, 5, AAEE. Nose, stored	BF	3-06
❑	XS216	Jet Provost T.4	ex Goole, Finningley, 6 FTS, CAW. Dam 7-5-73. Nose		3-06
❑	XS481	Wessex HU.5	ex Firbeck, Dishforth, Wroughton, Yeovilton, Culdrose, Yeovilton, 771, 707		3-06

❑	XS897		Lightning F.6	ex Firbeck, Rossington, Binbrook, 5,11,5,11,56,74. Stored	[13]	3-06
❑	XT236*		Sioux AH.1	ex Sunderland, Middle Wallop, MoAF, Sek Kong. Stored		3-06
❑	XW666		Nimrod R.1	ex Long Marston, Warton, Woodford, Kinloss, 51.		
				Crashed 16-5-95. Cockpit		3-06
❑	XX411		Gazelle AH.1	ex Chichester, 3 CBAS. Shot down 21-5-82, San Carlos		3-06
❑	E-424		Hunter F.51	ex Firbeck, East Kirkby, Tattershall, Cosford,		
				Dunsfold, G-9-445, Aalborg, RDanAF, Esk.724		3-06
❑	333		Vampire T.55	ex Barton, Chelford, Hadfield, Dukinfield, New		
				Brighton, Chester, Iraqi AF. Pod	CAC	3-06
❑	N-302		Hunter T.53	ex Firbeck, Chelford, Macclesfield, Leavesden, Elstree,		
				Hatfield, RDanAF Esk.724 ET-273, RNethAF N-302.		
				Repainted by 6-05. Nose	[5]	3-06
❑	162068*		AV-8B Harrier	ex Cottesmore 9250M, Wittering, AMARC, VMAT-203.		
				Nose. Arrived by 11-05	BF	3-06
❑	–		Tiger Moth	ex Spanhoe Lodge, Portugal (?). Fuselage	BF ®	3-06
❑	–		CG-4 Hadrian REP	ex Hatfield, *Saving Private Ryan*. Nose	BF	3-06

Yorkshire Helicopter Preservation Group: Congratulations to YHPG on winning the Transport Trust's Ron Wilsdon Award for 2004. Whirlwind HAR.10 XD165 arrived on site during November 2005 from Storwood, E Yorks, and was stripped of all useful parts. It then moved to Caernarfon, Wales, in exchange for the Dragonfly. In due course, WN499 will be restored to represent an HC.4 used in Operation FIREDOG, in Malaya [1]. The Skeeters are owned by YHPG member John Vose. They are under restoration by the Group, but off-site [2]. The Sioux is owned by YHPG's Alan Beattie and is a composite, with parts of XW179 included [3]. The group produce an excellent newsletter to keep members and 'rotorheads' in general in touch.

◆ *Alan Beattie, 18 Marshall Drive, Pickering, YO18 7JT e-mail info@yhpg.co.uk www.helicopter-preservation-yhpg.org.uk*

❑	WN499*	'Y'	Dragonfly HR.3	ex Caernarfon, Higher Blagdon, Blackbushe, Culdrose SF.		
				Arrived 3-06	[1]	3-06
❑	[XA862]*		Whirlwind HAS.1	ex Colerne, Weston-super-Mare, Coventry, Wroughton,		
				Lee-on-Solent A2542, Seafield Park, Haslar, Lee-on-S,		
				Fleetlands, 781, 771, 700, *Protector* Flt, 700, *Protector*		
				Flt, 705, G-AMJT ntu. Cockpit area. Arrived 2005		3-06
❑	XA870	'911'	Whirlwind HAS.1	ex Helston, Predannack, Lee-on-Solent A2543, *Protector*		
				Flt, 705, *Protector* Flt, 155, 848. Sectioned		3-06
❑	XJ398		Whirlwind HAR.10	G-BDBZ, ex Elvington, Oxford, Luton, XJ398, Culdrose		
				RAE, ETPS, Weston-s-M, DH Engines, AAEE, XD768 ntu		3-06
❑	XL738*		Skeeter AOP.12	ex Leeds, Ivybridge, Middle Wallop, Fleetlands, Middle		
				Wallop, Southampton, Middle Wallop 7860M, 651,		
				HTF. Boom of XM565	off-site ® [2]	3-06
❑	XL763*		Skeeter AOP.12	ex Leeds, Ivybridge, Ottershaw, Southall, Wroughton,		
				15/19 Hussars, 2 Div, 654, 1 Wing	off-site ® [2]	2-04
❑	XP345		Whirlwind HAR.10	ex Elvington, Storwood, Tattershall Thorpe, Lee-on-Solent,		
				8792M, Cyprus, 84 'B' Flt, 1563 Flt, 202, CFS. 84 Sqn c/s	®	3-06
❑	XT242	'12'	Sioux AH.1	ex Firbeck, Hooton Park, Warmingham, Long		
				Marston, Wimborne, Middle Wallop, 'Blue Eagles'	[3]	3-06

Museum and Art Gallery: The 'Flea' and the Bensen are displayed on the first floor.

◆ *Open Mon-Sat 10am to 5pm and Sun 2pm to 5pm. Chequer Road, Doncaster, DN1 2AE tel 01302 734293 fax 01302 735409 e-mail museum@doncaster.gov.uk www.doncaster.gov.uk/museums*

❑	'G-AEKR'	HM.14 'Flea'	BAPC.121, ex Breighton, Firbeck, Nostell Priory,		
			Crowle, Finningley		3-06
❑	–	Bensen B.7	BAPC.275, built by S J R Wood, Warmsworth		3-06

NETHERTHORPE AERODROME north of the A619, west of Worksop

By 2003, Apache G-ARJT and F.172K G-AYRG were flying again. Aztec 250C G-BCBM (last noted in September 2003) has moved on.

❏ G-AYXW	Evans VP-1	CoA 15-8-01. Stored	5-03

SHEFFIELD
Brimpex Metal Treatments: Work continues on the Campbell-Bensen and the 'Flea'. The former was involved in blade-tip propulsion experiments. The hunt is on for another gyroplane to restore.
◆ *Visits by prior arrangement only. 5 Devonshire Close, Dore, Sheffield, S17 3NX tel 0114 2366484 fax 0114 2620184 e-mail brimpex@demon.co.uk*

❏ –	BAPC.13 HM.14 'Flea'	ex Kirk Langley, Wigan, Peel Green, Styal, Urmston, Berrington, Tenbury Wells, Knutsford	® 3-02
❏ –	C-Bensen B.7	–	® 3-02

Others:

❏ XP558*	'20' Jet Provost T.4	ex Ipswich, Norwich, Honington 8648M, St Athan, Culdrose A2628, CAW, 3 CAACU, RAFC. Cockpit	12-05

WEST YORKSHIRE

BATLEY on the A652 north of Dewsbury
Northern Aeroplane Workshops (NAW): Make good progress with their Sopwith Camel, which will fly with the Shuttleworth Collection. The workshop is within the **Skopos Motor Museum**.
◆ *At Alexander Mills in Alexander Road, signed. Visits to see work in progress by a prior permission only. Alexander Road, Batley, WF17 6JA. tel 01924 444423. NAW c/o C Page, 20 Lombard Street, Rawdon, near Leeds, LS19 6BW e-mail r.hendrie4@ukonline.co.uk www.shuttleworth.org/collection/naw.htm*

❏ [G-BZSC]	Camel F1 REP	project under construction	4-06

BIRD'S EDGE on the A629 north-west of Penistone

❏ G-BKIR	SAN D.117	ex F-BIOC. CoA 28-8-92.	® 10-02

HALIFAX

❏ G-AIBY	J/1 Autocrat	ex Sherburn, 'Halifax'. CoA 13-4-81. Stored.	7-00

HUDDERSFIELD AERODROME or Crosland Moor, south of the A670 west of the city

❏ G-ANZU*	Tiger Moth	ex Godmanchester, L6938, Wyton SF, 25 RFS, 28 EFTS, 17 EFTS, 14 EFTS, 14 ERFTS. CoA 17-3-91. Spares	5-05
❏ G-AYKK	SAN D.117	ex F-BHGM. CoA 22-5-85	® 5-99
❏ G-BLYY	Archer II	ex OO-PAY, N9792K.Crashed 31-7-99. Stored	9-99
❏ C-GDQD	Thurston Teal	G-TEAL. Damaged 3-93. Fuselage	5-00

LEEDS
Leeds University: Have taken delivery of a training aid.

❏ G-BLLP*	T.67B Firefly	ex Eshott, Bagby. CoA 4-12-00. Inst	9-04

Others: A private owner *should* still keep a Bensen gyroglider in the area [1]. The Sea Harrier arrived at the Cross Green Industrial Estate [2]. The two Skeeters (XL738 and XL763) listed here in W&R19 (p272) are owned by YHPG member John Vose and can now be found under <u>Doncaster</u>, S Yorks.

❏ –	BAPC.200 Bensen B.7	ex Cheltenham, Long Marston, Stoke	[1] 11-93
❏ ZD613*	'122' Sea Harrier FA.2	ex Shawbury, 800, 899, 801, 899, 801, 800, 899, 801, 899, 801, 899. Arrived 8-11-05	[2] 11-05

LEEDS-BRADFORD AIRPORT (YEADON)
Cessna 150H G-AWES moved to Netherthorpe, S Yorks, and by mid-2005 was flying again.

❑ G-ATND	Cessna F.150F	crashed 9-12-72. Engine test-rig		12-05
❑ G-AWES	Cessna 150H	ex Blackpool, Glenrothes, N22933. Damaged 2-10-81	®	3-02
❑ EI-BPD	Short 360-100	ex Southend, Aer Arran, Gill, G-RMCT, Aer Lingus		
		EI-BPD, G-BLPU, G-14-3656. Dam 4-2-01.Fire crews		3-05

Locally: The Avian is under restoration, but 'off-site'.

❑ G-ACGT	Avian IIIA	ex Linthwaite, EI-AAB. CoA 21-7-39	®	11-04

PART TWO
CHANNEL ISLANDS

ALDERNEY AIRPORT
The overall yellow Aztec *should* still provide the fire crews with practice.

❑ G-ASHV	Aztec 250B	ex Guernsey, N5281Y ntu. CoA 22-7-85. Dump	12-99

GUERNSEY
The EAA Biplane is at Sausmarez Park, while the Noralpha is stored within St Peter Port.

❑ G-ATEP	EAA Biplane	CoA 18-6-73. Stored	5-03
❑ G-ATHN	Noralpha	ex F-BFUZ, French mil No.84. CoA 27-6-75. Stored	5-03

GUERNSEY AIRPORT
The firemen have had the nose of a former Predannack Hunter for non-destructive testing. It was last noted in the Cornwall fire pits in 1995 - how long has it been here? [1]

❑ G-BAZJ	Herald 209	ex Air UK, Alia 4X-AHR, G-8-1. Fire crews	2-04
❑ G-BBYO	Trislander	ex ZS-KMH, G-BBYO, G-BBWR. CoA 1-5-92. Fuse	10-01
❑ G-BDTN	Trislander	ex S7-AAN, VQ-SAN, G-BDTN. CoA 10-6-98. Stored	6-01
❑ N32625	Seneca 200	damaged 19-1-98. dump	10-01
❑ N97121	Bandeirante	ex City-Line, PT-SDK. Withdrawn by 4-97	11-02
❑ XM409	Jet Provost T.3	ex Firbeck, Moreton-in-Marsh, Halton 8082M,	
		Shawbury, 2 FTS. Nose.	10-01
❑ XS888	'521' Wessex HAS.1	ex Lee-o-S, Wroughton, Fleetlands. Dump	10-01
❑ XX466*	'830' Hunter T.7	ex ?, Predannack A2651 [2], Culdrose SAH A2738,	10-01
		FRADU, 1 TWU, Jordan AF, RSaudiAF 70-616,	
		HSA, XL620, 74, 66. Cockpit. See above	[1] 10-04

JERSEY AIRPORT
The fire service compound, located north of the Runway 09 threshold, has a steel airliner mock-up for 'burning' exercises..

❑ XP573	'19' Jet Provost T.4	ex Halton '8236M', Kemble, Shawbury, R-R, 1 FTS, CFS.	
		Really 8336M. Fire crews	1-06

PART THREE

SCOTLAND

Scotland's 'regions' comprise the following wholly 'single tier' unitary authorities: Bordersm Central, Dumfries and Galloway, Fife, Grampian, Highland, Islands, Lothian, Strathclyde and Tayside.

ABERDEEN

HQ Aberdeen Wing, Air Cadets / 2489 Squadron Air Cadets: Within the TAVR Gordon Barracks, Bridge of Don. The Phantom nose is dedicated to F/L Martin Owens.

❑ XV581	Phantom FG.1	ex Lossiemouth, Buchan 9070M, Wattisham,	
		43, 111, 43. Nose. 43 Squadron colours	1-03

Others: ARV Super 2 G-BNHC, last noted in December 1996, has moved on, perhaps to the Glasgow area.

ABERDEEN AIRPORT (DYCE)

The fire dump is occupied by a wholly 'synthetic' Sikorsky S-61 look-alike and an equally 'ersatz' Boeing 737-ish fuselage – the former for rescue/egress training, the latter for burning.

❑ G-TIGH	Super Puma	ex Bristow, F-WXFL. *City of Edinburgh.*	
		Crashed 14-3-92. Fuselage, rescue training	2-04

ABOYNE AERODROME south of the A93 west of Banchory

❑ G-BAHP	Volmer Sportsman	CoA 18-10-93. Stored	2-06

ALEXANDRIA on the A82 south of Loch Lomond

Russ Snadden: Russ was the leading light in the restoration of Bf 109 *Black Six*, star of the front cover of *W&R13* and now at the RAF Museum, Hendon. To keep his hand in, he's working on a Bestmann.

❑ G-CBKB*	Bestmann	ex F-PCRL, F-BCRU. Arrived 2002	12-05

ARBROATH

No.662 VGS: Stored inside the hangar is a former Portmoak Cadet.

❑ XE786	HLR Cadet TX.3	BGA.4033, ex Syerston, 643 VGS, 662 VGS. Stored	3-06

BALADO BRIDGE on the A91 west of Milnathort

❑ XM412	'41' Jet Provost T.3A	ex Ipswich, North Weald, Binbrook, Colsterworth,	
and '49'		Halton 9011M, 1 FTS, 3 FTS, 2 FTS	9-04

BANCHORY on the A93 west of Aberdeen

❑ G-ARXD	Airedale	ex Netherley. CoA 13-6-86	®	2-02
❑ G-ASAI	Airedale	ex Dundee, Islay. CoA 20-5-77	®	2-02

BORGUE on the B727 west of Kirkcudbright

Brighouse Bay Caravan Park: Displayed inside the camp is the former Carlisle Meteor.

❑ WS792	'K' Meteor NF.14	ex Carlisle, Cosford 7965M, 5 MU, 1 ANS, 2 ANS.	7-04

BRIDGE OF WEIR on the A761 north-west of Paisley

Neil Geddes: XK820 has wings from WZ754 and WZ778 and its own wings are at Kirton-in-Lindsey.

❑ XK820	Grasshopper TX.1	ex Strathallan, Aberdeen, Lancing, Locking. Stored.	10-02

CROSSHILL on the B7023 south of Maybole
A trailer-bound Prefect is resident at the bowling green.

❑ G-BVOD*	M-P Two-Place	Canx 23-11-00. Stored in rafters		8-05
❑ CKJ	1601 T.30A Prefect	ex PH-197. CoA 14-4-90. Stored		2-06

CRUDEN BAY on the A975 south of Peterhead
Hobson Home for Distressed Aeroplanes: A move of house in May 2004 brought about the scrapping of the 'fleet': Condor G-AVKM, FR.172J G-AXBU and AA-1B G-BCIL.

CULLODEN north-east of Inverness

❑ G-APOD	Tipsy Belfair	ex Dundee, OO-TIF ntu. CoA 23-8-88	®	2-01

CUMBERNAULD AERODROME north of the A80, north of Cumbernauld
George Cormack gifted Islander G-BELF to the Museum of Flight at East Fortune, Scotland. It was unveiled there on 7th July 2005. Super Cub 135 G-BWUC moved to Thornhill, Scotland.

❑ G-BEVV	Trislander	ex Bembridge, Cumbernauld, 6Y-JQK, G-BNZD, G-BEVV. Fuselage, stored	2-06
❑ G-BUTE*	EA-1 Kingfisher	ex G-BRCK. CoA 25-10-99. Stored	1-06
❑ G-BVER	Beaver 1	ex G-BTDM, XV268, Middle Wallop. CoA 23-4-95. Spares	2-06

CUPAR on the A91 west of St Andrews
In the area, a Bensen and a Cadet are stored and an enthusiast keeps a Victor nose.

❑ G-ARTJ	Bensen B.8M	ex East Fortune, Cupar, Currie, Cupar	5-03
❑ XA917	Victor B.1	ex Crowland, Barnham, Marham 7827M, AAEE, HP. Cockpit	9-05
❑ XE802	Cadet TX.3	ex Syerston, 624 VGS. Stored	2-06

CURRIE on the A70 south-west of Edinburgh
Robert Whitton: Gave Chipmunk WB670 to APSS and it moved to East Fortune, Scotland, by November 2004.

DIRLETON on the A198 west of North Berwick
A Grasshopper is stored at a strip in the area. It is a composite with the one at Carlisle, Cumbria - qv.

❑ WZ824*	Grasshopper TX.1	ex Strathaven, Ringmer, Dishforth, St Bees. Stored	2-06

DUMFRIES off the A701 north-east of Dumfries on the former airfield
Dumfries and Galloway Aviation Museum (DGAM): Run by the Dumfries and Galloway Aviation Group, the restored watch tower that forms the centrepiece of the museum contains a huge array of artefacts, all well presented. The tower and grounds continue to be refined and 2006 should see a new exhibition, 'Aviation in Scotland'. Still more airframes arrive; the Draken is on long term loan from the Imperial War Museum, Duxford [1]; the Gannet from Prestwick, Scotland, and the Lightning from Edinburgh, Scotland, are due [2].

    Notes: Trident G-AWZJ fuselage is open to the public and includes an extensive interior display and 30-seat lecture hall [3]. Chipmunk T.10 WD386 was fitted with the rear end of WD377. [4]. Canberra T.4 nose WJ880 is used as a travelling display [5]. Vampire XD547 has the wings of XD425 [6]. The damaged Spitfire FSM that had been in storage, has been deleted.

◆ *Open Sat and Sun 10am to 5pm 1st Apr (or Easter, if earlier) to Oct inclusive. Also Wed, Thu, Fri Jul and Aug, 11am to 4pm. Also open most Bank Holidays. Special visits by prior arrangement. Follow brown signs from A75 at the A701 roundabout. Former Control Tower, Heathfield Industrial Estate, Dumfries, DG1 3PH tel 01387 720487 e-mail info@dumfriesaviationmuseum.com www.dumfriesaviationmuseum.com*

☐	G-AHAT		J/1N Alpha	ex Firbeck, Exeter, Taunton, Old Sarum,		
				HB-EOK ntu. Crashed 31-8-74. Frame		4-06
☐	G-ARPP*		Trident 1C	ex Palnackie, Glasgow, Heathrow, BA, BEA.		
				CoA 16-2-86. Nose. Arrived 11-05		4-06
☐	G-AWZJ		Trident 3B-101	ex Prestwick, BA, BEA. CoA 12-9-85. Fuselage	[3]	4-06
☐	G-MMIX		Tiger Cub 440	ex Long Marston		4-06
☐	P7540		Spitfire IIa	ex Loch Doon, 312, 266, 609, 66. Cr 6-7-41	®	4-06
☐	WA576		Sycamore 3	ex East Fortune, Strathallan, Halton 7900M,		
				RAE, AAEE, G-ALSS ntu		4-06
☐	WD386	'O'	Chipmunk T.10	ex Firbeck, Cranfield, Tenby, St Athan, 1 FTS,		
				Ox UAS, 22 RFS , 2 BFTS. SOC 29-7-70	[4]	4-06
☐	WJ880		Canberra T.4	ex Firbeck, North Weald, Halton 8491M, 7, 85, 100, 56,		
				Laarbruch SF, RAE, 16, Laarbruch SF, Gütersloh SF, 104.		
				Nose	[5]	4-06
☐	WL375		Meteor T.7(mod)	ex West Freugh, RAE. RAE Bedford colours		4-06
☐	XD547	'Z'	Vampire T.11	ex Aberfoyle, Strathallan, Milngavie, Glasgow,		
				CATCS, 8 FTS, 1 RS, 263	[6]	4-06
☐	'XF506'	'A'	Hunter F.4	WT746, ex Saighton, Halton 7770M, St Athan,		
				AFDS. 'Black Arrows', 111 Sqn colour scheme		4-06
☐	XL497*	'041'	Gannet AEW.3	ex Prestwick, Lossiemouth, 849	[2]	**due**
☐	XP557*	'72'	Jet Provost T.4	ex Hemswell, Firbeck, Bruntingthorpe, Halton		
				8494M, 6 FTS, RAFC. Arrived 25-3-05		4-06
☐	XT280		Buccaneer S.2B	ex Dundonald, Birtley, East Fortune, Lossiemouth,		
				12, 208, 12, 16, 237 OCU. Nose		4-06
☐	XX483	'562'	Jetstream T.1	ex Welshpool, Weston-on-Trent, Shawbury, 750,		
				CFS, 5 FTS. Cockpit		4-06
☐	ZF584*		Lightning F.53	ex Edinburgh, Turnhouse, Warton, RSAF 53-682,		
				G-27-52. Gate	[2]	**due**
☐	FT-36		T-33A-1-LO	ex Sculthorpe, Belg AF, USAF 55-3047. *Little Miss Laura*		4-06
☐	318	'8-NY'	Mystère IVA	ex Sculthorpe, French Air Force		4-06
☐	Q497		Canberra T.4	ex Warton, Samlesbury, frustrated Indian AF B.52,		
				Bracebridge Heath, Samlesbury, Kemble, WE191, 231		
				OCU, 237 OCU, 231 OCU, 245. Fuselage		4-06
☐	Fv 35075*	'40'	J35A Draken	ex Duxford, RSwAF F16. Arrived 19-8-05	[1]	4-06
☐	42163	'005'	F-100D-11-NA	ex Sculthorpe, FAF. USAF colours, *Shillelagh*		4-06
☐	68-0060		F-111E	ex 20 TFW. Escape pod. Crashed 5-11-75		4-06

DUNDEE
AA-5A G-REEK, last noted in July 2002, is thought to have left in 2004, possibly for South Africa.

DUNDEE AIRPORT (RIVERSIDE)
The remains of Gulfstream I G-BNCE from the fire pit was removed by a scrappie in February 2006.

EAST FORTUNE AERODROME north of the A1, west of East Linton
National Museums of Scotland – Museum of Flight (MoF): Patricia Ferguson, Minister of Tourism, Culture and Sport, officially opened the 'Concorde Experience' on 15th March 2005. By prior booking *only*, visitors can inspect the inside of *Alpha-Alpha*. The expected demand to view the white hot-rod has determined the pre-booking, but this will probably ease when the 'mania' dies off. The supporting display for Concorde is well put together but the over-riding image, for at least the compiler, is the huge waste of display space within the rest of the hangar. A number of relevant and contrasting airframes could have been here, adding to the so-called 'visitor experience'. (And remember how much of the collection is in 'deep store' to allow for Concorde.) The Islander and the Tornado thankfully prove that collecting still continues post-Concorde. The Islander is a good example of the previously innovative collecting policy here. Sadly, it features a fanciful 'emergency services' colour scheme. What a pity, an early Loganair scheme would have been much more fitting.

STOP PRESS: As *W&R20* closed, the warned-of exodus of airliners from Cosford, Shropshire, was announced. British Airways are reported to be financing what they called the "deconstruction and reconstruction" of several of the former BA airliner collection and bringing them here courtesy of ASI of Alton, Hants. These are listed below in anticipation. The Viscount is a 'must', the BAC 111 far less so and doubtless chosen because it was the 'youngest' of the Cosford inmates – a mere 14 years outside. The Viscount (30 years outside at Cosford) *could* fit within the 'Concorde Experience' hangar, but we will have to wait until *W&R21* to see if this is the case. The Boeing 707 *and* Trident forward fuselages, seem excessive, but I suppose it is a case of not looking a gift horse in the mouth. The 707, one of two last vestiges of the Conway-engined breed in the UK, makes some sense, but the Trident probably was best put out of its misery at Cosford. However, it *appears* that further space has to be made for these, at the expense of the already ever-rarer light aircraft collection here – see below. (And yet, there seems to be several candidates that would not decay the 'sweep' of the collection at all. How about: an Air & Space 18A, a Jetstream, the awful 'B5577', VX185, WF259, XA109, the MiG cockpit, for example.)

Working in support of all aspects of the museum is the **Aviation Preservation Society of Scotland** (APSS) which was founded in 1973: Since April 2001, the team have been busy at work on a flyable Sopwith $1\frac{1}{2}$ Strutter, but it is too early yet to give it a 'formal' reference. Work was completed in October 2004 on the APSS Slingsby T.53 glider, which moved to Potmoak for flight test. It is the compiler's *understanding* that Auster TJ398 (in store) and the superb Monarch are to leave the site to give way for new inmates. I hope this all proves to be not the case [1]. APSS members receive copies of the excellent journal, *The Fortune Teller*. (c/o Museum of Flight, see below. email contact@apss.org.uk, www.apss.org.uk)

Notes: The Kay Gyroplane from Glasgow, Scotland, is on loan [2]. Fergus McCann donated the Eurowing Goldwing. Built as a kit by Eurowing at East Kilbride, assembled by a Scottish syndicate and operated in Scotland for 20 years, it is a highly appropriate item [3]. The Catto CA-16 microlight 'trike' was donated by Robin Henderson in 1983 and has the wing of G-MJEN [4]. Slingsby Gull I BED is *possibly* the former VW912 [5]. The Buccaneer cockpit is thought to be XK533 [6].

Departures: Weir W-2 BAPC.85 to Edinburgh, Scotland, by October 2005; the anonymous Beaufighter nose to Hendon, Gtr Lon, 17th December 2004.

◆ *Open daily (except Xmas and New Year) 10am to 5.30pm. Weekends only Oct to Mar. Pre-booking to view inside Concorde, via a 'Boarding Pass' is considered to be essential - contact the numbers below or book on-line. Parties by appointment. Guided tours of the storage hangar are possible, enquire prior to arrival. A series of regular events are staged – SAE for details. There is also a gift shop and the 'Aviator Café'. East Fortune Airfield, near Haddington, East Lothian, EH39 5LF tel 01620 880308 fax 01620 880355 e-mail museum_of_flight@sol.co.uk www.nms.ac.uk/flight*

❑ G-ACVA	Kay Gyroplane	ex Glasgow, Strathallan, Perth, Glasgow, Perth	[2]	4-06
❑ G-ACYK	Spartan Cruiser	ex Hill of Stake, Largs. Cr 14-1-38. Fuselage, stored		4-06
❑ G-AFJU	Miles Monarch	ex York, Strathallan, Lasham, Staverton, X9306, G-AFJU.		
		CoA 18-5-64	APSS [1]	4-06
❑ G-AGBN	GAL Cygnet II	ex Strathallan, Biggin Hill, ES915, MCCS, 52 OTU, 51 OTU,		
		23, G-AGBN. CoA 28-11-80		4-06
❑ G-AHKY	Miles M.18-2	ex Perth, Strathallan, Blackbushe, HM545, U-0224, U-8.		
		CoA 20-9-89		4-06
❑ G-AMOG*	Viscount 701	ex Cosford, Cardiff, BOAC, Cambrian, BEA *Robert*		
		Falcon Scott, G-AMNZ ntu. CoA 14-6-77. BEA c/s		**due**
❑ G-ANOV	Dove 6	ex CAFU Stansted, G-5-16. CoA 31-5-75		4-06
❑ G-AOEL	Tiger Moth	ex Strathallan, Dunstable, N9510, 7 FTS, 2 GU,11 RFS,		
		1 RFS, 7 RFS, 7 EFTS. CoA 18-7-72		4-06
❑ G-APFJ*	Boeing 707-436	ex Cosford, British Airtours, BOAC. CoA 16-2-82.		
		Airtours c/s. Forward fuselage		**due**
❑ G-ARCX	Meteor Mk 14	ex Ferranti, WM261. CoA 20-2-69		4-06
❑ G-ARPH*	Trident 1C	ex Cosford, BA, BEA. CoA 8-9-82. BA c/s. Forward fuse		**due**
❑ G-ASUG	Beech E.18S	ex Loganair, N575C, N555CB, N24R. CoA 23-7-75		4-06
❑ G-ATOY	Comanche 260B	ex Elstree, N8893P. Crashed 6-3-79. *Mythtoo*,		
		Sheila Scott's aircraft. Fuselage		4-06
❑ G-AVMO*	BAC 111-510ED	ex Cosford, Bournemouth, BA, BEA. *Lothian Region*		**due**
❑ G-AVPC	Turbulent	first flown 8-9-73. Donated by Stephen Sharp 4-03		4-04
❑ G-AXEH	Bulldog Srs 1	ex Prestwick, Shoreham. Prototype. CoA 15-1-77		4-06
❑ G-BBVF	Twin Pioneer 2	ex Shobdon, XM961/7978M, SRCU, Odiham SF, 230, 21.		
		Damaged 11-3-82		4-06

❑	G-BDFU		Dragonfly MPA	ex Blackpool Airport, Warton, Prestwick. Stored		2-00
❑	G-BDIX		Comet 4C	ex Lasham, Dan-Air, XR399, 216. CoA 11-10-81		4-06
❑	[G-BELF]*		BN-2A-26	ex Cumbernauld, D-IBRA, G-BELF. CoA 12-3-01.		
				Unveiled 7-7-05		4-06
❑	G-BOAA*		Concorde 102	ex London, BA, G-N94AA, BOAC. CoA 24-2-01.		
				Arrived 19-4-04		4-06
❑	G-BVWK*		A&S 18A	ex Kinnetties, SE-HID, N6108S. Canx 18-10-00.Arr 10-04		4-06
❑	G-BVWL*		A&S 18A	ex Kinnetties, SE-HIE, N90588, N6152S. Canx 18-10-00.		
				Arrived 10-04		4-06
❑	G-JSSD		Jetstream 3100	ex Prestwick, N510F, N510E, N12227, G-AXJZ. CoA 9-10-90		4-06
❑	G-MBJX		Super Scorpion	ex Halton. Acquired 1998. Canx 13-6-90		3-04
❑	G-MBPM		EW-21 Goldwing	CoA 21-8-98	[3]	3-04
❑	G-MMLI		Typhoon	BAPC.244. ex Glasgow. Canx 7-9-94. Stored		3-04
❑	[BED]	902	Gull I	ex Newbattle, 'G-ALPHA'	[5]	3-04
❑	[BJV]	1014	T.21A	ex Feshiebridge, SE-SHK		3-04
❑	–		Jetstream 1	ex Hatfield, East Midlands, N14234, N102SC, N200SC ntu,		
			(Super 31 EMU)	N1BE, G-BBBV, G-8-12. Fuselage		3-04
❑	–		BAPC.49 Pilcher Hawk	ex Edinburgh. First flown at Eynsham 1896, crashed at		
				Stanford Hall, Leics, 30-9-1899	off-site	3-04
❑	–		BAPC.160 Chargus 18/50 hg	ex Tranent. (Acquired 1975.)		3-04
❑	–		BAPC.195 Moonraker 77 hg	ex Edinburgh. Birdman-built, circa 1977		3-04
❑	–		BAPC.196 Sigma II Metre hg	ex Penicuik. Southdown Sailwings-built c 1980		3-04
❑	–		BAPC.197 Cirrus III hg	ex Edinburgh. Scotkites-built 1977		3-04
❑	–		BAPC.245 Electra Floater hg	ex Edinburgh. Built 1979. Stored		3-04
❑	–		BAPC.246 Hiway Cloudbase	ex Edinburgh. Built 1978, acquired 1995		3-04
❑	–		BAPC.247 Albatros ASG.21	ex Edinburgh. Built 1977, acquired 1995		3-04
❑	–		BAPC.262 Catto CA-16	ex Gifford. Acquired 1983	® [4]	3-04
❑	VH-SNB		Dragon I	ex Strathallan, VH-ASK, RAAF A34-13		4-06
❑	VH-UQB		Puss Moth	ex Strathallan, Bankstown, G-ABDW		4-06
❑	'B5577'	'W'	Camel REP	BAPC.59, ex Cosford, St Athan 'D3419', St Mawgan,		
				'F1921', St Athan, Colerne. Stored		4-04
❑	TE462		Spitfire XVI	ex Ouston 7243M, 101 FRS, Finningley SF		4-06
❑	'TJ398'		Auster AOP.5	BAPC.70, ex 'TJ472'. Inverkeithing, Currie, Perth,		
				Hamble, 'G-ALES'. Stored	APSS [1]	4-06
❑	TS291		T.8 Tutor	BCB / BGA.852, ex Portmoak, TS291		4-04
❑	VM360		Anson C.19	G-APHV, ex Strathallan, Kemps, BKS, TRE, AAEE	®	4-06
❑	VX185		Canberra B.5	ex Wroughton, South Kensington, 7631M, EE. Nose		3-04
❑	WB584		Chipmunk T.10	ex Manston, Kilmarnock, Edinburgh 7706M, Shawbury,		
			PAX	Debden CF, 11 GCF, Tangmere SF, Glas UAS, 8 FTS,		
				Bri UAS, 12 RFS, 22 RFS		3-04
❑	WB670*		Chipmunk T.l0	8361M, ex Currie, Southend, London Colney, Welwyn		
			PAX	Garden City, Hatfield, MoS, 5 FTS, LAS, 12 RFS,		
				5 RFS. Rear fuselage of WG303. Arrived 11-04	APSS	4-06
❑	WF259	'171'	Sea Hawk F.2	A2483, ex Lossiemouth SF, 736		4-06
❑	WV493	'29'	Provost T.1	G-BDYG, ex Strathallan, Halton 7696M, 6 FTS.		
				CoA 28-11-80. Stored		3-04
❑	WW145	'680'	Sea Ven FAW.22	ex Lossiemouth, 750, 891		4-06
❑	XA109		Sea Vampire T.22	ex Lossiemouth, 831, JOAC		4-06
❑	XA228		Grasshopper TX.1	ex Glenalmond School. Stored	APSS	3-04
❑	XL762		Skeeter AOP.12	ex Middle Wallop, Halton 8017M, 2 RTR, 9 Flt, 652,		
				22 Flt, 654, 651. Stored		3-04
❑	XM597		Vulcan B.2	ex Waddington, 50, 35, 101, 9, 50, 35, Wadd W, 12		4-06
❑	XN776	'C'	Lightning F.2A	ex Leuchars, 92, 19		4-06
❑	XT288		Buccaneer S.2B	ex Lossiemouth 9134M, AAEE, 208, 12, RN 800		4-06
❑	XV277		Harrier GR.1	ex Ipswich, Yeovilton A2602 [2], A2600 [2], Filton, HSA		4-06
❑	ZE934*		Tornado F.3	ex St Athan, 56, 111, 11, 43, 11, 111, 5. Arrived 13-9-05		4-06
❑	–		Buccaneer S.1 CIM	ex Lossiemouth	[6]	3-04

❑	9940		Bolingbroke IVT	ex Strathallan, RCAF 5 B&GS	℗	4-06
❑	3677		MiG-15*bis* SB	ex Cáslav, Ostravian Air Regt, Czech AF. c/n 613677		4-06
❑	309		MiG-15UTI	ex Polish AF. c/n 3309. Cockpit section.		3-04
❑	BF-10		Beaufighter TF.10	ex Swartkop, South Africa, Alverca, Lisbon, Port AF		
				RD220. Stored		4-06
❑	591		Rhonlerche II	ex D-0359		3-04
❑	–	'FI+S'	MS.505 Criquet	G-BIRW, ex Duxford, OO-FIS, F-BDQS. CoA3-6-83. Stored		3-04
❑	191659	'15'	Me 163B-1a	ex Cambridge, Cranfield, Brize Norton, RAE, Husum, II/JG400		4-06
❑	155848	'WT'	F-4S-MC	ex Yeovilton, VMFA-232, USMC.		4-06
❑	–		CG-4A Hadrian	ex Aberlady. Nose section. *The Bunhouse*		4-04

Others: To the west of the former airfield, a 'stub' of runway is used as a microlight strip.

❑	G-BEYN	Evans VP-1	Stored	2-06
❑	G-BSNO	Denney Kitfox	crashed 9-7-97. Wreck, stored	2-06
❑	G-MMBE	Tiger Cub 440	ex 'Fat Sam's', Edinburgh. Stored	8-05

EDINBURGH

Royal Museum of Scotland: Chambers Street. In a reversal of previous thinking, the 'parent' of the Museum of Flight at East Fortune, Scotland (qv) has taken back the Weir W-2 (and a section of Black Knight 'squib').

◆ *Mon to Sat 10am to 5pm; late opening Tues. Sunday noon to 5pm. Chambers Street, Edinburgh, EH1 1JF. 0131 2474027 fax 0131 2204819 e-mail info@nms.ac.uk www.nms.ac.uk*

❑	W-2*	Weir W-2	BAPC.85, ex East Fortune, Glasgow, East Fortune, Hayes,	
			Knockholt, Hanworth, Cathcart. On loan. Arr by 10-05	10-05

Ferranti / BAE Systems: Lightning F.53 ZF584 is being prepared to move to Dumfries, Scotland.

❑	ZF584	Lightning F.53	ex Turnhouse, Warton, RSAF 53-682, G-27-52. Gate	2-06

EDINBURGH AIRPORT (TURNHOUSE)

The **603 (City of Edinburgh) Squadron Association** look after the Spitfire FSM [1]. Cessna 310R G-BWYE was flying again by mid-2005.

❑	G-MALK	Cessna F.172N	ex PH-SVF, PH-AXF. Cr 23-7-97. Fuselage, fire crews		2-06
❑	'L1067'	Spitfire FSM	BAPC.227. ex 'L1070', 'XT-A', 603 Sqn colours.		
		'XT-D'	*Blue Peter*. Plinth-mounted near entrance	[1]	4-06

ELGIN on the A941 south of Lossiemouth and north of Elgin

Buccaneer Service Station: Ian Aitkenhead keeps the 'Brick' in excellent condition on the forecourt.

❑	XW530	Buccaneer S.2B	ex Lossiemouth, 208, 12, 208, 216, 16, 15, 16	10-05

ERROL south of the A90, east of Perth

SAN-built D.117 G-ATIN had gone by 2005, perhaps to the St Andrews area. The Buccaneer, Gannet and Vampire are kept by a *private* collector locally. The 'Bucc' was broken up at 'Lossie' in March 1994 [2].

❑	G-ATIN		SAN D.117	ex F-BHNV. CoA 18-4-96	℗	8-04
❑	'XE897'		Vampire T.11	XD403, ex Leuchars, Errol, Strathallan, Woodford,		
				Chester, 4 FTS, 1 FTS, 7 FTS, 8 FTS, 5 FTS, 4 FTS		8-03
❑	XG882	'771'	Gannet T.5	ex Lossiemouth 8754M, 845. Composite, parts from XA463. [1]		4-04
❑	XN981*		Buccaneer S.2B	ex Lossie', 12, 208, 12, 809, 12, 900, 801, 700B. F/n 9-02	[2]	9-03

FALGUNZEON on the A711 south-west of Dumfries

Dumfries and Galloway Gliding Club: Falke G-BFPA moved to Portmoak, Scotland, by December 2005. Three gliders listed here have been deleted: Ka.2B DCG (last noted 7-97), KA 2B DGT (9-01) T.45 DHP (5-95).

❑	BRQ	1177	EoN 460 Srs 1C	ex G-ARFU. CoA 8-96. Stored	8-04

FYVIE on the B947 west of Peterhead
Mark Reeder: Mark handed on all of his cache of Hornet parts to David Collins of Chelmsford, Essex.

GIRVAN on the A77 north of Stranraer
The Flix: A 'fun pub' in Bridge Street with a Tiger Cub 'flying' from the ceiling.
□ G-MJUH Tiger Cub 440 CoA 5-8-92 9-04

GLASGOW

Kelvingrove Museum: Courtesy of a team from Airframe Assemblies (Sandown, Isle of Wight) Spitfire F.21 LA198 was moved to its new home here. The team dismantled, moved and designed the suspension system and 'hung' the Spitfire in the newly-refurbished atrium. In flying trim, it was unveiled on 17th October 2005. The museum is due to complete its £27.9 million refurbishment in the summer of 2006.
◆ *In Kelvin Park in the West End of the city. Enquire regarding new opening times. Argyle Street, Glasgow G3 8AG tel 0141 2872699 e-mail museums@cls.glasgow.gov.uk www.glasgowmuseums.com*
□ LA198 Spitfire F.21 ex Kelvin Hall, East Fortune, Cardington, St Athan, Leuchars,
 'RAI-G' Locking, Worcester, 7118M, 3 CAACU, 602, 1. 602 Sqn c/s.
 Unveiled 17-10-05 3-06

Museum of Transport: The Pilcher was built by 2175 Squadron ATC, Glasgow, and awaits restoration. Spitfire F.21 LA198 moved to its new home at the Kelvingrove Museum by October 2005 – see above.
◆ *Mon to Thu and Sat 10am to 5pm. Fri and Sun 11am to 5pm. Nearest underground is Kelvin Hall. Kelvin Hall, 1 Bunhouse Road, Glasgow, G3 8DP tel 0141 2872720 fax 0141 2872692 e-mail museums@cls.glasgow.gov.uk www.glasgowmuseums.com*
□ BAPC.48 Pilcher Hawk REP Stored 3-06

No.2175 Squadron Air Cadets: Base a 'travelling' Bulldog at their Hillingdon HQ.
□ 'XX530' 'F' Bulldog T.1 XX637, ex Cranwell, St Athan 9197M, North UAS, 2 FTS 6-03

Others: A Nipper and an Airtourer are stored in the area. The reference for *Hotel-Tango* is decidedly ancient, and it could well be heading for LOST! [1]. Acollector has three microlights stored in the area [2].
□ G-AWJF Nipper T.66 ex airport and local area. CoA 7-6-88. Stored ® 12-01
□ G-AZHT Airtourer T3 ex airport and local area. Crashed 29-4-88. Stored. [1] 6-95
□ G-MBYI* Lazair IIIE CoA 8-8-05. Stored [2] 2-06
□ G-MWXA* Mainair Gemini CoA 15-8-97. Stored [2] 2-06
□ G-MWXU* Mainair Gemini CoA 23-1-03. Stored [2] 2-06

GLENROTHES on the A92 north of Kircaldy
□ G-AREH Tiger Moth ex Bridge of Weir, Lochwinnoch, Kilkerran, G-APYV ntu,
 6746M, DE241, 22 RFS, 22 EFTS. CoA 19-4-66 ® 8-01

GREENOCK west of Glasgow on the A8
James Watt College: Within the Aeronautical Eng Dept, Kingston Industrial Estate, in Port Glasgow.
□ XX690 'A' Bulldog T.1 ex Shawbury, Liv UAS, 3 FTS, CFS, York UAS,
 RNEFTS, EL UAS, RNEFTS, 2 FTS 2-03

HADDINGTON east of Edinburgh, south of the A1
Ian Sheffield: Keeps a two-seater Harrier cockpit in the general area.
▶ Viewable by prior appointment only: e-mail ian.sheffiled@tesco.net
□ -* Harrier T.2 or 4 cockpit 2-06

INSCH AERODROME west of the B992 at Auchleve

❑	G-BALK		SNCAN SV-4C	ex Aboyne, 'Cheshire', Liverpool, Littleborough,	
				F-BBAN, French mil No.387. Fuselage	10-05
❑	479781		L-4H Cub	G-AISS, ex D-ECAV, SL-AAA, 44-79781. CoA 25-6-97	® 10-05

INVERNESS

A Campbell Cricket has been stored in the area for a long time.

❑	G-AYHI	Cricket	CoA 19-8-86. Stored	8-03

INVERNESS AIRPORT (DALCROSS)

Highland Aviation Museum: The museum opened up in May 2005 and boasts an aircraft park and a detailed and well presented interior displays. Several airframes are on loan from a collector from North-East England - ¥.

Contrary to *W&R19* (p281), the deal for Wessex HU.5 XT480 fell through and it did *not* come here from Hixon, Staffs. The 'JP' T.4 nose is owned by Peter Westley and it will be used for instruction by Air Cadets and schools and as a travelling exhibit for the museum [1].

◆ *Open throughout the year, Sat, Sun and Bank Hols, 10am-5pm. Other times by appointment. 9 Dalcross Industrial Estate, by Inverness Airport, IV2 7XB tel 0167 461100 e-mail enquiries@highlandaircraft .fsnet.co.uk www.highlandaviationmuseum.co.uk*

❑	G-ASVO*		Herald 214	ex Glenrothes, Perth, Shoreham, Alto, Bournemouth,	
				Channel Express, PP-SDG, G-ASVO, G-8-3.	
				Damaged 8-4-97. Cockpit. Arrived 20-1-05	3-06
❑	WM145*		Meteor NF.11	ex Great Ayton, Rotherham, Finningley, 5, 29, 151, 219.	
				Nose. Due to arrive 3-06	**due**
❑	WT660		Hunter F.1	ex Inverness, Cullen, New Byth, Carlisle, 229 OCU,	
				DFLS. 43 Sqn colours	3-06
❑	WZ557*		Vampire T.11	ex Great Ayton, Huntingdon, Acaster Malbis, Woodford,	
				Chester, St Athan, 5 FTS, 16. Black c/s. Due to arr 3-06	**due**
❑	XD875		Valiant B.1	ex Winthorpe, Bruntingthorpe, Marham, Firbeck,	
				Coventry, Cosford, 7, 138, 207, 49, 207. Nose	¥ 3-06
❑	XK532	'632'	Buccaneer S.1	ex airport, Lossiemouth 8867M, Manadon, A2581,	
				Lossiemouth, 736	3-06
❑	XM169*		Lightning F.1A	ex Great Ayton, Thirsk, Leuchars 8422M, Leuchars TFF, 23,	
				Binbrook TFF, 111, AAEE, MoA, EE. Arr 23-6-04. Nose	¥ 3-06
❑	XN607*		Jet Provost T.3	ex Great Ayton, Leeds, 3 FTS. SOC 28-5-76. Nose.	
				All grey c/s. Arrived 23-6-04	¥ 3-06
❑	XS176*	'N'	Jet Provost T.4	ex Stamford, Luton, Solihull, Bruntingthorpe, Salford,	
				Halton 8514M, CATCS, 3 FTS, 2 FTS. Nose. Arr 18-6-05	[1] 3-06
❑	XV867*		Buccaneer S.2B	ex Great Ayton, Leeming, 208, 12, 208, 237 OCU,	
				FAA, 809, 736, 803. Nose. Arrived by 4-05	¥ 3-06
❑	ZA362*	'TR'	Tornado GR.1	ex Lossiemouth, 15, TTTE. Arrived 9-6-05	3-06

KILMARNOCK north-east of Ayr

No.327 Squadron Air Cadets: In Aird Avenue, off Dundonald Road. Those of Canberra T.4 WJ872 was scrapped circa 2002. The Hunter CIM, not noted since January 1998, has been deleted.

KINGSMUIR, or Sorbie, on the B9131 south east of St Andrews

❑	G-BRGO*	Air Command 532	CoA 13-2-91. Dumped	8-05

KINLOSS on the B9011 north of Forres

RAF Kinloss: The wreck of a Chipmunk is held at the base.

❑	G-AOSU*	Chipmunk 22	ex RAFGSA, WB766, 1 BFTS, 24 RFS. Cr 18-1-04	3-05

KINNETTIES on the B9127 south of Forfar
In October 2004 Air & Space 18As G-BVWK and G-BVWL moved to East Fortune, Scotland.

KIRKNEWTON on the B7031 west of Currie
❑ G-BRTC*	Cessna 150G	ex N3296J. Damaged 23-12-<u>91</u>. Canx 3-2-99. F/n 7-05	3-06
❑ G-BTVG*	Cessna 140	ex N2114N, NC2114N. CoA 15-4-99. First noted 12-05	3-06
❑ G-EEVA*	Aztec 250	ex G-ASND, N4800P. Arrived 9-05	® 3-06
❑ EI-APF*	Cessna F.150G	ex Perth, Sligo. CoA 8-98. First noted 9-05	3-06

KIRRIEMUIR on the A928, north of Dundee and west of Forfar
Kirriemuir Aviation Museum: Celebrating its 20th anniversary in 2005, this small, privately-owned museum was established by Richard Moss. Within can be found a wide array of artefacts.
◆ *Open 1st April to late Sept; Mon to Thu 10am to 5pm, Fri to Sun 11am to 5pm Bellies Brae, Kirriemuir, Scotland tel 01575 573233 www.kamrafa.co.uk*

LEUCHARS AIRFIELD on the A919, north-west of St Andrews
RAF Leuchars: The Harrier cockpit is on charge with **2345 Squadron**, ATC [1]. The Tornado on the gate is multi-faceted: it carries 43 Squadron colours on the port side of the nose, 111 Squadron colours on the starboard side and 56 Squadron colours on both sides of the tail [2].

❑ XR713	'C'	Lightning F.3	8935M, ex LTF, 5, 11, 5, LTF, 11, LTF, 5, 111, Wattisham TFF, 111. Displayed, officially ABDR	9-05
❑ XT864	'A''BJ'	Phantom FG.1	8998M, ex 111, 892, 767. Gate. 43 / 111 Sqn c/s	9-04
❑ XV582	'M'	Phantom FG.1	9066M, ex WLT, 43. *Black Mike*. All black c/s	9-05
❑ XV586	'AJ'	Phantom FG.1	9067M, ex 43, 893. 43 Sqn mascot	9-04
❑ XW265	'W'	Harrier T.4	ex St Athan, Cosford 9258M, Shawbury, 20, 233 OCU, AAEE. Cockpit [1]	7-03
❑ ZD906		Tornado F.2	ex St Athan, 229 OCU. Nose. ABDRT	9-01
❑ ZE256*		Tornado F.3	ex 56. Inst. First noted 9-03	3-04
❑ ZE967*		Tornado F.3	ex 56, 43, 111, 43, 25, 23, 25, 43, 11, 111. Unveiled 10-9-04 [2]	9-04

LOCHEARNHEAD on the A85 west of Crieff
❑ G-DHCB	Beaver 1	ex G-BTDL, XP779. CoA 16-9-97. Stored.	9-03

LONGSIDE on the A950 west of Peterhead
❑ G-BEJL	S-61N Mk.II	ex EI-BPK, G-BEJL, N4606G. CoA 30-9-98. Stored	9-03

LOSSIEMOUTH AIRFIELD south of the B4090, west of Lossiemouth
RAF Lossiemouth: Tornado GR.1 ZA362 moved to Inverness, Scotland, on 9th June 2005.

❑ XV863	'S'	Buccaneer S.2B	9145M, ex 9115M, 9139M, 16, 237 OCU, 208, 237 OCU, 208, 809. Pink c/s	5-05
❑ ZA324	'TAY'	Tornado GR.1	ex 15, TTTE. BDRT	9-03
❑ ZA355	'TAA'	Tornado GR.1	ex 15, TTTE. WLT	3-02
❑ ZA474	'AJ-F'	Tornado GR.1	ex 617, 12, 27, 20, 16. Spares	1-03
❑ ZA475	'FH'	Tornado GR.1B	9311M, ex 12, 27, 20, 17, 9, 16. Gate	10-03
❑ ZD900		Tornado F.2	ex St Athan, Warton, AAEE. Nose	9-03

MAYBOLE on the A77 south of Ayr
❑ OO-NAT	MS.880B Rallye	ex G-BAOK. Fuselage.	7-05

MINTLAW on the A950 west of Peterhead

❑ G-MBFZ	Goldwing	CoA 5-9-00. Stored.	1-01
❑ G-MJUF	Tiger Cub 440	Canx 27-4-90. Stored.	1-01

MONTROSE on the A92 north of Arbroath

Montrose Air Station Heritage Centre: By late 2004 the name had changed from the Montrose Air Station Museum to the current title with the Montrose Air Station Trust and the Montrose Aerodrome Museum Society becoming the **Montrose Air Station Heritage Trust**. A complete revamp over the winter of 2004/2005 merited a re-opening of the museum and this was carried out by author David Ross on 29th April 2005.

Notes: XE340 is on loan from the Fleet Air Arm Museum, Yeovilton, Somerset [1]. Vampire XE874 is fitted with the booms of XD528 (the rest of it is at Firbeck, S Yorks). The booms of XE874 are *also* present, just to confuse things! XE874 and the Sycamore are on loan from a private collector [2].

◆ *At Waldron Road, north Montrose. Open Sun noon to 5pm, other times by prior arrangement. Waldron Road, Broomfield, Montrose, DD10 9BB tel 01674 673107 tel / fax 01674 674210 e-mail rafmontrose@aol.com www.rafmontrose.org.uk*

❑ XD542	'N'	Vampire T.11	7604M, ex Edzell, Cranwell, 'XD429', Colerne, Melksham, FWS, CGS. Camouflaged		4-06
❑ XE340	'131'	Sea Hawk FGA.6	ex Strathallan, Wroughton, Staverton, Brawdy, 801, 898, 897, 800	[1]	4-06
❑ XE874	'61'	Vampire T.11	ex New Byth, Valley 8582M, Woodford, Chester, Shawbury, 1 FTS, 4 FTS, 8 FTS, 4 FTS, 1 FTS, 4 FTS, 7 FTS	[2]	4-06
❑ XJ380		Sycamore HR.14	ex New Byth, Drighlington, Finningley 8628M, Catterick, CFS, MoA, HS, 275	[2]	4-06
❑ XJ723		W'wind HAR.10	ex OPITB, Wroughton, 202, 228, 155		4-06

Neil Butler: Continues to work on the Prentice.

❑ G-AWSS	Condor	ex Fordoun. CoA 19-10-94. Stored		4-06
❑ VS356	Prentice T.1	G-AOLU, ex Stonehaven, Perth, Strathallan, Biggin Hill, EI-ASP, G-AOLU, VS356, CFS, 2 FTS. CoA 8-5-76	®	4-06

Oil Petroleum Training Industry Board:

❑ N116WG	WG.30-160	ex Weston-super-Mare, Yeovil, PanAm	7-03

OBAN

The Canberra nose here is believed to be moving on to an Air Training Corps unit.

❑ WJ721	Canberra TT.18	ex Dundonald, Bacup, Samlesbury, 7, 50, 40. Nose	12-05

ORPHIR near Kirkwall, Orkney Islands

It has been a long time - understandably - since there was a *physical* report of this one.

❑ G-ASRP	SAN DR.1050	ex F-BITI. Ditched 17-3-86. Canx 20-1-99. Stored	10-94

PALNACKIE on the A711 south of Dalbeattie, south west of Dumfries

James Halliday: The nose of Trident 1C G-ARPP moved to Dumfries, Scotland, by November 2005. In its place came a Boeing 737 cockpit, the rest of which was parted out at Prestwick early in 2005.

◆ *Visits by prior arrangement* only.

❑ EI-CJF*	Boeing 737-204	ex Prestwick, Ryanair, G-BTZF, G-BKHF, G-BKGV ntu. Nose. Arrived by 11-05	®	11-05

PATHHEAD on the A68 south-east of Edinburgh

❑ G-BOHN	Tomahawk 112 II	ex Edinburgh, Cardiff-Wales, N23593. Crashed 13-8-93. Cockpit, plaything	1-97

PERTH AIRPORT (SCONE)

Perth College: The cockpit of Herald 214 G-ASVO moved to Glenrothes, Scotland, by late December 2004 but stayed only fleetingly, before settling upon Inverness, Scotland, on 20th January 2005. Cessna F.150G EI-APF moved to Kirknewton, Scotland, by July 2005.

❏ G-AYGB	Cessna 310Q	ex N7611Q. CoA 23-10-87	1-06
❏ G-AZZG	Cessna 188-230	ex Blairgowrie, Lairg, Inverness, Southend, OY-AHT,	
		N8029V. CoA 1-5-81	1-06
❏ G-BCIE	Warrior 151	ex N9588N. Crashed 27-5-99. Dump	1-06
❏ G-BEWP	Cessna F.150M	crashed 4-10-83	1-06
❏ G-BTIN	Cessna 150C	ex N7805Z. Damaged 12-98	1-06
❏ G-NFLC*	Jetstream 1	ex Cranfield, G-AXUI, G-8-9. Arrived by 12-04	1-06
❏ XL875	Whirlwind HAR.9	ex Wroughton, Lee SAR Flt, CU SAR Flt, 847,848,815	1-06
❏ [XT140]	Sioux AH.1	ex Middle Wallop	1-06
❏ _*	HS.748 / ATP	nose. First noted 12-04	12-04
❏ _*	HS.748 / ATP	nose. First noted 12-04	12-04

Others:

❏ G-APXU	Tri-Pacer 150	ex Rochester, Bredhurst, N1723A. CoA 20-2-85	® 1-06

PETERHEAD on the A90 south of Fraserburgh

Score Energy Ltd: The Lightning 'guards' the GLEN Test Facility, which includes an overhaul facility for industrial Rolls-Royce Avons.

❏ XR749	'DA' Lightning F.3	ex Tees-side, Chop Gate, Leuchars 8934M, 11, LTF, 11, LTF,	
		Binbrook pool, 29, 226 OCU, 56, EE. Overstressed 17-2-87.	
		LTF colours. Arrived 26-7-04	7-04

PORTMOAK AERODROME, west of Glenrothes

John S Morgan and **Eoin MacDonald:** Have taken delivery of a Buccaneer cockpit. (For John's cockpit collection, see Pershore, Worcs.)

❏ G-BFPA*	SF-25B Falke	ex Falgunzeon, D-KAGM. CoA 13-8-98. Stored	® 12-05
❏ XX893*	Buccaneer S.2B	ex Blackpool, Birtley, East Fortune, Lossiemouth,	
		237 OCU, 208, 16, 15, 16, 12, 16. Nose. Arr 12-04	3-06

PRESTWICK AIRPORT

HMS *Gannet:* Predictably, Gannet AEW.3 XL497 was put up for tender in late 2005. It was acquired by the D&G at Dumfries, Scotland. As *W&R20* closed for press, its migration south was imminent.

❏ XL497	'041' Gannet AEW.3	ex Lossiemouth, 849. Gate of RN enclave	3-06

Others: Luscombe G-BNIP departed by road 18th December 2005 to continue its restoration south o' the border. GJD Services parted-out a series of former Ryanair Boeing 737s during 2005. Three nose sections went on to new lives: EI-CJE to Biggin Hill, Gtr Lon; EI-CJF to Palnackie, Scotland; EI-CKS to the Netherlands. The fuselages of EI-CKQ and EI-CKR moved to Bournemouth, Dorset.

❏ G-ATDB	Noralpha	ex Edinburgh, Skelmorie, Prestwick, F-OTAN-6,	
		Fr mil 186. CoA 22-11-78	® 2-06
❏ N250TB	Aztec 250D	ex G-VHFA, G-BZFE, G-AZFE, EI-BPA,	
		G-AZFE, N13962. Stored	7-05
❏ [N852FT]	Boeing 747-122	ex Polar Air Cargo, N4712U. Fire crews	12-05
❏ –	ATP/J61	fuselage. c/n 2068. Fire crews. c/n 2068	4-05

Locally: The Wagtail Flying Group continues to work on their Tipsy.

❏ G-AISC	Tipsy B	ex Cumbernauld, Henstridge, Yeovil. CoA 23-5-79	® 6-03

STONEHAVEN on the A90 north of Montrose
Pete Morris: By August 2005 Terrier 2 G-ASAX had moved to Chislet, Kent
| ❑ G-ASBU | Terrier 2 | ex Netherley, T.7 WE570, LAS, CFS,2FTS,CFS. Cr 12-8-80 | 1-00 |

STRATHALLAN AERODROME west of the B8062, north of Auchterarder
Cessna U.206F G-STAT moved to Grindale, E Yorks, by June 2004.
| ❑ G-BAGV | Cessna U.206F | ex N9667G. Crash 5-5-02. Para-trainer | 11-03 |
| ❑ R1914 | Magister I | G-AHUJ, ex Aboyne, Balado, Kemble, 137, 604, Middle Wallop SF, 604. CoA 9-7-98. Stored | 12-01 |

STRATHAVEN AERODROME on the A71 south-east of East Kilbride
Grasshopper TX.1 WZ824 moved to a strip at Dirleton, Scotland.
❑ G-AYFE*	D.62C Condor	CoA 6-12-01. Stored	8-05
❑ G-MMLE*	Goldwing SP	ex Glasgow. Stored, first noted 8-05	8-05
❑ –	Skycraft Scout	fuselage. Stored, unflown. Possibly G-MJDM	8-05
❑ –	Skycraft Scout	fuselage. Stored, unflown	8-05

STRATHDON on the A97 north of Ballater
| ❑ N15750 | Beech D.18S | ex Corgarff, 'CF-RLD', Lasham, G-ATUM, D-IANA, N20S. Cockpit section | 2-97 |

SUMBURGH AIRPORT Shetland Islands
| ❑ F-BMCY | Potez 840 | wheels-up landing 29-3-81. Fire dump | 2-01 |

TAIN north of Inverness
| ❑ G-ATWS | Luton Minor | CoA 26-3-69 | ® 7-01 |

THORNHILL AERODROME on the A873 north-west of Stirling
| ❑ G-BWUC | PA-18-135 | N719CS, ex Cumbernauld. SX-ASM, EI-1818, I-EIYB, MM54-2369, 54-2369. Stored Arrived late 2005 | 2-06 |

TOWNHILL east of the B912, north of Dunfermline
| ❑ XR627* | 'X' Scout AH.1 | ex Ipswich, Wattisham, Arborfield, Dishforth, Middle Wallop, Wroughton, Garrison Air Sqn, 3 CBAS | 2-06 |

WEST FREUGH AIRFIELD on the A715 south-east of Stranraer
Defence Science and Technology Laboratory (DS&TL)
| ❑ XN817 | Argosy C.1 | ex AAEE, MinTech, MoA. Fuselage, dump | 2-06 |
| ❑ XT852 | Phantom FGR.2 | ex Scampton, AAEE, HSA, AAEE, HSA, AAEE. Dump | 2-06 |

WICK AIRPORT north of the town on the A99
| ❑ G-BODH* | Motor Cadet III | ex East Fortune, BGA.474. CoA 13-8-02. Stored | 11-05 |
| ❑ G-BTUD* | CFM Image | ex G-MWPV. CoA 21-1-95. Stored | 11-05 |

YARROW on the A708 west of Selkirk
| ❑ G-ANOK | Safir | ex Strathallan, East Fortune, SE-CAH ntu. CoA 5-2-73 | 10-01 |

PART FOUR
WALES

☛ The 'regions' of Wales comprise the following wholly 'single tier' unitary authorities: Clwyd, Dyfed, Gwent, Gwynedd, Powys, Mid Glamorgan, South Glamorgan and West Glamorgan.

ABERGAVENNY on the A40 west of Monmouth

Restoration of the Tiger is thought to be continuing.

❑ N9191	Tiger Moth	G-ALND, ex Shobdon, Shipdham, N9191, 5 SoTT, 19 EFTS, Duxford CF, 6 CPF. Crashed 8-3-81	®	3-96

ABERPORTH AIRFIELD north of the A487, east of Cardigan

Defence Science and Technology Laboratory: The new Gallileo Avionica Mirach 100-5 drones can operate from the site here, hence the closure of Llanbedr. The remainder of the site here is being developed as a civil aerodrome and a science and industry park – Parc Aberporth. Hunter F.1 WT680 moved to Fleet Hargate, Lincs, on 25th July 2004.

❑ A92-255	Jindivik 3	ex DRA, RAE. Gate	5-02

AMMANFORD on the A483 north of Swansea

No.2475 Squadron Air Cadets: Still keep a Canberra nose.

❑ WH739	Canberra B.2	ex St Athan, 100, 85, 45, 75 RNZAF, Upwood SF, 50, 101. Nose	3-06

BRIDGEND on the A473 west of Cardiff

De Havilland Aviation wound down their store here – see under Bournemouth, Dorset, for the main entry. Vampire FB.6 'WL505' (G-MKVI) moved to Gainsborough, Lincs, in April 2004. The *real* WL505 (G-FBIX) moved to Bournemouth, Dorset, by October 2005. T.11 XE956 (G-OBLN) moved to Pen-Coed, Wales, by May 2003 and then to Rochester, Kent, 14th May 2004. T.11 XE985 pod to Cwmbran, Wales, by May 2004, but returned here; moving then to Exeter, Devon, on 29th January 2005. The anonymous and unflown, ex-Swiss, Vampire FB.6 pod is unaccounted for.

CAERNARFON AERODROME or Llandwrog north of the A487, south-west of Caernarfon

Caernarfon Air Museum: Dove 6 G-ALFT was scrapped on site by March 2004, corrosion having taken its toll over the years. By March 2004, the cockpit of Cessna 150 G-AWUK and Dragonfly HR.3 WN499 had gravitated to the fire dump – see below. The museum tells the story of aviation in general and aviation in North Wales in particular. The mountain rescue exhibit is a graphic story of wartime crashes, both Allied and Luftwaffe. The Weedhopper *may* be G-MJSM [1]. The Flea from St Athan is currently on show in uncovered form, but there are plans to restore it to taxiable condition [2].

◆ *Open Mar 1 to end of Oct, 10am to 5pm. Caernarfon airparc, Dinas Dinlle, Caernarfon, LL54 5TP tel 08707 541500 fax 08707 541510 e-mail info@caeairparc.com www.caeairparc.com*

❑ G-AMLZ	Prince 6E	ex Coventry, VR-TBN ntu, G-AMLZ. CoA 18-6-71		3-06
❑ G-MBEP	Eagle 215B	first noted 1-97. On loan from R W Lavender		3-06
❑ –	BAPC.201 HM.14 'Flea'	ex Talysarn. Fuselage, rudder, wing spars. Modded u/c		3-06
❑ –	BAPC.286 HM.14 Flea	ex St Athan, 'local area'. Scott A2S	® [2]	3-06
❑ –	Tiger Moth	ex Shobdon, Fownhope. Frame in 'workshop' scene		3-06
❑	Weedhopper	loaned from Ray Bancroft, Prestatyn	[1]	3-06
❑ WL756*	Shackleton AEW.2	ex St Austell, St Mawgan 9101M, 8, 204, 205, 37, 38. Nose. Arrived 10-2-06		3-06
❑ WM961	'J' Sea Hawk FB.5	ex Higher Blagdon, Culdrose A2517, FRU, 802, 811.		3-06
❑ WT694	Hunter F.1	ex Newton, Debden 7510M, 229 OCU, DFLS, 54		3-06

❑ WV781		Sycamore HR.12	ex Finningley, Odiham, Digby 7839M, HDU,	
			CFS, ASWDU, G-ALTD ntu. Forward fuselage	3-06
❑ XA282		Cadet TX.3	ex Syerston, 635 VGS	3-06
❑ XH837		Javelin FAW.7	ex Northolt, Ruislip 8032M, 33. Forward fuselage	3-06
❑ XJ726	'F'	Whirlwind HAR.10	ex Sibson, Wroughton, 2 FTS, CFS, ME SAR Flt, 22	3-06
❑ XK623	'56'	Vampire T.11	ex Bournemouth 'G-VAMP', Moston,	
			Woodford, Chester, St Athan, 5 FTS.	3-06
❑ XL618	'05'	Hunter T.7	ex Cottesmore 8892M, Shawbury, Kemble,	
			1 TWU, 229 OCU, Jever SF, Gütersloh SF	3-06
❑ –		Varsity T.1 EMU	ex Higher Blagdon	3-06

Airfield: Two former museum inmates had joined the fire dump by March 2004. One of these was Dragonfly HR.3 WN499 which was exchanged for the Whirlwind in March 2006 and moved to <u>Doncaster</u>, S Yorks.

❑ G-AWUK*		Cessna F.150H	ex Shobdon, Stansted, Oaksey Park, Bristol, Biggin Hill.	
			Crashed 4-9-71. Cockpit. Fire dump by 3-04	11-05
❑ G-AYPJ*		Cherokee 180E	ex Mona, N11C. CoA 1-10-04. Fuselage, stored. F/n 10-05	11-05
❑ XD165*	'B'	Whirlwind HAR.10	ex Doncaster, Storwood, Wattisham, Netheravon, Halton	
			8673M, SARTS, 202, 228, 22, 225, 155. Dump. Arr 3-06	3-06

CARDIFF AIRPORT (RHOOSE)

Airport: The fire crews here have a three-engined synthetic fire trainer as well as the real airframes.

❑ G-AVGH		Cherokee 140	CoA 5-12-91. Fuselage. Fire crews	2-01
❑ G-AVMT*		BAC 111-510ED	ex Bournemouth, European, BA, BEA. CoA 5-12-03.	
			Arrived by road 14-11-04. Fire crews	2-05
❑ –		Jetstream 41 EMU	ex WAM, Hatfield, Prestwick. Based on Srs 200	
			G-ATXJ. CoA 8-2-71. Fire crews	2-02

International Centre for Aerospace Training (Barry Technical College): Within the industrial and business park on the airport perimeter.

❑ G-BDAX		Aztec 250C	ex 5B-CAO, N6399Y. CoA 12-11-93	2-04
❑ XX672	'E'	Bulldog T.1	ex Shawbury, Birm UAS	1-05
❑ XX687	'F'	Bulldog T.1	ex Shawbury, EM UAS, Liv UAS	1-05

CAREW CHERITON on the A477 east of Pembroke

Carew Control Tower Group: Took delivery of an Anson for restoration and display at the former airfield.

❑ VM325*		Anson C.19	ex Gloucestershire, Bentham, Staverton, Coventry,	
			Halfpenny Green, WCS, NCS, WCS, TCCF, Upavon	
			CF, 173, 4 FP. Arrived 23-8-05	8-05

CHESTER AIRFIELD or Hawarden or Broughton, on the B5129 west of Chester

BAE Systems: The dump was cleared in September 2005. The anonymous HS.748 forward fuselage and Venom FB.50 'WE275' (G-VIDI) were removed to a local scrapyard and processed before the month was out. Prior to that the fuselage of ATP c/n 2075 had expired, or been removed: last noted in April 1998.

Hawarden Air Services and **North Wales Military Aircraft Services:** Bulldog 120 G-BHXB became G-JWCM in October 1999 and was flying shortly thereafter. The identity of the former Singapore ADC Strikemaster is *nearly* confirmed! [1] L29 Delfin 'Red 51' was supplied to the Real Aeroplane Company at <u>Breighton</u>, E Yorks, on 7th April 2005. How long had it been here?

❑ G-ASXH		Bensen B.8M	CoA 22-8-73	3-96
❑ G-BYED		Jet Provost T.5A	ex Londonderry, N166A, XW302, 6 FTS, 3 FTS,	
			RAFC, 1 FTS. Crashed 12-2-01	3-06
❑ G-OJCM		Rotorway Exec 90	crashed 25-9-95. Wreck	8-96
❑ G-UPCC		Robinson R-22	ex G-MUSS. Crashed 5-6-94	8-96
❑ CCCP-07268		An-2 *Colt*	YL-LEV, Latvia, USSR	3-06

☐	CCCP-17939	An-2 *Colt*	YL-LFC, Latvia, USSR. Dumped outside	5-05
☐	CCCP-19731	An-2 *Colt*	YL-LEU, ex Hooton Park, Chester, Latvia, USSR	3-06
☐	CCCP-19733	An-2 *Colt*	YL-LEZ, Latvia, USSR. Dumped outside	3-06
☐	CCCP-20320	Mi-2 *Hoplite*	YL-LHN, Latvia, USSR	3-06
☐	CCCP-20619	Mi-2 *Hoplite*	YL-LHO, Latvia, USSR	3-06
☐	CCCP-40748	An-2 *Colt*	YL-LFA, Latvia, USSR	3-06
☐	CCCP-40749	An-2 *Colt*	YL-LFD, Latvia, USSR	3-06
☐	CCCP-40784	An-2 *Colt*	YL-LEY, Latvia, USSR	3-06
☐	CCCP-40785	An-2 *Colt*	YL-LFB, Latvia, USSR	3-06
☐	CCCP-54949	An-2 *Colt*	YL-LEX, Latvia, USSR	3-06
☐	CCCP-56471	An-2 *Colt*	YL-LEW, Latvia, USSR	3-06
☐	–	Tucano T.1	ex Waverton, Belfast City. c/n S45/T42. Dam 1990 ®	1-05
☐	323*	Strikemaster Mk.81	ex Singapore ADC, S Yemen AF. Stored	3-06
☐	'03' r	Mi-24 *Hind-D*	ex Latvia, USSR. (3532461715415)	3-06
☐	'05' b	Yak-50	YL-CBH, ex Latvia. (832507)	11-97
☐	'05' r	Yak-50	YL-YAK, ex Strathallan, CIS. (832507?)	11-95
☐	'09' g	Yak-52	YL-CBI, ex Wrexham, Chester, Latvia. (811202)	11-96
☐	'20' b	Yak-52	YL-CBJ, ex Strathallan, CIS. (790404)	1-05
☐	'23' r	MiG-27 *Flogger*	ex Latvia, USSR. (83712515040). Dumped outside	3-06
☐	'35' r	Su-17M-3 *Fitter*	ex Latvia, USSR. ('25102')	3-06
☐	'54' r	Su-17B *Fitter*	ex Latvia, USSR. (69004/5). Dumped outside	3-06
☐	'56' r	Yak-52	ex Strathallan, CIS. (811506)	5-02
☐	–	Mi-24V *Hind*	ex Latvia, USSR. (3532424810853)	5-02

No.2247 Squadron Air Cadets: 'Parented' by Sealand, in Manor Lane to the east of the airfield.

☐	XE852	'H' Vampire T.11	ex Woodford, Chester, Shawbury, 1 FTS, 4 FTS	3-06

CHIRK on the A5 north of Oswestry

Not noted since October 1999, Bell 47J-2A G-ATFV is believed to have moved on – destination unknown.

☐	G-AJBJ	Dragon Rapide	ex Coventry, B'pool, NF894, 18 MU, HQ TCCF. CoA 14-9-61	3-06
☐	'G-AJCL'	Dragon Rapide	G-AIUL, ex Southend, British Westpoint, NR749, Kemble, 2 RS. CoA 29-9-67	3-06
☐	G-AKOE	Dragon Rapide	ex Booker, X7484, PTS. CoA 25-2-82	3-06
☐	G-ANFC*	Tiger Moth	ex DE363, 22 EFTS, 4 FIS. CoA 9-10-03	3-06
☐	G-BAYL	Norecrin VI	ex Ivychurch, Solihull, Bodmin, F-BEQV. Fuselage	3-06
☐	G-BEDB	Norecrin	ex Liverpool, Chirk, F-BEOB. CoA 11-6-80	3-06

CONNAH'S QUAY on the A548 west of Chester

North East Wales Institute, Dee-side College: (See also under Wrexham, Wales.). The Cessna 340 should be here, but as yet no reliable report of this.

☐	G-AZMX	Cherokee 140	ex Chester, Half' Green, SE-FLL, LN-LMK. CoA 9-1-82	8-03
☐	N66SW	Cessna 340	ex N5035Q	due
☐	XR658	Jet Provost T.4	ex Bournemouth, Wroughton, Abingdon 8192M, RAFEF, 6 FTS, CAW, 7 FTS	3-06
☐	XW423	'14' Jet Provost T.5A	G-BWUW, ex Little Snoring, RAF, Shawbury, 3 FTS, RAFC, 1 FTS, 3 FTS. CoA 14-2-02	3-06

Terry Parker: The Venom pod *could* be from J-1711.

☐	'J-1712'	Venom FB.54	ex Charnock Richard, Bournemouth, Thayngen, Swiss AF. Pod	2-04

COWBRIDGE on the A48 west of Cardiff

Task Force Paintball: The Whirlwind still battles it out at the paintball wargames park.

☐	XG592	Whirlwind HAS.7	ex Cardiff, Wroughton, 705, 846, 705, 700, C(A), HS, Westland	8-05

CWMBRAN on the A4051 north of Newport

Mark Gauntlett: See also Exeter, Devon, for Mark's Vampire T.11 pod.

❑ QA-12   Hunter FGA.78   ex Bournemouth, Qatar AF, G-9-284, RNethAF N-222. Nose   6-05

HAVERFORDWEST

The nose of 'JP' T.3A XN503 moved to Boscombe Down, Wilts, in October 2004.

HAVERFORDWEST AERODROME or Withybush, on the A40, north of Haverfordwest

Aeronca G-BPGK was flying by 2003. *Victor-Zulu* is a US-built Pietenpol, known as a Challis Chaffinch [1].

❑ G-ACZE	Dragon Rapide	ex Dorchester, G-AJGS, G-ACZE, Z7266, 3 FP,		
		6 AONS, G-ACZE. CoA 11-8-95	®	5-05
❑ G-ASAN	Terrier 2	ex Auster T.7 VX928, 661, HCEU, 661.CoA 28-6-96	®	4-01
❑ G-BMNV*	SNCAN SV-4L	ex Dorchester, Booker, F-BBNI. CoA 8-6-94.		5-05
❑ G-BSVZ*	Aircamper	G-KIRC, ex Kemble, N3265. CoA 6-9-93. Stored	[1]	7-05
❑ G-BTWU	Tri-Pacer 135	ex N3320B. Canx 15-5-03	®	10-99
❑ '5964'*	DH.2 REP	G-BFVH, ex Dorchester, Duxford, *Gunbus*, 'GBH-7'.		
		'4589', Land's End, Chertsey. CoA 20-7-01		5-05

HOLYWELL on the A5026 north west of Queensferry,

A Hobbycopter is stored in the area. It was built in the mid-1960s and flew, albeit unofficially!

❑ –   Hobbycopter   Stored   7-01

KENFIG HILL north of the B4281 east of Pyle

No.2117 Squadron Air Cadets: Off Main Street, and behind Pwll-y-Garth Street. The Hunter, 'parented' by St Athan, is hard to find! When found, it is overall grey and unmarked.

❑ WT569   Hunter F.1   ex St Athan 7491M, AAEE, Hawkers trials   3-06

LLANBEDR on the A496 south of Harlech

Maes Artro Village: The village closed for the second (ands what looks to be the final time, certainly as an aviation heritage venue) at the end of 2005. The Hunter nose had been acquired from the local 2445 Squadron, Air Cadets. It and Jindivik 203B A92-664 moved to Welshpool, Wales, by late 2005. The Spitfire FSM was acquired by a Northamptonshire company – no further details. The Anson is reported to have been sold, but is yet to leave the site [1].

❑ [VS562]	Anson T.21	ex Portsmouth, Llanbedr 8012M, AAEE, CS(A).	[1] 10-05
❑ XJ409	Whirlwind HAR.10	ex Grangetown, Cardiff-Wales, Wroughton,	
		Warton SAR Flt, 1310F, 228, 155, XD779 ntu	11-05

LLANBEDR AIRFIELD west of Llanbedr and the A496 on the road to Shell Island

Defence Science and Technology Laboratory: Meteor D.16 WK800 was ferried to Boscombe Down, Wilts, on 11th October 2004, making very probably the last-ever flight by a drone Meteor. The new Galileo Avionica Mirach 100-5 drones, that replaced WK800 and the Jindiviks, can operate from Aberporth, down the coast and the reason for this airfield to continue has therefore vanished. The final Jindivik sortie was carried out on 26th October 2004 by ZJ493 - the 7,747th in the UK which involved over 240 different 'Jins'. The airfield closed three days later and was handed over to Defence Estates on 11th February 2005. It is doubted that this fabulous airfield will see flying activity again.

Meteor D.16 WH453 was put up for tender in December 2004 and moved to Bentwaters, Suffolk, on 18th January 2005. Cronifer Metals of Clay Cross, Derbyshire, got the contract to process the scrap from here. A low-loader full of Jindiviks left in November 2004 and there were probably other such loads heading their way. Jindivik 4A ZJ493 (see above) was roaded out to Stafford, Staffs, on 25th January 2005.

Canberra B.2 WH734, TT.18 WH887 and B.2 WK128 were all scrapped in November 2004. The noses were all saved, WH734 and WH887 going to Basingstoke, Hants, and WK128 going to Pershore, Worcs. Phantom FGR.2 XV435 was scrapped in December 2004 and also moved to Derbyshire for destruction. No news on the Jindivik 203B gate guardian A92-480, last noted in October 2004.

No.2445 Squadron, Air Cadets: Have their HQ opposite the airfield entrance. By November 2005, they had gained a Jindivik (ex A92-908?). Their Hunter nose is at Llanbedr itself and was sold – see above.

❑ ZJ503*	Jindivik	trolley-mounted. First noted 11-05	11-05

LLANGEINOR on the A4064 north of Bridgend
Irvin-GQ: The rescue equipment manufacturer has a former Swedish Draken on display within the grounds.

❑ 35515*	'49' J.35F Draken	ex F10, RSweAF. Arrived 17-6-04	3-06

LLANGENNECH on the A4138 north-east of Llanelli
A MoD storage facility here holds two former SAAF Pumas pending possible use by the RAF.

❑ 173*	ZJ958 Puma	ex SAAF. Stored. First noted 9-03	3-06
❑ 184*	ZJ959 Puma	ex SAAF. Stored. First noted 9-03	3-06

LLANWRTYD WELLS on the A483 west of Builth Wells
'JP' XM358 is more accurately located at Newbridge-on-Wye, Wales.

MOLD on the A494 west of Chester.
Derek Griffiths: Derek runs the **International Cockpit Club** which serves to unite and inform anyone who owns, would like to own, or just likes the idea of cockpit collecting. The nose of Canberra B.15 WH984 moved to Norwich, Norfolk, on 30th November 2005. The nose of Buccaneer S.2B XW541 did not end up here, staying at Welshpool, Wales, stored on Derek's behalf.
◆ *Visits by prior arrangement* only. *21 Bryn-Y-Foel, Rhosemor, near Mold, CH7 6PW e-mail dgg.icc@btinternet.com www.internationalcockpitclub.org.uk*

❑ G-AYFA	Twin Pioneer 3	ex Carlisle, Hooton Park, Warmingham, Sandbach, Shobdon, Prestwick, G-31-5, XM285, SRCU, 225, Odiham SF, 230. Nose	3-04

NANTGARW on the A470 north-west of Cardiff
The Collection Centre: This is the large object store, for the National Museums of Wales. The Watkins is stored, destined for the Industrial Museum of Wales which will be set up in Swansea.
◆ Visits by prior appointment *only*.

❑ XM300	Wessex HAS.1	ex Cardiff, Cardiff-Wales, Farnborough, RAE, Westland. SAR colours. Stored	2-04
❑ –	BAPC.47 Watkins CHW	ex Cardiff, St Athan, Cardiff. Stored	2-04

NEWBRIDGE-ON-WYE on the A470 north of Builth Wells
(Previously listed under Llanwrtyd Wells.)

❑ XM358	Jet Provost T.3A	ex Twyford, North Scarle, Colsterworth, Halton 8987M, 1 FTS, 3 FTS, 1 FTS, CFS, RAFC, CFS, 7 FTS, 2 FTS	4-05

NEWPORT
No.210 Squadron Air Cadets: The Chipmunk *may* have moved to the Cardiff area.

❑ WD293	Chipmunk T.10 PAX	7645M. ex Caerleon, Cwmbran, QuB UAS, StA UAS, G&S UAS, StA UAS, Chatham Flt, SMR, 1 BFTS	10-98

PENDINE RANGES on the A4066 east of Tenby
Proof and Experimental Establishment: Still no news from the ranges.

☐ XV373   SH-3D Sea King   ex Foulness, AAEE, RAE   2-02

PETERSTONE on the B4239 north-east of Cardiff
☐ N5834N   Commander 114   force-landed 23-10-98. Hulk   1-04

ROSEMARKET north-east of Milford Haven
The Cub is stored on a local golf course! The others are stored elsewhere and are also getting very dated.

☐ G-AYCN	J3C-65 Cub	ex F-BCPO. CoA 27-1-89. Stored	8-95
☐ G-BBKR	Scheibe SF-24A	ex D-KECA. CoA 30-3-79. Stored	5-95
☐ G-BHPM	PA-18-95 S' Cub	ex F-BOUR, ALAT, 51-15501. Stored	5-95
☐ G-BJNY	Aeronca 11CC	ex CN-TYZ, F-OAEE. CoA 9-8-90. Stored	1-95

RUTHIN on the A494 south-west of Mold
Phantom Preservation Group: See also under Nantwich, Cheshire, for the group's 'showcase'.

◆ *Visits by prior arrangement* only. *Mark A Jones, Tyn Yr Erw, Llanfair Road, Ruthin, LL15 1BY e-mail mark3045@tesco.net*

☐ –   Phantom FGR.2   Nose section. Stored   3-06

ST ATHAN AIRFIELD on the B4265 west of Barry
RAF St Athan: The base is also home of the famed 'Crash-and-Smash' unit, more properly the **Aircraft Recovery and Transportation Flight**, itself part of the **Repair and Salvage Squadron**.

☐ 'XV498'   Phantom FGR.2   XV500 / 9113M, ex 56, 29, 23, 56, 111, 43, 54.
                                  92 Sqn colours. Displayed   4-06

Defence Aviation Repair Agency (DARA): It was announced in November 2005 that the fast-jet maintenance work carried out here would cease in April 2007. VC-10 work would continue until such time as the old girls finally throw in the towel. This will radically change the nature of what is left of the 'Roundel' presence here and another great 'name' in military *W&R* looks set to fade away. By the time of the announcement, the huge 'super-hangar' was already being used by airliner maintenance organisations and that *may* show the way forward. *W&R19* (p292) noted that 'JP' XS180 departed on 17th July 2002 and had not returned. Well, it snook back in by November 2004! The **Repair and Salvage Squadron**, operates an Aircraft Repair Flight (ARF) here; this unit has taken on the former Battle Damage Repair Training role.

With the wonderful **Sea Harrier** bowing out of service for good (with 801 Squadron on 28th March 2006), the remainder of the type will probably go through here (or Shawbury, Shropshire), but will very likely be too fleeting for a formal mention in these pages. (The Indian Navy has expressed interest in the last six machines in service when 801 'bowed out'.) Likewise, **Jaguars** are descending like migratory birds for spares recovery and disposal. These are also likely to be fast 'in-and-outs'. For completeness 'short-termers' are given separate treatment below.

Departures: (Some are fairly transitory, but included for completeness.) Gazelle AH.1 XZ322 to Cosford, Shrop, 25-1-06; HT.2 XZ941 to Cosford, Shrop, 25-1-06; **Harrier** GR.3 XZ991 to Cosford, Shrop, 24-1-06; GR.3 XZ993 departed 6-4-06, destination unknown; GR.5 ZD250 nose to Ipswich, Suffolk, by 12-05; AV-8B 162730 to Charlwood, Surrey, 25-5-05; **Jaguar** GR.1 XX722 put up for tender 9-05, removed by road 5-1-06 as scrap but the nose was saved and moved to 4 SoTT below; GR.3A XX723 to Coltishall 20-5-05 for return to service; T.4 XX845 arrived by 7-05, to Cosford, Shrop, 17-10-05; GR.1 XX977 up for tender 9-05, to Ipswich, Suffolk, 1-11-05; GR.3A XZ357 arrived by 6-05, to Ipswich, Suffolk, 27-10-05; **Sea Harrier** FA.2: XZ439 to Ipswich, Suffolk, 12-11-04; XZ459 to Charlwood, Surrey, 19-10-05; FA.2 ZD607 to Gosport, Hants, 6-05; FA.2 ZD611 to Culdrose, Cornwall, by 9-05; FA.2 ZH807 up for tender 6-05, left 1-9-05 for Basingstoke, Hants; **Sea King** HAS.6 XV643 to Cosford, Shrop, 24-1-06; **Tornado** GR.1 ZA399 to Cosford, Shrop, 10-1-06; F.3 ZE252 left 16-11-04, very likely for the yard at Hitchin, Herts; F.3s ZE290 and ZE339 left 9-3-06, also for Hitchin.

❑ G-BCWR		BN-2A-20	ex Bembridge, OY-RPZ, G-BCWR. Fuse, stored	5-03
❑ D-ASDB		VFW-614	ex Luftwaffe 17+03, D-BABS. Inst	7-05
❑ WJ717	'841'	Canberra TT.18	9052M, ex 4 SoTT, FRADU, 61, 15. Stored	1-06
❑ XS180	'21'	Jet Provost T.4	'8238M' [Really 8338M], ex Lyneham, St Athan,	
			Halton, Kemble, CAW, 6 FTS. Rescue exercises.	1-06
❑ XX254		Hawk T.1A	ex Brough, Chivenor, 7 FTS, 1 TWU, 2 TWU.	
			Front fuselage. Stored	1-04
❑ XX326		Hawk T.1A	ex Brough, 19, 92, 2 TWU. Front fuselage	1-04
❑ XZ106*	'FW'	Jaguar GR.3A	ex 41, 6, 41, 2. Arrived 3-5-05, spares recovery	7-05
❑ ZA140		VC-10 K.2	ex 101, A40-VL, G-ARVL. Cockpit	2-04
❑ ZA142	'C'	VC-10 K.2	ex 101, A40-VI, G-ARVI. Scrapping	4-05
❑ ZA325*	'TAX'	Tornado GR.1	ex Cosford, St Athan, 15, TTTE. Arr 12-12-05	ARF 12-05
❑ ZA411	'TT'	Tornado GR.1	ex 617, 15, 617, 2, 20, 16. Stored.	1-04
❑ ZD230*	'K'	VC-10 K.4	ex 101, BA, BOAC G-ASGA. Arr 16-12-05. Scrapping	8-05
❑ ZD240*	'M'	VC-10 K.4	ex 101, BA, BOAC G-ASGL. Arr 4-8-05. Scrapping	10-05
❑ ZD412		Harrier GR.5	ex Dunsfold, Brough, 3. Cr 30-9-01.NDT	1-03
❑ ZD462		Harrier GR.7	9302M, ex Cosford, St Athan, 1. Ditched 25-1-97	ARF 1-05
❑ ZD901	'AA'	Tornado F.2	ex 229 OCU. F.2-F.3 exchange. Dump 4-02	4-02
❑ ZD932	'AM'	Tornado F.2	ex 229 OCU. F.2-F.3 exchange	ARF 10-05
❑ ZG706	'E'	Tornado GR.1A	ex SAOEU	4-05
❑ ZG734		Tornado F.3	ex ItAF MM7231, RAF, 5, 29	4-05

Short-termers: For completeness, the following recent arrivals are briefly listed – serial, type, arrival. Should their stay be longer than a year, they will receive greater attention in *W&R21*.

❑ XR810*	VC-10 C.1K	4-11-05		❑ XZ356*	Jaguar GR.3A	2-06
❑ XX119*	Jaguar GR.3A	29-3-06		❑ XZ360*	Jaguar GR.3	8-11-05
❑ XX150*	Jaguar T.4	9-2-06		❑ XZ364*	Jaguar GR.3A	28-11-05
❑ XX720*	Jaguar GR.3A	24-6-05		❑ XZ366*	Jaguar GR.3A	4-11-05
❑ XX737*	Jaguar GR.3A	15-12-05		❑ XZ369*	Jaguar GR.3A	1-12-05
❑ XX838*	Jaguar T.4	29-11-05		❑ XZ372*	Jaguar GR.3A	5-7-05
❑ XX840*	Jaguar T.4	2-06		❑ XZ377*	Jaguar GR.3	16-3-06
❑ XX842*	Jaguar T.2A	29-3-06		❑ XZ385*	Jaguar GR.3A	27-9-05
❑ XZ106*	Jaguar GR.3A	3-06		❑ XZ396*	Jaguar GR.3A	4-11-05
❑ XZ107*	Jaguar GR.3A	4-1-06		❑ XZ400*	Jaguar GR.3A	6-7-05
❑ XZ113*	Jaguar GR.3A	15-3-06		❑ XZ459*	Sea Harrier FA.2	6-05
❑ XZ118*	Jaguar GR.3	29-9-05		❑ ZH807*	Sea Harrier FA.2	7-05
❑ XZ355*	Jaguar GR.3A	16-3-06				

No.4 School of Technical Training / Civilian Technical Training School: As with the rest of the station, the future is not looking bright and to underline this, seven out of the ten airframes were put up for tender in November 2005 – marked §. Dominie T.1 XS735 (last noted November 2005) is thought to have left going for 'adventure training' in the Brecon Beacons' – it has yet to send a postcard!

Departures: Bulldog T.1 XX626 became G-CDVV 1-06 and moved to Sleap, Shrop.

❑ XM419	'102'	Jet Provost T.3A	8990M, ex 7 FTS, 3 FTS, CFS, RAFC, CFS, 3 FTS, RAFC,		
			6 FTS, RAFC, 2 FTS	§	11-05
❑ XN551	'100'	Jet Provost T.3A	8984M, ex 7 FTS, RAFC, 1 FTS, 3 FTS, 6 FTS, RAFC	§	11-05
❑ XS735	'R'	Dominie T.1	ex Sealand, Cranwell, 55, 6 FTS, RAFC, CAW		11-05
❑ XX722*	'EF'	Jaguar GR.1	ex BDRT 9252M, Shawbury, Warton, Shawbury, 6, 54,		
			JOCU. Cockpit with Painters and Finishers by 3-06		3-06
❑ XW404	'77'	Jet Provost T.5A	9049M, ex 1 FTS	§	11-05
❑ XW409	'123'	Jet Provost T.5A	9047M, ex 7 FTS, 1 FTS		11-05
❑ XX635		Bulldog T.1	8767M, ex Ems UAS	§	11-05
❑ XX686	'5'	Bulldog T.1	9291M, ex CFS, 3 FTS, Gla UAS, Ox UAS, Gla UAS,		
			Liv UAS, 2 FTS	§	11-05
❑ XX763	'24'	Jaguar GR.1	9009M, ex Shawbury, 226 OCU. Open store 3-06	§	3-06
❑ XX764	'13'	Jaguar GR.1	9010M, ex Shawbury, 226 OCU, 14. Open store 3-06		3-06

SEALAND on the A550 south-west of Ellesmere Port
RAF Sealand - Defence Aviation Repair Agency (DARA): RAF Sealand held its official close down ceremony on 2nd February 2006. South Camp (with the airfield and the gliders) closed on 31st March 2006. A RAF presence will remain on site until 27th September 2006. The DARA element will continue in part of East Camp. The RAF element 'parented' a series of ATC airframes - eg Birkdale, Hawarden, Royton – difficult to consider which base will get the responsibility.

❏ 'WT720'	'B' Hunter F.51	8565M, ex Cranwell 'XF979', Brawdy, Dunsfold,	
		G-9-436, Esk.724, Dan AF E-408. 74 Sqn c/s, Gate	3-06

SWANSEA AIRPORT (FAIRWOOD COMMON)
Harvard II 'FT323' (1513) moved to Norwich, Norfolk.

❏ G-MJAZ	Ultravector 627	ex PH-1J1, G-MJAZ. CoA 23-9-93. Stored	6-04
❏ D-5084	Schleicher K.8b	EHA / BGA.2688. Stored	6-04

VALLEY AIRFIELD south of the A5, south-east of Holyhead
RAF Valley: The **Search and Rescue Training Unit** (SARTU) has two training airframes, the 'Huey' playing the role of a Griffin. A 'synthetic' Hawk fire training aid serves on the dump. The Hawk Composite Servicing School *should* still have a Hawk nose for instruction [1].

❏ WV396	'91' Hunter T.8C	9249M, ex Yeovilton, FRADU, 229 OCU, 20.		
		4 FTS red/white c/s. Gate		3-05
❏ XT772	Wessex HU.5	8805M, ex Wroughton, 781		SARTU 11-01
❏ XX300	Hawk T.1	8827M, ex Chivenor, 2 TWU, 1 TWU. Cr 2-10-82. Nose	[1]	4-98
❏ '998-8888'	UH-1H 'Huey'	ex Middle Wallop, Greenford, M Wallop, Fleetlands,		
		Stanley, Arg Army AE-406, 72-21491		SARTU 9-02

WELSHPOOL on the A483 west of Shrewsbury
Military Aircraft Cockpit Collection: Run by Sue and Roy Jerman. The Whirlwind HAR.10 cockpit is on loan from Dave Higgins [1]. The Harrier GR.1 nose is a 'spare' from the huge store at Stafford, marked '4 Spare Ser 41H-769733', which falls within the 'XW' range [2]. Correcting *W&R19* (p294), the nose of Buccaneer S.2B WX541 did not moved to Mold, Wales, but stayed here and is stored a behalf of Derek Griffiths.
◆ Private *collection, visits possible by prior arrangement* only. *e-mail cvrtsultan@aon.com*

❏ WH775	Canberra PR.7	ex Bruntingthorpe, Cosford 8868M/8128M, 100,		
		13, 31, 17, 31, 13, 82, makers. Nose		3-06
❏ WK102	Canberra T.17	ex B'thorpe, Cosford 8780M, 360, 45, RNZAF, 207. Nose		3-06
❏ WN957*	Hunter F.5	ex Llanbedr, Stafford, North Weald 7407M,RAE. Nose		3-06
❏ XJ758	Whirlwind HAR.10	ex Oswestry, Shrewsbury, Shawbury 8464M, CFS, 230, CFS,		
		217, 1360F, 22. Cockpit	[1]	3-06
❏ XM652	Vulcan B.2	ex Burntwood, Sheffield, Waddington, 50, 35, 44, 9. Nose		3-06
❏ XS923	'BE' Lightning F.6	ex B'thorpe, Cranfield, Binbrook, 11,LTF,5-11 pool. Nose		3-06
❏ XT277	Buccaneer S.2A	ex B'thorpe, Cosford 8853M, Shawbury, 237OCU,12. Nose		3-06
❏ XW541	Buccaneer S.2B	ex Ingatestone, Stock, Foulness, Honington 8858M,		
		St Athan, 12, 16, 15. Nose		3-06
❏ –	Harrier GR.1	ex Market Drayton, Stafford, Abingdon, Hamble. Nose	[2]	3-06
❏ A92-664*	Jindivik 203B	ex Llanbedr, DRA, RAE. Composite		3-06

WELSHPOOL AERODROME or Trehelig, south of the town at the A493/A490 junction

❏ G-BKCY	Tomahawk 112	ex OO-XKU. CoA 7-11-94. Fuselage	7-98
❏ G-BPER	Tomahawk 112	ex N91465. Crashed 21-7-98. Canx 31-8-99. Fuselage	10-01

WHITSON on minor roads south of the M4, south east of Newport
A long-lost Rallye is stored in the rafters at a strip here.

❏ G-ATWE*	Rallye Comm 150	crashed 29-3-81. Stored	6-05

WREXHAM
North East Wales Institute: Next to the football ground; see Connah's Quay for another NEWI site.
❏ [XP585] '24' Jet Provost T.4 8407M, ex Halton, St Athan, RAFC, 6 FTS, RAFC 3-06

YSTRAD MYNACH on the A472 south of Merthyr Tydfil
Jet Provost T.4 XP638 is believed to have been scrapped in September 2004.

PART FIVE
NORTHERN IRELAND

BALLYKINLER BARRACKS, Down
❏ XS865 Wessex HAS.1 ex Lee-on-Solent, A2694, Wroughton, 771. Camo 4-03

BALLYMENA, Antrim
Citabria G-BPMM was listed under this heading in *W&R19* (p296). It should have been under Ballymoney - see below. Tri-Pacer G-ARDV moved to <u>Newtownards</u>, N Ireland, by November 2004.
❏ VR-HJB* Scorpion 145 G-BMEB ntu. Stored 1-06

BALLYMONEY on the A26 south-east of Coleraine, Antrim
See Ballymena above for a slip of the 'cut and paste'!
❏ G-BPMM 7ECA Citabria ex N5132T. CoA 25-2-97. Canx 29-4-05. Stored 1-06

BANN FOOT north-west of Craigavon, Armagh
❏ G-BDWA*	Rallye 150ST	CoA 7-6-01	1-06
❏ G-PFAL	FRED II	CoA 27-7-88	1-06
❏ EI-AUT	F.1A Aircoupe	ex Cork, G-ARXS, D-EBSA, N3037G. CoA 30-7-76	1-06

BELFAST, Down
No.817 Squadron Air Cadets should still have their Devon fuselage [1]. Despite the wording in *W&R19* (p296), the Vampire 'pod' is *still* present at **Campbell College**, albeit shed-bound [2]. Former Flight Experience Workshop Canberra T.4 WT486 nose spent a long time stored in a shed on a golf course at Gilnahirk and moved to <u>Newtownards</u>, N Ireland, by August 2005.
❏ VP957	Devon C.2/2	8822M, ex Bishop's Court, Belfast Airport, Northolt, 207, 21, WCS, SCS, NCS, SCS, WCS, SCS, Andover SF, 38 GCF, AAFCE, 2 TAF CS, BAFO CS. Forward fuselage	[1]	1-06
❏ XD525	Vampire T.11	ex Holywood, Belfast, Aldergrove 7882M, 1 FTS, 4 FTS, 5 FTS, 7 FTS. Pod	[2]	1-06

BELFAST AIRPORT (ALDERGROVE), Antrim
Cessna F.150L G-BCBX moved to Newtownards and was flying again by mid-2004.
❏ G-AVFE	Trident 2E	ex BA, BEA. CoA 6-5-85. Fire crews	1-06
❏ G-AVYP*	Cherokee 140	ex N11C. CoA 14-2-04. Stored	1-06
❏ G-BBSC	Sierra 200	Damaged 4-12-97. Stored	1-06
❏ G-BFWK	Warrior 161	ex N9589N. CoA 8-12-99. Stored	1-06

☐ G-BGWW*		Aztec 250E	ex OO-ABH, N13971. CoA 28-9-01. Stored		1-06
☐ G-BNMK		Dornier Do 27A-1	ex OE-DGO, 56+04, BD+397, BA+399. Stored		1-06
☐ G-KNAP		Warrior II	ex G-BIUX, N9507N. Crashed 13-7-99	®	1-06
☐ G-OSNI*		Aztec 250C	ex G-AWER, N6556Y. CoA 22-504. Stored		1-06
☐ XT456	'XZ'	Wessex HU.5	ex 8941M ABDR, Wroughton, 847, 846, 845. Dump		1-06

RAF Aldergrove: The trailer-mounted nose sections are used by RAF Careers and do 'the rounds'.

☐ XE643		Hunter FGA.9	8586M, ex Abingdon, 208, 56, 63, 66, 92. Nose		1-06
☐ XR529	'E'	Wessex HC.2	ex 72, SARTU, 2 FTS, 18, 78, 72. Gate	®	1-06
☐ XR700		Jet Provost T.4	8589M, ex Abingdon, Shawbury, CATCS, 3 FTS, 1 FTS. Nose		1-06

BELFAST CITY AIRPORT (SYDENHAM), Down

Bombardier: Have taken delivery of a Tucano fuselage for canopy release tests. The Tucano EMU previously with UAS at Langford Lodge, has also returned to the fold.

| ☐ ZF167* | Tucano T.1 | ex Shawbury, 1 FTS, 7 FTS. Fuselage. Arrived 1-12-04 | 12-05 |
| ☐ –* | Tucano EMU | ex Langford Lodge, Belfast City, Shorts. Test rig. Arrived mid-2005 | 6-05 |

CASTLEROCK

| ☐ G-RORO | C.337B | ex G-AVIX, N5454S. Crashed 25-6-99. Spares, hulk | 1-06 |
| ☐ EI-AVC | F.337F | ex Abbeyshrule, N4757. Spares, hulk | 1-06 |

COALISLAND on the A45 north-east of Dungannon, Tyrone

A long out-of-use 'Volksplane' is stored in the area.

| ☐ G-BEHX* | Evans VP-2 | CoA 22-1-90. *Ulster Flyer*. Stored | 1-06 |

DROMORE on the A1 south west of Belfast, Down

| ☐ G-AJSN | Argus II | ex Cork, HB612, ATA, 43-14885. Crashed 10-6-67. *Barbara Ann*. Dismantled, stored | 1-06 |
| ☐ EI-ACY | J/1 Autocrat | ex G-AIBK. Crashed 6-4-67. Dismantled | 1-06 |

ENNISKILLEN on the A4 east of Sligo, Fermanagh

A Cessna 140 is stored at a private house in the area. It will be restored in due course.

| ☐ G-BPHX* | Cessna 140 | ex N2252N, NC2252N. Crashed 23-5-92. Stored | 4-05 |

FIVEMILETOWN on the A4 east of Enniskillen, Tyrone

Blessingbourne Carriage Museum: The Sioux is believed to have been ditched off Hong Kong [1].
♦ *Open by prior appointment only. Blessingbourne, Fivemiletown, Co Tyrone, BT75 0QS.*

| ☐ –* | Sioux AH.1 | cabin. See above | [1] | 1-06 |
| ☐ XW795 | Scout AH.1 | ex M Wallop, Almondbank, Wroughton, 659, 655, 669 | | 1-06 |

GORTIN on the B48 north of Omagh, Tyrone

Stored in a shed locally is a modified HM.14 'Flea' built circa 1973, taxied, but not flown. While we are on the hallowed subject of 'Fleas', the owner of this contemporary example has details of another example believed still extant - certainly in 2001 - of a 1937 example built at Moneymore by Captain R W Harris, not registered or flown. (The Flying Flea Archive has no details of this, but then again, details of 'Flea' activity in Northern Ireland are thin on the ground...) Worth scratching over...?

| ☐ –* | HM.14 'Flea' | Stored - see above | 6-04 |

HOLYWOOD on the A2 east of Belfast, Down

Ulster Folk and Transport Museum: On 8th March 2005, the 'Flight Experience', staged in association with Bombardier, was relaunched as the 'X2 Flight Experience'. The 'original' Ferguson REP, the Short SC.1 and the Sherpa cockpit are in this 'hands-on' gallery (FE). A workshop and conservation area is also part of the exhibition and visitors can gain a glimpse of the Sealand, which has started restoration. McCandless G-ATXX is displayed in an adjacent section showing achievements of local engineers and designers.

Other than those mentioned above, all other airframes are in store and not available for inspection. See under Dromod, Ireland, for a possible insight into Gemini G-AKEL and G-AKGE [1]. The registration G-ARTZ has been used twice, both times on Rex McCandless' products. See under St Merryn, Corn, for the second use [2].

◆ *Open daily, closed three days at Xmas. Telephone for details of opening times. Cultra Manor, Holywood, BT18 0EU tel 028 9042 8428 fax 028 9042 8728 www.magni.org.uk*

❏ G-AJOC	Messenger 2A	ex East Fortune, Strathallan, Dunottar. CoA 18-5-72		1-06
❏ G-AKEL	Gemini 1A	ex Kilbrittain Castle. CoA 29-4-72. Stored	[1]	1-06
❏ G-AKGE	Gemini 3C	ex Kilbrittain Castle, EI-ALM, G-AKGE. CoA 7-6-74.	[1]	1-06
❏ G-AKLW	Sealand	ex Bradley Air Museum, Connecticut, Jeddah, RSaudiAF, SU-AHY, G-AKLW.	®	1-06
❏ G-AOUR	Tiger Moth	ex Belfast, NL898, 15 EFTS. Cr 6-6-65. Stored		1-06
❏ G-ARTZ (1)	McCandless M-2	ex Killough. Stored	[2]	1-06
❏ G-ATXX	McCandless M-4	ex Killough. wfu 9-9-70.		1-06
❏ G-BKMW	Short Sherpa	ex Belfast City, CoA 14-9-90. Cockpit section	FE	3-05
❏ ALA 470	Nimbus I	ex Bishop's Stortford, Duxford. Stored		1-04
❏ – IAHC.6	Ferguson Mono	REP, ex Dublin	FE	1-06
❏ – IAHC.9	Ferguson Mono	REP, ex Belfast Airport, Holywood. Stored		1-06
❏ VH-UUP	Scion I	ex East Fortune, Strathallan, G-ACUX, VH-UUP, G-ACUX. Stored		1-06
❏ XG905	Short SC.1	ex Shorts, Sydenham, Thurleigh, RAE	FE	10-05

KILKEEL on the A2 east of Newry, Down

❏ OO-DFS*	PA-18-95	ex UK, ALAT 181637, 51-15637	®	1-06

LANGFORD LODGE AIRFIELD on the shores of Lough Neagh, west of Belfast, Antrim

Ulster Aviation Society Heritage Centre: In July 2004, the UAS announced that is was leaving the site. Negotiations for a new venue came to fruition during 2005 and the move of the collection started. UAS are very thankful to Langford Engineering for 13 years on the site and for their co-operation during the move. Removals were as follows: Short 330 G-BDBS (22-1-06); Tucano G-BTUC (9-9-05); Goldwing G-MJWS (24-8-05); G-RENT (26-10-05); Chargus Cyclone BAPC.263 (10-05); Rogallo BAPC.266 (10-05); Sea Hawker EI-BUO (9-05); Wildcat JV482 (28-9-05); Sea Hawk FB.5 WN108 (3-12-05); Vampire T.11 WZ549 (8-05); Jet Provost T.3A XM414 (23-9-05); Wessex HC.2 XR517 (arrived 31-3-04, left 3-12-05); Buccaneer S.2B XV361 (22-1-06) – all to Lisburn, N Ireland. Cessna 172A EI-BAG moved to Upper Ballinderry, N Ireland, early in 2005. The anonymous Tucano EMU returned to Belfast City, N Ireland, in mid-2005.

LARNE on the A2 north of Belfast, Antrim

❏ G-RWSS*	Kitfox Mk.2	crashed 18-8-92. Stored	4-05

LISBURN on the A3 south west of Belfast, Antrim

Ulster Aviation Society: From August 2005, the UAS moved its aircraft and artefact collection into a location in this area. A series of negotiations are underway to achieve a place of permanent exhibition and a new heritage centre will emerge. Because of these negotiations, the exact location is being with-held for what are hoped are obvious reasons. The Eurowing Goldwing, donated by Jeff Slater, is a very relevant airframe, having made its first flight from Langford Lodge [1]. The Robinson is on loan from Harold Hassard [2]

◆ *Airframes etc all in store.Research access only, by prior appointment until further notice. UAS publishes an excellent magazine, Ulster Air Mail, and stages a series of talks and other events. Ray Burrows, 33 Old Mill Meadows, Dundonald, BT16 1WQ www.ulsteraviationsociety.co.uk*

❑ G-BDBS*	Shorts 330	ex Langford Lodge, Belfast City, Short, G-14-3001.		
		CoA 2-9-92. Arrived 22-1-06		4-06
❑ G-BTUC*	Tucano	ex Langford Lodge, Belfast City, Short, G-14-007, PP-ZTC.		
		CoA 20-8-91. Arrived 9-9-05		4-06
❑ G-MJWS*	Goldwing	ex Langford Lodge. Canx 23-6-97. Arrived 24-8-05	[1]	4-06
❑ G-RENT*	R-22 Beta	ex Langford Lodge, Newtownards, N2635M. Dam 30-9-92		
		Arrived 26-10-05	[2]	4-06
❑ –*	BAPC.263 Chargus Cyclone	ex Langford Lodge, Ballyclare. Built 1979. Last flight 4-4-88.		
		Arrived 10-05		4-06
❑ –*	BAPC.266 Rogallo h-glider	ex Langford Lodge. Last flown 1978. Arrived 10-05		4-06
❑ EI-BUO*	Sea Hawker	ex Langford Lodge, Newtownards. Damaged 9-91. Arr 9-05		4-06
❑ JV482*	Wildcat V	ex Langford Lodge, Newtownards, Castlereagh,		
		Lough Beg, 882. Crashed 24-12-44. Arrived 28-9-05	®	4-06
❑ WN108*	'033' Sea Hawk FB.3	ex Langford Lodge, Newtownards, Belfast City, Shorts Apps,		
		Sydenham AHU, Bournemouth, FRU, 806, 895, 897, 800.		
		Arrived 3-12-05		4-06
❑ WZ549*	'F' Vampire T.11	ex Langford Lodge, Newtownards, Coningsby, Tattershall,		
		Coningsby 8118M, CATCS, 1 FTS, 8 FTS, FTU, C(A).		
		Arrived 8-05		4-06
❑ XM414*	'101' Jet Provost T.3A	ex Langford Lodge, Dundonald, Binbrook, Colsterworth,		
		Halton 8996M, 7 FTS, RAFC, 1 FTS, RAFC, 2 FTS.		
		Arrived 23-9-05		4-06
❑ XR517*	'N' Wessex HC.2	ex Langford Lodge, Shoreham, Ipswich, Fleetlands, 60,		
		72, 18. Arrived 3-12-05		4-06
❑ XV361*	Buccaneer S.2B	ex Langford Lodge, Lossiemouth, 208, 15, 208, 12, 15,		
		809, 800. Arrived 22-1-06		4-06

Others:

❑ G-AVCS	Terrier 1	ex WJ363, Odiham SF, AAC, 1900F. Cr 18-10-81	®	1-06
❑ EI-BGB	Rallye Club	ex Upper Ballinderry, Abbeyshrule, G-AZKB.		
		CoA 18-5-91		1-06

LONDONDERRY

W&R19 (p298) noted Champion 7DC G-BRFI going to the "East Midlands by mid-2003". The location was not short of the mark. It settled on <u>Leicester</u>, Leics, but it did so in <u>1998</u>!

❑ G-ARAP	7EC Traveler	ex Eglinton. Crashed 22-9-81	®	7-04

LOUGH FOYLE Londonderry

Just off shore can be seen the hulk of a Corsair.

❑ JT693	'R' Corsair II	ex 1837. Crashed 9-10-44	1-06

MONEYMORE on the A29, north of Cookstown, Londonderry

The 'Flea' fuselage is stored in a shed in the area. It was built by the late Robert Wilbert Harris in the town in 1937. It was powered by a converted Austin 7.

❑ G-BANF	Luton Minor	CoA 5-6-92. Stored	1-06
❑ G-NORD	SNCAC NC.854	ex F-BFIS. CoA 27-5-82. Stored	1-04
❑ –*	HM.14 'Flea'	fuselage, stored.	8-04

MOVENIS AERODROME near Garvagh, Londonderry

❑ G-AWJA	Cessna 182L	ex N1658C. Crashed 12-9-84. Fuselage	off-site	1-06
❑ G-BBRZ	AA-5 Traveler	ex Mullaghmore, EI-AYV ntu, G-BBRZ.CoA 30-4-99. Stored		1-06
❑ G-BIEW	Cessna U.206G	ex OO-DMA, N7344C. Crashed 31-12-88. Fuselage		1-06
❑ G-EESE	Cessna U.206G	ex N6332U ntu. Cr 29-8-89. Forward fuse	off-site	1-06

MULLAGHMORE AERODROME south-west of Ballymoney, Down
❑ G-BDRL	SA-3 Playboy	ex N730GF. CoA 17-6-98. Stored	1-06
❑ EI-BGA	Rallye 100ST	ex G-BCXC, F-OCZQ. CoA 7-01. Stored	1-06

NEWRY, Down
Two aircraft are stored at a location near here.
❑ G-MMJS*	MBA Tiger Cub	canx 7-9-<u>94</u>. Stored	1-05
❑ EI-BHW*	Cessna F.150F	ex G-ATMK. Canx 2-5-88. Stored since 1992	1-06

NEWTOWNARDS AERODROME south of the town, between the A20 and A21, Down
Super Cub G-ARCT was briefly away from the airfield under restoration in Bangor, Down, it is now back and well on the way to flight [1]. The Canberra nose is being restored by members of 664 VGS. Pitts N80BA left for storage off site.
❑ G-AJIH	J/1 Autocrat	CoA 19-11-94. Stored		7-05
❑ G-ARCT	PA-18-95	ex Bangor, Newtownards, EI-AVE, G-ARCT. Damaged 29-3-87	® [1]	2-06
❑ G-ARDV*	Tri-Pacer 160	ex Ballymena, EI-APA, G-ARDV, N10F. Cr 10-7-98. First noted 11-04	®	11-05
❑ WT486*	Canberra T.4	ex Gilnahirk, Belfast, Aldergrove 8102M, Wildenrath, 14, 17, 88, Wildenrath SF. Nose	® [2]	8-05

Locally: A Bensen is stored in an attic and a damaged Pitts is close by.
❑ G-BSNY	Bensen B.8M	CoA 6-9-01. Stored	1-06
❑ N80BA	Pitts S-2A	ex Newtownards. Crashed 7-11-99. Stored	1-06

OMAGH on the A5, Tyrone
David Shakespeare: Has acquired the former New Ross Dove.
❑ '176'*	Dove 6	VP-YKF, ex New Ross, Waterford, Cork, Dublin, 3D-AAI, VQ-ZJC, G-AMDD. Arrived by 1-05	1-05

RATHFRILAND on the A25, north-east of Newry, Down
Champion G-AVDT was flying again by 2004.

UPPER BALLINDERRY on the A26 west of Belfast, near Crumlin, Antrim
❑ EI-BAG*	Cessna 172A	ex Langford Lodge, Upper Ballinderry, Portadown, Enniskillen, Abbeyshrule, G-ARAV, N9771T. CoA 26-6-79	1-06

PART SIX
IRELAND

ABBEYSHRULE AERODROME Westmeagh, north-west of Mullingar
Some of the long-in-the-tooth wrecks here have been deleted as very likely scrapped: SAN DR.1050 EI-ARW (last noted August 1998); Rallye Club EI-AUJ (6-97); Rallye Club EI-AUP (5-99); Colt 108 EI-AYS (5-99); Rallye Club EI-BCW (6-97); Rallye Club EI-BGD (8-98); Rallye 180GT EI-BGS (5-96); Rallye; Rallye Club EI-BGU (8-98); EI-BIM Rallye Club (6-97); Rallye Commodore EI-BKU (5-99); AA-5 Traveler EI-BMV (8-98); Rallye Commodore EI-BOP (5-99); Rallye Commodore EI-BUJ (6-97).

❑ EI-ANN	Tiger Moth	ex Dublin, Kilcock, G-ANEE, T5418, 63 GCF, 24 EFTS,		
		19 EFTS, 12 EFTS. Crashed 18-10-64. Spares for EI-AOP		11-93
❑ EI-AOP	Tiger Moth	ex Dublin, G-AIBN, T7967, 18 EFTS, 1667 CU,		
		1 GCF, 16 PFTS. Crashed 5-5-74	®	11-93
❑ EI-ATK	Cherokee 140	ex G-AVUP. Crashed 14-2-87. Wreck		6-04
❑ EI-AWE	Cessna F.150L	Fuselage, stored		4-03
❑ EI-AYT	Rallye Minerva	ex G-AXIU. Crashed 12-11-89. Stored		4-03
❑ EI-BDP	Cessna 182P	ex G-AZLC, N9327G. Damaged 1998. Stored		6-04
❑ EI-BFI	Rallye 100ST	ex F-BXDK. Crashed 14-12-85. Spares		6-04
❑ EI-BHB	Rallye 125	ex F-BUCH. Stored, dismantled		6-04
❑ EI-BIC	Cessna F.172N	ex OO-HNZ ntu. Crashed 13-4-95		6-04
❑ EI-BJJ	Aeronca Sedan	ex G-BHXP ntu, EI-BJJ, N1214H		6-97
❑ EI-BNR	AA-5 Traveler	ex N9992Q, CS-AHM. Crashed 21-2-88		5-00
❑ EI-BPJ	Cessna 182A	ex G-BAGA, N4849D. *The Hooker.* Wreck		6-04
❑ EI-CAA	Cessna FR.172J	ex G-BHTW, 5Y-ATO. Damaged 12-93. Wreck		6-04
❑ G-BSUH	Cessna 140	ex N89088, NC89088. Damaged 6-93		6-04
❑ G-SKYH	Cessna 172N	ex A6-GRM, N76034. Crashed 21-7-91. Stored		4-03

ATHBOY on the N51, west of Drogheda, Meath

❑ G-BHMA*	SIPA 903	ex OO-FAE, F-BGBK. CoA 18-5-98. Stored	8-04

BALLYBOGHIL on the R122 north of Dublin, Co Dublin

❑ EI-AGJ*	J/1 Autocrat	ex G-AIPZ. Fuselage, stored	10-04
❑ EI-ALP*	Avro Cadet	ex Weston, Castlebridge, G-ADIE. CoA 6-4-78. Stored	10-04

BALLYJAMESDUFF on the R194 south of Cavan, Cavan
Norbert Reilly: Has no less than two Taylorcraft Plus Ds in his care.

❑ EI-ALH*	T'craft Plus D	ex G-AHLJ, HL534, 43 OTU, 651, G-AFTZ	8-04
❑ EI-ANA	T'craft Plus D	ex G-AHCG, LB347, 657, 655	8-04
❑ -*	Luton Minor	dismantled. Unfinished project	8-04
❑ XE808	Cadet TX.1	ex Syerston, 617 VGS, 645 VGS. Stored	8-04

CARLOW on the N9 south-west of Dublin, Carlow
Carlow Institute of Technology:

❑ 220	CM-170-1	ex Casement, IAC. Inst	8-01

CASEMENT AIRFIELD or Baldonnel, west of Dublin, Co Dublin
Irish Air Corps (IAC): CM-170 215 moved to Dublin, Ireland, on 25th November 2004; CM-170 217 was exported to Austria (where it served their air force as 4D-YL) for a museum by March 2005.

❑ 34	Magister	ex Dublin, Casement, N5392. Dismantled	12-05
❑ 141	Avro XIX	ex Dublin, Casement	12-05
❑ 164	Chipmunk T.20	stored	1-06
❑ 168*	Chipmunk T.20	stored. First noted 8-05	1-06
❑ 172	Chipmunk T.20	stored, dismantled	1-06
❑ 183	Provost T.51	ex Dublin, Casement	1-06
❑ 191	Vampire T.55	ex Gormanston, Dublin, Casement. Dismantled	1-06
❑ 198	Vampire T.11	ex 'gate', XE977, 8 FTS. Unflown by IAAC	1-06
❑ 199	Chipmunk T.20	ex Gormanston. Dismantled	1-06
❑ 202	Alouette III	ditched 20-10-95. Stored, dismantled	1-06
❑ 216*	CM-170-1	ex Cork, Casement, Aust AF 4D-YK. Dism. f/n 10-05	1-06
❑ 218	CM-170-1	ex Austrian AF 4D-YU. Stored	6-04
❑ 219	CM-170-1	stored	1-06

☐	221	'3-KE'	CM-170-2	ex French Air Force No.79. Dismantled	1-06
☐	229*		SF-260WE	stored. First noted 10-05	1-06
☐	233		SF-260MC	ex I-SYAS. Fuselage. Stored	9-03
☐	237		Gazelle	crashed 16-8-02. Wreck	1-06
☐	243*		Cessna FR.172H	crashed 6-5-04. First noted 8-05	8-05
☐	'98'		Cessna 172B	ex Southend, G-ARLU, N8002X. Dam 30-10-77. Rig	1-06
☐	[EI-BMM]		Cessna F.152 II	ex Weston. IAAC roundels	10-05
☐	[G-ASNG]		Dove 6	ex Waterford, Cork, (EI-BJW), Coventry, HB-LFF,	
				G-ASNG, HB-LFF, G-ASNG, PH-IOM. Stored	1-06
☐	-		Alouette III	instructional, non-flying, rig. c/no 1012	1-06

CELBRIDGE on the R403 west of Dublin, Kildare
☐	G-AHWO	Proctor V	ex Whitehall, Dublin, (EI-ALY). Cr 5-5-59. Stored	3-06

CHURCHTOWN south of Dublin city centre, Dublin
Nutgrove Shopping Centre: A Grob Astir 'flies' over the bargains.
☐	EI-124	G.102 Astir CS	displayed since 1993	8-04

CORK AIRPORT
CM-170 Magister 216 had returned to Casement, Ireland, by October 2005.
☐	-	Rallye	Fuselage	4-03

DELGANY east of the N11, south of Dublin, Wicklow.
Mick Donohoe: Is *thought* to still be at work on restoring the 'Flea'.
☐	IAHC 3	HM.14 'Flea'	ex Carbury	® 4-96

DROMOD on the N4 north of Longford, Leitrim
South East Aviation Enthusiasts Group (SEAEG): Thanks to the exceptional **Cavan and Leitrim Railway** the group have a new home and are busy consolidating it.
    Notes: See under Celbridge, Ireland, for Proctor G-AHWO which will also make the move. Leading light of the group is Phil Bedford; his aircraft are marked - PB. The 'Flea' is on loan from the Aviation Society of Ireland Preservation Group and is off-site having an engine and rudder fitted [1]. The identity of Gemini G-AKGE is confirmed - see Holywood, Northern Ireland) [2]. Phil is restoring T.8 Tutor CBZ to its original 1944 condition as a long-span Cadet TX.2. CBZ was converted into a motor glider with an enclosed cockpit and will use the cockpit of RA881 in the rebuild. Phil owns CBZ along with Damian Smyth [3]. The Chipmunk and Vampire are on loan from the Ministry of Defence [4]. Provost 184 is fitted with the wings of 183 and is on loan from the Ministry of Defence [5]. See also under New Ross, Ireland.
◆ *On the R202 out of Dromod village, east of the N4 Dublin-Sligo main road and alongside the mainline railway station. Open Sep to Jun 10am to 2.30pm; Jul to Aug10am to 5.30pm; Sun all year, 1pm to 5.30pm. Cavan and Leitrim Railway, Station Road, Dromod, Leitrim, Ireland tel 00 353 7838599 e-mail dromod@eircom.net www.cavanandleitrimrailway.com And for **SEAEG**: Phil Bedford, 10 Walled Gardens, Castletown, Celbridge, Kildare, Ireland. e-mail pbedford@tcd.ie*

☐	EI-BDM		Aztec 250D	ex New Ross, Waterford, Kildimo, G-AXIV, N6826Y	PB	3-06
☐	EI-100		SZD-12 Mucha	ex OY-XAN. CoA 1-7-97		3-06
☐	EI-139		T.31B	ex New Ross, Gowran Grange, BGA.3485, G-BOKG,		
				XE789. CoA 2-8-97	PB	3-06
☐	–	IAHC.1	HM.14 'Flea'	ex New Ross, Waterford, Dublin, Coonagh. *St Patrick*	® [1]	3-06
☐	G-AKGE		Gemini 3C	ex New Ross, Waterford, Kilbritain. Cockpit	PB [2]	3-06
☐	G-AOIE		Douglas DC-7C	'EI-AWA', ex New Ross, Waterford, Shannon, PH-SAX,		
				G-AOIE Caledonian, BOAC *County of Perth*. Forward fuse	PB	3-06
☐	G-BJMM*		Cremer Toy HAB	Cancelled 18-10-98. First noted 8-04	PB	3-06

❏	CBK	1410	Grunau Baby III	ex New Ross, Naas, Breighton, Stoke-on-Trent, Firbeck,		
				RAFGSA.378, D-4676	PB	3-06
❏	CBZ	1424	T.8 Tutor	BGA.1424, ex New Ross, Naas, Gowran Grange, Jurby,		
				RAFGSA.214, RA877	PB [3]	3-06
❏	VP-BDF		Boeing 707-321	ex New Ross, Waterford, Dublin, N435MA, G-14-372,		
				G-AYAG, N759PA. *Spirit of 73*. Nose	PB	3-06
❏	NC285RS		Navion	ex New Ross, Naas, Abbeyshrule, N91488.		
				Crashed 11-6-79. *My Way*. Cockpit and rear fuselage	PB	3-06
❏	173		Chipmunk T.20	ex New Ross, Waterford, Gormanston, IAAC	[4]	3-06
❏	184		Provost T.51	ex New Ross, Waterford, Casement, IAAC	[5]	3-06
❏	192		Vampire T.55	ex New Ross, Waterford, Casement, IAAC	[4]	3-06
❏	RA881		Cadet TX.1	ex New Ross, Breighton, ¹/₂d Green, RAFGSA 163. Nose	PB [3]	3-06

DUBLIN
Institute of Technology: In Bolton Street, has expanded its airframes.

❏	EI-BHM	Cessna F.337E	ex Farranfore, Weston, OO-PDC, OO-PDG. CoA 9-7-82 off-site	8-05
❏	EI-CGU*	Robinson R-22	ex G-BSNH, N9065D. wfu 16-4-97. DIT titles. F/n 8-04	8-05
❏	215*	CM-170-1	ex Casement, Aust AF 4D-YJ. Arrived 25-11-04	8-05

Former **Irish Aviation Museum** (IAM): Both references getting close to their 'sell by' date!

❏	EI-AOH	Viscount 808	ex Dublin Airport, Aer Lingus, PH-VII. Nose section	10-97
❏	G-ANPC	Tiger Moth	ex Edinburgh (?), Strathallan, Portmoak, R4950,	
			2 GS, Kirton SF, Hemswell SF, Oakington SF, 28 EFTS,	
			25 PEFTS, 17 EFTS, Benson SF. Crashed 2-1-67	4-96

Area: Brewster Buffalo BW-372 arrived at the National Museum of Naval Aviation at Pensacola, Florida, on 17th August 2004. Just when it left Ireland is another matter...

DUBLIN AIRPORT (COLLINSTOWN), Dublin

❏	EI-ABI	DH.84 Dragon ✈	ex EI-AFK, G-AECZ, AV982, EE, 7 AACU, 110	
			Wing, G-AECZ. *Iolar*. Aer Lingus 'Historic Flight'	12-03
❏	EI-BEM	Short 360-100	ex ALT, East Midlands, G-BLGC, G-14-3642.	
			St Senan. Crashed 31-1-86. Cabin trainer	9-93
❏	EI-BSF	HS.748-1/105	ex Ryanair, EC-DTP, G-BEKD, LV-HHF, LV-PUM.	
			Spirit of Tipperary. CoA 21-5-87. Fire crews	1-04
❏	EI-CJD*	Boeing 737-204	ex Ryanair, G-BKHE, G-BKGU ntu. Last flight 12-11-03.	
			Fire crews, and tow-training	7-05

FOYNES on the N69 west of Limerick, Limerick
Foynes Flying-Boat Museum: A grant of €1m from the Irish government will in part pay for a huge development at this superb museum. Plans, announced in the middle of 2005, will see a *tripling* of display space. Centrepiece to all of this will be a full-size model of a Boeing 314 'Clipper' floating out on the Shannon. This is due to be in place by July 2006. Located in the original transatlantic flying-boat terminal, the museum recalls the era of the great 'boats 1937-1945. Among other items at this nascent museum are the engines and other remains from BOAC Sunderland III G-AGES, which came to grief off Kerry on July 28, 1943. This is also a shrine to Irish Coffee, invented here by chef Joe Sheridan and first served up to revive passengers in 1942!
  ◆ *Open March 31 to October 31, 10am to 6pm – last visit 5pm. Foynes, Limerick, Ireland. tel 00 353 69 65416 fax 00 353 69 65600 e-mail famm@eircom.net www.flyingboatmuseum.com*

GALWAY
Eyre Square Centre: T.8 Tutor VM657 left for restoration to flying condition in 2003, destination unknown.

GALWAY AIRPORT (CARNMORE)

| ❏ | G-AFNG | Moth Minor | ex AW112, EAAS, Wyton SF, Binbrook SF, G-AFNG | | 8-04 |

GOWRAN GRANGE near Dublin, Kildare

❏	EI-102	Kite 2	ex IGA.102, IAC.102. Stored		8-04
❏	EI-123*	Phoebus C	wreck. Stored in trailer		8-04
❏	EI-128	Schleicher Ka 6CR –		®	8-04
❏	WZ762	Grasshopper TX.1	EI-135, ex Cosford, Rugby. (Wings of WZ756.)		3-05

HACKETSTOWN on the R747 east of Carlow

| ❏ | EI-BFV* | MS.880B Rallye | ex F-BVAH. Fuselage, stored, since circa 1994 | 6-04 |

KILRUSH AERODROME, Clare

| ❏ | EI-BIT* | Rallye 125 | ex F-BULQ. Stored | 8-04 |
| ❏ | G-AVSE* | Cherokee 180C | ex N11C. CoA 30-4-00. Stored | 8-04 |

LETTERKENNY on the N56, west of Londonderry, Donegal
Strains Scrapyard: A Rallye arrived here in August 2002.

| ❏ | EI-AWU* | Rallye Club | ex Rosnakill, G-AVIM | 4-04 |

LONGFORD on the N4, west of Mullingar, Longford

| ❏ | G-ANIS* | Auster 5 | ex TJ375, 1952 Flt. CoA 19-9-<u>76</u>. Stored | 8-05 |

NEW ROSS on the N25 north-east of Waterford, Wexford
South East Aviation Enthusiasts Group (SEAEG): See under Dromod, Ireland, for the bulk of the collection. The Aries (held off-site) and Vampire T.55 187 have yet to make the trek, although the latter is expected to move in April 2006 [1]. Dove 6 '176' (VP-YKF) moved to <u>Omagh</u>, N Ireland, by January 2005.

❏	G-AOGA	Aries 1	ex Casement, Dublin, Kilbrittain Castle,		
			EI-ANB, G-AOGA. Damaged 8-8-69	off-site [1]	4-03
❏	187	Vampire T.55	ex Waterford, Casement, IAAC	[1]	3-06

POWERSCOURT, Wicklow

| ❏ | EI-AUS | J/5F Aiglet Tnr | ex G-AMRL. CoA 2-12-75. Stored | 4-95 |

RATHCOOLE, Cork

| ❏ | EI-AFN | BA Swallow 2 | ex G-AFGV. Stored, off-site | 4-03 |
| ❏ | G-AXVV | L-4H-PI | ex F-BBQB, 43-29572. CoA 16-6-73. Stored | 4-03 |

SAGGART south of the N7, south west of Dublin
An owner has the cockpit section of a Trident 1, this was scrapped at Prestwick, Scotland, as far back as 1974!

| ❏ | G-ARPB* | Trident 1 | ex Prestwick, BA, BEA. Cockpit | 12-04 |

SHANNON AIRPORT, Clare
Boeing 707-123B YN-CCN was scrapped on 18th July 2003 and 737-2Q5C TN-AEE likewise on 7th July 2004.

| ❏ | EC-CFA* | Boeing 727-256 | ex N907RF ntu, Iberia. *Jeres Xeres Sherry*. Stored | 5-05 |
| ❏ | N285F | L.188CF Electra | ex N5012K. Damaged 1-3-99. Hulk | 8-02 |

SLIGO, Sligo

Gerry O'Hara: Gerry's homegrown aircraft are *believed* to be still stored here.

❏ –	IAHC.7	Sligo Concept	single seat low wing monoplane. Unflown, stored.	8-91
❏ –	IAHC.8	O'Hara Gyro	on Bensen lines. Unflown. Stored.	8-91

SLIGO AIRPORT (STRANDHILL), Sligo

❏ G-ECAT*	F-27-500	ex Euroceltic, G-JEAI, VH-EWY, PH-EXL.	
		Over-ran 2-11-02. Fire crews	11-05

TRIM on the R154 north-west of Dublin, Meath

❏ EI-ASU	Terrier 2	ex Rathcoole, G-ASRG, T.7 WE599, LAS, HCCS	®	10-04
❏ EI-BFO*	L-4J Cub	ex F-BFQJ, N79856, NC79856, 44-80405. F/n 10-04		10-04

WATERFORD AIRPORT, Waterford

❏ EI-BFE	Cessna F.150G	ex G-AVGM. Dismantled	1-05
❏ EI-BKK	JT.1 Monoplane	ex G-AYYC. Dismantled	4-99
❏ 207	Cessna FR.172H	ex Casement, IAAC. Fire crews	1-05

WESTON AERODROME near Leixlip, Kildare

Last noted here in June 2001, Avro Cadet EI-ALP moved to Ballyboghill, Ireland by October 2004. Rallye 100ST EI-BFP was flying again by February 2004. Tomahawk EI-BVK moved to Kilrush, Cork, by August 2004.

❏ EI-BBG	Rallye 100ST	CoA 1-12-83. Fuselage, stored	1-02
❏ EI-BBJ*	Rallye 100S	Stored. First noted 7-03	1-06
❏ EI-BCU	Rallye 100ST	Derelict by 8-01	9-05
❏ EI-BEA	Rallye 100ST	CoA 10-5-86. Fuselage, stored	1-02
❏ EI-BKN	Rallye 100ST	ex F-GBCK. CoA 5-98. Stored	1-02
❏ EI-BMB*	Rallye 100T	ex G-BJCO, F-BVLB. Stored. First noted 7-03	1-06
❏ EI-BUG	ST-10 Diplomate	ex G-STIO, OH-SAB. CoA 8-98. Dismantled	1-06
❏ EI-CGG	Aircoupe 415C	ex N2522H, NC2522H. CoA 10-00. Stored	1-06
❏ G-BTVV*	Cessna F.337G	ex PH-RPD, N1876M. CoA 12-1-03. Stored	1-06

PART SEVEN
RAF OVERSEAS

A listing of the British military aircraft in the *W&R* categories to be found on Crown territory or property. Please note that this section does *not* appear in any index.

CYPRUS – AKROTIRI AIRFIELD

RAF Akrotiri: The Sea Harrier was damaged on 23rd March 2005 and is not expected to return [1].

❏ XD184		W'wind HAR.10	8787M, ex 84 'A' Flt, 1563F, 228, 155. SAR c/s. Gate	7-05
❏ XR504		Wessex HC.2	ex 84, 22, SARTS, 18, 1 FTU. Spares	7-05
❏ XS929	'L'	Lightning F.6	ex Binbrook, 11, LTF, 11, 56, 11. 56 Sqn c/s. Gate	7-05
❏ XV470	'BD'	Phantom FGR.2	9156M, ex 56, 228 OCU, 19, 228 OCU, 92, 56, 92, 56, 17, 14, 27-05	
❏ ZH808*	'003'	Sea Harrier FA.2	ex 801, 899. Damaged 23-3-05	[1] 7-05

FALKLAND ISLANDS – MOUNT PLEASANT AIRPORT

RAF Enclave: The Phantom stands guard over the Tornados.

❏ XV409	'H'	Phantom FGR.2	9160M, ex 1435 Flt, 29, 228 OCU, 56, 111, 56,	
			111. *Hope*. Displayed	7-01

Appendix A
EXPORTS

Within the text, all known exports are of course listed, but not highlighted as such. The table here should help to tie all of this activity together. Column 4 gives the location under which it was to be found within *W&R* and Column 5 the destination.

G-AHMM		Tiger Moth	Southampton, Hants	Sweden, 2002
G-AKEZ		Messenger 2A	Great Waltham, Essex	New Zealand, 1-06
G-AVMN		BAC 111-510ED	Bournemouth, Dorset	Denmark 11-2-05
G-AWAH		Baron D55 ✈	Duxford, Cambs	USA 3-05
G-BTHD		Yak Yak-3U	Duxford, Cambs	USA 3-05
G-AXNZ		Pitts S-1S	Sandy, Beds	Turkey – unknown
G-BXSL		Scout AH.1	Chiseldon, Wilts	Germany, by 9-05
G-CEXG		F.27-500	Bournemouth, Dorset	Turkey 2004
G-HVIP		Hunter T.68 ✈	Bournemouth, Dorset	Switzerland, 8-3-05
G-WACO		Waco UPF-7	Gloucestershire, Glos	Belgium, circa 2000
BCF		Slingsby T.21B	Eaton Bray, Beds	Poland 12-10-05
LN-FOI		Electra nose	Pershore, Worcs	New Zealand 2-06
N44DN		Malibu 350P	Bournemouth, Dorset	USA, early 2005
N285RA		PBY-6A Catalina ✈	North Weald, Essex	Israel (destined) 28-5-04
N3455		C-47B Skytrain	North Weald, Essex [via Redhill, Surrey]	France 11-04
N25644		B-25D Mitchell ✈	Duxford, Cambs	USA, due to leave mid-2006
'MH415'		Spitfire FSM	Duxford, Cambs	Canada, 4-05
TD135		Spitfire XVI	Norwich, Norfolk	Belgium, circa 2005
VS562		Anson T.21	Llanbedr, Wales	Netherlands, by 9-05
WH734		Canberra B.2 nose	Basingstoke, Hants	New Zealand, by 2-06
WP515		Canberra B.2	Scampton, Lincs	Germany, 21-1-05
WV276		Hunter F.4	Scampton, Lincs	Germany, 22-7-05
XA286		Cadet TX.3	Rufforth, N Yorks	Netherlands by 3-04
XF358		Hunter T.8C nose	Exeter, Devon	Canada, 23-10-04
XF844		Provost T.1	Bruntingthorpe, Leics	Japan, 4-12-04
XG691		Sea Venom FAW.22	Gloucestershire, Glos	Malta, 12-9-05
XH568	(aka WG788)	Canberra B.6 nose	Bruntingthorpe, Leics	USA 28-3-06
XK482	G-BJWC	Skeeter AOP.10	Fyfield, Essex	Australia, beyond 2-01
XR442	G-HRON	Sea Heron C.1	Gloucestershire, Glos	USA 20-1-06
XS217		Jet Provost T.4	Bruntingthorpe, Leics	Germany, 7-05
XV399		Phantom FGR.2	Stock, Essex	Norway (?) 2004
XV710		Sea King HAS.6	Cosford, Shrop	Australia, late-2005 as spares for RAN
XV674		Sea King HAS.6	Gosport, Hants	Australia, mid-2005 as spares for RAN
XX657		Bulldog T.1	Colerne, Wilts	New Zealand, as ZK-WUF
XX948		Tornado P.06	Cosford, Shrop	Germany, early 2004
XX955		Jaguar GR.1A`	Ipswich, Suffolk	Germany, late-2005
XZ129		Harrier GR.3	Yeovilton, Somerset	New Zealand early 2005
XZ439		Sea Harrier FA.2	Ipswich, Suffolk	USA 1-06
ZH257		CH-47C Chinook	Odiham, Hants	USA mid-2005
–		Auster AOP.5 frame	Manston, Kent	"The Continent" by 8-04
BW-372		Brewster Buffalo	Dublin, Ireland	USA 17-8-04
'5429'	G-KAMM	Hurricane XII ✈	Sudbury, Suffolk	USA, due to leave mid-2006
7708		MiG-21MF	Boscombe Down, Wilts	USA 9-04
'LG+01'	G-AYSJ	Bü 133C ✈	Duxford, Cambs	USA 5-3-06
–	'4401'	Alpha Jet SIM	Boscombe Down, Wilts	USA, mid-2005
217		CM-170-1 Magister	Casement, Ireland	Austria 3-04
251457		B-24D Liberator nose	Duxford, Cambs	USA 23-4-04
51-14526	G-BRWB	T-6G Texan	Shoreham, W Sussex	Denmark, 2002
–		Lancaster nose REP	Gosport, Hants	Germany 3-05

Appendix B
'COCKPITFEST'

CockpitFest has established itself as a unique occasion in the aviation 'calendar'. The 'Best Cockpit' and 'Special' awards come from the judging team, while the 'Cockpiters' Cockpit' award is voted for by the attending 'cockpiters'. The *FlyPast* Readers Award is a vote from the attending public. Information is given as follows: Column 1 type and identity; Column 2 owner/keeper at that time; Column 3 location at that time; Column 4 awards, notes etc. Some of the very sophisticated and challenging 'cockpits' that attend *CockpitFest* are instrumentation clusters and as such would not get a mention in the main text and are equally not given here.

CockpitFest V, Winthorpe, 12th-13th June 2004

Cadet TX.3 XN238	Bill Fern	Doncaster, S Yorks	
Canberra B.2 WJ676	Simon Pulford	Hooton Park, Cheshire	
Canberra PR.7 WT536	Frank Lund	Southampton, Hants	
Canberra PR.9 XH177	Frank and Lee Millar	Resident	
Harrier GR.3	Roy Jerman	Doncaster, S Yorks	
Harvard II FX322	Naylan Moore	Doncaster, S Yorks	
Hunter F.1 WT684	Tony Collins	Lavendon, Bucks	
Hunter F.2 WN890	Naylan Moore	Doncaster, S Yorks	
Hunter FGA.9 XE597	Bob Dunn		
	Mick Boulanger	Bromsgrove, Worcs	*FlyPast* Readers' Best Cockpit
Hurricane I P3554	Tony Dyer	Boscombe Down, Wilts	Best Cockpit
Jet Provost T.3 XM474	1940 Squadron ATC	Levenshulme, Gtr Man	
Jetstream 200 G-ATXH	AeroVenture	Doncaster, S Yorks	
Lightning F.1 XM191	RAF EP&TU	Cranwell, Lincs	
Lightning F.6 XS898	Tony Collins	Lavendon, Bucks	Special award
Shackleton T.4 VP293	Shackleton Assoc	Resident	
Spitfire I P9451	Mike Davey	crash-site reconstruction	Special award
Spitfire IX REP	Stuart Gowans	Ingatestone, Essex	Cockpiters' Cockpit
Tiger Moth fuselage	Bill Fern	Doncaster, S Yorks	ICC 'In Progress' award
			Spirit of *CockpitFest* award
Vampire T.11 XD602	Karl Edmundson	South Shields, N&T	Best Cockpit, runner-up

CockpitFest VI, Winthorpe, 17th-18th June 2005

Bulldog T.1 SIM	Higgins Aviation	Resident	
Canberra B.2 WJ676	Sam Pulford	South Shields, N&T	
Canberra B(I).6 WT319	Tony Collins	Lavendon, Bucks	
Canberra PR.9 XH177	Frank and Lee Millar	Resident	
Hornet F.1	David Collins	Chelmsford, Essex	Best cockpit, runner-up
Hunter	Higgins Aviation	Resident	
Hunter F.1 WT684	Tony Collins	Lavendon, Bucks	
Hunter F.2 WN890	Tony Dyer	Boscombe Down, Wilts	
Hunter F.6	1986 Sqn ATC	Wymondham, Norfolk	{*FlyPast* Readers' Best Cockpit
			{Mike Doyle Award
Hunter FGA.9 XE584	{ Mike Davey	Hooton Park, Cheshire	
	{ Graham Sparkes		
Hunter FGA.9 XE597	{ Bob Dunn	Bromsgrove, Worcs	
	{ Mick Boulanger		
Hunter FGA.9 XG297	Bill Fern	Doncaster, S Yorks	
Hunter T.53 N-302	Mike North	Doncaster, S Yorks	
Jaguar GR.1A XX761	Boscombe Down AC	Boscombe Down, Wilts	Best cockpit
Jet Provost T.3 XM474	1940 Sqn ATC	Levenshulme, Gtr Man	
Lightning F.1 XM191	RAF EP&TU	Cranwell, Lincs	
Phantom SIM	Mike Davey	Hooton Park, Cheshire	
Spitfire IX REP	Stuart Gowans	Ingatestone, Essex	Cockpiters' Cockpit
Swift SIM	Higgins Aviation	Resident	
Vampire T.11 XD602	Karl Edmundson	South Shields, N&T	

Note that three broad types have been 'bundled' into 'families' for ease of reference: Balloons and Airships; Hang-gliders (modern examples only, classics such as Lilienthals, Pilchers etc are listed separately); and Ornithopters.

A6M *Zeke* (Mitsubishi)   25, 31, 153, 214
A-10 (Fairchild, Thunderbolt II)   22, 26
A-26 (Douglas, Invader)   164
A.109A (Agusta)   38
Adam RA-14   135
Addyman types   157, 274
Aero 145   214
Aero C-104 see Jungmann
Aerocar Mini-Imp   190
Aeronca 100   61, 267
Aeronca, other types   298
AFEE 10/42   75
Agricola (Auster)   174
AH-1 (Bell Cobra)   75, 180
Airbus A300   90
Aircamper (Pietenpol)   296
Air & Space 18A   285
Air Command gyros   266, 271, 288
Airedale (Beagle) 47, 86, 90, 170, 174, 281
Airtourer (AESL)   263, 287
Air Yacht (Loening)   263
Albacore (Fairey)   195
Albatros (Aero L39)   27, 163
Albatros D.Va   196
Albemarle (AW)   93
Aldritt Monoplane   217
Alouette II / III (Sud)   75, 76, 268
Alpha Jet (Dassault / Dornier)   262
Ambassador (Airspeed)   26
Andover – see HS.748
Antonov An-2   77, 160, 294, 295
ANEC II   13
ANEC Missel Thrush   160
Anson (Avro, inc XIX)   13, 24, 35, 147,
   160, 172, 176, 182, 204, 257, 271, 285,
   294, 296
Antoinette   152
Apache – see Aztec
Archaeopteryx (Granger)   13
Argosy (AW)   133, 177, 182, 223, 292
Argus – see Fairchild lightplanes
Arrow – see Cherokee
Arrow Active   267
Ashton (Avro)   177
ATP (BAe)   93, 94, 154, 156, 157, 291
Attacker (Vickers-Supermarine)   196
Audax (Hawker)   216
Auster (all high-wing types, inc Husky,
   Taylorcraft, Terrier)   10, 25, 26, 33, 35,
   40, 45, 46, 47, 54, 55, 56, 66, 73, 74, 75,
   76, 79, 85, 88, 90, 92, 93, 94, 129, 131,
   132, 133, 139, 140, 141, 143, 144, 148,
   153, 169, 170, 171, 174, 176, 177, 182,
   191, 199, 214. 257, 259, 262, 263, 268,
   270, 271, 274, 276, 279, 283, 285, 292,
   296, 302, 304, 305
Avian (Avro)   155, 280
Avro Cadet   61
Avro (and Roe) Triplane   13, 152, 155
Avro XIX - see Anson
Avro 504   13, 78, 79, 149, 152, 155, 157,
   210, 271
Avro 707   155, 182
Aztec (Piper, also Apache, Geronimo) 10,
   32, 33, 36, 56, 61, 64, 77, 85, 90, 142,

   145, 180, 202, 211, 222, 276, 280, 289
   291, 294, 302
B-17 (Boeing Fortress)   26, 28, 149
B-24 (Consolidated Liberator)   26, 148
B-25 (North American Mitchell)
   22, 26, 149, 214, 275
B-29 (Boeing Superfortress)   26
B-52 (Boeing Stratofortress)   26
Babe (Bristol)   65
Baby (Grunau)   11, 89, 203, 262, 266
Baby (Sopwith)   195, 273
BAC 111   27, 48, 50, 52, 59, 69, 71, 88, 181,
   210, 261, 284, 294
BAC 221   196
BAC (and Kronfeld) Drone   80, 173, 210
BAe 146 (inc RJX)   46, 59, 155, 156, 157
Baladou (and Super, Wassmer)   273
Balliol (BP)   160, 173, 182
BALLOONS and AIRSHIPS   17, 18, 24,
   88, 152, 155, 203, 219, 264, 265
Bandeirante (EMBRAER)
   59, 66, 69, 217, 280
Baron (Beech)   130
Barracuda (Fairey)   195
Battle (Fairey)   92
BE.2 (Royal A/c Factory)   89, 147, 153,
   170, 271
Beagle 206   61, 65, 221
Beaufighter (Bristol) 11, 29, 148, 224, 286
Beaufort (Bristol)   147
Beaver (DHC)   27, 75, 76, 224, 282, 289
Beech 17 'Staggerwing'   16, 29
Beech 18 (etc)   28, 58, 129, 284, 292
Bede BD-5 Micro   39, 82, 264
Belfast (Short)   59, 183
Bell 47 – see Sioux
Bell 212   214
Belvedere (Bristol)   148, 155, 193
Bensen gyros   44, 46, 155, 172, 193, 194,
   196, 203, 264, 278, 279, 282, 294, 305
Bestmann (Bücker)   212, 281
Beta (Rollason)   17
Beverley (Blackburn)   177, 269, 277
Bf 109 (Messerschmitt, inc
   Hispano Buchon)   16, 25, 54, 89, 149,
   150, 212, 220, 267, 271
Bf 110 (Messerschmitt)   149
Blackburn B-2   33, 214, 268
Blackburn Monoplane   13, 271
Blake Bluetit   58
Blanik (LET)   10, 49, 166
Blériot monoplanes 13, 51, 149, 150, 210
BN-1 (Britten Norman)   78
BN-2 (Islander) 38, 85, 151, 220, 285, 299
Bö 102 (MBB)   193
Bö 105 (MBB)   172, 193
Bö 208 (Bölkow Junior)   52, 77, 266
Boeing 247   264
Boeing 707   60, 181, 266, 284
Boeing 727   21, 50, 74, 134
Boeing 737   50, 60, 145, 156, 171, 290
Boeing 747   50, 68, 80, 91, 96, 212, 291
Boeing 757   66
Bolingbroke (Bristol - Fairchild)   27, 84,
   149, 286

Bonanza (Beech)   60
Boston (Douglas, inc A-20)   131
Boulton & Paul P.6   160
Boxkite (Bristol)   13, 61
Brantly types   15, 192, 193, 194
Brigand (Bristol)   65
Bristol 170   213
Bristol 173   65
Bristol 188   182
Bristol F.2b Fighter   13, 24, 29, 147
Bristol M.1   13, 149
Bristol Scout   159, 194, 262
Britannia (Bristol)
   12, 26, 65, 66, 181, 191
Brochet types   74, 135
Brown Helicopter   172
BT-15 Valiant (Vultee)   187
Buccaneer (Blackburn, HS) 25, 43, 47, 49,
   61, 64, 71, 72, 88, 91, 96, 129, 131, 134,
   142, 148, 161, 168, 177, 187, 196, 197,
   202, 205, 211, 224, 268, 277, 283, 285,
   286, 288, 289, 291, 300, 304
Bulldog (Bristol)   147
Bulldog (SAL)
   20, 27, 69, 86, 91, 177, 178, 182, 218,
   260, 262, 263, 269, 284, 287, 294, 299
C-47 - see Dakota
C-54 (Douglas Skymaster /DC-4)   56
C-119 (Fairchild Flying Boxcar)   56
Cadet (Slingsby, see also Avro and Piper)
   20, 25, 32, 44, 47, 61, 78, 91, 148, 157,
   160, 176, 201, 223, 262, 264, 271, 274,
   277, 281, 282, 294
Camel (Sopwith)
   51, 150, 153, 195, 210, 279, 285
Campbell Cougar   193
Canadair CL-44   50
Canberra (EE)   20, 22, 24, 32, 34, 38, 39
   40, 43, 49, 50, 63, 64, 68, 70, 71, 79, 87,
   91, 95, 130, 133, 139, 148, 150, 160, 161,
   163, 164, 165, 172, 173, 174, 177, 183,
   184, 204, 209, 211, 213, 224, 257, 259,
   261, 265, 266, 267, 271, 276, 277, 283,
   285, 290, 293, 299, 300, 305
Canso – see Catalina
Carvair (ATEL)   205
CASA 2-111 – see He 111
Cassutt Racer   191
Catalina (Consolidated, PBY, inc Canso)
   31, 74, 183
Caudron G.III   149
Cayley glider   265, 271
Cessna (single-engined, high wing)
   10, 12, 15, 18, 19, 22, 32, 33, 39, 40, 43,
   46, 47, 50, 59, 60, 61, 66, 67, 69, 74, 75,
   76, 77, 81, 82, 84, 85, 86, 89, 90, 93, 94.
   129, 130, 139, 142, 143, 145, 146, 152,
   154, 156, 162, 169, 175, 178, 179, 191,
   201, 202, 203, 208, 214, 221, 260, 266,
   268, 269, 270, 276, 279, 286, 289, 291,
   292, 293, 302, 304, 305
Cessna 188 Agwagon   291
Cessna 310 / 320 / 340
   22, 23, 67, 176, 221, 258, 291, 295
Cessna 303 Crusader   93

Cessna 336/337   22, 90, 167, 302
Cessna 400s   23, 165
CF-100 (Avro Canada)   25
CH-47 (Boeing Chinook)   76, 137, 209
Champion (7DC etc)   132, 301, 304
Cherokee (Piper, inc Archer, Arrow,
   Cadet, Dakota, Lance, Saratoga, Six,
   Warrior)   10, 31, 33, 44, 51, 52, 59,
   67, 68, 74, 77, 81, 87, 90, 93, 145, 154,
   166, 179, 191, 201, 211, 213, 221, 263,
   266, 269, 270, 274, 279, 291, 294, 295,
   301, 302
Chilton DW.1, DW.2   16, 79, 159
Chipmunk (DHC)   10, 14, 19, 21, 27, 30,
   32, 54, 55, 75, 78, 80, 83, 91, 95, 132,
   136, 143, 145, 146, 148, 151, 154, 157,
   160, 172, 175, 176, 178, 179, 182, 198,
   199, 200, 210, 214, 257, 259, 260, 262,
   267, 268, 275, 276, 277, 283, 285, 288,
   297
Chrislea Airguard   202
Cierva C.24   83
Cierva C.30 (inc Rota)   24, 147, 152, 193
Cirrus (Schemp-Hirth)   152
Civilian Coupé   145
Clarke TWK   150
Cmelak (LET)   264
Cody Type V   152
Colditz Cock   153, 203
Comanche (Piper)   77, 130, 284
Comet (DH.88)   13, 43, 82, 83, 84, 263
Comet (DH.106 jetliner)   11, 26, 62, 83,
   96, 138, 172, 181, 264, 284
Commander 112 / 114   168, 191, 298
Comper Swift   13, 38, 187
Concorde (BAC / SNIAS)   27, 38, 61, 62,
   65, 151, 156, 196, 210, 285
Condor (Druine / Rollason)
   74, 179, 220, 268, 290, 292
Constellation (Lockheed)   264
Convair CV-440   257
Cornell - see PT-19
Corsair (Vought, FG-1, F4U)   29, 196, 304
Cosmic Wind (Le Vier)   169
Cougar (GA)   10, 81
Coupé (Ord-Hume OH-7)   80
Cranfield Vertigo   194
Cricket (Campbell)   288
Cub (Piper, inc Super Cub et al)
   16, 17, 29, 70, 74, 132, 135, 190, 207,
   288, 292, 298, 303, 305
Currie Wot   45
Cygnet (GAL)   284
Cygnet (Hawker)   13, 181
Da Vinci glider   11
Dagling (RFD)   11, 274
Dakota (inc C-47, DC-3)   11, 26, 56, 67,
   68, 136, 147, 152, 183, 188, 257, 263,
   264, 271, 276
Dart 17R (glider)   274
Dauphin (SA.365N)   193
DC-3 - see Dakota
DC-6 (Douglas)   257
DC-7 (Douglas)   307
DC-8 (Douglas)   91
DC-10 (McDD)   156
Defiant (BP)   149, 160
Delfin (Aero L29)   187, 267
Demoiselle (Santos Dumont)   201, 210
Demon (Hawker)   11
Denney Kitfox   286, 303
Deperdussin   13

Desford Trainer (R&S)   131
Desoutter   13
Devon - see Dove
DH.2 (Airco)   259, 296
DH.9 (Airco)   147
DH.51 (DH)   13
DH.60 Moth – see Moth
DH.88 Comet - see Comet
Dickson Primary   274
Djinn (Sud)   194
Do 27 (Dornier)   302
Do 28 (Dornier Skyservant)   141
Dolphin (Sopwith)   183
Dominie – see Dragon Rapide or HS.125
Dove (DH, inc Devon and Sea)   26, 66,
   67, 68, 83, 176, 182, 214, 223, 257, 258,
   259, 265, 266, 276, 284, 301, 305
DR.400 (Robin)   10, 17, 66
Dragon (DH)   79, 264, 285
Dragon (microlight)   135, 267
Dragonfly (Viking)   179
Dragonfly (Westland)   87, 173, 181, 193,
   196, 197, 272, 278
Dragonfly MPA   285
Dragon Rapide (DH, inc Dominie)
   16, 17, 31, 48, 69, 83, 155, 158, 200,
   257, 264, 295, 296
Draken (SAAB)   140, 177, 283, 297
Drover (DHA)   74
Duet (Jordan)   21
EAA Biplane   280
EAP (BAe)   132
Edwards Helicopter   80
EE Wren   13
EH-101 (EHI Merlin)   36, 37, 148, 193
Eider Duck   85
Ekin Airbuggy   156
EKW D-3801   170
EKW C-3605 *Schlepp*   49, 140
Electra (Lockheed L.188)   258, 266
Emeraude (Piel, inc Linnet)   67, 88
Enstrom F-28, F-280   19, 50, 56, 154
EoN Baby   61
EoN Olympia   19
EoN Primary   11, 19, 203, 274
EoN 460   155, 286
Ercoupe 415 (Aircoupe, et al)
   84, 207, 276, 301
Eton (EoN)   200
Eurofightener – see Typhoon
Europa   271
Evans VP-1, VP-2   52, 77, 161, 165, 167
   209, 273, 274, 279, 286, 302
Excalibur (Wittaker MW-2B)   46
F6F (Grumman Hellcat)   29, 196
F7F (Grumman Tigercat)   29
F8F (Grumman Bearcat)   29
F-4 - see Phantom
F-5 (Northrop Freedom Fighter, Tiger II)
   22, 179
F-15 (McDD Eagle)   26, 207
F.27 (Fokker Friendship)
   46, 60, 165, 203, 266
F-84 (Republic Thunderstreak)   173, 184
F-86 (North American Sabre)
   28, 173, 183, 224
F-100 (North American Super Sabre)   26,
   90, 168, 173, 178, 204, 207, 224, 283
F-101 (McD Voodoo)   224, 258
F-104 (Lockheed Starfighter)   74, 140, 224
F-105 (Republic Thunderchief)   25, 168
F-111 (GD Aardvark)   26, 183, 207, 283

Fa 330 (Focke-Achgelis)
   25, 90, 197, 265, 267
Fairchild lightplanes (inc Argus)
   144, 167, 182, 203, 271, 302
Fairey IIIF   196
Fairey FD.2   182
Fairey ULH   64, 223
Falcon 20 (Dassault)   206
Falcon (Slingsby)   42
Falcon Major (Miles)   13
Farman F.41   183
Fauvel AV.36   13
FE.2b (Royal A/c Factory)   201
Felixstowe F.5   203
Ferguson Monoplane   303
Fi 103 V-1 (Fieseler)   24, 88, 89, 90, 149
   152, 153, 168, 183, 201, 273
Fi 156 Storch (Fieseler, inc MS.500 etc)
   25, 30, 183, 212, 213, 286
Fiat CR-42   29, 149
Fieldmaster (NDN)   86
Firefly (Fairey)   27, 158, 173, 194, 196
Fl 282 (Flettner Kolibri)   224
'Flea' - see Mignet
Fleet Canuck   260
Flexiform microlight   203
Flycatcher (Fairey)   194
Focke-Wulf Fw 44   212
Focke-Wulf Fw 189   220
Focke-Wulf Fw 190   148, 153, 163, 213
Fokker D.VII   150
Fokker D.VIII   38, 204
Fokker Dr.I   16, 89, 91, 196, 267
Fokker E.III   51, 152
Fournier RF-4   145, 201
Fox Moth (DH)   259
FRED (Clutton)   134, 176, 273, 301
Frelon (SA.321)   193
Fulmar (Fairey)   195
Fury (Hawker - biplane)   210
Fury (Isaacs)   48, 190
Gadfly HDW-1   192
Gamecock (Gloster)   64
Ganagobie (Avions Lobet)   52
Gannet (Fairey)   16, 19, 25, 37, 57, 79,
   210, 211, 224, 272, 277, 283, 286, 291
Gazelle (Westland / SNIAS)   14, 15, 16,
   69, 70, 72, 73, 75, 76, 80, 91, 137, 148,
   172, 177, 179, 185, 186, 188, 189, 190,
   196, 197, 198, 206, 207, 209, 259, 261,
   268, 270, 278
Gemini (Miles, inc Aries)   13, 35, 303
Gemini micolight   77, 259, 272
GenFly Mk.2   186
Gladiator (Gloster)   14, 29, 62, 64, 147,
   149, 197
Glaser Dirks DG-202   61
Gloster E28/39   64, 70, 132, 152
Gnat (Folland)   49, 54, 57, 66, 71, 73, 78,
   94, 141, 142, 151, 177, 178, 182, 184,
   187, 224, 265
Goevier 3   160
Goldwing microlight
   276, 285, 289, 292, 304
Gotha G.IV   91
Grasshopper (Cierva)   192, 194
Grasshopper (Slingsby)   14, 33, 40, 49, 51,
   61, 75, 78, 91, 132, 141, 148, 160, 165,
   167, 169, 170, 173, 177, 204, 206, 214,
   220, 224, 262, 264, 274, 277, 281, 282,
   285
Great Lakes Biplane   93

Grob G-109 93
Gugnunc (HP) 264
Gull (Slingsby) 210, 285
Gunbus (Vickers FB.5) 149, 170
GY-20 Minicab (Gardan) 47, 85
Gyro-Boat 193
HA-2 Sportster (Hollman) 15
Hadrian (Waco CG-4)
75, 188, 272, 278, 286
Hafner R-II 193
Halifax (HP) 65, 147, 153, 271
Halton Jupiter 217
Hamilcar (GAL) 50, 75
Hampden (HP) 139, 184
HANG-GLIDERS (h-g) 19, 21, 35, 64,
78, 88, 92, 155, 172, 197, 203, 210, 223,
260, 264, 285, 304
Hanriot HD.1 150
Harrier (HS, BAe, inc Sea and AV-8
- see also Kestrel, P.1127) 19, 25, 34, 37
39, 47, 63, 64, 65, 70, 71, 72, 82, 85, 88,
91, 94, 133, 135, 136, 137, 146, 150, 152,
153, 154, 159, 168, 175, 177, 179, 180,
185, 186, 187, 189, 196, 197, 198, 200,
204, 207, 210, 211, 212, 218, 224, 261,
262, 268, 272, 278, 279, 285, 287, 288,
299, 300
Hart (Hawker) 147, 150
Harvard (North American, T-6, SNJ etc)
26, 28, 29, 31, 48, 89, 129, 139, 147,
169, 176, 195, 222, 264, 276
Hastings (HP) 24, 176, 183
Hawk (Curtiss) 29, 95
Hawk (HS)
137, 212, 261, 267, 268, 289, 300
Hawk Trainer - see Magister
He 111 (Heinkel, inc CASA 2-111)
25, 149, 163
He 162 (Heinkel) 148, 153
Herald (HP)
19, 26, 44, 165, 220, 271, 280, 288
Hercules (Lockheed C-130) 23
Hermes (HP) 26
Heron (DH) 83, 146, 176
HH-43 Huskie (Kaman) 224
Hill Hummer 176
Hiller UH-12 (HT.1) 32, 172, 192, 197
Hind (Hawker) 13, 30, 182
Hiway microlights 155, 176, 276
HM.14 'Flea' – see Mignet
HM.280, HM.293 (Mignet) 41, 78
Hobbycopter (Adams-Wilson) 44, 296
Horizon (Gardan GY-80) 60, 179
Hornet Moth (DH) 83
Horsa (Airspeed) 44, 68, 75, 83, 188
Hotspur (GAL) 68, 75
Hoverfly (Sikorsky) 150
HP.115 (HP) 196
HR.100/HR.200 (Robin)
21, 169, 190, 211, 258
HS.125 (HSA, inc Dominie) 10, 50, 83,
91, 145, 151, 152, 171, 184, 185, 223
266, 276, 299
HS.748 (HSA, inc Andover) 22, 36, 60,
69, 93, 182, 192, 261, 291
Hudson (Lockheed) 148
Hughes 269 / 369 214
Hughes OH-6A Cayuse 194
Humber Monoplane 223
Humming Bird (DH) 13, 83
Humming Bird (1910) 220
Huntair Pathfinder 91, 264

Hunter (Hawker) 11, 20, 24, 25, 33, 35,
38, 45, 46, 49, 55, 57, 63, 64, 66, 67, 71,
74, 80, 86, 91, 130, 131, 132, 133, 134,
139, 142, 146, 148, 150, 155, 160, 161,
165, 168, 170, 173, 174, 177, 179, 182,
183, 191, 196, 202, 204, 208, 210, 211,
212, 213, 215, 218, 221, 222, 224, 258,
259, 261, 266,269, 272, 277, 278, 280,
283, 288, 293, 294, 296, 300, 302
Hunting 126/50 182
HUP-3 (Piasecki, Retriever) 194
Hurricane (Hawker, inc Sea) 13, 16, 24, 29
30, 35, 62, 79, 86, 87, 89, 90, 136, 138,
145, 147, 149, 152, 159, 161, 173, 182,
208, 210, 214, 221, 222, 261, 267, 271,
273
Husband Gyroplane 193
Husky – see Auster
Hutter H-17 260, 274
I-15 (Polikarpov) 29
Il-2 (Ilyushin) 140
IS.28M (ICA-Brasov) 141
Iskra (TS-11) 91, 96, 224
Jackaroo – see Tiger Moth
Jaguar (SEPECAT) 25, 47, 71, 91, 96
137, 161, 165, 182, 185, 186, 206, 211,
212, 261, 262, 268, 299
JAP-Harding Monoplane 152
Javelin (Gloster) 25, 64, 146, 177, 183,
204, 224, 272, 273, 294
Jenny Wren 203
Jet Gyrodyne (Fairey) 19
Jet Provost (Hunting, inc Strikemaster)
10, 20, 22, 25, 34, 41, 43, 48, 57, 67, 71,
78, 88, 93, 94, 95, 130, 132, 137, 138,
141, 148, 150, 154, 155, 156, 160, 162,
166, 168, 173, 177, 178, 179, 182, 184,
185, 197, 199, 200, 206, 207, 211, 214,
215, 259, 261, 266, 272, 273, 277, 279,
280, 281, 283, 288, 294, 295, 297, 299,
301, 302, 304
JetRanger (Bell, AB, inc Kiowa) 180, 276
JetStar (Lockheed) 79
Jetstream (HP, SAL, BAe) 10, 35, 39, 69,
93, 141, 157, 158, 159, 173, 177, 181,
183, 189, 199, 206, 221, 275, 276, 283,
285, 291, 294
Jindivik (GAF) 65, 71, 200, 293, 297, 300
JN4 Jenny (Curtiss) 208
Jodel lightplanes (CEA, SAN et al)
32, 55, 81, 93, 173, 179, 208, 270, 279,
286, 290
Ju 52 (Junkers, inc AAC.1, CASA 352L)
25, 181
Ju 87 (Junkers) 149, 212
Ju 88 (Junkers) 149
Jungmann (Bücker et al) 13, 31, 64, 149,
170, 267
Jungmeister (Bücker et al) 16, 212, 267
Jurca Sirocco 62
Ka-26 (Kamov, Hoodlum) 193
Kay Gyroplane 284
Kensinger KF 167
Kestrel (HS) 184
Kestrel (Slingsby) 61, 161
Ki 43 (Nakajima Hyabusa) 29
Ki 46 (Mitsubishi, Dinah) 183
Ki 100 (Kawasaki) 150
Killick Gyroplane 274
King Air (Beech) 60
Kingfisher (EA-1) 282
Kiowa – see JetRanger

Kite (Slingsby) 10
Kitten (Port Victoria) 271
Kittiwake (M-P) 180
Klemm L.25/ Kl 35 89, 212
Knight Twister 274
Kraguj (Soko P-2) 77
KZ.VIII (SAI) 187
Lafayette 1 80
Lake LA-4 82
Lakes Waterbird 201
Lancaster (Avro)
24, 136, 139, 147, 153, 212
Lansen (SAAB) 10
Lavi (IAI) 179
Lavochkin La-11 29
Learjet (Gates) 64, 151
Lee-Richards Annular 220
Leopard (CMC) 48
Leopard Moth (DH) 31, 85
Levi Go-Plane 85
Lightning (EE, inc P.1) 10, 20, 22, 25, 36,
38, 39, 40, 42, 49, 58, 64, 71, 90, 92, 95,
129, 130, 134, 135, 136, 137, 140, 144,
145, 146, 148, 155, 161, 165, 168, 173,
177, 182, 183, 199, 204, 208, 211, 213,
222, 224, 261, 262, 267, 270, 272, 277,
278, 283, 285, 286, 288, 289, 291, 300
Lilienthal glider 264
Lincock (Blackburn) 269
Lincoln (Avro) 163, 182, 275
Linnet – see Emeraude
Lockheed 10A 152
Lone Ranger 172
Luton Major 87
Luton Minor 11, 19, 55, 87, 154, 172,
263, 267, 292, 304
LVG C.VI 184
Lynx (Westland) 14, 15, 37, 72, 75, 76,
193, 194, 198
Lysander (Westland) 13, 24, 27, 148
McCandless M4 39, 303
Magister (Fouga CM-170) 306, 307
Magister (Miles, inc Hawk Tnr III)
13, 19, 24, 75, 200, 214, 167, 292
Mainair microlights 155, 271, 287
Manning-Flanders MF.1 51
Martin Monoplane 82
Martinet (Miles) 19
MB.339 (Aermacchi) 43
MD.600 (MDH) 56, 221
Me 163 Komet (Messerschmitt)
14, 152, 184, 286
Me 262 (Messerschmitt) 150, 163
Me 410 (Messerschmitt) 183
Mercury Dart 32
Messenger (Miles) 35, 179, 222, 303
Meteor (Gloster) 25, 31, 35, 40, 49, 53,
64, 65, 67, 74, 91, 134, 148, 156, 165,
168, 172, 173, 176, 177, 179, 181, 183,
197, 202, 204, 211, 222, 223, 224, 257,
259, 262, 265, 272, 276, 277, 281, 283,
284, 288
Mew Gull (Percival) 208, 267
Mi-1 (Mil, inc WSK SM-1) 194
Mi-2 (Mil, inc WSK SM-2) 193, 194, 295
Mil-4 Hound (Mil) 194
Mi-24 Hind (Mil) 25, 72, 194, 224, 295
MiG-15 (Mikoyan-Gurevich,
Fagot and Midget) 25, 183, 196, 286
MiG-17 Fresco 49
MiG-19 Farmer 179
MiG-21 Fishbed 54, 71, 169, 224

MiG-23, -27 *Flogger* 25, 54, 72, 178, 295
MiG-29 *Fulcrum* 168
Mignet HM.14 'Flea' 12, 13, 23, 41, 78,
146, 155, 172, 176, 181, 203, 210, 220,
223, 264, 266, 267, 271, 274, 276, 278,
279, 293, 302, 304
Miles M.18 284
Mirage III (Dassault) 272
ML Utility 75, 200
Mohawk (Miles) 11
Monarch (Miles) 19, 190, 284
Mong Sport 167
Monospar ST-12 65
Mooney M.20 etc 22, 166, 176
Morane BB 200
Morane Saulnier 'N' 51
Mosquito (DH) 24, 67, 83, 150, 163,
182, 271
Moth (DH) 13, 23, 79, 89, 150, 152, 271
Moth Minor (DH) 11, 51, 83
Motor Cadet (glider conversions)
10, 59, 160, 176, 292
MS.315 (Morane Saulnier) 139
MS.502 – see Fi 156
MS.733 (Morane Saulnier Alcyon) 170
Murray Helicopter 193
Musketeer (Beech, inc Sierra) 301
Mustang – see P-51
Mystère IVA (Dassault) 25, 41, 52, 90
96, 165, 173, 178, 204, 224, 283
Nakajima B5N2 214
Navajo (Piper) 50, 82, 93, 145, 202
NC.854 (Nord) 58, 304
Neptune (Lockheed P-2) 183
Newbury Manflier 264
Nieuport 17 91
Nimbus (Short) 303
Nimrod (Hawker) 29
Nimrod (HS) 40, 143, 201, 263, 268,
278
Nipper (Tipsy et al) 52, 173, 287
Noralpha (Nord) 212, 280, 201
Nord 1002 16, 27, 143
Nord 3202 141, 166
Nord 3400 166
Norecrin (Nord) 270, 295
Nulli Secundus (Santos Dumont) 150
Nyborg TGN.III 260
Ohka (Yokosuka MXY-7)
88, 155, 183, 196
Optica (Edgely) 56
ORNITHOPTER (wing flappers) 51, 141,
142, 155, 264
Otter (DHC) 83
OV-10 (Rockwell Bronco) 27
Oxford (Airspeed) 24, 148, 222
P.1A see Lightning
P.6 (B&P) 160
P-39 (Bell Airacobra) 29, 220
P-40 (Curtiss - Kittyhawk, Warhawk) 16,
29, 56, 147
P-47 (Republic Thunderbolt) 26, 29, 147
P-51 (North American Mustang) 16, 26
30, 31, 53, 56, 63, 150, 153, 159, 162,
183, 267
P-63 (Bell, Kingcobra) 214
P.68 (Partenavia) 134
P.111A (BP) 223
P.531 (SARO) 197
P.1052 (Hawker) 197
P.1121 (Hawker) 184
P.1127 (Hawker) 196, 210

Pacer (Piper, inc Colt, Cruiser,
Tri-Pacer etc) 19, 77, 79, 90, 167, 180,
191, 192, 211, 291, 296, 305
Parnall Elf 13
Pawnee (Piper) 17, 81, 144, 162
Pazmany PL-4A 162
Pegasus glider 203
Pegasus microlight 194, 259, 266
Pembroke see Prince
Penn-Smith Gyro 12
Percival Q.6 84
Phantom (McDD F-4) 22, 26, 31, 35, 36,
40, 54, 85, 88. 91, 95, 133, 137, 143,
148, 161, 171, 173, 178, 183, 184, 196,
207, 222, 224, 261, 273, 281, 286, 289,
292, 298
Piaggio P.149 262
Piaggio P.166 264
Pilatus P.2 21
Pilatus P.3 90
Pilatus Turbo-Porter 82
Pilcher Hawk 24, 134, 285, 287
Pioneer (SAL) 182
Pixie (Parnall) 223
Pitts (S-1, S-2)
38, 46, 77, 93, 152, 187, 305
Po-2 (Polikarpov) 13
Potez 840 292
Powerchute 176
Prefect (Slingsby) 184, 262, 276, 282
Prentice (Percival) 14, 74, 145, 176, 223
257, 276, 290
Prince (Percival, inc Sea, Pembroke)
40, 48, 69, 74, 182, 204, 211, 258, 259,
276, 293
Proctor (Percival)
24, 53, 139, 145, 200, 270
Prospector (Edgar Percival) 75, 214
Provost (Percival) 14, 18, 46, 49, 57,
177, 182, 190, 191, 200, 204, 260, 285
PT-17 (Boeing Stearman, PT-13 et al)
26, 67, 68, 167, 270
PT-19 (Fairchild, Cornell, inc PT-23,
PT-26) 163, 187, 201
PT-22 (Ryan) 14, 190
Pterodactyl (Hill) 152
Pucará (FMA) 25, 62, 173, 183, 204
Puma (Sud SA.330 etc) 72, 188, 281, 297
Pup (Beagle) 43, 69, 77, 81, 88, 154, 276
Pup (Sopwith, inc Dove)
13, 75, 149, 194, 223
Puss Moth (DH) 285
PZL Gawron 58
Queen Air (Beech) 61, 63, 221
Queen Bee (DH) 83
Quickie (QAC) 66, 201
Quicksilver MX 142
Rainbow Eagle 293
Rallye (MS, SOCATA, all types) 10, 48,
66, 81, 86, 140, 142, 155, 176, 191, 223
270, 289, 300, 301, 304, 305
Rand KR-2 64
Rans types 77, 269
Rattler Strike (Luscombe) 176
RE.8 (Royal A/c Factory) 24
Redwing (Robinson) 214
Rhonlerche (DFS) 61, 286
Robin DR.400 - see DR.400
Robin types (other) 203
Robinson (R-22, R-44) 15, 70, 147, 151,
161, 193, 214, 260, 276, 294, 304
Roe Biplane 210

Rolls-Royce TMR 152
Rooster 1 203
Rotachute III (Hafner) 75
Rotec Rallye 156
Rotodyne (Fairey) 193
Rotorway kit helicopter 294
Rutan types 52
SAAB J29F 224
SAAB 2000 69
Safir (SAAB) 18, 178, 292
Sandringham see Sunderland
SARO SR.53 182
Scheibe motor-gliders 154, 178, 298
Schleicher gliders
47, 61, 161, 218, 262, 274, 300
Schweizer TG-3A 25
Scimitar (Vickers-Supermarine) 20, 62,
78, 165, 196
Scion (Short) 214, 303
Scorpion (Rotorway) 54, 301
Scout (Westland, see also Bristol) 10, 14,
44, 47, 57, 70, 75, 76, 130, 162, 180,
190, 193, 195, 206, 209, 215, 261, 263,
277, 292, 302
Scud I 210
SE.5A (Royal A/c Factory) 13, 16, 70, 89
152, 210, 271
Sea Fury (and Fury, Hawker) 29, 49, 54,
164, 196, 198
Sea Harrier – see Harrier
Sea Hawk (Hawker) 25, 37, 42, 55, 71,
74, 158, 177, 187, 196, 198, 211, 224,
261, 265, 285, 290, 293, 304
Sea Hawker (Lavery) 304
Sea Hurricane see Hurricane
Sea King (Westland, Sikorsky, inc S-61)
36, 37, 39, 73, 185, 289, 298
Sea Prince see Prince
Sea Vampire - see Vampire
Sea Venom see Venom
Sea Vixen (DH) 20, 25, 46, 49, 78, 84,
130, 144, 177, 180, 196, 197, 204,
209, 211, 213, 222, 224, 260
Seabee (Republic) 47, 175
Seafire – see Spitfire
Seagull – see Walrus
Sealand (Short) 303
Sedburgh (Slingsby)
160, 175, 187, 200, 262, 276
Seminole (piper) 50
Seneca (Piper) 60, 67, 85, 90, 211, 280
SF-260 (SIAI-Marchetti)
Shackleton (Avro) 25, 37, 39, 155, 161,
167, 177, 211, 257, 259, 293
Shadow (CFM) 276, 292
Sherpa (Short) 92
Sheriff (Britten) 133
Short S.27 197
Short SB.5 182
Short SC.1 152, 303
Short 184 195
Short 330, 360 51, 52, 60, 69, 74, 91,
172, 183, 269, 280, 303, 304
Silvaire (Luscombe) 13, 40, 58, 70, 143
Sioux (Bell / Westland, inc Bell 47)
44, 75, 76, 88, 172, 173, 177, 193, 197
209, 263, 272, 278, 291, 302
SIPA 903 76
Sirocco 377GB 176
Skeeter (SARO) 12, 50, 75, 76, 78, 148,
152, 177, 193, 207, 209, 263, 277, 278,
285

Skua (Blackburn) 195
Skycraft Scout 44, 292
Skyraider (Douglas AD) 57, 197
Somers-Kendall SK.1 267
Sonerai (Monnet) 179
Sopwith Dove – see Pup
Sopwith Triplane 13, 150, 194
Sopwith 1½ Strutter 91, 149
Southampton (Supermarine) 147
Southern Martlet 13
SPAD types 26
Sparrowhawk (Miles) 61
Spartan Cruiser 284
Sperling (SF-23A) 273
Spitfire (Vickers-Supermarine, inc Seafire)
  13, 16, 21, 24, 27, 29, 30, 31, 35, 39, 43,
  45, 53, 54, 55, 56, 57, 63, 78, 79, 85, 86,
  87, 89, 90, 92, 131, 133, 136, 137, 138,
  139, 145, 146, 147, 148, 149, 150, 152,
  153, 155, 159, 164, 178, 180, 182, 187,
  190, 199, 200, 201, 204, 207, 213, 221,
  222, 260, 262, 264, 267, 271, 273, 283,
  285, 286, 287
Sprint (FLS) 56
Squirrel (Aerospatiale) 48
SR-71 (Lockheed Blackbird) 26
SR.A.1 (SARO) 78
Starduster (Stolp) 77, 90
Stearman – see PT-17
Stephens Akro 187
Stinson types 32, 86, 167, 191
Stranraer (Supermarine) 148
Strikemaster - see Jet Provost
Stitts Playboy 305
Student (Miles) 19
Su-7, -17, -22 (Sukhoi *Fitter*) 41, 142, 295
SUMPAC 78
Sunderland (Short, inc Sandringham)
  24, 78, 149
Super 2 (ARV) 77
Super Cub – see Cub
Super Guppy (Aerospacelines) 96
Supermarine S.6 78, 152
Supermarine 510 197
Supermarine 544 261
Surrey AL.1 45
SV-4 (Stampe et al) 11, 18, 21, 29, 44, 47,
  51, 70, 74, 190, 264, 270, 287, 296
Swallow (BA, inc Klemm) 16, 45, 81
Swallow (Slingsby) 198, 262
Swift (Globe) 58, 170, 201
Swift (Vickers-Supermarine) 78, 81, 173,
  177, 178, 222, 261
Swordfish (Fairey) 24, 194, 198, 200,
  268
Sycamore (Bristol) 61, 65, 75, 148,
  155, 172, 177, 182, 193, 204, 277, 283,
  290, 294
T-6 – see Harvard
T.21 (Slingsby) 141, 262, 273, 285
T-28 (NAA Trojan,inc Fennec) 28, 204
T.31 (Slingsby) 157, 202
T-33 (Lockheed, inc Silver Star) 26, 28,
  41, 58, 164, 165, 173, 178, 204, 222,
  224, 272, 283
T-34C (Beech, Turbo-Mentor) 197
T.45 (Slingsby Swallow) 269
T.49 Capstan (Slingsby) 178
T.61 (Slingsby, Falke) 166, 201, 291
T.67 (Slingsby, Firefly)
  44, 169, 260, 272, 279
Tabloid (Sopwith) 147

Tampico (TB-9) and Tobago (TB-10)
  211, 221
Taylorcraft – see Auster
TBM Avenger (Grumman) 26, 196
Teal (Thurston) 279
Team Minimax 94
Tempest (Hawker) 21, 139, 148, 150, 164
Terrier – see Auster
Thruster (TST) 77
Tiger (Eurocopter) 82
Tiger Cub (MBA) 53, 154, 160, 176,
  203, 283, 286, 287, 290, 305
Tiger Moth (DH, inc Jackaroo) 11, 13, 16,
  18, 24, 32, 44, 48, 51, 52, 70, 76, 77, 79,
  83, 86, 89, 139, 144, 146, 148, 164, 167,
  175, 176, 191, 196, 199, 223, 263, 276,
  278, 279, 284, 287, 293, 295, 303
Tipsy Junior etc 86, 139, 282, 291
Titch (Taylor) 203, 273
Tom Thumb (Crossley) 223
Tomahawk (Piper) 13, 32, 45, 47, 52, 69,
  70, 84, 175, 179, 202, 218, 258, 260,
  267, 270, 290, 300
Tomtit (Hawker) 13
Tornado (Panavia) 20, 25, 41, 43, 94, 95,
  137, 148, 163, 178, 182, 186, 221, 261,
  272, 273, 285, 288, 289, 299
Tourbillon (Chasle) 32
Travel Air 21
Traveler (AA-1, AA-5 etc) 50, 58, 74, 81,
  93, 147, 158, 258, 304
Trident (HS) 26, 52, 70, 71, 83, 155,
  156, 181, 264, 283, 284, 301
Triplane (see Avro, Sopwith)
Trislander (BN) 85, 90, 280, 282
TriStar (Lockheed) 55, 56
Tri-Traveler (Champion) 81, 199
TSR-2 (BAC) 25, 182, 210
Tucano (EMBRAER / Short)
  189, 295, 302, 304
Turbulent (Druine, inc Turbi) 13, 44, 45,
  154, 171, 223, 284
Tutor (Avro) 13
Tutor (Slingsby) 35, 138, 160, 262, 285
Twin Comanche (Piper)
  10, 50, 77, 81, 82, 130, 215
Twin Pioneer (SAL) 183, 257, 284, 297
Typhoon (Eurofighter) 150, 268
Typhoon (Hawker)
  25, 64, 89, 148, 190, 261
Typhoon (microlight) 285
U-2 (Lockheed) 26
UH-1 (Bell Iroquois, 'Huey' and AB.204)
  26, 57, 75, 193, 194, 197, 300
Valetta (Vickers) 184, 204, 277
Valiant (Vickers) 58, 183, 204, 210, 288
Vampire (de Havilland, inc Sea Vampire)
  20, 25, 34, 40, 41, 44, 45, 49, 50, 53,
  55, 58, 64, 78, 79, 82, 83, 84, 86, 87,
  90, 92, 134, 138, 139, 140, 146, 148,
  156, 168, 169, 172, 177, 178, 184,
  187, 196, 197, 199, 200, 201, 204, 223,
  224, 258, 259, 260, 266, 272, 275, 277,
  278, 283, 285, 286, 288, 289, 294, 295,
  301, 304
Vanguard (Vickers, inc Merchantman)
  49, 133, 210
Varga Kachina 59
Varsity (Vickers) 24, 133, 177, 182, 210,
  217, 269, 276, 294
VC-10 (Vickers, inc Super) 26, 179, 181,
  210, 299

Venom (DH, inc Sea) 16, 25, 48, 50, 57,
  78, 83, 84, 156, 173, 177, 183, 197, 201,
  211, 257, 258, 259, 277, 285, 295
Ventura (Lockheed) 184
VFW-614 299
Victor (HP) 25, 58, 91, 96, 130, 148, 163,
  183, 204, 211, 272, 282
Viggen (SAAB) 178
Viking (Dalotel) 16
Viking (Grob) 175, 179
Viking (Vickers, flying-boat) 210
Viking (Vickers) 210
Vimy (Vickers) 149, 152, 210
Viscount (Vickers) 11, 26, 27, 52, 60, 67,
  133, 134, 181, 210, 284
Voisin 210
Volmer types 155, 156, 176, 281
Vulcan (Avro) 25, 40, 49, 58, 59, 64, 96,
  134, 143, 148, 157, 165, 173, 177, 182,
  183, 204, 214, 224, 260, 277, 285, 300
WA.81 Piranha (Wassmer) 22
Wallace (Westland) 14, 147
Wallbro Monoplane 203
Wallis autogyros 151, 165, 166
Walrus (Supermarine, inc Seagull)
  78, 149, 195
Wanderlust (Broburn) 19
WAR Fw 190 202
Ward types 267
Warrior – see Cherokee
Watkins Monoplane 297
Wasp (Westland) 25, 38, 44, 57, 72, 73,
  82, 157, 193, 196, 197, 217, 261, 263
Watkinson CG-4 193
Watkinson Dingbat 158
Weedhopper microlight 92, 293
Weihe (DFS) 137
Weir W-2 286
Wellington (Vickers) 148, 210, 222
Wessex (Westland) 25, 38, 39, 49, 67,
  68, 72, 73, 74, 76, 77, 91, 134, 148, 157,
  161, 177, 178, 182, 184, 185, 189, 191,
  192, 193, 194, 196, 197, 198, 199, 200,
  206, 222, 266, 277, 280, 297, 300, 301,
  302, 304
WG.30 (Westland) 165, 193, 194, 290
WG.33 (Westland) 193
Wheeler Slymph 223
Whing Ding (Hovey) 92
Whippet (Austin) 276
Whirlwind (Westland, inc S-55) 25, 40, 41,
  52, 62, 70, 76, 80, 91, 94, 133, 134, 148,
  165, 173, 177, 191, 192, 193, 194, 197,
  199, 204, 211, 222, 223, 224, 259, 275,
  277, 278, 290, 291, 294, 295, 296, 300
Whitney Straight (Miles) 79, 187, 197
Whittaker microlights 258
Widgeon (Westland) 169, 172, 192, 203
Wight Quadruplane 78
Wildcat (Grumman, FM-2, and Martlet)
  29, 195, 304
Willow Wren 210
Woodhams Sprite 87
Wright Flyer 152, 271
Wyvern (Westland) 196
Yak (trainers, C-11, C-18 etc) 16, 21
Yak-1, Yak-3 (Yakovlev) 217
Yak-50, -52 (Yakovlev) 32, 260, 295
Yale (North American) 27
York (Avro) 26, 183
Zlin types 32
Zurowski ZP.1 176

Index II
LOCATIONS

Abbeyshrule 305	Bexhill 215	Casement 306	Cupar 282	Felthorpe 162
Abbots Bromley 199	Bicester 178	Castlerock 302	Currie 282	Fenland 139
Aberdeen 281	Bicton 80	Caterham 211	Cwmbran 296	Filton 62
Abergavenny 293	Bidford 223	Catford 146	Davidstow Moor 37	Fivemiletown 302
Aberporth 293	Biggin Hill 145	Celbridge 307	Deanland 215	Fleet 213
Abingdon 178	Binbrook 135	Chadderton 154	Debach 202	Fleet Hargate 139
Aboyne 281	Binfield 15	Chalgrove 179	Defford 266	Fleetlands 72
Accrington 92	Bird's Edge 279	Charlwood 211	Delgany 307	Flixton 203
Alconbury 22	Birkdale 157	Charnock Richard 94	Deopham Green 161	Ford 218
Alderney 280	Birkenhead Docks 157	Chatham 87	Derby 42, 43	Foulness Island 54
Aldershot 68	Birlingham 265	Chattenden 88	Digby 138	Foynes 308
Alexandria 281	Birmingham 158, 159	Chelmsford 53	Dinsdale 270	Framlingham 205
Altcar 157	Blackbushe 70	Cheltenham 62	Dirleton 282	Fyfield 54
Alton 68	Blackpool 93	Cheshunt 81	Diseworth 131	Fyvie 287
Ammanford 293	Bletchley Park 19	Chester 34	Dishforth 270	Gainsborough 139
Andover 69	Bodmin 36	Chester Airfield 294	Doncaster 275	Gallows Hill 51
Andrewsfield 52	Bodney Camp 161	Chesterfield 42	Donington 131	Galway 308
Arborfield 14	Bognor Regis 217	Chetwynd 180	Donnington 187	Gamlingay 32
Arbroath 281	Bolton 154	Chilbolton 70	Dorchester 51	Girvan 287
Armthorpe 275	Borgue 281	Chipperfield 81	Dover 88	Glasgow 287
Ashford 86	Boscombe Down 260	Chipping Camden 62	Dromod 307	Glatton 32
Ashington 217	Bosham 217	Chipping Ongar 53	Dromore 302	Glenrothes 287
Askern 275	Boston 135	Chipping Sodbury 62	Dublin 308	Glentham 140
Astley 180	Boulmer 171	Chirk 295	Dukinfield 154	Gloucester 63
Aston Down 61	Bourn 22	Chiseldon 262	Dulwich 146	Gloucestershire Apt 63
Athboy 306	Bournemouth 48	Chislet 88	Dumfries 282	Godalming 213
Attleborough 161	Bovington 50	Chorley 94	Dundee 283	Goodwood 218
Audley End 52	Braintree 53	Churchtown 307	Dunkeswell 44	Gortin 302
Awbridge 69	Bramley 70	Clacton on Sea 53, 54	Dunsfold 212	Gosport 72
Axbridge 190	Brampton 22	Clavering 54	Dunstable 10	Gowran Grange 309
Aylesbury 19	Branscombe 44	Clay Cross 42	Durham Tees Valley 52	Grainthorpe 140
Babcary 190	Bredhurst 86	Cleethorpes 135	Dursley 62	Gravesend 88
Bacup 92	Breighton 267	Clevedon 191	Duxford 23	Great Ayton 272
Balado Bridge 281	Brenchley 87	Clothall Common 81	Eaglescott 44	Great Dunmow 54
Balderton 173	Brenzett 87	Coalisland 302	Earls Colne 54	Great Waltham 54
Ballyboghil 306	Bridge of Weir 281	Coalville 130	East Dereham 162	Great Yarmouth 162
Ballyjamesduff 306	Bridgend 293	Cobbaton 44	East Fortune 283	Greenford 146
Ballykinler 301	Brierley hill 159	Cockerham 94	East Grinstead 217	Greenham Common 15
Ballymena 301	Brighton 215	Colchester 54	East Kirkby 138	Greenock 287
Bamburgh 171	Bristol 61	Colerne 262	East Tilbury 54	Grindale 268
Banbury 178	Bristol Airport 191	Colsterworth 136	East Winch 162	Guernsey 280
Banchory 281	Brize Norton 179	Coltishall 161	East Wretham 162	Hacketstown 309
Bann Foot 301	Bromsgrove 265	Comberton 23	Eaton Bray 11	Haddington 287
Barkham 15	Brooklands 209	Compton Abbas 51	Eccleshall 199	Hailsham 215
Barnstaple 43	Brough 267	Coningsby 136	Eccleston 94	Halesworth 205
Barrow-in-Furness 39	Bruntingthorpe 95, 129	Connah's Quay 295	Eckington 266	Halifax 279
Barton 154	Burbage 130	Corby 168	Edinburgh 286	Halstead 55
Basingstoke 69	Burnham on Sea 191	Cork 307	Egham 212	Halton 20
Basset's Pole 199	Burnley 93	Cosford 181	Elgin 286	Hamble 73
Bassingbourn 22	Burslem 199	Cottesmore 131	Elstree 81	Hanwell 146
Batley 279	Burton-on-Trent 199	Cove 70	Elvington 271	Hardwick 162
Bawtry 275	Burtonwood 34	Coventry 159	Ely 31	Harrington 168
Baxterley 222	Bury St Edmunds 202	Coventry Airport 223	Enniskillen 302	Harrogate 272
Beccles 202	Caernarfon 293	Cowbridge 295	Enstone 179	Haslemere 213
Beck Row 202	Callington 36	Cowes 85	Errol 286	Hatch 11
Bedford 10	Camberley 210	Cranfield 10	Eshott 171	Hatfield 82
Belfast 301	Cambridge 23	Cranwell 137	Eversden 32	Haverfordwest 296
Belfast City 302	Canterbury 87	Crawley 217	Evesham 266	Haverigg 40
Bembridge 85	Capel le Ferne 87	Croft 137	Ewyas Harold 80	Hawkinge 88
Benington 81	Capenwray 93	Crosshill 282	Exeter 45	Haxey 140
Benson 178	Cardiff 294	Croughton 168	Fairford 62	Haydock 158
Bentley Priory 145	Carew Cheriton 294	Crowland 137	Fairoaks 212	Hayward's Heath 218
Bentwaters 202	Cark 40	Croydon 146	Falgunzeon 286	Hednesford 199
Bere Alston 44	Carlisle 40	Cruden Bay 282	Farnborough 70, 71	Helston 37
Berkhamstead 81	Carlow 306	Culdrose 36	Farnham 213	Hemel Hempstead 82
Berkswell 158	Carlton Moor 270	Culham 179	Farnsfield 173	Hemswell 140
Beverley 267	Carthorpe 270	Culloden 282	Faygate 218	Hendon 147
Bewdley 265		Cumbernauld 282	Felixstowe 202	Henley-on-Thames 179

Henlow	11	Lancing	218	Market Harborough		Old Warden	12	Samlesbury	95
Henstridge	191	Larne	303		132	Oldham	156	Sandbach	36
Hereford	80	Lasham	74	Marksbury	191	Ollerton	36	Sandown	85, 86
Hibaldstow	140	Lashenden	89	Martham	163	Omagh	305	Sandtoft	142
High Wycombe	20	Lavendon	20	Martlesham	207	Orphir	290	Sandy	14
Hinckley	131	Leavesden	82	Maybole	289	Ottringham	269	Scampton	142
Hinton-in-the-		Lee-on-Solent	74	Melksham	262	Oxford	180	Scarborough	274
Hedges	169	Leeds	279	Melton Mowbray	133	Palnakie	290	Sealand	300
Hitchin	82	Leeds-Bradford Apt	280	Membury	16	Panshanger	84	Seaton Ross	270
Hixon	199	Leeming	272	Meppershall	12	Pathhead	290	Sedlescombe	217
Hockley Heath	159	Leicester	132	Messingham	141	Paull	269	Seething	166
Hollington	216	Lelant	38	Metheringham	141	Pendine	298	Selby	274
Holywell	296	Letterkenny	309	Middle Wallop	75	Pershore	266	Sevenoaks	92
Holywood	303	Leuchars	289	Mintlaw	289	Perth	291	Shanklin	86
Honington	205	Levenshulme	154	Mold	297	Peterborough	32, 33	Shannon	309
Hook	73	Lewes	216	Monewden	208	Peterhead	291	Shawbury	187, 188
Hooton Park	34	Lichfield	200	Moneymore	304	Peterstone	298	Shawell	134
Horley	213	Linley	269	Montrose	289	Plymouth	47	Sheffield	279
Horham	205	Linton-on-Ouse	273	Moreton-in-Marsh	67	Pocklington	269	Shenington	180
Houghton	32	Lisburn	303	Morpeth	171	Poole, Dorset	51	Sherburn-in-Elmet	274
Hucknall	173	Liskeard	38	Moston	156	Poole, Somerset	191	Shipdham	166
Huddersfield	279	Little Gransden	32	Movenis	304	Popham	76	Shrivenham	180
Hull	269	Little Snoring	162	Mullaghmore	305	Portishead	192	Shobdon	81
Humberside	141	Little Staughton	32	Mytchett	213	Portmoak	291	Shoreham, Kent	92
Hungerford	16	Littlehampton	220	Nantgarw	297	Portsmouth	77	Shoreham, W Sus	220
Husbands Bosworth		Liverpool	158	Nantwich	36	Powerscourt	309	Sibsey	142
	132	Llanbedr	296	Narborough	164	Predannack	38	Sleaford	142
Ingatestone	55	Llangeinor	297	Nayland	208	Preston, Lancs	94	Sleap	190
Ingleby Arncliffe	272	Llangennech	297	Neatishead	164	Preston, E Yorks	269	Sligo	310
Innsworth	64	Llanwrtyd Wells	297	Netheravon	262	Prestwick	291	Solihull	159
Insch	288	Lochearnhead	289	Netherthorpe	278	Purfleet	58	Somerford	51
Inverness	288	London	150	Newark-on-Trent	173	Quedgeley	67	Sopley	77
Ipswich	205	London Airport	151	Newbridge-on-Wye		Radcliffe	156	South Kensington	152
Isle of Man	84	London Heliport	151		297	Radcliffe on Trent	175	South Lambeth	153
Islington	150	London - Gatwick	220	Newbury	17	Rathcoole	309	South Molton	47
Iver Heath	20	London - Luton	12	Newby Wiske	273	Rathfriland	305	South Shields	171
Ivybridge	46	London - Stansted	55	Newcastle Airport	171	Rattlesden	208	South Woodham
Ivychurch	89	London Colney	82	Newcastle upon		Rayleigh	58	Ferrers	60
Jersey	280	Londonderry	304	Tyne	171	Reading	18	Southampton	77, 79
Jurby	85	Longford	309	Newhaven	216	Redditch	267	Southend Airport	59
Keevil	262	Long Marston	258	Newmarket	208	Redhill	213, 214	Southend-on-Sea	60
Kemble	65	Long Mynd	181	Newport, IoW	85	Reigate	214	Spadeadam	41
Kendal	41	Long Stratton	163	Newport, Wales	297	Rendcomb	68	Spalding	143
Kenfig Hill	296	Longside	289	Newport Pagnell	21	Retford	175	Spanhoe Lodge	170
Kesgrave	207	Longton	200	New Ross	309	Rettendon	59	Spark Bridge	42
Kew Stoke	191	Lossiemouth	289	Newry	305	Reymerston	165	Spilsby	143
Kidderminster	266	Loughborough	132	Newton Abbot	46	Ridgewell	59	Stafford	200
Kidlington	179	Lough Foyle	304	Newton-le-Willows		Ringwood	77	Stalbridge	51
Kilkeel	303	Louth	141		158	Robertsbridge	216	Stamford	143
Kilmarnock	288	Lower Stondon	12	Newtownards	305	Rochester	92	Stanford	134
Kilrush	309	Lower Upham	74	North Cave	269	Roehampton	151	Stannington	172
King's Cliffe	169	Lowestoft	207	North Coates	141	Romsey	77	Stansted – see London
King's Croughton	258	Ludlow	187	North Luffenham	133	Rooks Bridge	192	Stapleford Tawney	60
King's Lynn	162	Lumb	94	North Moreton	180	Rosemarket	298	Steventon	180
Kingsbridge	46	Luton – see London		North Stainley	273	Rougham	208	Stock	60
Kingsclere	74	Lutterworth	132	North Weald	55	Royton	156	Stockport	156
Kingsmuir	288	Lydd	90	Northallerton	273	Rufforth	273	Stoke-on-Trent	200
Kingston-upon-		Lyneham	262	Northampton	169	Rugby	259	Stone	200
Thames	150	Lytham St Anne's	94	Northolt	151	Rugeley	200	Stonehaven	292
Kington	80	Macclesfield	35	Norwich	164	Rush Green	84	Stoneleigh	259
Kinloss	288	Madley	80	Nottingham	175	Ruthin	298	Stoney Stanton	134
Kinnetties	289	Malmesbury	262	Nottingham East		St Albans	84	Storwood	270
Kirkbymoorside	272	Malpas	35	Midlands Apt	133	St Athan	298	Stowmarket	208
Kirknewton	289	Malton	273	Nuneaton	259	St Austell	39	Strathallan	292
Kirriemuir	289	Malvern Wells	266	Nympsfield	67	St Ives	33	Strathaven	292
Kirton-in-Lindsey	141	Manchester	153, 154	Oakham	134	St Leonards-on-Sea	216	Strathdon	292
Laindon	55	Mansfield	174	Oakley	21	St Mawgan	38	Stretton	36
Lakenheath	207	Manston	90	Oaksey Park	263	St Merryn	38	Sturgate	143
Lambourn	16	March	32	Oban	290	Saggart	309	Sudbury	208
Land's End	38	Marfleet	269	Odiham	76	Salford	156	Sumburgh	292
Langar	174	Marham	163	Okehampton	46	Salisbury	263	Sunbury-on-Thames
Langford Lodge	303	Market Drayton	187	Old Sarum	263	Saltby	134		214

Sunderland	171	Tolworth	153	Wannock	217	Weybourne	168	Woodhurst	34
Sutton	215	Topcliffe	274	Warminster	264	Weybridge	215	Woodley	19
Sutton Bridge	143	Topsham	47	Warton	95	White Waltham	19	Woolwich	153
Swansea	300	Torpoint	38	Warwick	259	Whitson	300	Worcester	267
Swanton Morley	166	Townhill	292	Washington	221	Whittlesey	33	Wrexham	301
Swindon	264	Tremar	38	Waterbeach	33	Wick	292	Wroughton	264
Syerston	175	Trim	310	Waterford	310	Wickenby	144	Wycombe Air Park	21
Tain	292	Tunstead	166	Wattisham	209	Wigan	157	Wymondham	168
Tamworth	200	Turweston	21	Watton	167	Wigston	135	Wyton	34
Tangmere	221	Twinwood Farm	14	Wellesbourne		Winchester	80	Yarmouth	86
Tatenhill	200	Twyford	21	Mountford	260	Windermere	42	Yarcombe	48
Tattershall Thorpe	143	Upavon	264	Wellingborough	170	Winthorpe	175	Yarnscombe	48
Tavistock	47	Upper Ballinderry	305	Welshpool	300	Wisbech	144	Yarrow	292
Terrington		Upper Hill	81	West Chiltington	222	Witchford	33	Yateley	80
St Clement	166	Upper Vobster	192	West Freugh	292	Withernsea	270	Yatesbury	265
Thatcham	18	Upwood	33	West Hanningfield	60	Witney	180	Yearby	52
Thirsk	274	Uxbridge	153	West Horndon	61	Wittering	34	Yeovil	194
Thornhill	292	Valley	300	West Thurrock	61	Woburn Sands	21	Yeovilton	195
Thorpe Abbotts	166	Waddington	143	West Walton		Woking	215	Ystrad Mynach	301
Thruxton	79	Wainfleet	143	Highway	167	Wolverhampton	159		
Tibenham	166	Wallington Green	153	Weston	310	Wolverhampton			
Tidenham	68	Walney Island	42	Weston-super-		Aerodrome	201	*Will you* please *stop*	
Tilstock	190	Walpole	208	Mare	192	Woodford	157	*farting while I'm trying to*	
Titchfield	79	Walton on Thames	215	Weston Zoyland	194	Woodhall Spa	144	*save the world!*	

We hope that you enjoyed this book . . .

Midland Publishing titles are edited and designed by an experienced and enthusiastic team of specialists.

Our associate, Midland Counties Publications, offers an exceptionally wide range of aviation, military, naval and transport books and videos for sale by mail-order around the world.

For a copy of the appropriate catalogue, or to order further copies of this book, and any of many other Midland Publishing titles, please write, telephone, fax or e-mail to:

Midland Counties Publications
4 Watling Drive, Hinckley,
Leics, LE10 3EY, England

Tel: (+44) 01455 254 450
Fax: (+44) 01455 233 737

E-mail: midlandbooks@compuserve.com
www.midlandcountiessuperstore.com

WRECKS & RELICS: THE ALBUM

Ken Ellis

The continuing popularity of the biennial *Wrecks & Relics*, recording preserved, instructional and derelict airframes in the UK and Ireland is well known. Ken Ellis has amassed an extensive archive of unpublished photos from the last forty-some years of *W&R* publication, and following a brief introductory narrative covering *W&R* itself, the body of the book is a gloriously nostalgic collection of photos with extended captions explaining the histories and linking the themes. As *W&R* was a b/w publication for so many years, most of the fascinating subject matter has not appeared in colour before.

The themes include: Airliners; Alas, No More (RIP Museums); Duxford's Early Days; Founding Fathers; Hulks; Light and General; Military Miscellany; Mr Nash; Mr Shuttleworth; Navy First!; Ones That Got Away; On Guard; RAF Museum; Time Capsule (Cranfield); V-Bombers; Warbird Origins; plus a types and locations index.

Softback, 280 x 215 mm, 128 pages
340 mostly colour photographs
1 85780 166 0 **£16.99**

1000 PRESERVED AIRCRAFT IN COLOUR

Gerry Manning

This book features aircraft of all types which have been preserved around the globe. The definition of the term 'preserved', in the context of the book, is a broad one. Aircraft recorded are either in museums, on display as gate guardians at military bases or other facilities, or have been kept in flying condition long after it would have been normal to retire them. Since most museums tend to preserve military aircraft rather than civilian ones, due to their history and availability, there is a bias towards these in the book. However, to balance this many of the vintage aircraft flying are civilian types. The book reflects today's growing trend to preserve classic airliners in flying condition, one which many aviation enthusiasts resolutely endorse.

The book aims to include as wide a selection of types and locations as possible from around the world. The thousand plus colour photographs are arranged in type order and are accompanied by informative captions.

Softback, 280 x 215mm, 160pp
over 1,000 colour photographs
1 85780 229 2 **£18.99**